SIR HENRY IRVING

.18. Irving .99.

Oliver Bath.
1 8 9 9

Silhouette of Sir Henry Irving, by Oliver Bath, 1899.

Sir Henry Irving

A Victorian Actor and his World

Jeffrey Richards

Hambledon and London
London and New York

Hambledon and London
102 Gloucester Avenue, London NW1 8HX

175 Fifth Avenue
New York, NY 10010
USA

First published 2005

ISBN 1 85285 345 X

A description of this book is available from the
British Library and from the Library of Congress.

Typeset by Egan Reid Ltd, Auckland, New Zealand,
and printed in Great Britain by Cambridge University Press.

Distributed in the United States and Canada
exclusively by Palgrave Macmillan,
a division of St Martin's Press.

Contents

For
John H.B. Irving
the keeper of the flame

Illustrations

Plates

Between Pages 148 and 149

Between Pages 308 and 309

Text Illustrations

Acknowledgements

I am grateful to Richard Foulkes who read several key chapters in the book and made constructive and helpful comments. The following friends and colleagues provided advice, suggestions and practical help of various kinds: Jennie Bisset, Jenny Brine, Peter Horton, Frances Hughes, David Mayer, Kate Newey, John Pick, Kristan Tetens and Stephen Wildman, and members past and present of the Irving Society and Lancaster University's Ruskin Programme. I am also indebted to Clare French, Joel Hockey and Pat Robinson for their word-processing expertise and to Martin Sheppard for his meticulous copy-editing. My greatest debt is to John H.B. Irving for his help and support. This book is dedicated to him in gratitude.

Publication of this book has been made possible by a grant from the Scouloudi Foundation in association with the Institute of Historical Research.

Introduction

Sir Henry Irving was the greatest actor of the Victorian age and also the best loved. He died on 13 October 1905 , so this year is the centenary of his death. The cultural heroes of an age are the measure of its mind, and Irving was undoubtedly one of the heroes of the Victorian age. His extraordinary centrality to Victorian culture can be demonstrated by a few examples, examples which could be multiplied many times over. W.E. Gladstone, 'The People's William', Victorian Liberalism incarnate, attended the Lyceum regularly from 1875 to 1893. Alfred, Lord Tennyson, the Poet Laureate, trusted Irving with the production of his apparently unstageable plays: by adroit cutting and staging Irving made them not only playable but, in the case of *Becket*, triumphant. Irving met the poet Robert Browning regularly for animated discussions of Shakespeare. Browning presented Irving with Edmund Kean's purse, which Irving cherished, for he was an avid collector of mementoes of his eminent predecessors on the stage, whose achievements he sought to emulate and if possible surpass. John Ruskin, the Sage of Brantwood, went to the Lyceum in 1882 to see *Much Ado About Nothing* saying 'Irving has so much power with the public that I want to see how he gets and how he uses it'. Oscar Wilde, with whom Ruskin went to see *The Merchant of Venice* in 1879, became one of Irving's greatest fans and addressed a sonnet, 'Fabien dei Franchi', to him in 1881 after seeing him in *The Corsican Brothers*. Irving collaborated with the leading composers (Sir Arthur Sullivan, Sir Alexander Mackenzie, Sir Julius Benedict, Sir Edward German) and the leading painters (Sir Lawrence Alma-Tadema, Sir Edward Burne-Jones, Ford Madox Brown, Seymour Lucas) of the age to ensure the visual and aural perfection of his productions. Finally, the Queen herself, who loved the theatre and for whom Irving staged several command performances, broke with tradition when she knighted Irving, saying 'We are very, very pleased, sir' as she conferred the accolade.

There were many biographies of Irving during his lifetime and there have been a number since his death, the most notable being the monumental *Henry Irving: The Actor and His World* (1951), by the actor's grandson Laurence. There have also been many studies of Irving's acting and stage production. Alan Hughes' *Henry Irving: Shakespearean* (1981) remains the definitive overview of Irving's Shakespearean productions. The present book, while it includes the full story of

Irving's life, is the first systematic attempt to locate him, his work and his reputation within the broader span of Victorian culture. Its aim is to explain how he achieved what he did and why he acquired such pre-eminence in nineteenth-century society.

I have drawn on two major collections of contemporary materials relating to Irving, the Bram Stoker Collection, currently held in the Shakespeare Centre Library, Stratford-upon-Avon, and the Percy Fitzgerald Collection, housed at the Garrick Club. The Stoker Collection, seventy-seven boxes of material, covers the thirty years during which Stoker was Irving's business manager and principal lieutenant. The Fitzgerald Collection is twenty-two scrap books of press cuttings, assembled by the journalist and author Percy Fitzgerald and utilised in the writing of his biography of Irving. Infuriatingly, Fitzgerald has systematically removed the names and dates of the newspapers and journals from which the clippings came. In addition, I have drawn extensively on the memoirs of those who were closest to Irving during his working life. Ellen Terry's *The Story of My Life*, Bram Stoker's *Personal Reminiscences of Henry Irving*, Sir John Martin-Harvey's *Autobiography* and Edward Gordon Craig's *Henry Irving* have provided particularly valuable insights. I was also very fortunate in being allowed access to the Irving family deed box which John H.B. Irving, the actor's great-grandson, generously opened up for me. He also acted as a kind and welcoming host while I studied the documents at his home.

It is my hope that, in this centenary year of Irving's death, I have thrown a new light on his celebrity and cultural significance.

Sir Henry Irving

In 1906 James Williamson, the first and last Lord Ashton, Liberal politician, philanthropist and linoleum magnate, financed the creation and erection, in the central square of his home town Lancaster, of the Queen Victoria Monument. It consists of a statue of the late Queen herself, four lions, groups of idealized figures representing Wisdom, Freedom, Truth and Justice and a frieze containing fifty-three depictions of the great and the good of the Victorian era. They include Gladstone and Disraeli, Livingstone and Shaftesbury, General Gordon and General Booth, Darwin, Dickens and Faraday, Ruskin and Carlyle, Florence Nightingale and George Eliot, Lord Tennyson and Sir Arthur Sullivan. There also, among this pantheon of the heroes and worthies who shaped and stamped the image of the Victorian age, is one actor – Sir Henry Irving.

The fitness of his inclusion had been demonstrated when he died on his farewell acting tour the previous year. Irving had played the title role in Lord Tennyson's *Becket* for the last time on Friday 13 October 1905 at the Theatre Royal, Bradford. Returning to the Midland Hotel, where he was staying, he collapsed in the foyer and died in the arms of his devoted dresser, Walter Collinson. When the *Daily Telegraph* (16 October 1905) reported the melancholy event and its aftermath and declared 'The whole nation mourns,' it was not exaggerating. Flags were flown at half mast, and all the London cabmen wore black bows on their whips. Tributes poured in from France, Germany, Russia, Greece and America.

In Britain the royal family led the mourning. On behalf of King Edward VII and Queen Alexandra, General Sir Dighton Probyn VC sent the following telegram to the Irving family:

> I am commanded to convey to Sir Henry Irving's family His Majesty's and the Queen's sincere sympathy on poor Sir Henry's death. Their majesties say, he will, indeed, be a great loss to the profession of which he was such a distinguished ornament.

Telegrams from the Prince and Princess of Wales, the Lord Mayor of London and the President of the United States were also received.

The *Daily Telegraph* reported that 'an immense crowd' had witnessed the removal of Irving's body from the Midland Hotel to the Great Northern railway station on the Saturday evening. Irving's sons, Harry and Laurence, had travelled by train to Bradford to collect the body and escort it back to London. 'There were many touching manifestations of grief and respect before the departure of the train', said the newspaper.

Irving's business manager Bram Stoker, who also accompanied the body, recalled the scene in Bradford in greater detail in his reminiscences of his time with Irving:

> Everywhere was a sea of faces, all the more marked as all hats were off as we drove slowly along. Street after street of silent humanity; and in all that crowd nothing but grief and respect. One hardly realised its completeness till when, now and then, a sob broke the stillness. To say that it was moving would convey but a poor idea of that attitude of the crowd; it was poignant – harrowing – overwhelming … It was the same at the railway station; everywhere the silent crowd, holding back respectfully, uncovered.[1]

Similar scenes accompanied the funeral in London. Irving's body was cremated in a small private ceremony at Golders Green Crematorium; and the urn of ashes, enclosed in a coffin, then lay in state at Baroness Burdett-Coutts's residence, 1 Stratton Street, London, where hundreds filed past it. The newspapers urged burial in Westminster Abbey as the most appropriate resting place for England's greatest and best-loved actor. The Dean of Westminster, Dr Armytage Robinson, encouraged by his stage-hating sister, initially refused.[2] But a petition signed not only by the leading actors of the day but by such major public figures as the Bishop of Ripon, the Duke of Devonshire, the Earl of Aberdeen, Joseph Chamberlain and Viscount Goschen caused him to relent. The funeral was held at the Abbey on 20 October, 1905. There were 50,000 applications for tickets but the Abbey could seat only 1200 people. Six hundred wreaths were received. Leading actors performed the duties of ushers. There were fourteen pallbearers: the actors Sir Squire Bancroft, Sir Charles Wyndham, Johnston Forbes-Robertson, George Alexander, John Hare and Herbert Beerbohm Tree; the painter Sir Lawrence Alma-Tadema, the composer Sir Alexander Mackenzie, Lord Tennyson (the son of the poet laureate), the playwright Arthur Wing Pinero, Professor Sir James Dewar, the Earl of Aberdeen (the former Governor-General of Canada and future Lord-Lieutenant of Ireland), Lord Burnham (the proprietor of the *Daily Telegraph*) and Mr Burdett-Coutts MP (husband of Baroness Burdett-Coutts). At the head of the catafalque stood a magnificent cross of white lilies and lilies of the valley from Queen Alexandra, with a card inscribed: 'To Sir Henry Irving, with deepest regret, from the Queen, "into Thy hands, O Lord, into Thy hands"'. The quotation was the last line spoken by Irving on the stage in *Becket* and it was much used in tributes to Irving, as if invoking divine blessing on both the actor and his profession. Another link with the stage was the inclusion in the order of service of the funeral march from Sir Alexander Mackenzie's incidental music for *Coriolanus*, Irving's last new Shakespearean production.

On Saturday 21 October 1905, the day after the funeral, *The Times* printed a third leader on the event, reflecting on Irving's national importance:

> Yesterday in the midst of a striking demonstration of the admiring affection of the public, all that remains of **HENRY IRVING** was buried in Westminster Abbey. It was a great sight and a clear proof that an actor of the first rank comes nearer to the heart of the people than do other great men. A statesman, or even a soldier, works for interests and causes of which the many can often understand but little, and a poet or a painter is not for them a real, vital human presence. When TENNYSON was buried the streets around the Abbey showed no signs of public mourning; people to whom DARWIN and BROWNING are mere names felt that they were saying farewell to a friend who had a score of times moved them to their inner fibre.

The writer noted that both actors and the public had agreed that the Abbey was the fitting resting place for Irving:

> To the former he was unquestionably the head of their profession, the man who had given new life to the stage, a new interest to the public, a new *status* to the performers. To the public, he was the man who had revealed **SHAKESPEARE** to them, and a score of other playwrights and poets, in a new and unforgettable way ... with **MISS ELLEN TERRY** to help him, and with his genius for stage-craft, he more than doubled the number of theatre-goers in London and in the provincial towns. The number of those who mourn him to-day is so large because his audience in life, by reason of his gifts and energies, was so immense.

It had been a long journey that had brought Irving to his last resting place in Westminster Abbey, the culmination of sheer ability, determination, dedication and unremitting hard work. In Victorian terms, Irving's life was a Smilesian success story. He had been born John Henry Brodribb in 1838 in the Somerset village of Keinton Mandeville, the son of a kindly but improvident travelling salesman Samuel Brodribb and his devoutly Methodist Cornish wife Mary Behenna. The young John Henry spent six years of his boyhood living in Cornwall with his maternal aunt while his parents tried to make a living for themselves. He rejoined them in London at the age of ten, studied at the City Commercial College and left at the age of thirteen to become a clerk. Inspired by visits to Samuel Phelps' Sadler's Wells Theatre, he became an enthusiastic amateur actor. At eighteen he decided to become a professional actor and embarked on his career at the Royal Lyceum Theatre, Sunderland, in 1856 under the stage name of Henry Irving. This provoked a permanent estrangement from his mother who regarded the stage as sinful.

There followed ten years hard labour for Irving in provincial stock companies as he learned his trade, playing 588 different parts. At times he was out of work and actually starved. But by the late 1860s he had begun to earn a reputation both as a villain in melodramas and as a character comedian. He made a particular impact in the role of the shabby genteel Digby Grant in James Albery's hit comedy *The Two Roses* at the Vaudeville Theatre, London, in 1870. On his benefit night, Irving performed his favourite recitation, Thomas Hood's macabre poem 'The Dream of Eugene Aram'. In the audience was the American impresario Hezekiah Linthicum Bateman, universally known as 'The Colonel', who had taken a lease on the Lyceum Theatre in order to showcase the acting talents of his daughter Isabel. Impressed by the power of Irving's recitation and his versatility in the role of Digby Grant, Bateman engaged him as the leading man of the Lyceum company. But the two opening productions, *Fanchette* and *Pickwick* failed, and Irving persuaded the sceptical 'Colonel' to put on a production of Leopold Lewis's version of a French melodrama, *The Bells*, with Irving playing the haunted Alsatian burgomaster Mathias. Irving's *tour de force* in the role made him an overnight star and Bateman now mounted a succession of plays to consolidate his stardom.

Irving starred in the newly commissioned plays *Charles the First*, *Eugene Aram* and *Philip*, in a revival of Bulwer Lytton's surefire historical warhorse *Richelieu* and, finally, again against Bateman's better judgement, in *Hamlet*. The production ran for a record two hundred performances and decisively established Irving as the leading actor of his generation. 'Colonel' Bateman died during the run of *Hamlet*, but his widow, Mrs Sidney Bateman, took over the lease and continued to promote productions starring Irving with Isabel Bateman as his leading lady. *Macbeth*, *Othello* and *Richard III* followed *Hamlet*. But in 1878, increasingly dissatisfied with the performances of Isabel, he asked Mrs Bateman to allow him to select a new leading lady. Mrs Bateman could not agree and a breach between them was inevitable. Mrs Bateman decided to withdraw. She sold the lease of the theatre together with the rights to many of the plays, complete with costumes and scenery, to Irving and took over Sadler's Wells Theatre in order to continue promoting Isabel's career. Irving remodelled and refurbished the Lyceum, engaged his own production staff, chose a new leading lady, Ellen Terry, who was to be his stage partner for the rest of the century, and inaugurated what came to be seen as a golden age of Lyceum productions, superbly staged, brilliantly directed and drawing on the talents of leading composers and painters to enhance their effect.

Irving set new standards of excellence in stage production. He did so with the aid of a large staff both on the stage and backstage. At its greatest extent in *Robespierre* (1899), he had a cast of sixty-nine actors and 235 supernumeraries. The backstage staff, musicians, gasmen, scenic artists, wardrobe people, property makers plus the front of house staff (ushers, pages, box office attendants) numbered some 350. All were carefully chosen and many stayed with Irving for years.[3] At the same time he embarked on a lifelong mission to establish the absolute respectability of the acting profession, long disparaged not least by the church. Irving's own career was the spearhead of this campaign as he became the first actor to speak at the Royal Academy Banquet, the first actor to lecture at Oxford University, the first actor to perform in the Chapter House of Canterbury Cathedral, and in 1895 the first actor to be knighted. One by one the bastions of the establishment succumbed to Irving's combination of personality, eloquence and integrity. Irving not only conquered the West End but, with the aid of railways and transatlantic steamships, he also conquered the provinces and the United States. He regularly toured Britain with his company and became as popular in Scotland, Wales and the English regions as he was in London. Perhaps even more significantly he undertook eight full-length tours of the United States, becoming the first actor to take his entire company and all his scenery with him – a mammoth undertaking. The impact of these tours both of Britain and the United States on artistic standards and cultural values was enormous. They were widely perceived as having helped to create both a national and an Anglo-American standard of taste and culture. It was Irving together with Dickens, Gilbert and Sullivan, Conan Doyle, Fenimore Cooper and Longfellow, all popular on both sides of the Atlantic, who between them created an Anglo-American culture which bridged the Atlantic. By the end of his career, with the costs of production mounting, it was the provinces and the United States that provided Irving with a financial lifeline.

By the end of the nineteenth century Irving's finances had become precarious. He had never stinted on costs and his productions were becoming increasingly large-scale and spectacular as he got older. In addition, a series of disasters overtook him: a catastrophic fire destroyed almost all his scenery; and a succession of illnesses undermined his health; and when he was not acting, Lyceum revenues collapsed. In the end in 1899 he surrendered the lease of the Lyceum to a syndicate, who employed him as its leading actor and director. But the syndicate broke up and dispersed his carefully built up and long-nurtured company of permanent staff, almost certainly to save money. Then in 1902 the insistence of the London County Council on £20,000 worth of alterations to the theatre to meet new fire regulations sent the syndicate into receivership. The Lyceum, long the recognized temple of dramatic art, was sold, gutted and turned into a music hall – the ultimate desecration of Irving's ideal. His last new production, *Dante*, mounted at the Theatre Royal, Drury Lane in 1903, was an expensive failure and Irving took to the provinces, touring continuously until having announced his retirement, he embarked on the final tour which ended prematurely with his death in Bradford.[4]

The basis of his eminence was of course his fame as an actor. It was, in terms of the West End, overnight fame. He had been a respected character actor in London and the provinces for some years when he opened in *The Bells* at the Lyceum in 1871, mesmerized the audience with his study of the haunted and

guilt-ridden Alsatian burgomaster and became a star. As one newspaper put it
on 26 November, 1892: 'On this morning twenty-one years ago Mr. Irving, like
Byron, awoke to find himself famous.' He rethought Shakespeare, presenting
imaginative new interpretations of classic roles, some of which (Hamlet, Shylock,
Benedick, Richard III) succeeded, while others (Malvolio, Othello, Macbeth)
failed. He sought to revive the tradition of English poetic drama, by staging the
verse dramas of the Poet Laureate Lord Tennyson (*Queen Mary*, *The Cup*, and
Becket) and by commissioning new poetic dramas from W.G. Wills and others
(*Charles the First*, *King Arthur*, *Vanderdecken*). He also revived the classic
Victorian melodramas, bringing them to a peak of artistic achievement (*The
Lyons Mail*, *The Corsican Brothers*, *Louis XI*). In all his roles, he created
continuous, carefully worked out, in-depth psychological portraits. It was called
naturalism but it was not what we would understand by the term. It was still
larger than life and it externalized emotion, but it was closer to reality than the
stylized form that had preceded it.

Irving thought and wrote much about acting, and was anxious to promote
good writing about the actor's art. He therefore suggested the republication of
the *Essay on the Actor's Art* by the French actor François Joseph Talma (first
published in 1825). Irving provided a preface to the 1883 English reprint. He
found much in Talma's essay with which to agree and he regularly quoted him
with approval. In particular, Irving endorsed Talma's preference for naturalistic
speech over declamation, his concern for historical fidelity in settings and
costumes, his belief in the need for a powerful, expressive and well-modulated
voice, and his stress on 'an extreme sensibility and a profound intelligence' as the
great qualities of a great actor. The sensibility allowed the actor to enter into 'the
most tragic situations and the most terrible of the passions' and the intelligence
allowed him to judge the impressions these created: 'It selects, arranges them,
and subjects them to calculation. If sensibility furnishes the objects, the
intelligence brings them into play.'

Similarly when *The Paradox of Acting* by Denis Diderot, the French *philosophe*,
was translated into English and published also in 1883, Irving again provided a
preface and this time found much with which to disagree. Diderot's entire work
was based on a series of propositions which Irving rejected fundamentally.
Diderot argued that actors were mimics and puppets of their writers. He rejected
the idea of sensibility because it led actors to rely on the inspiration of the
moment and ignore study, to wallow in morbid emotions and abandon the
intentions of the author. Irving, on the other hand, believed in the control and
direction of the actor's sensibility. Diderot supported formal declamation which
Irving rejected. Invited to speak on acting at Harvard University in 1885, Irving
contrasted the Talma and Diderot philosophies and proposed his own rules,
endorsing the requirement for sensibility and intelligence, urging close and

detailed study of the text, recommending the aspiring actor to pay great attention to elocution and pronunciation that should be 'simple and unaffected', to train the body and cultivate 'suppleness, elasticity and grace'. He praised ensemble playing, the careful development of 'business' and byplay, and he exhorted his audience above all to remember that 'excellence in any part is attained only by arduous labour, unswerving purpose and unfailing discipline'. His firm views embroiled him in sharp controversies about the nature of acting with such adversaries as the French actor Constant Coquelin and the poet George Barlow, fought out in the pages of the literary magazines.[5]

But Irving is rightly remembered not just as a great actor but as the dominant force in British theatre between 1870 and 1900, setting new standards in staging and production, and working tirelessly to elevate the art of acting and the status of the profession. Irving believed that 'the theatre must be carried on as a business, or it will fail as an art'. He gave people what they wanted but at the same time sought to educate them and elevate their artistic taste.

Irving's success in turning his theatre into a temple of high art is attested by a contemporary newspaper account of the Lyceum phenomenon inspired by the 1893 opening of *Becket*. For all its sneering metropolitan sophistication, it is sharply observed and has an air of accuracy about it.

> A Lyceum success, of course, is not exactly synonymous with a popular success, because the drama of the Lyceum and the acting of Mr Irving have passed out of the region of criticism and individual taste, and have become for thousands of middle-class householders a convention as firmly established as going to church on Sunday. The Lyceum is, in a sense, the cathedral of dramatic art, with Mr Irving for its high priest. Everybody goes there, and nearly everybody likes going there – those that don't are generally ashamed to confess it ... We desire to speak of Lyceum productions with at least as much respect as is due to the Equator. In sober earnest, there is nothing but the heartiest praise to be given to drama of the highest class, interpreted by the foremost actor and actress of our day, and staged with the nicest combination of refined taste with prodigal magnificence. Yet sometimes the idea will suggest itself that a taste for the Lyceum drama is acquired – that it is something like the bottle of old port that is opened with as much reverence as if it were a coffin, like the good clothes and good manners and good intentions the average man wears on a Sunday. Ordinary folk, it may be noted, do not 'drop in' at the Lyceum ... They go to that hallowed house of set purpose, putting their houses in order before they go, and reading up the book of the play (when obtainable) as a course of training for the entertainment. They enjoy themselves very much, and they come away telling each other what a wonderful actor Mr Irving is, what a charming play it was, and how much the British drama has been elevated of recent years. It is all quite genuine, quite sincere; but it is just a small bit funny.[6]

Herbert Swears, honorary secretary of the Irving Dramatic Club, the amateur actors who were inspired by their hero to stage an annual Shakespearean production, writing in 1939, confirmed the importance of the Lyceum to its audience:

> It is very difficult to-day for people to realize the position that the Lyceum held in the public estimation in the 'eighties and 'nineties of the last century. It was not then so much a theatre as a temple to be entered with bated breath. There was a sacerdotal air about the entire building. The entrance hall was covered with sombre hangings. The lighting dim. Small boys like acolytes distributed the programmes. When you entered the precincts you at once absorbed this rarefied atmosphere. A high priest, in the shape of Mr Joseph Hurst, sat remotely in the box office. If he smiled when rendering your change, it was a thing to be remembered.[7]

Alfred Wareing recalled the attentiveness of the devotees:

> The gallery audience at the Lyceum on first nights was unlike any other. The youthful enthusiasts were the minority, for those who had watched Irving from the beginning were always there, constant and loyal and enthusiastic, but always critical. There was the master boot-maker from Hoxton, the foreman compositor from Marylebone, the Soho dressing-case maker, and such like. We youngsters got to know them and their cronies well, and encouraged their stories of famous Lyceum first nights which they would repeat on the slightest prompting. They had found Irving, had helped him to climb to the position which they were determined he should maintain without a rival. To them, Beerbohm Tree was of no account, a fashionable actor with a lot of swell friends, and terribly jealous of 'the guv'nor', they said. One learned many things in the two or three hours wait, which was quite long enough to secure a seat in the centre of the third or fourth row. Our enthusiasm was not so very extravagant when it came to 'queuing up'. Irving inspired more affection and esteem than we can realize to-day, even those who criticized his mannerisms, admired him for his ungrudging efforts to give his very utmost. They knew he was as loyal a servant of the public as any actor of the day. He was a principal topic in the eighties, and continually discussed. There was Irving mania and Irving phobia lurking in every gathering. Long before I was taken to see him as Shylock I had learned a lot about him, and when I saw, and felt, too, the greatest personality I have known in the Theatre, I heard the Theatre calling me to its service.[8]

The received view of the history of Victorian theatre, first articulated in the nineteenth century and repeated in the standard theatre histories written in the twentieth century, is that in the early nineteenth century the middle classes deserted the theatre which remained until the 1860s resolutely plebeian, the haunt of noisy audiences, hack writers, crude melodrama and a broad external acting style. Then in the 1860s and 1870s the middle classes began to return *en masse* to the theatre, with the rise of society comedy and drama, the staging of spectacular and archaeologically accurate – therefore educationally improving – productions of Shakespeare and the sustained efforts of actor-managers like the Keans, Samuel Phelps, the Bancrofts and eventually Irving to raise the status of theatre and make it respectable. This resulted in a situation in which East End and West End theatre were different, distinct and separate both in audience and repertoires.

But Michael Booth, writing in 1991, warned: 'it is a serious over-simplification to picture the nineteenth-century theatre, as some still do, as climbing slowly out of a swamp of mob rule and working-class domination in the earlier part of the century to reach an eminence of profound Victorian decorum and middle-class and fashionable patronage of the theatre.'[9] Recent research suggests that the picture was far more varied and diverse.

The audiences for mid-Victorian theatres south of the Thames, in the East End and West End and in North London have recently been investigated with the aid of census returns, maps, playbills, transport timetables, local and national newspapers. It has been shown that 'London theatre audiences in the mid-nineteenth century were so diverse that generic definitions are clearly inappropriate.'[10] London theatre audiences were much more mixed, cross-class, more socially and physically mobile than previously allowed. Some of the cherished myths of Victorian theatre history, notably that Samuel Phelps tamed and gentrified the Sadler's Wells audience in Islington and that the Bancrofts virtually overnight transformed the Prince of Wales's Theatre from a rowdy 'dust-hole' into the harbinger of respectable upmarket theatre, have been exploded. It seems that Phelps's audience was already respectable and culture-hungry when he arrived at Sadler's Wells and the Bancrofts were building on reforms initiated by their predecessors at the Prince of Wales's. The story of the progressive taming and improving of theatre and its audience was a mythic construct of nineteenth-century commentators such as Dickens to vindicate the role of theatre as a vehicle for education, uplift and social improvement.

It remains the case, however, that West End theatre was moving towards greater respectability.[11] Actor-managers like Irving unquestionably saw theatre as precisely that vehicle for education and uplift that contemporary narratives of theatre history articulated. From the 1860s on more and more of the middle classes, along with the respectable working class, patronised the theatre. This theatre-going was facilitated by the completion of the suburban railway system which made it convenient, improved street-lighting and policing which made it safe, and the appearance of extended theatre coverage in the expanding popular press which made it fashionable.

Irving's audience was far from being exclusively middle and upper class. The critic William Archer, a regular attender at the Lyceum, wrote in his 1883 study of Irving:

> The Lyceum is more than fashionable; it is popular. There is probably no artistic institution in England which unites all classes as it does. The whole social menagerie of Du Maurier may be seen any evening in the stalls ... artists, men of science, men of letters, churchmen and soldiers, dons of the universities, magnates of the city, notables

of the bench and bar, meet there on common ground ... The intelligent foreigner is taken there as a matter of course, and the non-intelligent foreigner, the Prince of Crim Tartary or the Ambassador from Cariboo, is taken to the Lyceum just as to the House of Lords or Madame Tussaud's. Brompton and Bayswater congregate in the dress circle, Camberwell and Kentish Town in the upper boxes. In the unreserved places ... gather all who are not included in the above enumeration-the community as opposed to society ... Thus the whole of our modern London, not merely a play-going class, is attracted to the Lyceum; and the attraction is not temporary or fitful but constant.[12]

Irving similarly played to a cross-class audience on his regular provincial tours.

In terms of repertoires, the distinction between East End and West End, between provinces and metropolis has been too sharply drawn. Although there existed a distinctive body of home-grown working-class drama, audiences of all kinds shared certain tastes in common: a love of spectacle, a fascination with crime and criminals, a profound sentimentality and a belief in retribution. This taste embraced both melodrama and Shakespeare. In his first week as an actor at the Royal Lyceum Theatre, Sunderland, in 1856, Irving acted in *Richelieu* and *The Lady of Lyons*. Twenty years later he was starring in the same plays in his own Lyceum Theatre in London. When Irving did *The Lyons Mail*, *The Corsican Brothers* or *Louis XI* at the Lyceum, he was doing the same texts that were regularly done in theatres like the Britannia, Hoxton, and the Standard, Shoreditch. Irving in fact took his own production of *The Bells* to play at the Standard.

Adaptations of Dickens and Scott were produced in the East End, West End and throughout the provinces, as was Shakespeare. Far from being an exclusive preserve of upmarket audiences, Shakespeare was enjoyed by working-class audiences in Birmingham and Leicester.[13] Lavish Shakespeare productions were staged by Edward Saker in Liverpool and by Charles Calvert in Manchester.[14] In his memoirs, the working-class activist Frederick Rogers recalled: 'Shakespeare was always honoured by the working classes' and tells of troupes of working-class amateurs performing Shakespeare at the working men's clubs.[15] So when Irving put on a programme of Shakespeare and melodrama in London and in the provinces, playing to a cross-class audience he was working with the grain of popular theatrical taste.

But Irving's success also derived from the fact that he in many ways embodied the spirit of the age, was swimming with the intellectual currents of the era. His grandson Laurence said of him, 'he fashioned himself in the image of his own time'.[16] What was the image of his time? It was a combination of Evangelical Protestanism, an updated medieval chivalry and the gospel of hard work. Irving's strong commitment to Evangelicalism and chivalry dictated his dramatic repertoire. From Evangelicalism came the powerful concepts of the moral order, the linkage of guilt and remorse and the themes of respectability, domesticity and decency. From chivalry came the dominating and recurring ideas of gentlemanliness and the chivalric code.

As Sir John Martin-Harvey, long a member of his company, declared: 'His work was his life. He lived for nothing else. No man I ever met was so truly lonely as he.'[17] When Ellen Terry visited him in his last illness, she recorded this conversation.

'What a wonderful life you've had, haven't you?'
'Oh yes,' he said quietly. 'A wonderful life of work.'
'And there's nothing better after all, is there?'
'Nothing.'[18]

How he would have warmed to Carlyle's dictum on work, which encapsulates a central strand of the Victorian ethos:

There is a perennial nobleness, and even sacredness, in Work ... It has been written, a man perfects himself by working ... properly speaking, all true Work is religion ... Older than all preached Gospels was this unpreached, inarticulate, but ineradicable, forever-enduring Gospel: Work and therein have wellbeing ... Wheresoever thou findest Disorder, there is thy eternal enemy; attack him swiftly, subdue him; make order of him, subject not of Chaos, but of Intelligence, Divinity and Thee. But above all, where thou findest Ignorance, Stupidity, Brute-Mindedness ... attack it, I say; smite it wisely, unweariedly and rest not while thou livest and it lives.[19]

Irving never spared himself, supervising every aspect of production in his long management of the Lyceum and acting right up to the end in a fearfully demanding series of powerfully emotional roles.

In 1905 Charles Forshaw, an honorary official of the Actors Association and a fellow mason, collected and edited a selection of more than 100 poetical tributes that appeared in the week following Irving's death. He noted that the poems had been written by authors from all walks of life 'from gentlemen who have enjoyed all the advantages of a distinguished University career, down to men whose position in Society is of the humblest possible nature, from an octogenarian to a youth who has barely attained his sixteenth year'.[20] The collection amply attests the reverence with which Irving was regarded in the provinces, recognition of the years of touring which made Great Britain as a whole as familiar with his artistry as the West End of London. Thus alongside the tributes that appeared in *The Times*, the *Daily Telegraph*, *Punch*, and the *Pall Mall Gazette* are poems from the *Swansea Leader*, the *Aberdeen Gazette*, the *Bolton Chronicle*, the *Liverpool Courier*, and the *Huddersfield Examiner*.

This corpus of poems is bound together by recurrent themes, which underline Irving's cultural significance. He is, of course, hailed as a great actor, the greatest of his time, and as 'head of his profession.' He is compared to his great predecessors, Burbage, Betterton, Garrick, Macready, Kemble, Siddons, Phelps, the Keans father and son.[21] In particular he is praised for his dedication, hard work, thoroughness, his sense of artistic purpose, his ability to live his roles.[22] His many great performances form the basis of a large proportion of the poems.[23]

One poem (its author self confessedly 'a man of humble birth and lowly clan' anxious to pay 'my people's tribute') notes his cross-class appeal: 'For loved was he on every hand, by high and low throughout the land.' Another singles out his ability to depict the power of conscience. A third recalls the magnificence of his scenery, sets and *mise-en-scène*.[24]

A second recurrent theme is to celebrate him as an English or British hero or worthy – and here in this imperial age English and British are more or less synonymous.[25]

> Westminster Abbey – in that sacred place
> He is to sleep, to find a resting place,
> Among the great, the noble and the good –
> The finest and the best of England's race.
>
> (*Stockport Advertiser*)

> Broad were his views and keen his sense
> Of what in man was right or wrong,
> His influence was thus immense
> Throughout the land with old and young.
> Mourned by a nation for his worth
> Of character, which ever stood
> High 'mongst the sons of mother earth,
> In thwarting wrong and doing good.
> Then let his ashes 'mong the great
> Of British worthies be at rest;
> And may he in another state
> Be counted as a welcome guest!
>
> (*East Cumberland News*)[26]

He is specifically compared to others of England's greatest sons – to Garrick and Shakespeare but also to Gordon, Browning and Gladstone by one poet, and to Nelson by another.[27]

And what was it that made him a great British hero? It was the essential Victorian virtues which he was recognized as embodying. He is praised for his gentlemanliness and his knightliness. The *Somerset County Gazette*, taking understandable pride in his place of birth, calls him 'the Bayard of the stage, the mimic muse's Galahad, true knight of knights.' By others he is called 'a kindly, noble-hearted gentleman', 'a noble knight', 'a modern Bayard.'[28] *The Liverpool Courier*'s poem ran:

Mourn! England, for the knightly son whose life
Rung, link by link, the chain that binds thy race
In the firm bonds of human brotherhood.
He conjured up the past and made it live –
A lesson and a menace to our age;
He made articulate the thoughts that flit
Impalpably across the page of Time;
And through the mirror of his subtle art
We looked into the very heart of man.

This knightliness was linked specifically to his mission to purify the stage:

To lead thy country to the pure, the good,
Thine was the task so nobly done!
Thy mighty Art, unstain'd, for virtue stood
The laurel of thy Knighthood won:
Placed high by her, our Mother Empress Queen,
Amid her nobles round her throne,
Thy name, for thine unsullied Art, is seen
Marked as the Drama's knight, alone.
(Rev. W. Morgan B.A.)

We mourn a great redeemer of our stage
The long to be remembered Irving age;
Here gentleman and actor were combined,
With stage-craft mingled intellect refined;
Beloved not solely for his master art,
A lofty moulded mind and kindly heart,
Brought worship whence his calling bid him roam,
And won him love and reverence at home.[29]
(*Stockport Advertiser*)

Recurrently, his role as educator, purifier and ennobler of the stage, as moral instructor is singled out. 'The Educator falls – his work goes on' writes one. 'From lowly grade to its exalted height, he raised the art that he had made his bride' says another.[30]

The actor's world he lifted up
From base report and evil sway
Into the purer light of day
Where art and beauty rule the play.
(Laura Halliday)

> He touched the heart as with some potent spell,
> Life's drama he portrayed with master mind,
> He made emotions in the bosom swell,
> And in his words left lasting good behind.
>   (*Bradford Daily Argus*)[31]

Perhaps the most frequent reference is to the last words spoken by Irving upon the stage, 'into Thy hands, O Lord, into Thy hands' in that final performance of *Becket* at the Theatre Royal, Bradford. It made an enormous impact on the contemporary sensibility. It gave the life of Irving for the Victorian public a sense of symmetry, of fulfilment. The actor whose lifelong mission had been to purify and ennoble the stage, to educate and raise the taste of the people, to instil a value system based on Evangelical Protestantism and chivalry dies after playing a martyred archbishop and uttering the words of a still revered poet laureate. The Victorians were convinced that he would go to his heavenly reward. The *Birmingham Weekly Mercury* summed up that peculiarly Victorian sense of certainty, faith, hero-worship, dedication, work and duty that Irving had come to embody:

> 'Into Thy hands, O Lord, into Thy hands!'
> So the great actor breathes his final prayer
> In that last effort (little thought so then)
> Of work and witness for his fellow men,
> Ah! what a seal to his life's work is there!
> Out of that greatness, unto him God-given.
> Still greater heights of greatness he achieved;
> With steadfast purpose wrought what he believed
> To teach the people life's true meanings well,
> And help them to its riches. Is it strange
> His name should be a very household word?
> In every heart and home a chord be stirred
> At his great passing hence? O fitting way!
> Straight from the fervent, commendatory prayer
> He left us, with the words upon our hearts!
> No agonising scene to spoil the hush.
> Into the silence went to meet his call.
> And render up to God his task complete.
> Greatest of all in this. Could he have chosen
> Or those who loved him most, no better way
> For this transition to life's higher stage
> Might there be found. When history on her page
> Records this, with those nobly spoken words,
> 'The readiness is all,' their mighty spell
> Shall work in coming generations well,

No loud-voiced grief must fall beside that bier!
Simple, though great, our national mourning be;
Softly 'The Bells', in which his voice we hear,
Tell out their burden. And though he has passed
Beyond the veil, he still shall speak to us,
Bringing new treasures from our stores of old,
For we, with Irving, Tennyson behold
And Shakespeare moving in our midst to-day,
With soul-wrought messages to all mankind.
Till by such inspiration ever led
Higher and higher, shall we, too, some day find
Our little parts with theirs in God's light manifest.
The pattern-bearers these – we, workers with them blest![32]

2

Chivalry

Victorian society was strictly gendered with men and women expected to fill complementary roles. John Ruskin, citing as his authorities Shakespeare, Scott and Dante, outlined the ideal roles and relationships of men and women in *Of Queen's Gardens*. He insisted that the rights and responsibilities were inexorably linked and not to be considered separately.

> The man's power is active, progressive, defensive. He is eminently the doer, the creator, the discoverer, the defender. His intellect is for speculation and invention; his energy for adventure, for war, and for conquest, wherever war is just, wherever conquest is necessary. But the woman's power is for rule, not for battle, – and her intellect is not for invention or creation, but for sweet ordering, arrangement, and decision. She sees the qualities of things, their claims and their places ... By her office, and place, she is protected from all danger and temptation. The man, in his rough work in open world, must encounter all peril and trial; – to him, therefore, must be the failure, the offence, the inevitable error; often he must be wounded, or subdued; often misled; and *always* hardened. But he guards the woman from all this; within his house, as ruled by her, unless she herself has sought it, need enter no danger, no temptation, no cause of error or offence. This is the true nature of home – it is the place of Peace; the shelter, not only from all injury, but from all terror, doubt and division ... so far as it is a sacred place, a vestal temple, a temple of the hearth watched over by Household Gods, before whose faces none may come but those whom they can receive with love ... so far it vindicates the name, and fulfils the praise, of Home.[1]

Declaring that 'to the original purity and power of [chivalry] we owe the defence alike of faith, of law, and of love', Ruskin elevated the chivalric relationship, in which the knight is subject to the direction of his lady, as the highest form of manliness. As Walter E. Houghton wrote, 'this lecture of Ruskin's is the most important single document I know for the characteristic idealization of love, women and the home in Victorian thought'.[2]

This conventional wisdom of the Victorian age was summed up poetically by Tennyson in *The Princess*:

> Man for the field and woman for the hearth;
> Man for the sword and for the needle she;
> Man with the head and woman with the heart;
> Man to command and woman to obey;
> All else confusion.[3]

And by Kingsley even more succinctly in *The Three Fishers*: 'For men must work and women must weep.'

Manly men, womanly women, the sacredness of hearth and home, these were the cardinal elements of the Victorian world view. They were also Irving's values. The dominant ideology of Victorian masculinity was chivalry and its exponent was the chivalric gentleman.

What was a gentleman? Mark Girouard defines him:

> A chivalrous gentleman was brave, straightforward and honourable, loyal to his monarch, country and friends, unfailingly true to his word, ready to take issue with anyone he saw ill-treating a woman, a child or an animal. He was a natural leader of men, and others unhesitatingly followed his lead. He was fearless in war and on the hunting field, and excelled at all manly sports; but, however tough with the tough, he was invariably gentle to the weak; above all he was always tender, respectful and courteous to women, regardless of their rank. He put the needs of others before his own; as an officer he always saw that his men were looked after and made comfortable before thinking of himself, as landlord he took good care of his dependents. He was always ready to give up his own time to come to the help of others, especially those less fortunate than himself. He was an honourable opponent and a good loser; he played games for the pleasure of playing, not to win. He never boasted. He was not interested in money. He was an ardent and faithful lover, but hated coarse talk, especially about women.[4]

The emergence of the chivalric gentleman was no accident. The concept was deliberately promoted by key figures of the nineteenth century, such as Thomas Carlyle, Charles Kingsley, Edward Fitzgerald, Robert Baden-Powell, as a code of behaviour for the ruling elite. But it also filtered down through the rest of society by the agency of popular culture. It was not deemed to be class specific. As Samuel Smiles, one of the gurus of the nineteenth century, argued: 'Riches and rank have no necessary connexion with genuine and gentlemanly qualities. The poor man may be a true gentleman – in spirit and daily life. He may be honest, truthful, upright, polite, temperate, courageous, self-respecting and self-helping – that is, be a true gentleman.'[5] The concept was promoted to mitigate fears about mass democracy, the worship of money (a concomitant of the Industrial Revolution) and the placing of expediency before principle (which has ever been an element in politics).

The concept emerged as part of the reaction of the Victorian Age against what had gone before. It centred in this case on the definition of 'manliness'. The dominant idea of manliness in the early decades of the nineteenth century was the Regency sporting ethic, celebrated by writers like Pierce Egan. It involved physical prowess, courage and endurance but also drinking, gambling, violence and brutality. It was centred on such cruel pursuits as prizefighting, cockfighting and dogfighting. Appealing as they did to all classes, these pursuits were seen as democratic, patriotic and a source of national strength. This ethic was to be driven underground by the purification of society under the impact of Evangelical respectability. But it maintained its hold, in for instance the novels of G.A. Lawrence, which highlighted war, sport and fighting, and featured hard-riding, hard-drinking, two-fisted, anti-intellectual, godless aristocratic snobs. *The Saturday Review* on 12 September 1857, described Lawrence's Guy Livingstone as 'a hero of the iron kind, unequalled for strength of body, will and temper – in boxing and riding, a demigod to his sporting set and heroically and Byronically overbearing and insolent to the world in general'. But these characteristics, which would nowadays be called *macho*, also survived in a strand of working-class manhood, qualities which centred on sexual prowess, how much you could drink and how hard you were. It was a view that was almost invariably chauvinistic, sexist and racist. It was self-centred, self-gratifying, self-congratulatory.

It was to mitigate this prevailing ethic of barbaric yobbishness that alternative models of manliness were propounded and developed in the Victorian Age. One was Christian Manliness or as it was mockingly known by its critics 'Muscular Christianity'.[6] This was a tradition stretching back to St Paul but reinforced by the Cromwellian Puritanism rehabilitated by Thomas Carlyle. It was crucially developed by Charles Kingsley and Thomas Hughes and grew out of the views articulated by the 'Broad Church' liberal religious tradition of Samuel Taylor Coleridge, Dr Thomas Arnold and F.D. Maurice. This group challenged the social and political *status quo* of the early nineteenth century in a fundamental way, scorning the triumphalist doctrine of material progress associated with Macaulay and asserting more important moral, spiritual and cultural values. Coleridge laid particular stress on moral strength, in defining manliness.[7] F.D. Maurice, who advocated universal brotherhood and was a leading figure in Christian Socialism, saw life as a continual battle for righteousness and Christ as the champion of energy, manliness and nobility. Carlyle, the great advocate of heroes and hero-worship, also saw life as a struggle: 'Man is created to fight; he is perhaps best of all definable as a born soldier; his life "a battle and a march" under the right General.'[8] But he provided the rationale for the creation of the moral hero; someone who would triumph in the struggle over adversity but by the maintenance of the right moral qualities. Arnold stressed the importance of moral and spiritual education. From these different sources emerged a world view based on the gospel of work, the worship of heroes, the celebration of God in nature, an idealized vision of the past, and the promotion of cross-class sympathy. This world view produced the Christian Socialists, whose aim was the regeneration, purification and redirection of the nation through a loving, committed and socially active Christianity, creating the kingdom of God on earth.

Two of its most notable advocates and propagandists were Charles Kingsley and Thomas Hughes, whose view was sharpened and defined by the religious upheavals of the mid-Victorian period, in particular the dispute between Kingsley and John Henry Newman about the nature of Christianity. Kingsley could not accept the rejection of the physical world that Newman was advancing, stressing instead the importance of direct Christian action in the world. He was equally opposed to the promotion of celibacy, asceticism and what he saw as 'fastidious, maundering, die-away effeminacy'. So Kingsley articulated a comprehensive alternative world view in his novels, where discussions of contemporary social and political problems rub shoulders with satire, moralizing and *mens sana in corpore sano* propaganda. The principal elements in this world view were the promotion of physical strength, courage, health, the importance of married love and family life, the elements of duty and service to mankind, and the scientific study of the natural world to discover the divine pattern of the moral universe. Kingsley differed from other advocates of Christian manliness in laying stress on the particular importance of married love; something which undoubtedly proceeded from his own highly sexed nature.

Hughes was well aware of a boy's need to assert and demonstrate his masculinity. One of his objects in writing *Tom Brown's Schooldays*, one of the most famous and widely read books of the nineteenth century, was to advocate the particular form of moral manliness that he and Kingsley both articulated and themselves embodied. Dubbed 'Muscular Christianity', it was a term Kingsley disliked but Hughes readily embraced. He provided a very careful definition of it in *Tom Brown at Oxford*, distinguishing Muscular Christians from those whom he calls mere 'musclemen' and who are the barbarian yobs of all classes mentioned earlier. Hughes writes:

> The only point in common between the two being that both hold it to be a good thing to have strong and well-exercised bodies, ready to be put at the shortest notice to any work of which bodies are capable and to do it well. Here all likeness ends; for the 'muscleman' seems to have no belief whatever as to the purpose for which his body has been given him, except some hazy idea that it is to go up and down the world with him, belabouring men and captivating women for his benefit or pleasure, at once the servant and fomenter of those fierce and brutal passions which he seems to think it a necessity, and rather a fine thing than otherwise, to indulge and obey. Whereas, so far as I know, the least of the muscular Christians has hold of the old chivalrous and Christian belief, that a man's body is given to him to be trained and brought into subjection, and then used for the protection of the weak, the advancement of all righteous causes, and the subduing of the earth which God has given to the children of men.[9]

For Hughes, fighting included self-conquest, moral crusading, and self-defence. He also added with regard to physical combat: 'As to fighting, keep out of it if you can by all means. When time comes, if it ever should, that you have to say "Yes" or "No" to a challenge to fight, say "No" if you can.'[10] The idea put forward by his critics that Hughes advocated mere physical courage and athletic proficiency is bogus; that was the ethic of his rivals. He sought to channel Man's aggressive instincts into productive and morally defensible channels.

He elaborated further on his concept of manliness in *The Manliness of Christ*. Here he defined manliness as tenderness and thoughtfulness for others, readiness to bear pain and even death, unswerving loyalty to truth, subordination of the human will to one's sense of duty. Tom Brown embodied these qualities exactly. Hughes added: 'True manliness is as likely to be found in a weak as in a strong body ... a great athlete may be a brute or a coward, while a truly manly man can be neither.'[11] Nor was manliness an exclusive attribute of the upper classes: Hughes cited examples of true manliness shown by miners at Pontypridd, ordinary soldiers on the *Birkenhead* and a gambler in St Louis rescuing women and children from a fire.

But in the hands of Kingsley and Hughes, Christian concepts of morality and service became fused with what had become a dominant value system and that is chivalry. Hughes gives us the clue when he talks of muscular Christians embracing 'the old chivalrous and Christian belief'. Hughes and Kingsley were steeped in the idea of chivalry. Kingsley described himself as 'a joyous knight errant' and Hughes as 'a knight of the Round Table.' Preaching before Queen Victoria, Kingsley declared: 'The age of chivalry is never past so long as there is a wrong left unredressed on earth or a man or woman left to say: 'I will redress that wrong or spend my life in the attempt.'' In *Tom Brown's Schooldays* Hughes has Tom Brown's father say, 'If he'll only turn out a brave, helpful, truth-telling, Englishman and a gentleman and a Christian, that's all I want', and in *Westward Ho!*, Kingsley's hero, Amyas Leigh, declares it to be 'the finest thing in the world to be a gentleman'. They are endorsing the newly fashionable ethic of chivalry. This endorsement contrasts markedly with the comment of their mentor, Dr Thomas Arnold, who in 1829 wrote: 'If I were called upon to name what spirit of evil predominantly deserved the name of Anti-Christ, I should name the spirit of chivalry.' For he equated chivalry with feudalism, tyranny and class arrogance, all that was reactionary and needed eliminating. But within twenty years, it was seen as synonymous with true Christian manliness.[12]

Such beliefs were the end product of a process essentially initiated by Sir Walter Scott. Interest in matters medieval and chivalric had revived as part of the whole Romantic movement. Scott filtered his extensive historical research through his Romantic imagination to produce, in poems and novels like *Ivanhoe* and *The Talisman*, a stylized and idealized chivalric world. The medieval revival which these works triggered had enormous ramifications, which Mark Girouard in his book *Return to Camelot* explores with considerable relish and lavish illustration. At one extreme there was the staging of full-scale tournaments and the building of elaborate and fantastical imitation Gothic castles. In the arts, there was a massive revival of interest in the cycle of stories about King Arthur and the

Knights of the Round Table. Their potent mythic appeal and richly allusive imagery flow through Pre-Raphaelite painting, the poetry of Tennyson and Matthew Arnold, and the countless editions, adaptations and illustrations of Malory. But, in the practical field, there was also the elaboration of a code of behaviour for life – the reformulation of the image of the gentleman as the idealized medieval knight, the embodiment of the virtues of bravery, loyalty, courtesy, generosity, modesty, purity and compassion, and endowed with an indelible sense of *noblesse oblige* towards women, children and social inferiors. It was the now forgotten Kenelm Digby in his now unread *The Broadstone of Honour* (first published in 1822) who made the idealized medieval chivalry of Scott a living and meaningful code of life for the gentlemen of his own day. The basic ideas of Digby – that character is more important than intellect, that the training of the body in athletic exercise is vital to the inculcation of character, that money-making is squalid and that there was a natural affinity between gentlemen and the lower classes – formed dominant strands in Britain's national ideology for nearly a century.[13]

Norman Vance argues that the heyday of Christian manliness and Christian chivalry was essentially from the 1830s to the 1860s; thereafter manliness and Christianity became increasingly separated. There is some force in this. The secularization of chivalry can be seen in for instance the superseding of the muscular Christian juvenile fiction of Kingston and Ballantyne from the mid nineteenth century by the more straightforwardly imperial-military fiction of G.A. Henty and Gordon Stables at its end. It would also fit the superseding of Evangelicalism by Imperialism in the same period as the dominant ideology. It might be argued of course that Imperialism was itself a religion but it was a religion more of action than of theological discussion. Even if it was secularized, the ideal remained strong and intact. Chivalry continued as an essential thread of Imperialism and as the crucial definition of true manliness, as the constructive alternative to yobbery and barbarism. It was reinforced by the new cult of athleticism and found potent expression in the public schools.[14]

Chivalry infused every aspect of Victorian life, in particular the key institutions. Games, chapel and missions to the slums became significant elements in the new public schools, which were training and turning out the elite to run Britain and the Empire. As Mark Girouard writes, from the 1870s:

> Actual knights in armour appear as school trophies, and abound in the form of statues or stained glass figures, especially as memorials to the Crimean, Boer or Great Wars … In school magazines, the articles interspersed among the ever-increasing accounts of school games include ones on muscular Christianity, Kingsley, King Arthur, Tennyson's *Idylls*, chivalry and the *Nibelungenlied*.[15]

Sir Henry Newbolt, poet laureate of the public schools, claimed in 1917 that the public school system was essentially based on the codes and structures of chivalry.[16] In the second half of the nineteenth century the concepts of gentleman and sportsman became interchangeable with the rise of the cult of athleticism and transfer of the chivalric imagery to football and other fields. An entire genre of popular literature, the public school story, read by every class, promoted ideas of chivalry, athleticism and the public school code.[17]

From the 1870s onwards, the British Empire and Imperialism were linked with chivalry. It was seen as a duty to govern the undeveloped areas of the world, an idea powerfully advanced by Froude, Ruskin, Kingsley and Carlyle, key thinkers and publicists of the age. In 1891 the influential journalist W.T. Stead declared: 'The English-speaking race is one of the chief of God's chosen agents for executing coming improvements in the lot of mankind.'[18] The Empire was thus seen to have nothing to do with making money and everything to do with a chivalric mission. The heroes of the Indian Mutiny were cast in a chivalric mould, with General Outram, for instance, being dubbed 'The Bayard of India' after the celebrated medieval warrior. St George slaying the dragon became the symbol of the Empire; one of its influential bodies was the Round Table, an imperial propaganda organization; the imperialist Primrose League had chivalric divisions in its organization, its members being called 'knights and dames'. New orders of chivalry appeared to reward servants of the Empire: Knight Commander of the Star of India, Knight Commander of the Indian Empire, Knight of the British Empire.

The Boy Scouts, perhaps the most influential of youth organizations to emerge from the nineteenth century, was similarly steeped in chivalry. Baden-Powell, their founder, devoted a chapter of his *Scouting for Boys* to chivalry, encouraged the Scouts to read *Ivanhoe*, *The Broadstone of Honour* and Doyle's *The White Company*, based the qualities for good Scouts on his understanding of the chivalric code; he even at one time planned to call the Scouts, 'The Young Knights of the Empire'.

Popular fiction at every level was steeped in chivalry. It was there in the retellings of Malory and Froissart, in medieval romances such as those of Scott, Charlotte Yonge and Conan Doyle, which were all best-sellers, in the poetry of Tennyson, Newbolt and W.E. Henley, in the popular histories like Charlotte Yonge's *The Book of Golden Deeds* and W.H. Fitchett's *Deeds that Won the Empire*, in children's and juvenile literature from Marryat to Henty, and in the thrillers and romances of the late nineteenth century by Rider Haggard, Robert Louis Stevenson, Anthony Hope and Stanley Weyman.

Irving was strongly committed to the idea of gentlemanliness. He set out to turn himself into a gentleman. While still a clerk, he took elocution lessons, and, revealingly, drew up a list of fines to be imposed on other clerks to improve their English, eliminating cockneyisms, ungrammatical expressions and redundant aspirates. Accent and bearing were the outward and visible signs of innate gentlemanliness and Irving worked on this. His performances from an early date were praised for their gentlemanliness. Gentlemanliness was the keynote of many of his Shakespearean performances, Hamlet, Benedick, Othello, Malvolio, for instance. It was regularly commented on by the critics. Ellen Terry noted that Irving based his interpretation of Benedick on the Duke of Sutherland.[19] But this desire to gentrify his characters sometimes backfired. This was notably the case with Malvolio in *Twelfth Night*. The actor Frank Benson recalled his performance:

> Irving had far too strong a personality for Malvolio ... his Malvolio was distinctly a gentleman, not a buffoon; he was dignified, not heavy. It was inconceivable that that commanding presence should be a mere steward. He looked like some great Spanish hidalgo – a painting of Velasquez; never could he have become the butt of his fellow servants.[20]

In this his insight coincided with that of Ellen Terry, who wrote: 'Henry's Malvolio was fine and dignified, but not good for the play.'[21] Benson saw this as a continuing problem:

> All that Irving did was 'fine', so fine that, at times, it came near to defeating his end. Doctor Primrose, for example, was too fine for a country parson; Lesurques again was too fine for the bourgeois son of a village postmaster in the same way that Malvolio was too fine for the servants' hall.[22]

Irving sent his sons Harry and Laurence to Marlborough, to ensure the gentlemanly public school education for them that he had been denied. He would have been delighted to learn that Queen Victoria, upon meeting him for the first time, described him in her diary as 'gentleman-like'.[23]

The ultimate Victorian chivalric myth was the story of King Arthur and his Knights of the Round Table. Interest in Arthur had revived with the whole Romantic revival and the renewed interest in chivalry. Malory's *Morte D'Arthur*, last reprinted in 1634, went through three different editions in 1816 and 1817. Scott, who had studied Malory in detail, included an Arthurian tale in *The Bridal of Triermain* (1813). Bulwer Lytton published the first full-length Arthurian epic of the Victorian period, his poem *King Arthur*, in 1848. But it was Tennyson's poetic cycle *Idylls of the King*, published between 1859 and 1885, that exercised the greatest influence on the nineteenth century. The Arthurian stories were recast to appeal to Victorian ideals and sensibilities, with King Arthur, modelled on Prince Albert, depicted as the ideal ruler. The knights, with their code 'live pure, speak true, right wrong, follow the King', are prototype public school boys and the Lancelot-Guinevere story is told as a warning against the adultery and immorality that could undermine a society based on marriage, fidelity and

Christianity. Despite the dominance of the Tennysonian version, Victorian poets returned compulsively to the saga and there were Arthurian poems from Matthew Arnold, William Morris, Algernon Swinburne, Thomas Hardy, George Macdonald, Edmund Gosse, Laurence Binyon, George du Maurier and many lesser known writers.[24] The visual image of the knights inspired a whole raft of Victorian artists, notably the pre-Raphaelites. Arthur and the Round Table were a life-long obsession of Sir Edward Burne-Jones, but memorable images of the stories and characters were also painted by Dante Gabriel Rossetti, G.F. Watts, Joseph Noel Paton and Arthur Hughes.[25] Armoured knights, innocent maidens, evil sorcerers, designing sirens, banners, swords and lances populated the Victorian imagination. The Queen's Robing Room in the Palace of Westminster and the Oxford Union were decorated with Arthurian frescoes.

Irving had long wanted to put the legends on stage at the Lyceum. He suggested it to Tennyson, who refused, on the grounds that he had already tackled the subject in his *Idylls of the King*. He commissioned and paid for a *King Arthur* play from W.G. Wills (1890).[26] But after studying it, Irving felt it was unplayable, and secured another play from Joseph Comyns Carr (1893). He lavished on it the finest talents he could secure: scenery and costumes designed by Sir Edward Burne-Jones, music by Sir Arthur Sullivan and star roles for himself (Arthur), Ellen Terry (Guinevere), Johnston Forbes-Robertson (Lancelot) and Geneviève Ward (Morgan Le Fay). It was produced in 1895 and received ninety-one consecutive performances at the Lyceum, was revived briefly ahead of the fifth American tour (1895–96) where it was played seventy-four times and was given twelve times on a short provincial tour of England in June and July 1896.[27]

The play begins with a prologue in which Arthur is led by Merlin to the Magic Mere, where the sword Excalibur rises from the water and ethereal voices declare that the sword is given to the son of Uther Pendragon, who will rule the Kingdom, which is anachronistically called England rather than Britain throughout. Merlin tells Arthur he is Uther's son and will rule. At the same time he sees a vision of Guinevere and falls in love with her, declaring that he wants her as his Queen. The voices warn that, because of her beauty, great evil will befall the kingdom. But he takes the sword and resolves to rule.

Act 1, 'The Holy Grail', is set in the Great Hall of Camelot. A vision of the Holy Grail has caused many knights to take a vow to search for it. Mark of Cornwall and Ryons of Wales are plotting against Arthur, in league with Mordred, whose mother Morgan Le Fay wants to secure the throne for her son. Morgan reveals that she has divined that Guinevere loves Sir Lancelot and she wants to use this knowledge to break up the Round Table. Lancelot, returning to court, sees a vision of the Grail and resolves to join the quest. Elaine, the Fair Maid of Astolat, intercedes with Queen Guinevere to promote her cause with Lancelot, whom she loves. Despite her own love for Lancelot, Guinevere does so, but

Lancelot reveals his love for the Queen. This is one of the reasons he wishes to leave court. They cannot consummate their love because of 'the love of heaven, of honour and of – him' (Arthur). Arthur, however, forbids Lancelot to leave court and prevails on Guinevere to endorse his request. Act 2, 'The Queen's Maying', is set in a wood where lovers meet and express their feelings. Guinevere and Lancelot meet and embrace, and are seen by Mordred. Mordred knows that the rebels of Wales and Cornwall are besieging Caerleon and has killed the envoy bringing the news to Arthur. Morgan has stolen the scabbard of Excalibur and thrown it into the Mere. Act 3, 'The Black Barge', has Mordred confronting Lancelot with his knowledge of the love between him and Guinevere. He offers Lancelot Guinevere in return for his support in overthrowing Arthur in alliance with the rebels. Lancelot rejects the offer and Mordred threatens to expose him if he reveals Mordred's schemes to Arthur. Elaine, who has committed suicide out of unrequited love for Lancelot, is carried in, her body bearing a letter explaining that she dies because Lancelot loved another. Mordred tells the King that the object of Lancelot's affections is the Queen. Morgan confirms it. Lancelot denies the charge but Guinevere confesses. Arthur raises his sword but cannot bring himself to kill Lancelot. He dismisses him and sets out to raise the siege of Caerleon. Act 4, 'The Passing of Arthur', sees Guinevere in prison. Mordred comes to offer her the throne alongside him when he takes it. She rejects his offer. Arthur is rumoured to be dead, Mordred takes the throne and presides at Guinevere's trial, sentencing her to be burned. She calls for a champion. Arthur appears and fights for her, but is mortally wounded. Arthur gives Bedivere Excalibur to throw into the sea. News arrives that Lancelot has killed Mordred. Arthur dies, with the repentant Guinevere at his feet.

The production was for the most part received with great enthusiasm. One reviewer rhapsodized:

> The series of brilliant presentations which have raised the Lyceum to the position of the chief home in England of the poetical and imaginative drama reached their climax in the production of Mr Carr's play of *King Arthur*. It may be doubted, indeed, whether in any house in any country a vision so dreamlike in beauty, uniting so divinely all that is most elaborate and conscientious in detail with whatever is most passionately suggestive in poetry, has been realised. Some lengthiness of dialogue, which will shortly be excised, constitute all that can be urged against the play. To compensate for these, there are scenes exquisite in harmony, ideal in tenderness, and harrowing in pathos, together with a picture of feudal life so exact and so brilliant as to constitute an absolute revivification of history. No mere display of empty pageantry is exhibited … To realise how exquisite all is, a visit to the theatre is indispensable. Language is powerless to depict the grace and distinction of the life presented, the magic charm and allurement of successive scenes and the potent witchery of the whole. No stone has been left unturned to secure the result … A finer performance or more artistic and intellectual treat has not been seen in modern days, and the whole carries us back to the plays of the Elizabethan times.

The critic praised Sullivan for 'music sweet as love,' Burne-Jones for 'costumes of ravishing beauty' and Comyns Carr for 'a drama blameless, shapely, poignant'. He was evidently overwhelmed by the atmosphere of the production:

> There is about the performance that something undefinable, ineffable, impenetrable, that poets strive to express in phrases such as 'The light that never was on sea or land'. To see Mr Irving standing in the misty morning light, erect, triumphant, inspired, in his armour of sombre black, with the newly-won Excalibur held aloft to the skies, to watch Miss Terry, the very Guinevere of fact or legend, with a robe of indescribable richness and sheen rippling like water to her feet, and to contemplate the sad, virile, ascetic face of Lancelot … is to charge the memory with pictures that can never pass away.[28]

Terry and Irving were seen as ideal embodiments of femininity and chivalric masculinity.

One critic wrote of Terry:

> Ellen Terry has given performances in which there were greater moments than any that signalize her portrayal of Guinevere, but she has given no performance that was more definite, more smoothly rounded, or more evenly sustained. Her presentment of Guinevere is an explicit display of the true nature of what may, perhaps, be called the representative woman – a nature that rests not upon mind but upon emotion. Guinevere possesses attributes that make her individual and unique, but in this respect she is a type, and one of great significance. Thus portrayed, this is a woman who is not vicious but lives in sensation, not in thought, and who acts from feeling and not from principle … That personality, Ellen Terry, with her strange, wild beauty, her poetic frenzy, her endless caprice, her restlessness, her intuitional rather than intellectual methods, and her April temperament of smiles and tears, embodied without the least show of effort – making it superb.

Another critic wrote of Irving:

> Henry Irving's embodiment of King Arthur had in part been prefigured by his embodiment of Charles the First. The impersonations widely differ, but in both there are peculiar and identical attributes of majesty. Chivalry, sublimity and pathos … No actor of our time has so much distinction or can use the manner of lofty courtesy with a simpler grace. A man's love, when it is true, hallows its object and makes it sacred. Irving's King Arthur – perfectly poised, free, happy, resolute, calm, looking with clear eyes upon all the world and mighty with the purpose to make it pure and beautiful – was the vital image of that feeling.[29]

There were some more critical reviews. Some reviewers compared Carr's play unfavourably with Tennyson's *Idylls of the King*. Others thought Irving's role essentially subordinate to those of Lancelot and Guinevere. But against these, it even won over the normally severe William Archer, who wrote in *The World*:

A splendid pageant and a well-built folk play … these are the ingredients of the dish served up at the Lyceum … and hugely relished by the audience. *King Arthur* is a genuine success, of that there is no doubt; and it deserves its fortune. In producing such a work, Mr Irving is putting his opportunities and resources to a worthy use. In the historic or legendary pageant play he seems to have found the formula best suited to the present stage of his career.

He praised Comyns Carr's text:

Mr Carr writes creditable blank verse, correct, and by no means lacking in dignified sonority; and he knows how to put a play together much better than Tennyson ever did.

He lauded the acting:

The character of Arthur will undoubtedly be reckoned among Mr Irving's finer achievements. He embodies it with incomparable nobility and refinement, and speaks his verses with perfect distinction and purity of accent … Miss Ellen Terry is an ideal Guinevere to the eye; it is impossible to conceive a statelier or more gracious figure; and her performance is altogether charming. Mr Forbes Robertson is an etherealised Lancelot. His figure is absolutely beautiful; but it suggests an 'affable archangel' … rather than a knight of the Round Table; or if indeed a knight, then the stainless Galahad rather than the superbly human Lancelot … His acting, let me hasten to add, is perfect of its kind.

His only real criticism concerned what we would now call the special effects. 'The spectacle is gorgeous throughout; but the supernatural element, the *diablerie*, if I may put it so … is, from first to last, inferior.' By this he meant the appearance of Excalibur in the prologue and of the Holy Grail in Act One.[30]

Sir John Martin-Harvey, who played Sir Dagonet in the play, recalled in his autobiography:

The part of 'Arthur' allowed of no great profundity of expression, but Irving was a wonderfully Pre-Raphaelite figure in his black and gold armour. Indeed, the scenery, the costumes, the armour and the furniture, all designed by Burne-Jones, were a never-to-be-forgotten realisation of the semi-mythical age of Malory … The scenes of the Magic Mere, the Great Hall at Camelot, the view over the waters to the Isle of Avalon were all superb, and Irving, as the magnanimous Arthur, prototype of all that is mystical yet heroic in the British character, deceived and forgiving, and Ellen Terry – absolutely the perfect realisation of that beauty which men have dreamed and fought for since Homer sang of Troy and Helen – seemed to incarnate the very spirit of Romance and Chivalry.[31]

Regular theatre-goer Kate Terry Gielgud left her impressions of the play:

The Lyceum is perhaps the only theatre in which such a theme as this could be handled with due effect – the poetry, the chivalry, the romance, above all the picturesqueness of the subject fully appreciated and reverently treated. From a purely dramatic and literary point of view the play far exceeded my expectations. Mr Carr has kept his climax steadily in view. His main story of the love of Lancelot and Guinevere is complicated by remarkably few and slight digressions, and one can but admire this reticence when one thinks of the manifold temptations which must have presented themselves within the pages of Malory and Tennyson. Written throughout in blank verse its language has many a touch of genuine poetical feeling …

It has, of course, the great advantage of being spoken with intelligence and, in certain cases with marked elocutionary power: pictorially the play must please even the most critical, although probably every individual amongst the audience will take exception to some point or other which clashes with his or her previously conceived ideal.

She expressed some reservations about the appearance of Irving and Forbes-Robertson, but none about Ellen Terry:

> For my own part I cannot feel that either Mr Irving or Mr Forbes Robertson represent the physical personalities of Arthur and Lancelot. There is a lack of robustness, of virility in the King's careworn face, an absence of any suggestion of sensuality in the ascetic figure of the fair young knight, who is a very Sir Galahad in type. In the first act, and more especially in the prologue, one feels this, for Mr Irving relies on his voice alone to indicate the *young* king, with all the promise of his life and great prowess before him; the face, although Excalibur is not yet grasped, is shadowed in mystery, studious as Merlin's own. Later, when his life's ideal is shattered, his knights absent, his wife false, the sad eyes and tired face are very pathetic, and Mr Irving has never been more dignified than in the scene in which he learns the faithlessless of his wife and trusted comrade.
>
> Miss Terry's Guinevere is very lovely, very lovable in its true womanliness, *her* personality suits the part to perfection. I think the second act is, pictorially, the gem of the piece. The Burne-Jones atmosphere strikes me as being absolutely right here, while (to me) his individuality and strong peculiarities are too marked, and not quite appropriately so, in the more characteristically Arthurian scenes. It is always the same bloodlessness and asceticism that strikes me.

She echoed William Archer's disappointment with the special effects but concluded 'the whole ensemble is infinitely pleasurable, and I hope to see it again and again'.[32]

The theme of *King Arthur* is the destruction of the Round Table, the breaking up of the marriage of Arthur and Guinevere and the dissipation of the mystic vision. It shows at once the high point of chivalry and the beginning of its end. The counterpart of *King Arthur* in which chivalry remains meaningful is *Don Quixote* in which a demented Romantic tries to implement a chivalric vision in a world that has moved on. It was significantly another of the long-term cherished projects of Irving. His fascination is evidenced by the fact that he played Malvolio made up as Don Quixote.[33] He had successively commissioned two full-length plays on the subject from W.G. Wills (1888) and J.I.C. Clarke (1894). He concluded neither was playable but, as Stoker recorded, he was 'determined to essay the character', and he edited Wills's *Don Quixote* down to two scenes which he staged along with Pinero's *Bygones* and Conan Doyle's *Waterloo* in a Lyceum triple bill in 1895.[34] It was while he was playing Quixote that Irving's knighthood was announced (25 May 1895). When he uttered the line: 'Knighthood sits like a halo round my head', there were cheers of approval from the audience.

The play showed Quixote being inspired by books of chivalry to take up knight errantry and then arriving at an inn which he mistakes for a castle. He keeps vigil on his armour, fights a gang of muleteers, identifies a country wench as his lady fair and receives the accolade of knighthood from the innkeeper.

The critics generally agreed, as one put it, 'There is no need to dwell on this production in detail; in itself it is nothing; its sole interest is, of course, the opportunity it affords Mr Irving of appearing in a part for which nature – as everybody has been saying for years – has designed him.' It was agreed that Irving looked every inch the part and conveyed the essential dignity of it effectively. As another critic wrote of the play:

> it certainly introduced a Don Quixote who might have stepped straight out of a seventeenth-century Spanish picture. The sad earnestness underlying the knight's eccentricity, the grave dignity of his demeanour, even in the most grotesque of his flights, his outbreaks of genuine eloquence cut short by a humorous confession of his own mental confusion, his stately courtesy to women, and his patronising tone to men – these characteristics could not be better conveyed than they were last night.[35]

The fact that Irving long cherished the desire to play King Arthur and Don Quixote bespeaks a strong sense of identification with the roles. They are linked by a powerful commitment to the chivalric vision but also one that is doomed to end in failure.

As a self-made gentleman, Irving was always conscious of the fragility of gentlemanliness. Alongside his chivalric and gentleman heroes, he played a series of roles of shabby genteel con men clinging desperately to the remnants of gentlemanliness. One of his favourite roles in this line was Robert Macaire, bandit outcast and renegade gentleman, the great criminal anti-hero of Romanticism. It was one of the most famous roles of the great French actor Frédéric LeMaître, who, as a French equivalent of Irving, had played Edmund Kean, Napoleon, Hamlet, Othello and Cagliostro on the French stage.

The play featuring Macaire, *The Inn of Les Adrets* (*L'Auberge des Adrets*), written by three Boulevard hacks, Benjamin Antier, Saint-Amand and Paulyanthe, was a straight melodrama, but when it was produced at the Ambigu-Comique in Paris in 1823, LeMaître reworked the role, coming on in a costume of his own devising, patched trousers, bedroom slippers, battered grey felt hat, dirty white vest and scruffy green coat, and committing his misdeeds with sardonic quips, introducing a delicious line in black humour into the melodrama.

Eventually LeMaître completely rewrote the play as *Robert Macaire* (1834), 'transforming it from a play into a vehicle for topical extemporizations.'[36] So famous did the character become that the artist Honoré Daumier featured him in a series of satirical cartoons, portraying him as a master fraudster and confidence trickster.

Charles Selby, an actor who translated scores of plays from the French for the English stage, and who may have seen LeMaître play the part, adapted it for Covent Garden in 1834 where James Wallack played Macaire. Palgrave Simpson made a more scholarly version of the play called *The Roadside Inn* for Charles Fechter, which he performed at the Lyceum in 1865. It was this version which Irving used when he revived the play under the title *Robert Macaire* in 1883 at the Lyceum.

The two-act play takes place inside and outside the wayside inn. Two escaped prisoners, Macaire and Strop, turn up on the eve of the wedding of Charles, the adopted son of innkeeper Dumont, and Clementine, the daughter of farmer Germeuil. By a classic melodramatic contrivance, Charles is actually the son of Macaire, who had abandoned his wife and child fourteen years before. Then the wife, Marie Beaumont, also turns up, but fails to recognize Macaire. Macaire murders Germeuil and steals the dowry. The gendarmes suspect and accuse Marie and Macaire stands by, allowing her to be accused. But when their descriptions arrive, the gendarmes seek to arrest the two escapees. Macaire makes a break for it, but is shot by the gendarmes. Dying, he confesses to the murder and asks for forgiveness from his wife and son.

At the centre of the play is the comic double act of Robert Macaire and Jacques Strop, a kind of criminal Abbott and Costello, with Macaire, domineering, sardonic and bullying, putting on gentlemanly airs, flourishing handkerchief and snuffbox, and Strop, perpetually nerve-racked, cowardly, complaining, put-upon, and called upon to pose as a simpleton. When Irving had first performed *Robert Macaire* at the Theatre Royal, Manchester, in 1865, he specifically emphasized the gentlemanliness of the role, causing one critic to note:

> His 'make-up' is capital, and his assumption of gentlemanly ease and nonchalance is very clever. There are, however, natural obstacles in the way of Mr Irving's perfect realisation of the brave, bold ruffian of the genuine French stamp.

But it was evidently no part of Irving's plan to emphasize the ruffianly brutality. The critic went on:

> Coolness there was, and effrontery, but not of that devil-may-care sort necessary to throw out the prominent features of Macaire. Thus the earlier portions of Mr Irving's acting were most satisfactory, as requiring less energy and greater finish ... We ought not to omit a hearty recognition of the tact displayed in the dance with the village girl; the fine gentleman in rags changing his one glove from one hand to the other as his partner

changed sides and maintaining his severe politeness to the very close, was quite a masterly piece of acting.[37]

Irving had evidently rethought the character as one who retained the relics of gentlemanliness, hence the ingenious business with the glove. He repeated the role in Edinburgh later in 1865 and then in 1866 in Liverpool, where the journal *The Porcupine* described his Macaire as 'a Chesterfield and a gaol-bird in one, with a dash of Machiavelli and a dash of Jingle'.[38] He had evidently remained faithful to his interpretation, despite the strictures of the Manchester critic. He revived it in London in 1867. It was clearly a role to which he was much attached. On 14 June, 1883, he put on an all-star, one-off matinee production of *Robert Macaire*, on behalf of the Royal College of Music, raising £1002 for their funds. The cast was headed by the priceless double act of Irving as Macaire and his close friend, the leading farceur J.L. Toole, as Strop. Ellen Terry and William Terriss played the young lovers Clementine and Charles, Squire Bancroft the gendarme sergeant and Ada Cavendish played Marie Beaumont. In 1888 he revived it again in a double bill with *The Amber Heart*, alternating it with *Faust* in the Lyceum programme from 23 May to 7 July. Weedon Grossmith played Strop. Irving also performed it fourteen times on his autumn provincial tour that year.[39]

The impresario C.B. Cochran, who saw Irving as Louis XI, Mathias, Mephistopheles, Shylock and Robert Landry, recalled that:

> Robert Macaire comes more clearly to my mind than any of the great gallery of Irving characters ... Even to-day I can never see a drunken scene on stage without recalling Irving's Macaire. He was miserable and merry, thumping and generally ill-treating poor, frightened Jacques Strop. His pockets were stuffed with stolen property, and the comic business of dropping things, while odd articles slipped from his tightly buttoned coat, set the house in roars of laughter. It was sheer, broad, comedy with a masterly touch.[40]

The actor Fewlass Llewellyn thought the double bill of the black comedy melodrama with 'the sweet poetical romance', *The Amber Heart*, 'a masterstroke of managerial policy'. He never forgot Irving's appearance as Macaire, writing in 1939:

> What I saw was inevitably a shock; a gaunt, shabby figure in rusty black with a battered hat and a black patch over one eye, with the manner of a sinister Jingle, grotesque as a painting by Dégas. I soon realized that I was seeing the most wonderful dramatic personality that I had ever seen or was likely to see. He took my breath away.

He recalled the acting:

> The buffoonery in Act I was as near burlesque as I have ever seen in drama, but Irving carried it off with such enjoyment, and with such an air of conviction, that you accepted it without question. His business with the wooden snuff-box that creaked and squeaked

a warning when Jacques Strop's indiscretions threatened detection, had the air of inevitability that he gave always to the merest trifle. His dancing in the quadrille at the end of Act II, and the wild finale, were the apotheosis of extravagance. Then in Act II came the scene with his wife, the unfortunate Marie, an exhibition of the grossest callousness. The technical skill … in reconciling this side of the character with the grotesque demeanour of the thief in the earlier scenes, was a lesson I have never forgotten. This was paving the way to the end. The touch of humanity when he realises that Charles is his son and longs to beg his forgiveness, even to touch his hand, and how he contrived it, turning the episode again to burlesque – masterstrokes all. The thieves are discovered and arrested, Jacques Strop trembling, Macaire sullen and defiant. Suddenly he hurls the gendarmes from him and himself through the window. A volley is fired and he staggers back, bleeding, dying, to fall headlong down the staircase. All the batteries of his art were brought into requisition … His death scene as Macaire was a revelation; a mingling of despair and defiance, a thief, a murderer, passing unrepentant: 'I have foiled you, I shall die like a man' – terror and bravado – a gasp, a convulsive tremor, a choking sigh, and the wicked soul had fled. That is why I wiped the sweat from my forehead as I left the theatre.[41]

Weedon Grossmith, giving a detailed account of rehearsing and performing *Macaire* with Irving, recalled that Irving's realism was so 'horrible' that three women fainted before the end of the play.[42] Typically George Bernard Shaw in his famous review 'Mr Irving Takes Paregoric' denounced Irving's choice of 'the old third class version' of *Macaire* instead of the new version 'full of literary distinction', by W.E. Henley and Robert Louis Stevenson. He mocked Irving:

> What Mr Irving enjoyed, and obviously what attracted him to the business, was rushing Mr Weedon Grossmith upstairs by the back of his neck, breaking plates on his stomach, standing on a barrel boyishly pretending to play the fiddle, singing a *chanson* to an accompaniment improvised by himself on an old harpsichord, and above all – for here his glee attained its climax – inadvertently pulling a large assortment of stolen handkerchiefs out of his pocket while explaining matters to the police officer, and clinching his account by throwing one into his hat, which, having no crown, allowed it to fall through to the floor.[43]

The account, along with Llewellyn's, makes the performance sound irresistibly attractive and inventive. Ellen Terry confirms this view in her autobiography, rejecting Shaw's preference for the Henley-Stevenson version, which she dismisses as 'a burlesque, a skit, a *satire* on the real Macaire. The Lyceum was *not* a burlesque house! Why should Henry have done it?'[44]

The recurrent mentions of Jingle in connection with Macaire are significant. Jingle was one of the defining roles of Irving's career. He played the role in James Albery's *Pickwick* at the Lyceum on 23 October 1871. The journalist and playwright E.L. Blanchard thought it 'very bad indeed' and likely to sink the Bateman management. The *Daily Telegraph* called it 'a travesty'. Virginia

Compton, however, thought it 'remarkably good' and Irving 'absolutely a perfect Jingle'.[45] It was not a success but Irving's Jingle was thought strong enough to carry an entire play, and so *Pickwick* was cut, reworked by E.L. Blanchard and reduced from four acts to three, with new characters added and Jingle foregrounded. Later still it was cut from three acts to six scenes and re-emerged as *Jingle*, purely a vehicle for Irving. The play scenes illustrated Jingle the Stroller, Jingle the Lover, Jingle the Financier, Jingle the Dandy, Jingle the Swindler and Jingle the Penitent. *Jingle* was played in a double bill with *The Bells* in 1878. George M. Slater, who saw it, recalled that 'his performance was masterly. As Alfred Jingle, the voluble, tricky *Chevalier d'Industrie*: the strolling player masquerading as a gentleman, his humour and characterization were faultless; he acted not alone in speech, but with his hands; every gesture adding value to his words.'[46] Jingle, with his staccato speech, easygoing charm and self-confidence was a part that fitted Irving like a glove. He even deployed it off-stage. Ellen Terry recalled Irving addressing the American press in his 'best Jingle manner', 'a manner full of refinement, bonhomie, elegance and geniality.'[47]

There was yet another character in Irving's repertoire similar to Alfred Jingle. That was Jeremy Diddler in James Kenney's *Raising the Wind*. First performed at the Theatre Royal, Covent Garden, on 5 November 1803, this two-act comedy had been regularly performed ever since. It centred on the adventures and misadventures of Jeremy Diddler, a gentleman sponger, who by 'songs and bon mots' ingratiated himself with people to cadge money. He poses as an expected suitor to court a rich heiress, is pursued by the girl's spinster cousin and exposed as a fraud, but at the end inherits £10,000 from a conveniently deceased uncle which solves all his problems. Irving put on *Raising the Wind* in a double bill with *The Bells*, demonstrating his versatility by performing the grimmest melodrama and the lightest comedy on the same night.

Contemporary commentators noted the resemblance between Diddler and Alfred Jingle. Dickens, who drew much inspiration from the stage, may well have based Jingle on Diddler. But at least one commentator thought:

> It is not to be supposed that Irving was content to reproduce as Jeremy his successful performance as Jingle; in his hands Jeremy Diddler was a new creation and a vastly amusing one. Nothing but his extraordinarily ingratiating manner would ever have reconciled you to the idea that the scamp could be tolerated in any decent society, yet such was his charm, his address, his charming confidence, and that beneficent air of conferring a favour while he picked your pocket, that you welcomed his approach and regretted his departure.[48]

Clement Scott was less convinced about the difference:

> The characters of Jingle and Jeremy Diddler are themselves so similar, that it is no wonder we find unmistakable traces of the one in the other. The incessant restlessness, the

nervous, jerky, walk, the unblushing impudence, the 'seedy' get-up, the rollicking effrontery, are all common to the two parts and it is difficult to see how Mr Irving could efface, more than he has done, the necessary resemblance. Taking this for granted, no exception can be found to the latest representative of Jeremy Diddler. From first to last, Mr Irving's performance is instinct with power. His business, perfect in the minutest detail, must be the result of much hard study, and he shows thorough appreciation of the character. Many are the delicate touches which tell even more than the broad strokes in the general effect.[49]

Irving had demonstrated his attachment to the role by choosing it for his benefit in Manchester on 12 April 1865.

In James Albery's *The Two Roses*, the most notable success of a prolific playwright, Irving created the role of Digby Grant, the shabby genteel sponger, up to his ears in debt, asserting his links to a noble family, making dismissive references to plebeians ('You do not understand the feelings of a gentleman'), while cadging money off friends and neighbours. He inherits a property worth £10,000 and becomes very grand and condescending. He forbids his daughter Letty to marry her sweetheart Jack Wyatt. But, having been installed in a manor house and having lorded it over everyone, he is informed that he is not in fact the heir. The real heir is Caleb Deecie, the quick-witted blind friend of Jack. Digby resigns the estate to him and Deecie will marry Digby's other daughter, Ida, while Letty will marry Wyatt.

The character of Digby Grant seems to have been modelled directly on William Dorrit, 'Father of the Marshalsea' in Dickens's *Little Dorrit*, who undergoes the same character change the moment he inherits money. Irving first played the part at the newly built Vaudeville Theatre, which had opened under the direction of Tom Thorne, David James and H.J. Montague. First seen on 4 June 1870, the play ran for 294 nights. E.L. Blanchard saw the production, in which, alongside Irving, Thorne played Deecie and Montague played Wyatt, thought it 'a good piece, well written and excellently acted'.[50] For his benefit at the Vaudeville, Irving recited 'The Dream of Eugene Aram' and was recalled three times. It was the Aram recitation, coupled with the performance as Digby Grant, that persuaded 'Colonel' Bateman to sign Irving for the Lyceum. Irving revived *Two Roses* at the Lyceum on 26 December 1881, with a cast which included George Alexander as Deecie, William Terriss as Wyatt and David James as Jenkins the bagman. *The Times* thought that Irving's Digby Grant had 'improved with keeping'.[51] It ran for sixty performances. B.W. Findon recalled the famous cheque scene in the play: 'Those, and those only, who saw Irving in the shabby old dressing-gown, his heart bursting with self-adulation, handing to each of his former friends, with superb condescension "a little cheque" are able to appreciate Irving's subtle and complete realisation of the character'.[52] George M. Slater recalled that Irving's Digby Grant left an impression on my youthful mind never to be forgotten. In voice, deportment and action he made the character, so skilfully drawn, a living embodiment of a fascinating although contemptible personality ... that bombastic, pretentious, sly, ungrateful humbug who accepted favours when in embarrassed circumstances and who, during his temporary enjoyment of property, evinced such gross ingratitude.[53]

Both in his celebrations of a pure and ennobling chivalry and in his comedic explorations of the fragility of gentlemanly status, Irving captured perfectly two sides of the Victorian male psyche: the aspirational and the apprehensive. He did so in part because he himself embodied these traits.

3

Ellen Terry

One of Irving's shrewdest moves, and one which did much to ensure the continuing success of the Lyceum, was the recruitment of Ellen Terry as his stage partner. They complemented each other perfectly: her warmth, beauty and femininity offsetting and humanizing his aloof and chilly austerity. His fondness for tragedy and 'horrors' was matched by Ellen Terry's preference for comedy. Sarah Bernhardt thought her unequalled in comedy 'at any rate in the English-speaking countries'.[1] Her son, Edward Gordon Craig, an acute observer of acting, noted of their performances that Irving's were 'made', carefully crafted, built up; hers were 'spontaneous, genial, free'; Irving was 'so still, seldom moving'; she was 'all movement'; Irving's face commanded the attention, with Terry it was her whole body.[2]

Just as important as her style was her innate appeal. Bernard Shaw testified that 'every famous man of the last quarter of the nineteenth century – provided he were a playgoer – has been in love with Ellen Terry' – and that included himself.[3] Bram Stoker confirmed this: 'I think that Ellen Terry fascinated every one who ever met her – men, women and children, it was all the same.'[4] This contrasted strongly with attitudes to Irving, which were sharply divided and included a faction which disliked Irving to the point of vituperation. Having taken over the lease of the Lyceum, Irving was in need of a leading lady. He had decided to dispense with Isabel Bateman. The daughter of the previous lessees, 'Colonel' and Mrs Bateman, she had been imposed on Irving and it is clear that he did not rate her acting ability highly. Irving had acted with Ellen Terry once, at the Queen's Theatre, Long Acre, in 1867, in David Garrick's truncation of *The Taming of the Shrew*, called *Katherine and Petruchio*. Neither of them had been impressed with the other's acting. Irving recalled later: 'She was always bright and lively, and full of fun. She had a distinct charm; but as an artist was rather on the hoydenish side.'[5] She recalled: 'he played badly, nearly as badly as I did. He was stiff with self-consciousness; his eyes were dull and his face heavy.'[6]

But by 1878 she had conquered London. In 1875 she had appeared as Portia in a beautifully staged production of *The Merchant of Venice* at the Prince of Wales's Theatre, Charlotte Street, under the management of the Bancrofts. The press were ecstatic about her performance, The *Daily News* calling her:

the Portia that Shakespeare drew. The bold innocence, the lively wit and quick intelligence, the grace and elegance of manner, and all the youth and freshness of this exquisite creation can rarely have been depicted in such harmonious combination ... Miss Terry's figure, at once graceful and commanding, and her singularly sweet and expressive countenance, doubtless aid her much; but this performance is essentially artistic.[7]

But the Shylock of Charles Coghlan was totally inadequate. He had no real conception of the part and on the opening night his nerve failed. 'You could hardly hear a word he said', recalled Terry. 'He spoke as though he had a sponge in his mouth and moved as if paralysed. The perspiration poured from his face; yet what he was doing no one could guess.' The production closed after three weeks. But Terry's triumph as both an actress and a personality was undisputed. 'Everyone seemed to be in love with me!' she recalled. 'I had sweethearts by the dozen, known and unknown.'[8] This love was strengthened when she took the title role in a play specifically written for her, W.G. Wills's *Olivia*, an adaptation of Oliver Goldsmith's *The Vicar of Wakefield*. It was produced at the Court Theatre, Sloane Square, by actor-manager John Hare and proved to be the highlight of his management there. It caught a particular mood in the public. Clement Scott recalled that Hare had sought 'an English play, on an English subject, with an English setting, and acted by the best representatives of the English school' and in settling on *The Vicar of Wakefield* as a source for his play struck a chord:

A happier idea could not have occurred to mortal man. We were in the middle of a seventeenth century [sic] craze. We were all mad about blue china, Chippendale chairs, Sheraton sideboards, old spinets and brass fire-irons. George Du Maurier, with his *Punch* pictures, had started the fashion, and there was scarcely one in the artistic world who did not in their own home and belongings revert with joy to the modes and whims of their great-grandmothers. The men ransacked the bric-à-brac shops for last century china, clocks, and furniture; the women appeared wearing the mob caps, bibs, tuckers, fichus, and grills of their ancestors.[9]

Charles Hiatt concluded:

If a part was to be specially written for Ellen Terry at all, it is hardly conceivable that one more suited to her gifts than *Olivia* should have been produced. *Olivia* is by no means the most important of Ellen Terry's impersonations, but I question whether it is not the most charming of them.[10]

Freeman Wills, brother and biographer of W.G. Wills, called *Olivia* 'the most perfect study of woman's character conceivable, not tiresomely good, but yet divinely loveable'.[11] *Olivia* was a major popular success and Olivia caps, Olivia scarves and Olivia postcards became all the rage. Even Henry James, who dismissed the play as 'tame, dull and puerile', conceded that 'Miss Ellen Terry, whom it is greatly the fashion to admire, has a great deal of charm and an interesting, pathetic, even beautiful countenance'.[12] But his dismissal of the play was a minority view and the general praise for it and her led Irving to invite Ellen to the Lyceum to play Ophelia to his Hamlet.

Irving had not seen *Olivia* himself but had been advised by Lady Pollock that Ellen was the ideal leading lady for him.[13] Juliet, Lady Pollock, was the wife of Sir Frederick Pollock, barrister and holder of the ancient legal office of the Queen's Remembrancer. The Pollocks were both great devotees of the theatre. Sir Frederick had been an executor of the great actor Macready and had edited his *Reminiscences*. The Pollocks, along with critic James Spedding, painter Sir Frederic Leighton, poet Edwin Arnold and others, had proposed to the Bancrofts keeping the admired production of *The Merchant of Venice* going by subscription, but the plan had come to naught.[14]

Lady Pollock pointed out to Irving correctly that all London was talking about Ellen's Olivia, that she had acted Shakespeare well with the Bancrofts, and that she would bring to the Lyceum 'a personal following'. The arguments convinced Irving and he engaged her for Ophelia, initiating a partnership that would last for twenty years. Interestingly, of all her pre-Lyceum triumphs Irving would revive only two, *Olivia* and *The Merchant of Venice*, together with *The Lady of Lyons*, which she had done for one performance only, suggesting that he considered these productions in particular to showcase the essence of her talent.

The success of Irving's strategy is attested by Henry Labouchere, MP and theatre-owner, in his magazine *Truth* (3 January 1881). Writing of the production of *The Cup*, Labouchere shrewdly observed:

> At a time of affected aestheticism, of rapture and intensity, of sad wall paper and queer dados, what a stroke of genius it was to engage Miss Ellen Terry! This graceful and picturesque creature is the high priestess of the enthusiasts. She suits the dreams of the idealists. The age that gives us a Grosvenor Gallery must necessarily adore an Ellen Terry, for she is an embodiment of the aspirations of modern art. With her waving movement and skill in giving life to drapery, she is the actress of all others to harmonize with gold backgrounds, and to lounge under blossoming apple trees. The bait held out by Mr Irving took. The greedy public swallowed it. The empire of popularity was divided between the actor and actress without injuring either of them, and so one day the far-seeing manager bethought him of making the ideal priestess a priestess indeed.

Oscar Wilde, another Terry devotee and the author of three sonnets addressed to her in her roles as Portia, Camma and Queen Henrietta Maria, dubbed her 'Our Lady of the Lyceum', and there was something about her presence at Irving's 'temple of art' that seemed to sanctify her and to obliterate the knowledge of her spectacularly irregular private life.[15] In 1864 at the age of sixteen she had married the forty-six year old painter G.F. Watts and left the stage, where she had been performing since her debut in 1856 at the age of eight. But the marriage broke down after ten months and they formally separated on the grounds of 'incompatibility of temper', which meant that the high-spirited and untutored young girl had failed to fit into the reverential aristocratic circle surrounding and cosseting Watts, known to his admirers as 'The Signor'.[16] They eventually divorced in 1877. After a brief return to the stage, Ellen again retired in 1868, eloping with and setting up home with the architect E.W. Godwin, by whom she had two illegitimate children. They never married and Ellen was ostracized by her family and many of her friends. Poverty drove her back to the stage in 1874 and the relationship with Godwin ended. After they parted, and in order to legitimize her children and regularize her own position, Ellen married fellow actor Charles Kelly in 1877 as soon as her divorce from Watts, on the grounds of her adultery with Godwin, was finalized. However within two years her stage partnership with Irving was initiated. It seems likely that the professional relationship soon became more intimate. Certainly Kelly, who was conspicuously not invited by Irving to join his company, became more and more jealous, and the marriage ended in formal separation in 1881. Kelly died in 1885 and Ellen then remained unmarried until after Irving's death, when she entered a short-lived marriage with the much younger American actor James Carew, her third and final husband.

This record appears to confirm the commonly held view of actresses as 'loose women' who flouted the conventional rules of morality. Given the strict social conventions which prevented divorced persons being presented at court, for instance, the universal approbation that Ellen attracted after a divorce, two illegitimate children and a judicial separation is quite remarkable. It tends to substantiate the view that Victorians were able to separate those actresses who functioned in a competitive, co-sexual world of work, their evenings spent away from the home and exhibiting themselves before the public gaze as objects of desire, from their stage roles if those roles endorsed the dominant view of women and the prevailing perceptions of femininity. Ellen successfully did this and this apparently enabled her unconventional private life to be overlooked.[17] Her stage incarnation of feminine innocence and purity somehow purged her offstage reputation and redeemed her.

There has been much debate about the nature of her relationship with Irving and in particular whether they were in the physical sense lovers. This has been strenuously denied by Laurence Irving, Henry's biographer, and Roger Manvell, Ellen's biographer, among others.[18] There is no doubt that he fell deeply in love with her and that she reciprocated that love. Although most of the letters between them were destroyed, an instructive fact in itself, the fragments of Irving's letters that have survived testify to his adoration of her, 'My own dear wife for as long as I live', 'God bless you my only thought. Your own till death',[19] and Ellen's memoirs are eloquent testimony to her love for him. But they could never marry because Irving was already married, although formally separated from his wife Florence, and a divorce would have compromised his career-long commitment to raising the respectability of the acting profession. Contemporaries had little doubt that they were lovers. Dame May Whitty, who as a young woman was a member of the Lyceum Company, told her daughter, Margaret Webster, that she believed this to be the case.[20] Sir Edward Hamilton's diary reveals that when in 1883 Gladstone wanted to offer Irving a knighthood, the cabinet opposed the idea ('He is separated from his wife (not divorced) and there are stories about his too close intimacy with Ellen Terry') and the idea was dropped.[21]

Lucy, Lady Duff Gordon, became a friend of Ellen and recalled in her memoirs: 'It always struck me that their association was one of closest friendship rather than of love. She told me the same herself. "People always say that Henry is my lover of course. He isn't. As a matter of fact he never sees further than my head. He does not even know I have a body."'[22] But Ellen told a different story towards the end of her life. Marguerite Steen, an actress turned novelist, who wrote a collective biography of the Terrys, asked her point blank shortly after the First World War whether she had been Irving's mistress. 'She answered without hesitation. "Of course I was. We were terribly in love for a while. Then, later on, when it didn't matter so much to me, he wanted us to go on, and so I did, because I was very, very fond of him and he said he needed me."'[23] On other occasions Ellen told Steen that, because of her love for Irving, she was embarrassed at having to act love scenes with him on the stage; that she had told her daughter Edy about the relationship (Edy approved); and that Irving eventually left her for the journalist Eliza Aria, who was the companion of his final years and one of the three beneficiaries of his will (along with his two sons).[24]

Steen's account of the affair has the ring of truth about it. She writes:

It is difficult, in these days, to imagine the stress and strain, in Victorian days, of conducting a clandestine love-affair. Presumably they made their opportunities – which cannot have been without difficulty and anxiety for both. Irving had his rooms in Grafton Street, to which (according to her own account) Ellen never went except on formal occasions, as a guest among guests. Ellen was then established at Barkston Gardens, with her daughter Edy ... and living-in servants. When Irving bought the house at Brook Green as a place to entertain his friends, he never spent a night there; for some time the bedrooms were not even furnished ... The smallest indiscretion on Ellen's part would have brought down on her the malice of Irving's wife (this danger was eventually cancelled out by his agreement to pay Mrs Irving an allowance, instantly to be stopped if by word or action, she brought trouble to Ellen Terry). Yet – they made their opportunities: one of which was described by an American friend, a dear friend of both ... who with her husband entertained them frequently on Staten Island. They trusted her to preserve their secret, which she faithfully kept until both were dead. It is not conceivable that Mrs Alexander Shaw was the only friend to give them joint invitations, or to make convenient arrangements. Her description of Ellen lying on a white bearskin rug in front of the fire, of Irving holding out his hand to lead her up the stairs when midnight struck, is lively in the author's memory.[25]

Correspondence in the Folger Shakespeare Library between Irving, Terry and Mr and Mrs William Winter show the Winters treating and entertaining Henry and Ellen in America as a couple.[26]

One of Irving's favourite sayings was a line from Tennyson's *Becket*: 'Men are God's trees and women are God's flowers.' It is a saying that encapsulates a whole world view based on the separate spheres of men and women, and the separate attributes of masculinity and femininity. Irving clearly saw Ellen as the ideal woman, the embodiment of aesthetic beauty and femininity composed of grace, tenderness and charm. Intriguingly Ellen saw him as a tree, recounting in her autobiography a visit to his sick bed in Wolverhampton and describing him as looking 'like some beautiful grey tree that I have seen in Savannah'.[27]

Irving's view of women and of Ellen's qualities was widely shared in Victorian society. Femaleness and maleness are biological states but femininity and masculinity are cultural constructs. The image, attributes and behaviour associated with the idea of femininity like those of masculinity derived from three main sources: official culture – law, religious teaching, education; personal culture – the example and advice offered by parents, family and peer group; and popular culture – the concepts, fantasies, role models and images provided by such cultural forms as women's magazines, plays, films and books. These may sometimes be in conflict but frequently may have reinforced each other.[28] The most immediate and powerful agency of socialization is perhaps the family, even more in the nineteenth century than the twentieth and twenty-first centuries, because most girls then enjoyed only a relatively short period of schooling. So the relationship between parents and the patterns of behaviour and work in the home set the first model for girls to follow.

In all classes, men and women subscribed to a distinct separation of the spheres. There was the public world of business, work, politics, professional life – the male sphere, and the private world of love, emotions and domesticity – the female sphere. The cult of domesticity which grew up in the early nineteenth century, powerfully advanced by Evangelicalism, reinforced that separate female sphere and promoted an idealized view of womanhood, epitomized in Coventry Patmore's poem, *The Angel in the House*, and the triptych of paintings by George Elgar Hicks, *Woman's Mission*. The ideal woman was innocent, pure, gentle, submissive, self-sacrificing, dependent and home-based. The women played the key role in defining the social status of the family and preserving standards of gentility at all levels.

These ideals and images were relentlessly promoted both by the prescriptive and imaginative literature of the nineteenth century and contrasts were sharply drawn between the good, hardworking, devoted wife and the neglectful, untidy, selfish wife; and between the gentle, loving, self-sacrificing daughter and the lazy, sensual, vulgar daughter. Daughter figures like Florence Dombey in *Dombey and Son* or Little Nell in *The Old Curiosity Shop* filled the bill perfectly. From the mid nineteenth century onwards there was an increasing number of manuals on girl-rearing to help the Victorian mother, expected to perform the task of teaching her daughter, to conform to the dominant notion of femininity and to accept a position of inferiority to men. The manuals covered cleanliness, orderliness, correct matters of dress, exercise. The training of girls was seen very much in terms of inculcating skills. Dolls were prescribed as ideal toys for girls helping to promote the necessary feminine skills. The onset of puberty was believed to trigger the psychic manifestation of masculinity and femininity; and once her periods began, a girl developed modesty, timidity and dependence. Their clothes were often designed to constrain them – corsets, stays, tight bodices, long skirts, layers of petticoats. Mothers of all classes nursed the sick, raised the children, supervised domestic arrangements, provided the best kind of environment for the men; this set the example of service and sacrifice for their daughters.

After the family, school was an important influence. The Victorians saw education both as a means of social control and of individual betterment. Boys were undoubtedly shaped by the public school ethos, whether by attendance at the schools or by absorption of the ethos at second-hand through boys' papers. Far fewer girls went to school, however, than boys up to the First World War. In the later nineteenth century there was a move to set up girls' public schools. They did widen opportunities for some girls but they remained concerned with the ideal of femininity, and promoting decorum and cultural education, while accepting the girls' future was as wives and mothers. Ambition, determination, toughness and worldly success were still not thought ladylike. If cultured, well-educated wives were produced, they were still expected to channel their energies into the service of family and community. In the late nineteenth century, too, there was a move towards introducing higher education for women at the ancient universities. The opposition to this gives us insight into the prevailing view of woman's role. It was opposed on economic grounds: namely that women would take jobs from men and thereby neglect their home duties. It was opposed on intellectual grounds: that women were mentally inferior to men, incapable of prolonged thought, intuitive rather than inductive. It was opposed on physiological grounds: too much brainwork was dangerous to menstruating women and might lead to sterilisation, because women were physically delicate. It was opposed on religious grounds: the clergy supported the biblical idea of woman as descendant of Eve, who was created from Adam's rib, to be his helpmeet and supporter; that she was the cause of man's expulsion from paradise and therefore inferior and subordinate. A limited amount of university education did become available, but this led to the stereotype of the bluestocking, the dotty spinster academic, unfulfilled in her womanly instincts and therefore to be mocked and pitied by turn.

When girls began to go to school regularly in the later nineteenth century, the curriculum was directed towards supplying them with the appropriate womanly skills. Needlework was part of the school curriculum from the 1860s, and in 1878 domestic economy (cooking, laundry, household management) became compulsory for girls. But girls were often kept away from school to help with babyminding and household duties.

Towards the end of the nineteenth century, some of the physiological ideas about women began to change. Exercise and sport were seen as important in the new girls' schools, and hockey and callisthenics were encouraged. Middle-class women in particular took up bicycling and tennis. More women began to go out to work, particularly middle-class women, as the work opportunities increased for teachers, typists and upmarket shop assistants. A new model of femininity began to be developed, the 'modern girl', who had energy and independence, but this was carefully married to the older view of the woman's role.

Nevertheless, when Stanley Hall defined adolescence in the major theoretical work which set the understanding of the phenomenon for half a century, he argued that girls in fact never outgrow their adolescence and they always remain clothes-conscious, whimsical, flirtatious, faddish, fickle, weepy, giggling, coquettish, given to secrecy, disliking study. He rejected the idea of equality between the sexes and of coeducation, which he thought would have a deleterious effect on the boys, retarding their progress to manhood and feminizing them. He believed intellectual women were denying their natural role and fulfilment in motherhood.

The dominant views of the age in terms of gender roles were given vivid and powerful expression in popular culture, in books, plays, paintings and magazines which reinforced what was being taught in home, school and church. The popular success of theatres, plays and actresses was directly related to the extent to which they conformed to and expressed the majority views of the age.

Ellen Terry was a personality actress and it was a personality that the Victorians loved. As her long-time friend and admirer Bernard Shaw observed:

> Although she was soundly skilled in the technique of her profession she never needed to perform any remarkable feat of impersonation: the spectators would have resented it: they did not want Ellen Terry to be Olivia Primrose: they wanted Olivia Primrose to be Ellen Terry. Her combination of beauty with sensitive intelligence was unique: a disguise would have been intolerable. Her instinct was for beauty and sincerity: she had only to play a part 'straight', as actors say, to transfigure it into something much better than its raw self.[29]

From the time of her return to the stage in 1874, Ellen Terry was regularly described by the following adjectives: graceful, tender, womanly, charming.

Charles Hiatt published a celebration of Ellen Terry in 1898 in which he quoted extensively from contemporary reviews and their regular refrain is that Ellen was 'womanly'.

This was true even in her pre-Lyceum days. When in 1875 she played Clara Douglas in Lord Lytton's *Money* under the Bancrofts' management, the *Daily Telegraph* said: 'The actress paints for us the perfection of gentleness and maiden modesty … the whole nature of the woman is steeped in tenderness'; and the *Standard* said: 'Nothing will distinguish this revival so favourably as the exquisitely graceful, tender and charming performance … by Miss Ellen Terry … neither on our own stage nor on the French do we remember any exemplification of womanly self-sacrifice which surpasses Clara Douglas at the Prince of Wales's.'[30]

Hiatt thought her Lyceum Ophelia 'distinguished by the wonderful charm which is characteristic of all she does … complete innocence … intelligence … infinite pathos … bewitchingly tender and gentle.'[31] The extent to which she imbued the role with what contemporaries saw as the ideal is reflected in Dutton Cook's comment that 'An Ophelia so tender, so graceful, so picturesque and so pathetic, has not been seen in the theatre since Macready's Hamlet, many years ago, found his Ophelia in the person of Miss Priscilla Horton.'[32]

Frederick Wedmore of the *Academy* wrote of her Camma in *The Cup* that 'the part abounds in occasions for the display of her particular gifts which are gentleness, pathos and grace'.[33] William Archer of the *World*, one of the most consistent critics of Irving's acting, said of Terry's Queen Guinevere in *King Arthur*: 'it is impossible to conceive of a statelier or more gracious figure; and her performance is altogether charming.'[34]

Her Imogen in *Cymbeline*, which she played at fifty, was accounted one of her greatest triumphs. She herself, with her candid and critical view of her own career, wrote that, in the last ten years with Irving, Imogen was her only 'inspired performance'.[35] A.B. Walkley of the *Star* wrote that Imogen would:

> rank amongst her first-rate achievements. Sweet and tender, the soul of trust and innocence, full of girlish spirits in the few moments when cruel fate ceases to vex her, piteous beyond measure in her grief, radiant in her joy – here is a figure that dwells in the memory as one of absolute beauty … Miss Terry interprets beauty beautifully, and that is the long and short of it.[36]

The Times (23 September 1896) agreed, saying 'Miss Ellen Terry … with her airy grace and tender womanliness is Imogen to the life'.

But she conferred these qualities also on roles which were to her mind undeveloped. Clarice de Maluçon in *Robespierre*, a part she thought 'wretched', elicited from T. Edgar Pemberton the comment: 'she acted with her unvarying and invincible charm, at once arrested and held the sympathy of her audiences.

It was a sweet and womanly performance.'[37] The painter Graham Robertson recorded:

> I never realised the art of Ellen Terry more clearly than in the part of Rosamund in Tennyson's *Becket*. The character fairly puzzled her as she studied it. 'I don't know what to do with her' she said to me. 'She is not there. She does not exist. I don't think Tennyson ever knew very much about women, and now he is old and has forgotten the little that he knew. She is not a woman at all.' But she did her best for Rosamund and played her for all she was worth and more. I was particularly struck one night by her absolute identification (for the moment) with the character.[38]

William Archer, agreeing with Terry that the character was 'futile and out of place', nevertheless complimented her on a performance that was 'graceful, tender and altogether charming'. In other words she had imbued Rosamund with the Terry magic and made her another manifestation of ideal womanliness.[39] The adjective 'womanly' was first applied to her in her comeback play *The Wandering Heir* and, noted her biographer Christopher St John disapprovingly, it was an 'adjective which was to stick to her like a burr for the rest of her life'.[40] But in her autobiography, comparing herself and Irving, she said: 'I have always been more woman than artist. He always put the theatre first. He lived in it, he died in it. He had none of what I call my bourgeois qualities – the love of children, the love of a home, the dislike of solitude.'[41]

Her charm was regularly adduced, so regularly that it eventually palled on her: 'Blow that word charm!' she often exclaimed after reading her reviews, 'There is something more to my acting than charm.'[42] But the charm like the femininity was undoubted; it comprised her musical voice, her graceful movement, her physical beauty and an impression of almost permanent youthfulness.

All these qualities were used to project that idealized femininity which so entranced Victorian audiences. One of her most devoted critics, the American William Winter, identified the nature of the womanliness that she brought to one of her most celebrated roles, Portia, which he called 'magnificent' in its Lyceum incarnation. He argued that in Ellen Terry's Portia 'the essential womanhood of that character was for the first time in the modern theatre adequately interpreted and conveyed'. He went on:

> Upon many playgoing observers indeed the wonderful wealth of beauty that is in the part – its winsome grace, its incessant sparkle, its alluring … sweetness, its impetuous ardour, its enchantment of physical equally with emotional condition, its august morality, its perfect candour, and its noble passion – came as a surprise … Previous representatives of Portia had placed the emphasis chiefly if not exclusively upon morals and mind. The stage Portia of the past has usually been a didactic lady, self-contained, formal, conventional, and oratorical. Ellen Terry came, and Portia was figured exactly as she lives in the pages of Shakespeare – an imperial and yet an enchanting woman, dazzling in her beauty, royal in her dignity, as ardent in temperament as she is fine in

brain and various and splendid in personal peculiarities and feminine charm. After seeing that matchless impersonation it seemed strange that Portia should ever have been represented in any other light, and it was furthermore felt that the inferior, mechanical, utilitarian semblance of her could not again be endured.[43]

The appeal of this charming, sparkling femininity partially lay behind the choice of plays at the Lyceum. Irving and Terry both then and since have had their partisans. Terry's partisans have claimed that Irving deliberately tamed her independent spirit, denied her roles that would have expressed it, and subordinated everything to his own monstrous egotism.

> Always, Irving stifled the life in her, but it was not only inflexibility, or even competitiveness that led him to drag her down: once again, as he had when they first played together, he was taming a shrew.[44]

In this way, Irving's Benedick slowed down and thus tamed her Beatrice and his Shylock necessitated a complete rethink of Portia, 'the grim weight of his martyrdom crushed her comic triumph'. Ellen herself complained 'When Henry Irving put on *Much Ado About Nothing* – a play which he may be said to have done for me, as he never really liked the part of Benedick … he gave me little help. Beatrice must be swift, swift, swift! Owing to Henry's rather finicking, deliberate method as Benedick, I could never put the right pace into my part.'[45] When they did *The Merchant*, it was Irving's conception of Shylock which caused the problem: 'His heroic saint was splendid; but it wasn't good for Portia.'[46] But what is at issue here is acting styles and acting interpretations rather than gender ideology. It was not an attempt to neutralize Ellen. There was only one way in which Irving could do Shylock, given his particular vocal and physical limitations and that dictated to some extent the performance of Portia.

The grand *cause célèbre* in the case for Irving's deliberate downgrading of Terry's talent is his failure to cast her as Rosalind in *As You Like It*. She herself never ceased to lament this, writing in her *Four Lectures on Shakespeare*: 'I have been Beatrice! Would I could say that 'I have been Rosalind'. Would that opportunity to play this part had come my way when I was in my prime! I reckon it one of the greatest disappointments of my life that it did not! In my old age I go on studying Rosalind, rather wistfully, I admit.'[47] The view is shared by many commentators. Clement Scott spoke for many when he observed: 'The loss of such a Rosalind to the stage as Ellen Terry would and must have been, has ever formed a subject for regret with her warmest and most enthusiastic admirers. If ever woman lived who displayed in advance the temperament of Rosalind, it was Ellen Terry.'[48]

But this is rather disingenuous. *As You Like It* was rejected not because Rosalind was independent spirited – after all many Victorian actresses played the part. It was rejected because there was not a role of sufficient stature for

Irving to play. He toyed with the idea of playing Touchstone, but neither Touchstone nor Jaques, the other possible role, was big enough for the actor-manager. Bram Stoker says that Irving, far from being totally egocentric, staged *Romeo and Juliet, Much Ado, Twelfth Night, Olivia, The Cup, Iolanthe* and *The Belle's Stratagem* for Terry's sake.[49] He might have added *Madame Sans-Gêne* to this list.

Towards the end of their partnership suitable roles for her did become a problem. This was almost inevitable as she entered her fifties. Although Ellen played the large and important roles of Guinevere in *King Arthur* (1895), Imogen in *Cymbeline* (1896) and the title role of *Madame Sans-Gêne* in 1897, she grew increasingly dissatisfied with her roles. There had always been parts she disliked. She had considered the mother in *The Dead Heart* 'uninteresting' but did it because the play marked the acting debut of her son Edward Gordon Craig.[50] She also thought the role of Rosamund in *Becket* had nothing to it. But now the roles were getting smaller and even less appealing. In 1898 she wrote to Shaw complaining about her part in the forthcoming Lyceum production of *The Medicine Man* by Robert Hichens and H.D. Traill, but indicating her full awareness of her importance to the Lyceum:

> My part in it is just drivel. In the nineteenth century only a child of fourteen could express herself as I have to. If I'm not in a play at the Lyceum it does a good deal of harm to that play. If I play this part it will 'harm' me, inasmuch as I shall be simply ridiculous.[51]

She did play the part but it was withdrawn after twenty-two performances. In her memoirs she called it 'our only *quite* unworthy production'.[52] Her part in *Robespierre* she considered 'wretched', though the play was a success, running for ninety-three nights. Her part in *Peter the Great* was thin and she disliked her role of Volumnia in *Coriolanus*. Finally, when *Dante* was produced, she heard the play read and after pondering long and hard refused to appear in it 'in a part even worse than the one I had played in *Robespierre*'. Irving offered her £12,000 to go with him on his American tour with *Dante* as the main attraction, but she refused; and, while he went on tour, she went into production with her son.[53] As she wrote sadly:

> Henry Irving did not treat me badly. I hope I did not treat him badly. He revived *Faust* and produced *Dante*. I would have liked to stay with him to the end of the chapter, but there was nothing for me to act in either of these plays. But we never quarrelled. Our long partnership dissolved naturally. It was all very sad, but it could not be helped.[54]

There is, however, some evidence that her abilities were beginning to fray.

Jack Grein, not as entranced by Ellen Terry as Bernard Shaw, reported dispassionately on her performances in the later Lyceum productions. In *The Medicine Man*, he wrote:

> Miss Ellen Terry, a dream of youth on the stage, endeavoured to vanquish her nervousness, but hardly succeeded; she was very winning as the weak-headed girl, but somehow her performance was strained. It was an uneven battle between the woman, the actress and the emotions of an inauspicious first night.[55]

Of *Robespierre*, he recorded:

> her memory was vacillating and almost endangered the initial scene of the first act and the commencement of the fourth. Fortunately, Sir Henry was alive to all untoward events, and covered the tribulations of Miss Terry with his perfect routine.[56]

Ellen Terry herself admits that *Romeo and Juliet*, *Much Ado*, *Olivia* and *The Cup* 'all gave me finer opportunities than they gave Henry'.[57] She reveals that Irving positively disliked the roles of Benedick and Dr Primrose[58] but took on the roles to allow her to shine as Beatrice and Olivia. He knew he was miscast as Romeo but he put it on nonetheless. He wrote to Terry after the dress rehearsal:

> beautiful as Portia was, Juliet leaves her far, far behind. Never anybody acted more exquisitely the part of the performance which I saw from the front ... The play will be, I believe, a mighty 'go' for the beauty of it is bewildering. I am sure of this, for it dumbfounded them all last night ... I have determined not to see a paper for a week – I know they'll cut me up, and I don't like it.[59]

And cut him up they did. Also there is no reason why she should not have put on *As You Like It* herself. In 1879 and 1880 she toured with her husband Charles Kelly, playing Beatrice to his Benedick. If Rosalind was her dream role, surely then was the time to do it. Thanks to Irving, Terry got to play Ophelia, Desdemona, Portia, Juliet, Viola, Beatrice, Lady Macbeth, Cordelia, Imogen, Volumnia and Queen Katherine. They were seen by Victorian commentators to have symbolic significance as embodiments of womanliness.

John Ruskin in *Proserpina* (1879) identified Shakespeare's heroines as being incarnations of various kinds of love. Isabella is 'Shakespeare's only "Saint" in whom all earthly love and the possibilities of it' are 'held in absolute subjection to the laws of God'. Queen Katherine, by comparison, is 'only an ordinary woman of trained religious temper'. Cordelia's 'earthly love' consists 'in diffused compassion of the universal spirit; not in any conquering, personally fixed feeling'. In Portia, 'the maidenly passion' becomes 'great and chiefly divine in its humility' and absolute subordination to her duty, but she is 'highest in intellect of all Shakespeare's women'. Hermione is 'Fortitude and Justice personified, with unwearing affection', Virgilia 'perfect type of wife and mother', Imogen 'the ideal of grace and gentleness', Perdita and Miranda 'rather mythic visions of maiden beauty than mere girls', Desdemona, Ophelia and Rosalind, 'creatures of fate utterly devoted to heroic figures with no free will', Viola and Juliet, 'Love the ruling power in the entire character: wholly virginal and pure'.[60]

Mrs Anna Jameson, the feminist writer, published the influential *Characteristics of Women: Moral, Poetical and Historical* (1832), in which she discussed Shakespeare's heroines as types of woman. It was issued in an enlarged edition in 1833 and reissued in 1847, 1858, 1879, 1897, 1901, 1904 and 1905, thus enjoying a very long shelf-life. Ellen possessed a copy of the 1833 edition, with many passages marked, and Jameson clearly influenced Ellen's interpretations. She divided Shakespeare's heroines into 'characters of intellect' (Portia, Isabella, Beatrice, Rosalind), 'characters of affections' (Hermione, Desdemona, Imogen, Cordelia), 'characters of passion and imagination' (Juliet, Helena, Perdita, Viola, Ophelia, Miranda) and 'historical characters' (Lady Macbeth, Katherine of Aragon, Cleopatra, Octavia, Margaret of Anjou, Constance of Brittany, Blanche of Castile).

Of Portia, Mrs Jameson wrote:

> besides the dignity, the sweetness, and tenderness which should distinguish her sex generally, she is individualized by qualities peculiar to herself; by her high mental powers, her enthusiasm of temperament, her decision of purpose, and her buoyancy of spirit. These are innate.

But from her circumstances as a wealthy heiress, 'there is a commanding grace, a high-bred airy elegance, a spirit of magnificence in all that she does and says'. It was Mrs Jameson's view that 'warm and generous affection, that tenderness of heart ... soften, strengthen and purify' the intellect. So she is intelligent but feminine. She also adds that a Portia in the present day 'would find society arm'd against her'.

Beatrice, she thought, unites 'wit and imperious temper' with 'a magnanimity of spirit' and 'high sense of female virtue and honour'. Juliet is 'love itself. The passion is her state of being, and out of it she has no existence.' Viola is characterized by 'sentiment and elegance', 'exquisite refinement' and 'sweet consciousness of her feminine nature'. Ophelia is a 'young, fair, inexperienced girl, facile to every impression, fond in her simplicity, and credulous in her innocence ... exquisitely delicate'. Desdemona is 'modesty, tenderness and grace ... artless devotion to the affections ... ethereal refinement and delicacy'. Imogen is 'of all his women ... the most perfect'. Mrs Jameson writes of her:

> In her we have all the fervour of youthful tenderness, all the romance of youthful fancy, all the enchantment of ideal grace ... The conjugal tenderness of Imogen is at once the chief subject of the drama and the pervading charm of her character.

In Cordelia, 'the whole character rests on the two sublimest principles of human action, the love of truth and the sense of duty' but Shakespeare has 'wreathed them round with the dearest attributes of our feminine nature, the power of feeling and inspiring affection'. Katherine of Aragon is characterized by truth and integrity and is above all 'a *good* woman'. In Volumnia, 'her lofty patriotism,

patrician haughtiness, her maternal pride, her eloquence, and her towering spirit'
are there, 'yet the truth of female nature are beautifully preserved … her maternal
pride and affection are even stronger than her patriotism'. Lady Macbeth is, 'cruel,
treacherous and daring' and her 'amazing power of intellect, her inexorable
determination of purpose, her superhuman strength of nerve, rendered her as
fearful in herself as her deeds are hateful'.[61]

Ruskin was looking at the characters from a male perspective and Mrs
Jameson from a female, but what they were agreed on is that there is something
called a feminine nature, a specific set of female qualities; and Ellen seems to
have incarnated them better than any other actress of her generation.

Two of the lectures on Shakespeare that Ellen delivered during a ten year
period (1911–21) in Britain, America, Australia and New Zealand, and subsequently published as a volume of essays in 1932, were on Shakespeare's women.
She declared characteristically:

> An actress does not study a character with a view to proving something about the
> dramatist who created it. Her task is to learn how to translate this character into herself,
> how to make its thoughts her thoughts, its words her words.[62]

She divided the characters into 'triumphant women' and 'pathetic women'. In
the first category came Beatrice, Portia and Rosalind. Ellen declared that the
majority of Shakespeare's heroines were 'women of strong character, high-
mettled, quick-witted and resourceful'.[63]

Beatrice, she believed, must be 'a pleasant-spirited lady' and since 'her repartee
can easily be made to sound malicious and vulgar … it should be spoken as the
lightest raillery, with mirth in the voice and charm in the manner'. Complaining
as she did in her autobiography that she had never been swift enough in her
performance because 'I had a too deliberate, though polished and thoughtful
Benedick in Henry Irving', at least she said, 'I did not make the mistake of being
arch and kittenish'.[64]

Rosalind, the role she was still lamenting never having played, had 'all the
qualities of the well-bred at all times'.[65] Portia, she said, she had played five or six
different ways but always came back to the 'Renaissance way', stressing her beauty.
But she believed that 'in spite of her self-surrender to love there is something
independent, almost masculine in her attitude to life'. She is intelligent,
responsible and animated by 'noblesse oblige'.[66]

The 'Pathetic Women' include Viola, Juliet, Desdemona, Ophelia, Cordelia,
Imogen and Lady Macbeth. Viola must be young; she has 'a lovely rather than a
brilliant mind. She seldom says a clever thing. She often says a beautiful thing.'
She has 'a golden heart as well as a golden voice'.[67]

Desdemona, generally regarded as a ninny, is in fact a woman of strong rather
than weak character and the role requires 'a great tragic actress with a strong

personality'. Juliet, though young, is fearless and morally strong, Cordelia is a 'wonderful study of a daughter'. Lady Macbeth is defined contrary to the ferocious female tiger played by Sarah Siddons. Ellen, defending her controversial Lyceum interpretation, sees her not as a robust, muscular woman, but 'a small, slight woman of acute nervous sensibility'.[68]

Her favourite part among Shakespeare's heroines was Imogen. 'She enchants me, and so I can find no fault in her.' She approvingly quotes Shaw, who said she was 'an enchanting person of the most delicate sensitiveness, and of the highest breeding and courage. She needs the highest courage, for she is made to suffer trial after trial.'[69]

Ophelia is 'Shakespeare's only timid heroine ... her brain, her soul and her body are all pathetically weak' and she is 'really mad, not merely metaphorically mad – with grief'.[70] It is fascinating to see that the charm, intelligence, beauty and ladylike good breeding which she sees as characterizing these roles are precisely those characteristics which audiences and critics so applauded in her performance, and saw as specifically feminine.

A look at three of Terry's own non-Shakespearean vehicles, in all of which she achieved popular success and which figured for many years in her repertoire, confirm the qualities that lay behind her enduring success. On the occasion of her benefit, on 20 May 1880, the last act of *The Merchant of Venice* was omitted and a one-act play by W.G. Wills was substituted. It was *Iolanthe*, a new version of the lyric drama *King René's Daughter* by the Danish poet Henrik Herz. In previous versions, it had proved a successful vehicle for Mrs Stirling (1849), Mrs Charles Kean (1849) and Helen Faucit (1850). It was a 'Sleeping Beauty' story in which a blind princess in a beautiful and picturesque garden is restored to sight by the love of a gallant nobleman. It was described by its author as an 'Idyll', and the pathos that was the keynote of *Iolanthe* was perfectly attuned to Terry's gifts. Irving, on the other hand, who took the role of the lover Count Tristan, was not well cast. Terry declared frankly, 'Henry was *not* good in it. He had a Romeo part which had not been written by Shakespeare'.[71] It was, however, so popular that it played with *The Merchant* for the rest of the run. The choice of the subject, the care with which it was staged (its setting 'amongst the finest stage pictures which Mr Hawes Craven has painted for the Lyceum'),[72] and Irving's own miscasting as the lover, all point to this as a dramatic love offering by Irving to his partner, and one which would showcase her femininity. Indeed Irving wrote to Clement Scott: 'Ellen Terry is simply exquisite in the part and her simplicity of method a lesson to all artists.'[73]

A similar role was provided for her in *The Amber Heart*, a 'poetical fancy in three acts' by Alfred Calmour, which saw Ellen Terry as the pathetic Ellaline dealing with abandonment by a false lover. The critics were enraptured. Typical were the comments of the *Athenaeum* critic: 'The picture presented by Miss Terry was delightful, and her acting had singular delicacy, refinement, and pathos, and no small measure of power'; and the *World*'s William Archer: 'Miss Terry has perhaps done nothing more moving than her soliloquy in the second act and her performance throughout was instinct with grace and feeling.'[74] Some thought it her greatest performance. It was a play which she admitted she believed in and it was a part she liked.[75] Irving, who did not appear in it and watched it from the front – the first time he had actually seen her give an entire performance from the stalls – wrote to her afterwards: 'I wish I could tell you of the dream of beauty that you realized.' He purchased the copyright of the play and presented it to her, and she continued to perform it '"on and off" here and in America until 1902'.[76]

It was Terry herself who purchased Charles Reade's one-act play *Nance Oldfield*, performing in it first in 1891 as part of a double-bill with *The Corsican Brothers*. Later it formed part of a double-bill with *The Bells*, in which there was no role for her, just as there was no role for Irving in *Nance Oldfield*. The play dramatizes a fictional episode in the career of the real-life eighteenth-century actress Anne Oldfield. A young poet and dramatist, Alexander Oldworthy, falls in love with the fascinating actress. His father, a prejudiced old attorney, implores her to cure him of his folly, which she does by making herself out to be worldly, heartless and slatternly and disparaging his compositions. The young man is driven to suicidal despair and the father now begs her to revive his son's love for her, which she succeeds in doing. It was so popular it was to be constantly revived and she recalled playing it 'hundreds of times'.[77] In the first production, her son Edward Gordon Craig played the young man. The *Birmingham Daily Post* (29 September 1891) recorded that she played the part with 'irresistible charm', adding 'before the play was over the majority of the audience were in the plight of the poor young Alexander Oldworthy – hopelessly in love with the bewitching actress'.

Taken together, the popularity of *Iolanthe*, *The Amber Heart* and *Nance Oldfield*, all of which played to Ellen's particular strengths, confirmed the image of femininity which her public demanded that she incarnate: tender, gentle, self-sacrificing, charming, wistful, graceful. As for Irving taming and somehow devitalizing Terry, Irving never actually directed her, something which both infuriated her and unsettled her. Auerbach says that Irving reinvented Terry as a womanly actress whom audiences could love without fear or unease.[78] But she was already regarded as occupying that role before she joined Irving. Her performances in pace and timing certainly had to complement his and his interpretations were to a great extent dictated by his limitations. But as to his shaping her performances, we have Ellen Terry's own testimony to the opposite. It began with *Hamlet* in 1878. Irving read the whole play and acted out every part except Ophelia, which he skipped. He rehearsed the entire cast rigorously and meticulously but not Ellen, apparently having confidence in her own understanding of the part.[79] Her habitual first night nerves were exacerbated by her concern at the lack of rehearsal, and she was convinced that she had failed. In fact the critics bathed her in praise, as they were to do for much of what she did. The *Saturday Review* compared her to Sarah Bernhardt and proclaimed her a genius.[80] Her regularly favourable press was what made adverse criticism sting. It was comparatively rare. Irving, on the other hand, endured continual criticism.

One famous example of adverse criticism featured in the pages of *Blackwood's Magazine*, in which Sir Theodore Martin, who was married to Helen Faucit, the Portia of the previous generation, used the opportunity of an article (published anonymously) on the idea of a national theatre to deliver a detailed critique of the Lyceum *Merchant*. While praising Irving's Shylock ('his best Shakespearean performance. It is based upon a broad, clear conception, and carried out in all its details with great finish and great picturesqueness'), and his treatment of the trial scene ('excellent'), he attacked all the other performances and in particular Ellen Terry's Portia, which had otherwise attracted almost universal critical approval: 'she is not the great lady of Belmont, the self-possessed queenly creature, whose very presence turns men of ordinary mould into poets, and attracts, even while she holds them at bay in admiring reverence'. He stressed the intellectuality of the role: 'She is the ideal of the high-born woman, gloriously endowed in body and in mind.'[81] In particular he felt she was far too forward in her attitude to Bassanio, holding him caressingly by the hand while urging him to wait a day or so before trying his fortune with the caskets. John Ruskin and Henry James shared this view. James wrote: 'Miss Terry's mistress of Belmont giggles too much, plays too much with her fingers, is too free and familiar, too osculatory in her relations with Bassanio.'[82]

Terry was so stung by this attack that she took it up in her 1908 autobiography, saying 'The suggestion that I showed too much of a 'coming-on' disposition in the casket scene affected me for years and made me self-conscious and uncomfortable ... Any suggestions of *indelicacy* in my treatment of a part has always blighted me.' She went on to defend her interpretation, citing in support the views of F.J. Furnivall, who had written to her saying:

> Your whole conception and acting of the character is so true to Shakespeare's notes that one longs he could be here to see you. A lady gracious, handsome, witty, loving and wise, you are his Portia to the life.[83]

In her *Four Lectures on Shakespeare* she summed up her approach to Portia:

> But from my point of view no interpretation entailing a sacrifice of beauty, whether to mirth or realism can ever be satisfactory. Portia is the fruit of the Renaissance, the child of the period of beautiful clothes, beautiful cities, beautiful houses, beautiful ideas. Wreck that beauty and the part goes to pieces.[84]

In an important article comparing the interpretations of Portia by Faucit and Terry, Richard Foulkes puts his finger on the essential difference:

> The difference lay in the 'tone and manner' in which they played the part. Helen Faucit based her characterization on Portia's breeding and intellect and sought to anchor each scene in its underlying reality … For Ellen Terry Portia's beauty was paramount to the extent that even in her disguise her audience, on the whole willingly, remained conscious of her charm and femininity. Her performance belonged to the realm of comedy.[85]

Irving's practice of not offering her direction continued throughout their association. Ellen wrote to Bernard Shaw on 24 September 1896, after he had criticized elements of her performance as Imogen in *Cymbeline*:

> You must understand I am the one person at the Lyceum who is never advised, found fault with, or 'blackguarded' before the production of our plays! Henry finds fault with everyone and rehearses and rehearses and rehearses and (da capo) them over and over and over again. Then our scenes (his and mine) come on, and he generally says 'Oh, we'll skip these scenes', and I am to be found up in the scene-dock doing it all by myself, or being heard words by some girl or boy. Then Henry's scenes come on, and I watch those, and find fault with them(!), and this great advantage is lost *only* to me … It is *frightful* not to be found fault with.[86]

Robert Hichens, co-author of *The Medicine Man*, observed Irving's failure to direct Terry at first hand:

> She kept saying 'What is there for me to do here?' and 'I don't see what I'm to make of this!' Irving didn't seem to care in the least what she thought. He seemed entirely intent upon his part as the doctor. I have never seen any other actor apparently so indifferent to the feelings and needs of his leading lady on the stage. Sometimes Miss Terry wrung her hands. He remained completely impassive.[87]

In her autobiography Ellen says he 'never spent much time on the women in the company, except as regard to position. Sometimes he would ask me to suggest things to them, to do for them what he did for the men.'[88] Why this failure to offer direction or criticism on Irving's part? Probably because she was doing, and he knew she would do, what he wanted in terms of imparting to the roles her distinctive qualities. She records that her acting as Desdemona was so imbued with pathos that, when he was playing opposite her as Iago, his eyes filled with tears.[89] Terry was an actress who needed constant reassurance, was regularly convinced that she had failed and was intensely self-critical. After the first performance of *Romeo and Juliet* she wrote to a friend:

> A thousand thanks for your letter. The fact remains that Juliet was a horrid failure. *And I meant so well!* I am very sad, but I thank you. *It is not the critics.* I knew it all on Wednesday night[90]

When he was preparing *Romeo and Juliet*, Irving revived *Two Roses* but released Ellen from the role of Lottie in which he had cast her to allow her to concentrate on studying Juliet: 'You've got to do all you know with it', he told her.[91] Irving, we know, thought her performance perfect and told her so. She evidently brought to it everything Irving wanted in the role. The critics were rather less enthusiastic. Joseph Knight in the *Athenaeum* said: 'To the stronger scenes of Juliet she is ... unequal ... There is no point at which the intensity is realized ... Portions of her rendering have her known grace, beauty, and intelligence; but her Juliet is altogether inferior to her Ophelia, and far below her Portia.'[92] Frederick Wedmore in the *Academy* said: 'the latest scenes are wanting in the imagination of tragedy. Nothing is called out of the depths. The actress deals with tragedy like an eighteenth-century portrait painter ... The first word is grace – but so is the last.'[93]

Charles Hiatt notes that these views were echoed by the daily paper critics with 'striking unanimity', praise for some parts of the interpretation but not for others.[94] But none of this can be put down to Irving, for Terry was regularly unable to sustain tragic intensity in a role, which is why she interpreted Lady Macbeth to fit her range. She was a highly conscientious actress, who thought out her parts, annotating her scripts profusely.[95] Another personal reason for Irving not rehearsing her may be her admission that, while they were in love, she actually found it embarrassing to act out love scenes with him on the stage. Perhaps he felt the same or perhaps he sought to reduce her embarrassment.

If she could not master the depths of tragedy, pathos was certainly her great strength. When she appeared as Ellaline, the heart-broken maiden abandoned by her lover, in Alfred Calmour's *The Amber Heart*, and the critics united in finding it the perfect vehicle for her grace and charm, she wrote to the author:

> I hope you are pleased. I am so sorry about one thing yesterday. From nervousness my acting of the first act was strained and artificial, and I confess that I entirely ruined and *missed* your first beautiful soliloquy in the second act! I am *truly* sorry! I know that you are a good creature, and view all my efforts from the point of view of my *intentions* since I succeeded better in some bits. Although I may never play the part again, I never will cease to love the play for its own sake, and to regard and esteem my friend who wrote it – *for me* – I do believe.

Her biographer T. Edgar Pemberton commented on this: 'Poor, self-tormenting lady! From first to last she had played the part to perfection – and everyone but herself knew it.'[96] The critics saw it as a role perfectly suited to her 'grace and charm.'[97] Edward Gordon Craig, analysing her approach, wrote:

> She did not depend much on bits of business, as we call them; her power lay in entering any character and making herself one with it – 'getting under the skin of the part' is the

phrase used by the profession. And it came to be said of her that she possessed in the very highest degree the art which conceals art.[98]

So she found something of herself in the part or put something of herself into it. Ellen revealingly recalled that before playing Ophelia she visited a madhouse to study the lunatics and received no enlightenment:

> There was no beauty, no nature, no pity in most of the lunatics. Strange as it may sound, they were just too *theatrical* to teach me anything … My experiences convinced me that the actor must imagine first and observe afterwards. It is no good observing life and bringing the result to the stage without selection, without a definite idea. The idea must come first, the realism afterwards.[99]

Ellen had a very clear and precise knowledge of her own strengths and weaknesses and those of other actors, especially Irving. She told her son Gordon Craig what her faults were: 'I always lacked concentration – could not restrain tears – could not easily achieve repose – could not sustain any feeling for very long.'[100] She expanded on this in her autobiography. She realized she could never be a great tragic actress like Sarah Siddons:

> It has never been in my power to *sustain* … On the stage I can pass swiftly from one effect to another, but I cannot fix *one*, and dwell on it, with that superb concentration which seems to me the special attribute of the tragic actress.[101]

The strain of playing the tragic Margaret night after night in *Faust* was so great that she had to surrender the part to Winifred Emery during the run.[102] She wrote of her performance as Camma in *The Cup*: 'The first act was well within my means; the second was beyond them, but it was very good for me to try and do it.'[103] Where possible and where the intensity of a role was beyond her, she transformed it. According to Gordon Craig, she loathed the part of Pauline in Lytton's *Lady of Lyons*.[104] Joseph Knight, seeing her one-off performance as Pauline Deschappelles in 1875, and realizing that the power and fury of the character were beyond her, presciently noted:

> It seems probable that Miss Terry's powers will be restrained to depicting the grace, tenderness and passion of love. In the short scene in the third act, in which Pauline chides her lover for treachery, the actress scarcely rises to the requisite indignation … Juliet in her stronger scenes would be, we should fancy, outside the physical resources of the artist. Beatrice, Rosalind, Viola, Imogen, Miranda, and a score other characters of the most delicate and fragrant beauty are, however, all within what appears to be her range.[105]

As it turned out, the critics did indeed find the stronger scenes of Juliet beyond her, but Beatrice, Imogen and Viola among her successes. Clement Scott also provided a shrewd analysis of her performance as Pauline, a part written as proud, haughty and scornful – and played that way by Helen Faucit. Ellen solved her problem with the part, he noted, 'by turning Pauline into a French Olivia' and playing her as 'tenderly fragile, constantly fainting and tearfully pathetic'.[106]

Similarly she softened the character of Lady Macbeth in a performance that was as controversial as Irving's new reading of Macbeth. Ellen wrote in her diary:

> It is a success, and I am a success, which amazes me, for never did I think I should be let down so easily. Some people hate me in it; some, Henry among them, think it my best part, and the critics differ, and discuss it hotly, which in itself is my best success of all! Those who don't like me in it are those who don't want, and don't like to read it fresh from Shakespeare, and who hold by the 'fiend' reading of the character … One of the best things ever written on the subject, I think, is the essay by J. Comyns Carr. That is as hotly discussed as the new 'Lady Mac' – all the best people agreeing with it.[107]

Gordon Craig attributed the transformation rather more to Ellen's desire to be loved by her public. Depicting her saying: 'Now, my dear, dear people, you won't *really* think I am a horrid woman like that, will you?', he tartly encapsulated the interpretation:

> In the sleepwalking scene, you did not shudder at the thought beneath the words: 'The Thane of Fife had a wife – where is she now?' You only felt: 'Poor Ellen Terry – she is so sorry for the Thane of Fife's wife, and is wondering where she can possibly be now, poor, poor dear. What a *nice* woman.'[108]

The celebrated portrait by Sargent of Ellen as Lady Macbeth in the famous dress of blue, green and gold, and the red tresses, crowning herself proud, taut and ambitious, eyes blazing, 'filled top full of direst cruelty' stands in mute reproach to the performance that failed to highlight these qualities. As Christopher St. John pointed out: 'The Sargent portrait criticizes her on canvas better than anyone managed to do on paper.'[109] But Ellen knew only too well that she could never sustain the 'fiend' performance.

Similarly of her Queen Katherine in *Henry VIII*, a part Terry herself disliked, and another favourite of Sarah Siddons, Hiatt wrote:

> It may safely be asserted that Miss Terry's reading of the part differed widely from that of any of her predecessors. Queen Katherine , as interpreted by Miss Terry, was first of all a woman infinitely tender, infinitely loveable. It is open to doubt whether Miss Terry did not go further in this direction than the author or authors of the play intended, whether she was not a trifle too winning, too graceful, too obviously attractive.[110]

Perhaps one of her most 'feminine' traits was her readiness to weep. And as Gordon Craig observed: 'The English public has always loved to cry if it could get someone to cry with – it will not cry until the actress cries.'[111] 'My real tears on the stage have astonished some people, and have been the envy of others, but they have often been a hindrance to me. I have had to *work* to restrain them', she wrote. She claims to have cried too much in *Olivia* (though her tears reduced the author W.G. Wills, watching from the wings, to tears), in the nunnery scene of *Hamlet* and the last act of *Charles the First*. She explained her tears in *Olivia* by saying that 'Olivia, more than any other part touched me to the heart'.[112] This could well be because in it she found herself recreating her own life. Olivia, one of a large family, the beloved daughter of a doting father, elopes with Squire Thornhill, is betrayed and abandoned but rescued and brought home by her father, Dr Primrose, the Vicar of Wakefield. Ellen, herself, similarly one of a large family with a doting father, had herself eloped to live with E.W. Godwin in a state of unwedded bliss, being reconciled with her family only when the liaison ended. The action of the play must have struck many chords for her.

If at one level she was the Victorians' ideal woman, bringing her celebrated feminine charm and tenderness to a succession of ideal daughters (Olivia, Cordelia), dutiful wives (Queen Henrietta Maria, Camma, Imogen, Queen Katherine of Aragon) and noble mothers (Catherine Duval, Clarice de Maluçon), she was also their aesthetic ideal. Just as often as she was described as the embodiment of femininity, Ellen was described as the embodiment of Pre-Raphaelitism. Graham Robertson said she was 'the accepted type of the Pre-Raphaelite School and an embodiment of all the romance and glamour of their favourite literature'.[113] Clement Scott said 'she was the ideal of every Pre-Raphaelite painter'.[114] In his 1900 biography Clement Scott recalled seeing her in 1863: 'I never saw a more enchanting and ideal creature. She was a poem that lived and breathed and suggested to us the girl heroines that we adored in poetry and the fine arts generally.'[115] He compared her to Elaine, the Fair Maid of Astolat, Vivien, Rapunzel, Tennyson's Princess and Browning's Porphyria. Graham Robertson called her '*par excellence* the Painter's Actress'.[116]

In writing of Ellen, critics constantly turned to painting for their descriptions. Writing of her performance as Camma in *The Cup*, Frederick Wedmore in the *Academy* said: 'Aided by draperies arranged with the most singular skill, the figure, in its freedom and suavity, recalls the Elgin marbles and the designs of the artist who has learnt the best use from them – Mr Albert Moore. In hue and line the actress is a realization of Mr Moore's painting.'[117] When she played Queen Katherine, she reminded Charles Hiatt of 'one of those portraits of patrician ladies which Rembrandt painted in his earlier and more minute manner'.[118]

The *Daily Telegraph* said of her 1875 Portia that she 'looked as if she had stepped out of a canvas by Mr Leighton'.[119] Clement Scott said of her Pauline in the Lyceum *Lady of Lyons* that she looked as 'if she were sitting for a picture by Marcus Stone or Orchardson'.[120] Joseph Knight said of her Lyceum Portia that she was 'got up in exact imitation of those stately Venetian dames who still gaze down from the pictures of Paolo Veronese'.[121]

Terry fitted perfectly into an age when plays were staged, framed and designed as pictures, when famous paintings were 'realized' on the stage and when acting was pictorial.[122] For Henry James, this pictorialism actually disguised a limited talent. He wrote rather caustically:

> By many intelligent persons she is regarded as an actress of exquisite genius ... This is not, in our opinion, the truth ... The difficulty is that Miss Terry has charm – remarkable charm; and this beguiles people into thinking her an accomplished actress. There is a natural quality about her that is extremely pleasing – something wholesome and English and womanly ... Miss Terry has that excellent thing, a quality; she gives one the sense of something fine. Add to this that though she is not regularly beautiful, she has a face altogether in the taste of the period, a face that Burne-Jones might have drawn, and that she arranges herself (always in the taste of the period) wonderfully well for the story. She makes an admirable picture and it would be difficult to imagine a more striking embodiment of sumptuous sweetness than her Ophelia, her Portia, her Pauline, and her Olivia.[123]

Ellen was aware of the source of her appeal and cultivated it. Her aesthetic taste had been trained by Godwin and she was able to advise Irving on costumes and settings with confidence. She wrote in her autobiography of her early triumph as Portia: 'The aesthetic craze, with all its faults, was responsible for a great deal of true enthusiasm for anything beautiful. It made people welcome the Bancrofts' production of *The Merchant of Venice*.'[124] It was her appearance that struck the first night audience at the Bancrofts' *Merchant*. Alice Comyns Carr, the wife of Joseph Comyns Carr, the editor of the *English Illustrated Magazine*, drama critic of the *Pall Mall Gazette* and director of the Grosvenor Gallery, friend of Whistler and Burne-Jones, recorded in her *Reminiscences*:

> Joe and I were present on the first night, and as the curtain rose on Nell's tall and slender figure in a china blue and white brocaded dress, with one crimson rose at her breast, the whole house burst forth in rapturous applause.[125]

Joe was so moved he rushed out between acts to Covent Garden to buy a bouquet which he threw at her feet at the end of the play. Alice Comyns Carr eventually replaced Patience Harris (the sister of Sir Augustus Harris) as Ellen's dress designer. Patience had favoured 'elaborate pretentious gowns' but Alice preferred much more simple and stylized fashions. So from *The Amber Heart* (1888), for which she devised a flowing white long-sleeved gown, Alice designed all her dresses for the next twenty years in line with prevailing costume ideas. These included the famous Lady Macbeth gown in which she was painted by Sargent and which Ellen in a letter to her daughter said had 'Rossetti-rich stained-glass effects' and the heavy brocade gown of 'steely silver and bronzy gold' worn by Queen Katherine in *Henry VIII*.[126] Graham Robertson also invoked Rossetti when describing her Rosamund in *Becket*: 'she looked her loveliest, especially in the rich gown of her first entrance, a wonderful Rossettian effect of dim gold and glowing colour veiled in black, her masses of bright hair in a net of gold and golden leaves embroidered on her robe'.[127]

This painterly beauty was one reason why at sixteen she had captivated G.F. Watts, who married her and painted her in five works, one of them as Ophelia, fifteen years before she actually played the part. He even painted her after their divorce in 'The Madness of Ophelia', inspired by the Lyceum production. Although she was the Pre-Raphaelite ideal, none of the Pre-Raphaelites painted her. The most celebrated painting of her is Sargent's full-length portrait of her as Lady Macbeth. But she was also painted by Johnston Forbes-Robertson, W. Graham Robertson, Mortimer Menpes, Solomon J. Solomon and the Duchess of Rutland. She was also photographed regularly, in idealized poses, by among others Julia Margaret Cameron and Lewis Carroll.

When Sir Edward Burne-Jones and Lord Leighton went to see Ellen in *The Amber Heart* (1888), she enraptured their painterly sensibility. Burne-Jones wrote: 'It is the most inspiring work to a painter – and Miss Terry's performance a revelation of loveliness. It is not acting – it is a glimpse into Nature itself', and Leighton wrote: 'Beautiful! Beautiful! Acting and play beautiful! A sweet and abiding memory.'[128]

While the usual way of referring to Ellen Terry was to invoke painterly comparisons, Gail Marshall has argued for the application of a sculptural metaphor to actresses, a metaphor validated by the popularity in Victorian culture of the Ovidian myth of Pygmalion and Galatea.[129] Ellen Terry was a clear case in point: an emblematic choice for her thesis, as Ellen's acting career began and ended with *The Winter's Tale*, in which the heroine poses as a statue. In 1856 Ellen played Mamilius and in 1906 Hermione.

Sculpturally informed aesthetic judgements and criteria became possible in the nineteenth century because of the large numbers of classical sculptures appearing in museums, two of the most popular being Venus de Milo and Venus de Medici. They achieved tremendous exposure and popularity. Classical sculptures inspired the paintings of Watts, Poynter, Alma-Tadema, Albert Moore, Frederic Leighton and Burne-Jones. The statues of Venus made Venus at the same time 'sexually available and angelically idealized'. So the language of the Venus statue informs descriptions of real-life beauties like Lillie Langtry and of the attitudes of men to women in fictions like Henry James' *Portrait of a Lady* and George Meredith's *The Egoist*. The obsession with statues of women became a classifiable form of erotomania, dubbed by Havelock Ellis as 'Pygmalionism'.

The myth of Pygmalion and Galatea was central to Victorian culture. Galatea is a male image of female subjection. In the many Victorian poetic reworkings of Ovid's original story, Galatea usually returns to stone at the end, whereas in the classical texts she remained alive. The reason for the change of ending was the

Victorian concern about women stepping down from their domestic pedestal to become liberated. They are returned to immobility at the end.

Actresses fulfilled the Galatea model by speaking words given to them by men and taking on the role of isolated and desirable spectacles like Galatea: desirable and unattainable. G.F. Watts, inspired by classical statues, painted *Pygmalion's Wife* (1868), and sought to act as Pygmalion to Ellen's Galatea, explicitly outlining this mission in a letter: 'I have determined to remove [Ellen Terry] from the temptations and abomination of the stage, giving her an education and if she continues to have the affection she now feels for me, marry her ... To make the poor Child what I wish her to be will take a lot of time and most likely cost a great deal of trouble.'[130] After ten months the project foundered and she proved untamable.

Victorian actresses' relationship to the Pygmalion-Galatea narrative had its roots in the early nineteenth-century manifestations of the link between sculptures and the stage. Between 1800 and 1817 white muslin dresses, modelled on classical sculptures, were all the rage. Emma Hamilton became famous for her 'attitudes' – poses imitating classical sculptures and mythological characters which gave rise to a long-running tradition of *tableaux vivants* and *poses plastiques*, scantily clad women in classical postures.

Classical purity continued to be a desired model on the stage. Helen Faucit, seen as the epitome of chaste womanhood, praised for her Antigone and Hermione, was regularly compared to Greek statues. Sir Frederic Burton sketched her as 'The Greek Muse'. Faucit's 'passive desirability is allowed to exist hand-in-hand with her modesty and virtue'.[131] The 1880s saw a vogue for toga plays with leading actresses arrayed in classical draperies.

There are references to Ellen Terry in George du Maurier's *Trilby*, a best-selling romance which Gail Marshall identifies as a variant of Pygmalion and Galatea. Du Maurier's drawings of Trilby resemble Ellen. Trilby is explicitly compared to Ellen's Camma. What she does not go on to say is that on this interpretation, Irving is her Svengali. There is much irony in this for in the stage version of *Trilby*, Svengali was played with great success by Irving's greatest rival, Sir Herbert Beerbohm Tree, and Trilby by Irving's future daughter-in-law Dorothea Baird. He was clearly so taken with the part that he commissioned an imitation, the mesmerist Dr Tregenna in *The Medicine Man*, which failed. Contrary to Tracy Davis, who sees the Victorian actress as transgressive and liberated, Marshall sees her as 'highly conservative'.[132]

The 1890s were a time of change. It was the decade of 'The New Woman' when the arrival of Ibsen, the Independent Theatre of J.T. Grein and the 'theatre of ideas' represented by Pinero and Henry Arthur Jones led to the demand voiced by William Archer and Bernard Shaw for literary and intellectual drama. Ibsen's heroines are the opposite of Galatea. Marshall argues that 'Ibsen's principal gift to the actress was to allow her to exceed the possibilities of the spectacular stage, and the constraints, moral, intellectual and creative, embodied in the sculptural metaphor previously applied to her. This is iconographically represented in the multiple possibilities of movement embodied by his female characters.'[133] Ibsen was credited by contemporaries with changing the perceptions of actresses. Women were prominent in the new movement as managers, playwrights and independent actresses. Eleanora Duse is seen as an example of the new actress, the producer of her own intelligence and executive ability. But this development should not be overstressed. There had always been female actor-managers (Madam Vestris, Marie Wilton, Sara Lane) and Ellen remained the favourite actress of her age.

Feminists have argued that when she joined Irving, Terry became a queen consort not a queen, deliberately denied any managerial responsibility.[134] Irving directed, produced and oversaw all aspects of the Lyceum programme. But when Terry attempted direction on Laurence Irving's play *Godefroi and Yolande*, she could not manage it and Irving had to step in to save the production. And when she went into management at the Imperial Theatre and produced Ibsen's *The Vikings at Helgeland* at the behest of her son Edward Gordon Craig, the production was a failure and she lost much of her savings.

Her career at the Lyceum had given her unparalleled financial security. Irving paid her far more than he paid himself. She was earning £200 a week in her heyday.[135] She was able to play a range of Shakespearean roles unlikely to have been available to her elsewhere. The idea that she was imprisoned by the Lyceum, devitalized, projected as a womanly ideal that she herself rejected, is not borne out by the facts. She excelled in comedy and pathos and played both at the Lyceum. She herself wrote: 'I have sometimes wondered what I should have accomplished without Henry Irving. I might have had 'bigger' parts, but it doesn't follow that they would have been better ones, and if they had been written by contemporary dramatists my success would have been less durable.'[136]

In an 1888 letter to Clement Scott, which highlights her own modesty but also her credo, Ellen wrote: 'I am quite surprised to find that I am *really* a useful actress – for *I really am*!! To be able to *get through with* such difficult parts as – Ophelia – Olivia – Beatrice – Margaret – and Lady M. and my aim is *usefulness* to my lovely art and to H.I.'[137] In her autobiography she wrote: 'I have been happiest in my work when I was working for someone else. I admire those impersonal people who care for nothing outside their own ambition, yet I detest them at the same time, as I have the simplest faith that absolute devotion to another human being means the greatest *happiness*.'[138] It was this belief that led her into marriage with G.F. Watts, her liaison with E.W. Godwin and her long and productive partnership with Irving. Ellen's friend Graham Robertson perceptively wrote in 1931:

As to her career being sacrificed to him [Irving] – does anyone in their senses suppose that she would have gained her unique position without him? She had little ambition – no 'push' – little business capacity. She loved to serve and would always have served *somebody*.[139]

Her son Edward Gordon Craig recorded that when she left Irving, far from being 'liberated from his paternalist tyranny,' she was left 'rudderless': 'She could not take and abide by the counsel of any one person, after she left Irving – she had preferred to consult dozens of people about everything, and to annoy them by never entirely following their advice.'[140]

In her memoirs, she assessed the nature and strength of the Irving–Terry partnership with clear-eyed realism:

Henry could never have worked with a very strong woman. I might have deteriorated in partnership with a weaker man whose ends were less fine, whose motives were less pure.[141]

Although latterly surrounded by militant feminists (her daughter Edy and her circle), Ellen was not a political animal. When women got the vote, she never exercised her right to vote. Her interests lay elsewhere. Edward Gordon Craig said she believed 'the whole purpose of life is happiness' and she was 'convinced of the goodness of loving things and the hatefulness of hating things'.[142] Tom Prideaux called his biography of Ellen *Love or Nothing* and it is clear that she was a woman for whom love was vital. After all she deserted the stage to marry G.F. Watts and to live with E.W. Godwin, and returned to it only because of financial necessity. She married three times and cultivated romantic friendships with attractive men, but she also needed a succession of father figures to guide her career – from her own father Benjamin Terry through the painter G.F. Watts, the dramatists Tom Taylor and Charles Reade, to Irving himself, who was both lover and father. It is her character and her needs that dictated the nature of her relationship with Irving and the Lyceum: it is her positive feminine attributes and dramatic limitations that governed her theatrical interpretations, and it is her happy congruence with the gender ideals of the age that ensured her long and unbroken hold on the affections of the public.

4

The Victorian Stage

The second half of the nineteenth century saw a major transformation in the status of the theatre and the standing of the actor. Irving played a central role in this process. In his analysis of nineteenth-century social progress, *Social Transformations of the Victorian Age* (1897), journalist T.H.S. Escott included a chapter on the stage, acknowledging this development in terms which enshrined the arguments which had been advanced consistently in favour of the stage:

> The organisation of the stage into a wholesome agency of popular amusement and teaching began with Macready, the earliest of that line of considerable actors who have served their generation during the Victorian epoch. But the prejudices against the play prevailing among other than the austerer classes long survived the work of this great reformer of the English stage. The company which fills a theatre today in respect of ethics and behaviour is not inferior to the fashionable occupants of an opera box on a subscription night.[1]

Macready was followed by Samuel Phelps, Walter Montgomery and Charles Kean with whom began 'the improvement in stage scenery, costume, and in all incidental accessories that has been brought to so high a point of perfection by the genius, industry, and well-judged lavishness of Henry Irving'.[2]

The drama revived under the impact of the plays of Tom Robertson, which substituted 'the realities of contemporary life in drawing room, club, shooting field and camp for the threadbare traditions, stilted sentiment and fustian talk of conventional melodramas'. As a result of this, the middle classes returned *en masse* to the theatre and acting as a profession became respectable.[3]

> The theatre with us was firmly established as an honourable and lucrative institution directly men of intellectual power and of competent education began to throw their energies into it as they might have done into the law, the legislature or any other of the liberal professions.[4]

The drama's popularity was evidenced by the increasing number of Etonians and Oxford graduates entering the profession and Irving's knighthood was 'just recognition' of his achievements.

Escott declared the theatre 'an integral part' of the life of the 'most respectable portion of the middle classes' and praised 'the far more amusing repertory ... at the end of this century that at any previous epoch' and declared 'the surprising success of the new religious drama' to be evidence of 'its utility as an agency of mental improvement and moral teaching'.[5] Taken together, the themes highlighted are the ones that became the commonplaces of theatrical history: the achievements of a succession of actor-managers in improving the quality, literacy, naturalism and respectability of the drama, the return of the middle classes and the educational and improving role played by the stage.

The return of the middle classes and the increasing respectability of the stage and the acting profession were part of a major cultural change in the mid nineteenth century: the rise of the middle-class professionals to meet the needs of an increasingly urbanized society; the growth of mass commercialized leisure industries to meet the increased desire for recreation facilitated by higher wages and shorter working hours; the modification of traditional religious beliefs and attitudes towards the stage; the establishment of a mass circulation popular press able to promote the theatre; and improvements in transportation and social mobility

The actor in 1830 was a social and artistic outcast, a rogue and vagabond.[6] The arts were seen not as a profession but as a raffish and bohemian avocation. This changed during the second half of the nineteenth century in the context of the rise in the wider society of the idea of professionalism. By 1860 the three chief principles on which the modern profession is based were already recognized: qualification by examination; legal acknowledgement of the right to practice; and the right of a professional body to internal self-regulation. In the 1861 census the arts began to be classified as a profession for the first time.

The Romantic concept of the artist as an elite figure with a heightened sensibility was widely accepted by mid century. But the role of the actor was still highly problematic. There was no recognized means of entering the profession, there were no acting schools, there were no professional institutions, and there had been no award of honours. Polemics against the stage were regularly issued by clerics, moralists and reformers. Intellectuals accused the stage of being unoriginal and immoral. It was argued that great plays were better read than seen performed. Theatres were linked to prostitution, juvenile delinquency, idleness, drunkenness and frivolity. It was all the antithesis of the Victorian world view which prized respectability, gentility, decency, education and uplift. Samuel Phelps's daughter was expelled from her school when it was discovered her father was an actor.

Within the theatrical profession, various leading figures took steps to meet this agenda, by raising the moral tone and respectability of the stage. Macready was ashamed of his profession and abandoned it as soon as he was able to. But Charles Kean, whose Etonian education was made much of by defenders of the stage, was given a dinner by fellow Etonians where he was hailed for making the theatre 'into a gigantic instrument of education ... and edification'. The Bancrofts prided themselves in their joint autobiography for paying actors a proper wage for the first time and making the stage 'a worthy career for refined and talented people'.[7] The theatre readily accepted the censorship system which enshrined the conventional Victorian morality. The rise of society drama and a gentlemanly acting style were seen as important contributions to the increasing acceptability of the stage.

In the early nineteenth century, actors were marginal figures, working unsocial hours, lacking security of employment but strongly bound together by family traditions and involvement. Actors had their own rituals, language, jokes and habits. In London they tended to live in defined areas, such as Brompton and Bloomsbury. By the 1880s the position of the actor was changing. Actors had become members of clubs and mixed with other professionals. The wealthier actors moved to St John's Wood, leaving the poorer ones in South and East London, something which showed the stage mirroring the class divisions of the wider society. A growing number of educated and middle class figures were entering the profession. The theatre was becoming centralized and stabilized with long runs, national tours and greater regularity of employment. Twenty-four new theatres were built between 1880 and 1914, ensuring more work.

Actresses had traditionally been even more disreputable than actors. They were seen as working women, exposed to the public gaze, painting their faces, displaying their bodies, often deemed little better than prostitutes. But during the second half of the nineteenth century, with a growing number of women in public life as teachers, authors, doctors, artists and musicians, and with the fashion for polite society dramas giving better opportunities to ladies (such as Mrs Lillie Langtry and Mrs Patrick Campbell) the status of the actress began to improve, though more slowly than that of the actor.

The rise in professional status did not bring the actor security. He remained a casual labourer in an unregulated and extremely precarious market. Unemployment was always high, working conditions were often bad, exploitation by crooked managers and promoters rife. There was, however, some improvement by 1890. There remained disparity between earnings in London and the provinces, and, despite higher wages and an increase in status for those in work in the last decade of the nineteenth century, unemployment and marginality remained the common experiences of many in the profession. A rank and file actor might hope to earn twenty-five shillings a week, the equivalent of a skilled artisan.

If not necessarily wealth, the rise of the acting profession did bring status, and a distinction was carefully drawn between 'legitimate theatre', the stage functioning in theatres under the control of the Lord Chamberlain, and 'illegitimate theatre', travelling players, the music hall and irregular shows. Stress was increasingly laid on the gentility of the profession. The Bancrofts wrote that in the 1860s, although a few notable figures such as Charles Kean, Alfred Wigan, Charles Mathews and Leigh Murray 'were significant for their gifts, both as gentlemen and histrions [ie actors], they visibly contrasted with others of their order unhappily lacking the marks of breeding and education'.[8] In the second half of the century, there was a marked influx of public school and university men into the profession. Drama societies were set up at Oxford (OUDS, 1884) and Cambridge (ADC, 1854). Although there was no coherent professional structure, national theatrical bodies developed to give the profession an institutional base. The General Theatrical Fund was established in 1839 to provide pensions for actors and actresses, receiving a royal charter in 1853. Other charitable bodies developed in the 1850s: the Dramatic, Equestrian and Musical Sick Fund Association (1855), merged in 1904 with the Royal General Theatrical Fund; the Dramatic College (1858); Actors Benevolent Fund (1882). These were organized with self-conscious professionalism as corporate bodies with regular meetings, periodic fund-raising events and official sanction. The ideas of a national theatre and a national drama school were regularly canvassed from the 1870s.

Actor-managers Henry Neville and Ben Greet set up their own dramatic academies in London, in 1884 and 1896 respectively; and Sarah Thorne, sister of actor-manager Thomas Thorne, ran a respected school of acting in Margate from 1885. Frank Benson had a touring academy from 1901. Eminent elderly actors such as Hermann Vezin and Walter Lacy took on acting pupils and the London Academy of Music and Guildhall School of Music taught elocution.[9] Irving was initially opposed to drama schools, believing that actors should learn their craft on the job. But from 1894 he advocated municipal theatres, among whose duties would be the systematic training of actors.[10] Eventually the Academy (later Royal Academy) of Dramatic Art (RADA) was set up in 1904 and the Central School of Speech and Drama in 1906. They became the principal formal drama schools.

There was a move to set up an acting union, but this was deflected into the more genteel-sounding Actors' Association. The idea originated with two young actors in Manchester, Robert Courtneidge and Frank Benson. They wanted some form of protection for actors against bogus managers who exploited and swindled actors. Irving, fearful that it would set actors against managers, was opposed to the idea as 'destructive of our best traditions of comradeship and understanding'. But Benson persuaded him that an Actors' Association was the best means to avoid a trade union. Irving agreed to become president and made the Lyceum available for meetings. It was launched in March 1891.[11] It originally had 320 members but by 1895 had 1063, a small proportion of the estimated 20,000 actors in Britain. Irving's presence meant that all the leading actor-managers joined. In 1895 Irving was able to report that the association had undertaken 153 cases on behalf of actors who had been defrauded. Irving put on an all-star matinee of *The Merchant of Venice* in 1903 to clear the Association's debts, raising £800. It was the Actors' Association that took the lead in promoting the Irving Memorial after his death. After Irving's death, however, there were problems. Pressure to exclude managers and go for a closed shop led in 1907 to the managers resigning *en masse* and forming The Society of West End Managers. The more radical actors broke away to form the Actors' Union in 1907. But in 1910 the Actors' Union was wound up and its members rejoined the Association. The Actors' Association voted to readmit the managers and Sir Herbert Beerbohm Tree became president. This remained the actors' union until it became moribund and was replaced in 1929 by the British Actors Equity Association.

The stage acquired leadership in the struggle for recognition and responsibility. When in 1871 Irving burst onto the London theatrical scene and was proclaimed the new stage star, the position of the leader of the profession was effectively vacant. Charles Kean had died in 1868 and Samuel Phelps's reign at Sadler's Wells had ended in 1862; ageing and ailing, he was touring the provinces and making intermittent London appearances.

It was Kean and Phelps who had contested the leadership of the profession in the mid-Victorian period following the retirement of Macready in 1851. Each had made his mark with a distinctive theatrical regime. Kean, the Eton-educated son of the great tragedian Edmund Kean, had embarked on his management at the Princess's Theatre, Oxford Street, in 1850 and for nine years created a succession of lavish and spectacular productions that long remained in the memory. Charles Pascoe claimed that in one season alone £50,000 was expended on plays.[12] *King John, Richard II, Henry VIII, Henry V* and *The Winter's Tale* were all produced with the emphasis on spectacle, effects and historical and archaeological accuracy. In addition, Kean, with good taste, care, refinement and skill, mounted English versions of successful French melodramas with great central acting roles. He put on Dion Boucicault's versions of *Faust and Margaret, Louis XI* and *The Corsican Brothers* and Charles Reade's *The Courier of Lyons*. Despite his production achievements, Kean himself was not highly regarded as an actor. Macready called him 'a mere pitiful quack'.[13] Irving did not rate Charles Kean highly except in the role of *Louis XI*. Chance Newton recalled that Irving 'used to give me sundry imitations of Charles Kean's evidently "code id the dose" method of delivery'.[14]

Although Edmund Kean was his idol, Irving had never seen him act. His immediate model in acting was Phelps. Newton recalled that Irving said of Phelps: 'He was the greatest actor I ever saw – or ever shall see. And you and I well know, old friend, that whatever is best in my work at the Lyceum – not only in playing but also production – you and I both know, damned well, that is *all* Phelps.'[15] Irving had seen Phelps at Sadler's Wells play on successive nights

Hamlet, King Lear, Timon of Athens, Christopher Sly and Sir Giles Overreach and had never forgotten the experience.

Phelps's achievements prefigure those of Irving. He dispensed with the truncated, rewritten and amended Shakespeare texts that had held the stage until his time – Colley Cibber's version of *Richard III*, for instance, Garrick's *Taming of the Shrew* and Davenant's *Macbeth* – and returned to the original Shakespearian texts. He produced thirty-one Shakespearian plays, many of them not acted since Shakespeare's own day. He laid emphasis on the whole play as an entity and not just the star part. He coached and trained actors to improve their skills. He insisted on artistic and historically accurate settings, though nothing on the same scale as Kean. He sought to promote the poetic drama and put on new plays in the Shakespearean verse tradition. He edited, with the help of the critic and playwright E.L. Blanchard, his own edition of Shakespeare's plays. During the eighteen years of his management (1844–62) he made Sadler's Wells a centre of cultural uplift and he himself lived an impeccably respectable life.

In all of these activities, Irving emulated him. In two things he did not. Where Phelps produced thirty-one Shakespeare plays at Sadler's Wells, and with extraordinary versatility played the leading tragic and comic roles in most of them, Irving produced only twelve. But by Irving's day the long run had replaced the nightly changing repertory system that Phelps had operated. Phelps was an ensemble actor, choosing plays which suited his company as then constituted and he was willing to take subordinate roles in the interest of the play and the company (Jaques in *As You Like It*, Mercutio in *Romeo and Juliet*, Don Adriano in *Love's Labours Lost*), something Irving never did. Irving was always the star and the centre of attraction.

So why is it Irving and not Phelps who is today remembered? Always a great actor, Phelps never became undisputed leader of his profession as Irving did. For one thing, he was continually losing the actors he coached and brought on at Sadler's Wells to the West End. For Sadler's Wells, unlike Irving's Lyceum, was not in the West End; it was in unfashionable Islington. At a time when social patronage was a vital element in theatrical success, Phelps, though strongly favoured by the intelligentsia and literati, never gained the aristocratic and royal patronage enjoyed by Charles Kean. Phelps did several command performances at Windsor Castle but Queen Victoria never visited Sadler's Wells. She did, however, visit Charles Kean's theatre several times, amid maximum publicity, and appointed him her master of the revels. Where the Queen went, high society followed. Last and equally significantly, Phelps, a shy and modest man, who disliked socializing, preferred after performing to have supper with his family and retire to bed. He had 'a special distaste for anything that might be construed as currying favour with the press or men of influence in other spheres'.[16] The actor J.H. Barnes confirmed this: 'He was in no sense a society man. He had not the time … No speeches, no paragraphs, no interviews, no photographs, no bunkum of any sort! Just honest straightforward work for the public when the curtain went up.'[17] In this he differed markedly from Irving. Irving was a master of publicity. He cultivated the sympathy and support of the royal family and high society, and he loved entertaining and regularly played host to the celebrities of the day. He was a clubman and socializer until the early hours, his separation from his wife allowing him to lead a more bohemian bachelor existence than Phelps, with his loving wife and six children, either could or wanted to. Most of all Irving cultivated good relations with the press, where possible, as part of his business as a theatre manager. Despite these temperamental differences, what has been said of Phelps, that he had 'seriousness of purpose, moral convictions, devotion to hard work and intellectual approach to art', is equally true of Irving.[18] Irving and Phelps were never at their best on their first nights, both suffering seriously from nerves. Their ends were also curiously parallel. Phelps was on his farewell tour before retirement when he collapsed on stage at the Aquarium Theatre, London, playing Cardinal Wolsey. He had just delivered the last line: 'Farewell, a long farewell to all my greatness.' He died on 6 November 1878, aged seventy-four. Irving was also on his farewell tour, performing at the Theatre Royal, Bradford. Although ailing, he got through his performance of *Becket*, speaking the last line: 'Into Thy hands, O Lord, into Thy Hands', before collapsing. He returned to his hotel and died in its lobby on 13 October 1905, aged sixty-seven.

Chance Newton, who knew both Irving and Phelps well, called Phelps 'the greatest English actor of the Victorian Era – perhaps the most startlingly versatile player of any age'.[19]

J. H. Barnes, who acted with both Irving and Phelps, wrote: Phelps

> Irving was the best actor I ever saw, or ever expect to see, in a great number of parts. In *The Bells, Louis XI* or *The Lyons Mail* he was incomparable! His *Charles I* was a most beautiful performance. Much of his *Hamlet* was very fine indeed. In parts of the more physical nature he may not have been quite so satisfying. His King Lear, Othello, Macbeth, Coriolanus were open to criticism. Most certainly his Malvolio, Richelieu and Wolsey were not equal to Phelps'. In many comedy character parts, such as Digby Grant (*Two Roses*), Dick Chevenix (*Uncle Dick's Darling*), Jingle (*Pickwick*), he was quite splendid. In Romeo and Claude Melnotte he was not at his best.

Put another way, Irving was an excellent melodrama and comedy character actor, but Shakespeare was largely beyond him. On the other hand, Barnes proclaimed Phelps his 'ideal'.

> By many actors of the modern school, whose reverence is not their strongest point, I have been thought quite mad in my worship of Samuel Phelps … I have never seen such

an actor ... He played more parts, and a wider range of parts – well, than any actor who ever spoke the English language ... Phelps's reputation rests on sixty [parts] – and more ... Apart from his own individual acting his ideas of our art were all broad and grand. Nothing little or narrow-minded found a place in his nature ... To talk with him on any play or theatrical subject was an intellectual treat. On the stage he was fairness itself, and he would, (and did, constantly) show anyone who was in earnest how to make the most of his part, even when it would seem to score against himself ... In the course of my life I have never met an artist in any profession whose ideals were higher and whose sympathies were broader.[20]

The two greatest performances Barnes says he ever saw on the stage were Madame Ristori as Queen Elizabeth I and Phelps as Sir Pertinax MacSycophant in *The Man of the World*.

Sir Johnston Forbes-Robertson, who also acted with both Irving and Phelps, wrote warmly in his autobiography of Irving's generosity and humour but revealingly said little about his acting. Of Phelps he wrote:

> Phelps was a most versatile actor. He could ring the changes from tragedy to character parts, and from high comedy to low. I supported him in his Sir Peter Teazle, John Thornbury, Sir Pertinax MacSycophant ... Bottom, Wolsey, Falstaff, Shylock, Henry IV, Richelieu, Anthony Absolute, and Malvolio, all masterly performances ... Samuel Phelps' dignity of mind, his high ideals, his pride in his calling, his contempt for wire-pullers, left a lasting impression which remained with me through all my stage career.[21]

The reputation that Phelps gained lived after him. Irving and Tree both told Chance Newton that 'for years ... they "funked" playing Wolsey' because Phelps had been so great in the role. Irving, who rarely commented on other actors, made a notable exception in the case of Phelps, describing him as 'a most venerated member of our profession'. He paid a generous tribute to Phelps' work in an 1878 address, praising his dedication, enthusiasm, taste, skill and commitment to Shakespeare. Irving concluded that under Phelps's management Sadler's Wells

> became, by force of mere popular success, a classical national theatre more truly than was ever established by means of royal patronage or imperial subventions. Mr Phelps has much to be proud of in the artistic creations of his histrionic power, and scarcely less in this great historic encouragement, secured for ever by his faith and patience, to all who labour in the same cause.[22]

Interestingly Phelps did not do melodrama, with the notable exception of *Louis XI*, an irresistible part for an actor. What Irving did was to combine the qualities, agendas and repertoires of Phelps and Charles Kean. He did his lavish and spectacular Shakespeare and his modern poetic drama (the plays of W.G. Wills and Lord Tennyson, where Phelps had performed the plays of Tom Taylor and Robert Browning); but he also revived those melodramas in which

Kean had scored, taking over the roles of Mephistopheles, Louis XI, the Corsican Brothers, Louis and Fabien dei Franchi, and Lesurques and Dubosc. He did all the off-stage things that Phelps scorned: the socializing, the addresses, the interviews, the 'bunkum'. It was the combination of his acting, his production techniques and his repertoire, his public appearances, speeches and addresses, his cultivation of the leaders of society, his promotion of theatrical commemoration and his publicity management that made him the best known and best remembered actor of the Victorian era.

Irving was anxious to cultivate the support and patronage of the ruling classes, believing that this would go a long way to breaking down anti-theatrical prejudice. Queen Victoria had been a regular theatre-goer until the death of Prince Albert in 1861, after which she retired into her long seclusion. But after twenty years she revived the habit of command performances. Between 1881 and 1901 there were twenty-eight held variously at Windsor, Sandringham and Balmoral. The majority were for operas but nine were theatrical. The Kendals appeared in *Sweethearts*, John Hare and the Bancrofts in *Diplomacy*, and Beerbohm Tree in *The Red Lamp*. Irving and Ellen Terry did two command performances.

The Queen had never seen Irving and Ellen Terry act until 1889 when she was staying at Sandringham as the guest of the Prince of Wales. He arranged for a performance of *The Bells* and the trial scene from *The Merchant of Venice*. The Lyceum was closed for the evening, special scenery and backdrops prepared for the occasion, and the company was transported entirely at Irving's expense to perform in the great drawing-room at Sandringham. Afterwards Irving and Ellen Terry supped with the royal guests. Queen Victoria, who retired early, nevertheless spoke to the stars before doing so. She recorded in her diary of *The Bells*: 'The hero [Irving] though a mannerist of the Macready type, acted wonderfully'; and of *The Merchant*: 'Irving played the part of Shylock extremely well – Miss Ellen Terry that of Portia beautifully.' She added: 'I waited a moment in the Drawing Room to speak to Irving and Ellen Terry. He is very gentleman-like, and she very pleasing and handsome.'[23] Irving always defrayed all the expenses of the command performance himself, Stoker commenting: 'Irving was only too proud and happy to serve his Queen and future King in all ways of his own art to the best of his power.' But there is also another reason. In the days of Charles Kean, actors in command performances had been paid by the Privy Purse and there had once been an unfortunate misunderstanding when a leading actor had been seriously underpaid and had sent the derisory salary to the police court poor box as a contribution from himself and Queen Victoria. The Queen had been incensed. By paying the actors himself, Irving avoided any repeat of such an episode.[24]

His second performance before the Queen was a production at Windsor of *Becket* on 18 March 1893. The Queen wrote of the performance: 'Irving acted well, and with much dignity, but his elocution is not very distinct, especially when he gets excited', and pronounced Ellen as Rosamund, 'so graceful and so young – looking in her lovely light dress – quite wonderfully so, for she is forty-six!!' Of the production, she wrote: 'The staging is magnificent and Irving had all the scenery (there were many scenes) painted on purpose. The dresses and every detail were so correct and exact … The last scene where Becket refuses to fly and defies his murderers is very fine, and his death and the way he falls down the steps very striking'. At the end of the production, the Queen complimented Irving and Ellen Terry on the 'perfection and beauty of their playing'. To Irving she said: 'It is a very noble play! What a pity that old Tennyson did not live to see it. It would have delighted him as if has delighted us.'[25] All the leading newspapers asked for permission to be present. This was refused 'as it was purely a private affair'. But Stoker was given special permission to send a five hundred word telegram to the press from Windsor Castle telegraph office reporting on the event.

In 1902 Irving had a special request from King Edward VII for a command performance of *Waterloo* at Sandringham during the visit of the Kaiser. The King stipulated that it should be a surprise and no news should get out until after the event. Irving and his company were performing *Faust* in Belfast. After the performance on the night of November 13, Irving, his small cast and his production crew sailed by the fastest boat of the Belfast line to Liverpool and then by one of the royal saloons attached to expresses of the London and North Western and Great Eastern railway companies who took them via Crewe, Rugby and Peterborough to King's Lynn, where they boarded a special for Wolferton, the station for Sandringham. After performing the play to an audience of 350 at 10 p.m., they left at 1 a.m., did the journey in reverse and reached Belfast at 5 p.m. in time for the evening performance of *Faust*.[26]

Given the Queen's relatively sparse patronage of the theatre, her place was taken as the active head of society by her son, Edward, Prince of Wales. Under the influence of the Prince of Wales the nature of society and social acceptability changed dramatically. His biographer Sir Sidney Lee recalled:

> English society over which the Prince assumed virtual sovereignty near the date of his wedding 'season' [1863], rapidly acquired a character sensibly differing from that on which his parents had, through the previous generation, set their hallmark. Queen Victoria and the Prince Consort strictly limited their social circle to their kinsfolk, with a select infusion of officialdom and of the old nobility … a rigid code of etiquette … governed the Queen and her husband's relations with society, and deprived them of breadth or vivacity. Under the Prince of Wales's ruling auspices London society defied the old and narrow barriers which his parents had carefully guarded. Political, ethical and economic tendencies were soon deflecting the centre of social gravity and were giving

the interests of sport and of wealth and of heterogeneous fame social recognition – a recognition which was ampler than that enjoyed by birth conditioned by virtue or by dignified political office in the days when those qualifications constituted the sole passports to Queen Victoria's social circle … Social enfranchisement was conferred on the nobility and gentry – young and old of both sexes – who made pleasure and sport their main pursuits; on plutocrats of middle class or plebeian origin, deriving their fortunes from finance, commerce, or manufacture; and on ambitious and prosperous members of the professions – the Civil Service, medicine, law, art, journalism and the stage. (Literature was the sole branch of culture which the new society failed readily to assimilate) … With unswerving loyalty the Prince conformed to the customs and pursuits of society in its broadened reach. At banquets, garden-parties, and balls, at the Italian opera and at the theatres which were the homes of lighter forms of drama, no less than in the hunting-field or at shooting parties, he was in his element.[27]

Lee attributes the rise in social status of the drama directly to the Prince's conspicuous patronage of the drama. Admitting that 'Books never played any appreciable part among the Prince's diversions', Lee went on:

Music and drama always stood with the Prince on a footing very different from literature. In the opera and the play he found through life one of the most effectual means of relief from the monotonies of ceremonial routine. In his leisure hours at home and abroad he welcomed, too, the society of leading members of both the dramatic and musical professions. The Prince's theatrical tastes, while they inclined to the lighter forms of entertainment (he was particularly fond of Adelphi and Drury Lane melodrama and the farcical comedies of J.L. Toole), were, in middle life, comprehensive … In England the Prince personally interested himself in a wide range of drama and in its leading interpreters. On Sir Henry Irving, the serious-minded chieftain of the English stage through the latter half of Queen Victoria's reign, the Prince bestowed much attention. He witnessed most of Irving's Shakespearian productions at the Lyceum Theatre from 1872 onwards, and maintained with him friendly social relations … The social standing of actors was sensibly raised by the Prince's theatrical zeal … To the Prince's influence may be attributed the bestowal of official honours on leading actors … The Prince's persistence as a playgoer and his interest in actors could not fail to provoke unfavourable remark in some old-fashioned quarters, but the theatre in England and elsewhere was a national institution and a purveyor of amusement for the people at large, which deserved in unprejudiced minds, all the encouragement the Prince gave it.[28]

It was an epoch-making event when the Prince gave a dinner at Marlborough House in 1882 for the leading actors and managers of the day. Thirty-eight sat down to dinner, the theatricals present being Squire Bancroft, then the senior manager in London, Henry Irving, J.L. Toole, John Hare, Charles Wyndham, Charles Coghlan, W.H. Kendal, John Clayton, David James, Arthur Cecil, Henry Neville, Lionel Brough, Hermann Vezin and George Grossmith the elder. It was, recalled Squire Bancroft, 'one of the many acts by which he endeared himself to the theatrical profession'.[29] He gave a similar dinner a year or two later at the

Marlborough Club and accepted in return an invitation from the actors to dine at the Garrick Club. Bancroft confirms Lee's perception that 'the stage has never found among Royal heads a firmer friend than was the late King; his gracious words and acts went far to conquer a decaying prejudice'.[30] The profession recognized this on 10 November 1891, when a delegation of leading actors and managers (Bancroft, John Hare, Beerbohm Tree, Sir Augustus Harris and D'Oyly Carte) travelled to Sandringham to present him with a cigar and cigarette box in gold, with the Prince of Wales feathers mounted in brilliants, to mark his fiftieth birthday the day before.[31] Irving was in America at the time.

In addition to his theatre-going, the Prince also was an inveterate clubman and this provided him with another opportunity to mingle with actors. He became patron of the Garrick Club and several times attended the Savage Club dinners. 'Few opportunities did he neglect of meeting in the convivial atmosphere of clubs men who could be counted on to amuse or interest him.'[32]

The Prince's interest in the theatre was not just confined to being out front. On 18 October 1880, he went backstage for the first time at the Lyceum during *The Corsican Brothers* and described in detail to Irving how Charles Kean had staged his production of the play.[33] In 1883 the Prince suggested a benefit on behalf of the Royal College of Music which he was then promoting. Irving put on an all-star production of *Robert Macaire* entirely at his own expense. The house was packed, the Prince of Wales attended, and £1002 8s. 6d was raised for the college.[34] On 7 May 1883, during the run of *Much Ado*, the Prince was guest of honour at a dinner on the stage of the Lyceum with fifty guests. For the 1897 Diamond Jubilee Irving gave a reception on the Lyceum stage for all the colonial premiers, Indian princes and all the officers taking part in the celebrations. He repeated this for the coronation of Edward VII in 1902.[35] Although the coronation was postponed due to the King's appendicitis, the festivities went ahead and Stoker recalled it as the swansong of the Lyceum:

> That Coronation reception was certainly a most magnificent sight … When one entered at the back of the stage the *coup d'oeil* was magnificent. The place looked of vast size; the many lights and the red seats of the tiers making for infinite distance as they gleamed through the banks of foliage. The great Crown and Union Jack seeming to flame over all the moving mass of men and women, nearly all the men in gorgeous raiment, in uniform or Court dress, the women all brilliantly dressed and flashing with gems; with here and there many of the Ranees and other various nationalities in their beautiful robes. Everywhere ribbons and orders, each of which meant some lofty distinction of some kind. Everywhere a sense of the unity and the glory of Empire. Dominating it all, as though it was floating on light and sound and form and colour, the thrilling sense that there, in all its bewildering myriad beauty, was the spirit mastering the heart-beat of that great Empire on which the sun never sets. That night was the swan-song of the old Lyceum, and was a fitting one; for such a wonderful spectacle none of our generation

shall ever see again. As a function it crowned Irving's reign as Master and Host. Two weeks later the old Lyceum as a dramatic theatre closed its doors – for ever.[36]

Stoker concludes:

> The King was always a most gracious and generous friend to Irving. Throughout the whole management of the Lyceum and to the time of Irving's death, King Edward, both as Prince and King, extended to him the largest measure of approval. He gave him a position by his very courtesy and by the hospitalities which he graciously gave and accepted ... He showed that he considered the Player in his own way to have brought some measure of honour to the great nation that he rules and whose countless hearts he sways ... And whether as Prince or King, his Most Gracious Majesty Edward VII R and I had no more loyal, no more respectful, no more believing, no more loving subject than Henry Irving.[37]

This favour took the form of invitations to the wedding of George, Prince of Wales, son of Edward VII, to the funeral of Queen Victoria and the coronation of Edward VII. Stoker records that whenever Lord Burnham, the proprietor of the *Daily Telegraph*, entertained the Prince of Wales at his home, Hall Barn, he always included Irving in the party. ('Such a friendship is a powerful help to an artist.')[38] Interestingly too, he relates that the Prince went three times to see *Peter the Great*, one of Irving's later failures. It may be that he hoped to boost the box office by his presence but the Prince may also have felt some sympathy with a story about an heir to the throne whose parents contrived to keep him out of power.[39]

Taking their lead from the Prince, many prominent aristocrats regularly patronized the Lyceum, and they were religiously listed in the society column reports of the opening nights. The Duke of Fife and the Duchess of Sutherland were among the regulars. Irving's fans included Baroness Burdett-Coutts and Mr Gladstone.

W.E. Gladstone, who was Prime Minister during the years 1868–74, 1880–85, 1886 and 1892–4, was born in Liverpool in 1809 and brought up in a strict Scottish Presbyterian atmosphere. He inevitably imbibed the evangelical distrust of the theatre. He recorded in his diary, on 19 December 1832, his belief that the races and the theatre 'involve the encouragement of sin'.[40] But at Eton and Oxford he was required to study the repertoire of classical plays and the standard texts on rhetoric and gesture. When he took up politics, he turned these studies to good effect, as well as harnessing his natural gifts, and became a renowned orator. In the 1850s Gladstone underwent something of a conversion to theatrical performance. This may have been due to the regime of his fellow Etonian Charles Kean at the Princess's Theatre.

There is no doubt that Gladstone found Kean's regime at the Princess's Theatre very much to his taste. He went there to see *The Winter's Tale* (3 July 1856),

Richard II (22 April 1857), *The Tempest* (8 August 1857), *King Lear* twice (29 May and 10 June 1858), *The Merchant of Venice* (13 July 1858), *Henry V* (5 May 1859), *The Corsican Brothers* and *A Midsummer Night's Dream* (6 August 1859)[41] His interest in that theatre was demonstrated by the fact that he arranged for Kean to show him all over the building (12 May 1857) and they had a long conversation about government subvention for the theatre, though nothing came of it.[42] He went backstage too after *Richard II* (16 May, 1857).[43] He rarely commented on the plays but, when he did, the comments were usually favourable: *Richard II* 'some good acting and wonderful spectacle'; *King Lear* (10 June), 'Kean's is a very considerable performance'; *Henry V*, 'the melodrama was admirable and Shakespeare a mighty poet.' He spoke at the Kean retirement dinner on 20 July, 1859. He apologized that his parliamentary duties kept him from attending the theatre more often. Gladstone said that Kean 'had laboured in the noble and holy cause of endeavouring to dissociate the element of the drama from all moral and social contamination'. He expressed the hope that others would follow Kean 'in endeavouring to improve the tone and elevate the character of the English stage'.[44]

Gladstone's conversion extended to his writing an open letter advocating the establishment of a National Theatre.[45] By the 1860s and 1870s he was going regularly to plays. In particular Irving's regime at the Lyceum became a favoured destination. Stoker recalls his visits covering the period 1881-95, declaring that a visit to the double bill of *The Cup* and *The Corsican Brothers*, on 3 January 1881, was Gladstone's first.[46] He went on stage to congratulate Irving and Terry on their performances and was shown around backstage. Ellen Terry, who noted that 'one of the best' audiences 'that actor or actress could wish for was Mr Gladstone ... he could always give his whole mind to the matter in hand', recorded her impression of him as a 'suppressed volcano'.[47] Whenever Gladstone went to the Lyceum, he used Irving's private entrance in Burleigh Street and his family sat in Irving's private box. They used also to visit Irving and Terry after the play either on stage or in his dressing room.[48] Irving also socialized with the Gladstone family.[49]

After his first visit, says Stoker, 'he seemed ever afterwards to take a great interest in Irving and all he did'. In addition, 'the public seemed to take a delight in seeing him at the theatre, and he appeared to take a delight in coming'. When he came to the Lyceum on 10 April 1886, two days after making his great speech introducing the Home Rule Bill, he received 'an immense ovation.'[50]

Gladstone himself recorded his Lyceum visits and his impressions of Irving and Terry in his diaries. He had attended much earlier than the 1881 visit remembered by Stoker. His first visit on 16 April 1875 was to *Hamlet*, during the Bateman regime, when he wrote: 'to the play. Irvine's Hamlet [*sic*] though a work of ability is not good; but how marvellous are the drama and the character'.[51]

Interestingly, he had seen Fechter's *Hamlet* at the Princess's Theatre in 1861 and wrote: 'it is a finished work.'[52] But he went back for the revival of *Hamlet* with Ellen Terry on 19 February 1879, commenting: 'what food for thought'.[53] In the meantime his opinion of Irving's acting had risen. He went to *Othello* on 19 February 1876: 'Mr Irving's remarkable study; Iago good.'[54] He saw *Richard III* on 4 May 1877 in which he thought Irving's Richard 'a great performance'.[55] He was also prepared to take in melodramas: seeing *The Lyons Mail* ('a notable melodrama, well got up and acted') on 5 March 1878 and *The Lady of Lyons* on 19 June 1879 ('acting very good, drama has I fear a central fault' – though tantalisingly he does not say what it is).[56] Parting company with other great Victorians like Ruskin, Carroll and Shaw, he proclaimed *The Merchant of Venice*, seen on 28 February 1880, 'Irvine's [sic] best, I think'.[57] For 3 January 1881 Gladstone recorded 'to unbend after the strain [of working on the Queen's speech] we went to the Lyceum and saw *The Cup* and *The Corsican Brothers*, with a kind of interlude which Mr Knowles and I had behind the scenes. *The Cup* had some very fine passages with a beautiful *mise-en-scène*. I can't quite estimate it as a drama until after reading it.'[58] When he went to *Romeo and Juliet*, on 8 July 1882, he noted that he had met Irving and Ellen Terry afterwards. 'She acted beautifully', he said, but did not mention Irving.[59] On 25 October 1882 he was at *Much Ado* ('admirable'), again seeing the stars afterwards.[60] He was to see it again on 29 January 1891, when he brought a cheque for £10 for the Actors' Benevolent Fund.[61]

On 10 April 1886 Gladstone was at *Faust* ('most remarkable as to both performances and *mise-en-scène*'). This time the performance prompted him to write directly to Irving the next day, thanking him for 'the performance of last night; especially for your own share in it, the most remarkable part of a remarkable whole'. He noted that Miss Terry's cold had been announced at the beginning but that there had been nothing to apologize for in her performance and he thought Mrs Stirling gave the best performance he had ever seen her give. Finally, 'the *mise-en-scène* could not have been done better'.[62] On 2 December 1890 he was at *Ravenswood*: 'a striking piece. Miss Terry fine in the great scene.' He wrote to Stoker saying he was 'so fond a lover' of the story that he had requested permission to sit at the side of the stage so he could hear the play better. Irving arranged it and thereafter he always sat in the same place.[63] 11 May 1892 found him at *Henry VIII* complaining that, although he was sitting on the side of the stage, 'I heard but ill.'[64] On 22 November 1892 he was at *King Lear*. 'She admirable; he of great power and skill, but wanted measure.'[65] His final Lyceum diary entry is for *Becket* on 25 February 1893: 'capital'. Stoker noted 'he was delighted with *Becket*, and seemed to rejoice in the success of Tennyson's work'.[66] Increasing deafness put an end to Gladstone's theatre-going.

The evidence of Gladstone's own diaries can be supplemented by that of his daughter, Mary. Mary Gladstone (1847-1928), the fifth of Mr Gladstone's eight children, was intelligent and highly cultured, counting among her friends Tennyson, Browning, Ruskin, Burne-Jones and Lord Acton. For a time she acted as her father's secretary. With her father she attended the Lyceum regularly. Her diary entries show a greater partiality for Ellen than for Henry, his Benedick and Mephistopheles being the performances of his she most favoured. On 18 February 1876, she was at *Othello*:

> Felt it all, every word, marvellous. It hardly seemed to matter how it was acted. It is almost too awful a story to see, so infinitely more terrible than when read. 'Oh, the pity of it.' All one's breath seemed taken away in awe and admiration of the conception. Iago's characterisation specially strikes one as a superhuman masterpiece. On the whole it was well done, Irving a little exaggerated perhaps. It is awfully sad.[67]

On Saturday 9 March 1878, she dined with Tennyson ('uncommonly crusty with lumbago and bit my nose off') and missed the first act of *Louis XI* but saw the rest: 'much too horrible and ghastly throughout, except when it became hideously vulgar. The finest piece of acting on Irving's part I ever saw; but the last two Acts are entirely occupied with men hard dying, and he looks unutterably ghastly in gorgeous blue velvet robes and crown sparkling with jewels. Lasted till past 12.'[68]

On Wednesday, 19 February 1879, she accompanied her parents to see *Hamlet*:

> It felt quite an epoch in my life, first seeing and hearing this great, wonderful play, and on the whole the performance is great too, specially Ophelia. Ellen Terry certainly gives a new idea of the character one had thought decidedly milk-and-water, and fills it with the tenderest grace and most touching pathos. There could not be a more striking contrast than the Hamlet and his lady-love. He with that shock of coal black hair, and she with the fairest golden, wavy locks … The mad scene is quite wonderful … Hamlet in parts very fine, specially when quiet, but he spoils the part by his extraordinary pronunciation and exaggeration generally. It is a great strain on what one is pleased to call one's intellect and immensely long. Came home pumped out.[69]

Hamlet

She went back to see it again on Tuesday 25 February:

> This time Ophelia carried me more off my feet and I could not take my eyes off her. It's awful the pathos of it – her voice, countenance, attitudes, gestures etc, perfect. He [Irving] too, is almost inspired in the great scene with her, the struggles between bitterness and love, the cruel taunting words, and then the outstretched arms trembling with passion, the paroxysms of conflicting feelings that fly across his face. The whole scene keeps one breathless, and know it as you may, you still have a hope that she may conquer him. She cries really, especially in the mad scene – she comes shrinking in with terrified, hunted look, long white garments clinging to the slight graceful form, great shadowy tearful eyes, pale wet cheeks, and the sudden childlike illumination of countenance as he catches sight of the flowers in her hands, and the relapse into terror, and the wailing song. It certainly all is most wonderful.[70]

On Friday 23 April 1880, Mary and her brother Harry went to see *The Merchant of Venice*:

> Under present circs, it dragged a little (they were waiting to hear if the Queen would ask Mr Gladstone to form a government). Still the scenery was lovely and made me so wistful over last October and my lovely Venice. Ellen Terry was a perfect Portia and her clothes were gorgeous.[71]

On Wednesday 12 January 1881, Mary dined with Lord Acton at the St James's Hotel but left in the middle to go to the Lyceum with her brother Herbert and Alfred Lyttelton for *The Cup* and *The Corsican Brothers*. She wrote:

> *The Cup*, very short, very exciting, and horrible, very splendid in stage effects and here and there fine in writing. Ellen Terry's acting of it is beautiful, though scarcely powerful enough. It is more perfection of grace than tragic power. *The Corsican Brothers* afterwards, has a splendid ghost. I enjoyed the whole thing greatly.[72]

She went again to the double bill of *The Cup* and *The Corsican Brothers* on Wednesday 26 January: 'Thought the former boundlessly beautiful. It grows wonderfully.'[73]

On Wednesday 15 June 1881, she was at the Lyceum for *Othello*: 'It was some of it too awful, for Ellen Terry is the most lovely heartbreaking Desdemona. Booth has not quite the physique for *Othello*. Irving as Iago shows how he can act in his relations with Emilia.'[74] On 19 April 1882, she was at *Romeo and Juliet*: 'Her acting is almost perfection, and he is so little to the fore. The scenery is wonderful, the clothes and the minor parts mostly admirable. Mrs Sterling [*sic*], especially, also Mercutio. Nothing could be tenderer and lovelier than she is throughout.'[75] Then, on 25 October 1882, to *Much Ado*:

> It is the best part that Irving ever did. Benedick's dry humour and irony suit him exactly, and the by-play and facial acting are capital. All the men are more or less good, Hero the poorest of all the parts; scenery and dressing magnificent. Went behind the scenes afterwards. Irving had spectacles on, which looked odd in his gorgeous attire. She seemed full of go and fun. They disappear off the stage dancing a delicious jig. There is a lovely organ in the Church scene, which he has bought for the play.

On 7 July 1885, she went to *Olivia*: 'all wept freely. It was beautiful and heartbreaking because of what it represents.'[76] On 30 January 1886, she was at *Faust* with Winifred Emery replacing Ellen Terry, who was ill. Mary recorded:

> A blow, but perhaps Marguerite gained in the girlishness and simplicity of her substitute, Miss Emery. Irving's Mephisto carries one right off one's feet as he never has before. It's the subtle sardonic humour wh. is so astonishing. The whole management of scenery etc is A1, and the great climax when Gretchen spurns Mephisto and flings herself on the cross and the Angels float over her is very overpowering.[77]

On 23 November 1892, Mary went with her father and others to *King Lear*: 'The fourth Act too lovely. Ellen Terry pathetic and graceful beyond words. King Lear overdone throughout. Going on stage after was most interesting. Found E.T. overwhelmed with emotion, Irving satisfied with having surpassed himself in dying.'[78]

Irving, who as a struggling young actor had starved, never forgot the plight of the less fortunate members of his profession. He maintained a private list of pensioners to whom he paid a weekly allowance. Irving's mistress Eliza Aria recalled 'no week elapsed without £50 being distributed among the needy'.[79] Sir Charles Villiers Stanford recalled that stage manager Henry Loveday told him that when Mrs Bateman surrendered the Lyceum lease to Irving, he dispensed with many of her stagehands and brought in more efficient successors. But he continued to pay the dismissed their full wages.[80] He was also much involved with official charitable organisations. The most prominent was the Royal General Theatrical Fund, which was funded by charitable donations, annual subscriptions, investments and the profits of theatrical benefits and annual dinners, and paid out annuities to elderly and ailing thespians. Irving was elected a trustee in 1874 in place of W.C. Macready, who had died. His election is a measure of how rapidly he had established himself as a major star since *The Bells*. In 1875 Irving took the chair at the thirtieth annual dinner of the fund, raising a record amount.[81] He took the chair again in 1881, 1884 and 1894. In 1879 when the fund was in financial difficulties he donated £50. The 1881 dinner, which he chaired, raised £933 17s. 5d., the largest amount since he previously took the chair. He regularly gave his services to the all-star theatrical matinees which the fund staged at Drury Lane to raise money. In 1881 he and Ellen Terry performed the trial scene from *The Merchant of Venice* in a bill which also included Johnston Forbes-Robertson, J.L. Toole, Edwin Booth, Helena Modjeska and William Creswick. The show raised £806 0s. 2d. In 1886 and 1889 he performed in scenes from *Louis XI*. He filled the gap left by the death of its earlier moving spirit, Charles Dickens and 'no one showed a more practical interest'.[82]

Not content with his Royal General Theatrical Fund activities, Irving was one of the trio, along with Bancroft and Toole, who at a dinner party in 1882 decided to set up the Actors Benevolent Fund 'to relieve distress in the dramatic profession'. They were later joined by Hare, Wyndham, Kendal and Barrett, who all agreed to donate £100 annually. Irving acted as president. By the time of their first dinner in 1891 they had distributed £18,000 to relieve 700 cases of distress.[83] It was at Irving's suggestion that in 1891 a series of public dinners was inaugurated to raise donations. It began at the Whitehall Rooms of the Metropole Hotel with Irving in the chair. A series of theatrical benefits at London theatres with all-star casts also contributed to funds.[84] Irving regularly gave performances at the Lyceum in aid of the fund. He performed in the church scene from *Much Ado* on 21 July 1885. On 24 July 1886, he gave a special performance of *The Bells* and *Raising the Wind* in the presence of the Prince and Princess of Wales. On Thursday afternoon 9 June 1887, he performed *Louis XI*. On 2 June 1889, he performed *The Bells* at the Lyceum for the fund, in a bill in which J.L. Toole, Sims Reeves and Constant Coquelin also appeared. It raised £450.

Irving was in constant demand during the years of his eminence to write articles, give speeches and make addresses. These were invariably reported in the newspapers, usually with a complete text of the speech. Laurence Irving recalled: 'He attached great importance to these speeches. They were the medium through which he 'kept close to the people' and of his advocacy of his profession.'[85] The speeches, even if intended to be impromptu as at last nights in the theatre, were always written out and learned by heart. For formal dinners, they were printed in very large type, so that, as Stoker records, 'He would not seem to read it, and of course he would be familiar with the general idea. But he read it all the same; with a glance he would take in the whole sentence of the big type and he would use his acting power not only in the delivery but in the disguising of his effort.' If there was not time to get the speeches printed, Irving would write them out himself 'in a big hand with thick strokes of a soft pen.'[86] His formal lectures were a vital element in his continuing campaign to secure intellectual respectability and social recognition for his profession. He was the first actor to be invited to lecture at Oxford and Harvard Universities. He delivered the prestigious Rede Lecture at Cambridge University and the Trask Lecture at Princeton. He lectured on *Macbeth* at Owens College, Manchester, Columbia University and Chicago University. He lectured to the Royal Institution, the Philosophical Institution of Edinburgh and the Goethe Society of New York. He addressed the Royal Academy and the Royal Society of Musicians.

Who wrote Irving's speeches and articles? With characteristic mischievousness Shaw raised the question in a *Saturday Review* article (9 February 1895):

> Who writes Mr Irving's lectures? Of course, I must not altogether exclude the hypothesis that he writes them himself; but I had rather flatter him by assuming that he contents himself with jotting down a scenario, and orders some literary retainer to write the dialogue, enjoining him to put in plenty of art and learning and not to forget some good declamatory passages, in the manner of the late Mr Wills, for elocutionary display.

There is plenty of evidence to support this view. In the Stoker papers there are just such scenarios sketched in Irving's almost indecipherable handwriting, and Laurence Irving prints a letter from Irving in Boston in 1884 to his secretary Louis Austin in England:

Jot down and send me something for the last night in New York and afterwards send me a speech for the Theatrical Fund Dinner – which is just after our return. Get the books from the Secretary of the Fund … and cull what you can from the different chairmen. I have taken the chair twice – that should be alluded to – also the American tour and the bounteous hospitality of the people – and of course particularly the object of the Fund. The speech will be an important one – for it will be the first I make after my return.[87]

But against this Laurence Irving later reports:

Despising insincerity in any form, these speeches expressed the promptings of his heart and mind at the moment, so that notes which had been prepared for him were often useless. The farewell speech, for example, which he gave in New York, included hardly a word from the painstaking draft which Austin had prepared for him.[88]

The speeches were often the result of prolonged debate between Irving and his associates. Austin complained: 'We are always wrangling over little words concerning the meaning and importance of which he has eccentric and not altogether literary ideas.'[89] The Stoker papers contain several different drafts of important speeches, some in Irving's hand, some in Stoker's, some in both. In 1891, Irving was the first actor to speak at the annual Royal Academy banquet. Sir Frederic Leighton, President of the Academy, invited Irving, together with Sir Arthur Sullivan, to reply to the toast to Music and the Drama, being proposed for the first time. The speech Irving actually gave (and which he presumably wrote himself) is much lighter and funnier than the solemn and serious one prepared for him, presumably by Stoker. It had been printed and proofread, but Irving only used one sentence from it.[90]

Ellen Terry, implicitly rebuking her old friend Shaw, and recalling Irving's entirely spontaneous response to the critical and sarcastic speech from Lord Houghton at the dinner to mark the one hundredth performance of *The Merchant of Venice* (14 February 1880), wrote:

Henry Irving's answer was delightful. He spoke with good sense, good humour and good breeding, and it was all spontaneous. I wish that a phonograph had been in existence that night, and that a record had been taken of the speech. It would be so good for the people who have asserted that Henry Irving always employed journalists … to write his speeches for him! The voice was always the voice of Irving if the hands were sometimes the hands of the professional writer. When Henry was thrown on his debating resources he really spoke better than when he prepared a speech, and his letters prove, if proof were needed, how finely he could write! Those who represent him as dependent in such matters on the help of literary hacks are just ignorant of the facts.[91]

This seems as good a summary of the situation as we are likely to get at this remove. Irving considered his addresses to be significant enough for four of the most important of them to be collected in a slim volume, *The Drama*, in 1893. They were his lectures 'The Art of Acting' (1885) delivered at Harvard University,

'Four Great Actors' (1886) delivered at Oxford University, and two lectures to the Philosophical Institution of Edinburgh: 'The Stage as It Is' (1881) and 'The Art of Acting' (1891). Many of his other addresses were printed in periodicals.[92]

The first of his many addresses on the subject of the social function of the drama was delivered to a conference of the Church of England Temperance Society at Shoreditch Town Hall on 31 March 1876. It is a key statement of Irving's beliefs in the educative and improving role of the theatre and was subsequently published in the magazine *All The Year Round* (22 April 1876). He began by acknowledging the importance of religion and recognizing the opposition to the stage within the clerical profession:

> No one can be more conscious than a thoughtful member of my profession of the value of profound religious emotion; and I believe it is a thing almost unknown ... for actors to speak otherwise than with respect, even of those extreme types of religion which are most hostile to our art. Still we must not shut our eyes to the fact that the feelings of a more active and personal religion have been attended by a certain alienation of the ministry of the Church from general culture, and, therefore, from the stage ... The truth seems this, that the clergy ... found the theatre surrounded and infested with many abominations ... it is certain those abominations have been, now, absolutely swept away, and that the audience portion of any decently conducted theatre is as completely free from immoral, or even indecorous associations, as Exeter Hall during the performance of the *Elijah*.

But he believed that clerical prejudices against the theatre were wearing down and it was a sign of the times that an actor had been invited to address them. He argued for the importance of the stage as an agent of moral improvement for the masses:

> I ask you to reflect how little the masses of our great towns are under the active influence of religion; to what a poor extent they are educated; how limited is their reading; and comparatively, how much they frequent the galleries and pits of the minor theatres ... Much in these theatres is vulgar, and there may even be things that are deleterious ... Nonetheless, however, is it true that the main stream, of dramatic sentiment in all veins is pure, kindly, righteous, and, in a sense religious ... what forms the basis of almost every standard play, but some moral lesson forcibly impressed by the aid of fable?

He called upon them to work with the theatre and not against it, so that the stage could become 'a most powerful mundane influence for the exaltation of virtue and depression of vice'. He believed that on the stage 'as much as in the noblest poetry and teaching' were to be found:

> bright lights for guidance, sweet words of encouragement, comprehended even by the most ignorant, glowing pictures of virtue and devotion which bring the world of high thoughts and bright lives into communion and fellowship with the sphere of simple, and, perhaps, coarse, day-to-day existence ... What we want is an entertainment which

the middle and lower classes can enjoy together, and happily the dramas most in credit amongst us precisely answer that description. They gratify every taste, and afford scope for every kind of managerial enterprise, spectacular or otherwise.

He argued that, whatever its faults, the theatre was a far better way of spending time than the gin-palace or the pot-house. He called upon the church to recognize and utilize this:

> Make the theatre respected by openly recognising its services. Make it more respectable by teaching the working and lower middle classes to watch for good or even creditable plays, and to patronise them, when presented. Let members of religious congregations know that there is no harm, but rather good, in entering into ordinary amusements, so far as they are decorous. Use the pulpit, the press, and the platform to denounce, not the stage, but certain evils that find allowances on it. In England attendance at the theatre – I know this well, for I was brought up in Cornwall – is too commonly regarded as a profession of irreligion. Break down this foolish and vicious idea, and one may hope that some inroads may be made on the dominions of the drink demon, and some considerable acreage annexed to the dominions of religion and virtue.

He concluded with a rousing call to co-operation:

> Gentlemen, change your attitude towards the stage, and, believe me, the stage will co-operate with your work of faith and labour of love. It will help you in disarming and decimating the forces which make for moral evil, and in implanting and fostering the seeds and energies of moral good.[93]

Irving returned to the theme in an address on 'The Stage' delivered to the Perry Barr Institute in Birmingham. The Birmingham and Midland Institute was set up in 1854 with the aim of providing scientific, literary and philosophical education for the workers by way of evening classes. It was a classic Victorian embodiment of the commitment to self-improvement. Its presidents over the years included Charles Dickens, Charles Kingsley, J. A. Froude, John Tyndall and Sir Arthur Sullivan. Its clientele tended to be for the most part clerks and artisans.

As Birmingham expanded, there was a demand from the suburbs for similar provision and a cluster of suburban institutes was created. The first was the Perry Barr Institute, opened in 1874. It was joined later by Institutes at Acocks Green, Erdington, Harborne and Edgbaston, King's Heath, Moseley and Sutton Coldfield. In 1878 Irving was elected president of the Perry Barr Institute and gave an address at the Institute on 6 March 1878. On 12 August of the same year he laid the foundation stone of the Harborne and Edgbaston Institute. Irving's address was reprinted in *Theatre* (13 March 1878) and issued as a pamphlet, price sixpence, with all profits going to the building fund of the Perry Barr Institute.

His theme was 'the immemorial and perpetual association of the stage with the noblest instincts and occupations of the human soul'. He outlined the virtues of the stage:

To efficiency in the art of acting, there should come a congregation of fine qualities. There should be considerable though not always systematic culture. There should be delicate instincts of taste cultivated, consciously or unconsciously, to a degree of extreme and subtle nicety. There should be a power at once refined and strong, of both perceiving and expressing to others the significance of language, so that neither shades nor masses of meaning ... may be lost or exaggerated. Above all there should be a sincere and abounding sympathy with all that is good and great and inspiring.

But the acting profession had been disparaged in the past because of 'the tendencies of art-life', 'the tenacity of sanctimonious prejudices' and the exigencies of an art 'dependent on the favour and money of the public'. But the state of the stage in the past could not be blamed on the actors for 'those who live to please must please to live' and 'their power of sustaining the taste and tone of their patrons is sharply and narrowly limited by the very conditions of their existence and their work'. All this had led to a state of affairs when 'it is thought by some to be a mark of superiority to say that one appreciates Shakspere [*sic*] far more in reading him than in seeing him acted'. Irving rejected this view wholly, quoting the critic Theodore Martin, who had written in the *Quarterly Review*: 'Plays are written, not to be read, but to be seen and heard. No reader, be his imagination ever so active, can ... thoroughly understand a finely-conceived character or a great play until he had seen them on the stage.' It is seeing rather than reading a play which has the greater effect on 'the unimaginative many of all ranks'.

They are not inaccessible to passion and poetry and refinement, but their minds do not go forth, as it were, to seek those joys, and even if they read the works of poetic and dramatic fancy, which they rarely do, they would miss them on the printed page. To them, therefore, with the exception of a few startling incidents of real life, the theatre is the only channel through which are ever brought the great sympathies of the world of thought beyond their immediate ken ... it follows from all this that the stage is, intellectually and morally, to all who have recourse to it the source of some of the finest and best influences of which they are respectively susceptible. To the thoughtful and reading man it brings the life, the fire, the colour, the vivid instinct, which are beyond the reach of study. To the common, indifferent man, immersed as a rule in the business and socialities of daily life, it brings visions of glory and adventure, of emotion and of broad human interest. It gives him glimpses of the heights and depths of character and experience, setting him thinking and wondering even in the midst of amusement. To the most torpid and unobservant it exhibits the humorous in life and the sparkle and finesse of language, which in dull ordinary existence is stupidly shut out of knowledge or omitted from particular notice. To all it un-curtains a world, not that in which they live and yet not other than it – a world in which the interest is heightened and yet the conditions of truth are observed, in which the capabilities of men and women are seen developed without losing their consistency to nature, and developed with a curious and wholesome fidelity to simple and universal instincts of clear right and wrong.

He went on to give an account of his appearance at the Church of England Temperance Conference, summarizing the arguments he had put forward there on behalf of the stage. Irving conceded that sometimes the stage fell below the highest standards, portraying vulgarity, indecency and 'moral un-healthiness' but he believed those faults to be rare. By contrast with these evils, 'the stage whose cause I plead is that which Shakspere [sic] worked for and made immortal'. The theatrical manager must 'suit the taste of the day sufficiently to fill his theatre but he is no more entitled to offer the public coarse and indelicate, or insidiously immoral entertainment, than a grocer to sell arsenically tinted tea, or a brush-seller to vend stolen brooms. Common morality must enter into all businesses.'[94]

Irving developed his arguments on the ennobling and educational role of the stage further in an address to the opening session of the Edinburgh Philosophical Institution on 8 November 1881. He began by expressing the hope that the idea that you can appreciate Shakespeare more by reading him than seeing him acted ('a gross and pitiful … delusion') has 'almost absolutely died out'. He argued instead for the paramountcy of acted Shakespeare. While there is only one Shakespeare,

> there is a great deal of average dramatic work excellently suited for representation. From this the public derive pleasure. From this they receive – as from fiction in literature – a great deal of instruction and mental stimulus. Some may be worldly, some social, some cynical, some merely humorous and witty, but a great deal of it, though its literary merit is secondary, is well qualified to bring out all that is most fruitful of good in common sympathies.

The theatre used to be shunned for fear of moral contamination, the theatre of fifty years ago certainly needed reforming but it was successfully reformed. There may still be moral contamination from what is performed on the stage, but so there is from books, dances and lawn tennis clubs. The solution is not to avoid the theatre but to bring public opinion to bear upon it.

> Depend upon two things – that the theatre, as a whole, is never below the average moral sense of the time; and that the inevitable demand for an admixture, at least, of wholesome sentiment in every sort of dramatic production brings the ruling tone of the theatre, whatever drawbacks may exist, up to the highest level at which the general morality of the time can truly be registered. We may be encouraged by the reflection that this is truer than ever it was before, owing to the greater spread of education, the increased community of taste between classes, and the almost absolute divorce of the stage from mere wealth and aristocracy. Wealth and aristocracy come around the stage in abundance, and are welcome, as in the time of Elizabeth; but the stage is no longer a mere mirror of patrician vice hanging at the girdle of fashionable profligacy as it was in the days of Congreve and Wycherley. It is now the property of the educated people. It has to satisfy them or pine in neglect.

He went on to elaborate on the positive value of the stage and the increasing respectability of the acting profession, with the disappearance of the old Bohemian habits 'so far as they were evil and disreputable' and the recruitment of educated and earnest young men into the ranks of the actors.

> The stage is now seen to be an elevating instead of a lowering influence on national morality, and actors and actresses receive in society, as do the members of other professions, exactly the treatment which is earned by their personal conduct.

Declaring that the theatre 'must be carried on as a business or it will fail as an art', he rejected interference by quixotic 'dramatic reformers' who did not know what they were talking about:

> If the noble fascination of the theatre draws to it … an immortal poet such as our Tennyson … if a great artist like Tadema is proud to design scenes for stage plays; if in all departments of stage production we see great talent, and in nearly every instance great good taste and sincere sympathy with the best popular ideals of goodness; then, I say, the stage is entitled to be let alone – that is, it is entitled to make its own bargain with the public without the censorious intervention of well-intentioned busy-bodies … the right direction is public criticism and public discrimination. I say so because beyond question, the public will have what they want.

He argued that managers could not force on the public either very good or very bad drama; they follow the public taste. If the people wanted Shakespeare – 'and I am happy to say that they do, at least at one theatre in London, and at all the great theatres out of London, to an extent unprecedented in the history of the stage', they got Shakespeare. If they want modern dramatists – and he listed Albery, Boucicault, Byron, Burnand, Gilbert and Wills – they got them. If they wanted opera bouffe, they would have it. Those who wanted the higher drama 'in the representation of which my heart's best interests are centred', should make themselves a majority and if they did, the higher drama would be produced.

He went on, in words lifted from his Birmingham address, to insist on the intellectual and moral value of the stage, the role of theatre as a counter-attraction to the pub, the glories of Shakespeare, concluding rousingly: 'If you uphold the theatre honestly, liberally, frankly and with wise discrimination, the stage will uphold in the future, as it has in the past, the literature, the manners, the morals, the fame, and the genius of our country.'[95]

Ever on the alert for attacks on the stage and ready to use his speeches to rebut criticisms, he chose a banquet by the Pen and Pencil Club of Edinburgh, held on 2 October 1888, to respond to an article in the *Universal Review* by George Moore entitled 'Mummer Worship', attacking acting both as an art and a profession. Dismissing Moore as a 'flippant lampooner', Irving declared that the average of acting was better than it had ever been, the presentation of plays 'incomparably better' and the theatres and actors had increased thirty-fold since the days of Garrick and Kean. Acting was, he said, 'a great and beautiful and delicate art'.

> But if a spiteful and irresponsible writer … wishes to call his actors 'mummers' by way of opprobrium and to drive them all back into the squalor and outlawry of bad old days by the flail of his abuse, then it is necessary for such a man to deny indiscriminately to all histrionics any valid status or grade in art. You have only to realise the meaning of such a contention – you have only to recall a few of the great names of the stage – nay you only have to remember a few of your own experiences of emotion and of intellectual finesse, and of humorous merriment in the theatre to feel that this scandal merchant's necessary basis for his structure of affront is as grossly unsound as his assault is malicious and impertinent. The hater and scorner of the stage is simply at war with the finest instincts of humanity.[96]

Irving's speech, greeted by prolonged applause, was widely reported in the press. Harry Quilter, founder and editor of the *Universal Review*, replied in a letter to *The Times* defending Moore's position and declaring 'the present social worship of the stage is a bad thing. The dramatic profession is, generally speaking, a dangerous one for women, an undesirable one for men.' Irving struck back with another robust defence of the stage in the speech he made after laying the foundation stone of the new Theatre Royal, Bolton, on 17 October 1888, declaring acting 'a beautiful art, priceless to civilisation in the solace it yields, the thought it generates, the refinement it inspires'. Irving was at this time performing in Manchester and while he was there he received a letter from Frank Burnand of *Punch*, telling him of a scandal involving a stage manager and some chorus girls which had again caused some newspapers to comment adversely on the moral failings of the theatre. Irving wrote back to Burnand furiously:

> The actor's art is a great art and when suggestions are made of bullying stage managers and slatternly ballet girls, of masher young men and brainless idiots of women, and that these make up the stage – I say it is unjust and not to the purpose. These do not make up the best of the stage, the stage that we love. Neither Toole, Hare, Kendal, Tree, Bancroft nor Irving and others are responsible for the abuses of the theatre … the majority of theatres in London are, I believe, well conducted.[97]

It was in this state of righteous indignation that he penned the address he was to give to the Manchester Arts Club on 26 October 1888. He declared:

> I must confess that I have been filled with astonishment on reading the attacks upon hundreds and hundreds of good women, for assail the few and you assail the many, mothers, daughters, wives and sisters, who earn their daily bread upon the stage in the honourable practice of their calling. The theatre has been and always will be assailed … and there are plenty to defend it – the public and the mighty press of our country are ever ready to defend the right. But it has certainly been left to this year of grace 1888 to see a deliberate attack made upon the women of the stage, not a very chivalrous campaign

to enter upon, gentlemen, not work that a knight of the Round Table would care to engage in.[98]

On 15 June 1898, Irving received an honorary degree (Doctor of Letters) from the University of Cambridge. His fellow honorary graduands included the Italian Ambassador General Annibale Ferrero, the Master of the Rolls, Sir Nathaniel Lindley, the Deputy Speaker of the Commons Leonard Courtney MP, Albert Venn Dicey, Vinerian Professor of English Law at Oxford, James Bryce, the historian and former President of the Board of Trade, Sir Edward John Poynter the painter, Dr Edward Caird, the moral philosopher and Master of Balliol, Francis Cranmer Penrose, former President of the Royal Institute of British Architects and first Director of the British School of Archaeology in Athens, and Charles Booth, the pioneer sociologist and compiler of *Life and Labour of the People of London*. On the same day Irving delivered the Rede Lecture at the Senate House, Cambridge. The prestigious lectureship dated from 1524, when it had been instituted by Sir Robert Rede, Lord Chief Justice of Common Pleas. Irving was the first actor to deliver the lecture and followed in the footsteps of such luminaries as Ruskin, Huxley and Matthew Arnold. Stressing the educational role of theatre, Irving called for the state to encourage the stage as it encouraged the other arts. His text was printed in the *Fortnightly Review* (July 1898):

The aim and purpose of the drama is to cultivate the imagination, and through this means to bring home to heart and mind the lessons which tend to advance the race. Imagination is one of the most potent factors of human progress. It stimulates effort; it enlarges the bounds of thought; it creates for the individual new realms of possibility; it clears away the intellectual mists of sordid reality; it harmonises the seeming divergences in the great scheme of creation; it reconciles, by its restful change, poor humanity to the wearisome details of life; it brightens, invigorates and freshens the jaded faculties. To the suffering it brings anodyne to pain; for the weary it affords a healthy and noble stimulation, generous in aim, immeasurable in scope and myriad in detail. Surely in the well-being of a nation all that tends to such a wholesome and useful end is of prime importance. Surely a medium of education such as this ... should have fitting recognition. It is hardly sufficient that in the economy of the State such exercises with their economic difficulties should be left entirely to the chance of personal enterprise. To cultivate sympathy ... to widen the understanding of it; to train the minds of the young to its beneficial exercise, and to stimulate in all high and unselfish feeling is a good office in the government of men. And for this end I say the theatre ever makes ... the Theatre is an item of vast potentialities – a natural evolution of the needs and thoughts and wishes of the people – an institution which has progressed for good unaided by the State, and which in future should distinctly be in some degree encouraged by the State or by municipalities.[99]

These remained his themes throughout his career.[100] But Irving was not alone in his campaign to establish the respectability of the stage and the actor. He had been preceded by Henry Neville. Henry Neville delivered, on 13 July 1871, a jeremiad in the form of a lecture 'The Stage: Its Past and Present in Relation to Fine Art' to the Society for the Encouragement of the Fine Arts. It was published in 1875 in a revised and expanded form. Neville (1837-1910) was the popular star of romantic melodrama. He created the role of Bob Brierly in Tom Taylor's *The Ticket of Leave Man* (1863), eventually playing the role two thousand times. But he also painted and carved as well as acting. From 1873 to 1879 he was actor-manager of the Olympic Theatre and in 1878 set up the Dramatic Studio in Oxford Street to train actors. In his lecture he lamented the state of the theatre, denouncing the 'taste for tinselled and spangled nudity taking the place of the ancient reverence for the instructive, elevating and ennobling drama', and the 'want of interest in the grand works which constitute our national drama'. This had caused 'our theatres to degenerate into mere places of amusement'. He stressed the antiquity of the drama, the contributions to the stage of the greatest authors from Aeschylus, Sophocles and Euripides to Lord Byron, Lord Lytton and 'a host of others – all of them containing lessons valuable in themselves, and sparkling with gems of wit and eloquence'. He stressed the educational role of plays: 'to excel in dramatic composition has always been peculiarly gratifying. Not on account of the pecuniary profit ... but because of the popularity gained by it, and the satisfaction of *instructing* the mass of the people'.[101]

He complained, 'the present generation forgets how greatly it is indebted to the Stage for all the blessings of civilization it enjoys. Everything worth knowing was taught from the Stage ... it is absurd to shut our eyes to its vast intellectual and moral power.' Giving an account of the growth of the theatre from Ancient Greece onwards, he claimed that Shakespeare represented the pinnacle of dramatic achievement. But he lamented that only about seven of his thirty-seven plays were known on the stage 'and when the seven are spasmodically brought out they are not supported or cared for as they deserve'. He added a footnote to say that, since that paragraph was written in 1871, he was glad to observe a Shakespearean revival due to Mr Irving's *Hamlet*.[102]

Comparing the stage with painting and sculpture, Neville argued:

> In one sense the Stage has indeed the advantage. For while in Sculpture we have form, actual relief and expression, and in Painting the additional beauty of colour, light and shadow, on the stage we have all these perfections combined; crowned with that grandest of human gifts, the power of language; which harmonizes them, and gives to the observer living pictures that instruct the unlearned while they are the pleasure and delight of the educated and refined.[103]

It thus had a holistic aesthetic and educational potential. But he complained about the lack of proper training for actors, the eclipse of acting by scenery, costumes and accessories of various kinds, and a decline in the quality of the drama over the previous seventeen years:

> Our living authors (with a few noble exceptions) ... aim only at a shallow and meretricious excellence; and ... content themselves with the evanescent delights of a new sensation, which degrades alike the amuser and the amused.[104]   Note

He asked for the stage to be made – with government backing – 'a National Institution' with 'an Academy, a Discipleship, a Home' like the other arts, and demanded to know. 'Why should there not be a Sir Samuel Phelps as well as a Sir Joshua Reynolds?' This would mean that the stage could become:

> one of the brightest luminaries of the age and of the world, and mingle its rays with the press and the pulpit for the enlightenment of the ignorant, the elevation of the degraded, the reproving of vice, the encouragement of virtue, and the dissemination of those principles of public morality which consolidate a nation and glorify a throne.[105]

The celebrated actress Mrs Madge Kendal caused a sensation with an address she made to the Congress of the National Association for the Promotion of Social Science in Birmingham in September 1884. She was the first woman to address such a gathering and her comments on the current state of the theatre, republished as a pamphlet, provoked what William Archer dubbed 'a storm in Stageland'.[106] Madge Kendal (1848–1935) was the sister of the playwright Tom Robertson and the wife of actor-manager W.H. Kendal. An actress of great verve and charm, a noted comedienne and the favourite actress of John Ruskin, she was dubbed and rejoiced in the sobriquet 'the matron of the drama'. With her husband and John Hare, she successively ran the Court and the St James's theatres. After her marriage in 1869, she identified herself totally with the career of her husband. St John Ervine tartly characterized him as:

> dull and pompous, both as player and a private person, a solemn, sententious man, whose heavy utterances were received by his wife as the most delicious sallies of wit; and he made a cult of respectability which although it earned appreciation for him and his far abler wife, made them both disliked in many quarters because of the ostentation with which the respectability was displayed.[107]

Retiring from the stage in 1908, she was appointed Dame of the British Empire in 1926.

She declared in her address that 'there never was a time when the theatre was more popular, or so much a topic of conversation, as now' and she set out to list its improvements and deteriorations. First, there was the improvement in the staging of plays:

> It was not until the present generation that correctness in costume, fidelity in scene-painting, and attention to every little detail connected with the action, came to be looked upon as absolutely essential to the proper production of a play. Nowadays, indeed, that which is theatrically known as the 'staging' of a play is in itself a work of true art, and in its own way gives rise to as much thought and care as the author has for his dialogue or the actor for his part.

She concluded 'if the surroundings and minutiae of … scenes are correct and in good taste they must add not only to the enjoyment but to the education of an audience'.

There had been improvements in conditions for the audience: 'good light, attention to warmth and ventilation, soft cushions, ample room, good music, and, above all, cleanliness'. There were many and excellent playwrights at work and 'the improved condition of the theatre has made the most famous literary men of the day anxious to identify their names with it'. But 'the playwright of today is hardly appreciated as he should be. The most remarkable change, however, was 'the fact that there is at last a recognized social position for the professional player'. Compared to the past when the Theatrical Profession was regarded with 'something like contempt', it was now 'acknowledged to be a high and important one, and the society of the intelligent and cultivated actor is eagerly sought after … the terms of actor and gentleman may now be regarded as synonymous'.

Another advance she claimed for the Drama was in 'its influence as a teacher – for as a teacher it always has been and ever will be … it is quite certain that many hundreds – nay thousands of people have been influenced for good or for evil by what they have seen portrayed upon the stage'. So it was important that the stage should be 'really wholesome and useful'. She listed 'honest self sacrifice', 'manly effort', 'womanly devotion' and 'contempt for the portrayal of meanness, treachery and snobbery' as the virtues taught.

She moved on to the ways in which the theatre had deteriorated. The first was what she calls 'advertising'.

> Neither the painter nor the poet thinks it advisable to fill the columns of the daily papers with the monotonous repetition of what this or that critic has said of his work … true art in every branch advertises itself.

She denounced in ringing tones 'the absurd mania' of some members of the Theatrical Profession (capitalized throughout her address) for keeping their name before the public, which 'assuredly does not add to their dignity'.

In what looks like a shaft aimed directly at Irving she listed the modern methods of advertising – 'what are known as "receptions" at theatres, in railway station "demonstrations", by photography, and by speech-making, and one and all are degrading to the Drama … Advertising nowadays is an art, but it is *not* the art of acting'. Interestingly there are only two passing references to Irving in her autobiography – silence perhaps suggesting distaste.[108] This implication of dislike is confirmed by Jessie Millward who, having worked unhappily for the Kendals at the St James's Theatre, moved on to join Irving's company at the Lyceum. She recalls that on one occasion Mrs Kendal, who was in a box at the Lyceum, sent for her between the acts:

'I dare say you think you have done better for yourself, Miss Millward', she observed consolingly, 'Personally I think him laughable, and I sit in the box and smile and wonder at his success.'[109]

She denounced as 'absolutely debasing to the profession', 'the flippant and what may be termed "personal style" of theatrical journalism … in which leading artists of the Stage are alluded to by their Christian names, and where insolent and generally untrue gossip and tittle-tattle take the place of honest criticism'. The result is that performers' popularity is gauged not by their talent but the amount of publicity they get:

> It is the actor who lets the public know through the newspapers, everything that he does, from the entertainment that he gives to his friends and admirers, down to the goose he sends to his gasman at Christmas, that seems to get the largest following. 'Bunkum' of this description has of late years been practised to an extent which is absolutely nauseating.

She denounced the 'suggestiveness' of modern farce, blaming the French, and the deterioration in the quality of burlesque. She criticized the level of press criticism. 'Existing critics generally rush into extremes, and either over-praise or too cruelly condemn.' She urged the public to make its own judgment of plays and not be dictated to by the critics and by fashion. She concluded by propounding her gospel of 'respectability':

> It is more than a necessity that actors and actresses of position, who have the true interest of their noble art in view, should make their lives an example to those with whom they are associated, and to those who are to come after them. By this means, and by this means only, can the Theatrical Profession expect to maintain its dignity and to secure the high position it should hold in the estimation of the public. It behoves actors and actresses of every degree, while cultivating their talents to elevate and amuse, to lead such lives that those who have regarded the Stage with a suspicious eye will at last give it its proper place in the world of Art.[110]

In her 1933 autobiography Mrs Kendal recalled that several of the daily papers had been 'very appreciative and even laudatory' in their criticism, but the appreciation had not been universal. She was in fact roundly denounced in the theatrical press both for her criticism of the press and for raising issues that were better left unventilated. She rather disingenuously said 'the address, so carefully planned, so discreetly worded as not to give offence, was actually twisted from its purpose by certain members of the press'.[111] But she declared that even after the passage of nearly fifty years she still stood by her text.

The *Theatre*, the unofficial organ for Irving's views, fulminated in an editorial that instead of letting sleeping dogs lie, Mrs Kendal had stirred up 'such a barking and growling … as were never heard before in the history of the modern stage'.

Before Mrs Kendal stepped forth into the arena to deliver herself of her undesirable platitudes ... the stage question was fairly at rest. Prejudice was gradually disappearing. The church and the stage, like righteousness and peace, were kissing one another. Society consented to be smoothed down when the profession was mentioned. Old sores were being healed, stale contentions were at an end, charity and good faith reigned supreme. Unquestionably one of the wisest guides and counsellors in this matter of peace and toleration was Henry Irving. Quietly, seductively, undemonstratively the good seed was being sown at the Lyceum. Never since the days of Macready had been felt all round such a strong influence for good. Irving conquered by strategy. He became, almost before he was aware of it, a leader of men. Youth elected him as their champion: women chose him as their friend: the dramatic profession voted for him as their chief: the public yielded to his power and wise administration. All that Irving and the stage wanted was support from influential members of the dramatic profession. At this vital moment Mrs Kendal stepped into the breach, and brandishing her shillelagh of indiscretion, she overturns the silent work of years. She managed to tread on every corn that could well be trodden on ... She selected Henry Irving and his work as a target for her acidulated sarcasm. She saddened the discreet members of her own profession; she offended the critics of the press, men who have worked as hard, and harder, than she has ever done to uphold the dignity and honour of her profession. There was scarcely one error in judgment that partisan could make, which Mrs Kendal did not succeed in accomplishing. And what is the result?..all the distasteful controversy about the stage and stage morals, which is simply disastrous in its effect. This is exactly what the Puritans wanted ... it is a pity these questions were ever raised at this moment.[112]

Battle was well and truly joined in the periodical press. In an article in the *Fortnightly Review*, journalist and playwright Frank Burnand absolutely refuted Mrs Kendal's contention that acting had now been accepted as a profession and the terms actor and gentleman were now synonymous. Burnand maintained that: '*prima facie*, for a man to be an officer, a barrister, or a clergyman, was in itself a passport to any English society. Wherever he is personally unknown, it is assumed that he is a gentleman ... and this assumption is on the strength of his profession only.' It was very different for the actor. Acting was the only profession in which a man changed his name when entering it. Going on the stage almost always incurred the disapproval of relatives. 'Let his parents be small or large tradesmen, civil servants, clerks in the City, no matter what, they rarely took kindly to their son "going on the stage" ... The bourgeois is as dead against his son becoming an actor as he ever was. Scratch the British bourgeois and you'll come upon the puritan.'

It was even more serious with women. 'Would any of us wish our daughters to "go on the stage"? There can be but one answer to this: "No". They will encounter bad company, free and easy conduct and bad language. If they possess a histrionic temperament, they will be 'impulsive, passionate, impressionable, self-willed, impatient of control, simple, confiding and vain ... desirous of applause ... illogical, inconsistent, full of contradictions, fond of variety, and unable to live without excitement' and therefore be likely to succumb to 'the first schemer that throws himself in her way'. So he argued: 'public life has great dangers for young women of the artistic temperament'. Acting was not a profession because it involved no course of training or certificates of qualification. It was an art. It was open to anyone who wanted to take it up. As far as he could tell, there were no more actors received in society than thirty years ago and only a handful of university men had taken to the stage.

He praised the desire to raise the status of actors and actresses. But did not think it had made any headway. 'There is a strong leaven of Puritanism amongst us, and, in some respects, so much the better; but also among very excellent people of various religious opinions, there has always been, and it exists now, a sort of vague idea that the stage has always been under the positive ban of the Church.' He refuted this belief but was forced to conclude that to claim for acting: 'the social status of the recognized professions, and to be fussily indignant with society at large for refusing to acknowledge this groundless claim, is degrading to an art which should be as independent, and as exalted, as virtue, and content with virtue's reward'.[113]

This prompted replies from the playwright Hamilton Aidé in the *Nineteenth Century* and the actor-manager John Coleman in the *National Review*. Aidé argued:

> Great and good men recognise more and more that the theatre may be fully as potent a factor for morality as the pulpit. Certain men and women are born into this world with a capacity for representation ... it cannot be 'unworthy' to pursue the path that Nature indicates.

He said that Burnand's statement that the Stage was not regarded as a profession in the same light as the Bar, the Army, the Navy or the Church was self-evidently true but class prejudices existed against other professions. He condemned those men or women who went on the stage with no other qualifications than good looks. But he added: 'when some measure of ability is combined with strength of character and ambition of the best kind, why should not the stage be as laudable as it is a lucrative means of employment to the youth of both sexes'. As to women on the stage, he opined that with:

> our enormous female population and the greater emancipation from conventional trammels, which a closer intercourse with America has helped to produce, a wider range of employment has opened out for ladies of intelligence and independence. Why should the stage, which demands more special qualifications than many of these occupations, be the only one shut to those who possess characters and capacities that fit them for the career? ... I feel very sure that there is a number of well-educated, high-principled girls, with an aptitude for representation, who run no greater risks here than they do in any other arena where prudence and vigilance are needed.

He concluded:

> Those who have at heart the real welfare of the stage in England … will do nothing to repel enthusiastic young worshippers who bring cultivated gifts and all the fervour of youth to serve at this altar. If the reviving taste for the poetical drama is to be fostered, it must be by the educated and refined of both sexes being encouraged to devote their talents to the cause. The tendency of Mr Burnand's article is distinctly to discourage such … by the omission of that which I have endeavoured briefly to put forward in vindication of the stage, he has produced an effect not only derogatory and unjust to the profession at large, but hurtful to the true interests of the Drama.[114]

John Coleman, surveying the history of acting since the time of Elizabeth I, rejected Burnand's contention that a stigma still attached to the profession:

> The honours paid to Charles Kemble when the Queen commanded his return to the stage; the repeated honours paid to Macready, to the Keans, Charles Mathews, and Phelps, to Fanny Kemble, and Helen Faucit, in the past; and in the present, the tributes to English art which accompany Mr Irving's triumphal march through America, the high claims to social distinction accorded in the case of Mr and Mrs Wilson Barrett, Mr Barry Sullivan, Mr Toole, Mr Vezin, Mr Hare, the Kendals, the Bancrofts, Miss Mary Anderson and many others whom I could name, appear strangely at variance with Mr Burnand's theory of 'the social stigma'. Of course he will maintain that these honours have merely been accorded to certain individual artists. I admit it; but these individual artists are representative people, and whether the President of the United States calls on Mr Irving, or the late Viceroy of India invites Wilson Barrett and his accomplished wife to Knebworth, or Professor Ruskin compliments the actors or authors of *Claudian*, they are simply paying homage to the art of which the actor and the authors are, for the time being, representative. Similarly, when the first gentleman in England invites a number of distinguished actors to Marlborough House, he pays a natural compliment to the art the whole world loves and admires.

He pointed out, contrary to Burnand, that the simple fact of being a clergyman, barrister, officer in the army or navy was not in itself a passport to social acceptance and that equally many of the most respected actors of the day were self-made men of humble origin: Irving, Toole, Wilson Barrett, Barry Sullivan, Lionel Brough, Henry Neville, Thomas Thorne. The same was true of actresses: Mrs Kendal, Mrs Bancroft and Helen Faucit among them.

But Burnand's most serious allegation, he believed, was that the stage was such that 'if a girl remains pure in heart, it is a miracle of grace'. He rejected the idea that the scantily clad girls in burlesque could be classified as actresses. He pointed out that the chorus at the Savoy Theatre for the D'Oyly Carte operas were 'charming, modest, well-educated, and were all more of less accomplished musicians. Some of them … were daughters of poor clergymen, doctors and retired military men, while others belonged to the middle class.'

He rejected Burnand's suggestion that there were moral dangers for young women in London theatres or on tour. He described the routine on tour, from twenty-five years' experience as actor and manager, pointing out that the single men and women of the company travelled in separate railway carriages and stayed in separate lodgings.

He rejected Burnand's allegation that actresses required no special training: 'To attain any distinction in the higher range of art it is essential that the aspirants should understand the principles of elocution, and the art of intoning verse rhythmically; they should be able to dance and fence, and the mere art of moving with ease and grace is in itself one of the most difficult accomplishments to acquire.' The doctrine of 'the survival of the fittest' made short work of those who did not train and work hard.

He concluded by saying that, as in every walk of life, there were black sheep but the majority of actresses were 'devoted daughters, faithful wives, and the best of mothers' and that 'actors and actresses, with all their foibles and their faults will compare favourably, with a similar number of any particular section of the community, for propriety of conduct, humanity, and benevolence ... despite Mr Burnand's dictum to the contrary'.[115] This controversy petered out but the argument resurfaced periodically, causing a storm whenever it did. One of the most serious and inexplicable of these crises arose when Clement Scott, doyen of the corps of London critics and at the height of his power after thirty-seven years in the profession, gave an interview to the magazine *Great Thoughts*, in which as Laurence Irving noted: 'he committed professional suicide'.[116] Headed 'Does the Theatre Make for Good?', it was published on 1 January 1898. In the interview, Scott announced: 'stage life, according to my experience, has a tendency to deaden the finer feelings, to crush the inner nature of men and women, and to substitute artificiality and hollowness for sincerity and truth'. Warming to his theme, he went on:

> It is nearly impossible for a woman to remain pure who adopts the stage as a profession. Everything is against her ... I marvel at any mother who allows her daughter to take up the theatrical career, and still more am I astonished that any man should calmly endure that his wife should become an actress ... He must be either a fool of a knave. Nor do I see how a woman is to escape contamination in one form or another. Temptation surrounds her in every shape and on every side; her prospects frequently depend upon the nature and extent of her compliance, and, after all, human nature is very weak.

Actors did not escape his strictures, as he denounced them as vain and egotistical: 'Actors, and very particularly actresses, cannot bear a word of dispraise ... unless you feed their insatiable vanity with continual praise, the average actor, and still more, the average actress counts you as their bitterest enemy.' He concluded his denunciation of actors and actresses by saying, 'there is no school on earth so bad for the formation of character, or that so readily, so quickly and so inevitably draws out all that is worst in man or woman as the stage'. If this was not bad enough he went on to reject out of hand the idea of a rapprochement between church and stage, which Irving among others had been advocating for years: 'everyone who knows the stage must realize how absolutely futile any attempt must be which strives to reconcile the two … The stage is of the earth, earthy – very earthy. The Church is spiritual – or so she is supposed to be.' This was a root and branch denial of the gospel according to Irving.[117]

Sensing that what they had was dynamite, *Great Thoughts* sought to stimulate controversy, sending out proofs of the article to leading actors and actresses inviting their comments. *Figaro* (16 April, 1898) caustically observed that the editor's 'object was, and successfully so, to increase the circulation of a semi-religious journal, by supplying the greedy appetites of his "goody goody" readers with prurient pabulum, the printing of which could do no good … save in the sale of the journal'. Perhaps recalling the furore over Mrs Kendal's speech, the recipients declined to get involved. So the *Daily Mail* sent out a hundred copies of the magazine to members of the profession, eliciting replies from Mrs Adelaide Calvert, Joseph Jefferson and Edward Chester among others, all of whom conceded that the profession was not perfect but that Scott had gone much too far in his denunciation.

The formal reply from the leaders of the profession came at a dinner for actor Charles Cartwright, who was leaving for a tour of Australia. Two actor-managers, having seen the proofs of the article, made speeches denouncing it which were faithfully reported in the press. Charles Wyndham said: 'a man whose livelihood and position have depended so largely on the profession, who has been received for years into comradeship with us, has thought proper in, I sincerely hope, a fit of mental aberration, to gratuitously hurl the foul, false and treacherous slander on our inner life'. Beerbohm Tree, declaring that 'a more flagrant attempt to betray those among whom he moved and lived could scarcely be made by any man for thirty pieces of silver', noted that the attack had been met by 'a splendid outburst of contemptuous silence' but this had been misunderstood in some quarters and he endorsed Wyndham's rejection of the slanders. Playwright Robert Buchanan, writing in the *Stage*, argued that the profession was suffering from an excess of respectability rather than a plethora of immorality. Scott's attack was widely reported and discussed in the press on both sides of the Atlantic.[118]

Irving, on behalf of the Actors' Association, conveyed the formal protest of the profession to the editor of the *Daily Telegraph*, though, out of friendship for Scott, he had urged his colleagues to moderate their protest. But the storm was so great that Scott was compelled to resign and retire to the Continent, after issuing an apology. He wrote to Irving, saying: 'I did an idiotic thing, but I was dragged into it when I was sick, ill, racked with pain and quite demoralized.' But he thanked Irving for 'his loyal and affectionate championship' of him.[119]

But there were still those to perpetuate the view Scott had espoused and, as Irving approached the end of his life, yet another attack was launched, this time by the journalistic crusader and controversialist W.T. Stead. As early as 1886 Irving had urged Stead to undertake an investigation of the stage – doubtless in the confidence that he would acquit it of the calumnies alleged against it. But in 1904 when Stead decided to undertake such an investigation, he began with an essay 'First impressions of the Theatre' published in his journal, the *Review of Reviews*. He recalled his childhood as the son of a Congregationalist minister, when he had been taught that the stage was a waster of time and money and 'often in its results ... disastrous to the moral sense of its votaries'. He argued that 'which was, which is, and perhaps ever will be the one great outstanding objection to the stage' is that by inflaming the senses it exposes the spectators to temptation. He quoted Scott's statement that 'it is impossible for a woman to remain pure who adopts the stage as a profession'. He ignored Scott's recantation, instead repeating it and arguing:

> Not until the standard of morality is as high on the stage as it is, say, among members of a church choir ... I do not see how it will be possible to overcome the reluctance of a very great number of very good people to recognise the theatre as an indispensable agency for the moral and intellectual elevation of the community.[120]

The essay provoked responses from actresses Gertie Millar and Marie Studholme, actor Frank Benson and playwrights Sydney Grundy and Bernard Shaw. But its very appearance indicates that the struggle to which Irving had devoted a large part of his career was still not finally won.

It was, however, well on the way to being won. When he surveyed the development of the theatre in *The Art of the Victorian Stage* (1907), the Manchester architect Alfred Darbyshire could write:

> The effect of Irving's work on the present generation has been extraordinary, the prejudice against the Theatre has been entirely removed; the Lyceum ... as long as it was under the control of Irving was the rallying place of all classes of society and the common ground of culture, refinement and art. I know of nothing in the history of modern civilisation that can compare with the revolution in thought and idea caused by Irving's work in connection with the Theatre as a national institution.[121]

The Victorians were obsessed by the past. They looked to history to give them lessons about how to deal with the present, a present that was constantly changing and over which hung the looming shadows of two revolutions, the French Revolution, which had created a continuing fear of massive upheaval, social division and class hatred, and the Industrial Revolution, which prompted fears of the alienation, demoralisation and deracination of a swelling urban populace and the selfishness, materialism and philistinism of the commercial and industrial classes.

One of the by-products of this increased interest in the past was the invention of the tradition of commemoration. Centenary commemorations were rare before 1800 and uncommon before the mid-nineteenth century. They grew so rapidly in scope and number in the later nineteenth century that the *Pall Mall Gazette* (20 June 1885) referred to the 'present rage for centenaries' and Roland Quinault has pronounced it 'a cult'.[122] The growth of centenary commemorations was 'primarily caused by an increased public interest in the past, which was encouraged by current developments in literature, art and politics'. Local patriotism and commercial interest also provided stimuli.

But in one branch of the arts the cult of commemoration played a different though equally important role – and that was in the theatre. The context of this was the battle for respectability that a succession of leading members of the acting profession waged over the course of the nineteenth century. One means of raising the respectability of theatre was to stress its glorious history by means of commemoration. A start had been made in the eighteenth century with the elevation of Shakespeare as 'England's supreme culture hero'.[123] He was proclaimed the great native genius, the representative man of English letters and thought, the patriot poet. His birthday fell with symbolic convenience on St George's Day, 23 April. It was all part – and a very important part – of creating a defined and special British culture.[124] But as yet theatre could not claim him as a patron saint. It was as a literary genius that he was celebrated. His bicentenary passed off without commemoration in 1764 but in 1769 David Garrick, the leading actor of the day and a man as committed as Irving would later be to raising the respectability level of the profession, was made the first freeman of Stratford-upon-Avon, Shakespeare's birthplace. He announced a three-day Shakespeare Jubilee for September 1769 to celebrate Shakespeare's memory. The event involved song recitals, banquets, balls, a performance of the oratorio *Judith* and the recitation of an ode to Shakespeare specially written by Garrick and set to music by Dr Thomas Arne. But the last two days of the Jubilee were seriously affected by torrential rain, a pageant was cancelled, a firework display washed out and the specially built Rotunda was flooded. Garrick who had underwritten the whole event himself, because the council refused to put up any money, lost £2000. The most singular fact about the event – and one which was a sign of the times perhaps – was that the Jubilee featured no performances of the plays and was timed to coincide with the Stratford races. Garrick left Stratford and never returned, but recouped his losses by staging at Drury Lane the aborted Shakespeare pageant from Stratford. According to one theatre historian the Shakespeare Jubilee was no more than 'a freak, an amiable oddity, a short-lived wonder'.[125] What came to be called Bardolatry picked up in the nineteenth century. There was a one-day festival in Stratford in 1816 to celebrate the bicentenary of Shakespeare's death. There were festivals in 1827 and 1830, and in 1847 the Shakespeare birthplace was purchased for the nation. The next big event was the Shakespeare tercentenary in 1864. This was an altogether grander affair than Garrick's. It had a fortnight's programme of events both in Stratford and in London. But the different organizing committees had different objectives and there were constant quarrels between them. The event failed to secure royal patronage but the National Shakespeare Committee recruited two dukes, nine earls, a viscount and nine barons, with the Duke of Manchester as President and Dickens and Bulwer Lytton as Vice-Presidents. Most significantly, there were three bishops on the committee. This church participation continued, for along with concerts, banquets, fancy dress balls, readings and pageants, there was a performance of Handel's *Messiah*, and there were sermons at Stratford from the Archbishop of Dublin on Shakespeare's God-given gifts and from the Bishop of St Andrews on the moral and spiritual significance of his work. This time too there was a programme of plays both in London and Stratford but the leaders of the profession did not emerge very well from it. Charles Kean was away touring Australia during the event and the other two leading actors, Samuel Phelps and Charles Fechter, had quarrelled. The proposal that Fechter, the French actor whose *Hamlet* had been a sensation, should play it in Stratford outraged Samuel Phelps, who regarded the part as peculiarly his and who detested Fechter ('that bloody Frenchman', he called him). Phelps would have nothing to do with the festival in Stratford and opposition mounted to a Frenchman taking the lead in this celebration of the English genius, and at the last minute he also withdrew and a double bill of *The Comedy of Errors* and *Romeo and Juliet* was substituted. This caused leading actress Helen Faucit also to withdraw from a production of *As You Like It* because the French actress Stella Colas was playing Faucit's old role of Juliet. Both London and Stratford had eventually decided that they would raise money for a statue, but in the event none was forthcoming.[126] However in 1873 Albert Grant MP commissioned a statue of Shakespeare for Leicester Square Gardens in London and in 1888 Lord Ronald Gower, the society sculptor, presented a bronze statue of Shakespeare seated and surrounded by Hamlet, Falstaff, Prince Hal and Lady Macbeth to Stratford.

In 1887 Henry Irving travelled to Stratford by special train to inaugurate a handsome new drinking fountain presented to the town by G.W. Childs, a Philadelphian philanthropist, as a memorial to Shakespeare and to mark the Queen's Golden Jubilee. It was a genuinely Anglo-American occasion, celebrating Shakespeare as a link between the two nations, as a message from the poet James Russell Lowell stressed: 'I am glad to think that this memorial should be the gift of an American, and thus serve to recall the kindred blood of two great nations, joint heirs of the same noble language and of the genius that has given it a cosmopolitan significance.' Irving read out some verses specially composed for the occasion by Oliver Wendell Holmes and a telegram was received from the

Queen expressing her pleasure at the handsome gift to Stratford. British and American flags flew from public buildings and a band played patriotic tunes from both countries. Irving delivered the dedicatory address, stressing Anglo-American kinship but also arguing for the intellectual and moral value of the stage:

> It is above all things as the poet of the people that Shakespeare is supreme. He wrote in days when literature made no appeal to the multitude. Books were for a limited class, but the theatre was open to all. How many Englishmen, to whom reading was a labour or an impossibility, must have drawn from the stage which Shakespeare has enriched some of the most priceless jewels of the human mind! ... It is not only because Shakespeare is the delight of scholars, or because he had infinite charm for the most refined taste, that he wields the unbroken staff of Prospero over the imagination of mankind. It is because his spell is woven from the truth and simplicity of nature herself. This after all is the heart of the mystery. Without an effort the simplest mind passes into the realms of Shakespeare's fancy ... Learned and simple, gentle and humble, all may drink from the inexhaustible wisdom of this supreme sage.

Replying to the toast made to him at the Town Hall luncheon following the inauguration, Irving made a point of linking Shakespeare with the acting profession:

> It is the lasting honour of the actor's calling that the Poet of all Time was a player, and that he achieved immortality by writing for the stage. Of all the eloquent tributes which have been paid to Shakespeare, one ever recalls the words of his fellow-actors, to whose loving care we owe the first edition of his works, and who tell us that 'as he was the happy imitator of nature, he was a most gentle expresser of it'.

He went on to quote with approval Emerson, who claimed Shakespeare taught manners, morals, economy, philosophy, religion, taste, love, conduct, duty and gentlemanliness. He ended by saying that today's ceremonies would 'make every actor in the world-wide sphere of Shakespeare's influence prouder than ever of the calling which I have the privilege of representing here'. The speeches were widely reported in the press and were typical of Irving's message wherever he spoke. It was occasions such as these that helped to transform the popular attitude towards the stage.[127]

Statues are another way of commemorating the famous and inscribing them in the popular consciousness. Mrs. Sarah Siddons was one of the legendary stars of the British stage. Famous for her Lady Macbeth and Volumnia, she had died in 1831. When the Shakespeare Reading Society, of which Irving had been the first president, proposed a public memorial to her, he lent the idea his enthusiastic support. He took the chair at a public meeting, on 17 May 1895, at Paddington Vestry Hall to promote the project. In his speech to that meeting, he spoke of her influence living on beyond her lifetime, her work helping 'to make the name of

England illustrious throughout the world'. He pointed to her starting out with 'no advantage of fortune or station, but the possessor of great powers and great purpose, and she used them well and honourably', serving a long apprenticeship in the provinces and then animating her stage roles with 'a soul and a passion' of which the authors sometimes never dreamed. In all this she prefigured Irving. He concluded 'it is right and fitting that such a career should be remembered in a way as to keep it ever prominently before the eyes of the young'. Irving was also on hand on 14 June 1897 to unveil on Paddington Green the statue of Mrs Siddons, sculpted by Léon-Joseph Chavailliaud and based on a Reynolds portrait *The Tragic Muse*. Irving repeated his account of her career, pointing out that it was the first statue of an actor to be erected in London. There were statues of Shakespeare celebrated as a poet, though Irving reminded his listeners that 'the dramatic profession does not forget that Shakespeare was an actor, and that but for his connection with the stage it is improbable that he would have enriched our dramatic literature'. But Irving also commends that 'public spirit which has sacrificed an ancient social prejudice in homage to a great actress' and the 'enlightened tolerance' which led the Paddington vestry to donate the site and the basement of the statue.[128]

On 15 July 1896, a monument to John Heminge and Henry Condell, who had brought out the first collected edition of Shakespeare's plays in 1623, was unveiled in the churchyard of St. Mary Aldermanbury, near the Mansion House. Heminge and Condell and their wives were buried in the churchyard. The monument was the gift of Charles Clement Walker of Lilleshall Old Hall, Shropshire. It took the form of a red granite monument with a bronze bust of Shakespeare at the top and a reproduction in stone of the title page of the first folio, with an inscription recording its creation. The Lord Mayor of London, the American Ambassador and Sir Henry Irving attended among others. Lord Ronald Gower was also there and recorded in his diary that 'the ceremony was well-ordered' and that the Ambassador's speech was 'rather indistinct, but one heard every word of Irving's address; he was loudly cheered when leaving by the crowd outside'.[129] Irving paid tribute to the work of Heminge and Condell, fellow actors of Shakespeare, in publishing his work:

> They had as little expectation of (immortality) as of being invited to the table of the Lord Mayor of London some three centuries ago. The hospitality of the city had wider amenities now, and the Lord Mayor had graciously shown how fitting was the civic pride which honoured the memory of these two citizens – these two players – who lived in affectionate friendship with a fellow player, a playwright and player, William Shakespeare, and handed on to future ages the glory of this supreme genius of literature.[130]

On 17 February 1905, Irving unveiled a tablet on the house in Bath occupied by the eighteenth-century actor James Quin (1693–1766). Irving enthralled his listeners with a series of colourful anecdotes about Quin's career and later was entertained by the Mayor and Corporation to luncheon at the Guildhall, where he was presented with a silver smoker's combination, hardly the most appropriate gift for a man dying of emphysema. The very fact of Irving commemorating Quin emphasized how far the profession had come since the eighteenth century. Dr Lionel Weatherly, proposing a toast to Irving, summed up what many felt:

> He set himself to elevate the drama, and to elevate the tastes of the play-going public. It would be ever remembered to his credit how he introduced to that play-going public historical, poetical and romantic dramas, but above all he would be remembered for his wonderful revival of the plays of the immortal Shakespeare ... Those sumptuous revivals of Shakespeare, always in thorough and perfect good taste, had inculcated a love, a new love, in the English public for that marvellous dramatist – a love which they knew burned fiercely at this very day ... Surely they could truly say that they left a play of that sort realising full well that their higher mental faculties had been improved, that their wonderful storehouse of memory had been replenished with something worth thinking about, and that the moral side of their nature had been stimulated – all for the making of good. What could he say to Sir Henry Irving as a man? What had he not done as a man for the social position of the profession which he adorned? ... it would be incredible to adequately describe the difference between the social position of the actor in the old days ... and what it was in the present day. He said without fear of contradiction that to Sir Henry Irving the profession was indebted to a very great extent as an actor, as a manager and as a man, for the position that the profession now held.[131]

The contrast between Irving and Quin was not lost on the trade paper the *Era* which reported (18 February 1905):

> There is a strong contrast between the character of Quin and that of the great actor who unveiled the tablet to Quin's memory in the city of Bath yesterday. For if Quin was 'a child of his time', no less is Sir Henry a thorough representative of the present age. He is the antipodes of Quin in many respects. He fights no duels because he has no enemies. He is 'clean-built' – Quin was corpulent; abstemious – Quin was a winebibber. In several points, however, Sir Henry and the actor whose memorial he unveiled yesterday are alike. Sir Henry is generous, almost to a fault; like Quin he will brook no slight of the profession to which he belongs. The present generation, with its keen sensitiveness, its intellectual activity, its moderation, its humanity, and its self-control, paid honour on Friday to the eighteenth-century ideal of an actor; the three-bottle or rather six-bottle man, the rake, the duellist, and the beau. How much humanity has improved and advanced since those days of limited ablution and unlimited paint, powder and perfume; of foolish fighting and intemperate indulgence; of heartless repartee, and scandalous epigram, it is hardly necessary to note.

It was not always possible to accommodate theatrical figures of earlier eras to Victorian sensibilities. On 16 September 1891 Irving unveiled a memorial to Christopher Marlowe in his birthplace, Canterbury. It took the form of a life-size bronze statue of the Lyric Muse, the work of Onslow Ford, who had also sculpted the figure of Irving as Hamlet. As *The Times* reported, however, 'Owing to the inadequacy of funds, only one of the four niches intended to receive statuettes of the leading characters in Marlowe's plays – that allotted to Tamburlaine – is at present filled'. The lack of enthusiasm for Marlowe is not perhaps surprising considering that Marlowe's plays were not performed on the Victorian stage and Irving himself had never appeared in a Marlowe play. It is an interesting case of an attempt to reconstruct a very un-Victorian figure, a homosexual atheist intriguer who died in a tavern brawl in Deptford, to fit the Victorian age and to play an inspirational role. Irving stressed that he was not concerned with Marlowe the man but Marlowe the poet, the man 'who first captured the majestic rhythms of our tongue, and whose "mighty line" is the most resounding note in England's literature'. But he could not resist the temptation to boost his own profession:

> His reputation should be an abiding element to our national pride. And … as an actor, I am proud to remember that Marlowe's work, like Shakespeare's, was written primarily for the stage; that, if not an actor himself, Marlowe was intimately associated with the actor's calling, and that Elizabethan dramatists, with Shakespeare the actor at their head, employing the stage as the first medium of their appeal to posterity, linked it for ever with an imperishable glory.

But that Marlowe was not a sufficient figure to inspire the great and the good of the age is evidenced by the fact that, despite the presence of Irving, Ellen Terry and a group of writers, critics and poets, apologies for absence were received from Lord Coleridge, the Duke of Westminster, the Marquis of Ripon, the Earl of Derby, the Earl of Lytton, Lord Aberdare, Leslie Stephen, Sir Frederic Leighton, the Dean of Canterbury and 'many others'.[132]

Irving as principal representative of the British theatre was also anxious to participate in other commemorations, associating theatre with the national past. In 1901 the thousandth anniversary of the death of Alfred the Great was celebrated in Winchester by the King Alfred Millenary. Alfred was revered as the founder of the English Navy, as scholar and ideal ruler, as Anglo-Saxon folk hero. His biography had been written by Thomas Hughes, Liberal MP and author of *Tom Brown's Schooldays*. Edward Augustus Freeman in his *History of the Norman Conquest* called him 'the most perfect character in history', and J.R. Green in *The Conquest of England* said: 'He stands … in the forefront of his race, for he is the noblest as he is the most complete embodiment of all that is great, all that is lovable in the English temper.'[133] The Millenary was celebrated in Winchester by pageants, parades, an address by the Prime Minister, Lord Rosebery, and the unveiling of a statue of Alfred by Hamo Thorneycroft. A new battleship was also named the HMS *King Alfred*. Irving offered his services. There was a play *Alfred the Great* by Sheridan Knowles, in which Macready had starred in 1831, but Irving had never appeared on the stage as King Alfred. One of his greatest successes, however, had been in the title role of *Becket*, a play by another candidate for the title Alfred the Great, the Poet Laureate Alfred, Lord Tennyson. So on 18 September 1901, he interrupted a provincial tour to travel to Winchester and gave a reading in the Castle Hall of the text of *Becket*. Bram Stoker recalls that 'Winchester was then thronged with strangers from all parts of the world, a large number of whom were accredited representatives of some branch or interest of the Anglo-Saxon race'. Irving received an ovation and made a patriotic speech appropriate to the occasion:

> A thousand years of the memory of the great King, who loved his country and made her loved and respected and feared, is a mighty heritage for a nation ... The work which King Alfred did he did for England, but the whole world benefited by it. And most of all was there benefit for the race which he adorned. In the thousand years which have elapsed since he was laid to rest in that England in whose making he had such a part, the world has grown wiser and better, and civilisation has ever marched on with mighty strides. But through all extension and advance the land which King Alfred consolidated and the race which peopled it, have ever been to the front in freedom and enlightenment; and today when England and her many children, east and west, and north and south, are united by one grand aspiration of human advance, it is well that we should celebrate the memory of him to whom so large a measure of that advance is due.[134]

It is worth noting in this context that on 31 May 1897 Irving had given a similar reading of the text of *Becket* in the Chapter House at Canterbury Cathedral in support of the restoration fund.[135]

It is appropriate to end this survey of theatrical commemoration with two events which seem to signal the final acceptance of the acting profession. On 5 December 1910, outside the National Portrait Gallery in Charing Cross Road, before 'an assembly of many hundreds of Irving's colleagues and admirers – among them, as he would have devoutly wished, representatives of all the arts including, in spite of the not-too-conspicuous absence of G.B.S., literature', a bronze statue of Irving nine feet high cast by Thomas Brock was unveiled by actor-manager Sir John Hare.[136] The entire cost had been met by subscriptions from members of the acting profession. Significantly, Irving was not costumed in any of his great theatrical roles but dressed in his doctoral robes, intellectual respectability personified. It remains along with Mrs Siddons's statue the only statue of an actor in London.[137]

On 2 May 1916, the tercentenary of Shakespeare's death was celebrated at Drury Lane Theatre, in 'a tribute to the genius of William Shakespeare, humbly offered by the players and their fellow-workers in the kindred arts of music and painting'. The contrast with the Garrick Jubilee and the 1864 Tercentenary was marked. The King and Queen were patrons of the event, the Prime Minister, Mr

Asquith, was Honorary President of the organising committee and all the leading actors of the day were on the actors' committee. A programme of music associated with the works of Shakespeare was arranged by Sir Hubert Parry and Sir Alexander Mackenzie and conducted by Sir Alexander Mackenzie, Sir Henry Wood, Hamilton Harty, Edward German and Norman O'Neill. A commemorative book of pictures and drawings of scenes from and actors associated with Shakespeare was published with contributions from many leading painters, headed by Sir Edward Poynter. There was an all-star production of *Julius Caesar* and a pageant of tableaux from eight Shakespeare plays. In the royal box during the intermission Frank Benson, who directed and starred in productions at the Shakespeare Memorial Theatre in Stratford for thirty years, was knighted by the King while still in costume as Julius Caesar.[138] Frank Benson was not of course the first theatrical knight.

The award of a knighthood was the ultimate act of Establishment recognition. Mrs Charles Kean had petitioned unsuccessfully for a knighthood for her husband and Henry Neville had publicly called for one for Samuel Phelps. But it was Irving who received the first theatrical knighthood in 1895. By a cruel irony, the day that Irving's knighthood was announced, 25 May, was the day Oscar Wilde was convicted at the Old Bailey of gross indecency. It was a salutary reminder of the taint of immorality which for many people still attached to the stage. But following Irving's knighthood there had been knighthoods for Squire Bancroft in 1897, Charles Wyndham in 1902, John Hare and Herbert Beerbohm Tree in 1907, George Alexander in 1911 and Johnston Forbes-Robertson in 1913 – all of them members of the Tercentenary Committee – but Benson was the first to be knighted actually in a theatre, in costume and with a theatrical sword. The battle had been won and won in part by an appeal to history and in particular to Shakespeare, whose significance as actor as well as playwright was stressed once again in the foreword to the Commemoration Book of the Tercentenary by W.L. Courtney.

> To all artists the memory of the Great Englishman is as dear as to those who recall with gratitude his patriotic love of his native land ... But actors have a special claim to pay their homage to one who was himself an actor and playwright – whose works, apart from their contribution to philosophic thought and their 'wood notes wild' of divinest poetry, were written primarily for the stage and can best be seen on the boards.[139]

As the festival was being staged at the height of the First World War, Courtney was effectively reminding his readers that it would be unpatriotic to doubt the artistic *bona fides* of actors, especially since the greatest of English playwrights had also been an actor.

Irving in *The Bells*, cartoon by Alfred Bryan, *Entr'acte*, 5 December 1896.

5

The Victorian Repertoire

History is famously written by the victors and there is a received view of nineteenth-century drama, endlessly reproduced in the standard works on the subject, which is in essence that nothing of any value was produced before the last years of the century. This view is summed up in *The Old Drama and the New* (1923), the published version of a course of lectures delivered in 1920 and 1921 by the eminent critic William Archer. Archer believed that the gold standard in drama was represented by realism, intellectuality and seriousness of purpose. Literally a theatrical Puritan, he spoke of the 'process of purification' of the drama, its gradual purging of excess and exaggeration and the acquisition of seriousness. This meant Archer had to dismiss 'the great mass of Elizabethan, Restoration and eighteenth-century plays' because they 'have nothing to say to modern audiences, because they exemplify primitive and transitional types of art, portray ... gross and unpleasing manners, and call for forms of virtuosity in representation which are well nigh extinct on the modern stage'. The exception is 'the towering genius of Shakespeare' who 'overcame the imperfections of the form in which he worked, and gave to the stage and the whole world a series of ever-living masterpieces'.

In what became a commonplace of theatre history Archer saw the whole course of British drama from 1590 to 1915 as an evolutionary process: 'the sloughing off from drama of lyrical and rhetorical elements, both tragic and comic, and the conventions associated with them, until at last we reach a logical and consistent art-form, capable of expressing ... not only the social but the spiritual life of the modern world'. In what would now be seen as an extreme version of the Puritan position, he dismisses all Elizabethan drama, apart from Shakespeare, as 'rude, incult, unpolished' and Restoration drama as 'gross ... cynical, corrupt' and proclaimed the eighteenth century 'a dreary desert broken by a single oasis', the comedies of Sheridan and Goldsmith.[1]

The period 1810–35 he sees as 'the winter solstice of English drama. There had been no such lean years since 1590, if we except the short period during which Civil War and Puritanism silenced the stage.' He went on:

> In comedy nothing of any note was produced, and tragedy was represented by dismal and stodgy productions; inspired by the worst traditions of the seventeenth and eighteenth centuries. How deep was the decline appears clearly from the fact that

Sheridan Knowles ... was incontestably the leading playwright of the period ... I know of few men who have made any considerable success on the stage with less genuine talent to account for it. His art lay wholly in stodgy rhetoric.

He did, however, concede some success to Bulwer Lytton, 'for all their faults cannot ... annul the fact that *The Lady of Lyons, Richelieu* and even *Money* have given me a great deal of pleasure'. So 1835–65, though almost as barren as 1810–35 was 'redeemed from utter insignificance by the plays of Bulwer'.[2]

One after another he dismissed the leading playwrights of the era: Douglas Jerrold wrote 'pleasant trivial comedies and domestic dramas'; Charles Reade 'contributed nothing of permanent interest to the stage'; Tom Taylor 'an industrious playwright without a spark of inspiration'; Dr Westland Marston, 'an eminently respectable writer of uninteresting plays, mostly in blank verse', and Dion Boucicault 'an industrious adapter from the French'. The mark of legitimate drama was blank verse and Archer declared it was much easier to write this stilted archaic stuff than good colloquial modern dialogue.[3]

The first signs of Renaissance came in 1865. Tom Robertson's *Society* and the ensuing plays before his early death at forty-two established an everyday reality in settings and speech in place of stagy artificiality. But 1870–85 was 'almost as barren as the period which preceded the advent of Robertson'. Henry Irving did 'practically nothing for the living drama'. The last thirty years of the period from 1885 to 1923 had, however, seen 'a greater efflorescence of English drama than any similar period since the thirty years from 1590 to 1620 which included the whole life-work of Shakespeare'.[4]

The 'regenerator of the English drama' was Pinero and in his wake Henry Arthur Jones, Haddon Chambers, R.C. Carton, Oscar Wilde and, after them, Stanley Houghton, John Galsworthy, Harley Granville-Barker and Bernard Shaw. The influence of Ibsen was 'indirect' but 'pervasive', more pervasive than anything since Byron, inspiring 'Free Theatre' and encouraging 'problem plays'. The Independent Theatre, the Stage Society and the Vedrenne–Barker regime at the Royal Court Theatre all helped to bring to the stage the first real, pure 'theatre of ideas' since Shakespeare.[5] Archer's interpretation of theatre history was also shared by other influential critics such as Bernard Shaw, A.B. Walkley and J.T. Grein, and has left its imprint on much subsequent writing.

But that this is a critical orthodoxy rather than an objectively factual account is evidenced by the fact that of Archer's pantheon only Wilde and Shaw are now regularly performed, Pinero and Galsworthy rarely and Chambers and Carton never. By contrast, the last few years have seen triumphantly successful revivals of Bulwer Lytton's *Money* and Boucicault's *London Assurance, The Shaughraun* and *The Colleen Bawn*, suggesting that there is still theatrical life in the despised standards of the Victorian repertoire.

Archer hinted at an alternative interpretation of the Victorian theatre in writing of Lytton's 'stagey' *Richelieu*. He conceded of the famous 'Curse of Rome' scene:

> Edwin Booth's rendering of this passage was one of the few performances I can recall which enabled me to realise the *kind* of effect which the great actors and actresses of the great age of rhetorical acting used to produce. It was thrilling, startling, electrifying, beyond anything dreamt of in our humdrum realistic stage. It was not imitation – it was passion incarnate.

Then of Irving he wrote:

> He had very little literary or dramaturgical sense, and his talent and training both led him back to the rhetorical tradition. He produced in the seventies two notable works inspired by that tradition, *Charles the First*, by W.G. Wills, and *Queen Mary*, by Alfred Tennyson; but neither took a permanent place on the stage.[6]

All the things that Archer detested – rhetoric, Romanticism, theatricality, blank verse – characterized much of nineteenth-century drama and constituted an alternative theatre to Archer's 'theatre of ideas' – a theatre of feelings and emotions, a theatre of performance and dramatic devices, a Romantic Theatre. It was precisely the input of actor William Charles Macready to Bulwer Lytton's scripts that made them not only playable but long lived.

Unlike the 'theatre of ideas', which was pre-eminently a writer's theatre, the Romantic Theatre was an actor's theatre. As Willson Disher, biographer of one of the last great romantic actors, Sir John Martin-Harvey, wrote:

> At the zenith of acting its leading exponents did not choose their parts. The stars had their courses fixed for them. Several of Shakespeare's tragic roles had to be essayed; not Hamlet, Lear, Macbeth, Othello, Iago and Romeo alone but Richard III, Shylock, Coriolanus and Iachimo as well. Which part suited which player best the audience decided with faculties trained by constant comparison … If a player did find a new part, then other actors must act it. They had to act, almost like prizefighters, *against* each other.[7]

Besides Shakespeare, the Romantic repertoire included Sir Giles Overreach in Massinger's *A New Way to Pay Old Debts,* Jaffier in Otway's *Venice Preserv'd,* Rolla in Sheridan's *Pizarro,* Young Norval and Sir Edward Mortimer in *The Iron Chest* (George Colman's adaptation of William Godwin's *Caleb Williams.*)

What Archer was rejecting *tout cour* was Romanticism, the movement which dominated art and letters from the 1760s to the 1850s. The humanism of the Renaissance had given way in the early eighteenth century to the Age of Enlightenment, in which reason and common sense prevailed, when science was believed to provide rational explanations for everything and when an ordered, measured classicism prevailed in the arts. But this *Weltanschauung* eventually provoked a violent reaction. It was bold, challenging, unconventional. It exalted the imagination, the emotions, dreams and fantasies, mysticism; everything that was alien and abhorrent to the prevailing classicism. Change was in the air, political revolution in France and America, industrial revolution in Britain, and from this turbulence burst forth the Romantic Movement.

It is difficult to define Romanticism precisely because it was so all-embracing and so widespread. But it had at its roots a burning desire for freedom from restraint and the unshackling of the imagination. Once this was done, then the human spirit could fly in all directions: to wild excess or morbid introspection, to an idealized past or a fantasized future. It had certain basic fascinations: the past, especially the medieval past, the cult of naturalism and spontaneity, heroic individualism, the occult – but above all the primacy accorded to the imagination. It produced the historical novel, the lyric poem, the Gothic tale, the romantic melodrama; the poetry of Byron, Keats and Shelley; the music of Berlioz, Liszt and Wagner; the paintings of Delacroix, Turner and Goya; the novels of Walter Scott, Alexandre Dumas and Victor Hugo.

As a movement, Romanticism took different directions in different countries. Allan Rodway discerned in the movement two wings, the radical and the reactionary, writing:

> What radical and reactionary romantics have in common – in addition to their anti-rationalism – is the feeling that they are Outsiders – and feeling an outsider in your own society naturally leads to … subjectivism, utopianism and extremism. The difference is that reactionaries think society is, or rather *was*, natural, and therefore they want to be insiders, but in a society of an older type. Hence their support of feudalism or an authoritarian monarch and Church. The radicals think society is or was *un*natural and therefore do not wish to be insiders. They would be at one only with the universe.[8]

So in Germany, Romanticism found expression in a passionate defence of 'throne and altar'; absolute monarchy and the Catholic church; and in France, in republicanism, atheism and a revolt against the established order.

Irving falls into the category of reactionary Romantic, not a supporter of absolute monarchy and Catholicism but, in the context of Victorian England, a convinced supporter of monarchy, empire, aristocracy, state censorship and Evangelical Christianity. He was the classic outsider, a poor provincial who by effort and dedication turned himself into a gentleman, sought to make himself an insider in the society he found and to achieve social acceptance for his profession. Artistically he was drawn inexorably to the key elements of Romanticism – the past, individualism, the occult, the idea of the brooding Byronic anti-hero, the grand gesture. His work was permeated by these ideas. But he placed them in a framework that asserted the dominant values of a settled Victorian society – the assertion of order, family values, retribution for evil. The *Times* critic A.B. Walkley identified Irving's artistic personality with absolute precision:

To touch the imagination in the playhouse world of Romance and, withal, to bring the great outer Philistine world to its knees – to set our ears ringing with the 'chink-chink' of the Polish Jew's sleigh bells, and to get elected to the Athenaeum Club *honoris causa* – is an achievement verging on the paradoxical; it is running with the hare and hunting with the hounds. Alone among actors, Mr Irving has taken this double-first: a success on the stage and off it ... Burke's phrase comes naturally to the mind, for there is something chivalric in the man as in the player – a dignity, a gusto, a touch of the hidalgo. When a quarter of a century ago Henry Irving, after ten years' rustication, was permanently enrolled in a London company, the prospects of the English stage were ... aleatory. The die might have come down drab; our next great actor might have been a John Kemble or an elder Farren, a classic, a depository of 'correctness' and the traditions ... When it was finally cast, it came down flamboyant. The actor approached his proper goal of the romantic, the fantastic, in Digby Grant, in Jingle, and reached it, amid a roar of astonished applause from the crowd, in Burgomaster Mathias. This was his first great assault on Philistia. It roused the average sensual man to the disquieting consciousness of a nervous system. Contrast it with M. Coquelin's impersonation of the same part, and you have the pass-key to Mr Irving's method. The one is of imagination all compact, a common Alsatian innkeeper transfigured by romance, seen, as it were, by flashes of lightning; the other is plausible, logical, correct; a figure of cold daylight, leaving you cold. In a word, the one is flamboyant; the other only drab.

It was evident from the first that he had not the fluid or ductile temperament which makes your all-round actor, your Betterton, your Garrick ... Mr Irving's individuality is too strongly marked ... As soon as he attacked Shakespeare we saw that he was not going to sweep the board. He began – of course, they all do – with Hamlet. It is a part in which no actor has ever been known entirely to fail; but it will never be linked with Mr Irving's name as it is, for all time, with Betterton's – the classic impersonation ... His Othello, his Richard, were only half-successes ... Over the recollection of his Romeo one passes hastily, suppressing a chuckle ... His Macbeth, even in its second version, revised and improved, was rather romantic than tragic. So it was in the romantic rather than the tragic repertory of Shakespeare, in the figures painted from the rich fantastic palette of the Italian Renaissance, the one that waited for him confidently. Shylock, Iago, Malvolio, Benedick, these are all flamboyant parts, and he took possession of them by right of temperament ... His Iago was daringly Italian, a true compatriot of Borgias ... The remembrance of those grapes which he plucked and slowly ate still sets the teeth of Philistia on edge. His Malvolio had an air of *hidalguia*, something of Castilian loftiness, for all the fantasy of its cross-gartering; Don Quixote turned Major Domo. Quite the best of his Renaissance flamboyants is his Benedick, as gallant a picture of the courtier-scholar-soldier as anything in the pages of Cellini, or the canvases of Velasquez. But, grateful as we are for these things, his greatest services to Shakespeare, most of us will think, have been less immediate than mediate, less as actor than as manager ... His series of Shakespearean land and sea-scapes, Veronese gardens open to the moonlight, a Venice unpolluted by Cook's touristry, groves of cedar and cypress in Messina, Illyrian shores, Scotch hillsides, and grim castles, Bosworth field – what a panorama he has given us! The sensuous, plastic, pictorial side of Shakespeare had never been seen before as he showed it. Here you have the flamboyant artist outdoing Delacroix on his own ground.

Nevertheless man cannot live by Shakespeare alone, least of all this man. His most permanent triumph has been in melodrama – which is Philistia's name for the stage-flamboyant expressed in prose. His prototype in this was Lemaître; and his conquest of the Lemaîtrist repertory is complete. His Robert Macaire, his Dubosc, are the most effective of stage sudorifics. French melodramas, too, have yielded him Louis XI, the two Dei Franchi, while two of Macready's greatest parts – played in a manner widely different from Macready's – have furnished him with Richelieu and Werner. These are all his studies in the lurid, the volcanic, and they are amongst his strongest; but two at least of his best things are figures of repose, if not of still life – his Charles I and his Dr Primrose. Over them all, the just and the unjust, his romance has gleamed impartially.

But … this romantic actor could not hope to escape the special danger of his temperament. Like the Don Quixote with whom I have compared him, he has now and then mistaken spavined hacks for Rosinantes and flocks of sheep for armies. His Vanderdecken, his Eugene Aram, perhaps his Philip, and his Court Tristan, were among these errors. His Mephistopheles, too, and, as some think, his Edgar of Ravenswood. The fault was not all his own. His authors played him false. There one touches him between the joints of his harness; he has failed to create a great modern playwright. Let him crown his career by doing that, and I, for one, will vote for his canonisation.[9]

There is room for disagreement about individual performances but this account of Irving's career is full of acute insights.

Although Britain as a nation eschewed radical and revolutionary Romanticism, English theatre was decisively influenced by the Romantic theatre of France, by the writers Hugo, Dumas, De Vigny and Delavigne and the actors Talma and LeMaître. Edmund Kean who embodied the wildness and imaginative excess of Romanticism in England became himself the subject of a play originally called *Disorder and Genius* but rewritten by Dumas as *Kean* (1836). In it Frédèrick LeMaître played an Edmund Kean who defies the decadent monarchy and aristocracy of England. In England, however, the plays about actors which held the stage were *David Garrick* and *Nance Oldfield*, both adaptations from French stories in which famous eighteenth-century actors behave properly, gently dissuading besotted admirers from running away from home to pursue them.[10]

Interestingly both James Agate and A.B. Walkley saw Irving as an English counterpart of LeMaître. Irving played two of the roles LeMaître made famous – Edgar of Ravenswood in *La Fiancée de Lammermoor* and Robert Macaire, the sardonic criminal rejoicing in his crimes, in *L'Auberge des Adrets*. LeMaître also played Hamlet, Othello, Mephistopheles and Napoleon, all roles later taken up by Irving. But there were other similarities. LeMaître's partnership with the actress Marie Dorval prefigured the Irving-Terry partnership. The critic Jules Janin wrote of LeMaître and Dorval: 'Together they undoubtedly formed a bold, skilful and all-powerful combination … He had strength, she had grace; he had violence, she had charm'.[11] When Robert Baldick wrote of LeMaître's method he might also have been writing of Irving:

> 'Study' is the operative word; and Frédèrick's surviving scripts show that in fact he pored over every line of his parts, rehearsed every intonation, practised every entrance and exit. Only when he had mastered a part intellectually did he bring his emotions into play, first thinking and then feeling himself into his role, so that he became to all intents and purposes one with the character he was representing.[12]

It is small wonder then that, as the actor Frank Archer recalled, when Irving appeared in *The Bells*, 'Colonel' Bateman 'excitedly and fiercely ... swore that the acting was equal to LeMaître's, and the American was a judge of theatrical art'.[13]

From France, too, came the series of plays that Charles Kean turned into successes on the English stage and versions of which Irving went on to produce – *Louis XI*, *The Courier of Lyons*, *Faust and Margaret* (originally Michel Carré's 1850 *Mephistopheles*) and *The Corsican Brothers*. So great was the influence that even original English plays like Lytton's *The Lady of Lyons* and *Richelieu* dealt with French subjects.

The French actor Charles Fechter brought grand Romantic acting to London, during his tenure of the Lyceum (1863–67) appearing in Shakespeare, but also playing Robert Macaire in *The Roadside Inn*, the Dei Franchi brothers in *The Corsican Brothers*, Claude Melnotte in *The Lady of Lyons* and Edgar in *Master of Ravenswood* (Palgrave Simpson's adaptation of Scott's novel which ran for 106 performances in 1865–66).[14] Together with the Courier of Lyons, Ruy Blas, Vanderdecken the Flying Dutchman, Faust and Louis XI in various versions, these Fechter roles constitute what Willson Disher calls 'Neo-Gothic Shakespeare', the classics of the Romantic repertoire that were played alongside the works of the Bard. Irving played in them all at the Lyceum with the single exception of Ruy Blas. Their linking characteristic, 'the secret sorrow ... the sense of guilt or the feeling of despair', was a major feature of the roles Irving selected for himself at the Lyceum.[15]

But it was worth recalling that French theatre had in its turn been galvanized and transformed by the impact of Shakespeare and Schiller. In his preface to *Cromwell* (1827), a five act play too huge to be staged, Victor Hugo published a manifesto of Romantic drama. In this he rejected the unities of time and place in favour of the unity of theme, stressing the need for verse, insisting on the presence of comedy and grotesquerie, and declaring:

> The drama is a mirror in which nature is reflected. But if this mirror is an ordinary one ... It will reflect only a dull and flat image ... The drama must therefore be a concentrating mirror which ... picks out and intensifies those which turn a glow into a bright light, a light into a flame ... Everything that exists in the world in history, in

life, in man, everything can and must be reflected in it, but subject to the magic wand of art.

He insisted that historical drama is not the same as history:

> But it will be said that the drama also depicts the history of nations. Yes, but in terms of everyday *life*, not of *history*. The drama leaves to the historian the precise series of general facts, the chronological order of dates, mass movements, battles, conquests, the splitting up of empires, everything external in history. The drama takes the internal events. What history forgets or disdains, details of costume, customs, faces, the underpinnings of events, life, in a word, belongs to the drama; and drama can be immense in aspect and in overall picture when small things are taken into a great hand … But one must be careful not to look, even in the *historical* drama for pure history. The drama writes down legends, not archives. It is a chronicle, not a chronology.[16]

Just as the English stage was peopled by characters from French history, so the French theatre was inspired by English historical figures, with Hugo writing *Cromwell* (1827) and *Marie Tudor* (1833), Alfred de Vigny *Chatterton* (1835), Delavigne *Les Enfants d'Edouard* (1833) about the Princes in the Tower, and Dumas *Kean* (1836) and *Catherine Howard* (1834).

Irving laid out in an article for an American journal the *Spirit of the Times*, the reasons dictating his choice of plays. They were 'the possibility of finding a satisfactory cast', 'the time of year or season must be taken into consideration, as a prudent manager must calculate the period over which his original outlay is to be spent', 'the political and social conditions of the day … prudence demands the postponement of subjects of a possible disturbing nature', 'the development of the various characters and the possibilities of picturesque effect … All that can be learned by the eye alone – all that colour and form and light can present – plays an important part in the living pictures of the modern stage'. So the majority of his considerations are purely theatrical.[17]

In fact Irving's repertoire was absolutely in the mainstream of the Romantic tradition as it held the stage from the days of Edmund Kean onwards. Irving believed that the poetic drama as perfected by Shakespeare was the acme of the theatre and devoted much time to finding the nineteenth-century successor to Shakespeare in that genre. In an address given in 1878 he quoted Byron's poetic denunciation of 'the degradation of our vaunted stage', only to reject it. He pointed out that Macready had successfully staged Byron's *Werner* and *Sardanapalus*. 'And the world remembers Bulwer's *Richelieu*, Milman's *Fazio*, Talfourd's *Ion*, Taylor's *Van Artevelde* and a host of other fine plays, among the subsequent fruits of a tree which Lord Byron had considered dead.'[18] But in fact most of these blank verse dramas were as dead as doornails and the only one Irving revived was *Richelieu*. He turned, however, to Tennyson and Wills to provide new examples of the poetic drama. At the Lyceum he alternated

Shakespeare and the poetic drama with melodrama, but the latter refined and stylized to conform to the style defined by the critic George Lewes in his celebrated review of Charles Kean's *The Corsican Brothers* as 'gentlemanly melodrama'. During his own artistic control of the Lyceum, Irving produced thirty-seven plays, only twelve of which were Shakespeare. The standard Shakespeare repertoire in Irving's day consisted of *Hamlet, Macbeth, Othello, Romeo and Juliet, Richard III, Henry VIII, Henry V, King John, As You Like It, Much Ado About Nothing* and *Merchant of Venice*.[19] Irving produced them all except for *As You Like It, Henry V* and *King John*. Disher lists the showy roles which an actor needed to take on to be compared with his great predecessors as: Macbeth, Othello, Hamlet, Lear, Iago, Romeo, Richard III, Shylock, Coriolanus and Iachimo.[20] Irving played them all. The absence in particular of popular patriotic tub-thumpers *Henry V* and *King John* is intriguing. Despite his personal sense of patriotism, this was evidently not part of his theatrical agenda, which was dictated more by the Evangelical morality of the mid-Victorian period than the imperialist mentality of late Victorian Britain.

It was in the middle of the eighteenth century that Shakespeare became indisputably the English national poet and playwright. It was part of a conscious creation of an English artistic identity independent of France. By the Victorian era the Bible and Shakespeare were being mentioned in the same breath and according to Matthew Arnold were 'imposed upon an Englishman as objects of his admiration'.[21] In his volume on heroes and hero-worship Thomas Carlyle included Shakespeare and Dante in the lecture on 'The Hero as Poet'. Carlyle himself called him 'the chief of all Poets hitherto, the greatest intellect who, in our recorded world, has left record of himself in the way of literature'.[22] Charles and Mary Lamb's story versions of the plays for children, *Tales from Shakespear* [*sic*], and Thomas and Henrietta Bowdler's expurgated *The Family Shakespeare*, brought Shakespeare directly into the Victorian home as an instrument of cultural uplift and educational improvement. During the nineteenth century a major scholarly industry developed around Shakespeare and his work. It was characterized by 'a sense of progressive order and intense moral purpose'.[23]

Victorian Shakespeare criticism was dominated therefore by a desire to establish the moral lessons in the plays and to gather as much factual evidence as possible to place Shakespeare securely in his historical context. There was a passionate desire to establish the correct chronology of the plays and to produce authoritative versions of the texts. Shakespeare became the dominant voice in the new subject of English Literature, which entered the university curriculum in the later nineteenth century.[24]

Irving had a passion for Shakespeare. According to Ellen Terry, in his lonely boyhood the Bible and Shakespeare were his principal companions.[25] Irving saw him as the supreme English dramatist, his great roles as the major challenge to any actor. Irving told Squire Bancroft: 'No actor can be remembered long who does not appear in the classical drama',[26] and at the head of the classical drama was Shakespeare. The great actors of the past were remembered for the successes they made in the great roles and the new generation sought to measure themselves against the remembered achievements of the likes of Garrick, who had triumphed as Hamlet, Macbeth, Richard III and King Lear, Edmund Kean, remembered for his Shylock, Richard III and Othello, and John Philip Kemble, who was noted for his Hamlet, Coriolanus and Hotspur.[27]

Irving sought continuously to promote the value of Shakespeare, both to culture and society. He regularly lectured on the importance of Shakespeare to British culture.[28] He leant his name to a handsome eight-volume collection of the complete works of Shakespeare. It was initiated and edited by his old friend Frank Marshall, playwright, scholar and journalist. The eight volumes were issued between 1888 and 1890. But Marshall fell ill during the final stages of the work and died in 1889, leaving the final volume to be finished by others. Irving contributed an essay on Shakespeare as playwright to the first volume in which he took the opportunity to argue that Shakespeare should be seen on the stage rather than just read in the study. It was a recurrent theme of his lectures and aimed at those polemicists who accepted Shakespeare's credentials as a poet but rejected the stage. Irving argued that Shakespeare was both a practical and a popular dramatist. He singled out Shakespeare's handling of dramatic situations and delineation of character as his great strengths. He denounced the rewriting of Shakespeare by the likes of Dryden, Davenant, Crowne and Cibber. He was not against cutting: 'In many plays of Shakespeare the omission of passages, the modification of certain words or phrases, and the transposition of some scenes, are all absolutely necessary before they can be acted; but the popular taste nowadays would not permit an actor to take such liberties with the text as were once thought not only pardonable but commendable; and, indeed, the more the actor plays Shakespeare, the more he must be convinced that to attempt to improve the language of our greatest dramatist is a hopeless task.'[29] He defended the use of spectacle in staging the plays, something which had been regularly criticized since Charles Kean had pioneered it.

> Much objection has been made to the employment of the sister arts of music and painting in the stage representation of Shakespeare, and to the elaborate illustrations of the countries in which the various scenes are laid, or of the dress and surroundings of the different characters. I do not contend that a play, fairly acted, cannot be fully effective without any of these aids and adjuncts. But, practically, their value has ceased to be a matter of opinion; they have become necessary. They are dictated by the public taste of the day – not by the desire for mere scenic display, but that demand for finish in details which has grown with the development of art in all its phases ... The stage has become not only a mirror of the passions, but also a nursery of the arts, for here students of the

past learn the form and colour of the costumes and the decorations of distant ages. To all this there are clear limits ... the resources of the picturesque must be wholly subordinate to the play. Mere pageant apart from the story has no place in Shakespeare, although there may be a succession of truthful and harmonious pictures which shall neither hamper the natural action, nor distract the judgment from the actor's art. In fine, there is no occasion to apologise for the system of decoration.[30]

He ended by reminding his readers that Shakespeare had been an actor and quoting James Orchard Halliwell-Phillips who said: 'there is among the defective records of the poet's life ... one feature demanding special respect, it is the unflinching courage with which, notwithstanding his desire for social position, he braved public opinion in favour of a continuing adherence to that which he felt was in itself a noble profession, and this at a time when it was not merely despised but surrounded by an aggressive fanaticism that prohibited its exercise even in his own native town'. This if nothing else made him a man after Irving's heart. In Irving's open glorying in England's great man of letters being both an actor-manager, not highly educated but with a deep understanding of human nature, and a Warwickshire country boy made good, we can see Irving, the Somerset boy made good, interpreting Shakespeare in his own image: one explanation perhaps of the great affinity he had with Shakespeare.

Most significantly, Irving conscientiously studied, researched and rethought all the major roles, presenting often controversial new readings which divided the critics. Lecturing to the Goethe Society of New York in 1888, Irving declared:

To play Shakespeare with any measure of success, it is necessary that the actor shall, above all things, be a student of character. To touch the springs of motive, to seize all the shades of expression, to feel yourself at the root and foundation of the being you are striving to represent – in a word, to impersonate the characters of Shakespeare – this is a task which demands the most exacting discipline, and widest command of all the means of illustration. Of all the triumphs of the stage there is none so exalting as that of a representation of Shakespeare which gives to the great mass of play-goers a strong and truthful impression of his work, and a suggestion of the ideal which his exponents are honourably struggling to attain.[31]

Having established himself as an undoubted star in *The Bells* and *Charles the First*, Irving was anxious to prove himself in the great classical role that was the agreed test for all aspiring thespians – Hamlet. The English stage did not have a reigning Hamlet. All the great actors attempted the role, though theatre historians still looked back to the Restoration actor Thomas Betterton as the definitive interpreter of the role. It was generally agreed that Hamlet had not been among the great achievements of Irving's immediate predecessors as leading London actor, William Charles Macready, Charles Kean and Samuel Phelps. Irving pressed 'Colonel' Bateman to allow him to do Hamlet at the Lyceum. Bateman was extremely reluctant. Irving explained: 'What I did play, by my own desire, and against his – Bateman's – belief in its success was Hamlet; for you must know that at that time there was a motto among managers – "Shakespeare spells ruin".' The phrase 'Shakespeare spells ruin and Byron bankruptcy' had been coined by F.B. Chatterton, who in September 1873 had produced spectacular and expensive productions of *Antony and Cleopatra* and *Sardanapalus*, which had both failed. It had rapidly become an axiom of theatrical management. But Irving was insistent and Bateman agreed but allocated a meagre £100 for production and Irving was forced to use the churchyard backdrop from *Eugene Aram* as part of an extremely economical production.[32]

Irving had never played Hamlet in London, though he had played it in Manchester, Oxford and Buxton, and had played Laertes to the Hamlets of both Edwin Booth and Charles Fechter on their provincial tours. The approaches of both men influenced him. Booth had played the part for a hundred nights in New York in 1864 and Fechter for 115 at the Princess's Theatre in London in 1861.[33] The theatre critic John Ranken Towse recalled Booth's Hamlet as 'dignified, courteous, meditative and deeply sympathetic', but noted that 'it absolutely bristled with points, each of which seemed in itself absolutely sound and full of illumination as it was presented, but which could not, when assembled be made to harmonize'.[34] Fechter, who in 1861 had astonished the world by playing the role with his native French accent and in a blonde wig, which he deemed appropriate to a Dane, had captured the imagination of the young. Clement Scott, looking back at his career in *The Drama of Yesterday and Today*, said: 'I candidly own that I never quite understood Hamlet until I saw Fechter play the Prince of Denmark. Phelps and Charles Kean impressed me with the play; but with Fechter I loved the play, and was charmed as well as fascinated by the player.'[35] *The Times* (22 March 1861) highlighted its revolutionary nature:

> With the conventions of our stage, with the "points" which to us, seem almost as needful to the play as the words of the text, he has nothing to do. He goes straight from the book to the boards ... There is no doubt that to him the meditative element in Hamlet's nature has seemed the most essential. The manner in which he throws out his answers, like one unwilling to awaken from a continued abstraction, into which he presently relapses, is admirably truthful and the pretense of madness little changes this manner, beyond the addition of a light tone of irony ... the novelty of this rendering consists in the peculiarity that the stronger passions intrench as little as possible upon his solitude, and that he is chiefly occupied with a play of intellect. The birth of his thoughts is more visible than the influence of his emotions. The gentleman-like side of Hamlet stands also high in the considerations of Mr Fechter. Throughout the whole tragedy he is the very perfection of courtesy.

Irving clearly learned from Fechter and applied some, though not all, of his ideas to his own reading.

Irving selected Hamlet as one of his four favourite roles in an article for the *English Illustrated Magazine* (September 1893), writing:

> For Hamlet I have that affection which springs naturally in the actor towards the most intensely human of Shakespeare's creations ... All the striving, all the most lovable weaknesses of humanity, the groping after thoughts beyond the confines of our souls, the tenderest attributes of our common nature, fate and free will, love and death, passions and problems, are interwoven in the character of Hamlet, till he touches us at every point of our strange compound of clay and spirit. To achieve so complete a command over all these elements as to place the impersonation beyond cavil has been given to none of us. But to represent in Hamlet the type of filial love, to suggest that sense of the supernatural which holds the genius of romance like a veil, and that haunted look of one who is constantly with the spirit which has 'revisited the glimpses of the moon', to disentangle the character from traditions which are apt to overlay with artifice one of the most vividly real of all the conceptions in art, to leave upon your generation the impression of Hamlet as a man, not as a piece of acting – this is, perhaps, the highest aim which the English-speaking actor can cherish. This is why one or two Hamlets – Edwin Booth for instance – have an enduring hold upon the memories of playgoers. Something of the chivalry, the high-strung ecstasy, the melancholy grace of the man clings to the mind when the sterner grandeur of other creations of the poet may have lost its spell.[36]

Chivalry, high-strung ecstasy, melancholy grace, were all clearly elements in Irving's interpretation but so too was a high sense of intellectuality.

Irving's Hamlet opened on October 31 1874, to considerable popular and critical acclaim, and ran for an unprecedented 200 consecutive performances. Irving revived the play with Ellen Terry as his Ophelia on December 30 1878, as the first play under his personal management of the Lyceum. It remained in his repertoire until May 8 1885, when he gave his last performance in the role. He became the Hamlet of his generation, not to be supplanted until Johnston Forbes-Robertson took on the role, at Irving's prompting, in 1897. Writing in her autobiography in 1908, Ellen Terry still remembered Irving's as the finest Hamlet she had seen:

> The success on the first night at the Lyceum in 1874 was not of that electrical, almost hysterical splendour which has greeted the momentous achievements of some actors. The first two acts were received with indifference. The people could not see how packed they were with superb acting – perhaps because the new Hamlet was so simple, so quiet, so free from the exhibition of the actors' artifice ... In *Hamlet*, Henry Irving did not go to the audience. He made them come to him. Slowly but surely attention gave place to admiration, admiration to enthusiasm, enthusiasm to triumphant acclaim ... When I read *Hamlet* now, everything that Henry did in it seems to me more absolutely right, even than I thought at the time ... He kept three things going at the same time – the antic madness, the sanity, the sense of the theatre. He was never cross or moody – only melancholy. His melancholy was as simple as it was profound. It was touching, too, rather

than defiant ... I knew this Hamlet both ways – as an actress from the stage, and as ... one of the audience – and both ways it was superb to me.[37]

The critic Clement Scott, writing immediately after the first night, confirms Ellen Terry's memory. He was conscious of seeing something revolutionary which it took the audience two acts at least to understand. Scott, identifying Hazlitt's characterisation of Hamlet as a gentleman and a scholar as the key to Irving's interpretation, confirmed that the first two acts left the audience disappointed. Irving was not making the familiar actors' points. He was 'neglecting his opportunities'. Only the discerning like Scott could see what he was doing: 'Mr Irving's intention is not to make points, but to give a consistent reading of a Hamlet who 'thinks aloud' ... He is not acting ... he is an artist concealing his art: he is talking to himself; he is thinking aloud. It was in Act 3, Scene 1 in his scene with Ophelia that he finally won over the audience, a scene, in which as Irving explained in a published article, he gives us Hamlet feigning madness but carried away by his excited temperament, that combination of sanity and antic madness that Ellen Terry noticed. Scott recalled 'Every voice cheered, and the points Mr Irving had lost as an actor were amply atoned for by his earnestness as an artist. Fortified with his genuine and heart-stirring applause, he rose to the occasion. He had been understood at last.' His success was confirmed by his rendering of the speech to the players and then the play scene which he acted 'with an impulsive energy beyond all praise'. By the end, the actor had 'in the teeth of tradition, in the most unselfish manner, and in the most highly artistic fashion, convinced his audience'.[38]

Joseph Knight, recognising Irving's debt to Fechter, called his performance 'revolutionary, and that would have appeared more so but for the previous experiment of Mr Fechter'. He nevertheless conceded that the production was 'noteworthy as marking a stage in the history of theatrical art, since it shows the final abandonment of old traditions of acting and of conventions of declamation'.[39]

The always hard-to-please Dutton Cook was less enthusiastic than Scott and Knight about Irving's Hamlet. He thought the audience's enthusiasm for his performance 'excessive', and called Irving's Hamlet 'the conscientious effort of an intelligent and experienced player', but curiously, in view of his colleagues' recognition of innovation, he argued 'his rendering of the part ... does not ... differ much from that adopted by preceding Hamlets'. He thought its apparent differences due to Irving's marked peculiarities of manner: the limited compass of voice and lack of strength, which prevented him from fully sustaining so arduous a character, and the angularity of movement. He concluded 'if Mr Irving scarcely impresses us so completely as did some earlier interpreters, he yet rarely fails to interest ... here is a *Hamlet* who is always zealous and thoughtful; often very adroit; who spares no pains to please; who has at command a certain feverish impetuosity … and who is, in short, as complete a representative of the part as the modern theatre can furnish'.[40]

Edward Russell of the *Liverpool Post*, in a lengthy appreciation of the part, subsequently published in pamphlet form, and reprinted in his collected essays, thought it was the physical peculiarities that added to the originality of Irving's Hamlet and entirely suited to the troubled prince who is constantly debating his motivations and actions and full of nervous energy: 'such a physique as Irving's – nervous, excitable, and pliant, suggestive of much thought and dreamy intellect, yet agile and natural and individual in its movements – comes nearer the normal English preconception of such a character than one more characterized by physical beauty and gesticulatory and elocutionary grace'. Russell recognized that what you had in Irving was 'a bold combination of tragedy with character acting' and he saw Irving as the 'first to essay' this.[41]

We are fortunate in having the reminiscences of ordinary theatre-goers too. Richard Dickins, describing 31 October 1874 as 'a day in my life to be marked for ever with a white stone', recalled his reaction to the opening night of Irving's Hamlet:

> I found to my intense surprise and joy, that I was watching the Hamlet of my imagination, that Hamlet, but with a thousand beautiful thoughts and touches added. At last I saw, not a dignified reciter speaking the wonderful lines with more or less grace and skill, but the living man, his soul wracked with anguish, groping blindly for the light, feeling up to God and yearning for human love; sweet, gentle, dignified, intellectual, most lovable, tinged with melancholy, but with a keen sense of humour: such was the Hamlet conceived and embodied by Henry Irving … I have seen it many times, and in my opinion, Irving's Hamlet was, not the most perfect, but the greatest and most beautiful performance of my experience.[42]

What Irving had done was to study the text exhaustively, to consult the work of critics and commentators, draw on theatrical tradition and to evolve his own interpretation, which involved discarding the making of points and the delineation of a rounded and entire character in all its psychological complexity and the working out of that character's dilemmas. Alan Hughes, who has examined the successive versions of the text utilized by Irving, has underlined this concentration on the central character:

> No doubt he undervalued language, which he entirely subordinated to character. He was determined to show what every word meant rather than to recite beautiful sounds. Inevitably his own part was over-emphasized by omissions, simplifications and the sheer focusing power of his genius, but the production was probably not as oversimplified as most we see today, and Irving's Hamlet was a complex, mysterious but believable human being.[43]

Irving devised new business to improve this character-based approach:

abandoning the tradition of producing two miniatures of Hamlet senior and Claudius when he urges Gertrude to 'look here upon this picture and on this', substituting imaginary pictures on the fourth wall which the audience cannot see: scribbling down new speeches for the players to underline the parallels between the murder of Gonzago and the murder of Hamlet senior, and nervously shredding Ophelia's fan as he watches the play. He never stopped refining and developing his performance or the acting text of the play.

It is hard to overestimate the impact of the success of Irving's *Hamlet* upon theatrical London and even more so of the succession of ever more lavish Shakespearean revivals that he staged at the Lyceum. By 1875 there were four other starry Shakespeare productions showing in the West End. At the Gaiety there was Samuel Phelps in *The Merry Wives of Windsor* followed by Mrs Kendal in *As You Like It*. The great Italian actor Tommaso Salvini gave his *Othello* at Drury Lane and Ellen Terry entranced London as Portia in the Bancrofts' production of *The Merchant of Venice* at the Prince of Wales's Theatre. The boom continued, so that William Archer in an article in *Time* in December 1884, declared Shakespeare 'unquestionably, the popular dramatist of the day'. He went on:

> What other playwright can boast of two five-act plays running simultaneously at the two leading theatres of London? What other playwright is studied so scrupulously or mounted so sumptuously? If he now 'spells ruin' to any one, it is not to the managers who act him, but to the modern dramatists who have to compete with him.[44]

Archer recognized that 'the present theatrical revival undoubtedly dates from Mr Irving's historic performance of *Hamlet*, by which the stage was magnified and made fashionable. It was that performance, and its successors, which induced in the world of letters, art, and fashion, the habit of theatre-going, so that the Lyceum now ranks with the Grosvenor Gallery, the Princess's with the popular concerts, among the statutory topics of conversation at every well-regulated aesthetic tea. For this change we have to thank Shakespeare.' But Archer being Archer wondered if Shakespeare was popular with an 'understanding, discriminating, abiding popularity, or only with a temporary unreasoning vogue'.[45]

Referring to the 1884 revivals of *Twelfth Night* at the Lyceum with Irving and Ellen Terry, *Hamlet* at the Princess's with Wilson Barrett, and *Romeo and Juliet* at the Lyceum with Mary Anderson and William Terriss, Archer argued that all three produced only one piece of perfect acting – Mrs Stirling's Nurse in *Romeo and Juliet*. Much of the rest of the acting he deemed mediocre. He felt that spectacle was being indulged in for its own sake and that artistic effect was being subordinated to mere ostentation. He complains that only a handful of Shakespeare's plays were regularly revived and that no one could now speak Shakespearean verse properly. The audience was not trained sufficiently to appreciate the plays as they should be appreciated nor the actors to act him as he should be acted. He contrasted it with the old days of the patent theatres when, in for example 1777–78, fourteen Shakespeare plays were produced at Drury Lane and nine at Covent Garden. 'What wonder that the public with its attention frittered away between the melody of Offenbach, the humour of Byron, and the pathos of Sardou, should fail to acquire a sensitive taste for the melody, the humour, and the pathos of Shakespeare.' He concluded by calling for a theatre exclusively dedicated to Shakespeare and his contemporaries with a repertory company of actors who could master poetico-romantic acting. Such a theatre would educate the public too. He called upon some wealthy philanthropist to establish it not for profit but for education. As it happens just such a philanthropist had created the Shakespeare Memorial Theatre at Stratford in 1879 to house an annual Shakespeare festival. In due course it would grow into precisely the institution demanded by Archer.[46]

In 1875 the Italian actor Tommaso Salvini had taken London by storm with his Othello, a powerful, passionate portrayal of the Moor as 'noble savage'. It exactly fitted Victorian preconceptions about the essentially barbaric nature of the African. When Irving came to do the part in 1876, he may have sought to distance himself from this portrayal but then again 'noble savage' was simply not within his range. He had the wrong physique and more important the wrong acting temperament. Refined intellectuality and morbid introspection were his strengths and he sought to recast Othello in this mould. His Othello was a Moorish gentleman, so he adopted a light bronze makeup and Venetian dress instead of the usual Oriental robes. This was the first cause of astonishment to critics. Clement Scott noted that there was 'no turban, no white burnous, no sooty face, no "thick lips" and "no curled hair"'.[47] Joseph Knight observed 'a studied absence of Oriental colour, and … more of European culture and refinement than of African imagination and heat of temperament'. But more seriously, the interpretation was found wanting. Knight declared 'his Othello is as far from his Macbeth and farther from his Hamlet, from conveying the idea of one capable of forming and expressing a great conception of a heroic character'. He complained of a deficiency of colour and individuality and felt that Irving was 'too plaintive and lachrymose'. He noted the wide gulf between 'the undraped animalism of … Salvini and the moral and intellectual stays and starch' of Irving, clearly preferring the former.[48] Scott said that Othello should be played as soldier and lover but Irving's Othello was 'without dignity … destitute of command … and, in the expression of love, singularly undemonstrative. We scarcely think of him either as a soldier or a lover.'[49] Dutton Cook echoed these comments, saying of the performance that: 'its imperfections and infirmities are many and grave', and putting his finger precisely on the reason: 'Othello has long enjoyed popular admiration for the very qualities Mr Irving is least enabled to impart to his stage portraitures.'[50] It was in fact Henry Forrester's Iago who walked off with the notices, winning universal praise.

Then in 1881 when the great American actor Edwin Booth was giving a Shakespeare season with a scratch company to poor houses at the Princess's Theatre, Irving, in one of his characteristic masterstrokes of showmanship, invited him to the Lyceum and suggested they act together in any piece he chose. According to Stoker it was Booth who proposed that they alternate the roles of Othello and Iago.[51] Irving reverted to the traditional makeup and a succession of exotic Oriental robes, presenting 'as superb an appearance as an Eastern King pictured by Paolo Veronese'.[52] But the *Athenaeum* (14 May 1881) complained that he was still 'the most civilized specimen of a Moor that has yet been seen in history or fiction'. Dutton Cook noted of this Othello that 'he is now a far more disciplined performer than he was five years ago; his art has been tempered and chastened; he is able to concentrate his forces, and to endow his effects with a completer sense of climax', but he added: 'That this *Othello* is wholly satisfying I do not pretend to say; but certainly his performance exhibited fewer defects, is altogether more sustained and even than once it was.' Nevertheless in the later passages of the play, Dutton Cook missed 'the poetic grandeur and profundity of Othello's passion, his extremity of perplexity, his leonine fury, his demonic frenzy, his exquisite pathos and dreadful despair', which is a fairly damning indictment of an actor missing the essential points of the character.[53]

Dutton Cook's judgement was echoed by Ellen Terry (whose Desdemona Dutton Cook had pronounced 'very sympathetic, graceful and picturesque'). She recorded that his Othello was 'almost … universally condemned' and she agreed: 'He screamed and ranted and raved – lost his voice, was slow when he should have been swift, incoherent where he should have been strong. I could not bear to see him in the part.' Like so many others, she preferred Salvini's Othello: 'his Othello was the grandest, biggest, most glorious thing … his groan was like a tempest, his passion huge'.[54] Irving knew he had failed as Othello and Ellen thought 'his failure was one of the unspoken bitternesses of Henry's life'.[55]

It was very different when Irving came to play Iago. Ellen recorded: 'Everyone liked Henry's Iago. For the first time in his life he knew what it was to win unanimous praise.'[56] Scott thought 'Mr Irving has never done anything better' and even the demanding William Archer said it came 'as near perfection as anything he has done'.[57] Irving chose Iago as one of his four favourite Shakespeare roles and wrote of him:

> Manifestly, such a character should be played with a devilry not writ large in every look and action. The quality of youth, moreover, is all important. Iago I take to be a young man about eight and twenty … not embittered by disappointments which have come in middle age, but instinct in all his manhood with the duplicity which belongs to his temperament and his generation. To me he has a slight dash of the bullfighter, and during

the brawl between Cassio and Montano, I used to enjoy a mischievous sense of mastery by flicking at them with a red cloak, as though they were bulls in the arena. To impersonate the veritable spirit of a creation so foreign to our native thought and atmosphere demands an abstinence from some obvious devices of the stage which enhance a moral monstrosity at the expense of the intellectual *vraisemblance*. Iago is no monster, but perfectly human and consistent, which needs to be represented with more delicacy of suggestion and less rhetorical artifice if we are to saturate the imagination with a cold and constant purpose.[58]

He became the definitive Iago of his generation. Ellen recalled:

One adored him, devil though he was. He was so full of charm, so sincerely the 'honest' Iago, peculiarly sympathetic with Othello, Desdemona, Roderigo, *all* of them – except his wife. It was only in the soliloquies and in the scenes with his wife that he revealed his devil's nature. Could one ever forget those grapes which he plucked in the first act, and slowly ate, spitting out the seeds, as if each one represented a worthy virtue to be put out of his mouth, as God, according to the evangelist, puts out the lukewarm virtues. His Iago and his Romeo in different ways proved his power to portray *Italian* passions – the passions of lovely, treacherous people, who will either sing you a love sonnet or stab you in the back – you are not sure which.[59]

In general critics preferred Booth's Othello to Irving's and Irving's Iago to Booth's, though to many Booth's technique of making dramatic points and acting toward the audience was beginning to look old-fashioned compared to Irving's rounded and in-depth character studies.

Macbeth was one of the great tragic roles of Shakespeare and one of the tests of the great tragedians. It had been memorably played by Betterton, Garrick, Kemble, Kean, Macready and Phelps, while Mrs Siddons had definitively established the interpretation of Lady Macbeth as ferocious and dominating, a 'Scottish Clytemnestra'. Macbeth was generally played as a bluff manly soldier who is led into evil by a scheming wife.

When Irving first attempted Macbeth in 1875, with Kate Bateman playing Lady Macbeth in the approved Siddons manner, he attempted a new reading, seeing Macbeth as 'a moral coward' and 'one of the most bloodyminded and hypocritical villains in Shakespeare'. It was an interpretation that had been advanced in essence by Coleridge, who saw Macbeth as that archetypal figure of Romance, the conscience-haunted, brooding individual. This was the emphasis Irving gave the role in a lecture on the character of Macbeth which he delivered at Owens College, Manchester in 1894:

A poetic mind on which the presages and suggestions of supernatural things could work; a nature sensitive to intellectual emotion so that one can imagine him even in his contemplation of coming crimes to weep for the pain of the destined victim; self-torturing, self-examining, playing with conscience so that action and reaction of poetic thought might send emotional waves through the brain whilst the resolution was as grimly fixed as steel and the heart as cold as ice; a poet supreme in the power of words with vivid imagination and quick sympathy of intellect; a villain cold-blooded, selfish, remorseless, with a true villain's nerve and callousness when braced to evil work, and the physical heroism of those who are born to kill; a moral nature with only sufficient weakness to quake momentarily before superstitious terrors; a man of sentiment and not of feeling. Such was the mighty character which Shakespeare gave to the world in Macbeth.[60]

When he revived the play in 1888, he told Ellen Terry that he had come to this interpretation in 1875 by intuition, but it was confirmed by subsequent study, in particular of an 1844 interpretative essay by George Fletcher, which was reprinted and reissued by Longman in 1888 as a result of the interest generated by the play.

It has generally been thought that Irving reinterpreted the part the way he did because the physically powerful barbaric warrior chieftain portrayed by Garrick, Kean, Macready and Phelps was simply not within his range. Alan Hughes denies this: 'He did not avoid the conventional interpretation of Macbeth because he was incapable of playing it; he avoided it as utterly foreign to his artistic nature'. Certainly the rereading was in line with his reinterpretation of Othello, but that was almost certainly because the 'noble savage' interpretation was beyond him. It seems likely that an awareness of his physical limitations reinforced his natural artistic predisposition, and both figured in his thinking.[61]

He revived *Macbeth* in 1888 in a spectacular production which not only featured his rereading of Macbeth but a Lady Macbeth by Ellen Terry that was softer and more feminine than audiences had been used to and far from the 'Scottish Clytemnestra'. Ellen Terry saw the 1888 production as peculiarly significant: 'My mental division of the years at the Lyceum is *before Macbeth* and *after*. I divide it up like this, perhaps, because *Macbeth* was the most important of all our productions, if I judge by the amount of preparation and thought it cost us and by the discussion which it provoked.'[62] It ran for 151 performances and was revived for an American tour in 1895.

Ellen was right about the discussion it provoked. The letter columns of newspapers and journals were filled with correspondence about the interpretation. Joseph Comyns Carr wrote a pamphlet *Macbeth and Lady Macbeth* defending the new interpretations (reprinted as 'Sex in Tragedy' in his collected essays) and Ellen called it 'One of the best things ever written on the subject ... that is as hotly discussed as the new "Lady Mac" – all the best people agreeing with it'.[63] Although Irving's Macbeth character reading convinced some of Ellen's 'best people' such as critics Clement Scott, Edward R. Russell, William Archer and Bernard Shaw in 1875 and 1888, the majority of the critics disagreed with both new interpretations of Macbeth and Lady Macbeth.[64] Almost all united in praising the spectacle and power of the production.

Richard III was the ideal role for Irving. He named it one of his four favourite parts and Ellen Terry thought he was perfect in it. As Joseph Knight observed in his review, 'in the whole range of the Shakspearian [*sic*] drama ... no part of serious interest could be found so suited to Mr Irving as Richard'.[65] It was a role that had been tackled by all Irving's illustrious predecessors. Garrick had made his name in the part and it had been part of the repertoires of George Frederick Cooke, Junius Brutus Booth, Edmund Kean, W.C. Macready, Samuel Phelps and Charles Kean. But they had all played not Shakespeare's *Richard III* but the version by Colley Cibber. Cibber had streamlined and partially rewritten Shakespeare's play, eliminating the characters of Edward IV, Clarence, Hastings, Queen Margaret and the Woodvilles, adding a scene of the murder of the Princes in the Tower, only reported in Shakespeare. The Richard of this version was a blustering bully. As Clement Scott put it, he was 'a truculent tyrant who has so long stamped about the stage in scarlet doublet and flapping, russet boots, with black ringlet wig and bushy eyebrows, supposed to symbolize in their hue the darkness of his deeds of villainy' and, as Dutton Cook described him, he was a 'petulant, vapouring, capering, detonating creature'.[66]

On January 29 1877 Irving produced *Richard III* utilizing only Shakespeare's text and dispensing with the Cibberian accretions. Phelps had tried to reintroduce it into the repertoire in 1845 but had reverted to Cibber in 1861. After 1877 it was Shakespeare's *Richard III* rather than Cibber's who held the stage. Dutton Cook, noting that Irving's Othello and Macbeth had not been as successful as his Hamlet, saw Richard III as a spectacular return to form. He recorded that Irving's audience were 'carried away by his superb force of character' and he commanded 'the favour, admiration, and even a measure of the sympathy of his audience.' Irving played Richard, reported Cook, 'as an arch and polished dissembler, the grimmest of jesters, the most subtle and the most merciless of assassins and conspirators, aiming directly at the crown ... and gifted ... with a certain diabolical delight in his own enormities'.[67] Knight thought that Irving's mannerisms and individuality fitted the part and that he played 'to perfection the soured, malignant and ambitious man, to whom men are of no account, who plays with them as though they were dice ... and sweeps them away when they have served his purpose'.[68] Scott thought Richard Irving's 'greatest triumph as an actor', intelligent, carefully wrought and convincing.[69]

Choosing Richard III as one of his four favourite roles, Irving wrote of the role: 'Shakespeare's Richard is a Plantagenet with the imperious pride of his race, a subtle intellect, a mocking, not a trumpeting duplicity, a superb daring which needs no roar and stamp, no cheap and noisy exultation. Moreover, the true Richard has a youthful audacity very different from the ponderous air of the "heavy man". In this character, as in Iago, the great element is an intrepid calculation.'[70] The play ran for three months and was universally acclaimed as a success.

Veteran theatregoer Richard Dickins found Irving's Richard a revelation. He found the change 'startling from the coarse, loud, swaggering bully, who had done service as Richard in the former stage version, to the refined, fascinating Plantagenet Prince imagined by Shakespeare, and embodied by Henry Irving ... The fact that Richard was a Plantagenet was never lost sight of.' He said, 'There can be no doubt Richard ranks amongst the actor's greatest triumphs'.

Irving chose to revive *Richard III* in 1896 with all the advantages of staging that he had developed during his own management. It was not as well received as the 1877 production. He had a bad fall after the first night, damaged his knee ligaments and was laid up for weeks recovering. He resumed the role but it had only a short run, making way for the long-planned production of *Madame Sans-Gêne*. Richard Dickins went to see *Richard III* four times and reported: 'I think it doubtful whether a finer performance of a tragedy by Shakespeare has ever been seen on the English stage.' Comparing it with the 1877 performance, which he had also seen, he said: 'It was now even more subtle, if possible more marvellously intellectual, stronger, and in the scenes of intense emotion the actor had his powers more completely under control. The performance from first to last was a wonderful example of consummate art, conceived and portrayed by an extraordinary magnetic personality.'[71] Kate Terry Gielgud, though complaining that the elaborate scene changes protracted the production until nearly midnight, conceded that 'Pictorially it was quite beautiful, and the production in its entirety showed all the care and infinite attention to detail that has made the Lyceum famous', but of Irving's performance she criticized 'a too marked Satanism of manner, a tendency to repeat the character of Mephistopheles, an over-redundancy of gesture and certain mannerisms of delivery and speech'.[72] The novelty of 1877 had worn off and Irving's Mephistopheles had perhaps become too familiar to theatregoers.

Romeo and Juliet was presented on 8 March, 1882 and was long remembered as the first of the Lyceum spectacular Shakespeares. At this time Irving was forty-four and Ellen Terry thirty-five. The critics competed with each other to bestow superlatives on the production and staging. Clement Scott called it 'probably the grandest production of a play by Shakespeare that the stage has ever seen',[73] and *The Times* (9 March 1882) said that with regards to staging and production, '*Romeo and Juliet* reaches a height of perfection that has seldom been approached, and that certainly has never been surpassed'. But the critics found fault with both Irving and Terry as Romeo and Juliet. Sympathetic Irvingites made allowances for Irving. Scott noted 'Mr Irving has ... two very marked manners, gloomy and comic, but naturally neither of these adapts itself to the lighter and more ecstatic side of Romeo's character ... In his intense desire to be fervent he becomes spasmodic and loses self-command ... Romeo has other things to do besides making love. He was at his best when the tragic notes were sounded, and constraint was cast aside; he rose to the occasion at the moment that Romeo's life became fate-haunted and bordered with despair.' Despite this, he concluded that 'it would be an exaggeration to declare that the actor is shown in the truest light or in his best manner as Romeo'.[74] Others did not mince their words: 'He was of course picturesque, but Romeo is not likely to remain in the chronicle as one of his greatest parts.' 'He is ... as far from being a typical Romeo as any of his predecessors, and this in a man of Mr Irving's mark cannot be regarded as a success.'[75] Once again, Ellen's perceptive comments allow us to appreciate best Irving's Romeo. She wrote:

> Henry Irving's Romeo had more bricks thrown at it even than my Juliet! ... I am not going to say that Henry's Romeo was good. What I do say is that some bits of it were as good as anything he ever did. His whole attitude before he met Juliet was beautiful ... I know they said he looked too old – was too old for Romeo ... He was not boyish; but ought Romeo to be boyish? ... He couldn't catch the youthful pose of melancholy with its extravagant expression. It was in the repressed scenes, where the melancholy was sincere, the feeling deeper, and the expression slighter, that he was at his best. [76]

Whatever the imperfections of the leading players, it ran for 160 performances.

Irving's 1882 production of *Much Ado* established it securely in the modern Shakespeare repertoire. The play had not been seen much on stage before because Victorians thought Beatrice too shrewish and forward and preferred the Rosalind of *As You Like It*. But the teaming of Irving and Ellen Terry succeeded in making the sparring couple so acceptable that the play ran initially for 212 performances and it remained in the Lyceum repertoire until 1895, as popular in America as Britain. As a result of this success Hughes concludes: 'The rehabilitation of *Much Ado* as a popular comedy has been complete and enduring.'[77]

In the view of several influential critics Irving and Terry achieved their success by transforming the characters from Shakespeare's originals to conform with Victorian sensibilities. The American William Winter, who saw them act the play in New York, thought Irving made Benedick 'a higher and finer character' than Shakespeare's original and Ellen made Beatrice 'a more lovely and tender woman' than the original. He saw Shakespeare's Benedick as 'buoyant, brilliant, dashing, aggressive ... he is not a man of sentiment and there is no romance in his nature' and Beatrice as 'strong, bold, brilliant, but untender and devoid of woman-like gentleness'. But in the hands of Irving and Terry, Benedick was invested with 'high-bred ease, intellectual repose, and demure gravity' and a basic goodness concealed by pretended cynicism, and Beatrice was imbued with 'an indescribable charm of mischievous sweetness ... There is no hint of the virago here, and even the tone of sarcasm is superficial.'[78] Clement Scott, who thought they were 'a revelation', recorded:

> At once both Mr Irving and Miss Ellen Terry caught the spirit of the play; they filled it with gaiety and with humour … It was the very light breath and fragrance of true comedy. Beatrice was no shrew, but the most light-hearted, pleasant-spirited lady in the world. Benedick was no boor, but a refined, whimsical, humour-loving gentleman.[79]

For an audience reaction, we may turn again to Richard Dickins, who saw all the important Shakespeare productions in London over a forty year period. He writes:

> If *Romeo* was the most beautiful production, its successor *Much Ado About Nothing* was in its entirety the most perfect representation given of a Shakespeare play during the last forty years. In the way of production *Much Ado* presents less opportunities than *Romeo* but on 11 October the series of pictures were wholly satisfactory and the Church scene a triumph alike for the artist and stage manager. If individually the company had not been at 'the top of their form' in *Romeo*, each and all made up for it in *Much Ado*, there was not a weak spot and throughout it is hardly an exaggeration to say the representation was faultless. The Benedick and Beatrice were perfect examples of bright poetic comedy, and their acting was so easy and effortless that it is only since I have seen the dismal failures of others in the same parts, that I have fully realised how extraordinary their performances were. The comedy sparkled with merriment from beginning to end, the fun literally bubbled over, and you sighed with regret when the curtain fell.[80]

If *Much Ado* was a major triumph, then the Lyceum production of *Twelfth Night* (1884) was a major setback. It suffered from a combination of blows from which it never really recovered. *Twelfth Night* was not a popular play with the Victorians, its incongruous mix of Italianate and English characters in an unidentifiable fantasy land offended their sense of historical and geographical literalism. One critic called the play 'involved, improbable and wearisome' and another said it was 'devoid of strong dramatic interest and suffering in some parts from a certain obsoleteness of humour'.[81] This was avoided in *Much Ado* by drastically cutting back the appearances of the English watch in sixteenth-century Messina, but it was central to *Twelfth Night* and inescapable. The production opened in a heat wave. On the first night Ellen Terry was suffering badly from an infected thumb and eventually, having developed blood poisoning, had to be replaced after sixteen performances by her sister Marion. The play was, unusually for Irving, seriously miscast. John Martin-Harvey recalled: 'The cast was quite a remarkable example of square pegs in round holes.' Irving had imported outside actors into the company, all of whom were inadequate: the veteran comic actor David Fisher as Sir Toby was now elderly and inarticulate, Rose LeClercq was too old for Olivia and inaudible, Stanislaus Calhaem playing Feste was handicapped by the fact that his 'dental accoutrement rendered his speech almost unintelligible', and 'a particularly charming dancer Frank Wyatt' was out of place as the ungainly Sir Andrew. Ellen agreed about the widespread miscasting, adding that 'Terriss looked all wrong as Orsino'.[82] On top of all this Irving's Malvolio was more tragic than comic and this undercut the comedy. The result was that at the end a section of the audience booed. Irving reprimanded the audience in his curtain speech. Ellen thought his speech 'the only mistake that I ever saw him make. He was furious and showed it.' Irving subsequently admitted that it was a mistake to attempt *Twelfth Night* without three great comedians.[83] *Twelfth Night* ran for just thirty-nine performances in London and was never revived.

Irving learned the lesson of the London production and, when he took it to America, recast, from within his company, Tom Wenman as Sir Toby, Norman Forbes as Sir Andrew, Sam Johnson as Feste and Winifred Emery as Olivia. The result was a much more successful production. 'In America *Twelfth Night* was liked far better than in London, but I never liked it' recalled Ellen, 'I thought our production dull, lumpy and heavy.'[84] But she admitted that she could never dissociate the production from the physical pain she suffered during it. Laurence Irving believed that the London failure of *Twelfth Night* convinced Irving to turn his back on comedy as thereafter none of his new productions saw him in a straightforward comic role.[85]

The London critics praised the staging and the beauty of the pictures evoked and Ellen got her customary ecstatic notices. Typical of the reviews is this one: 'In Viola, assuredly one of the sweetest, gentlest, most womanly of Shakespearian ladies, Miss Ellen Terry has a part suited to her style – a style which is nothing if it is not sweet, gentle and womanly ... No one could be more passionately yet at the same time more prettily in love. Her voice, even, silvery and plaintive, gave to her earnestness the requisite tone of tenderness, and her manner, feminine in the sweetest sense of the word, seemed to gain in womanly charm by the very contrast with her boyish garb.'[86] But there were reservations about Irving's Malvolio, one critic noting that he was 'everywhere and always a gentleman', austere, punctilious and moral and evoked pity rather than laughter. Another noted that his pathos at the end almost reduced the women in the stalls to tears and a third thought him too serious and realistic.[87]

Of the four Shakespearean roles he selected as his favourites, King Lear comes as the greatest surprise, given the problems it presented and which he frankly outlined:

Of Lear, I may candidly say that I doubt whether a complete embodiment is within any actor's resources. For myself the part has two singular associations. It broke down my physical strength after sixty consecutive nights, and when I resumed it after a brief rest I was forced reluctantly to the conclusion that there is one character in Shakespeare which cannot be played six times a week with impunity. On the first night I had a curious experience. As I stood in the wings before Lear makes his entrance I had a sudden idea which revolutionized the impersonation and launched me into an experiment unattempted at rehearsal. I tried to combine the weakness of senility with the tempest of passion, and the growing conviction before the play had proceeded far that this was a perfectly impossible task is one of my most vivid memories of that night. Lear cannot be played except with the plenitude of the actor's physical powers, and the idea of representing extreme old age is futile.

His reading of the part was that Lear was already failing mentally before the start of the play, so 'the actor has to represent the struggles of an enfeebled mind with violent self-will, a mind eventually reduced to the pathetic helplessness of a ruin in which some of the original grandeur can still be traced. This is without doubt the most difficult undertaking in the whole range of the drama.'[88]

Irving's *Lear* ran for seventy-six performances and has retrospectively been deemed a failure. But this was a record run for a play that was never popular with the Victorians. Garrick had made a success of the part in the eighteenth century, but in the version rewritten by Nahum Tate with a happy ending in which Lear and Cordelia survive and she marries Edgar and inherits the kingdom. Macready had dispensed with Tate's version in 1838 and Shakespeare's had held the stage since then. Victorians found the play too uncompromisingly tragic, unrelievedly bleak and overfull of horrors. The actor-managers who staged it saw it as essentially a domestic tragedy and that is how Samuel Phelps and Charles Kean played it. According to J.S. Bratton, Irving's version, 'historicized, sentimentalized and domesticated … carried the appeal to family feeling and domestic sentiment to an extreme'.[89] But this is what will have appealed to Irving, who responded readily to stories of family break-up and the effects upon its members. It may be this which explains why Irving had planned a production as far back as 1883. Bram Stoker recorded in his diary for 5 January 1883, that Irving announced his intention to produce *Lear* on his return from America, noting significantly: 'Gave rough idea of play-domestic.'[90] In the event, he did not produce it until 10 November 1892. He attempted to make it as palatable as possible for his audience. He set it in an effectively and atmospherically recreated ancient Britain soon after the departure of the Romans. He announced in his acting edition of the play that 'all superfluous horrors have been omitted' and that included notably the blinding of Gloucester, which now took place offstage. Irving played the part for pathos and both he and the production, despite the problems of the opening night, received glowing reviews. Some critics mentioned his inaudibility and one commented that 'he must, as a "voice" from the gallery after curtain told him, 'speak up"'.[91] He corrected his vocal interpretation after the first night and played the part in a stronger voice for the rest of the run. 'A representation of the very greatest intellectual interest and dramatic power', 'one of Mr. Irving's greatest artistic triumphs', 'unquestionably this noblest of tragedies receives a more luminous interpretation than it can ever have enjoyed saving, perhaps, at the hands of Charles Kean', 'Mr Irving had come triumphantly through this great ordeal'.[92] Interestingly other actors had a high opinion of it, J.L. Toole thought Lear Irving's greatest performance and A. Acton-Bond, who played Burgundy, thought it 'one of his greatest performances'.[93] Both Irving and Ellen received praise for their performances. 'She has never been more exquisite in her art', said the *Pall Mall Budget* (17 November 1892). There were, as ever, some dissenting voices. One of them pulled out all the stops, denouncing the production ('conventional and restrained') and laying into Irving and even the normally sacrosanct Ellen. Of Ellen, the critic said: 'Miss Terry, as is her wont, fluffed her way through the part, spoke the blank verse with her old familiar awkwardness, and though undistinguished, was never distressing.' Of Irving, he wrote: 'Throughout a weary, long-drawn performance, "our leading actor" murmurs, grunts and groans, but never speaks ... that an actor should have some power of speech has the sound of an axiom' and thought the performance 'wholly lacking in beauty, suppleness, or rhythm.'[94]

Cymbeline, a fantastical Romance set partly in Ancient Britain and partly in Renaissance Italy, perplexed the literal-minded Victorians. The reaction to the play by William Archer of the *World* is typical. He called *Cymbeline* 'Anything but a good play ... it is constructed in plain defiance not merely of any and every set of canons, but of rudimentary common sense.'[95] Bernard Shaw in the *Saturday Review* went further, dismissing it as 'for the most part stagey trash of the lowest melodramatic order, in parts abominably written, throughout intellectually vulgar, and judged in point of thought by modern intellectual standards, vulgar, foolish, offensive, indecent, and exasperating beyond all tolerance'.[96] But it contained one of the best-loved of Shakespeare's female roles, Imogen, the model of the ideal faithful wife. It was a perfect role for Ellen Terry.

When Irving revived it in 1896, suitably cut to minimize the indecency and set with the aid of Alma-Tadema in a stylized Rome and Roman Britain, it was the first major production for thirty-one years and would not be done again until 1923. Predictably Ellen enchanted the critics. 'What could be more charming, more captivating, more true than Miss Ellen Terry's rendering of one of the most beautiful of Shakespeare's heroines, it was absolutely flawless' was typical.[97] It would be 'difficult to overpraise' Ellen's Imogen, thought Warwick Bond.[98] William Archer said hers was 'a delightful performance, certainly one of the most charming things she had ever done'.[99] Ellen herself thought it her 'only inspired performance in her last ten years at the Lyceum'.[100]

The leading male role had hitherto been considered to be Posthumus, but Irving took on the part of Iachimo and fashioned out of it another of his Machiavellian Italian villains and it won over his sternest critics. Bernard Shaw, who rarely had a good word to say of him, recorded with evident astonishment that Irving had transformed Iachimo who in Shakespeare's version was 'a mere *diabolus ex machina'*. He called it 'a true impersonation, unbroken in its life-current from end to end, varied on the surface with the finest comedy, and without a single lapse in the sustained beauty of its execution'.[101] William Archer declared: 'Iachimo is quite in Sir Henry Irving's line, and he makes a striking and memorable figure of him. Shakespeare probably conceived a younger, lighter, more irresponsible villain – a stinging gad–fly rather than a rattlesnake … Sir Henry Irving's Iachimo is not "a slight thing" at all. He is a subtle, tenebrous, deadly creature, beside whom Posthumus, in the person of Mr Frank Cooper, is a very "slight thing" indeed. His acting is extremely artistic, both in what he does and in what he refrains from doing.'[102] Clement Scott recorded wonderingly:

> Henry Irving's Iachimo was another extraordinary study … different from anything of the kind that had been seen before … No lady-killer of Rome, no butterfly of the Forum, no fantastic dandy was the Iachimo of Henry Irving. He was an intellectual lover, not an empty sensualist. If he had to win Imogen it would be by his brain, not by his fastidiousness or good looks. Earnestness and brain power stamped every line of the new Iachimo … It is a subtle and weird idea of a well-known Shakespearian character. Iachimo seems to embark on his enterprise not touched by passion but by a devilish love of mere mischief.[103]

As a result of the performances and the staging it ran for eighty-eight performances.

Henry VIII was a play about which doubts were expressed concerning the extent of Shakespeare's contribution. It was deemed badly constructed. Clement Scott in the *Daily Telegraph* called it 'one of the most difficult of the historical plays of Shakespeare' and declared 'Every student is perfectly well aware that it is a succession of pageants, a series of spectacular tableaux, with a thin thread of story very loosely connecting them'.[104] This was a generally held view. The story basically comprised the divorce of Queen Katherine and the downfall of Wolsey. Wolsey was the role the actor-managers went for and it had been played by Charles and Edmund Kean, Macready and Phelps. The last major production had been Charles Kean's spectacular 1855 revival, which was the major point of comparison with Irving's Lyceum production which opened on 5 January 1892. Most critics echoed the *Saturday Review*: 'We do not hesitate to say that never before have such stage pictures been exhibited upon any stage.'[105]

Irving's Wolsey was one of those roles perfectly suited to his talents. Clement Scott recorded:

> Never before in our memory has Mr Irving made so wonderful a picture. He is swathed from head to foot in what is miscalled the cardinal's scarlet. It is not scarlet at all, but an indescribable geranium-pink, with a dash of vermilion in it. The biretta on his head is of the same blush-rose colour, and it hides every inch of hair, bringing into relief the pale,

refined and highly intellectual face. We see at once, at the first glance, how Mr Irving intends to read Wolsey. He is to be far more like Richelieu than the humble trader's son of Ipswich. This is no man of ignoble birth who has risen by his brains to power. He is not coarse in feature, he is not gross, there is nothing of the vulgarian about him. There is majesty in his lineaments, a little foxiness in his face, but the power is that of the lynx, and not the British bull-dog. For the purposes of playing, Wolsey can be read anyhow ... Henry Irving's Cardinal Wolsey is a cultured and crafty ascetic, not a man of dogged determination and of iron will. So fascinating, however is this picture at the entrance of the Cardinal that the audience, if consulted, would have liked to stop it for a few moments. It was like so many of its fellows, 'a living picture' that exactly fascinated the eye.[106]

The intellectuality and refinement were the features picked up by most critics. The *Observer*, for instance, said:

Mr Irving elects, and quite legitimately, to emphasise the intellectual side of the great political priest, his subtlety in exercising control, his courteous dignity as host and his skill as diplomat. It is hard to imagine a more impressive figure than he makes in the wonderful robes and biretta of pink silk. It is harder still to call to mind the achievement of any finer effect in the familiar and famous farewell speeches than the line scored by the actor.[107]

Another critic evoked comparisons with Irving's predecessors in the role:

No more vivid portrait – as a portrait – can have been given of the crafty Churchman than that of Mr Irving's. From what we know of the physical characteristics of the Keans it must be superior to theirs. Mr Phelps' Cardinal was a striking figure, but Mr Irving's has more native asceticism, more subtlety, conveying in truth the sense of a malignity which is almost Mephistophelian – an effect heightened by the scarlet of the Cardinal's robes. The greater part of his great soliloquy after his fall he delivers seated, as if crushed by his reverse ... At this supreme moment ... the habitually sinister aspect of the Cardinal has departed from him; he is a feeble old man – the most pathetic figure, perhaps, which Mr Irving has ever portrayed.[108]

The refinement and intellectuality not to mention the hint of Mephistopheles links Irving's Wolsey directly to his previous characterisations. *Henry VIII* ran for 203 performances.

Irving's last and least successful Shakespeare revival was *Coriolanus*, which ran for a mere thirty-six performances in 1901. It had never been popular with playgoers and neither Irving nor Ellen were ideal casting for Coriolanus and his mother. The critics' reactions were summed up by the *Morning Post* (16 April 1901), which praised the production, thought Irving's Coriolanus 'a figure of striking dignity and power' and Ellen's Volumnia 'not the stern Roman mother of classical tradition; she has the strength and authority of the matron, but it is wielded in and through a woman's tenderness'. But the critic pointed out about the play: 'its weak point for the modern reader as well as for the modern spectator is that the pride and temper of the hero estrange him from that sympathy without which no tragic hero can exist. We do not sympathize except with those whom we recognize as men of like passions with ourselves.' Ellen noted in her diary that on the final day of the run of *Coriolanus*, 20 July 1901, 'H.I. for the first time played Coriolanus *beautifully*. He discarded the disfiguring beard of the warrior that he had worn during the run ... and now that one could see his face, all was well.'[109] The most successful and long-lasting of Irving's Shakespearean creations was Shylock. He was still playing it on his farewell tour.*

Irving certainly considered other Shakespeare plays but for various reasons did not proceed to production. As Ellen Terry observed, there was always 'reasons against'. She believed 'we ought to have done *As You Like It* in 1888, or *The Tempest*'. Squire Bancroft thought the same. After the success of *Much Ado*, Bancroft urged Irving to stage *As You Like It*, enthusing about the possible Lyceum cast: Ellen Terry as Rosalind, William Terriss as Orlando, Johnston Forbes-Robertson as Jaques, James Fernandez as the Banished Duke, Henry Howe and Tom Mead as Adam and the old shepherd. Irving replied: 'Good – very good – but where do I come in?' Touchstone, said Bancroft, arguing 'for certain comedy parts, he was a brilliant actor, raising them to great prominence'. Terry confirms that he considered Touchstone but eventually decided against it. She gives no reason but it is hard to avoid the conclusion that the part was simply not big enough or dominating enough for the actor-manager. To Terry's eternal regret, *As You Like It* was never played at the Lyceum. He also did not do *The Tempest*, although attracted to the part of Caliban. 'The young lovers are everything, and where are we going to find them?' said Irving to Terry, on one occasion. On another he said he could not do it without three star comedians in the company, the lack of whom had sunk his production of *Twelfth Night*. This confirms his statement about casting being a central fact in decisions about play selection.

Terry considers that he ought to have done *Julius Caesar*, *King John*, *Antony and Cleopatra*, *Richard II* and *Timon of Athens*. Bancroft also urged *King John* and *Richard II* on him: 'It seemed to me that he was singularly gifted to pourtray [*sic*] the characters of both monarchs.' But as Terry observed of her list: 'There were reasons "against" of course.' *Richard II* was planned for 1899 but abandoned because of Irving's illness, after he had prepared an acting text and commissioned set designs from painter Edwin Abbey and music from Sir Alexander Mackenzie. But it remained on his agenda as a vehicle for either himself or his son H.B. Irving. He considered *King John* inferior to *Becket*. Neither *Timon* nor *Antony and Cleopatra* were popular in the nineteenth century. But he seriously considered and planned for *Julius Caesar*. He prepared an acting edition, discussed set design with Alma-Tadema and promised George Henschel the commission for the incidental music. Bancroft lamented that:

---

* See below, Chapter 14.

He allowed all his own wealth of ideas concerning a great production of *Julius Caesar*, for which he had splendid help from Alma-Tadema, to slide away and vanish, losing eventually, the opportunity of playing Brutus and casting Forbes-Robertson and Terriss for Cassius and Marc Antony.

Irving, who wanted to play Brutus, explained to Ellen Terry:

> That's the part for the actor ... because it needs acting. But the actor-manager's part is Antony – Antony scores all along the line. Now when the actor and actor-manager fight in a play, and when there is no part for you in it, I think it's wiser to leave it alone.[110]

So once again acting considerations prevailed.

Another problem was that Tree, Irving's great rival, was also producing spectacular Shakespeare productions at the Haymarket Theatre and later on at Her Majesty's Theatre – and Irving tended to avoid those Shakespeare productions that Tree put on. Irving planned to play Falstaff and showed W.H. Pollock a sketch of himself in costume and demonstrated to him how he intended to play the part:

> He became for a moment Falstaff himself; his face seemed to broaden and develop into the very semblance of the fat knight; and he spoke some of Falstaff's words in a deep rich voice with wondrous unctuousness of tone and expression, and ... he called up for a brief minute not only Falstaff himself, but with him all the strange company at the Boar's Head.

But when Tree took on the role in *The Merry Wives of Windsor* (1889), Irving dropped it.[111] Interestingly, Tree also produced *The Tempest*, *A Midsummer Night's Dream*, *King John*, *Julius Caesar*, *Richard II*, and *Antony and Cleopatra*, all of them plays which Irving did not produce.

The only eighteenth-century plays that Irving revived at the Lyceum were Mrs Cowley's *The Belle's Stratagem* and George Colman's *The Iron Chest*. Unlike Phelps, he revived nothing from earlier centuries aside from Shakespeare. But he long contemplated reviving some of Phelps's successes. The theatre critic H. Chance Newton recalled: 'Sir Henry and I often talked for hours together at his flat or at the Garrick Club over plays old and new which he seemed to fancy trying.' He pondered reviving *The School for Scandal*, in which he had been a success as Joseph Surface in his early days as the St James's Theatre. Latterly he was contemplating the part of Sir Peter Teazle but would exclaim to Newton: 'And there we are up against Phelps ... *What* a Sir Peter! Marvellous!!'[112] After Irving's death in 1905, however, Sir Charles Wyndham revealed that five years earlier Irving had suggested a production of *School for Scandal* with Irving as Teazle, Wyndham as Charles Surface, Mary Moore (Lady Wyndham) as Maria and Ellen Terry as Lady Teazle: 'It was seriously considered for some time' but their managerial commitments could not be squared.

Two of Phelps's other virtuoso roles attracted him too, Luke Frugal in Massinger's *The City Madam* and Sir Giles Overreach in *A New Way to Pay Old Debts*. He had actually seen Phelps as Overreach, though not as Frugal. Newton recalled:

> So obsessed was Irving, especially with the part of the tyrannical monster, Overreach …
> that he had read and reread everything he could lay his hands on concerning Edmund
> Kean's Overreach. Many a lunch time, or supper time, at the Garrick Club have Irving
> and I sat beneath Kean's portrait as Sir Giles … while he held forth on what he (and I)
> had read of the Great Little Edmund's evidently electric outbursts. Undoubtedly of all
> the actors of the past whom he had never seen, *the* Kean was Irving's idol.

But Irving never played Overreach and it is possible that he concluded that it was beyond his powers in the same way that Othello so evidently was.

In 1879 he announced an intention to produce *The Stranger* and *The Gamester*, powerful but gloomy eighteenth-century plays that had been standards in his youth. They were of the same vintage as Colman's *The Iron Chest*. Stoker recalled 'Irving had considerable faith in Colman's play and intended to give it a run'. He had played the role of the secretary Wilford early in his career. But the failure of *The Iron Chest* to appeal to the public sealed the fate of the other two plays, which were abandoned.[113]

In the choice of melodramas, which he alternated with his Shakespearean production and to which he applied the same degree of lavishness and spectacle, he was guided by the established popularity of the pieces and the acting opportunities they offered. He revived all the great French-derived melodramas which Charles Kean had made into hits: *The Courier of Lyons* (renamed *The Lyons Mail* in Irving's version), *Louis XI* and *The Corsican Brothers*. He also had a new version of *Faust* written for him rather than revive Kean's *Faust and Margaret*. He revived the venerable melodramas in which even earlier great actors had scored hits: *The Iron Chest* (a success for Edmund Kean), *Richelieu* and *The Lady of Lyons* (Macready triumphs) and *Robert Macaire* (the star vehicle of the great Frédèrick LeMaître). He commissioned new plays from the great French melodramatist Sardou (*Robespierre*, *Dante*). He added to the melodrama repertoire the play that became peculiarly associated with him, Leopold Lewis's *The Bells*, based on the French play *Le Juif Polonais* by Erckmann-Chatrian.

Irving's continuing commitment to the Romantic poetic drama is evidenced in his desire to stage the dramas of Byron, his cultivation of Tennyson and his regular recourse to W.G. Wills. Although the nineteenth century is remembered as a low point in the history of British drama and much of its output is dismissed as irredeemable hack work, not enough credit is given to those who shared the stated aim of Macready 'of advancing the drama to a branch of

National Literature and art'.[114] The work of commissioning new plays and of seeking to make the works of the great poets playable in theatrical terms that Macready began was continued by Phelps at Sadler's Wells and Irving at the Lyceum.

Almost all the great poets of the nineteenth century wrote plays: Byron, Keats, Shelley, Wordsworth, Blake, Coleridge, Landor and Swinburne. But they wrote them to be read rather than acted and almost all of them lacked a sense of theatre, seeing their works essentially as dramatic poems. Each of the great actor-managers took up and persevered with the work of a great poet with the aim of enhancing the prestige of the stage: Macready with Byron, Phelps with Browning and Irving with Tennyson. With the exception of Byron's *Werner*, it was really only Irving with *Becket* and *The Cup* who succeeded in making popular and successful theatre out of the work of the great poets.

Byron

Byron loved the theatre but the low level of public taste and dramatic writing in his era deterred him from actively seeking to write directly for the stage. But there were innate problems with his plays anyway for any potential producer. He sought to maintain absolute historical accuracy, and gave his characters long scenic descriptions to speak and long explanatory soliloquies. As a result, his plays lacked dramatic tension. In addition the dictates of running time meant that most of Byron's plays had to be cut in length by half and were subject to the demands of the theatrical censor to remove all political comment, criticism of church, state and monarchy and explicit sexual references. This meant the foregrounding of private dilemmas, such as the conflict of love and duty.[115]

Byron, believing the Shakespearean Jacobean model employed by most aspiring writers of verse plays to be exhausted, turned for inspiration to Greek drama with its dramatic unities of time, place and theme and classical simplicity. He declared his desire to eschew melodrama and avoid 'the rant of the present day'. His aim was rather to explore the political and moral dilemmas at the heart of his subject, to create a theatre of ideas. The problem was that the audience in the nineteenth century wanted melodrama, rant, action and spectacle. So those seeking to stage Byron cut down his monologues and intellectual debates, instilled action and drama and turned his 'mental theatre' into historical melodrama.[116]

Despite all these problems, theatrical managers persisted in trying to put Byron on the stage. Of Byron's eight plays, six reached the stage in the nineteenth century, his Venetian conspiracy dramas *Marino Faliero* and *The Two Foscari*, his Assyrian drama *Sardanapalus*, his metaphysical drama *Manfred* and his melodrama *Werner*. *Marino Faliero* was produced at Drury Lane by R.W. Elliston in 1821. Cut by half, shorn of its political comment, and with its final scene removed, it became a story of conflict between 'private affections and public duty'. It failed. Macready took it up and produced it in 1842. He cut for pace and dramatic effect, eliminated criticism of the priesthood and the sexual references, simplified the plot, emphasized conventional sentiment and created a passionate hero and sentimental heroine. It was well received on the first night, acted three more times and on tour in the USA, but then dropped. In 1867 a musical version of *Marino Faliero* retitled *The Doge of Venice* adapted by William Bayle Bernard and starring Samuel Phelps was produced at Drury Lane. It was based on Casimir Delavigne's 1829 French adaptation which had introduced a new character to the drama, and changed motivation, to make it more melodramatic. The music was by Donizetti, who had based an opera on the play. It ran from 2 November to 17 December but lost £5500.

Sardanapalus appealed because of the opportunities for spectacle. The play dramatizes the fate of the indolent but idealistic Assyrian philosopher-king, who tries to create an earthly paradise. But when rebellion breaks out against him, he dies on a massive funeral pyre. It was produced by Alfred Bunn at Drury Lane in 1843 and the scenery painted by Clarkson Stanfield included a reproduction of John Martin's epic canvas *The Fall of Nineveh*. It starred a reluctant Macready, who claimed that he could not 'work myself into the reality of the part'.[117] Macready cut the text substantially and the emphasis was placed on the spectacle, in particular the final conflagration. It was well received and played for twenty-three performances, and Macready subsequently performed it on tour.

Where Macready disliked the play, Charles Kean responded much more positively. He saw in it the possibilities for one of his grand spectaculars. Using Macready's cut text, he played it to great applause in Birmingham in 1832 and revived it at the Princess's Theatre, Oxford Street, in 1853, after Macready had retired. He capitalized on the excitement created by Sir Austen Layard's excavations at Nineveh. Kean employed a diorama of Nineveh and the River Tigris, a sunset effect, a lavish banquet and the destruction of Nineveh. It ran initially for sixty-one performances and later for another thirty-two.

Charles Calvert undertook a new production of the play in Manchester in 1875, bringing it to London in 1877. He argued in the preface to the published text of his stage version:

> Surely the theatre is put to no ignoble use, when, in addition to the vivid representation by accomplished performers, of one of the happiest dramatic effects of Byron's genius, it becomes an arena where its cognate arts – painting, music, history, archaeology – combine harmoniously to show 'the very age and body of a time' coeval with Josiah's restoration of Solomon's temple.[118]

It is the axiom of those theatre managers who saw the stage as educational and directly foreshadows Irving's credo. Calvert made cuts, interpolated scenes and dialogue and built up the spectacle. It did well in the provinces but not in London where the reviews criticized the acting (the unknown Arthur Darley played the lead) and they agreed that Kean's version was superior and not less gorgeous. The play was not seen again in London. Its success anyway was more due to music, dancing and spectacle than to Byron.

The dramatic poem *Manfred*, inspired by the myth of Prometheus, was a meditation on the human spirit. Manfred wanders the Alps tormented by guilt for a secret crime. In search of oblivion, he tries suicide but fails. He conjures up the spirits of the universe, the witch of the Alps, and Arimanes on the throne of fire. He refuses submission to the spirits of evil and has a vision of the woman he wronged, Astarte. She foretells his death. He rejects the consolations of revealed religion, defies the demons who come to claim him, and dies. Alfred Bunn saw it as a conventional Gothic drama and adapted it as such in 1834 with Sir Henry Bishop setting Byron's lyrics. He removed all controversial political and religious references, and much of Byron's philosophy. In this version Manfred's secret sin is having killed the woman he loved, rather than incest with his sister, as in the poem. The key features of the production were Alpine scenery, witches and demons, Arimanes on his throne inspired by John Martin's *Satan in Council* and *Paradise Lost* and a finale involving thunderbolts, a storm and falling glaciers. Henry Crabb Robinson complained that although the poem had merit, as a drama it was poor – no action, no light relief, merely a set of monotonous monologues.[119] It ran for thirty-three performances.

In 1862 Phelps chose *Manfred* for his first production at Drury Lane after leaving Sadler's Wells. It was much less extensively cut than Bunn's adaptation but still depended on Henry Bishop's music, the Alpine scene-painting and the spectacle of dances, Arimanes on his throne of fire and the spirit appearances. Despite its essentially undramatic nature, it ran for sixty-three performances. Charles Calvert produced a version in Manchester in 1867, cutting the monologues even further, playing the lead, reducing it to two acts and providing lavish scenery. But it did not enjoy the success of his *Sardanapalus*. Charles Dillon took the lead in an 1873 production at the Princess's Theatre which ran for fifty-four performances. It was the music, dancing and scenery which kept it in the repertoire essentially.

The Two Foscari, Byron's other Venetian conspiracy play, was put on by Macready for his benefit night in 1838. Macready cut it and trimmed the speeches, playing Francis Foscari the Doge. He turned it into a drama of paternal love, the conflict between devotion to duty and the love of a son who is imprisoned for treason. It was so completely forgotten that, when Charles Calvert produced it in Manchester in 1865, he believed it was the first production. He produced a 'vivid replica of Venetian life', condensed the text to three acts, and utilized the music from Verdi's operatic version of the play. He starred as the Doge. It was critically well-received but replaced after only six performances. The public did not take to it.

The most popular of Byron's plays on the nineteenth century stage was *Werner*.

Byron had based it on a melodramatic tale by Harriet Lee published in 1801. Byron was attracted by the story as a study in guilt. It is set at the end of the Thirty Years War. Count Siegendorf (alias Werner) is reunited with his long-lost son Ulric. But, after Siegendorf's old enemy Baron Stralenheim (whose gold Werner had stolen) is murdered, he learns that Ulric did it. He helps the innocent man wrongly accused of the murder to escape and sees his son depart for a bandit's life declaring 'the race of Siegendorf is past'. Byron declared in a preface to the 1822 published version: 'The whole is neither intended, nor in any shape adapted, for the stage.'

But it had all the elements of Gothic melodrama (ruined castle, secret passage, hidden guilt, bandits) and, in Werner, a study in parental anguish and guilt. Macready seems to have been drawn to stories of parental love and bereavement, perhaps a reflection of the fact that as a devoted husband and father he saw several of his children die. It is a recurrent theme, in the way that Irving was drawn compulsively to stories of guilt. As has been pointed out, *Werner* is 'tedious in the extreme. It abounds in very long speeches and unnecessary scenes, which make it impossible for production without considerable cutting, and neither the sensationalism of the plot nor the improbable characters provide dramatic tension or action.'[120]

Macready cut the text by half, made the dialogue more brisk, added a final death scene for Werner, made a mystery of Stralenheim's death, which initially points to Werner, and devised a new ending with Ulric arrested for murder. All this had the effect of emphasizing the paternal love and anguish of Werner. It became one of Macready's most popular parts, along with *Hamlet*, *Macbeth*, *The Lady of Lyons* and *Virginius*. He performed it seventy-six times in London and more on tour. The critic Joseph Knight in the *Dictionary of National Biography* called it his 'masterpiece'. Phelps played it in his first Sadler's Wells season and almost every season thereafter, notching up fifty-one performances. One critic called Phelps' Werner 'as noble a work of art as ever came from the mind of man ... it is no acting, it is perfect transformation'.[121]

It is perhaps significant that of all these productions the two Irving wanted to put on were *Manfred* and *Werner*, both in-depth studies of Romantic anti-heroes haunted by guilt. An added motive would have been the success in the roles of his great predecessors, Macready and Phelps, whom he was seeking to emulate and indeed surpass.

If Chance Newton is to be believed, he saved Irving from 'both a professional and pecuniary failure' in staging *Manfred*. He recalled that Irving confided in him his plan to revive *Manfred*: 'A play by Lord Byron, a tragedy which hasn't been revived for many years – together with my first appearance in the character – all should help to attract. Eh?' he said. Newton argued strongly against it: 'Even in my time I have known Charles Dillon, Creswick, and Phelps attempt that morbid monologue, for it is almost a monologue, and even Phelps – *your* great exemplar – who gave a magnificent performance, couldn't make it either profitable or palatable ... And *you*, Irving, can't act that dreary, declamatory, introspective "rotter". That night in his column in the *Referee* he mentioned Irving's plan and said he hoped he wouldn't do it! 'Not only is he utterly unsuited to the part, and, moreover, there is no money in *Manfred*.' A few days later Irving said to him that his paragraph in the *Referee* had persuaded him. 'Irving unsuited. No money in *Manfred* ... That foiled me.'[122]

Despite the strictures of Chance Newton, Irving never completely abandoned hopes of producing *Manfred*. Stoker believes he came closest to a definite decision to produce it in 1884 after seeing a performance of Schumann's *Manfred* in Boston.[123] Sir Alexander Mackenzie recalls in his memoirs that 'Byron's *Manfred* ... had a perpetual fascination for Irving, and, knowing that I had witnessed the run of Phelps' assumption of the part and could describe the production scene by scene, he frequently discussed the possibilities of an exceptionally brilliant revival with me.' Twice Irving asked Mackenzie to provide the incidental music for *Manfred* and twice cancelled the order to start writing it. Then in 1897 he announced at short notice that he intended to put on the play at once. By now Mackenzie had completed most of the score apart from 'The Hall of Arimanes'. But two days later Irving wrote to say that 'there are impediments in the casting of *Manfred* (as my company now stands) which would make the production impossible'. Mackenzie concludes that 'again he was overruled by the advice of his friends', which appears to have been the case every time he proposed to produce it. But three years later in a speech at the Annual Prize Distribution of the Royal Academy of Music at the Queen's Hall, he again alluded to his plans to produce *Manfred*. In the event he never produced the play.[124]

His other cherished ambition to put on *Werner*, attracted by its success in the hands of Macready and Phelps, its prestigious poetic status and its haunted Gothic hero, he realized on one occasion only. This was in 1887 at a special benefit performance for the aged and penurious playwright Westland Marston. It is significant that he chose not to revive one of Marston's irretrievably dead plays. He put on a full production of *Werner*, complete with Hawes Craven scenery, Seymour Lucas costumes and a cast which included Ellen Terry as Josephine, George Alexander as Ulric and Winifred Emery as Ida von Stralenheim. It is hard to avoid the impression that he was testing the waters ahead of a decision to add it to his permanent repertoire.

Fitzgerald says Irving had intended to perform it on his forthcoming American tour.[125] Macready's acting text was adapted for Irving by Frank Marshall. He condensed its five acts into four, modernized some of the language, cut most of the comic relief and wrote two new scenes, one of them showing Ulric murdering Stralenheim and thus removing the 'whodunnit' element;

the other was 'a very pretty episode' between Werner and Ida replacing a scene of Werner's penitent gift of the stolen money to the Prior. Irving then trimmed and revised Marshall's version.[126]

Irving was quoted as saying of the play:

> The play follows the story closely, but the concealment from the reader of the murderer's identity, which is perhaps, the strongest point in the story, becomes a blemish in the play. An audience unacquainted with the play of *Werner* or with the tale of *Kruitzner* would either be entirely in the dark as to the connection of Ulric with the murder, or, at the best, would be enabled to make but a vague guess as to his guilt. The true tragic interest of *Werner* may be said to lie in the proud and passionate love which ... Werner has for his son, of whose real character he has not the slightest suspicion, and it is the shock of the discovery that Ulric is a robber and a murderer, which actually proves fatal to the agonised father.[127]

This makes it clear that the changes were instigated by Irving himself. But for one critic this created a new problem – Ulric's motivation. Observing that in the original version the audience were kept in ignorance of the identity of Stralenheim's murderer until the end and that suspicion was thrown on Gabor, who had a grudge against the dead man, the critic said:

> Mr Irving and Mr Marshall have altered all this. Gabor, in his midnight exit by the sleeping baron's room, is seen to be preceded by Ulric, who proceeds to better Werner's crime of theft by assassination. For the purpose of the stage much may be said for the change. It is risky to keep an audience long in the dark – to play tricks, as it were, with its intelligence. And it must be said that, if the scene had to be added, the addition could not have been more neatly or graphically made. On the other hand, it may be urged that this more realistic and logical treatment robs the drama of much of its mystic power. Moreover by leaving so little to the imagination it concentrates attention somewhat inconveniently upon Ulric, whose motive in his sudden change of mood is left unexplained and apparently inexplicable.[128]

Clement Scott, reviewing the play, recalled that the followers of Macready and Phelps each claimed their hero had triumphed in the part but remarked that the followers of Macready 'candidly owned that *Werner* was a very dull play'; and the followers of Phelps admitted 'that not much of the sparkle of Lord Byron's verse, and very little of his impulse or vivacity, could be found in the heavy text of the play'.

Scott went on: 'to the surprise of everybody ... the interest that was started at the outset was sustained to the finish. The scenes were dark, but the play was never dull; the story was sad, but every actor in it was picturesque.' Its success was due to the fact that *Werner* was produced 'with loving care, with lavish expense, and with unerring judgement'. He praised Frank Marshall's adaptation ('infinitely preferable to any that the stage has ever seen'). He praised Irving's

1. Henry Irving, an early photographic portrait.

2. Ellen Terry as Imogen in *Cymbeline*.

3. Henry Irving, photograph.

4. The Lyceum Theatre, exterior.

5. The Lyceum Theatre, interior.

6. Saturday night at the Savage Club, Irving with cigar (front third from right), from painting by W.G. Bartlett.

7. Leaving the stage door, followed by Bram Stoker.

8. Sir Henry Irving, a photographic portrait.

9. Sir Henry Irving, 1899.

10. Statue of Sir Henry Irving. (*Jennie Bisset*)

Werner ('in this example of what may be called the poetry of paternity, he has given us few more beautiful or thoughtful pictures'.) He praised Ellen Terry, seen grey-haired for the first time, 'the part is nothing, but … it was made valuable by the assistance of such an actress'. He praised George Alexander ('in every way suited to this hot-headed, impetuous youngster, whom the act of murder changes from a frank and affectionate youth to a morose young savage').[129]

If Irving had been intending to add *Werner* to his repertoire, the general critical reaction dissuaded him. There was widespread praise for the production and the performances: 'The interpretation of the gloomy and rather morbid tragedy … left very little to be desired. Indeed, Mr. Irving's embodiment of Werner was truly remarkable for the pathetic dignity with which the actor contrived to invest a character not in itself either elevated or impressive.' 'The play in every detail was as perfectly done as if it were destined for a run.' 'It is probable that no play has ever been "dressed" with more scrupulous accuracy or with greater sumptuousness, even at the classical Lyceum, than *Werner*.'[130] But the problem was the play: 'depressing and monotonous … gloomy and rather morbid'; 'all this art is in a great measure wasted, for the reason that the story cannot be made interesting … there are probably few persons who would desire to see *Werner* twice.'

Ellen Terry noted in her diary that the production had been 'a triumphant success due to the genius and admirable industry and devotion of H.I. for it is just the dullest play that ever was! He made it intensely interesting'.[131] Fitzgerald summed up the general reaction in his Irving biography:

> The play gave little satisfaction, and was about as lugubrious as *The Stranger*, some of the acts, moreover, being played in almost Cimmerian gloom. What inclined the manager to this choice it would be difficult to say. He had rather a *penchant* for those morosely gloomy men, who stalk about the stage and deliver long and remorseful reviews and retrospects of their lives.[132]

Fitzgerald has answered it in a nutshell: Werner was another of Irving's long line of guilt-ridden and curse-haunted heroes. But it was no longer to the public's taste any more than the similar character in *The Iron Chest* which Irving also revived without success.

More significantly, Irving was to produce and star in three plays by the Poet Laureate, Alfred, Lord Tennyson: *Queen Mary*, *The Cup* and *Becket*. Bram Stoker recalled:

> He loved Tennyson – really loved the man as well as his work – and if for this reason alone exerted all his power to please him. Moreover as a manager he saw the wisdom of such a move. Tennyson's was a great name and there had been a lot of foolish argument in journals and magazines regarding 'literature' in plays, and also concerning the national need of encouraging contemporary dramatic literature. Rightly or wrongly the public interest has to be considered and Tennyson's name was one to conjure

with. Moreover he came to depend on the picturesque possibilities of Tennyson's work.[133]

As always with Irving, there is the combination of the theatrical potential, the publicity angle and the national significance along with personal partiality.

In his endless search for prestige dramatic projects, Irving even considered Swinburne's *Bothwell*. Published in 1874, it was another of those poetic works unable to leave anything out and displaying absolutely no theatrical sense. Swinburne's biographer Harold Nicolson pronounced it "intolerably dull" and "diffuse".[134] In 1875 and 1876 Theodore Watts-Dunton undertook a revision of the text in consultation with Swinburne with a view to making it playable.[135] Swinburne had a meeting with Irving to discuss staging *Bothwell* at the Lyceum but, says Harold Nicolson, found Irving's mood "taciturn".[136] Irving had probably read the play and decided it was unstageable.

Swinburne wrote to Lord Houghton, on 13 March 1875, that "having exchanged hospitalities of club and chambers with him last autumn, I have had occasion to find him one of the nicest fellows I have ever met for a long time. Indeed I liked him so much that I never would go – and never yet have been – to see him act Hamlet", though in 1885 he referred to the occasion when he and Irving had discussed Irving's Hamlet interpretation until 5 a.m. in Swinburne's chambers.[137] They evidently remained on good terms, despite Irving's failure to stage *Bothwell*, for in 1887 Swinburne served on the Westland Marston Testimonial Committee for which Irving staged his production of *Werner*. Swinburne had been a great friend of Marston's son Philip, the blind poet.[138]

Swinburne despised the Lyceum production of *Queen Mary* with what looks like a touch of professional rivalry with Tennyson. He wrote to Theodore Watts on 7 July 1875:

> As for Tennyson's "play" my first and last remark on it was and is that it has a very pretty song in it. The last two scenes in which the Queen appears seem to me well above the somewhat low level of the rest – really rather effective and pathetic. But isn't the press fun – above all the incomparable *Spectator* [*Spectator*, 26 June, 1875] which sets it high above the ordinary work of Shakespeare and only a little lower than his highest. And yet I am not very much alarmed at the advent of this conquering rival and I am very sorry for poor Irving.[139]

In his choice of repertoire, Irving returned obsessively to the same subjects and they were subjects that were rooted in his own troubled past. The psychological drives which impelled him towards certain subjects in many cases intersected with the preoccupations of the wider Victorian society which explains the enduring success of some of his most popular vehicles.

Melodrama, the genre in which Irving excelled, was a way of making sense of a confusing world. In the last decades of the nineteenth century society was troubled by the rise of ideas which threatened the secure and stable Victorian world view based on home, family, religious faith, love of country, bourgeois respectability, class hierarchy and defined gender roles. Socialism and anarchism threatened the established social and political order, Darwinism undermined the foundations of the Christian faith, feminism and Wildean decadence threatened male and female gender archetypes, and Zolaism and Ibsenism intruded an unwelcome realism into the sentimental pieties of the Victorian world view.[140]

In Michael Booth's classic definition, melodrama functioned as a reassurance that whatever the difficulties, in the end all would be well:

> One of the great appeals of this world is clarity: character, conduct, ethics and situations are perfectly simple, and one always knows what the end will be. The world of melodrama is a world of certainties … where vice and virtue coexist in pure whiteness and pure blackness … where good triumphs over and punishes evil and virtue receives tangible rewards.[141]

Following the demise of theatrical melodrama around the time of the Great War, the form came to be mocked. But Peter Brooks reinterpreted the genre, focusing specifically on melodramatic excess not as a cause for criticism but for appreciation and understanding of how melodrama operated:

> The desire to express all seemed a fundamental characteristic of the melodramatic mode. Nothing is spared because nothing is left unsaid; the characters stand on the stage and utter the unspeakable, give voice to their deepest feelings, dramatize through their heightened and polarized words and gestures the whole lesson of their relationships … the world is subsumed by an underlying Manichaeanism, and the narrative creates the excitement of its drama by putting us in touch with the conflict of good and evil played out under the surface of things.[142]

So strong emotions, overt villainy, moral polarisation, extreme behaviour and extravagant expressions are all part and parcel of the form. Brooks claims further than melodrama becomes the principal mode for "uncovering, demonstrating and making operative the essential moral universe in a post-sacred era", in recognising and confronting, combating and expelling evil to purge the social order.[143] Melodrama thus functions as ritual and catharsis. This definition clearly applies to those classic melodramas that Irving made his own and retained in his repertoire throughout his career: *The Bells*, *The Lyons Mail*, *The Corsican Brothers*, *Faust* and *Olivia*. But they and other plays in his repertoire had a more personal meaning.

Irving's dedication to his craft had resulted in two powerful and long-lasting psychological blows – rejection by his mother and by his wife. When he decided to go on the stage in 1856, he was cast off by his ferociously Methodist mother, Mary Brodribb (née Behenna). She believed the stage to be sinful and her son to be damned. She never accepted his choice of career and died unreconciled with him on 23 January 1862, aged fifty-four, of tuberculosis. Irving's father, Samuel, by contrast was proud of his son and, having returned to Bristol to live with his brother Thomas following the death of his wife, from 1865 to 1871 he pains-takingly and lovingly copied out by hand reviews of his son's performances in a little notebook (now in the possession of J.H.B. Irving). He died on 20 June 1876.

If the rejection by his mother was not enough, worse was to follow. Early on the morning of 26 November 1871, Irving and his wife Florence, the daughter of Army Surgeon General Daniel O'Callaghan of the Indian Army, whom he had married in 1869, were driving home following Irving's greatest triumph to date, his debut as Mathias in *The Bells* which made him an overnight star. Florence turned to him and said: "Are you going to go on making a fool of yourself like this for the rest of your life?" Irving stopped the coach, got out and left his wife. He never spoke to her again and they never met again. He took refuge with the Batemans and Mrs Bateman eventually found him bachelor rooms in Grafton Street.[144] At the time of the split, Florence was heavily pregnant – the result of an earlier rapprochement after Irving had temporarily moved into lodgings following marital problems. Their second son, Laurence, was born in late December, 1871. Irving did not attend the christening. Whatever else happened, the marriage failed because of Florence's rejection of his chosen career. They never divorced, which would have been social suicide, but there was a legal separation. Irving supported his wife and their sons, H.B. 'Harry' Irving and Laurence, throughout his life. He sent her tickets for every first night at the Lyceum and Mrs Irving was regularly there, sometimes accompanied by her sons. Irving paid for them to go to preparatory school (Linton Hall) and public school (Marlborough), but expressed the hope that neither would go on the stage, intending Harry for the bar and Laurence for the Foreign Office. In the event, both went on the stage and Irving became reconciled to the fact.

Raised by their mother, the two boys were subjected to 'the persistent ridicule and denigration of the husband who had deserted her'.[145] Matters were made worse when Irving engaged Ellen Terry as his leading lady. Rumour had it that they were lovers and Florence extended her detestation to Ellen, whom she called 'the wench'. Florence's persistent denigration of Ellen led to a formal remonstration from Irving, telling her to stop slandering Ellen or he would cease to support her financially.[146] Relations between father and sons were uneasy and intermittent during their boyhood – tuck hampers to the school, theatre tickets and occasional visits to the rooms in Grafton Street. But gradually they achieved a rapprochement with their father, whom they dubbed 'The Antique'. As H.B.'s son Laurence described it, Harry:

with cool detachment ... judged his father for himself, and decided the terms on which he could accept him without surrendering his independence. His admiration for the consummate actor was tempered by his distaste for the sycophancy that hedged in 'the

Chief' of the Lyceum. Nothing would have induced him to accept professional favours from his father. But they soon discovered that in sharing a sardonic sense of humour, a taste for criminology and an aversion to humbug, they could pass the time agreeably enough in each other's company. Harry's marriage to Dorothea Baird ... induced a new intimacy between them ... [Irving] found Harry a congenial companion; and to be welcome in such a happy home was a new and delightful experience.[147]

Irving engaged Dorothea, the star of *Trilby*, for the Lyceum company.

Laurence, intellectual, vegetarian and republican, had a much more ambivalent relationship with his father, but they were brought together by – of all people – 'the wench'. Ellen Terry, while on tour in the United States, persuaded Irving to let her appear in Laurence's one-act play *Godefroid and Yolanda* with its famous opening direction 'Enter a chorus of lepers'. It was Ellen too who persuaded Irving to stage Laurence's full-length play *Peter the Great*. She thought Laurence 'a born ready-made genius'.[148] Thereafter he became a regular member of the Lyceum family as actor and as translator of Sardou's *Robespierre* and *Dante*. Lady Irving deeply resented the new closeness between her sons and their father but could do nothing about it.

The double blow of rejection and separation had upon Irving a twin effect. It fuelled his passionate desire to make his profession respectable, a life-long crusade, but it also filled him with feelings of guilt and remorse. This drew him to that succession of tormented figures with whom he had made his name. It is no coincidence that he had two favourite recitations, performed throughout his career on innumerable occasions. One was Henry Glassford Bell's 'The Uncle', in which an uncle confesses to his nephew the crime that has haunted him – murdering his brother, the boy's father, because of love for his brother's wife:

> He was a man of gloomy mind,
> And few his converse sought;
> But, it was said, in solitude
> His conscience with him wrought,
> And there, before his mental eye,
> Some hideous vision brought.[149]

This might be a description of the succession of haunted characters Irving inhabited on the stage. The second recitation was Thomas Hood's 'The Dream of Eugene Aram', a poetic account of the crime, guilt and remorse of the historical schoolmaster murderer, which electrified audiences whenever he performed it.

Irving's name was made in *The Bells*, in which the Alsatian burgomaster Mathias, haunted by memories of the murder he has committed years before, undergoes a supernatural trial and dies of his guilt. This set the pattern for several of his subsequent vehicles and for a recurrent theme in his *oeuvre*. Guilt and remorse were the keynotes of the murdering schoolmaster in *Eugene Aram*, the jealous Spanish count who thinks he has killed his brother in *Philip*, the Flying Dutchman in *Vanderdecken* and the benevolent country squire Sir Edward Mortimer concealing the knowledge of a murder he committed in the past in *The Iron Chest*. In historical plays, such as *Macbeth*, *Richard III* and *Robespierre*, Irving was confronted by the ghosts of his victims, precipitating grand displays of guilt and remorse.

Olivia

The destruction of a happy home and family is a major theme of *Charles the First*, *The Bells*, *The Lyons Mail* and *Olivia*. *Olivia* was a particular favourite of Victorian audiences. It was W.G. Wills's adaptation of his fellow Irishman Oliver Goldsmith's *The Vicar of Wakefield*. *The Vicar of Wakefield* had inspired over one hundred canvases before 1900. From no other novel had so many different episodes inspired painters.[150] The artists included Daniel Maclise, Richard Redgrave, W.P. Frith, William Mulready and Ford Madox Brown. Sir Walter Scott had written: 'We read *The Vicar of Wakefield* in youth and in age. We return to it again and again and bless the memory of an author who contrives so well to reconcile us to human nature.'[151] It is a view that seems to have been shared by a large section of the nineteenth century reading public. It had been commissioned by John Hare, then managing the Court Theatre and was produced there in 1878 with Ellen Terry as Olivia Primrose, Hermann Vezin as the Vicar, and William Terriss as Squire Thornhill. It was, said W. G. Wills' brother Freeman, 'pronounced one of the most tender and charming plays that ever graced the English stage. The dramatist used to say that he never wrote with the same ease and buoyancy.'[152] He dictated it in a pleasant house to two ladies who were 'admiring disciples'.

It emerged as a classic Victorian morality tale of domestic bliss, family break-up and sentimental reunion. It opens in the vicarage gardens with the Vicar, Dr Primrose and his wife celebrating their silver wedding, children playing and neighbours gathering to felicitate the couple. Squire Edward Thornhill is courting Olivia, while Mr Burchell (actually the Squire's uncle, Sir William Thornhill) is courting her sister Sophy. News arrives that the Vicar is ruined, as the London merchant he has lodged his money with has absconded with it.

Act 2, set in the vicarage parlour, has the Vicar and his wife making an inventory of their belongings for the sale of their possessions, which is due to take place. The family is breaking up under the impact of the ruin. Son Moses is to go to work for Farmer Flamborough; daughter Olivia will go to York as companion to an old lady. But Thornhill persuades Olivia to elope with him, intending a fake marriage by a bogus parson to allay her scruples. Burchell, who knows his nephew to be a scoundrel, has warned the Vicar that he is a 'profligate and practised seducer' but the Vicar refuses to believe him. Olivia asks Sophy not to be ashamed of her and asks her two younger brothers Dick and Bill to say their prayers and movingly departs. The song 'Happy Morn' by Sir Arthur

Sullivan is sung. Then the Vicar learns that Sir William Thornhill, an unexpected benefactor whom he does not know (being unaware that he is Burchell), has made over the vicarage to him and bought all his furniture for him. 'Mine!', exclaims the Vicar joyfully surveying the home that has been saved. But on the back of this news, comes the word that Olivia has eloped; everyone is distraught.

Act 3 takes place at the Dragon Inn three months later. It is Christmas and Olivia is thinking sadly of her home and family, of Moses cutting holly and ivy, and her father composing his Christmas sermon. She has tired of the artificial and shallow London round and continuous travelling that has characterized her life with Thornhill. She expresses a desire to go home. Thornhill reveals that they are not really married, for the ceremony was a fake. She is devastated by the news. Burchell arrives, tells them that he is really Sir William Thornhill and cuts off his nephew. The Vicar arrives and embraces his daughter. Olivia, overcome by shame, cannot face her family. He tells her they will go away together and live 'like lepers among the tombs'.

Act 4 is set in the vicarage parlour on Christmas Day. 'Home Sweet Home' is played. Olivia and the Vicar enter; 'Home!' is her first word. The Vicar tells her that he has kept a light burning in the window for her during her absence. The family is reunited: Moses is to marry Polly Flamborough and Sophy is to marry Burchell, now revealed as Sir William. Mrs Primrose refuses to welcome Olivia: 'Have you presumed, madam, to return to your innocent home that you have disgraced? It is the first time guilt has ever entered this door.' But the Vicar urges her to follow the Bible's teaching: 'She is penitent, and Heaven is rejoicing.' Mother succumbs: 'Your father is right, child, I forgive you. May heaven wash away your guilt.' But at this point Sir William reveals that he had arranged for a real parson to be substituted for his nephew's fake one and the marriage is legal. A penitent Squire Thornhill turns up to ask forgiveness. The Vicar places his hand in Olivia's: Thornhill kneels and kisses it. The final words are the Vicar's: 'She gives you hope. 'Tis Christmas. 'Tis merry gentle Christmas. On every little cloud around the sun methinks I see a herald angel sing "Peace and goodwill to men".'

The play had an extraordinary personal meaning both for Wills, since, according to his brother, he wrote it in the spirit of fond remembrance of his own happy childhood in the family of a country parson. For Ellen, it carried even more potent memories. She had eloped with E.W. Godwin and had lived with him 'in sin'. She had as a result been cast off by the Terry family. Only when the relationship ended and she returned to the stage, marrying her fellow actor Charles Kelly, was she received back in the bosom of her family, her own life exactly echoing the story-line of the play.

The success of the play lay in the way in which Goldsmith's eighteenth century original had been refined to bring it into line with Victorian sensibilities. Freeman

Wills concluded:

> The characters of Mrs Primrose and Olivia are altered for the better in Mr Wills' play.
> The one fact that in the original Olivia did not believe marriage was in question, and in
> the drama such belief is the mainspring, involves an essential difference in character. In
> the play, she is the most perfect study of woman's character conceivable, not tiresomely
> good, but yet divinely loveable. Her womanly waywardness, her spoiled child's petulance,
> her little penitent ways, her huffs and her relentings, her feminine want of logic and
> illogical loyalty, her playful wit and tenderness, her womanly heroic impulses of self-
> sacrifice, and her change to stone under the last deadly affront, all these fibres of character
> make up one of the creations of flesh and blood which the author of *Olivia* put on the
> stage. But it is not only in its characterisations, in atmosphere, and incident the play
> differs widely from the novel. In the play there is more refinement of language and
> sentiment, and the broad drollery is toned down to quaintness. The ruin of the family is
> but an incident ... there are no fine ladies from London, and no prison scenes. The
> language is not borrowed except in one passage, but it is exactly such as would have been
> used by the characters of the time to which the play belongs. The author's reading in
> early days was so much in the books of that period ... that he was imbued with the
> language and spirit of Johnson's and Goldsmith's day, and wrote for this reason the real
> and not the Wardour Street imitation of eighteenth-century English; and the retired
> vicarage in Ireland of his youthful associations was not so remote in its *genius loci* from
> Dr Primrose's vicarage, that it would not have helped him to enter into the spirit of
> the latter.[153]

That classic trope of Victorian drama – the immoral village squire seducing,
betraying and abandoning the innocent maiden – is here rehearsed against a
background of family break-up and reunion, financial ruin and restoration
thanks to an aristocratic *deus ex machina*, Christmas and Christian forgiveness.
In 1885 Irving revived the play at the Lyceum, with Ellen as Olivia and himself as
Dr Primrose, but William Terriss (as Thornhill) and Norman Forbes (as Moses)
were recalled from the Court Theatre cast. It remained in the repertoire until
almost the end. Of a 1900 revival, the *City Leader* (1 June 1900) recalled: 'There
can, in truth, be little danger of the public growing tired of Sir Henry's exquisite
portrait of the kindly Vicar of Wakefield, or of the touching story unfolded by
Mr W.G. Wills in the play he so successfully fashioned out of Goldsmith's
immortal tale.' For Irving, the appeal was the celebration of the family, divided
and then reunited, something which he would only experience in part later in
life upon the rapprochement with his sons.

Stormy relationships between fathers and sons, and the reunion of fathers
with long lost children, again in reflection of reality, featured in several of Irving's
later productions: *The Dead Heart, Robespierre, Dante* and *Peter the Great*, for
example. Indeed Sir Henry's grandson and biographer Laurence Irving saw in
his uncle Laurence's play *Peter the Great* 'a reflection of their own unhappy

relationship – a strong, self-willed, intelligent, but ruthless father and his sensitive, visionary and vulnerable son'.[154]

The tenacity with which Irving clung to plans to produce plays which all his advisers warned were uncommercial can only be fully understood in the context of psychological compulsions. In 1879 Irving announced his intention to produce *Coriolanus* and it remained in his plans until he eventually brought it to the stage in 1901. But it was a play that had never been popular. Coriolanus was not a hero the Victorian public could identify with. The part had been a success for John Philip Kenble and Macready, but the last major production of it prior to Irving's had been in 1860 when Samuel Phelps staged it at Sadler's Wells. Irving himself had never seen it.[155] So why was Irving determined to do it? The answer perhaps lies in his conception of the play. It has been argued that Irving took neither the 'political' plot (the class conflict between the aristocratic general and the proletariat) nor the rivalry with Aufidius as the central conflict. Irving saw it rather as 'a tragedy of filial love', centring on the conflict between mother and son about his duty to Rome.[156] He cut and constructed the play, eliminating for instance the battles, to emphasize this. Given his own experience of rejection by his mother when he went on the stage, this looks like the explanation for his determination to put on this production as the dramatic working-out of that mother-son conflict in his own life. Similarly throughout his management he was looking for the opportunity to stage Byron's *Manfred*, the classic tragedy of a man seeking to expiate a secret sin for which he has been tormented by guilt and remorse. He came close to doing it in 1884 and 1897 but in the end he was saved from what would very likely have been as much of a box office disaster as *Coriolanus*.

There is another important psychological dimension to Irving's choice of roles. Henry Arthur Jones the playwright wrote of Irving:

> He was supremely great in what was grim, raffish, ironic, crafty, senile, sardonic, devilish; he was equally great in what was dignified, noble, simple, courtly, removed, unearthly, saintly and spiritual. The core of them was in himself. The sly impishness, the laconic mockery, and grim *diablerie* that were the underwoof of his character were the strange, harmonious complements of his hauteur, asceticism and spirituality.[157]

There is a prevailing idea of doubleness about the Victorian Age. It was in the broadest sense a divided age, torn between confidence and anxiety, respectability and unrespectability, reason and unreason. Its literature is full of secret lives, double identities, family secrets.[158] Many of its leading figures led double lives. Wilkie Collins, George Cruikshank and W.P. Frith all had two families, the existence of each unknown to the other. Dickens famously had an actress mistress in Ellen Ternan. Oscar Wilde and other leading Victorian homosexuals led secret lives in the sexual *demi-monde* of Victorian London. From time to time the existence of these other facets of life broke through the carapace of respectability to shock the citizenry: the Dilke Case, the Cleveland Street Scandal, the Wilde Case, Jack the Ripper, W.T. Stead's exposure of child prostitution and so forth. By the end of the century, writers were searching for the forces of darkness within as well as outside man, in anticipation of Freud. Many of the most potent figures of late Victorian literature explored this fascination, notably Stevenson's *Doctor Jekyll and Mister Hyde* (1886), where the evil battles against the good within a respectable doctor; Wilde's *The Picture of Dorian Gray* (1891), in which a beautiful young aristocrat lives a secret life of such depravity that his portrait ages and disfigures hideously; and Bram Stoker's *Dracula* (1897), where even in the most respectable dark desires are unleashed by the bite of the vampire.

Interestingly all these fictions had links with the Lyceum. Most famously the author of *Dracula* was Irving's business manager and steeped in the supernatural atmosphere of such productions as *The Corsican Brothers*, *Faust* and *The Bells*. Even if Irving dismissed *Dracula* as 'dreadful', there are those who have seen Dracula as a portrait of Irving himself, product of the subconscious resentment of Stoker at the way Irving drained the creative life out of all those around him. Wilde penned odes to Irving and Ellen Terry and offered a poetic drama to the Lyceum which Irving turned down. Perhaps most significantly, Irving purchased a stage adaptation of *Doctor Jekyll and Mister Hyde* by Oliver Booth and John Dixon in 1894 but never produced it, perhaps because Richard Mansfield had achieved a notable success in a different adaptation in 1888 at Irving's own theatre, the Lyceum, while Irving was touring the United States.

If doubles and duality were an obsession of late Victorian culture, Irving was its embodiment. He was the first knight of the theatre, the friend of Prime Ministers and princes, but he was separated from his wife and successfully conducted two long-lasting extra-marital affairs with married women (Ellen Terry and Eliza Aria). While preaching the virtues of domesticity, marital fidelity and family life, he lived a classic Bohemian bachelor existence of late nights, convivial clubland dinners, cigars, wine and masculine conversation.

His greatest stage successes came, as Jones implied, in his gallery of sardonic villains (Iago, Iachimo, Mephistopheles, Synorix, Richard III) and spiritual saints (Becket, Charles I, Doctor Primrose, Shylock). Even more notably he actually played doubles in two of his most popular vehicles, *The Corsican Brothers* and *The Lyons Mail*. In *The Corsican Brothers* he played twins, Fabien and Louis dei Franchi. They are identical twin brothers each of whom experiences the sensations of the other. Fabien is raised in Corsica, Louis in Paris, but when Louis is killed in a duel, Fabien travels to Paris to exact vengeance on the killer. Audiences were fascinated by Irving's playing of the brothers. As the painter Graham Robertson recalled:

Irving sought no aid from make-up in creating the separate identities of the twins; Fabien and Louis were physically identical, yet, after the first glance, no one would have mistaken them. Fabien was the noble savage, Louis the finished product of civilization, exquisite in manners, meticulous in costume, gentle and courteous, chivalrous and charming.[159]

Similar virtuosity was required from Irving in *The Lyons Mail.* This play was based on a true story. In 1796 Joseph Lesurques was guillotined for robbing the Lyons Mail. But he was the victim of mistaken identity. He strongly resembled the real criminal Dubosc, who was only caught many years later. In 1850, with the permission of the family, the story was dramatized as *Le Courier de Lyons* by Moreau, Giraudin and Delacour. Their play which premiered on 16 March, 1850 at the Théâtre de la Gaîté had an unhappy ending, with Lesurques executed. This so upset audiences that a happy ending, sparing Lesurques, was written and the two different endings were played on alternate evenings. It was an immediate success and translated into English, with the happy ending preferred, by Lewis Phillips and performed at the Standard Theatre, Bishopsgate, on 10 March, 1851. The most famous English version was the one made by novelist Charles Reade for Charles Kean and performed with great success at the Princess's Theatre in 1854. In 1870 Hermann Vezin did it with success at the Gaiety Theatre. Irving made the two parts his own when he revived it at the Lyceum in 1877 in a production which he kept in his repertoire for the rest of his career.

Act 1 of *The Lyons Mail* establishes the contrasting lives of the central figures. Joseph Lesurques, a rich and respectable self-made bourgeois, arrives in Paris to oversee the marriage of his daughter Julie to her fiancé, the merchant Didier. He meets old college friends at an inn where associates of the escaped convict Dubosc, drunkard, thief and brute, are also gathered. After Lesurques leaves, Dubosc arrives. He encounters Jeannette, whom he has seduced and abandoned, leaving her with a child. He rejects her and plans with his associates the robbery of the Lyons Mail. Lesurques' father Jerome, an innkeeper facing bankruptcy, but too proud to ask for help, leaves his inn to seek a purchaser. Lesurques arrives and secretly leaves money for him. Dubosc and his gang then rob and murder the couriers with the Mail and make off also with the money left by Lesurques. Jerome returns, confronts Dubosc, recognizes him as his son and is shot and wounded.

Act 2, at Lesurques' house in Paris, sees Julie befriending and giving employment to the abandoned Jeannette. Lesurques is then identified by the tavern boy Joliquet and other witnesses as the robber of the Mail and arrested, along with Courriol and Choppard, accomplices of Dubosc. In a new scene, introduced by Reade, Jerome believing his son guilty, offers him the escape of suicide but Lesurques rejects the proffered pistol and is denounced by his father for cowardice.

In Act 3, as Lesurques faces trial, Julie wants to break her engagement with Didier, so as to spare him disgrace. He refuses her offer and produces evidence of Lesurques' innocence. However, Dubosc enters the house secretly and destroys the evidence. Jeannette appears and tries to stop him leaving but he stabs her and flees. In the prison where Lesurques, now condemned, awaits execution, Jeannette who has survived the attack, arrives to explain the mistaken identification. Choppard and Couriol confirm it. The judge hastens to secure Lesurques' release, and Jeannette leads the authorities to Dubosc. In the final scene, a drunken Dubosc, who has taken a room in a tavern to watch the execution, waits as the procession of the condemned passes. But the gendarmes, led by Jeannette, turn up, arrest him after a struggle and Lesurques is freed and reunited with his daughter. With its contrasting portraits of nobility and depravity in identical-looking characters, played by the same actor; its theme of redemption for a fallen woman; its picture of happy family life, filial piety and marital devotion, threatened with destruction but preserved at the eleventh hour, it had all the elements of an enduring Victorian success.

John Martin-Harvey, who played Joliquet in the 1891 and 1893 revivals of the play and was to take on the leading roles after Irving's death, recalled of Irving's performance:

> Lesurques in his hands bore very little resemblance to a hero of melodrama; he was typical of all that is implied by 'middle class respectability', though perhaps a trifle too distinguished, and might very well have passed for a younger brother of Doctor Primrose, whom he more nearly resembled than any other of his impersonations.

By contrast, Dubosc was callous, brutal and at the climax, savage. The contrast was striking.

> I have known the audience 'stagger' on the first apparition of Dubosc. Lesurques is hardly out of sight when Dubosc is there in the doorway, grim, sinister, the embodiment of wicked intent. His accomplices cower as he comes among them chewing his straw, and regarding them with contemptuous, insolent tolerance. Then, peremptorily, he issues his orders and from that moment dominates.

Martin-Harvey recalled that to emphasize Dubosc's cruelty Irving would hum some bars of *La Marseillaise* as he searched the dead body of the courier. 'One night in a fit of fantastic humour he almost shocked us by substituting "Nearer, my God to Thee". The effect was appalling.' As for the finale, 'it is hardly possible to exaggerate the savagery of Irving's performance in that scene, yet never did he overstep the truth of nature and degenerate into extravagance. Dubosc though a monster was a credible human being and it was that fact that gave the play its lasting popularity.'[160]

Up until the end of his career, Irving retained in his permanent repertoire

Becket, The Bells, Charles the First, Louis XI, The Lyons Mail, Waterloo and *The Merchant of Venice*. Until only a couple of years before his death, he also maintained *Olivia, Faust, Robespierre* and *Madam Sans Gêne*. Significantly, there was only one Shakespeare play and, apart from his recent commissions (*Robespierre* and *Madame Sans Gêne*) and Tennyson's poetic drama *Becket*, they were all melodramas. This was the repertoire he fell back on whenever a new production failed or ran out of steam. These were the sure-fire titles with which he could fill the theatre.

After 1903, and the failure of *Dante*, he mounted no new productions. In an interview he gave on the eve of embarking on his farewell tour, in answer to the question about whether there was to be production of a new play, he said:

> Even were I disposed to try something novel, it is the old familiar pieces which the public appears to want. I can conceive that as generation has followed generation, parents have talked over the subjects of these with their children, and the desire of the latter to see what their fathers enjoyed formerly serves to fill the theatre. And I dare say there are many staunch friends who are quite willing to repeat their experiences of twenty or thirty years ago. What satisfies them ought surely to satisfy me.[161]

What was it about this group of works that they exerted such enduring fascination on audiences? On a purely theatrical level there were showy parts that enabled Irving to demonstrate to the full his acting abilities. But perhaps even more important, these plays spoke to and for the Victorian world view. There were the heroic saints (Charles I, Becket, Shylock, Lesurques in *The Lyons Mail*) who evoked sentiments of sympathy and admiration and the demonic villains who got their come-uppance (Mephistopheles, Robespierre, Louis XI, Dubosc). Together they represented a clear-cut black and white morality. There were the celebrations of domesticity and family life (*Olivia, Charles the First*). There was the drama of conscience and retribution (*The Bells*). There was the eternal battle between the forces of good and those of evil for the soul of Mankind (*Faust*). It was in his regular exploration of these cardinal principles of the Victorian outlook that Irving won a permanent place in the affections of Victorian theatre-goers of every age, class and condition.

6

Playwrights

For much of the nineteenth-century playwriting remained one of the jobs of the man of letters. Many were journalists and not a few theatre critics. These theatre critics turned playwright, who continued to combine the two professions, included William Bayle-Bernard, E.L. Blanchard, Leicester Buckingham, John Heraud, John Hollingshead, Westland Marston, H. Chance Newton, John Oxenford, Tom Taylor, George R. Sims, F.G. Tomlins and Edmund Yates. But playwriting was also a sideline for lawyers, clerics, civil servants, and clerks. The most remarkable career was that enjoyed by Tom Taylor, who was variously Oxford don, professor of English at London University, art critic of the *Times* and the *Graphic*, leader writer on the *Morning Chronicle* and the *Daily News*, for twenty years a civil servant at the Board of Health and finally editor of *Punch*. He also wrote eighty plays.[1]

The main source of playwrights was the tribe of prolific journalists, who functioned in a Bohemian world, revolving around clubs like the Arundel, the Savage and the Garrick, where they enjoyed dining, drinking, smoking, literary conversation and late nights amid a convivial company of actors, writers and painters. On 1 January 1880, the *Theatre* magazine ran a symposium on 'The Dearth of Dramatists: Is it a fact?' perhaps prompted by the fact reported in the February issue:

> The dramatic year of 1879 will be memorable on account of its disastrous history of failures at almost every theatre in the metropolis. The successes may be easily counted on two hands ... Of these plays five are from the French, and two from America.

Irving made the first contribution and he said: 'dramatists were numberless ... but they possess one characteristic in common – they are wholly unadapted to the stage ... The reason ... why there is a dearth of good dramatists ... is, in my opinion, that although many people are anxious to write for the stage, few will take the trouble to study the technique, which is essential to an acting play.' He points out that our greatest dramatist Shakespeare was an actor and two of the most popular modern playwrights, T.W. Robertson and H.J. Byron, were both actors. He added the caveat that you did not have to be an actor to be a successful playwright. 'Mr Tom Taylor is not professionally an actor, and yet there is no dramatic author who more thoroughly understands his business.' In fact, Irving never staged one of Taylor's plays at the Lyceum and his own input was often essential to making submitted scripts playable or to dictating the structure and content of plays as they evolved.[2]

Irving's playwrights were frequently chosen from that Bohemian brotherhood, the men of letters, some of them without much of a record for playwriting. It is instructive to examine them to establish the context of the drama. Frank Marshall (1840–1889) was the son of the MP for Carlisle and later East Cumberland, William Marshall (1796–1872). He was educated at Harrow and Oxford University but did not take a degree. A clerk in the Audit Office for several years, he resigned in 1868 to become a full-time writer. He was the drama critic of the *London Figaro* but also wrote eight plays, mainly comedies, plus *A Study of Hamlet* (1875). He became one of Irving's circle, editing the *Henry Irving Shakespeare*, adapting Byron's *Werner* for the Westland Marston Benefit and writing the eventually unproduced *Robert Emmet* as a vehicle for Irving. He collaborated with W.G. Wills on *Cara*. He also wrote *Henry Irving: Actor and Manager* under the pseudonym 'an Irvingite.' His second wife was the actress Ada Cavendish (1839–1895). Sir Frank Burnand recalled him as

> one of the kindest-hearted, best read, and most eccentric young men within my fairly large circle of friends at the time … He was very well off, and came up to town, after a gay career at Oxford, with the curly locks of an Apollo, a taste for brilliancy in attire, evidenced by the shiniest patent leathers in constant use, and as much white waistcoat as he could carry. He was naturally of a very pale complexion, wanting in tone, but was rarely without a cheery smile, and never without a hearty word of welcome. His white waistcoat and creamy face earned him the sobriquet … of 'The Boiled Ghost'.

Burnand assessed him as 'a bit of an author, light and serious, but first and foremost he was a scholarly student and this fact won him the lasting friendship of John Oxenford'. Oxenford, twenty-five years his senior, and drama critic of the *Times* 'belonged to what would now be considered an old-fashioned school of journalistic critics, whose real opinions were to be found … in the higher class magazines and most erudite quarterlies'.[3] But Marshall's commitment to scholarship did not prevent his involvement in the Bohemian life of parties, dinner and japes.

Percy Fitzgerald, another of the Irving circle, recalled as 'pleasant' and 'not without a dash of eccentricity', a mercurial figure who had 'many friends who thoroughly believed in him and liked him'. He started out with energy and spirit and had a fortune of his own and later inherited his brother's estate. But Fitzgerald then proceeded rather dismissively, and with a distinct whiff of sour grapes, to observe that he wrote nothing more than 'a play or two' (actually eight), *A Study of Hamlet* and edited the Irving Shakespeare:

He did little to win a reputation. Yet reputation he had; he was well known, and looked upon as an authority. Reputations in London are often made in a most mysterious way. It would all seem to depend on personality ... it depends a good deal on friends – friends who write in books, journals, society papers and the like ... In the writing world ... it is not writing alone that gets you on. Frank Marshall was a striking illustration of this. He was a squire and independent ... and hospitable. To Irving he attached himself. He was presumed to be his adviser and director in matters of nice criticism. He had written on 'The Bard' and used to prefix criticisms to acting editions of Irving's plays. I doubt, however, if his Shakespeare views were to be taken very 'seriously'. He was too flighty for sober judicial criticism.

Of the Irving Shakespeare, which he edited, Fitzgerald, while conceding it was 'a handsome and useful addition', disparaged Marshall's contribution:

It need not be said that an edition of Shakespeare is a work of so gigantic a kind as properly to engross the labour of a life, requiring an equipment of the most extensive kind, perfect familiarity with the contemporary literature, together with the English scholarship of a Skeat. This Frank Marshall could scarcely be said to possess. Like so many of his friends and companions, he was destined before the close of his life to experience the decay which ... often attends an erratic career. He fell into bad health and suffered much; he seemed to be rather forgotten, and to have fallen out of his old place ... He somewhat surprised his friends by his marriage with that popular actress and excellent woman, Miss Ada Cavendish. In his fortunes he was not so prosperous as he had been.[4]

But Marshall did make it into *The Dictionary of National Biography*; though Fitzgerald did not. When the final volume of the Irving Shakespeare was published in 1890, Irving paid tribute to him, arguing that he was the first practising playwright to edit the works of Shakespeare and that he was able to apply to his criticism his practical knowledge of stagecraft. Of the man himself, Irving recorded:

Frank Marshall was a friend of my life. We were brought together and linked by the golden band of a common love for the Great Englishman whose work he endeavoured worthily to set forth; and from the hour we first met our friendship ripened, till in all the world I had no warmer friend.

In a passage cut at proof stage, he praised Marshall's 'wit and humour ... his intensity of thought and purpose ... his tenderness of heart and geniality'.[5]

Percy Fitzgerald himself was another polymathic man of letters. Fitzgerald (1834–1925) was willing to turn his hand to anything. For a time dramatic critic of the *Observer* and for many years dramatic critic of the *Whitehall Review*, he also wrote novels, biographies, travel books, works of criticism. He wrote books on the art of acting, music hall land, the Savoy Operas and the story of Bradshaw's *Guide* as well as a study of the London suburbs dedicated to the Queen. For

Irving he collaborated with W.G. Wills on *Vanderdecken*, whose genesis he recounted in his biography of Irving. He records that Irving encouraged him to persist with the subject, and in 1881 he published his own version *The Spectral Ship*, but it was not taken up by Irving.

Herman Charles Merivale wrote *Edgar and Lucy*, an adaptation of *The Bride of Lammermoor*, which Irving produced and starred in as *Ravenswood*. Herman Charles Merivale (1839–1906) was the son of the eminent civil servant, Herman Merivale (1806–1874), Permanent Under-Secretary at the India Office. Herman Charles was educated at Harrow, where the headmaster, C.J. Vaughan, 'became much attached to him', and Oxford University. To please his father he worked as a barrister from 1864 to 1874 but disliked it. As soon as his father died, he abandoned the law for his real love – the stage. He had been a keen amateur actor, had walked on as a super in some of Charles Kean's productions, and he now became a prolific playwright. He wrote burlesque and farces, literary adaptations and a highly regarded poetic drama, *The White Pilgrim*, produced by Hermann Vezin in 1883. Also notable were his adaptation of *A Tale of Two Cities* called *All For Her* (1875), written with Palgrave Simpson, *Forget-Me-Not* (1879) co-written by F.C. Grove, which Geneviève Ward performed two thousand times, and an adaptation of Sardou's *Fedora* for the Bancrofts (1882), 'one of the biggest of the many successes' of that regime. He wrote novels, one of them *Faucit of Balliol*, winning great praise, and a stream of articles for such journals as the *Spectator*, *Punch*, *The Saturday Review*, the *World* and *Truth*. A brilliant speaker, he refused many invitations to stand for Parliament, but as an active and ardent Liberal he worked energetically for the party from 1880 to 1890. He lost all his money in 1900 as a result of the fraud of his solicitor, undertook two years of court action which failed and in consequence his health broke down. He sailed to Australia to recuperate – only to be shipwrecked. Eventually he was awarded a Civil List pension and the proceeds of a benefit performance at Her Majesty's Theatre.[6] J.B. Booth recalled him as 'temperamental to a degree, highly strung, excitable, vociferous in argument, poor Merivale was a man who required appropriate handling and a certain degree of understanding'.[7] This temperament led Merivale to sue Martin-Harvey for breach of contract when he rejected his *Don Juan* play, which Martin-Harvey said had 'an atmosphere of false and heavy Victorian sentiment which made me feel slightly sick'.[8]

That demanding critic William Archer paid tribute to Merivale in *English Dramatists of Today*:

> Though Mr Merivale has scored several successes, he can scarcely be called one of the popular dramatists of the day. He writes too well and too carefully for that bad eminence. In farce, in so-called tragedy, in romantic drama, and in modern drama, he has given the stage some of the best work it can boast.

The White Pilgrim, he called, 'perhaps the very best poetical play of the past ten years' and *Forget-Me-Not* 'an interesting and powerful work'.[9]

Charles Hamilton Aidé (1826–1906) was an exotic figure. He was born in Paris and grew up fluent in both French and English. His father was the son of an Armenian merchant and his mother the daughter of a British admiral. His father was killed in a duel when Charles was four and his mother brought him to live in England. He was educated at the University of Bonn and served for a time in the British army, emerging as a captain in 1853. He never married but lived with his mother at Lyndhurst until her death in 1875. Thereafter he took rooms at Queen Anne's Gate where he hosted a celebrated salon which drew 'the chief figures in the social and artistic world of France as well as England'. Later in life he lived with married cousins near Ascot in Berkshire.

The *Dictionary of National Biography* describes him as 'a man of versatile accomplishments and with abundant social gifts, who devoted himself with equal success to society, music, art and literature'. He wrote several volumes of poetry, composed songs, exhibited the sketches made on his regular foreign travels at various galleries. He wrote nineteen novels dealing with fashionable society which 'enjoyed some vogue'. His drama *Philip* was produced with Irving in the lead at the Lyceum in 1874 and his comedy *A Nine Day's Wonder* was produced by John Hare and the Kendals at the Court Theatre in 1875.[10] Robert Hichens paints a more intimate portrait of him, describing him as:

> a short, bearded man who ... seemed to have met everybody of note in all the countries of Europe, and to have become friends with most of them ... he advised 'promising' young men how to work and to live. And he gave parties ... where many celebrities were to be met with. For he knew all the duchesses, all the actresses, all the (successful) novelists and musicians.

Mrs Patrick Campbell nicknamed him 'the world's governess' and he took up Hichens, then a young journalist who had achieved a certain notoriety with his anonymously published novel *The Green Carnation* (1894), satirising Oscar Wilde and his circle.

> Mr Aidé wanted to guide me, and I was touched by his kind interest, but I felt from the very beginning of my friendship with him that his temperament was hardly akin to mine. He was too anxious about 'What will society say?' to be the right guide for me. I had to go my own way without thought of the Dowager Duchesses, who were all his intimate friends. I think some of my writings rather shocked him, but to the end of his long life he remained my very good friend. He was a highly accomplished man, but he had not the touch of greatness that makes men defiant of the conventions ... A lot of talent was his – facile talent.[11]

Like his mentor Aidé, Robert Hichens also wrote a play for Irving but not through Aidé's influence. Hichens (1864–1950), a clergyman's son, was educated at

Clifton and studied at the Royal College of Music. But he turned to journalism and short story writing to earn a living. He succeeded George Bernard Shaw as the music critic on the *World*. Not only was he taken up by Aidé, he was also taken up by another older man, the journalist H.D. Traill. Henry Duff Traill (1842–1900) was a respected journalist and author. He was leader writer, columnist and essayist for the *Pall Mall Gazette* (1873–80) and then for the *St James's Gazette* (1880–82). From 1882 to 1897 he was chief political leader writer of the *Daily Telegraph*. From 1897 to his death he was the first editor of *Literature*. He wrote monographs on Lord Shaftesbury, William III, Strafford, the Marquis of Salisbury and Lord Cromer, and biographies of Lawrence Sterne, Samuel Taylor Coleridge and Sir John Franklin. The *Dictionary of National Biography* describes him as 'a fine and penetrating critic' with 'an admirable style – easy, fluent, dignified and correct'. Evidently he was also an aspiring playwright, but had produced only a blank verse tragedy *The Diamond Seeker* 'of no great merit', privately published in the early 1870s, and a comic extravaganza *Glaucus*, acted at the Olympic Theatre in 1865.[12]

For some reason, Irving thought him capable of providing a new play for the Lyceum and asked him to do so. Traill invited Hichens to collaborate with him. Hichens recalled their association:

> I made the acquaintance of a famous journalist, Mr H.D. Traill, who took a kind interest in me and in what I was doing, encouraged me and now and then wrote plain words of critical warning. He was an elderly man, much older than I was, and was married but had no children. He and his wife had a large house in Bloomsbury, and gave there occasional tremendous luncheon-parties, like banquets, at which many great guns of the literary and newspaper world assembled.

The Traills invited Hichens to supper to meet Irving. They talked till dawn and Irving drove Hichens as far as Grafton Street. Hichens, who already considered Irving 'by far the greatest English actor', wrote in his autobiography:

> Few men have fascinated me as much as Sir Henry Irving. He was absolutely unlike any man I had ever encountered. He made upon me in private life, as he did on the stage, the impression of possessing genius. He looked and seemed like a being apart. Yet I never found him at all difficult to deal with. He was invariably kind to me, polite and presently friendly.[13]

Traill and Hichens came up with the idea of a play set in Ancient Egypt and prepared a scenario, but Irving rejected it, saying he would like a modern play and 'I wouldn't mind playing a doctor ... But he mustn't be an ordinary doctor'.

Hichens outlined the process by which the play emerged: 'After several meetings and discussions, in none of which Miss Terry took part and in which her name was seldom mentioned, we decided what we would do, and we wrote ... *The Medicine Man*.' In his autobiography, Hichens called it the worst failure of his career, 'I am convinced it was a very bad play … But the strange thing was that Irving liked it, even liked it very much.' Hichens first met Ellen Terry at rehearsals and concluded correctly that 'she hated the play.' It was produced before a brilliant audience, headed by the Prince and Princess of Wales. Traill and Hichens were summoned on stage at the end and applauded. But the next day 'the critiques were pretty bad. And soon in the *World* Mr William Archer gave the play what I consider to have been the *coup de grâce*'. Despite some pleasing elements of social satire, *The Medicine Man* emerged as a distinctly underpowered imitation of *Trilby*. Irving played Dr Tregenna, a sardonic and egotistical nerve specialist, who controlled his patients by willpower. He seeks revenge on the man he believes has stolen his sweetheart by using his power to turn the man's daughter against him. He ends up being murdered by another of his patients. It had only a short run and was soon withdrawn but to Hichens's surprise Irving's manner towards him never changed. 'It was invariably kind and friendly' and they continued to exchange social invitations.[14]

Hichens did go on in later years to achieve stage success, notably with an adaptation of *Becky Sharp* for Marie Tempest. But his greatest success came with his exotic novels dealing with forbidden love in far-off climes, the most famous being *The Garden of Allah* (1904), which he also adapted for the stage. He spent much of his life travelling and died unmarried. The reason Irving never blamed him for the failure of the play is probably because Irving blamed himself. He had chosen the theme and encouraged the authors, had ignored Ellen Terry's unhappiness with her part and had pressed on regardless. It is clear that what he wanted was a part to emulate Tree's success as Svengali. In this he failed, but he was satisfied to have made the attempt. He tried no more modern dress parts after this. In view of Hichens's subsequent success, Irving might have been better advised to take the Egyptian scenario.

Joseph Comyns Carr (1849–1916) was an extraordinarily versatile man about the arts. The son of a businessman, he studied for the bar and graduated from London University with a First in Jurisprudence and Roman Law. He was called to the bar in 1872 and became a junior barrister on the Northern Circuit. But his interests lay in the arts. He began reviewing for the *Dramatic and Musical Review* and then became drama critic of the *Echo*. He joined the permanent staff of the *Globe* but at the same time he became art critic of the *Pall Mall Gazette* as well as contributing essays to the *Saturday Review*, the *Examiner* and the *World*. He later also became the critic of the *Manchester Guardian*.

In his autobiography he recorded that in any given week he would work all morning at the *Globe* and would write an article each for the *Saturday Review*, the *Examiner* and the *World*. In addition there would be three or four columns of art criticism for the *Pall Mall Gazette* and the *Manchester Guardian*, as well as occasional articles for other journals. He became editor of the English version of

L'Art and from 1883 to 1886 was editor of the *English Illustrated Magazine* for Macmillans.

In addition to all this journalism, he was from 1876 to 1887 director of the Grosvernor Gallery; and, after he resigned due to a disagreement with Sir Coutts Lindsay, the owner, about policy, he co-founded The New Gallery. He went into theatre management running the Comedy Theatre and he also found the time to write plays. With his wife Alice, he prepared an English version of the French classic *Frou-Frou*, called *Butterfly*, which Ellen Terry and her husband Charles Kelly performed in the provinces. Together they also did an adaptation of Thomas Hardy's *Far From the Madding Crowd*, in which Marion Terry played Bathsheba Everdene in the provinces and later in London. In 1884 Carr had a great success with his adaptation of Hugh Conway's novel *Called Back*, which was produced in London with Beerbohm Tree in the lead. A follow-up also based on Conway, *Dark Days*, produced in 1885, was less successful. Together with Sir Arthur Pinero, he provided the libretto for Sir Arthur Sullivan's opera *The Beauty Stone*. He cultivated the friendship of great men: Rossetti, Millais and Burne-Jones, Browning and George Meredith, Sullivan and Irving. He had an indirect connection with the Lyceum in that he had been at school with the son of 'Colonel' Bateman, Dick Bateman, who was later drowned off the coast of Japan on a business venture. But Dick introduced him to the Lyceum and to Irving. For Irving, he prepared the English language version of *Madame Sans-Gêne*, and when he found himself unable satisfactorily to revise W.G. Wills's *King Arthur*, he wrote his own version of the story which Irving staged at the Lyceum. Carr also wrote *Nerves* for the Comedy Theatre, *My Lady of Rosedale* for Sir Charles Wyndham, and adaptations of Dickens's *Oliver Twist* and *Edwin Drood* for Tree. In 1899, as Irving's debts mounted, it was Carr who put together a syndicate to take over the Lyceum and to hire Irving as their leading actor. But the syndicate failed and the Lyceum was turned into a music hall.[15]

Irving told an American interviewer that Carr was the wittiest man in England ('the most sparkling man I have ever met'). After he died, Carr was paid many tributes. The novelist Anthony Hope called him: 'A man of rare gifts, a splendid companion, a generous, kindly, gracious friend'. The novelist W.J. Locke called him 'an eminent art critic, a theatrical manager with high ideals, an editor of fine discernment, and a distinguished playwright ... one of the finest after-dinner speakers of his generation'. The publisher Sir Frederick Macmillan called him: 'One of the most gifted and brilliant creatures I have ever known, and had such a kindly nature that no one could come across him without loving him.'[16]

Irving commissioned W.L. Courtney to prepare an English version of Ludwig Fulda's play *The Bloody Marriage*. William Leonard Courtney (1850–1928), son of an Indian civil servant, had been an Oxford philosophy tutor at New College (1876–90). But while in Oxford he also coached the boat club and helped produce plays at the Oxford University Dramatic Society (OUDS), founded in 1884. Through OUDS he became friends with H.B. Irving and through H.B. he met Sir Henry, whom Courtney brought to Oxford to lecture. He was already writing articles for the *World* and the *Fortnightly Review*. In 1890, embittered by his failure to get the Whyte Chair of Moral Philosophy at Oxford, and tiring of academic life, as he says in his autobiography *The Passing Hour*, he left Oxford and took a full-time post on the *Daily Telegraph* where in the mid 1890s he became chief drama critic and literary editor, a post he held until 1925. 'His scholarly training and dramatic experiences, his wide interests and resource in emergency made him a fine journalist', says *The Dictionary of National Biography*. From 1894 until his death, he was editor of the *Fortnightly Review*, and for many years was chairman of Chapman and Hall, the publishers. The *DNB* recalls him as a fine soldierly figure who was 'a genial companion and loyal friend'. He published several studies on philosophy. He also wrote plays. His one-act play *The Death of Kit Marlowe*, was produced by Sir George Alexander with *The Importance of Being Earnest* at the St James's Theatre. His play *Undine* was performed by Mrs Patrick Campbell in 1903 for a very short run. *On the Side of Angels*, a play about the effects of drug addiction, was performed at the Royalty Theatre in 1906 by the Pioneers. But, notes the *DNB*, 'his plays had little success'. He published his version of the Fulda play as *The Bridals of Blood*, but it was never acted.[17]

Irving announced that *Charles IX*, as Courtney's play was then called, would succeed *King Arthur* on the Lyceum stage, but, as Courtney recalled in *The Passing Hour*, 'unfortunately for myself, the play was postponed for a short version of *Don Quixote*, and then disappeared indefinitely'.[18] Courtney's memory is at fault. *Quixote* had already been played when, at the end of the 1895 season, Irving announced that after his forthcoming American tour he would produce *Coriolanus*, Courtney's play and *Madame Sans-Gêne*. Instead, when he returned to the Lyceum in late 1896, he produced *Cymbeline* and *Richard III*, before sustaining the knee injury that kept him off stage for two months. When he came back, it was with *Madame Sans-Gêne*.[19] Courtney regretted Irving's failure to play *Charles IX*:

> The part of Charles IX is one which ought to have suited him well, for it included certain saturnine elements, together with an original weakness of character, interrupted by moods of insensate cruelty and an intense fear of his mother, Catherine de Medici. The Bartholomew massacres form a splendid subject for a fine drama; there are so many characters which all have an importance of their own. Beside Charles IX, there is Henry, King of Navarre, the Cardinal of Lorraine, Admiral Coligny, Margaret de Valois, and the superb masterful woman who wove most of the plots to entrap the Huguenots, the great Catherine de Medici.[20]

It may be the very fact that there were so many important characters that eventually dissuaded Irving from producing it. He might not have been the main focus of attention. It is intriguing to note how frequently Irving turned to upmarket journalists, many of them drama critics, to provide him with new plays, and also how frequently they failed. He seems to have felt that the combination of literary ability, dramatic knowledge and respectability within the profession – most of them appear in *The Dictionary of National Biography* – would pay off. It did not and he turned back to a proven master of stagecraft in Victorien Sardou.

Victorien Sardou (1831–1908) was the veteran French master of the 'well-made play'. He also had a reputation for fashioning successful star vehicles for such luminaries of the French stage as Sarah Bernhardt (*La Tosca, Theodora, Fedora*) and Réjane (*Madame Sans-Gêne*). All these qualities must have commended him to Irving. He was the inheritor of the mantle of Hugo and Dumas, dividing his output between social comedies and historical dramas. It is no coincidence that several of Sardou's plays were transformed into operas (*Tosca, Fedora*). They are steeped in the French Romanticism that so appealed to Irving. In 1877 Sardou was elected a member of the Académie Française. He also made a very handsome living from his plays, earning a nightly 10–12 per cent of the profits on the productions. He made an estimated 250,000 francs a year and his most successful plays such as *La Tosca* and *Madame Sans-Gêne* netted him over half a million francs apiece.

Sardou's grandfather had served as a surgeon with Napoleon's Army of Italy and Sardou himself became an authority on the French Revolution, no fewer than six of his plays dealing with that period: *Monsieur Garat* (1860), *Les Merveilleuses* (1873), *Thermidor* (1891), *Madame Sans-Gêne* (1893), *Robespierre* (1899) and *Pamela* (1898). Irving saw a French company playing *Madame Sans-Gêne* in London and acquired the English rights. Joseph Comyns Carr prepared the English language version and it proved successful. This led Irving to commission two further vehicles from Sardou, *Robespierre* (1899), translated into English by Laurence Irving, and *Dante*, co-written with Emile Moreau, his collaborator on *Madam Sans-Gêne* and again translated by Laurence Irving. Sardou declined to travel to England to see *Robespierre*: 'He dreaded the prospect of the dinners and speeches to which he would be compelled to submit. "That no longer agrees at my time of life. Besides, I have never had much taste for such things".'[21]

Towards the end of his career, Irving, recognising the continuing importance of America to his career, employed American actors in his plays, and he let the Lyceum to a succession of visiting American stars when he was on tour. He even commissioned an American playwright to provide him with a script.

Joseph Ignatius Constantine Clarke (1846–1925) was born in Ireland but had migrated to England in 1858. Having been active in Irish republican organisations, he was forced to flee to America in 1868 and there embarked on a journalistic career. He was managing editor of the *New York Morning Journal* (1883–95), the editor of *Criterion* (1898–1900) and Sunday editor of the *New York Herald* (1903–1906). In addition to his journalistic career, he was a poet and a playwright, responsible for among others *For Bonnie Prince Charlie*, a vehicle for Robert Taber and Julia Marlowe, *The First Violin*, written for Richard Mansfield, and *The Prince of India*, starring William Farnum. Irving commissioned two dramas from him, *Don Quixote* and *George Washington*, but he produced neither. Clarke, however, remained a friend and left an affectionate account of Irving in his memoirs.[22]

William Gorman Wills, known to his intimates as 'Willie' and to his public as W.G. Wills, was perhaps the leading purveyor of the romantic, poetic, historical drama to the British theatregoer in the 1870s and 1880s. His brother and biographer, the Rev. Freeman Wills, in his 1898 biography of Willie, described him as 'the poetic dramatist of the Victorian era' and claimed as his achievements:

> He restored poetry to the stage at a time when the poetic drama was supposed to be dead. He successfully took up the thread of history plays when managers were saying that Shakespeare spelled ruin. His dramas were literature to the cultivated, while they were human nature to the crowd, thus acquiring among all classes a widespread popularity.[23]

These are strong claims but there is some evidence to support them, in the long runs of his best plays and the fact that they remained in the repertoire of such leading actors as Henry Irving and Wilson Barrett throughout their careers and were thus performed not just in London but throughout the provinces and in America.

Percy Fitzgerald, who collaborated with Wills, painted a more balanced picture. He recalled Wills as 'a strange, incoherent combination ... of good nature, hurry, cleverness, and sensitiveness'. He wrote 'never was there a more good-natured yet inconsequent being ... he lived at a studio in the Fulham Road, with a number of his countrymen and others 'hanging loose on' him, to whom his purse and shelter too, was always open'. Of his work, Fitzgerald said: 'He overflowed with poetry and could turn on streams of blank verse with wonderful facility. There was within him a soft, tender and romantic vein.' But 'the author was strangely deficient in managing the construction of his dramas ... it always seemed a mystery how he contrived to put together *Olivia* which is a marvel of construction and judicious arrangement'.[24]

Wills was born on 28 January 1828, in Blackwell Lodge near Kilmurry. He was the third of the seven children of a Church of Ireland minister and scion of an Anglo-Irish gentry family prominent in the church, the law and letters – Oscar Wilde was a cousin. Educated at Trinity College, Dublin, where he was a 'respectable athlete' and won the Vice-Chancellor's prize for poetry, he was destined for the law but 'destined himself for art and literature', devoting himself to painting, drawing, flute-playing and poetry writing, where his influences were Goethe, Heine and the Brontës. He grew up to be 'the great Bohemian of his day', whimsical, warm-hearted, generous and unworldly. He had 'the eccentricity of genius without its affectations ... he met the highest or lowest on a footing of good-natured equality'. He was personally 'extremely abstemious' and heedless of what he ate, drank or wore. 'While for many years of his life he was making large sums of money, he was so surrounded by parasites and harpies that he was always poor and sometimes penniless.' He regularly forgot engagements. He was loved by children, 'his simplicity, akin to theirs, and his tenderness and gentleness making them at once his friends'.[25] His lack of concern about his appearance had one exception. His hair went very thin on top in his thirties and he took to wearing a very obvious wig, prompting the nickname of 'Willie Wiggs'. He went to London in 1855 and settled there permanently in 1862. Initially he earned his living as a novelist (*Notice to Quit, The Wife's Evidence, David Chantry*, 'a striking and original work', according to Percy Fitzgerald.)[26] In 1863 he saved a blind boy from drowning in the Thames. He became a member of London's Bohemian club life, joining the Arundel Club in 1863 and actually living there from 1867 to 1871. He joined the Garrick in 1872. He regularly attended the salon of Dr Westland Marston and had a brief romance with Marston's daughter Nellie, which led to nothing and she married the poet Alfred O'Shaughnessy. In 1868 Wills's father died and for the twenty years of her widowhood he supported his adored mother, setting her up in a house in Dublin and paying all her expenses. It was this which spurred him to take on lucrative employment. He took a studio, at 15 The Avenue, Fulham Road, and set up as a fashionable portrait painter in pastels, painting among others the Marchioness of Bute, Lord Garmoyle, Lady Granville and Lady Wenlock. His fame was such that he was summoned to Osborne by Queen Victoria to paint the royal grandchildren. Haunted by the idea of Ophelia, he painted four studies of her, including *Ophelia and Laertes* which Irving purchased for the vestibule of the Lyceum. In 1867 he took to writing plays. He wrote *The Man o' Airlie* for actor-manager Hermann Vezin. He dictated the play to Vezin and benefited from Vezin's advice and help on dramatic construction and stagecraft. It was a critical rather than a popular success when Vezin starred in it. He wrote two more plays for Vezin, *Hinko* (adapted from the German novel by Ludwig Storch) and *Broken Spells* (co-written with Westland Marston).

In 1871 Wills took on Alfred Calmour as his secretary and Calmour, learning from his master, became himself a successful poetic playwright. In 1871 Vezin introduced Wills to 'Colonel' Bateman who commissioned him to write a version of *Medea* for his daughter, Mrs Crowe, based on Legouvé's version of Euripides, prepared for but rejected by Rachel and eventually performed with success by the Italian tragedienne Ristori. *Medea in Corinth* was a success and Bateman, who declared Wills the greatest poetic dramatist since Shakespeare, engaged him for five years at £300 a year as the Lyceum's resident dramatist. It was Irving's idea that Bateman commission a play on the subject of Charles I. This was a subject that strongly appealed to Wills, for, as his brother recalled, 'although he was curiously out of touch with modern politics, he was very strongly imbued … with the old-fashioned Tory faith and the feelings of the Cavalier'; he was also a monarchist.[27] The impact of *Charles the First* put Irving at the forefront of actors and Wills at the forefront of dramatists. Freeman Wills recalled:

> For the time being, he stood foremost among contemporary dramatists. Thousands who saw *Charles I* carried away the printed edition sold at the theatre doors to study in private; passages from it were recited by high and low, in drawing rooms and workmen's clubs; and hardly ever did a simple play do so much to make its author celebrated.[28]

Despite his fame, Wills shunned publicity, hardly ever going to first nights. 'He greatly disliked personal publicity, and one rule that he was inflexible in observing was never to appear before the curtain.' He was acutely sensitive to criticism and took to not reading hostile notices: 'The disadvantage of this was that he deprived himself of the wholesome lessons to be learned from it.'[29] Commissions poured in but they were not all effectively executed: 'He was impatient of much of the dramatic work he was commissioned to do, and when this was the case, he did it badly, selling his name and not his talents. It was when writing for worthy interpreters that his genius awakened.'[30]

It is clear that many of Wills's best plays reflected his own experiences and character. He responded directly to stories involving happy families and maternal love. Dutton Cook noted of his *Medea in Corinth*: 'unusual stress is laid upon Medea's maternal love, and her children are permitted to figure more prominently than heretofore upon the scene.'[31] He responded directly to the family scenes in *Olivia* and the dramatisation of a clerical family that falls on hard times directly echoed his own childhood experiences. The focus of *Charles the First* was the King as family man, loving husband and father. All this chimed precisely with the Victorian celebration of the family, domesticity, hearth and home, as a central element in their world view.

The pathos which was the keynote of his work was a feature of the man himself. He wrote the last act of *Charles the First* at one sitting; his landlady found him bathed in tears as he was doing so. His parents were apparently given to weeping when reading emotional passages. Freeman Wills says:

> The son, in writing, was always moved to tears by pathetic passages … No writer ever caused so many tears in others; and, for the same reason, his own flowed – because the pathos of his plays came straight from his heart. He did not … resent being thus moved; for he has told me that it was the test of truth to nature when your composition drew tears.[32]

He lived in conditions of chaos and increasing squalor, surrounded by cats and a monkey. He worked on his plays from 5 a.m. to noon and then painted until dusk.

Wills smoked his pipe continuously throughout. He hated revising and rewriting: 'his best work was done at the first intention, and with great rapidity; but his most slovenly work would also pass without revision'.[33] The habit no doubt explains why some of his commissions remained unproduced. He wrote *Icenia* for Mary Anderson. It centred on the love between a Roman general and a captive British princess, a relative of Boadicea. It was not produced, says Freeman Wills, because Mary Anderson married and retired from the stage. Mary Anderson recalled that the first acts were very good but the '*dénouement* being commonplace, this was abandoned'. She also abandoned his scenario *The Young Cleopatra* – 'not one of his happier efforts.'[34] He had no practical knowledge of the stage, put in few stage directions and was mainly concerned with a poetic vision: 'he disliked realism, and saw everything through a veil of poetry'. His method of work was not conducive to dramatic structure. He wrote on scraps of paper and on the backs of envelopes, began plays in the middle and wrote the first act at the end. He liked to compose his plays to music and had a music box continuously playing *Trovatore* and *Lucia*. He took to writing in bed, spending so much time there, avoiding both exercise and fresh air, that his health was eventually undermined. He then began dictating his plays to a secretary. He also composed in the bath, in South Kensington Museum and on Brighton Pier. He collaborated from time to time with other, more experienced figures who provided narrative structure, while he furnished the poetic dialogue: Henry Herman (*Claudian*), who insisted he rewrite and rewrite until they got it right, Percy Fitzgerald (*Vanderdecken*) and Sydney Grundy (*The Pompadour*). He had to be pressed to take on and finish projects, and would turn aside from his writing to paint. Allegedly the final scene of *Sappho* was produced only on the day the play was due to open.[35]

For the Lyceum and 'Colonel' Bateman he wrote *Eugene Aram* and *Vanderdecken*. The arrangement with the Lyceum ended with the end of the Bateman management. But although Irving did not retain him as resident dramatist, he commissioned five new dramas from him (*Rienzi, Iolanthe, Don Quixote, King Arthur* and *Faust*), only two of which Irving actually produced in their original form, *Iolanthe* and *Faust*. Wills had a succession of romantic attachments to women, none of which came to anything. Ellen Terry recalled in her autobiography:

> I had known Wills through the Forbes-Robertsons. He was at one time engaged to one of the girls, but it was a good thing it ended in smoke. With all his charm, Wills was not cut out for a husband. He was Irish all over – the strangest mixture of the aristocrat and the sloven. He could eat a large raw onion every night like any peasant, yet his ideas were

magnificent and instinct with refinement. A true Bohemian in money matters, he made a great deal out of his plays – and never had a farthing to bless himself with. In the theatre he was charming – from an actor's point of view. He interfered very little with the stage management, and did not care to sit in the stalls and criticise. But he would come quietly to me and tell me things which were most illuminating, and he paid me the compliment of weeping at the wing while I rehearsed *Olivia*.[36]

J.B. Booth the journalist reports that his success with *Charles the First* came too late: 'The girl he had long loved in silence, because of his poverty, was dead', a feeling Wills commemorated in an ode.[37] But his brother reports a series of failed romantic attachments.

> He studied the heart, and sometimes in playing on its strings drew forth feelings towards himself, which he felt when he discovered them, involved him in a difficulty. His manner of life was not of a kind which predisposes to marriage; nor did he, though he sometimes perhaps persuaded himself that he did, fall a genuine victim to love.[38]

The journalist Richard Whiteing suggested women were attracted to him 'by the sheer sense of his want of mothering rather than wifeing'.[39]

In the wake of *Charles the First*, he wrote many historical plays. In February 1874, he penned *Mary, Queen of Scots* for 'the beautiful Mrs Rousby'. But, says Freeman Wills, 'a play full of his own charming and characteristic poetry and sentiment' was ruined by Mrs Rousby, who was 'for the most part inaudible and when audible expressionless'. *Buckingham* (November 1875), written for Henry Neville, 'failed entirely to realize the complex nature of the madcap duke' and recast him as 'the dignified counterpart of *Charles I*'. *Jane Shore*, written without commission but later picked up by Wilson Barrett, was a success in the provinces and ran for a year in London. Although the critics thought it gloomy, the public was moved by the plight of the innocent and ill-used heroine. *England in the Days of Charles II*, was a Drury Lane pageant play based on Scott's *Peveril of the Peak* (September 1877). *Nell Gwynne* (1878) was more in Wills's line: 'the dialogue was sparkling, and the madcap heroine is invested with the sympathy to which, in spite of her failings, her goodness of heart entitled her.' *Sedgmoor*, although attributed to W.G. was written largely by Freemen Wills, as his brother was out of the country. He wrote *Sappho* for Geneviève Ward but no copy of it survives. His last play, *A Royal Divorce* (1891), about Napoleon and Josephine, toured the provinces for years and inspired the immortal line 'not tonight, Josephine', though most of the script was rewritten and Wills's contribution much reduced.[40]

Freeman says 'One of Willie Wills' great fortes was adaptation. He could rapidly extract the pith from a novel, grasping the main facts and all that was essential, arranging the perspective and preserving the characteristics.'[41] So *Cora* and *Camille* were adapted from the French. *Ellen*, although it contained much of his best writing, failed because eclipsed by *Olivia* and by having a flawed heroine. He wrote *Jane Eyre* for Mrs Bernard Beere in 1882 and *Clarissa*, based on *Clarissa Harlowe*, for Isabel Bateman in 1888. *Olivia*, based on Oliver Goldsmith's *The Vicar of Wakefield*, was perhaps his greatest success in adaptation. He was not partial to one-act plays but did several, *Iolanthe* for Irving and Terry, *Elizabeth* dealing with the death of Elizabeth I intended for Terry and never played, and *Gringoire*, adapted from Theodore de Banville's play.

Wills's idealisation of women and creation of the Victorian archetype of womanly women is what made his plays so appealing to Victorian sensibilities. Many of them were about women and contained strong roles for actresses: *Mary, Queen of Scots, Medea, Olivia, Nell Gwynne, Jane Shore, Sappho, Cora, Camille, Juana, Iolanthe, Pompadour* and *Jane Eyre*. It is significant that the bulk of his plays with male characters were written or intended for Irving (*Charles the First, Eugene Aram, Vanderdecken, Rienzi, Don Quixote, King Arthur* and *Faust*). Several of his plays were written with happy and unhappy endings (*Jane Shore, Ninon* and *Clarissa*); Victorian audiences invariably preferred the happy ending. Freeman Wills writes of *Ninon*, 'as in the case of *Jane Shore*, the happy ending meant success and the tragic a great falling off in the receipts'.[42] This practice of trying out different endings prefigures the established Hollywood practice of shooting alternative endings to films, with audiences invariably preferring the happy one.

The death of his beloved mother on 3 April 1887, broke Wills's heart. He had dedicated the published version of *Charles the First* to his mother as a token of the 'deepest love, admiration and respect'. He lost all motivation, aged rapidly and his health gave way. He earned only £200 in 1891 and died virtually penniless on 13 December that year. J.B. Booth, who remembered seeing him when a boy, recalled him as 'an excessively untidy old gentleman with an unkempt beard, and an obvious wig', but said 'Everyone I met who had known him spoke of him with affection and a kindly remembering smile. "Poor Willie Wills" seems the invariable epitaph.'[43]

James F. Stottlar considers that Wills was a significant figure in rehabilitating the classics, leading to long runs: *Charles the First* (180 nights), *Jane Shore* (278) and *Olivia* (131 and 135 nights). Stottlar attributed their success to a change in the composition of audiences in the 1860s and 1870s and the rise of a middle-class social tone. *Olivia* moderates the villainy of the squire, eliminates boisterous rough and tumble, has no spectacle or sensation, crowd scenes or mechanical effects. *Charles the First* and *Eugene Aram* are eventless; *Jane Eyre* notably quiet. In Wills's plays, domesticity, with wives and children prominent, and strong sentiment all appealed. Wills was hired by the Kendals to revise Douglas Jerrold's rumbustious nautical melodrama *Black Ey'd Susan* to suit late Victorian tastes. Wills opted to retain the third act but to write two completely new acts to go before it. Wills eliminated the drinking and swearing, removed all the low comedy characters and the physical action, stressed the early happy domesticity, and refined and sentimentalized it.[44]

William Archer applied his critical scalpel to Wills in *English Dramatists of Today* (1882):

> His is one of those self-contradictory talents which seem made for definition in rhymed paradoxes. He is so strong and so weak, so manly and so puerile, so poetic and so common-place, so careful and so slovenly, that one hesitates whether to regard him as the greatest or the worst of modern dramatists. In truth, he is neither. He is a man of poetic and artistic temperament, with occasional moments of dramatic inspiration. Unfortunately he does not always wait for these moments to take up his pen and, when he writes without inspiration, his deficient taste and lack of genuine dramatic instinct betray him into deplorable solecism.

He lists his defects – 'his lack of firm taste, his lack of moral force and purpose. His greatest possible defect is that he is a writer of dramatic scenes, not an inventor or constructor of dramas'. Archer declared *Charles the First* to be his finest work, despite its calumny on Cromwell: 'it will probably live as long as any poetic play of this century.' Of his other plays for Irving, *Eugene Aram* 'consists of a good first act, an excellent second act and a very feeble third act'. Of *Olivia*, it 'has been praised much above its deserts. It contains some beautiful touches, but also several errors of taste and the last two acts … are extremely faulty.' With *Medea in Corinth*, he thought 'Wills narrowly escaped producing a great play … it deals with a genuinely tragic theme, and … deals with it in a really able fashion'. Of his rewrite of *Black Ey'd Susan* called *William and Susan*, he said: 'He refined both the humour and the pathos of the older play, and gave it a touch of delicate and fanciful poetry. The honest sentiment and homeliness remained with an added grace and charm. This is the style of work in which Mr Wills excels.' But Archer gave short shrift to the rest of his output: *Hinko*, 'a heavy German melodrama of the most old-fashioned type'; *Jane Shore* 'was rendered a great success by means of a snow-scene but was a tedious and inartistic play'; *England in the Days of Charles II* 'was, and deserved to be, an enormous fiasco, only equalled in this respect by the lugubriously poetic *Ellen*'; *Sedgmoor* was 'a bad play on a good subject'. In the event, none of Wills' plays has survived in the repertoire, the result perhaps of their being geared to a specific Victorian sensibility which post-Victorian audiences have rejected.[45]

Two criticisms levelled against Irving are that he did nothing to encourage contemporary British playwrights and that he underpaid his writers. Both criticisms need to be qualified. The idea that he did nothing to encourage contemporary playwrights is refuted by his business manager Bram Stoker, who recorded:

Irving was always anxious for good plays, and spared neither trouble nor expense to get them. Every play that was sent was read; very many commissions were given and purchase-money or advance fees paid. In such cases, subjects were often suggested, scenario [a detailed outline] being the basis.[46]

He purchased or paid fees for twenty-seven plays none of which was eventually produced. He laid out £9000 on unproduced plays. Among them Stoker listed: *Rienzi, Mephisto, King Arthur, Don Quixote* by W.G. Wills, *Robert Emmet* by Frank Marshall, *Schuldig* by Richard Voss, *George Washington* and *Don Quixote* by J.I.C. Clarke, *The Vestal* by Fergus Hume, *The End of the Hunting* by Penrhyn Stanlaws, *The Jester King* by H.T. Johnson, *Saviolo* by Egerton Castle and Walter Pollock, *Jekyll and Hyde* by O. Booth and J. Dixon, *The Professor's Love Story* by J.M. Barrie, *The Isle of St. Tropez* and *The Count* by F.C. Burnand, *The Balance of Comfort* by H. Guy Carleton and *The Bloody Marriage* by Ludwig Fulda (adapted as *Charles IX* by W.L. Courtney). In addition to these Irving 'made efforts regarding plays by other authors,' including Mrs F.A. Steel, K. and Hesketh Prichard, Marion Crawford, Conan Doyle, Henry Arthur Jones, W.L. Courtney, Miss Mary Wilkins, and Robert Barr. Several of these were for dramatisations of novels. Irving always hoped that Arthur W. Pinero, who had begun his career as an actor in Irving's company and whom Irving regarded as 'a great intellectual force', would produce a vehicle for him, but Pinero was never able to come up with a subject suited to Irving. There was no shortage of authors anxious to submit plays to the Lyceum. They came, says Stoker, not only from professional playwrights but from 'historians, lyric poets, divines from the curate to the bishop ... professional men, merchants, manufacturers, traders, clerks ... domestic servants, and from as far down the social scale as a workhouse boy'.[47]

Irving had no compunction about turning down offerings from even the most eminent names. He rejected Oscar Wilde's *The Duchess of Padua*, Conan Doyle's *The House of Temperley*, Bernard Shaw's *The Man of Destiny* and Anthony Hope's *Nell Gwyn*. Reasons for not proceeding even with commissioned projects varied. He rejected *The House of Temperley*, a Regency boxing drama, because he thought it unseemly to put prize fights on the stage.[48] In the case of J.M. Barrie's *The Professor's Love Story*, he liked it very much but concluded that the leading role was not within his range. Nevertheless he took it upon himself to try to persuade two other leading actors, J.L. Toole and John Hare, to do it. Neither of them felt it was within their range either. But E.S. Willard took it on and 'made with it both a hit and a fortune'. Stoker agreed with Irving's judgement: 'The play is an excellent one, but wants to be exactly fitted. Irving was naturally too strong for it.'[49] (We get a particularly well-informed insight into Irving's dealing with plays and playwrights from the reminiscences of Bram Stoker, who was privy to many of Irving's plans and discussions.)

Even when he had purchased a play, Irving would often sit on it for years, while thinking about how best to produce it. In 1882 Irving purchased outright the acting rights to Herman Merivale's *Edgar and Lucy*, a new dramatisation of Sir Walter Scott's novel *The Bride of Lammermoor*. He did not produce it for eight years. Stoker recorded:

> For seven years after Irving had possession of Merivale's play he had thought it over. He had in his own quiet way made up his mind about it, arranging length and way of doing the play and excogitating his own part till he had possession of it in every way.

Then on 25 November 1889, he read the play out to Stoker and his stage manager Loveday. Stoker recorded in his diary: 'It was delightful. Play very fine. Literature noble. H.I. had cut quite one-half.' The play was presented under the title *Ravenswood* on 20 September 1890, and ran for 102 performances. But business collapsed after the failure of Baring's Bank. It was hastily replaced by the more cheerful *Much Ado About Nothing* and business at once picked up. A play which Stoker describes as 'lugubrious' was clearly not appropriate for the times. It had also put a great strain on Ellen Terry, who could only play it in the evenings with no matinees because of the physical and emotional demands of the role.[50]

When it came to commissioning plays, Irving remained wedded to the idea that the poetic drama was the mainstay of the legitimate theatre. His choice of play themes was strongly dictated by the Romantic sensibility and the now traditional themes of the school. Seeking a new play from Tennyson during the 1880s, Irving suggested to him the ideas of Enoch Arden, Dante, King Arthur, and Robin Hood. Tennyson, having considered them, rejected both Enoch Arden and King Arthur as he had already written poems on the subjects, and of Dante, replying: 'A fine subject! But where is the Dante to write it'. Irving then plied Tennyson with books and plays about Robin Hood. 'He had hopes that the romantic side of the outlaw's life would touch the poet.' Tennyson did eventually produce a Robin Hood play, *The Foresters*, but Irving rejected it, complaining to Tennyson that it was not in tune with the mood of the public ('public taste is, I fear, in a very "sensational" condition'). It was produced with great success in America in 1892 by Augustin Daly. But Daly's London production ran for only two weeks before closing. Peter Thomson characterized the play as an 'unresolved mixture of pastoral romance, domestic melodrama, light opera and heroic legend' which 'dithers between prose and verse.'

The American critic William Winter, reviewing the American production of the play, while hailing Tennyson as the greatest poet since Byron and rhapsodising about the performance of Ada Rehan as Maid Marian, nevertheless conceded:

> *Robin Hood*, as technical drama, is frail ... it contains no single scene in which its persons can amply put forth their full histrionic powers with essentially positive dramatic effect. Its charm resides more in being than in doing, and therefore it is more a poem than a play ... It is not one of those works that arouse, agitate, and impel.[51]

Irving rarely abandoned a theme, once he had set his heart on it and indeed Dante became the subject of his last new play, staged in London in 1903 in a commission from the ever-reliable Sardou. The first suggestion was made in 1894, and there was extensive correspondence between Irving and Sardou over the next seven years before a scenario was produced in 1901. Initially minded to reject it, Irving changed his mind and commissioned the play, which was delivered and translated into English by Laurence Irving. Nor did he give up on King Arthur. Having failed with Tennyson, he commissioned a King Arthur play from W.G. Wills. He purchased it from him in 1890 but 'he did not think it would act well', and in 1893 asked Comyns Carr to revise it. Instead, Carr wrote his own new King Arthur play, which Irving duly staged on 12 January 1894. It ran in Britain and America for 191 performances.[52]

Another cherished project was Don Quixote. He suggested the subject to Wills, who duly produced a play. Irving purchased the entire rights from him in 1888. He worked on it himself but remained dissatisfied with it. Chance Newton recalled:

> Among the unproduced plays which Irving frequently talked over with me were three of Wills's namely *King Arthur*, *Don Quixote* and *Rienzi*. The last-named always seemed to me a fine play. *King Arthur* wasn't ... *Don Quixote*, originally in five acts, always seemed to worry Irving. Knowing that I was a fellow-enthusiast concerning Quixote, Irving talked this play over with me again and again, eventually shortening it from time to time.

When Irving reduced Wills's play to one act, carved out of the first of his five acts, and put it on in 1895, Chance Newton concluded: 'it proved a failure although Irving was a highly realistic Don'.[53] So he commissioned another Don Quixote play from J.I.C. Clarke, the American journalist and playwright. Clarke recalled its genesis in his memoirs. He had become a friend of Irving on his American visits. 'The seed of Irving's praise, at one of our meetings, of Don Quixote as a character for a play and his desire to play in it had been stirring within me.' He prepared a scenario, which Irving accepted, and he began work on the play, writing for two hours every morning before setting off for his full-time job as a newspaper managing editor. 'It grew rapidly, ending with the death of the Don. It depicted him as a wholly noble, idealistic madman, pathetic in his state as in his fate, and offset, as Cervantes intended, by rough, hardy, everyday commonsense in his burly squire, Sancho Panza.' Irving read it, told him 'how fine the lines were, how the characters stood out, but the personality of the dear old Don himself was so lifting, so lovable and amusing'. Irving told him Wills's version was 'rubbish'.[54] He purchased Clarke's play in 1894 for £500 ($2500).[55] On 14 July 1894, Clarke wrote to Irving:

I do love and reverence my gentle Knight of La Mancha, and I do hope and trust in his early deliverance from the dusk of the library and I pray for his emergence into that mystic sunlight which comes from below, and literally lights up nobility on the stage. I often cheer myself picturing you bringing out the charm and inspiration of the immortal character that the great Spaniard limned for us. May my dream be realized.[56]

Although Irving had the text printed by the Chiswick Press in 1895, it was not produced. On 26 March 1895, Clarke wrote to Irving to say he had received the bad news that Irving was doing a one act version of Wills's drama, which would effectively kill any chance of him producing Clarke's version. He offered to pay back the fee in return for the rights to the play. 'You know, dear Mr Irving, that the entire attraction for me was your production of the play. The money was a small matter in my eyes.' On 19 July 1895, Clarke confirmed that he had received the rights back but did not propose to offer them to anyone until he had discussed it on Irving's next visit to America, in case there was a chance of Irving still doing it.[57] Stoker explained that the one-acter had been 'a mere *ballon d'essai* sent up to see if they would take to the character'. But Irving said, 'Huh, they did not care for it', and that was the end of Clarke's *Quixote*.[58] Stoker recalled: 'There were some very fine points in this new play, especially in illustrating the gravity of the Don's high character and his deep understanding of a noble act.' He believed that the problem with both plays lay with the central character: 'The character was too simple and too fixed for the necessary variety and development of character in a long grave play.'[59] For a while Irving held the English rights to Edmond Rostand's *Cyrano de Bergerac*, another of those quixotic romantic characters that so appealed to him, but he never produced it and sold on the rights to Ellen Terry in 1898 for £500, which presumably represented his original investment.[60]

It was very rare that a play reached the stage unaltered. Tennyson's *The Cup* did with only minor alterations; and so did Conan Doyle's *A Story of Waterloo*. Stoker recalls: 'Irving fell in love with the character and began to study it right away.' He asked Doyle 'to consolidate the matter of the first few pages into a shorter space. The rest of the manuscript remained exactly as written.' It premiered in Bristol on 21 September 1894, in a double bill with *The Bells*, and was an instant success. Irving eventually played it 345 times in all in Britain and America. Stoker considered it 'as an acting play ... perfect; and Irving's playing in it the high-water mark of histrionic art'.[61] But in the case of other plays, he often suggested the themes, individual scenes and bits of business. Roles were written specifically for him, the plays built around his known strengths. The writing of the plays was often a collaborative process, much like the writing of modern film scripts, something which involved endless story conferences. This was a procedure that was anathema to the proponents of 'writer's theatre'.

Irving's own input into the play was crucial. He rarely played the texts as they stood, whether they were Shakespeare or melodramas. Even when the texts had been thoroughly revised, they continued to evolve during performances, with bits of text added or taken away. Irving prepared his own acting versions of Shakespeare, having them privately printed and distributed among the cast. When reviving old plays he had them thoroughly revised. Charles Reade revised his text of *The Courier of Lyons*, and it was renamed *The Lyons Mail*. Frank Marshall revised and partially rewrote Byron's *Werner*. Walter Herries Pollock revised *The Dead Heart* and Joseph Comyns Carr translated and adapted Victorien Sardou's *Madame Sans-Gêne* – but this was always done under Irving's direction and with his active participation. Even when he had Pollock revise *The Dead Heart*, Irving further amended it himself, writing to Ellen Terry:

> It's tiresome stuff to read because it depends so much on situations. I have been touching the book up though, and improved it here and there, I think … I shall send you another book soon to put any of your alterations and additions in. I've added a lot of little things with a few lines for you – very good, I think, though I say so as shouldn't – I know you'll laugh. They are perhaps not startlingly original, but better than the original, anyhow. Here they are – last act:
>
> 'Ah, Robert, Pity me. By the recollections of our youth, I implore you save my boy!' (*Now* for 'em)
>
> 'If my voice recalls a tone that ever fell sweetly upon your ear, have pity on me! If the past is not a blank, if you once loved me, have pity on me!' (Bravo!)
>
> Now I call that very good and if the 'If' and the 'pitys' don't bring the house down, well it's a pity.[62]

These are the words of a man who knew precisely how to manipulate the emotions of his audience to create the right theatrical effect.

Sometimes, however, even a rewritten version was judged unplayable. Walter Herries Pollock was commissioned by Irving to revise *Pauline*, a French-derived melodrama in which Charles Kean had achieved success at the Princess's Theatre. Pollock wanted to humanize the villain as part of his modernisation of the text. Irving refused, saying: 'He must be an out-and-outer'. Pollock recorded:

> In this he certainly showed the judgement which so seldom failed him. He showed it yet more in completely shelving the play. For an English version, unless it had gone right away from the original, keeping only the central idea, common enough in fiction and drama, of a secret villain and bandit who, to the world and even to his wife, seemed to be a wealthy man of birth, breeding and charm, could not possibly have appealed to the audiences whose taste had been nurtured by Irving's care and education.[63]

In 1996, the London solicitors Langton and Passmore were clearing out their cellars and discovered a long-forgotten deed box which had belonged to H.B. Irving, the actor son of Sir Henry, who had died in 1919. Eventually this deed box was returned to John H.B. Irving, H.B.'s grandson. The deed box proved to contain letters, memoranda and agreements throwing important new light on Sir Henry Irving's dealings with playwrights and composers.

The documents confirm the process by which scripts were developed as a result of script conferences between Irving and the writers, and continuing rewrites until a final script approved by Irving emerged. A dozen letters, covering the period June 1897 to June 1898, from H.D. Traill and Robert Hichens, reveal a process of plot development, amendments, cuts, explications of character and motivation, characterising the writing of the play that eventually came to be called *The Medicine Man*. The play was originally called *Doctor Elton* after its leading figure, but he was renamed Dr Tregenna at the direct suggestion of Irving. This is, intriguingly, a name which recalls Irving's Cornish boyhood and echoes the name of his Cornish mother, Mary Behenna.[64]

A further series of six letters, covering the period September 1896 to September 1897, from J.I.C. Clarke to Stoker and Irving, reveal the development of a commissioned play, *George Washington*. It was to cover the major events of the Revolutionary War, with plot themes involving star-crossed lovers and the activities of a traitor Llewellyn (partially based on Benedict Arnold). We learn that Irving had specified that the play should begin with a scene at Mount Vernon to show aspects of Washington's domestic life, thus humanising the great man. Irving had complained that he was not being given enough to do. The letters detail cuts, developments and rewrites. Clarke indicates a willingness to carry out whatever Irving wants and asks for more specific instructions. Eventually he announces that he has written an entirely new third act. This active involvement by Irving was a feature of his career from the start of his management.[65]

The story of *Robert Emmett* is in many ways typical. It had often been suggested to Irving when he was in Ireland that he should play Robert Emmet (not Emmett). 'He bore a striking resemblance to the Irish patriot … and his story was full of tragic romance.'[66] Emmet had been executed in Dublin in 1803, aged twenty-five, after leading an unsuccessful uprising against the English. Young, idealistic, romantic and gentlemanly, he became an icon of Irish nationalism.[67] The play is called *Robert Emmett* throughout Stoker's account of its genesis. In 1878, the first year of his management, Irving suggested the subject to the dramatist Frank Marshall. 'He was delighted with the idea, became full of it, and took the work in hand. In the shape of a scenario it was so far advanced that at the end of the second season, Irving could announce it as one of the forthcoming plays.' The success of *The Merchant of Venice* postponed the production for another year. Marshall adopted a more leisurely pace in his writing. In the autumn of 1881 a version was ready but the production of *Romeo and Juliet* meant that it was again postponed until 1882. By then an upsurge of Fenianism caused the censors to intervene:

> The government of the day considered that so marked and romantic a character as Robert Emmett, and with such political views portrayed so forcibly and so picturesquely as would be the case with Irving, might have a dangerous effect on a people seething in revolt.

At the request of the Lord Chamberlain, Irving abandoned plans to produce it.

The play had evolved over those years as a result of a series of meetings between Marshall, Irving and Stoker, himself of course Irish. Each scene was sent in by Marshall as it was written and revised in the light of lengthy discussions by the trio. At one point in the play, Irving wanted the writer to convey a sense of fear and surprise in his characters when faced by the fury of a mob. So, waiting until Marshall was not looking, he hurled half a dozen wine glasses at the door, causing Marshall almost to collapse with shock. Irving declared to the fainting Marshall:

> You are in a rare position now, my dear Marshall, of the dramatist who can write of high emotion from experience. The audience are bound to recognize the sincerity of your work. Just write your scene up to that effect. Let the audience feel even an indication of the surprise and fear that you have just felt yourself, and your play will be a success.[68]

Chance Newton liked the play: 'Marshall had written some really beautiful scenes around the Irish patriot, Emmett', though he added, 'but somehow Irving could never get the play to "shape" to his liking'. That, plus the censors' intervention, led Irving to hand the play over to Dion Boucicault, who rewrote it and produced it in America in November 1884, starring in it himself. The production failed, though more due to the chaotic nature of the production than the quality of the script, as Boucicault reported to Irving, and the fact that the play's opening coincided with a presidential election.[69]

The process by which 'Willie' Wills' plays reached the stage was recalled by playwright and journalist Percy Fitzgerald. He confirmed the importance of the input initially of both 'Colonel' Bateman and Irving. Of Wills's greatest success, *Charles the First*, Fitzgerald recalled:

> There are many stories current as to the progress of the manufacture of this piece, Wills carrying in whole sheafs of blank verse. None of which was found satisfactory or dramatic. The old 'Colonel' and the actor, however, used their pruning knives freely, and by consultation the play was at last fashioned into proper shape.[70]

The 'Colonel' famously complained that in early drafts there was too much politics. He suggested more concentration on the domestic scene, recommending that Wills model his last act on the farewell scene in the popular old tear-jerker *Black-Ey'd Susan*. Wills's *Faust* had enormous success but was written in the theatre 'under strict and sagacious direction', this time by Irving alone.[71] The critic William Winter revealed a similar process at work in *Eugene Aram*: 'In the construction of the piece Henry Irving made many material suggestions. The treatment of the character of Aram was devised by him, and the management of the close of the second act denotes his felicity of invention.'[72]

Percy Fitzgerald was directly involved with W.G. Wills in the writing of Irving's Flying Dutchman play *Vanderdecken*:

> Irving was much attracted by the subject, and induced the old 'Colonel' to give us both a commission to undertake the work. On such occasions Wills gave way to his full enthusiasm. I see him now in council, pouring out all kinds of suggestions, each of which was 'to fetch 'em', 'bring down the house' etc. We contrived a scenario, but it did not give satisfaction, and the whole plan was laid aside. After a time it was entrusted to Wills alone, to be once more laid aside. After the 'Colonel's' death it was once more taken up and entrusted to myself, it was again put aside, and finally taken up to be given to Wills and myself once more ... I wrote the whole of the first act, and a portion of the second; Wills, and another concealed hand, the rest ... After many delays and changes, the aid of other 'hands' and collaborators was invited, and at last ... the piece was produced.[73]

One of these unnamed collaborators was Bram Stoker, who recalled that, the day after he arrived in London to take up his post as Irving's business manager, he saw him in the opening night of *Vanderdecken*:

> Irving was fine in it, and gave one a wonderful impression of a dead man fictitiously alive ... But the play itself wanted something. The last act, in which Thekla sails away with the phantom lover whose soul has been released by her unselfish love, was impossible of realisation by the resources of stage art of the time. Nowadays, with calcium lights and coloured 'mediums' and electricity, and all the aids to illusion which Irving had himself created or brought into use, much could be done. For such acting the play ought to have been a great one; but it fell short of excellence. It was a great pity; for Irving's appearance and acting in it were of memorable perfection. On the next day, Sunday, I spent hours with Irving in his rooms in Grafton Street, helping him cut and alter the play. We did a good deal of work on it and altered it considerably for the better I thought. The next morning I breakfasted with him in his rooms; and, after another long spell of work, on the play, I went with him to the Lyceum to attend rehearsal of the altered business. That even I attended the Lyceum again and thought the play had been improved. So had Irving too, so far as was possible to a performance already so complete. I supped with him at the Devonshire Club, where we talked over the play and continued the conversation at his own rooms till after five o'clock in the morning.[74]

Irving was fascinated by the subject and according to Fitzgerald: 'himself furnished some effective situations, notably the strange and original suggestion of the Dutchman's being cast up on the shore and restored to life by the waves', and the Dutchman's first appearance, standing beside the sailors who are unconscious of his presence. The play failed in its first manifestation because, according to Fitzgerald, audiences found it 'too sombre', there was an 'unusual sultry spell of summer weather' which clearly affected box office takings, and Mrs Bateman had economized on some of the effects – the unveiling of the picture upon which much dramatic effect hung revealed 'a sort of grotesque daub' which provoked titters in the audience. But Irving 'never lost faith in the subject' and a couple of years later encouraged Fitzgerald to try again, added to which 'Miss Terry has always been eager to attempt the heroine, in which she was confident of producing a deep impression'. But no playable new version came from Fitzgerald.[75]

Stoker also believed in the subject and recalled: 'I ... always wanted him to try it again ... The character, as Irving created it, was there fit for any setting, and so long as the play should be fairly sufficient the result ought to be good.'[76] It became one of the subjects Irving discussed with the Manx novelist Hall Caine. A friendship developed between Irving and Caine following a meeting in 1874. Stoker too became a friend, dedicating *Dracula* to Hall Caine under his childhood nickname 'Hommy Beg'. Stoker was well placed to observe the friendship between the two men. He recorded:

> Caine seemed to intuitively understand not only Irving's work, but his aim and method. Irving felt this and had a high opinion of Caine's powers ... The two men were very much alike in certain intellectual ways. To both was given an almost abnormal faculty of self-abstraction and of concentrating all their powers on a given subject for any length of time. To both was illimitable patience in the doing of their work, and in yet another way their powers were similar: a faculty of getting up and ultimately applying to the work in hand an amazing amount of information.

Irving saw the dramatic possibilities in Hall Caine's novel *The Deemster* (1887), but Wilson Barrett acquired the rights first and turned it into a stage success. 'From that time on, Irving had a strong desire that Caine should write some play that he could act.'[77]

Irving had long wanted to act the part of Mahomet. The publication in France of a play on the subject by De Bornier stimulated him to implement this interest. Finding the De Bornier play unsuitable for his purpose, he asked Hall Caine to write him a Mahomet play. Caine established a scenario by 1890. Irving was pleased with it and it was developed into a full play, entitled *The Prophet*, only to be vetoed by the Lord Chamberlain on the grounds of likely offence to the Moslem subjects of the Empire, who believed it was sacrilege to depict images of the Prophet. Caine refused to accept a fee from Irving for his work and promptly turned the play into a novella. In 1892 Irving pressed him to tackle the subject of the Flying Dutchman. Instead, Caine adapted his poem *The Demon Lover* into a scenario which he submitted to Irving in 1895. Irving was impressed by it but thought the leading role too young for him and asked him again to tackle the

Flying Dutchman. In 1896 Caine produced a scenario. Irving asked him to make the character more sympathetic and less brutal at the start. But no play emerged. Caine offered Irving his new play *Home, Sweet Home*, but Irving concluded that the leading character was too young for him in the first act, too rough in the second and too tall in the third act. ('There is no general sympathy on the stage for tall, old men.') So Caine never succeeded in producing a play for Irving.[78]

Hall Caine gave his own version of his attempts to provide a vehicle for Irving in his autobiography:

> During many years thereafter I spent time and energy and some imagination in an effort to fit Irving with a part, and the pigeonholes of my study are still heavy with sketches and drafts and scenarios of dramas which either he or I or our constant friend and colleague Bram Stoker ... thought possible for the Lyceum Theatre. I remember that most of our subjects dealt with the supernatural, and that 'The Wandering Jew', 'The Flying Dutchman', and 'The Demon Lover' were themes around which our imagination constantly revolved. But in spite of the utmost sincerity on all sides our efforts came to nothing, and I think this result was perhaps due to something more serious than the limitations of my own powers.

He thought that the problem lay with Irving.

> The truth is that, great actor as Irving was, the dominating element of his personality was for many years a hampering difficulty. When in my boyhood I knew him first, he was about thirty, very bright, very joyous, not very studious, not very intellectual, full of animal vigour, never resting, never pausing, always rushing about and hardly ever seen to go upstairs at less than three steps at a time. At the end of his life he was a grave and rather sad old man, very solemn, distinctly intellectual, and with a never-failing sense of personal dignity. Between his earlier and his later days he had done something which I have never known to be done by anybody else – he had created a character and assumed it for himself ... It was a character of singular nobility and distinction, but a difficult character too, not easy to put on, and having little in common with the outstanding traits of his original self – a silent, reposeful, rather subtle, slightly humorous, detached and almost isolated personality, with a sharp tongue but a sunny smile and certain gleams of the deepest tenderness – in short, a compound of Voltaire and Cardinal Manning.

This, he believed, stood in the way of Irving sinking his own individuality into a stage role. No man could sink a personality like that of Henry Irving, and, towards the end of his life, with the ever-increasing domination of his own character and the limitation of choice which always comes with advancing years, it was only possible for him to play parts that contained something of himself. He was painfully conscious of this for a considerable time.[79]

In an interview he gave shortly before embarking on his farewell provincial tour, Irving recalled that many years before, Charles Dickens the Younger, journalist son of the novelist, had brought him a scenario based on his father's novel *Dombey and Son*: 'We worked together upon it. The thing came to nothing but I recall one scene in particular, not in the book, which we rather prided ourselves upon. It was in the days when the advent of the first hansom cab upon the stage caused an extraordinary sensation.' The plan was for a scene to be set in a hall in Dombey's house with large central doors; the doors would be flung open to admit a brougham carrying Dombey and his new wife, Edith. 'Here, you see, we trusted to impress the spectator, not so much by a dramatic situation but by a novel spectacular effect.'[80]

When Irving decided he wanted to do a Robespierre play, he contacted Sardou in 1896 to provide it and, after a scenario was submitted and approved, the completed play was submitted in 1898, translated into English by Laurence Irving and produced on 15 April 1899. Irving not only suggested the subject but even suggested a scene based on something he had read – Robespierre in his lodgings 'shaving himself whilst listening to a matter of life and death for many people and all the time turning to spit.'[81]

A question has been raised about Irving's lack of generosity when it came to paying for plays. The distinctive profession of playwright did not really emerge until the 1890s. The nineteenth century was an actors' theatre – and the rapid turnover of plays, the low status of theatre and the lack of copyright protection combined to keep the playwright down. It was possible for a playwright to earn a living from the theatre in the 1830s but not in the 1840s and 1850s when the conditions of work in the theatre reflected the depressed economic state of the nation. Money was to be made writing novels. So Bulwer Lytton, one of the most successful playwrights of the 1830s, gave up the stage to write novels. The situation improved in the 1870s and 1880s with the rise in the status of the theatre, and a change in the payment system, pioneered by Dion Boucicault, by which writers got a share in the profits from the run of the play rather than an outright payment for the play. Long runs could make a fortune for writers, and Pinero, Wilde and Henry Arthur Jones made an excellent living from their plays in the 1890s.

The trend in the 1880s and the norm in the 1890s for playwrights, was profit-sharing. John Russell Stephens suggests that Irving held out against profit-sharing for more than twenty years, clinging to the outdated system of the outright purchase of all rights or much later a fixed royalty. He concludes that Irving was either an atavist or a skinflint, quoting Henry Arthur Jones, who had had dealings with Irving, that his priority was 'cheap plays' and that he 'would probably have grudged a thousand pounds to an English author as an extravagance'. This latter comment may be a specifically chauvinistic remark directed at Irving's very generous settlements with Victorien Sardou, far and away the best paid of Irving's authors. But then, as the fees he paid Sir Arthur Sullivan, nearly double what other composers got, suggest, he would pay over his usual rates for those he considered the best.[82]

The picture is not quite as clear-cut as this. The playwright usually cited as having been exploited by Irving is the unworldly 'Willie' Wills. His brother and biographer Freeman Wills, writing in 1898, complained that although he had written thirty-two plays, he had made only £12,000 over his entire career, the sum which could be earned by a single play 'in modern times'.[83] He received royalties for *Ninon*, *William and Susan*, and *Pompadour*; and, although Wilson Barrett bought all the rights to *Jane Shore*, he still paid Wills a royalty when it was performed in London.[84] But the Irving deed box yields evidence of a rather more complex situation. In a letter to Wills, dated 2 July 1880, Stoker offered him, for the play *Rienzi*, either a royalty of £5 per performance, if the play were produced in the next five years, or £500 for complete acting rights for five years or £700 for all rights to the play. Wills, who was notoriously careless about money and was exploited by a crowd of hangers-on, settled for the largest amount immediately available. He assigned all rights to Irving for £700 in a letter to Stoker dated 19 July 1880.[85] Freeman Wills says the play was actually written in 1887 after a visit to Italy and Irving paid £800; this may represent an additional later payment, as Irving pronounced the play 'magnificent'.[86] Irving in fact never produced the play, though he had it printed up and corrected in 1894, suggesting that it was still on his agenda. The fact that he considered it playable is indicated by his assigning the rights to his son, H.B. Irving. Chance Newton thought it 'a fine play' and Freeman Wills thought it one of his brother's greatest works, 'a drama of extraordinary power and poetic beauty'.[87]

In 1891 a question about the rights of *Charles the First* arose and Wills wrote to Isabel Bateman to clarify the situation. Isabel Bateman replied on 26 February 1891 to confirm that her mother, Mrs Bateman, had purchased the rights to *Charles the First* for a ten-year period (1877–87), but that those rights had passed to Irving when he purchased the Lyceum lease and a variety of dramatic properties from Mrs Bateman in 1878. (A document in the deed box reveals that Mrs Bateman paid Wills £100 for the rights for ten years from 14 September 1877). But that period had now expired and the rights had reverted to Wills. She added: 'May I venture to counsel you *very strongly* not to part with the copyright of any of your plays.' She pointed out that she had paid Wilson Barrett £1500 in royalties over three years to play Wills's *Jane Shore*, money which would have been Wills's if he had not sold the rights outright to Barrett. She also suggested that she might be willing to take on *Charles the First* herself on a royalty basis. She had after all been Irving's original Queen Henrietta Maria, and to snatch one of his favourite properties from under Irving's nose would have been sweet revenge. The upshot of this was that Wills, ignoring her advice, wrote to Irving (2 March 1891) to say that 'of course I have been loyal to you and refused as civilly as I could to let the play to her'. Evidently Wills then offered to let Irving have the rights to *Charles the First* as a gift. Irving insisted on paying him £500 for the rights, the same sum he had paid him for *Olivia*. A memorandum dated 13 March 1891, confirms the granting of all rights in *Charles the First* to Irving for £500.[88]

This seems to confirm the story told by Wills himself to his cousin Harry Plunket Greene, the singer, and recounted by Greene in his biography of Stanford. Greene described Wills as 'the only real British Bohemian I ever knew, totally oblivious of time and money, and the lifelong prey of duns and harpies in general'. Shortly before his death, he was 'on the rocks' and Irving heard of it, asked him to lunch at the Garrick Club and said he wanted to buy complete rights to *Charles the First* for £200 and *Olivia* for £200, and that he still owed him £100 for *Faust*. None of this was true. He had already acquired complete rights in the two plays and owed no money on *Faust*. Irving said he would not pay the £500 at once, but rather at the rate of £5 a week, to prevent the bloodsuckers falling on Wills and draining him dry again. In this way he supported the playwright until his death.[89] The original rights to *Charles the First* had not covered America and Irving had had to pay Isabel Bateman £500 in 1883 to secure American rights in *Charles the First* for the duration of the existing lease of rights.[90]

Irving was willing to meet Wills's demands when made for plays he really wanted. Wills wrote on 6 December 1886 asking for £800 for writing *King Arthur*, pointing out that he had received £900 from Wilson Barrett for *Claudian*, which in part covered the demand that the script be completed in fourteen weeks. Irving gave Wills his £800, and a memorandum dated 25 October 1890 indicated that £650 of it had already been paid. In the end Irving did not use the play and in 1893 paid Joseph Comyns Carr £500 for a completely new script. The flat fee to Carr was perhaps a result of the large amount he had already paid out on the project. Irving paid Wills £600 for all rights in *Don Quixote*, but eventually only produced one of the five acts. Wills considered himself generously paid because only a few theatres wanted poetic dramas and he evidently appreciated regular large infusions of ready cash.[91]

Irving purchased in 1882 all acting rights in Herman Merivale's *Edgar and Lucy* (later renamed *Ravenswood*), paying Merivale £600. Merivale wrote to him on 21 December 1882 to say 'I wish all theatrical negotiations were as plain and straightforward as with you'. Irving did not produce it until 1890. He paid Frank Marshall £450 to write *Robert Emmett*, which he never produced. He purchased entire rights to *The Amber Heart* from Alfred Calmour in 1887 for £250.[92]

If you leave out of account W.G. Wills, who appears to have preferred payment in cash rather than by royalty, Irving seems in fact to have regularly paid a royalty earlier than Stephens implied. During the 1880s, Irving staged *Othello*, *Romeo and Juliet*, *Much Ado* and *Twelfth Night*, which were all in the public domain, and Wills's *Faust* and *Olivia* for which he had purchased rights. In addition to these he staged Boucicault's version of *The Corsican Brothers* (1880), for which he paid Mrs Charles Kean and later her heirs £20 a month.[93] He paid James Albery six guineas a performance for the 1881 revival of *Two Roses*, though this may indicate generosity to a playwright who had attained little success since the original production of the play and was perpetually hard up. Irving paid Tennyson for his two act play *The Cup* £4 per performance, netting Tennyson £508 for a run of 127 performances in 1881.[94]

Throughout the 1880s Irving was paying a royalty for performances of Charles Reade's *The Lyons Mail* which had been in his repertoire since 1877. On 6 May 1891, Charles L. Reade, the heir of the original author, wrote to ask for an accounting of the amount due for fees on *The Lyons Mail*. Stoker calculated he was owed £37 16 shillings for twelve performances, suggesting a performance royalty of around £3. He calculated that Reade had previously received £72 9 shillings on 22 June 1883 and £44 2 shillings on 24 July 1887 for the performances of the play. Reade also asked Irving to quote him a figure for buying the acting rights completely. Again, the initiative was not coming from Irving but the rights holder who wanted to sell.[95]

During the 1890s a royalty was the norm at the Lyceum. Irving produced three Shakespeare plays (*Henry VIII*, *Cymbeline* and *Coriolanus*), which required no authorial payment. He produced *Becket* (1893), for which Tennyson agreed a royalty of ten guineas per performance, its run of 112 performances netting the family £1165. Irving calculated the royalty on the basis that the production had already cost him £2000 and would probably not enjoy a long run.[96] For *Peter the Great* (1898), by his son Laurence, there was a royalty of £10 per performance, netting him £380 for the thirty-eight performances.[97] For *The Medicine Man* (1898), Irving agreed a royalty of £12 per performance for authors Hichens and Traill, paying them £250 on account (12 July 1897).[98] When he purchased from a theatrical agent the rights for Richard Voss's *Schuldig*, he did so on 14 April 1891 paying £100 in advance on a proposed performance royalty of £10 each performance. He paid Sydney Grundy, a leading English playwright, £300 to provide an English version of the play.[99] But the play was never produced. Against this run of royalties he agreed in 1896 to pay J.I.C. Clarke £500 ($2500) for *George Washington*, but again this may have been at the author's request, for he is to be found asking for an advance during the writing as a result of financial reverses, receiving $1000 to add to the £250 he had previously received as an advance. The money was paid but the play was never produced.[100] Irving also paid Clarke £500 for his *Don Quixote*. Clarke recalled: 'I was overjoyed. What did I care about the terms? What it meant to me outweighed money.'[101] Irving had already paid £600 to Wills for his *Don Quixote*.

Irving paid Conan Doyle a royalty of two guineas a performance for the one-act *Waterloo*.[102] But mainly he continued to pay outright for one-act plays. In 1879 and 1880 he purchased all rights in Pinero's one-act plays *Daisy's Edge* and *Bygones*. He paid £100 to Egerton Castle and Walter Herries Pollock for their play *Saviolo* (24 May 1893) and £100 to his son Laurence for *Godefroi and Yolande* (21 July 1894).[103] But it is evident that he sometimes acquired plays for purely charitable reasons which he had no intention to perform. On 14 March 1901, Mrs Evelyn Bayle-Bernard, the widow of the playwright William Bayle-Bernard, who had died in 1875, wrote to Irving enclosing a copy of her late husband's play *Frederick the Great*, which had been written for Mr Wallack, who had died before it could be performed. She did not want any profit and was willing to donate any fee to the Actors Benevolent Fund. She just wanted to see it acted. On 6 April 1901, Irving thanked her for the 'charming play', offered her £100 and said that, although he was currently tied up with *Coriolanus*, he hoped he might produce it in the future. On 8 April 1901, Mrs Bayle-Bernard accepted his terms and donated the money to the Actors Benevolent Fund. The play was never produced.[104] There is also an agreement dated 10 July 1895, giving James Mortimer £50 for all rights in *Father Gabriel*, a play he claimed to have written specifically for Irving, with promise of another £50 if performed. It never was. A letter of 8 July 1895 from Mortimer to Irving confirms that he was using the money to settle his debts.[105] The Belfast journalist and playwright F. Frankfort Moore, who was Stoker's brother-in-law, wrote to Stoker on 17 February 1881 saying he was very hard up and offering Irving his play *A Lover's Tale* for £20. Irving sent him £20 by return. The play was not performed.[106]

Even when he had acquired rights to plays, Irving sometimes returned them. On 23 March 1885 Irving paid £150 to F.C. Burnand and Montagu Williams for the play *The Isle of St Tropez*, probably a one-act play, given the fee. But on 14 April 1888, he wrote to Burnand to say that he did not see the prospect of producing the play because he had to do a new Shakespeare and to follow it with 'something big – which I believe from experience to be a necessity', so he offered to pay him for the extra work he had done on the play and return the rights to him.[107] He also returned to J.I.C.Clarke the rights to his *Don Quixote* on repayment of the fee.

If he was less generous than other producers in paying playwrights, one has to consider his expenses. He laid out large sums on plays he never produced: £3000 in his first four years of management; £9000 over his entire career. Irving's own input into commissioned plays was considerable and he received nothing for that. Although the leading actor-manager of the day, he paid himself only sixty pounds a week. He, for instance, had worked on *Becket* cutting and rearranging until it was playable, which Tennyson's original had not been. His outlay on productions was large and got larger as in his later career he staged more and more spectacular productions.

The exception to all of Irving's customary arrangements was Victorien Sardou. Sardou was one of the best-paid playwrights in Europe and made his fortune from profit-sharing. But he accepted a fixed royalty of £14 a performance for Irving's production of *Madame Sans-Gêne* which brought him £1190 for the eighty-five performances. When it came to commissioning Sardou to provide a new play, the arrangements recognized his pre-eminence. For *Robespierre* Irving offered £500 for the scenario, another £500 on receipt of the script, £1000 in the event of Irving deciding to take the play to America, plus 5 per cent of gross receipts, the first case of profit-sharing in Irving's career. In the event, after a ninety-three night run, Sardou received £2604, though Stephens thinks that on the basis of the regular and consistent payments this was on a nightly royalty of £28 per performance rather than a percentage of gross receipts. This made *Robespierre* the most expensive play ever purchased by Irving.[108]

Irving enforced his exclusive rights to scripts he had purchased. On 18 May 1888, Stoker wrote to Alfred Calmour refusing him permission to publish *The Amber Heart*, reminding him that he had sold all rights to Irving. An aggrieved Calmour wrote back to Irving (19 May, 1888), expressing his deep disappointment at not being allowed to publish, saying that he thought he had sold only acting rights ('perhaps it was foolish of me to sign the agreement without having read it') and lamenting the great monetary loss he had sustained. He had had 500 copies of the play printed at his own expense and was out of pocket to the tune of £45. Irving did not change his mind but, on 18 June 1888, he did send Calmour £20 as partial recompense for his loss.[109]

Irving's attitude was not just perversity or proprietorial *amour-proper*. He had sound business reasons for not permitting publication of what had become a standard part of the Lyceum repertoire. On 16 August, 1883, Wills had written to Irving asking for copies of the scripts of *Charles the First* and *Olivia* because he was planning a collected edition of his plays, which the publisher Samuel French had agreed to bring out. Stoker replied on 17 August 1883:

> Mr Irving thinks it would not do to publish *Charles the First* as he knows from experience that when once a play is published it is shortly acted by unscrupulous persons. He has lately had to pay to Miss Isabel Bateman £500 to secure his American rights and under the circumstances it would be detrimental to his interests to make it public property.[110]

Evidently the same position still applied long after Wills's death. His brother and heir, Freeman Wills (who had received from Irving £200 to renew American rights to *Charles the First* and *Olivia*), sought Irving's permission to publish his brother's plays in a collection.[111] He complained that a previous letter on the subject had been ignored.[112] No permission was forthcoming and the plays remained unpublished.

Mr John Ruskin criticises Sir Henry Irving.

7

Ruskin and Ruskinism

John Ruskin, the pre-eminent art critic of the Victorian age, laid out in *Modern Painters* III what he considered to be the characteristics of Great Art. He wrote:

> Great art dwells on all that is beautiful ... great art accepts Nature as she is, but directs the eyes and thoughts to what is most perfect in her ... High art, therefore, consists neither in altering, nor in improving nature; but in seeking throughout nature for 'whatsoever things are lovely, and whatsoever things are pure'; in loving these, in displaying to the utmost of the painter's power such loveliness as is in them, and directing the thoughts of others to them by winning art, or gentle emphasis. Art is great in exact proportion to the love of beauty shown by the painter, provided that love of beauty forfeit no atom of truth. The next characteristic of great art is that it includes the largest possible quantity of Truth in the most perfect possible harmony. If it were possible for art to give all the truths of nature, it ought to do it. But this is not possible. Choice must always be made of some facts which *can* be represented from among others which must be passed by in silence, or even in some respects, misrepresented.[1]

He went on to give Rembrandt and Veronese as examples of artists whose use of colour, light and shade create a harmonious whole, which conveys truth and beauty. This Ruskinian creed can be seen to lie behind the philosophy of the stage and the drama articulated by Sir Henry Irving.

Irving wrote: 'in the consideration of the Art of Acting, it must never be forgotten that its ultimate aim is beauty. Truth itself is only an element of beauty, and merely to reproduce things vile and squalid and mean is a debasement of Art.' He was committed to a great cause: 'We go forth, armed with the luminous panoply which genius has forged for us, to do battle with dullness, with coarseness, with apathy, with every form of vice and evil.' He declared:

> Truly the actor's work embraces all the arts. He must first have the gift or faculty of acting ... His sympathy must then realise to himself the image in the poet's mind, and by the exercise of his art use his natural powers to the best advantage. His form and emotions are, in common with the sculptor's work, graceful and purposeful; his appearance and expression heightened by costume and pictorial preparation, are in common with the efforts of the musician – to arouse the intelligence by the vibrations and modulations of organized sound.[2]

Here is the same concern for compositional harmony as Ruskin expounded in discussing painting.

Was Irving familiar with Ruskin's ideas? He certainly possessed a good range of Ruskin's works. When he fell on hard times at the end of his career and was forced to sell off part of his library, he sold among many other works his five-volume set of *Modern Painters*, his three-volume set of *The Stones of Venice* (1873–4) and his nine-volume set of *Fors Clavigera* (1871–87).[3] But he retained until his death a single volume containing Ruskin's 'Pre-Raphaelitism', 'Notes on the Turner Gallery at Marlborough House', 'The Nature of Gothic Architecture' and 'Notes on the Royal Academy', numbers 3, 4, and 5.[4] This was sold with the rest of his library after his death.

John Ruskin had been raised as a strict Evangelical and the Evangelicals famously disapproved of the theatre, which they saw as a distraction from religion, as a vehicle for a Bohemian lifestyle and value system antithetical to their own, and as a promoter of frivolity, vanity and female forwardness. These views were clearly shared by Ruskin's mother Margaret, who disapproved of the theatre and never visited it. But, somewhat surprisingly, Ruskin's father John James loved the theatre, had been an enthusiastic boy actor at school and introduced his son to playgoing at the age of twelve. In 1882 Ruskin jocularly listed as among the pleasantest things to do 'going to all manner of wicked plays and pantomimes'.[5] Ruskin recorded his theatre visits in his diaries. Unlike his father, he did not on the whole go to tragedies and dramas, apart from Shakespeare, in whom he had a long and abiding interest, but chiefly to comedies, pantomimes and French plays in the original language.

Why did Ruskin go to the theatre? One reason is that he was a fan. A particular favourite of his was the actress Madge Robertson, later Mrs Madge Kendal and later still Dame Madge Kendal, who acted regularly with her husband W.H. Kendal. The *Theatre* magazine wrote of her: 'No living actress has done more by means of her art to teach men to be true and women to be tender.'[6] This is something likely to have commended her to Ruskin, with his strictly defined views on gender roles.[7] Another reason Ruskin went was that theatre took him out of himself. It was a sort of therapy. He regularly recalled in his diaries that, after a day of lassitude or depression, he would go to the theatre to be cheered up.[8] But plays also caused him to think about his work. In 1871 he wrote to the actor-manager Squire Bancroft to thank him for the pleasure afforded him by Bancroft's production of Tom Robertson's play *Ours*, saying: 'I get more help in my own work from a good play than from any other kind of thoughtful rest.'[9] So there was more than just escape in the theatre, there was intellectual stimulation. In his diary for 26 January 1872, Ruskin recorded: 'At French play last night. Saw the dreadful *Frou-Frou* – the best views of Venice I ever saw.'[10] The author of *The Stones of Venice* was clearly being inspired by the backdrops and scene-painting in an otherwise disappointing play. This confirms a view he later expressed about the educational value of the stage. In 1888 he was quoted as saying: 'I have always

held the stage quite amongst the best and most necessary means of education –
moral and intellectual.'[11] This was entirely in line with his strong commitment
to the artistic and cultural instruction of the masses.

This shared commitment inevitably drew him to Irving. He wrote to
Ellen Osborne, who had been the first May Queen at Whitelands College, on
14 December 1882, to say that he was going on Friday to the Lyceum to see Irving,
'who has so much power with the public. I want to see how he gets and how he
uses it.'[12] He recorded in his diary on 16 December 1882:

> Yesterday, at Lyceum, to Irving and Helen Terry's *Much Ado* [he always called Ellen Terry
> Helen], which taught me a good deal in Beatrice that I had not felt, but I am not sure
> how truly. Irving's Benedict of course offensive only, yet suggestive.[13]

He had first seen Ellen Terry in a revival of Tom Taylor's *New Men and Old Acres*
in 1877 and declared her 'very delightful – but a different creature from Madge
Robertson; a wonderful study in what the difference is. Much, I think, in the
continued ease of a soul at unity with itself in a lady, and the abruptness of one
broken in two, in those who are less than ladies.'[14] This is a clear reference to the
well-known irregularity of Ellen's private life: separation from G.F. Watts,
elopement with E.W. Godwin and the bearing of two children out of wedlock. It
was all a pointed contrast to Ruskin's adored Madge Robertson, a pillar of
respectability who came to rejoice in the sobriquet 'the Matron of the Drama.'
Indeed she may have rejoiced in it rather too much. The play agent Elizabeth
Marbury recalled: 'virtue was carried to such an excess by the Kendals that
gradually a rebellious reaction set in … Madge Kendal particularly was a whole
vice commission in herself … I had barely known her when she warned me
against certain promiscuous actresses with whom I should never be seen in
public'.[15]

Then in 1879 Ruskin became embroiled in a public controversy with Irving
about his interpretation of Shylock in *The Merchant of Venice*. Despite their
disagreements about the portrayal of Shylock, Irving continued to preach an
essentially Ruskinian gospel about the uplifting and ennobling role of the stage:

> Not for a moment is the position to be accepted that the theatre is merely a place of
> amusement … it is a living power, to be used for good, or possibly for evil; and far-
> seeing men recognise in it, based though it be on the relaxation and pleasures of the
> people, an educational medium of no mean order. Its progress in the past century has
> been the means of teaching to millions of people a great number of facts which had
> perhaps otherwise been lost to them. How many are there who have had brought home
> to them in an understandable manner by stage-plays the costumes, habits, manners, and
> customs of countries and ages other than their own; what insights have they thus
> obtained into facts and vicissitudes of life – of passions and sorrows and ambitions
> outside the narrow scope of their own lives, and which yet may and do mould the

destinies of man. All this is education – education in its widest sense, for it broadens the sympathies and enlarges the intellectual grasp. And beyond this again … there is that higher education of the heart, which raises in the scale of creation all who are subject to its sweetening influences.[16]

He was not the first actor-manager to propound this doctrine. Charles Calvert declared something similar in the published text of his 1877 adaptation of Lord Byron's *Sardanapalus*.[17]

They were both part of the tradition of stage management initiated in the 1850s by Charles Kean, which combined the acting of the drama with the spectacular recreation of times and places and the conscious desire to educate and inform an audience. Irving's theatre represented what has been called 'the final full achievement of the nineteenth-century pictorial mode,' the idea of the stage as a series of living pictures, with the text embellished and explicated through visual spectacle.[18] In addition to his staff of scene-painters headed by Hawes Craven, Irving actually employed distinguished contemporary artists to help design his productions. But it was not just the use of painting that characterized Irving's *mise-en-scène*. There was also the use of lighting, the deployment of space, the choreography of crowds and performativity, all of which came into consideration when critics viewed Irving's productions. A perfect example of this is Irving's production of Tennyson's *The Cup*.

There was a vogue in the 1880s and 1890s for what came to be called 'toga plays', plays set in Ancient Rome and the Roman world. They were melodramas which were often billed as educationally valuable by virtue of their archaeological accuracy and faithful reconstruction of the buildings, costumes and manners of the Ancient world. More importantly, they had an ideological purpose, delivering a set of warnings to late Victorian Imperial Britain. They frequently stressed the value of Christianity as a corrective to the profligacy and sensuality of the ruling class; the need for ethics in the running of an empire rather than the naked exercise of absolute power; and the correct role for females in a society troubled by the notion of the liberated and independent 'New Woman'.

Perhaps the most significant success of the 1880s was *Claudian* (1883), a play written by Henry Herman and W.G. Wills and starring actor-manager Wilson Barrett, who went on to write, produce and star in the later toga plays *The Sign of the Cross* (1895) and *Quo Vadis* (1900).[19] The story was a variation on the 'Flying Dutchman' and 'Wandering Jew' myths. A decadent aristocrat of the fourth century called Claudian pursues a young married Christian woman, fatally injures a holy man who intervenes to protect her, and causes the young woman to die of shock. Dying, the holy man curses him with everlasting youth and beauty. A century later, still youthful, he survives an earthquake, but finds an opportunity for expiation. A blind girl with whom he has fallen in love is swept away by the earthquake and he restores her life and sight by sacrificing his own.

This very moral tale unfolded amid spectacular scenes set in Byzantium and Bithynia with lavish costumes and musical accompaniment. It was designed by E.W. Godwin and he and Barrett published a pamphlet describing the measures they had undertaken to ensure the archaeological accuracy of the play.

The play delighted Oscar Wilde, who called it 'perfect in its picturesqueness ... and showing ... the whole nature and life of the times'.[20] It also delighted John Ruskin, who normally avoided drama and tragedy in the theatre. Ruskin said in an interview:

> I was immensely pleased with *Claudian* and Mr Wilson Barrett's acting of it; indeed, I admired it so much that I went to see it three times from pure enjoyment of it, although as a rule I cannot sit out a tragic play. It is not only that it is the most beautifully mounted piece I ever saw, but it is that every feeling that is expressed in the play, and every law of morality that is taught in it, is entirely right.[21]

What is fascinating here is Ruskin's delight in both the beauty and the moral message. The play exposes the decadence of the Roman Empire, preaches a tale of individual moral redemption and sets the whole thing among beautifully realized and archaeologically accurate sets. It became one of the earliest plays which clergymen were able to recommend their flock to see because of its Christian message. Its ability to enthral Ruskin, given the importance to him of Rose La Touche, the young girl he had loved and hoped to marry but who had died in 1875, may also lie in its theme of a dead girl being brought back to life by the power of love.

W.S. Gilbert's blank verse comedy *Pygmalion and Galatea* was a precursor of the toga vogue. It was first produced in 1871 and revived in 1877. Dame Madge Kendal created the role and recorded in her memoirs: 'Mr John Ruskin liked the play very much and came often to see it.'[22] It was then performed by the beautiful American actress Mary Anderson in 1883, 1884 and 1888. Gilbert's version has Pygmalion making Galatea an idealized version of his wife. The statue comes to life and causes chaos by her inexperience and interference and is turned back to stone. It has been argued that the Pygmalion myth was central to Victorian culture. Galatea was a male image of female subjection. She is created by man, remains only and always the image of his desires, but when liberated from her marble subjection causes chaos and has to be returned to her immobile state on her pedestal.[23]

Evidently Ruskin went to see this production too. Mary Anderson recorded in her autobiography: 'Ruskin once said to me that he had never cared for plastic art; and was good enough to add that my Galatea had given him more of an appreciation of it than he had ever expected to have.[24] It seems likely that Ruskin saw the 1883 revival starring Mary Anderson which ran from December 1883 to April 1884, for he told the art critic M.H. Spielmann in early 1884 that he was 'a critical admirer ... with many reservations, of Miss Mary Anderson ... a sweet lady and an excellent person, but not, I think, a great actress', – a view held by many contemporaries.[25] On 25 February 1884, Ruskin wrote to Charles Eliot Norton observing gnomically, 'I'm beginning to reform the drama – by the help of Miss Anderson', suggesting that he saw *Pygmalion and Galatea* as putting his principles into action on the stage, much as he saw *Claudian* doing this.[26]

Whereas he evidently saw both *Claudian* and *Pygmalion and Galatea* in 1883 or 1884, when he was much in London and Oxford and visiting the theatre again, it seems unlikely that he saw *The Cup*, which ran in London from January to April 1881. In late autumn 1880 there was a deterioration in his mental condition. He suffered a complete mental collapse at the end of February 1881, was manic for a month and spent the rest of the year recovering. But *The Cup* was the first in the cycle of toga plays and it conformed to the principles that Ruskin later praised in *Claudian*.

Irving was to produce and star in three plays by the Poet Laureate, Alfred, Lord Tennyson: *Queen Mary*, *The Cup* and *Becket*. Irving was committed to maintaining the English tradition of poetic drama and Tennyson was Britain's leading poet. In 1879 Tennyson offered the completed *Becket* to Irving. Tennyson reported to the poet William Allingham that Irving 'said it was magnificent, but it would cost him £3000 to mount it: he couldn't afford the risk. If well put on the stage it would act for a time and it would bring me credit (he said) but it wouldn't pay'. He said: 'If you give me something short I'll do it.'[27] Austin Brereton wrote in his 1908 biography of Irving that this was actually a polite evasion: 'he knew that *Becket* was unsuitable for the stage, and at the time, it would have been injudicious to have suggested the drastic compression which he himself afterwards made'. He supported this contention by pointing out that *Becket* actually cost Irving £4723 to put on.[28]

Tennyson came across a paragraph in W.E.H. Lecky's *History of European Morals* which recounted a story from Plutarch about a noble Galatian woman Camma who, after the murder of her husband, poisoned herself and his murderer in order to avoid marrying him. Tennyson rapidly turned this into a short two-act play *The Cup*, which he sent to Irving. It was not in fact the first play on the subject. The Italian playwright Montanelli had turned it into a full-length tragedy for the great Italian actress Adelaide Ristori. It was a paean to the sanctity of marriage and of marital fidelity. Excited by the manuscript, Irving invited Tennyson to read the text to himself and the company. Irving would play Synorix, Ellen Terry Camma and William Terriss Sinnatus. Tennyson, clearly anxious for stage success, agreed not to publish the text until after the play had been performed, and accepted the few changes suggested by Irving to improve its playability.[29] Hallam Tennyson listed them in his biography of his father: 'Three short speeches for Synorix, Act I scene 3; and at the end of Act II [he means scene 2 here], the quarrel between Sinnatus and Synorix was lengthened by two lines, and Camma made to interrogate Sinnatus as to what Synorix had said, and three or four entrances were made less abrupt.'[30] Tennyson's letters show him willingly amending and adding to speeches.[31] Hallam Tennyson wrote to Irving on behalf of his father: 'Here are all the alterations. I think them great improvements. Your enthusiasm is infectious, and has made us happy. We are grateful to you for all your trouble ... My father will alter anything – or pray omit any of the lines which you think superfluous.'[32]

In Tennyson's play Synorix, the former tetrarch of Galatia, ousted by his people because of his record of debauching local women, returns to the province, now ruled by Rome, in pursuit of Camma, the wife of the present tetrarch Sinnatus. The Roman general Antonius, although he despises Synorix, commissions him to uncover a rumoured conspiracy headed by Sinnatus and aimed at overthrowing Roman rule. Antonius holds out to Synorix the prospect of the crown if he is successful. Posing as a visiting Greek called Strato, Synorix goes hunting with Sinnatus, is entertained by him to dinner and in discussion advocates submission to Rome. Camma prefers war even though it may mean defeat ('In wars of freedom and defence the glory and grief of battle won or lost solders a race together'). Synorix, recognized by one of his victims, is thrown out by Sinnatus. Next day Camma comes to the temple of Artemis to intercede with Antonius for her husband, but Synorix, who has lured her there under false pretences, presses his suit. Sinnatus appears, seizes Synorix and is stabbed to death. Camma takes refuge in the temple, where she becomes the priestess of Artemis. Synorix is proclaimed king of Galatia by the Romans. He repeatedly requests Camma's hand in marriage. She finally agrees but at the wedding ceremony presents him with the cup which he had given her. They both drink from it and both die, as she has poisoned the wine. Dying, she declares that it had been her intention to poison Antonius also, but is glad she has failed because, if Galatia has to be ruled by Romans, he is gentle and worthy. Antonius forgives her for her act of killing the Roman-nominated king. The play clearly conforms to the themes of the later toga plays, here focusing on the proper role for women, the celebration of marital fidelity, but also hinting at the conflict of ethics and political necessity in imperial rule.

Irving was determined to present his play as artistically as possible and as archaeologically faithful as the demands of theatre permitted. So intensive research was undertaken. Bram Stoker recalled the work:

James Knowles reconstructed a Temple of Artemis on the ground plan of the great Temple of Diana. The late Alexander Murray, then Assistant Keeper ... of the Greek section of the British Museum, made researches amongst the older Etruscan designs. Capable artists made drawings from vases, which were reproduced on the great amphorae used in the Temple service. The existing base and drum of a column from

Ephesus was remodelled for use, and lent its sculptured beauty to the general effect. William Telbin painted some scenes worthy of Turner; and Hawes Craven and Cuthbert made such an interior scene of the Great Temple as was surely never seen on any stage.[33]

Stoker was concerned enough with the play's archaeological accuracy to defend some modifications made in the designs. The *Architect* criticized the columns, saying they were not the right proportions. But Stoker argued that correctly proportioned they would have looked skimpy in the stage picture; perspective and the need for the columns to appear 'to tower aloft in unimaginable strength' dictated the proportions. To criticism from Alexander Murray that the great amphora had red figures on a black background instead of black figures on a red background, Stoker declared that both forms were used by the Etruscans.[34]

Irving wrote to Tennyson: 'I hope that the splendid success of your grand Tragedy will be followed by other triumphs equally great', and Ellen Terry thanked him for 'his great little play', a view she endorsed in her autobiography.[35] Browning wrote to Tennyson congratulating him on the play.[36] Hallam Tennyson thought Ellen played Camma 'magnificently' and Alfred Tennyson addressing her as 'my dear Camma', wrote 'you did it beautifully – not only the wifely and tender part of the character, but the talk about the patriots and the cry to the Goddess, which, if I recollect rightly, you had some fear of falling short in … I was so entranced that I lost my spectacles – my reading ones – I heard them fall off and forgot to pick them up'.[37] Hallam reported, however, that his father had said: 'Irving has not hit off my Synorix, who is a subtle blend of Roman refinement and intellectuality and barbarian self-satisfied sensuality.'[38]

E.W. Godwin, the architect, artist and designer, who had been Ellen Terry's lover before she joined Irving and had fathered her two children as well as educating her aesthetic taste, and who was a key figure in the toga play movement, was involved in this production. He designed Ellen Terry's costumes, which she called 'simple, fine and free', and the cup itself, a replica of which Ellen presented to Tennyson on the hundredth night of the production.[39] But for all its archaeological accuracy, it was Irving's stagecraft that made the production come alive, that animated the pictures. Stoker says:

> It was to Irving that the scene owed most of its beauty and grandeur. Hitherto, in all pagan ceremonials on the stage – and, indeed in art generally – priestesses and votaries were clothed in white. But he, not finding that there was any authority for the belief, used colours and embroideries – Indian, Persian, Greek – all that might add conviction and picturesque effect. Something like a hundred beautiful young women were chosen for Vestals; … Irving himself devised the procession and the ceremonies; in fact he invented a ritual … The effect of the entry into the Temple of the gorgeously armoured Roman officers was peculiarly strong.[40]

Ellen Terry confirmed the importance of Irving's artistic vision. Calling it 'one of the most beautiful things that Henry Irving ever accomplished', she wrote:

> A great deal of the effect was due to the lighting. The gigantic figure of the many-breasted Artemis, placed far back in the scene-dock, loomed through a blue mist, while the foreground of the picture was in yellow light. The thrilling effect always to be gained by the simple expedient of a great number of people doing the same thing in the same way at the same moment, was seen in 'The Cup', when the stage was covered with a crowd of women who raised their arms above their heads with a large, rhythmic, sweeping movement and then bowed to the goddess with the regularity of a regiment saluting.[41]

The combination of sets, stage movement and lighting was completed by costume and make-up. Terry did not share Tennyson's dissatisfaction with Irving's interpretation:

> With a pale, pale face, bright red hair, gold armour and a tiger-skin, a diabolical expression and very thin crimson lips, Henry looked handsome and sickening at the same time. *Lechery* was written across his forehead.[42]

Irving spent £2369 4s 1d on the production.[43]

The Cup was first produced on 3 January 1881, and ran for 127 performances, but, too short to stand on its own, it was coupled first with the melodrama *The Corsican Brothers* and later with the comedy *The Belle's Stratagem*. The audience at the first night included the Prime Minister, Mr Gladstone (an admirer of both Irving and Tennyson) and his family. Stoker noted with satisfaction that audiences for the play included many High Church clergymen, attracted no doubt by the recreation of religious ritual and the impeccable moral tone. Tennyson went to see it first on 26 February 1881.

The critics were entranced by the visual splendours of the production. Clement Scott invoked Sir Frederic Leighton and Alma-Tadema as the inspirations for the temple scenes. 'The pictures that dwell on the memory are countless, and not to be effaced in spell or witchery by any of the most vaunted productions of the stage, even in an era devoted to archaeology.' Of Act Two, he said: 'As for the second act, with its groupings, its grace, its centre figures and surroundings, its hymns to Artemis, its chants and processions, we are inclined to doubt if the Stage has ever given to educated taste so rare a treat.'[44] William Archer, in *English Dramatists of Today*, said Irving:

> mounted the piece with a taste and lavishness positively unexampled. Each scene was a masterpiece in itself. I doubt if a more elaborate and perfect stage-picture of its kind has ever been seen, and if so, certainly not in England. It almost seems as if stage-decoration could go no further.[45]

Metropolitan sophisticates tended to sneer at the overtly educational bent of the Lyceum Theatre. *Truth* (13 January 1881), for instance, said of *The Cup*:

There is a learned air about the whole thing that suits the sham culture of society, and the era of high schools and advanced education. The play is dated at least three centuries before St Paul preached to the Galatians, and enables people to prate about Ionia and the Ephesian Artemis and Pagan ritual. They swell with information concerning Tetrarchies and tributary kings of Rome and the wars of Mithridates, and dinner tables wax eloquent concerning the lovely Camma and the fate-haunted Synorix.

The Times (5 January 1881) seems to have captured the general reaction to the play, acknowledging the beauty of the staging, praising Ellen Terry and offering respect to the Poet Laureate, but finding it somehow insubstantial and unsatisfying. *The Times* declared it an improvement on his previous play *The Falcon*, which was a poem rather than a play. *The Cup*, acknowledged the critic, 'may claim to be a play'. But the reviewer suggested respectfully that there was still too much dialogue, not enough action and a lack of human interest in the characters:

> The great fame of the writer, the repute of the theatre and the principal actors, the beauty of the scenery, the splendour and finish of the general furnishing – which it may be said here surpasses all the theatrical magnificence that even our pampered age has seen, and the propriety of which few probably will be found bold enough to dispute – this happy combination of circumstances cannot but serve to raise the whole performance out of the common groove, to invest it with a halo of romance, perhaps of poetry which for the moment at least will render a dispassionate examination a work to many minds of more than ordinary difficulty. But when all these facts are claimed for ... the question remains, what proportion of substance is there behind all the external splendour and show? ... how far will it be found that the story of these men and women of the old Pagan world, their love and hate, their passion and revenge, has touched the heart and stirred the feelings of the people?

This prompted criticism of Ellen Terry's performance as Camma couched in familiar terms:

> Miss Terry presents her as a wondrously picturesque and graceful personage, and the earlier scenes allowed the actress full scope for all the womanly tenderness and feeling which are the most agreeable qualities of her art. But the second act, with its set plan of vengeance and dying cry of triumph, seems to demand more majesty and power than the lady is able to supply. She makes, indeed, a striking figure in a magnificent scene, the crowning glory of a series of scenic masterpieces; but she impresses us rather with a sense of pity for the woman than awe for the avenger.

Interestingly Terry's own view of her performance echoed this criticism directly: 'The first act was well within my means; the second was beyond them, but it was very good for me to try and do it.'[46]

Of Irving, the *Times* critic wrote that his speech was 'unintelligible to the larger part of the audience' and he created 'a picturesque if somewhat quaint figure. It is not easy to gather from his appearance what manner of man this Synorix is intended to have been.' William Terriss was declared 'a manly and vigorous Sinnatus ... but despite his ancient and most fantastic garb, he is an essentially modern figure in the picture, his robust style seems out of place in that elegant and artificial atmosphere'. Some of the criticism reflected an unfamiliarity with what were to become the conventions of the toga play, but other reviewers echoed *The Times*'s principal comments.

The *Weekly Dispatch* (9 January 1881) criticized Tennyson ('Mr Tennyson's work is more remarkable for dignity of outline and beauty of word-painting than for mere stage effect such as we should obtain from a more practised dramatist') and Irving ('many of the lines ... were lost in consequence of the faulty enunciation of the actor'). But the newspaper praised Ellen Terry ('Miss Ellen Terry has seldom appeared to greater advantage than as the faithful and avenging wife of Sinnatus. Her attitudes are grace itself and her speech delicious in its gentleness and womanly charm'). But when it came to the production itself, the critic declared:

> Words fail us in attempting to describe the scenic perfection of this remarkable production. The lovely landscape of Mr Telbin, with its vine-clad slopes, its glistening mountains, ever-changing in tint, and its marvellous atmosphere, is a picture to gaze on with delight; but it is thrown into the shade by the representation of the Temple, by Messrs Hawes Craven and W. Cuthbert. This we consider the greatest triumph of scenic art within our remembrance. When the doors are thrown open, and the bright crimson rays of the morning sun stream on the strangely solid columns and throw into deeper shade the mysterious recesses of the building where the colossal figure of Artemis looms darkly on all, as the procession of torch-bearing men and flower-laden maidens and children assumes every instant some new groupings of beauty and picturesqueness, we surrender ourselves delightedly to the spell, and feel that the eye and the intellect are receiving equal gratification.

Truth (13 January 1881) declared:

> *The Cup* ... is destined to please the eye more than it satisfied the mind. It is as a spectacle that it is a success, and I am bound to say that nothing more complete of its kind has ever been seen in this country. Where, indeed, could anything be found better in the mechanical and pictorial arts of decoration? There are only two scenes of major importance, one a wooded ravine in Asia Minor, faultless in colour, with a distant view of snow-capped mountains, that change to rose colour at sunset and to gold at dawn. But it is the inner set of the Temple of Artemis concerning which the Art world is raving; and, indeed, one can forgive the excitement occasioned by the impressive picture. The really striking thing of this scene is the arrangement of light; that, I own, quite puzzles me. The temple is dark, but still luminous; there is a weird mystery about the sacred statue in the background, but little less than marvellous is the effect of the sudden rays and waves of light when the temple doors are opened ... It is the most astonishing bit of

deception I have ever seen, and the eye can scarcely believe it is not all real and solid. The only objection that could be urged to the picture when complete is the introduction of the boy-girls, or girl-boys, with their obvious tights and baskets of flowers. They may be correct – doubtless they are, for the British Museum would revolt at any anachronism at the Lyceum – but the frivolous mind refuses to disassociate then from the vulgarities of pantomime and Flora's haunt among the fairies. They jar upon the scene, and are the one blot on a picture that looks like Alma Tadema in action. In this gorgeous temple, filled with incense that is wafted into the theatre, among all these draperies and torches and statues and marbles and flowers, stands Miss Ellen Terry, with her fair hair, her ideal presence, and her picturesque figure robed in stuff that seems spun out of the wings of a dragon-fly and close to her Mr Irving in a regal Roman robe and tawny hair, make the picture complete and the illustration perfect ... Never before were the favourites placed in so gorgeous a frame.

Calling the play 'a banquet of sensuous delicacies', *Pan* rhapsodized about the work of William Telbin in painting the scenery for Act One.

Without comparison, there can be no doubt that no scene painter, either in London or Paris, could have produced anything more completely a picture than the first set in *The Cup*. The stone pines, the rocky inland cliffs which dominate the olives and myrtles of the woods and uplands of a classic ground, which, far as the eye can reach, stretches in pastoral beauty till it terminates in a line of purple hills whose snowy tops are tinged with the roseate light of breaking day; while among the broken columns and vine-covered stairs the flowering aloe, the yucca and the gladiolus lend life and reality to the scene. On one side the massive steps and peristyle of the Temple of Artemis lend grandeur and width to the splendid stage. Up on the grass-grown marble steps among trellised vines a laughing boy with bronzing limbs and blue-black curls sits like a living 'Leighton' glowing in the sun. Claude and Turner seem to have presided over nature, and schooled the loveliest elements of creative composition to a glorious whole.

The critic went on to revel in the aesthetic beauty of the appearance of Irving's Synorix and Ellen Terry's Camma.

The figure might have been drawn by Salvator Rosa and dressed – probably had been by Alma-Tadema. Indeed, there is evidence in many places of this artist's advice, for no one has ever studied the Gallo-Roman archaeology as he has. The ruddy locks, the leopard spoils and iron scales, the harmonious tintings of the silken fleshings, all denote the true artistic temperament of the wearer. The eye is soon attracted to something as picturesque and yet more fascinating, for down from the cliffs by the same stone path among the sunny vines and creeping plants, Camma, the witching heroine, appears in all her plastic beauty. She might have stepped from out some Elgin marble. There are the undulating draperies, the sloping forms Zeuxis would have joyed to paint and Phidias to carve. The pale amber and sea-green tints, just broken by Persian fancy with embroidered flowers, harmonize admirably with Ellen Terry's blue eyes and sunny waved hair. From first to last Camma is a dream of poetry, an ever varying picture of classic grace and old-world imagery. She is not asked to be powerful, her vengeance is not the outpouring of passion, but the justice of overwrought tenderness. All she says and does, her every motion and her varied charm is like the seductive melancholy of Shelley's verses, carrying you on from one scene to the other, till all culminates in the loving faith of her broken heart speeding to the spirit of her waiting husband. I do not think I can be often accused of 'gush', but it would be easy to write line upon line on the perfectly artistic beauty of this actress's conception of Camma.[47]

The *Daily Telegraph* (11 January 1881) even ran an entire editorial on the Temple set, in which it praised fulsomely the work of James Knowles, Alexander Murray and Henry Irving in recreating the Temple of Artemis, complete in every aspect.

We see for the first time at the Lyceum the pagan temple adequately and harmoniously furnished; we say harmoniously, because the paraphernalia of the ritual, the vestments of the priests and priestesses, the very fumes of the incense, the glow of the flowers, the glare of the torches, and the solemn strains of the antique psalmody, all combine with and are absorbed in the general and magnificent architectonic whole. The great charm of the Temple of Artemis scene is its subtle Asiatic suggestiveness. It is not the paganism of Hellas, not the paganism of Rome – it is Oriental paganism which shall one day become Christian and Byzantine ... Technically, as well as artistically, this Artemisian tableau must be held to constitute, so far as modern times are concerned, a new departure in the decoration of the stage. The Temple at the Lyceum is not only actually built up and out, instead of being painted on one plane surface with 'wings' or side scenes, and draperies hanging from the 'flies' to complete its perspective effect, but it is actually and solidly modelled. The shafts of the columns are really round and fluted; the capitals and cornices are really moulded; the plinths are real plastic bas-reliefs. It is as though the accomplished scholars who have combined thus nobly to illustrate the verse of Tennyson had been imbued with that deep-thinking spirit of artistic fitness which led Augustus von Schlegel to institute his famous parallel between sculpture and Homeric Epos ... No English dramatist has had the advantage of such constructive services as those which Mr Knowles has rendered to Mr Tennyson and Mr Irving, since the illustrious architect Inigo Jones aided Ben Jonson in the production of the Royal Masques at Whitehall.

There were one or two dissentient, not to say irreverent voices raised. Among them was the *Referee* (9 January 1881) which reported:

If the thing had not been written by the Poet Laureate, and produced at a theatre which has a strong following, and which would fill nightly even if Mr Irving proposed to play the part on his head, the whole affair would be ridiculed. I wonder what the Miss Nancy critics who gush slush about this flabby production with its stagiest of stagy acting, would have said of it if it had been written by an ordinary author and produced by ordinary mortals. There are two fine passages in the play, and only two ... nearly all the rest is twaddle.

But, having said this and sent up the production something rotten, the anonymous critic added: 'With all the faults of *The Cup*, you should pay your

money and have a pull at it, if only to get a peep at the beauties of the surroundings and at Ellen Terry, who in some lovely robes looks loveable.'

It was a visual experience, however, that those who saw it would never forget.
In his 1906 biography of Irving, Percy Fitzgerald recalled of *The Cup*:

> It still lingers in the memory with an inexpressible charm, breathing poetry and romance.
> We shall ever look back fondly to *The Cup*, with its exquisite setting, and lament heartily
> that others did not so cordially or enthusiastically appreciate it. There was something so
> fascinating about the play, something so refining, and also so 'fantastical', that though
> lacking the strong thews and muscles of a regular drama, it satisfied the eye and ear …
> On the two chief characters, both full of tragic power, the eye rested with an almost
> entrancing interest. Never did Irving *act* better – that is, never did he convey by his look
> and tones the evidence of the barbaric conception within him. There was a fine, pagan,
> reckless savagery, yet controlled by dignity. Miss Terry's Camma returns to the memory
> like the fragment of a dream. The delightful creation was brought before us more by her
> sympathetic bearing and motion than by speech; but what music was there is in those
> tones, pitched in low, melodious key, interpreting the music of Tennyson! Her face and
> outline of figure, refined and poetical as they were, became more refined still in
> association with the lovely scenery and surroundings. She seemed to belong to the
> mythological past.[48]

After its initial run, however, Irving did not revive it. In 1887–88 Mary Anderson
had lengthy discussions with Tennyson, planning to revive *The Cup* (for which
Tennyson wrote four new scenes) and to produce *The Foresters*. But in 1890 she
married Antonio de Navarro and retired permanently from the stage and the
plans remained unfulfilled.[49] The toga cycle, however, continued on the stage
until the end of the century.

The significance of such plays is attested by none other than John Ruskin,
who wrote directly to Wilson Barrett after seeing *Claudian*: 'You know perfectly
well, as all great artists do, that the [play] is beautiful, and that you do it perfectly.'
He said it 'gave me not only delight at the time, but were a possession in memory
of great value', and he urged him to produce a series of revivals of classically set
plays as an educational experience for English audiences, saying: 'And with scene-
painting like that the Princess's [theatre] might do more for art teaching than all
the galleries and professors of Christendom.'[50]

In a true Ruskinian sense, Irving was strongly committed to the spread of culture
to the people. He regularly accepted invitations to open libraries, galleries and
exhibitions. By so doing, he was implicitly linking theatre to libraries and art
galleries as a cultural and educational force.

From the 1830s and 1840s onwards, there was growing concern about
working-class leisure within the middle classes. It was born of concern about the
effects of urbanisation and the demoralisation of the work force by sex, drink

and violence in a culture centred on the pub and the street. It was born too of fear of revolution, the lingering shadow of the French Revolution but also a fear revivified by the upheavals of 1848 and the activities of the Chartists. This stimulated a desire in the middle classes to control, discipline and regulate working-class leisure and make it useful, respectable and improving. The fundamental Puritan view that all leisure was inherently bad and corrupting and took you away from the work and the prayer that were your God-given duties gave way to a drive for rational recreation which was a mixture of enlightenment and self-interest.

Leisure was redefined as recreation, a time in which people refreshed and restored themselves, enabling them to work better when they returned to work. The idea of the moral and educational value of leisure was promoted. Culture was portrayed as socially cohesive with exposure to it desirable on the grounds of shared values. There was a social control element, too, with an ordered, disciplined and improving culture deliberately promoted to replace a culture that was violent, emotional, spontaneous and drink-centred. As has been pointed out, this should not be over-stressed for the idea of rational recreation grew, not just out of the desire to control, but out of the middle-class experience itself. Middle-class reformers had found their own system of leisure to be good and wanted to extend it to the working class: a home-centred world (reading, playing the piano, singing); an improvement-centred world (excursions to museums and galleries, reading, nature study); and a health-centred world (seaside trips, walking). Rational recreation was seen as personally fulfilling. At the same time, there was in some quarters of the working class an ethic of self-improvement, with contemporary accounts of learning how to read and the opening up of the whole world of knowledge having the sense of a religious experience and working men getting together to organize reading groups and to visit lectures and exhibitions.[51]

The practical expression of this gospel was a network of mechanics institutes, mutual improvement societies and working men's clubs, all providing adult education. This was also catered for by increasing numbers of art galleries and museums. There were also public libraries funded both by the local authorities after the 1850 and 1855 Library Acts, which authorized a penny rate to pay for them, and by individual philanthropists. Ruskin was the most influential figure linking art, society and religion. John Ruskin wrote in 1867: 'Every one of our principal cities ought to have a permanent gallery of art of which the function should be wholly educational, as distinguished from the historical and general purpose of the collections of the British Museum and National Gallery.' In 1880, he added 'the first function of a Museum ... is to give example of perfect order and perfect elegance, in the true sense of that test word, to the disorderly and rude population'. Ruskin wanted them well-warmed, well-lighted and accessible to all classes, but he proposed a small entrance fee to discourage mere idlers, though overwhelmingly the advocates of museums and galleries argued for free access. He also believed that minor as well as major artists should be included, if they had a moral lesson to teach.[52] As with libraries, the move to provide museums and art galleries was partly due to local government initiative and partly to private philanthropic enterprise. In 1870 there were only the National Galleries in London and Edinburgh and a group of university galleries and private institutions. By 1914 every English and Scottish town of any consequence boasted a municipal art gallery. The earliest established were Birmingham (1876) and Nottingham (1878). Because of an inadequate local government system in London, museum and gallery provision in London was poor. So philanthropic enterprise filled the gap, for example the South London Art Gallery, founded in 1878 by William Rossiter, a self-educated Holborn trunkmaker who became a teacher at the Working Men's College, and the Whitechapel Art Gallery, which grew out of the annual Whitechapel Fine Arts exhibitions established in 1881 by the Reverend Samuel Barnett and his wife Henrietta.

J. Passmore Edwards (1823–1911) was a classic Victorian philanthropist. A working-class autodidact from Cornwall who became a journalist in London, he took over the *Echo* as editor and proprietor in 1876, running it until 1896 when he sold it to a syndicate. Under his leadership, the *Echo* stood for liberal politics and social reform. Passmore Edwards himself served on committees campaigning for the abolition of capital punishment, taxes on knowledge, flogging in the army and navy, and the opium trade. He was also president of the Anti-Gambling League. He served as Liberal MP for Salisbury from 1880 to 1885 but gave up Parliament, impatient at his ability to get things done. He turned to philanthropy, devoting his funds to the foundation of free libraries and hospitals – eventually seventy institutions owed their existence to his beneficence. He turned down the offer of knighthoods from both Queen Victoria and King Edward VII.[53] The laying of a foundation stone for a Passmore Edwards institution was always a public event, performed by a well-known figure and covered by the press. When, on 24 October 1896, the foundation stone of the latest Passmore Edwards Library was laid at Dulwich, the celebrity doing the honours was Henry Irving. Passmore Edwards was donating the £5000 necessary to pay for the construction but Dulwich College was donating the land. This allowed Irving not only to praise the munificence of Passmore Edwards but also to pay tribute to Edward Alleyn, the Elizabethan actor who founded Dulwich College and was a role model for the actor, who was also devoted to the public good. Irving praised the role of the public library:

> The mechanism for good which public libraries afford is of incalculable value, and the
> influence must be vast, especially as their use becomes the help of the young. What can
> be better for a young mind – or for an old mind either – when wearied by the old

commonplaces of life and labour, than to seek peace and refreshment in the isolation of the organized and completed thought of others; to feel that sweet sympathy and companionship of those, whose experiences, both good and bad, have been turned into examples or warnings for those that follow – whose cultured imaginations can lead the weary and jaded or eager mind into new realms of intellectual delight.[54]

When the South London Gallery declared its intention of moving from Camberwell to a new building in Peckham Road, to be paid for by an anonymous benefactor, the gallery launched an appeal for £1200 to purchase the site and a further £1000 for fixtures and fittings. Irving took the chair at a public meeting held on Friday 18 July 1890 at the Suffolk Street Gallery of the Royal Society of British Artists. In his speech Irving set out the classic rationale for the public funding of art galleries:

Anything which takes people out of the joyless humdrum of their daily existence, and anyone who sheds a gleam of art in the wintry face of toiling poverty is a benefactor ... It has always seemed strange to me that in a country where so much has been done for education, and where there are so many agencies for the diffusion of moral truth, so little in comparison has ever been attempted to spread the influence of art ... Yet I venture to say that in the greatest city of the world we have the gravest responsibility for everything which is calculated in any degree to elevate and refine the public taste ... for all art ranks among the missionary influences of civilisation. Art has its pulpit, and pictures are often very excellent sermons.[55]

The project ran into difficulties, however, when the anonymous benefactor reneged and stumped up only £500. The distinguished members of the Council of the Gallery had to step into the breach with funds, and eventually the redoubtable Passmore Edwards contributed £3000 to pay for the Gallery's lecture room and library.

Irving enlarged upon the civilising affect of paintings for the masses, when he opened the eleventh annual exhibition of paintings at St Jude's School, Whitechapel, on 17 March 1891, and again when he opened a free exhibition of pictures at the town hall, Stratford East, on 3 May 1897. He said at Whitechapel:

The good which can be done by exhibitions of this kind is incalculable. It is at all times wise to wake in the minds of all, both young and old, new ideas, more especially when such ideas tend to the lovely and imaginative side of life. There is too much sad and squalid realism already, and what we want is now and again a glimpse of that ideal which we all yearn for, and yearn in proportion to the exacting nature of our lives.

He made a direct link between theatre and gallery:

One cannot help thinking there is much in common between my art – the art of the player and the art of the painter. From canvas and sculpture actors have often caught the inspiration of vivid action, and their ambition has been kindled by studies of the statuesque; whilst the theatre has sometimes afforded painters subjects for their work, and also that stimulus and enthusiasm which the living, breathing action of the player may sometimes inspire. The fields of history and fancy are open to the actor, as to the painter; the actor perhaps having one advantage – inexact and fading though his work may be – of directly moving a multitude of spectators in the mimic scene. Art has its pulpit, and picture galleries and clean and wholesome theatres preach very often very excellent sermons.[56]

In his Stratford East speech, Irving praised the munificence of West Ham Borough Council in providing municipal institutions for public use: a public hall, free libraries, two recreation grounds and public baths.

> You are rapidly extending the means and opportunities of rational and aesthetic recreation. These pictures have already enlarged the horizons of many minds. They have done incalculable good by giving impressions of beauty to men and women who toil amidst conditions not always helpful to conceptions of the beautiful. They are true missionaries of civilization, ministering to that eternal need of the ideal, which is as instinctive in us as the craving for material happiness.[57]

Late in the nineteenth century Irving began to campaign for municipal theatres as an extension of the civic gospel. He expounded the argument for the first time in his presidential address, on 26 September 1894, to the Walsall Literary Institute; it was published in the *Theatre* (December 1894). Arguing that 'we may congratulate ourselves that so much has been done to dispel social prejudice against the theatre, and successfully to assert its claim to a place amongst the liberal arts and the refining graces of life', he asked 'if all the agencies now at our command are adequate to the purpose of maintaining a high standard of the drama?' Every theatre in Britain was conducted by voluntary free enterprise and he personally had no reason to be dissatisfied with that. But on the Continent the stage was recognized as an integral part of the education of the community, and in Germany the cultivation of the drama was seen as a part of civic duty. As a result, theatre received public subventions. In England this meant confronting the ratepayers and Irving observed that 'the wealthier the ratepayer ... the less inclined he is to subscribe to works of common utility.'

Describing the drama as 'the Cinderella of the arts', he called for a fairy godfather, either municipality or millionaire, to endow a theatre which would train actors, 'uphold a consistently high standard of dramatic literature, and to preserve the distinction between the true form of the drama and the various entertainments which pass under its name'. But since millionaires bestow their money elsewhere, there are the municipalities who already provide for libraries, museums and picture-galleries – so why not theatres? He noted the paradox that 'you may burn municipal gas, consume municipal water, sleep in municipal lodging, travel on a municipal tramway, study municipal pictures; but you cannot go to the municipal play and applaud the municipal actor'. He believed that municipal theatres would encourage the study and practice of elocution, enrol the dramatic art among the pleasures of citizenship, provide a training ground for new actors and writers, stimulate the imagination and elevate public taste. He was convinced that, even from the commercial point of view, such theatres would be profitable in the long term. He quoted Mr Gladstone as supporting the idea and urged on the burghers of Walsall that they had the opportunity to provide the municipal leadership and thus earn 'the honourable distinction of having enlarged the influence of a noble art'.[58]

He returned to the subject in an address to the Edinburgh Pen and Pencil Club on 31 October 1894, observing that his suggestion that certain great cities might build municipal theatres 'has been widely discussed and I cannot truthfully say that it has provoked a whirlwind of enthusiasm'.[59] In a retrospective essay on the stage in the Victorian era, written in his capacity as president of the drama section of the 1897 Victorian Era Exhibition at Earl's Court, Irving lamented: 'for years I have advocated municipal theatres without converting a single town clerk'.[60] Irving may not have lived to see it but he had been prophetic, for the twentieth century was to see the establishment of municipal theatres.

MR. HAWES CRAVEN.

A HOST OF DELIGHTFUL STAGE PICTURES HE HAS GIVEN US.

Hawes Craven.

8

The Arts

In his 1891 essay, 'The Soul of Man under Socialism', Oscar Wilde, noting that there had been 'a certain advance' in drama in the previous twenty years, wrote:

> It is important to point out that this advance is entirely due to a few individual artists refusing to accept the popular want of taste as their standard, and refusing to regard Art as a mere matter of demand and supply. With his marvellous and vivid personality, with a style that has really a true colour – element in it, with his extraordinary power ... over imaginative and intellectual creation, Mr Irving, had his sole object been to give the public what they wanted, could have produced the commonest plays in the commonest manner, and made as much success and money as a man could possibly desire. But his object was not that. His object was to realise his own perfection as an artist, under certain conditions and in certain forms of Art. At first he appealed to the few: now he has educated the many. He has created in the public both taste and temperament. The public appreciate his artistic success immensely. I often wonder, however, whether the public understand that that success is entirely due to the fact that he did not accept their standard, but realised his own![1]

Art, education, taste, these would have been music to Irving's ears as they sum up his mission in the staging of plays at the Lyceum.

Irving summarized his holistic view of the stage in a lecture given at Harvard University in 1885:

> Today we are employing all our resources to heighten the picturesque effects of the drama, and we are still told that this is a gross error. It may be admitted that nothing is more objectionable than certain kinds of realism, which are simply vulgar; but harmony of colour and grace of outline have legitimate sphere in the theatre, and the method which uses them as adjuncts may claim to be 'as wholesome as sweet, and by very much more handsome than fine.' For the abuse of scenic decoration, the overloading of the stage with ornament, the subordination of the play to a pageant, I have nothing to say. That is all foreign to the artistic purpose which should dominate dramatic work. You perceive that the nicest discretion is needed in the use of the materials which are nowadays at the disposal of the manager. Music, painting, architecture, the endless variations of costume, have all to be employed with strict regard to the production of an artistic whole, in which no element shall be unduly obtrusive.[2]

He warned that the actor too must be incorporated into this whole:

> It is most important that an actor should learn that he is a figure in a picture, and that
> the least exaggeration destroys the harmony of the composition. All the members of the
> company should work towards a common end, with the nicest subordination of their
> individuality to the general purpose. Without this method a play when acted is at best a
> disjointed and incoherent piece of work, instead of being a harmonious whole like the
> fine performance of an orchestral symphony.[3]

It was in the 1880s that a fully pictorial stage was achieved in Victorian England,
blending actor and crowds in the setting with a sustained atmospheric and
compositional unity.[4]

That this was the best way of presenting plays had become an article of faith
for many by the end of the century. Typically, architect Alfred Darbyshire in his
The Art of the Victorian Stage (1907) began by noting that the two greatest eras
in stage history were the reigns of two great queens, Elizabeth whose era had
'produced the greatest dramatist the world has ever known' and Victoria, during
whose reign the stage became 'the medium of the *true* and beautiful method of
expression of a Shakespeare drama'.[5] He was here making the same equation
between truth and beauty that Irving regularly made and he invoked the memory
of Irving to justify his interpretation, recalling a visit they had made together in
1902 to Robert Courtneidge's pictorial production of *As You Like It* at the Theatre
Royal, Manchester. Irving observed: 'I have seen exactly what Shakespeare saw as
he wrote the immortal comedy'.[6] Darbyshire attributed to a succession of actor-
managers, Kean, Phelps, Calvert, Tree, Courtneidge, Benson and Irving, the
realisation of the ideas of 'true and beautiful stage expression of the
Shakespearian creations'.[7]

The final responsibility for achieving the compositional harmony, artistic
cohesion and dramatic flow of the Lyceum productions was Irving's. For not
only was he the star, he was what we would now call the director and what was
then known as stage manager. However divided they may have been about his
acting, the critics were generally agreed about one thing – he was a great director.
He had directed plays at the Queen's Theatre and the St James' theatre before
joining the Lyceum and he personally directed all the Lyceum productions
thereafter.

As H.A. Saintsbury wrote: 'Irving possessed in the highest degree the gift of
the superlative stage-manager, the gift of co-ordinating, single-handed, all the
various entities that make a stage production; the actors, the scenery, the
costumes, the lighting, the music, the effects.'[8] Tighe Hopkins in the *Westminster
Gazette* confirmed this concern with every aspect of the productions:

> Scenery, costumes, properties, music, are matters scarcely less important than the correct
> delivery of speeches and the management of scenes; and if it be nothing graver than the

always
note music

size and shape of a footstool, the extent to which a door should stand open, or the position of a book on a table, the main source of inspiration is still Sir Henry himself. He knows instinctively what music will convey the apt suggestion of a particular scene, as he knows where a splash of colour in a costume is inharmonious; and his skill in the disposition of lights is extraordinary.[9]

Edward Gordon Craig, who studied Irving's production methods closely, listed the influences upon his stage vision.[10] He said that in seeking to establish the atmosphere and style of a production Irving would turn to illustrators: John Gilbert, Honoré Daumier and in particular Gustave Doré. Doré (1832–1883) had made famous illustrated editions of Cervantes's *Don Quixote*, Dante's *Divine Comedy*, Tennyson's *Idylls of the King* and Milton's *Paradise Lost*. These works undoubtedly provided Irving with inspiration for the visuals in his own productions of *Don Quixote*, *Dante*, *King Arthur* and *Faust*. In the scale and nature of his productions, he was influenced by the spectacle achieved by Charles Kean and the melodramatic effects that resulted from the theatrical experimentation of Dion Boucicault. In Irving's own acting, Craig saw the greatest influences as Samuel Phelps, the acknowledged master of Shakespearean interpretation, and Charles Fechter, who had perfected the style of romantic melodrama in many of the popular vehicles Irving subsequently took over. Then there was Dickens. As an actor, Irving played the parts of David Copperfield, Bill Sikes, Jonas Chuzzlewit, Daniel Quilp, Montague Tigg, Wackford Squeers, Ralph Nickleby, James Steerforth, Mr Dombey, John Peerybingle, Mantalini and Alfred Jingle. Craig observed: 'One master who without doubt served him as he has done a hundred others, was Charles Dickens ... all Dickens was especially wonderful to Irving; and when he is *Dubosc* he is Dickens, and when he is *Lesurques* he is Dickens. He is guided by Dickens in *Richard III* and in *Charles the First*, as well as in *Eugene Aram* and *Robert Landry*!'[11] There is something peculiarly satisfying to learn of the dominance of Dickens and Doré in Irving's thinking, because Dickens and Doré have done more than any other artists to shape the popular image and folk memory of Victorian England. This may be another explanation of why Irving and his work struck so many chords with his audience.

Craig cited one final influence on Irving – E.W. Godwin. The great prophet of the marriage of archaeological accuracy and artistic effect was E.W. Godwin (1833–1886), whom Oscar Wilde called 'one of the most artistic spirits of this century in England'.[12] Architect, archaeologist, antiquarian, furniture designer, textile and wall-paper designer and drama critic, Godwin had considerable influence on the thinking about stage production in the later nineteenth century, bringing it in line with the tenets of the Aesthetic movement. He had been strongly influenced by the ideas of Ruskin. In 1874 and 1875 he published a series of seminal articles in the *Architect* entitled 'The Architecture and Costume of Shakespeare's Plays', in which he sought to identify precisely the historical period of each play and discussed the appropriate contemporary sources to illustrate the correct costumes and scenery.[13] But he entered an important caveat. The archaeological accuracy had to be in harmony with acting and staging to create the perfect 'illusion'. This also became the gospel according to Irving. Godwin advised the Bancrofts on the design of their celebrated 1875 production of *The Merchant of Venice*. They visited the locations in Venice that Godwin recommended and studied the paintings of Titian and Veronese for costume ideas. The result was an aesthetic if not a box office triumph. Looking back in 1913, Tree called it 'the first production in which the modern spirit of stage management asserted itself'.[14] Godwin was a great friend of W. G. Wills and through him got to design the scenery, costumes and properties for his historical drama *Juana* (1881), produced by Wilson Barrett. He fulfilled a similar function on Barrett's subsequent productions, *Claudian* (1883), *Hamlet* (1884), *Junius* (1885) and *Clito* (1886), plays set respectively in the Byzantine Empire, Medieval Denmark, Ancient Rome and Ancient Athens. These productions earned the critical accolade of equalling in splendour and accuracy Irving's productions at the Lyceum, where Godwin's principles were being implemented. But Godwin worked only once for Irving, designing the costumes for *The Cup*. This was at the suggestion of Ellen Terry, who had been Godwin's lover. Despite their similarity of outlook, Irving was perhaps reluctant to have permanently on hand the former partner of his leading lady with whom he was now in love. In 1883 Godwin did a whole set of costumes and designs for Wills's *Rienzi*, which had been commissioned by Irving, perhaps in the hope of participating in the forthcoming production. In the event Irving never produced the play.

Godwin was often at loggerheads with the actor-managers, with whom ultimate responsibility for production lay. There was a famous row with Barrett over his refusal to use a Byzantine litter Godwin had designed. Godwin finally gained complete control over production and design in a series of largely amateur productions, *As You Like It* (1884), *The Faithful Shepherdess* (1885), *Fair Rosamund* (1886) and *Helena in Troas* (1886), which were for the most part enthusiastically reviewed. But a venture into commercial management with *The Fool's Revenge* (1886) failed and Godwin's death in 1886, from complications following an operation to remove kidney stones, cut short his career in production.[15]

His aesthetic and ideological legacy remained. Tree, in *Thoughts and After-Thoughts*, listed the productions staged in the Godwinian spirit as Irving's *Hamlet, Macbeth, Othello, Much Ado, King Lear, Romeo and Juliet, The Merchant of Venice, Henry VIII, Richard III* and *Cymbeline*; Mary Anderson's *A Winter's Tale*; John Hare's *As You Like It*; Wilson Barrett's *Hamlet* and *Othello*; George Alexander's *As You Like It* and *Much Ado*; and his own *Hamlet, The Merry Wives*

of Windsor, Henry IV, Julius Caesar, King John and *A Midsummer Night's Dream.*[16]
Tree, like both Irving and Godwin, argued that 'worthily to represent
Shakespeare, the scenic embellishment should be as beautiful and costly as the
subject of the drama being performed seems to demand; that it should not be
subordinate to, but rather harmonious with, the dramatic interest, just as every
other element of art introduced into the representation should be, whether those
arts be of acting, painting, sculpture, music or what not.'[17]

Irving was one of the key figures in establishing among the arts of Victorian
England – the art of the stage. Although archaeological accuracy was regularly
stressed in accounts of his work and was part of his gospel of the stage as a vehicle
for education, Irving was far from being a slave to accuracy. He wrote: 'Nor do I
think that servility to archaeology on the stage is an unmixed good. Correctness
of costume is admirable, and necessary up to a certain point, and when it ceases
to be 'as wholesome as sweet,' it should, I think, be sacrificed.'[18]

What mattered to Irving, as Edward Gordon Craig recalled, was what worked
theatrically. Craig was cast as Arviragus in *Cymbeline*:

> The leopard-skin he gave me to wear (in spite of Alma Tadema's presence, and Tadema
> was a stickler for correct costume) was utterly incorrect: the old black velvet suit I wore
> in *Henry VIII*, when playing *Cromwell* to his *Wolsey* was equally incorrect. What seemed
> fitting, that was best with him. All the correctness in the world was not worth a fig to
> Irving, unless it *seemed* all right.[19]

Bram Stoker tells a similar story regarding *Romeo and Juliet*:

> In the beginning Irving had asked Mr Alfred Thompson, known as a popular designer
> of dresses for many plays, to design the costumes. This he did; but as they were not
> exactly what was wanted, not a single one of them was used in the piece. Irving himself
> selected the costumes from old pictures and prints, and costume books. He chose and
> arranged the colours and stuff to be used. Nevertheless, with his characteristic generosity,
> he put in the playbill and advertisements Mr Thompson's name as designer.[20]

This attitude got Irving into trouble with Henry Herman, the co-author of
Claudian. In an 1888 article in the *Magazine of Art*, entitled 'The Stage as a School
of Art and Archaeology', Herman took as his text the 1884 opinion of John Ruskin
about *Claudian*: 'With scene-painting like that, this Princess's Theatre might do
more for art-teaching than all the galleries and professors of Christendom.'
Herman complained bitterly that, while many actor-managers claimed to be
doing this, they were not.

> It is given only to men of deep research and honest self-denial in the cause of art to
> penetrate behind the veil of popular glamour, of gaudy impressiveness, with which the
> best spectacles of the stage of the present day are shrouded, and to find there the germ of
> a new school of art, a *popular* school of art, a school-mind what our great art-teacher

says – that '*might* do more for art-teaching than all the galleries and professors of Christendom'.

He denounced the critics for taking at face value the claims from actor-managers that their productions were archaeologically accurate: 'As a matter of fact … not one out of twenty among them knows the difference between a Greek and a Roman helmet, and not one in ten could tell you whether his own countrymen fifteen or sixteen hundred years ago wore boots, or shoes, or sandals, or what … In the innocence of their hearts, a great scene-painter's name or the name of a costumier was sufficient absolution for any number of incongruities, and what the eye does not see the heart does not grieve for.'

He singled out for criticism as an example of 'the strange incongruities foisted upon an unsuspecting public by the very best of our stage-managers' (ie Irving) the Lyceum *Romeo and Juliet* in which the actors wore a mixture of costumes ranging over a period of a hundred years.[21] But, as Irving argued, archaeological accuracy had to be melded with artistic harmony. That was the variety of accuracy so often hailed by the critics. Wilde, for instance, rejecting an argument advanced by Lord Lytton for freedom from archaeological accuracy, wrote: 'The most lively scenes that have been produced on our stage have been those that have been characterized by perfect accuracy, such as Mr and Mrs Bancroft's eighteenth-century revivals at the Haymarket, Mr Irving's superb production of *Much Ado About Nothing* and Mr Barrett's *Claudian*.'[22] It was an illusion of 'perfect accuracy' that Wilde was in fact praising.

The journalist J.B. Booth recalled Irving's production method on a play, which remained the same throughout his career:

> Once he had determined on its production he lived with it and in its period. Authorities bearing on it were studied, precedents and traditions examined, to be accepted or discarded as they fitted in with the scheme which was maturing in his mind. And so at last he saw the play precisely as he meant it should be played – as a whole, clearly, precisely. There was no fumbling, no groping. In his mental vision all was clear-cut and finished when he summoned his company to hear the play read and to have their parts allotted them. He had passed the whole production through his mind, before the first rehearsal. He knew exactly what he intended, and what if it was humanly possible, he meant to have.[23]

Irving then realized his concept through long and intensive rehearsal.[24]

Irving knew precisely how he wanted every part played. Edward Gordon Craig recalled: "He told us all who we were, why and what we had to do'. When Craig was cast as Oswald, the steward, in *King Lear*, Irving said one word to him: 'Malvolio' at the first rehearsal ('With that in my pocket I knew what to do and I didn't hesitate').[25]

One of the most notable features of Irving's *mise-en-scène* was his handling of crowds. His mastery dated from *Romeo and Juliet*. Ellen Terry recalled it as the most elaborate of all the Lyceum productions, very sumptuous, impressive and Italian. 'In it Henry first displayed his mastery of crowds. The brawling of the rival houses in the streets, the procession of girls to wake Juliet on her wedding morning, the musicians, the magnificent reconciliation of the two houses which closed the play, every one on stage holding a torch, were all treated with a marvellous sense of pictorial effect.'[26]

Romeo and Juliet was produced in 1882 and it seems that Irving had learned lessons from the celebrated visit to London in 1881 of the Saxe-Meiningen Company. They performed in German a series of Shakespeare plays, beginning with *Julius Caesar*. The Saxe-Meiningen Company were renowned for the 'extraordinary accuracy and picturesqueness of stage-management, especially in the handling of mobs or other great masses of humanity'. George Odell concluded that their visit had a lasting effect on the English stage and in particular on Irving.[27] He was certainly familiar with the company who were the ducal players. Irving entertained the Duke of Saxe-Meiningen to dinner and in 1897 he received jointly from the Duke of Saxe-Meiningen and the Duke of Saxe-Coburg the honour of Commander of the Ernestine Order (Second Class), the first time a foreign decoration had been conferred on an English actor.[28] From 1882 onwards, Irving's handling of crowds was invariably singled out for praise, and as he moved into putting on larger and larger spectacles, the crowds of the French Revolution, the Italian Renaissance and the Roman forum came to life on the Lyceum stage.

Irving became a master of stage lighting. When he took over the lease of the Lyceum in 1878 he undertook a major reconstruction of the theatre, bringing up to date all the lighting appliances: the footlights, the wing lights, the battens (the lights run along the top of the stage), the ground rows, and special lights designed for specific items of built scenery. Eventually at the Lyceum, the auditorium and the footlights were lit by electricity. But for Irving, stage lighting meant gaslight and limelight, and Irving developed an increasingly sophisticated means of lighting scenes by applying coloured lacquers to the limelight mediums, and dividing the footlights into independently controlled colour circuits.[29] This meant, says Stoker, that Irving could use 'the media of coloured lights as a painter uses his palette'.[30]

Ellen Terry, writing in 1908, attributed much of the beauty of Lyceum lighting to gas and limelight. 'Until electricity has been greatly improved and developed, it can never be to the stage what gas was. The thick softness of gaslight, with the lovely specks and motes in it, so like *natural* light, gave illusion to many a sense which is now revealed in all its marked trashiness by electricity.'[31]

Percy Nash, who stepped in to stage manage *Robespierre* in 1899 when H.J. Loveday fell ill, recorded:

Irving would never use electric lighting; he argued rightly that when you dim an incandescent lamp you obtain an orange-red effect, whereas the argand burner (a circular flame protected by a glass chimney) could be easily controlled and to its last flicker is blue. The calcium, or limelight, too, is soft and mellow and can be concentrated at will. Scenes lit by Irving had always the effect of oil-paintings, the boundaries lost in shade, highlights focussing the points of greatest interest.[32]

One of these points of greatest interest was Irving's face. Nash says: 'A special operator always followed the chief's face with a small 'pin' light of steel-blue; however dark the scene was you always saw Irving's face.'[33] This explains why so many accounts of his acting describe in such detail his facial expressions. H. A. Saintsbury confirms: 'Irving would have no electric light, it glares: his six rounds of argand burners in the float glowed softly and gave depth; electric flattens. He performed miracles with gas and calcium lights; the sunset on the quicksand in *Ravenswood*, the dawn in *Romeo and Juliet*, the mystic lake and apparition of *Excalibur*; they have never been rivalled ... We have seen nothing in design or lighting since his time that he did not anticipate'.[34]

Irving was essentially creating three-dimensional paintings. He was fond of particular effects, for instance sunlight falling diagonally through a window, particularly a stained glass window, an effect used in the church scene in *Much Ado*, the christening scene in *Henry VIII* and the arrest of Hastings in *Richard III*, and blood-red sunsets (the battle of Bosworth in *Richard III*, the opening scenes of *Macbeth*, the finale of *King Lear*).[35]

The new sophistication of lighting effects also seems to date from *Romeo and Juliet*. Edward R. Russell noted: 'Throughout the play the management of lighting is a thing wholly new in its perfect and accurate graduation, and here we have in the first scene the first example of it, in the creation of what the *Spectator* well described as 'an atmosphere'.'[36] He expanded on the meaning of 'atmosphere' in a later article. Calling *Romeo and Juliet* 'a matchless realisation of Italian beauty – light, real and artificial, architecture of uncommon reality and grace, foliage fresh and umbrageous, exquisite interiors dimly seen or glowing and brightly lit, the chill majestic gloom of the marble mausoleum – all these lent exquisite atmosphere to the old sweet story'.[37]

Costume was a vital part of Irving's theatrical ensemble. H. A. Saintsbury provided a devastating comparison between Irving's attitude to costume and Tree's. Where Tree sought a striking effect, Irving went for authenticity. Saintsbury, writing in 1939, recalled:

Irving would have nothing white, it was too crude, every shirt cuff and kerchief, every scrap of lace was tea-tinted. The clothes were lived in. Don Pedro, Don John, Claudio and Benedick, returned from the war (in *Much Ado About Nothing*), each commander with his staff and colour, bore evidence of campaigning; richly apparelled as the period and their station demanded but worn, slashed and cobbled; their boots had known service. The troopers came at the double to the King's tent at Newark (in *Charles the First*), road-stained, grimed, bespattered, with jingling spurs and clatter of accoutrements. The halt in a cloud of dust, is electric. In *Joseph and His Brethren* Tree marched Egyptian soldiers across the desert *in gilt armour*! In *The Belle's Stratagem* powder was worn and the manner that goes with it; bearing and gait matched the red-heeled shoe. That meticulous care is no longer practised. An historical drama or period comedy is a happy excuse for fancy dress as worn at the Chelsea Arts Ball … If armour is borne all is burnished – no dent, no tarnish, no rust, even after battle; no tattered standard, no bandaged limb.[38]

Irving did not hesitate to call in specialists to get his costumes correct. Seymour Lucas (1849–1923) was both a Royal Academician known for his genre and historical paintings and a Fellow of the Society of Antiquaries. He painted for the Royal Exchange, a fresco of William the Conqueror granting the first charter to the City of London. His many historical canvases included *The Armada in Sight*, *Philip II Receiving News of the Armada* and *The Surrender of Don Pedro de Vargas to Drake aboard the Revenge*. So his knowledge of Tudor costume and accoutrements obviously qualified him to be historical adviser on Irving's production of *Henry VIII*. His paintings of *Charles I before Gloucester*, *A Whip for Van Tromp*, *From the Field of Sedgemoor*, *Charles II visiting Christopher Wren* showed his mastery of seventeenth-century costumes and settings. His sympathy with Irving's repertoire is manifested by paintings of *Romeo and Juliet*, *Louis XI* and *Peter the Great*.

Seymour Lucas wrote an article for the *Magazine of Art* on 'Dressing an Historical Play'.

> The adequate 'dressing' of a play is now considered by all theatrical managers of first rank to be a matter of the highest importance … The playgoer of today expects that his enjoyment shall be enhanced by correct pictorial presentment; and the expectation is likely to grow. The public is even now in a position sufficiently to appreciate artistic excellence … It must surely be to everyone a source of genuine delight to watch the performance of a play well-mounted and carefully dressed. Well-painted scenery and accurate costume not only assist the imagination of the onlooker, they cannot fail to be a very real help to the actor. On the other hand, garish and inharmonious colouring, bad grouping, inaccurate costume and all sorts of historical and antiquarian anachronisms inevitably tend to weaken in the minds of the educated the illusion produced by the very highest histrionic talent.

This was very much in line with Irving's philosophy, so it was no coincidence that, of the four plays that Lucas had dressed to date, three (*Werner*, *Henry VIII* and *Ravenswood*) were for Irving (the fourth, *Richard III*, was for Richard Mansfield). Lucas argued that the artist had two concerns when designing costumes: colour and accuracy. The colour scheme must be in sympathy with the mood and atmosphere of the play. 'As a rule a play will assert with unmistakable clearness its own claims in this respect – it will suggest its own colour. *Ravenswood*, for instance, calls for a treatment in sombre greys, whilst *Henry VIII* at once suggests gold and brilliant reds.' The costumes of the leading actors set the key and the rest of the cast are clothed 'with an eye to relative chromatic value'.

Research was essential. For *Henry VIII*, Lucas consulted the paintings of Holbein, the Calendar of State Papers, the letters of the Spanish Ambassador, the Warwick Roll of the College of Heralds and a portrait of Henry VIII owned by the Duke of Rutland, who kindly permitted a copy to be made. For *Ravenswood* the Print Room of the British Museum was a principal source. Having assembled his research materials, the artist made drawings of the individual costumes – there were 138 for *Henry VIII*, which were then executed by costumiers. Lucas expressed his frustration that some of the actors ('the females in subordinate positions being the greatest sinners') persisted in wearing wigs, coifs and dresses that would make 'the most effectual display of personal charms' rather than the historically accurate costumes prescribed. Some, particularly when using armour, put it on back to front or the wrong way round. 'Again and again it has been necessary to point out how the entire character of an important piece of costume, such as a hat, has been altered by the ignorant way in which it has been put on.'[39] When *Henry VIII* was produced in 1892, a critic wrote:

> It is impossible to overstate Mr Irving's genius as a great stage painter. Stage-night and stage-day, stage-men and women, canvas properties, music – all are merely pigments used by this Michel Angelo of his art. Unlike any other London manager, he does not want all that he has on the stage to be seen. He is content to let much opulence of detail, much beauty of accessory, be lost in mysterious half light, if only he can obtain his Rembrandtesque effects of chiaroscuro by so doing. Note with what an artist's eye he chooses his people. Bluff Mr Terriss – broad, brusque and virile, to make up as one of Holbein's portraits of the tyrannic Tudor. Mr Forbes Robertson to touch with fire the aristocratic and scholarly Buckingham; fragile Miss Vanbrugh, with long, graceful swan neck, suggestive of a headsman's easy task, for Anne Bullen.[40]

The references are all to the stage as painting, as composition, a play lit, dressed and mounted like a canvas. The critics laid stress both on the spectacle and its educational value:

> 'It was', said Mr. Irving to a Scotch interviewer, 'a splendid time; and I shall endeavour to give it a splendid setting'; and, with consummate knowledge, taste, and splendour, this most generous and cultured artist has worked his will. He has executed his project in thirteen matchless tableaux – a series divided, for convenience sake, into five separate acts. He has used the best actors and actresses in London, priceless stuffs, the talent and taste of master harmonists in rich colour, stage scenery, architecture, and furniture, made by the most skilful hands, and light itself, just as the painter uses his pigments, never sparing expense over detail, but aiming always at the impressiveness of the general effect

... No Tudor Exhibition at the New Gallery ever taught us half so well how King Hal and his Court lived and had their being as these thirteen, never, once seen, to-be-forgotten, pictures at the Lyceum. There is but one man who could have directed their composition and sustained throughout their unity of intention.[41]

Another critic observed: 'The Tudor court seems to live again in all its sumptuousness and splendour ... Under the spell of Mr Irving's stage management, the slightest mental effort transports one back to the England of 300 years ago, so complete is the picture in itself and so accurate its details, if not to the actual truth, at all events to the conception which the historians and the painters have enabled us to form of it.'[42]

Fascinatingly one critic compared Irving's staging of *Henry VIII* to the exhibitions of Imre Kiralfy and the Drury Lane pantomimes of Sir Augustus Harris.

Mr Imre Kiralfy has astonished London at Olympia, Sir Augustus Harris has delighted it at Drury Lane, and now with the waning of the holiday season, comes Mr Irving to show these masters of spectacle what can be done by an accomplished stage-manager who is also an artist, a scholar, and ... a poet. The new show at the Lyceum is not as big as *Venice in London* and not as glittering and many-coloured as *Humpty Dumpty*, but it has the advantage of illustrating a most interesting period of English history, and presenting on the stage real persons, real costumes, and real scenes, with a lavish magnificence of display and a most conscientious accuracy of detail. There are no fewer than fourteen scenes in its five acts, every one of them artistic in design and perfect in execution, and many of them marvellously elaborate and beautiful. The dances ... are very quaintly and ingeniously arranged, the processions are as costly as anything Drury Lane has ever seen, and far more picturesque and interesting than any stage combination of 'dolls', or 'gems', or 'nations', known to pantomime, and its fairy transformation scene is a masterpiece of poetic feeling, and dexterous manipulation of the limelight. These are high terms of praise, but no visitor to the Lyceum will be disposed to cavil with them, for Irving has set himself down to beat contemporary spectacular triumphs, and has completely succeeded.[43]

Despite his strictures on the archaeological inaccuracy of actor-managers, Henry Herman ended his article on the art of the stage by declaring 'In the art of scene-painting England stands paramount and alone among nations'. He listed W. R. Beverley, William Telbin, Hawes Craven, Walter Hann, T.E. Ryan, Stafford Hall and William Harford as 'artists in the truest and best sense of the word, and it is to their work that John Ruskin principally refers when he speaks of the stage as a possible school of art'. He ended by calling upon the star actors and actresses to make it their business to ensure that the stage became 'a home of true art'.[44] Three of Herman's list (Craven, Telbin and Hann) worked for Irving.

Scene-painting had a long history. In the eighteenth century Garrick, although he performed his Shakespeare in contemporary costume, engaged the painter Philippe de Loutherbourg to design appropriate scenes for his productions and de Loutherbourg, strongly influenced by the picturesque, contributed Romantic landscape backgrounds. In the early nineteenth century Clarkson Stanfield (1793–1867) and W. R. Beverley (1814–89) painted large back cloths for the historical plays of Shakespeare produced by Macready and Phelps respectively.[45]

It was Charles Kean who combined the scene-painting of leading painters like Thomas Grieve, William Telbin the elder, William Gordon, William Cuthbert and Frederick Lloyds, with architectural and antiquarian research into costume, building styles and accessories by Charles Kean himself (which earned him a Fellowship of the Society of Antiquaries) in pursuit of a defined philosophy of stage art. He summed it up in his retirement speech after his final performance at the Princess's Theatre in 1859: 'I have always entertained the conviction that, in illustrating the great plays of the greatest poet who ever wrote, historical accuracy might be so blended with pictorial effect, that instruction and amusement would go hand in hand.'[46]

It was his series of spectacular Princess's theatre revivals that led Darbyshire to dub Kean 'the pioneer of the reformation of the art of the Victorian stage'.[47] Moelwyn Merchant also attributed the beginnings of artistic Shakespeare to Charles Kean, saying 'Irving continued, though with greater genius and more refined sensibility, the tradition of Charles Kean'.[48]

The productions in which Irving starred for the Bateman management were tastefully but economically staged on the whole. It was when Irving took over the lease of the Lyceum himself that he was able to put into effect his grand artistic vision. The Bateman *Hamlet* cost only £100 to stage and netted £10,000. When Irving restaged *Hamlet* under his own management, he had completely new scenery painted and costumes made.[49]

Irving employed what was by common consent the finest team of scene-painters in London, Hawes Craven, William Telbin the Younger, Walter Hann, William Cuthbert and Joseph Harker. In an article written for the *Magazine of Art*, William Telbin stressed that scene-painters needed wide archaeological, artistic and mechanical knowledge, confidence in execution and an understanding of what was and was not possible: 'We must avoid powerful greens, which become coarse, strong blues, which become black, and exaggerate our yellows, which are robbed of their strength by the gas; and we must paint solidly. Distemper, like thin oil-colour, always looks poor.'

He defended the lavish mounting of plays: 'In the illustration of Shakespeare too much cannot be done if done with a true feeling of admiration and veneration for his work. Here is the best of all food for the mind, and it cannot be served in too tempting a form.' He claimed popularity for the scene-painter's work: 'Whatever the status of scene-painting may be as an art, that it is very popular with the public is certain.' He saw their role as an essentially collaborative one: 'those who are responsible to the public for the production of plays must surely mount them as well as they can afford to do; and we whom they trust and make responsible for the pictorial illustration of them, must not leave a thing undone that may assist in making the illusion more complete'. But the scene-painter had limitations which the picture-painter did not:

> In this scenic art the more pronounced effects of nature are those most suited to the stage. Sunrise, noon, sunset, and moonlight tell best. The subtler effects of nature are likely to fall short of the satisfactory – that very prejudiced illuminator, gas, would deprive the quiet greys of dawn of much of their value, and twilight also would be disappointing. And above all, the uncertain proceedings of the gas men (though, as a rule, very intelligent and attentive fellows) might, as like as not, help to mar an effect of the gentler character.

In terms of influences, he singled out Turner's great panoramas such as *Dido Building Carthage* and *Bay of Baiae* as 'magnificent lessons to the scene-painter in colour, composition, and poetry'. He outlined the procedure followed by scene-painters. When the scene-painter receives his commission, some managers give an idea of what they want, others leave the artist a free hand. So the first step is to create a scale model, showing composition, colour and lighting scheme. Once the model is approved great bales of canvas are stretched on frames and the painting begins, ending with the foreground. Once it is finished, a day or two is spent on the stage lighting it. Lighting is vital. 'The best scene ever designed and painted can be ruined by injudicious lighting; for the illumination is the last and most important touch to the picture – its very life.'

He ended his article by asking rhetorically if the stage would ever draw recruits from the Royal Academy or vice-versa. His conclusion was that the technical demands of scene-painting meant that 'it is exceedingly improbable that a highly talented Academician would do anything worthy of his reputation in a theatre … From the stage to the Academy is a refining, concentrating, and clarifying process – vice-versa is a process of undoing.'[50]

The specialist nature of scene-painting is confirmed by Stoker. During the run of *Faust*, Irving was preparing his next great Lyceum production for 1888 – *Macbeth*. Irving who admired the work of the painter Keeley Halswelle (1832–1891) invited him to do the designs for the play. Halswelle had painted a notable picture of the play scene from *Hamlet* (1878), inspired by Irving's performance, and he had begun his painting career in Edinburgh. So he must have seemed an appropriate artist for *Macbeth*. His sketches were pronounced excellent. He declared a desire to paint the scenes himself and Irving engaged the paint room at Covent Garden Opera House. The canvas cloths, framed pieces, borders and wings were prepared by the Lyceum carpenters and 'primed' for the painting. Time passed and Stoker went to inspect the work only to find acres of white untouched even by a charcoal outline. 'The superb painter of pictures, untutored in stage art and perspective, had found himself powerless before those vast solitudes. He had been unable even to begin his task', recorded Stoker.[51] The work was undertaken by Irving's regular team headed by Hawes Craven, Joseph Harker, Walter Hann and T.W. Hall. But Halswelle's work on the production inspired a painting, *Spirit Scene: Irving's Macbeth* (1889), a highly atmospheric composition with a grim hill, gnarled trees and forbidding rocks, overlooking a cauldron and a procession of cowled figures. Telbin found an ally in his desire for scene-painting to be taken seriously in Oscar Wilde. He argued, in what must have been music to Telbin's ears, that critics should 'exert whatever influence they possess towards restoring the scene-painter to his proper position as an artist. I have never seen any reason why such artists as Mr Beverley, Mr Walter Hann and Mr Telbin should not be entitled to become Academicians. They have certainly as good a claim as have many of those RA's whose total inability to paint we can see every May for a shilling.'[52]

Irving's leading scene painter was Hawes Craven (1837–1910), who had originally practised his art at the Theatre Royal, Dublin, where, according to Percy Fitzgerald, 'his scenery attracted attention for its brilliancy and originality. It had the breadth and effect of rich water-colour drawings of the Prout school.' At the Lyceum, he devised the 'medium' principle – 'the introduction of atmosphere, of phantasmagoric lights or different tones, which are more satisfactory than the same tones when produced by ordinary colours. The variety of the effect thus produced has been extraordinary'.[53] Among other achievements, Craven developed a new pigment which created the effect of the clear blue Italian sky in *Romeo and Juliet*. He was also a key figure in the process by which sliding painted flats were supplemented on the stage by built-out and moulded three-dimensional sets to create an even greater illusion of reality. A rare interview with Hawes Craven was published in *Sala's Journal* (4 March 1893). This was a newly-founded (1892) weekly newspaper which was the latest venture of the prolific and influential journalist George Augustus Sala (1828–1895). Significantly, he had been one of the earliest advocates of the work of the scene painter, claiming in an article published thirty years earlier that they were 'better architects, landscape painters, professors of perspective' than the established artists who looked down on them. The new article argued:

> a great deal of the enjoyment which we derive at the theatre is due to the artistic efforts of the scene-painter. He has played an important part in assisting to popularise our places of amusement. He it is who silently but successfully educated us in the matter of artistic surroundings. Nowadays the manager who would win public favour and achieve success must provide not only good plays and good players, but also effective scenery. The one has become as much a necessity as the other. There

must be Art in the painting-room of the theatre, as well as in the studio of the picture-painter.

Craven explained that he had been born in Leeds of a theatrical family, his mother a writer, his father an actor. His early partiality for drawing led to his being sent to the School of Design at Somerset House and the School of Art at Marlborough House, where he had won the bronze medal. He was then apprenticed to the scene-painter John Gray at the Britannia Theatre, Hoxton, and after three years he went with him when he was appointed chief scene painter at the Olympic Theatre. From the Olympic, he went on to be a scene-painter at the Adelphi, Drury Lane and the Theatre Royal, Dublin. He returned to London as chief scene-painter at the Olympic 'where I remained until its collapse' and after that joined Mr Bateman at the Lyceum: 'I have been here ever since and ... here I intend to remain as long as Mr Irving thinks fit to retain my services.'

He expressed the view that there had been a great advance in scene-painting not only in the theatre of the West End but also on the Surrey Side:

> It is the sumptuous way in which Irving has produced his pieces, combined with his own genius, that has gained for them such unparalleled success, and Beerbohm Tree and other managers are now following his lead and producing their plays on the finest possible scale. Irving is doing what Charles Kean did, only in a much more liberal manner. And the public expect it; they will not be satisfied with anything less. It is the same in the provinces. Most of the companies that go on tour take with them the principal part of the scenery. The consequence is the provincial audiences get accustomed to that which is of the very best and decline to patronise anything that is on a lower scale.

He explained that 'Mr Irving is always desirous that everything shall be as perfect as possible, and when a new play is decided upon and there is occasion to travel in the locality from which the scenes are taken, I invariably accompany him in order to make sketches'. He spent five or six weeks in Germany for *Faust*, visited Scotland for *Macbeth*, went to Venice prior to *The Merchant of Venice* and to Paris for *The Bells*. 'It is only in this way that it is possible to attain anything approaching reality. Irving is also careful to supply such archaeological works as may assist with information, and models are prepared of each scene and submitted before the actual work itself is commenced.' It was enormously hard work, sometimes requiring the scene-painter to be at it for sixteen hours without a break. The scenery for *Faust* necessitated him working sixteen Sundays, and *Becket* required five. 'Still, there is to me a fascination in the work and I am never so happy as when I am in full swing.' Asked what he considered his best work, he replied that it was generally held that the view of Hampton Court he painted for *Charles the First* was his best work and he would not demur from that. He stayed with Irving until *Coriolanus* (1901). *The Dictionary of National Biography* pronounced him 'probably the greatest scene-painter of his century'.[54]

Irving would never accept anything less than perfection in his scene-painting. It was this perfection that gave the Lyceum its reputation for artistic beauty and led, for instance, to every scene in *King Arthur* being applauded as the curtain rose.[55] Ellen Terry recalled:

> He never hesitated to discard scenery if it did not suit his purpose. There was enough scenery rejected in *Faust* to have furnished three productions, and what was finally used for the famous Brocken scene cost next to nothing. Even the best scene-painters sometimes think more of their pictures than of scenic effects. Henry would never accept anything that was not right *theatrically* as well as pictorially beautiful. His instinct in this was unerring and incomparable.[56]

Ellen cultivated the friendship of the scene-painters, remembering a play early in her career, *The Antipodes*, a bad play in which she had a bad part, but recalling the scenery by William Telbin as 'lovely':

> Telbin was a poet, and he has handed on much of his talent to his son, who is alive now, and painted most of our *Faust* scenery at the Lyceum – he and dear Mr Hawes Craven, who so loved his garden and could paint the flicker of golden sunshine for the stage better than anyone. I have always been friendly with the scene-painters, perhaps because I have always taken pains about my dresses, and consulted them beforehand about the colour, so that I should not look wrong in their scenes, nor their scenes wrong with my dresses.[57]

Irving's total involvement in his productions is illustrated by Stoker's account of the genesis of *The Merchant of Venice*. He had not intended producing it. The 1879–80 season had already been announced as *The Iron Chest*, *The Gamester*, *The Stranger*, *Coriolanus* and *Robert Emmett*. But two weeks into the run of *The Iron Chest*, he called in his business manager, Stoker, and H.J. Loveday, his stage manager, and announced that he intended to put on *The Merchant of Venice* and to do so in three weeks' time. He had been on a Mediterranean cruise during the summer and had been inspired by what he saw with a vision of how to do the play. Stoker recounted the scene:

> 'I have it in my mind. I have been thinking it over and I see my way to it. Here is what I shall have in the "Casket" scene.' He took a sheet of notepaper and made a rough drawing of the scene, tearing out an arch in the back and propping another piece of paper in it with a rough suggestion of a Venetian scene. 'I will have an Eastern Lamp with red glass – I know where is the exact thing. It is, or used to be two or three years ago, in that furniture shop in Oxford Street, near Tottenham Court Road.' Then he went on to expound his idea of the whole play; and did it in such a way that he set both Loveday and myself afire with the idea. We talked it out till early morning.

The whole Lyceum machine swung into action at once.

Scenes had to be talked over, entrances and exits fixed and models made. Four scene-painters bent their shoulders to the task. Craven did three scenes, Telbin three, Hann three, and Cuthbert one. The whole theatre became alive with labour. Each night had its own tally of work with the running play; but from the time the curtain went down at night till when the doors were opened the following night full pressure never ceased. Properties, dresses, and 'appointments' came in completed perpetually. Rehearsals went on all day. On Saturday night, 1 November just over three weeks after he had broached the idea, and less than three from the time the work was actually begun – the curtain went up on *The Merchant of Venice.*[58]

The eventual production's initial cost was £1200.[59] The work paid off and the scenery received its due meed of praise. Percy Fitzgerald recalled:

The scenery alone would take an essay in itself, and it is hard to say which of the three artists engaged most excelled. The noble colonnade of the ducal palace was grand and imposing; so was the lovely interior of Portia's house at Belmont, with its splendid amber hangings and pearl-grey tones, its archings and spacious perspective. But the Court scene, with its ceiling painted in the Verrio style, its portraits of Doges, the crimson walls with gilt carvings, and the admirable arrangements of the throne etc, surely for taste, contrivance, and effect has never been surpassed. The whole effect was produced by the painting, not by built-up structures. The dresses too – groupings, servants and retainers – what sumptuousness: the pictures of Moroni and Titian had been studied for the dove-coloured cloaks and jerkins, the violet merchant's gown of Antonio, the short hats ... and the frills. The general tone was that of one of Paolo Veronese's pictures – as gorgeous and dazzling as the *mélange* of dappled colour in the great Louvre picture.[60]

But as Ellen Terry pointed out, 'The Lyceum production of *The Merchant of Venice* was not so strictly archaeological as the Bancrofts' had been, but it was very gravely beautiful and effective. If less attention was paid to details of costume and scenery, the play itself was arranged and acted very attractively and always went with a swing.'[61]

On 18 February 1898 Irving suffered an irreparable loss. The Lyceum storage depot in Bear Lane, Southwark, beneath two railway arches over which ran the London, Chatham and Dover line, caught fire. Irving, whose finances were by now precarious, had ordered the insurance cover for the store reduced from £10,000 to £6000. Stored in the depot were over 260 scenes from forty-four plays which the Lyceum had produced, more than two thousand individual pieces of scenery and 'bulky properties without end'. They were totally destroyed. Stoker estimated the value of the lost properties at over £30,000 (in today's money £1,869,000). He added:

But the cost price was the least part of the loss. Nothing could repay the time and labour and artistic experience spent on them. All the scene painters in England working for a whole year could not have restored the scenery alone[62]

Given the failure of a succession of new productions at the Lyceum, *Peter the Great*, *The Medicine Man*, *Coriolanus*, Irving increasingly depended on his tried and true repertoire which people would always come to see. In order to perform his standard repertoire, Irving had to have the scenery repainted for *Louis XI*, *Charles the First*, *The Bells*, *The Lyons Mail*, *Olivia*, *Faust* and *Becket* at an aggregate cost of over £11,000.

Despite the fact that Irving had at his disposal the most eminent scene-painters in the business, he also saw the publicity value in drawing on the services of established artists who were revered by the intelligentsia and also had popular appeal. The first one he called on was Sir Lawrence Alma-Tadema (1836–1912). At the close of his second season as manager, 25 July 1879, Irving announced his intention of producing *Coriolanus*. Anxious to secure archaeological accuracy, he turned to Alma-Tadema, celebrated for his visually stunning, meticulously accurate pictures of life in the ancient world and who was, moreover, an expert not just on ancient architecture but also on statuary, arms and armour, furniture and lighting, the implements of domestic life and the staging of ceremonial. Stoker recalled: 'Irving felt that with such an artist to help – archaeologist, specialist, and genius in one – he would be able to put before an audience such work as would not only charm them by its beauty and interest them in its novelty, but would convince by its suitability.'[63] Throughout 1880 and 1881 Alma-Tadema worked on the designs and, although he announced it again at the end of the 1881 season, Irving continually postponed the production. Stoker suggests that this was because Ellen Terry was too young to play the leading female role, Coriolanus' mother Volumnia, and he wanted to put on plays that would showcase her youth and beauty. In fact it was not until 1901 that Irving staged *Coriolanus*, almost certainly in a bid to emulate Tree's success with *Julius Caesar*.

Before *Coriolanus* came to life, Alma-Tadema had also designed *Cymbeline* for Irving in 1896 and *Hypatia* (1893) and *Julius Caesar* (1898) for Tree. Irving wrote to Alma-Tadema's biographer Percy Cross Standing that Alma-Tadema's designs for *Cymbeline* and *Coriolanus* were 'one and all, exquisite works of the highest art, full of imagination, poetry and learning and they must all live. In every case they were accurate lessons in archaeology. No praise could, to my mind, be too great for Sir Lawrence's work for the stage.' Ellen Terry also wrote to Standing about the costumes Alma-Tadema designed for her:

> The costumes were very very beautiful, but I can give you no adequate idea of the *colours* – the colour could only be expressed by Sir Lawrence himself! He contrived to make me look like a young girl, which was a wizard's work, for it is not so very long ago that I played Imogen.[64]

Alma-Tadema also clearly admired the effects achieved by Irving in his stage productions. Alfred Darbyshire was sitting next to Alma-Tadema at Irving's production of *The Cup*, which received rapturous applause for its classical sets and backdrops. Darbyshire reported that: 'With a sigh and a shrug of his shoulders, he exclaimed: "Ah! How poor my art is after this." The great artist repeated this opinion to the great actor-manager. Irving, with that sad smile which sometimes passed across his features, said "Ah! Tadema, when I am dead and gone my art is gone, while yours lives for ever".'[65]

But on another occasion, Alma-Tadema was provoked by Irving's approach. When Irving was planning to produce *Julius Caesar* with music by George Henschel and designs by Alma-Tadema, he outraged the artist by asking him to imitate Jean-Léon Gérôme's paintings, particularly *The Death of Caesar*, for particular scenes. Alma-Tadema wrote angrily to Henschel: 'I am very sorry indeed that we are not going to be associated with *Julius Caesar* at the Lyceum. I too find it incredible that a man like Irving should lack judgment in what is due an artist. He already bothered me to imitate Gérôme's pictures among my scenes ... As if I could be brought to copy another and make what you rightly call a patchwork.'[66] It is clear that Irving planned to 'realize' several classical paintings in his staging, a common occurrence at the time, but failed to take into account the distinguished artist's *amour-propre* in explaining it. In the end, he abandond the planned production.

Interviewed by the *Daily News* (16 April, 1901), Alma-Tadema admitted to taking some dramatic licence in a way Irving would have approved. He declared that *Coriolanus* presented particular difficulties that other plays did not. One was the lack of detailed knowledge of the period and another was the need for dramatic contrast in the staging of the play. Early Roman civilisation, he had discovered, was largely Etruscan in character.

> It was from the Etruscan that the toga was derived, the tombs of the Romans and Etruscans are closely similar. But it was necessary in this play to mark a contrast between the inhabitants and the builders of Rome and Corioli, and to make the Rome of Marcius more distinctively Roman, and I was obliged to avail myself of a little artistic or poetic license. In the Volscian scenes I have made some attempts ... to reconstruct the known characteristics of Etruscan architecture. In the Roman scenes, while partly preserving the same character, I have allowed myself a little latitude in bringing the date of the play in architecture a little nearer to a period which can be recognised as definitely Roman, while I have sometimes assumed that the earliest forms of furniture and other accessories were not so different in earliest Rome than in earliest Greece.

Irving had condensed the play into three acts and ten scenes and this called for sets and backdrops representing the forums in Rome and Antium, the interior of the Senate House in Rome, the interior of Coriolanus' house, the interior and exterior of Tullus Aufidius' house and two streets in Rome. For guidance, Alma-

Tadema turned to Vitruvius' description of an Etruscan temple, the design of Etruscan and Lycian tombs, and recent archaeological discoveries in Volterra, Vulci and Cervetri. He also rejected the idea of simulating marble, which had not in the period he had chosen been commonly utilized in buildings, preferring wood and brick, which were more authentic. Alma-Tadema's designs were faithfully executed by Hawes Craven, Joseph Harker and Walter Hann.

The results were nothing less than sensational. Standing suggests that Alma-Tadema's designs for the Forum in Rome and the less elaborate Forum in Antium were 'among the most effective of his stage pictures,' while 'perhaps the most brilliant successes of the whole series' were his models of the interiors of the various houses.[67]

The *Era* (20 April 1901) declared: 'A visit to *Coriolanus* ... is a liberal education in the attire, the furniture, the weapons and the architecture of Rome five hundred years before Christ.' Richard Phené Spiers FRIBA, FSA, calling the designs 'a revelation', devoted a lengthy article in the *Architectural Review* to an analysis of them, an article subsequently published as a free-standing pamphlet.[68]

Coriolanus was almost fore-doomed to failure, despite the splendour of its mounting. Critic after critic lined up to dismiss it: 'Neither in the study nor on the stage is *Coriolanus* an attractive work ... For the theatre there has never been 'money' in *Coriolanus*; the play is no tragedy; Coriolanus is no hero ... the whole play shows signs of half hearted and unfinished workmanship ... Much of the verse is clumsy and careless'; 'I venture to assert that the modern man cannot find himself sufficiently in sympathy with Coriolanus to care much about him and his well-deserved fate.'[69]

But there was general praise for the production: 'thanks ... to the valuable artistic help of Sir Lawrence Alma-Tadema for the designing of the Ancient Roman scenes and dresses, Sir Henry has presented the most marvellous stage picture of masses of moving crowds ever seen on any stage. It is *mise-en-scène*, indeed, that would make the reputed author of the tragedy rub his eyes and exclaim, "Can such things be?"'; 'Sir Lawrence Alma-Tadema's work in relation to the scenery has produced some of the finest scenic effects ever given at the Lyceum, and presents a remarkably interesting series of pictures of Roman life.'[70]

Ellen Terry was generally seen as too sympathetic for the role of Volumnia: 'Her personality made it impossible for her to adopt the 'commanding' reading of the character which is handed down by the Mrs Siddons tradition.'[71] This will have been underlined by Geneviève Ward's triumph in the role in Frank Benson's otherwise disappointing February 1901 production at the Comedy Theatre and of which Shakespeare aficionado Richard Dickins said he could imagine nothing finer: 'she was the ideal embodiment of the Roman mother who loved her son beyond everything in the world, except only her country'. Of Ellen Terry's Volumnia, he said rather dismissively 'she was little more than Ellen Terry in

Roman attire.'[72] But the attire received detailed attention in one newspaper. 'Our lady correspondent', reviewing the dresses, praised Volumnia's costumes, the "beautiful chiton of pure silk, with the wide full sleeves caught together with gold ornaments", the tunic of apple green bordered with gold, and "a veil of shimmering grey silk," and later in the play, a flame-coloured chiton, white tunic embroidered with gold and with large uncut rubies in her hair.[73] Writing in 1939, Frederick Harker recalled *Coriolanus*:

> The production was the finest I had seen at the Lyceum. The scenery, some of the best work of Hawes Craven and Joseph Harker, from the designs of Sir Alma-Tadema, was of rare beauty, using that word in the sense that Keats used it ... 'beauty is truth, truth beauty', for the archaeological accuracy of the mounting was a great feature of the revival. One scene I can still visualize, remarkable for its simple grandeur – 'The Capitol'. Against grey stone walls, with little ornamentation, tier upon tier of seats filled the whole back of the scene, on which were seated the white-robed, grey-bearded senators, whose interest in the proceedings was intense. When at the close of the scene, wishing him good speed, they exclaimed with one voice: 'To Coriolanus come all joy and honour', one felt it was no ordinary crowd just speaking in unison, but that there was individuality in it, as if each senator was speaking for himself.[74]

But equally significant is Harker's statement that, in his entire theatre-going experience, he had never seen *Coriolanus* before or since that Irving production. Its unpopularity as a text doomed it with the public. It flopped and was withdrawn after thirty-six performances.

When Irving decided to produce *King Lear* in 1892 there was only one artist he could turn to – Ford Madox Brown, who had had a career-long interest in the play. Irving had an engraving of Brown's painting *Cordelia's Portion* on his dressing room wall and, according to the painter Graham Robertson, he 'admired it immensely'. He also acquired sixteen pen and ink drawings of scenes from *King Lear* that Brown had executed in the 1840s. These, together with the painting *Lear and Cordelia* (1848–54), set the style of the production. In addition, Irving engaged Brown to design the Romano-British interiors of Lear's palace and Albany's hall, as well as the exterior of Gloucester's castle with a Roman temple in the background.[75]

Graham Robertson, who noted the inspiration provided by Brown, recorded: 'The result was fine; sombre and austere throughout until the final heart rending scene of the old king's death beside the body of Cordelia, which was enacted amongst flowery down-lands where white chalk cliffs towered out of a sea of dazzling blue under skies full of pitiless sunshine; a daring and most poetical touch which seemed to isolate the two tragic figures and to intensify the darkness of their doom.'[76]

Macready had presented Shakespeare's original text of *King Lear* in 1838 for the first time in 150 years, supplanting Nahum Tate's 'happy ending' version. He also sought to give it a definite historical setting, vaguely the Anglo-Saxon period, with pagan halls and Druid stone circles. Irving too opted for a period just after the Romans left Britain, so he could utilize a semi-derelict Roman palace and a Roman temple.

For *King Arthur*, the obvious painter to turn to was the man who had made the Arthurian legends his own particular subject – Sir Edward Burne-Jones, Bart. Stoker recalled that Irving enormously enjoyed working with Burne-Jones:

> This man had such mighty gifts that in his work there was no waste; all the creations of his teeming brain were so fine in themselves that they simply stood ready for artistic use. His imagination working out through perfected art, peopled a whole world of his own and filled that world around them with beautiful things ... There was simply no end to his imaginative ideas, his artistic efforts, his working into material beauty the thoughts which flitted through his mind. As a colourist he was supreme, and he could use colour as a medium of conveying ideas to the same effect as others used form. His own power of dealing with the beauties of form was supreme.[77]

Burne-Jones designed the armour and the costumes and made sketches for the scenery. His wife Georgiana recalled that they 'were but slight, with a rough suggestion of colour' and Burne-Jones's ignorance of the theatre initially led to some difficulties with Irving's regular scene-painters Hawes Craven and Joseph Harker.[78] Stoker recalled: 'When it was objected that the suggested scenes were impossible to work in accordance with stage limitations, Irving pointed out that there was in itself opportunity for the ability of the scene-painters' skill and invention. Burne-Jones suggested the effect aimed at; with them rested the carrying it out.'[79]

The problems were overcome. Burne-Jones went to see Hawes Craven painting the backdrops, but his daughter recalled: 'Father seemed to have nothing to suggest or criticize, only to wish to be shown things, and they talked like brother artists.' The resulting scenes were applauded each time the curtain went up.[80] Stoker wrote of them: 'To my own mind it was the first time that what must in reality be a sort of fairyland was represented as an actuality. Some of the scenes were of transcendent beauty, notably that called 'The Whitethorn Wood'. The scene was all green and white – the side of the hill thick with blossoming thorn through which, down a winding path, came a bevy of maidens in flowing garments of tissue which seemed to sway and undulate with every motion and every breath of air. There was a daintiness and a sense of purity about the whole scene which was very remarkable.'[81] The scene-drops were destroyed in the great fire of 1898 and the costumes designs were lost until recently, many of them only turning up in 1982 and enabling scholars to compare Burne-Jones's originals with the eventual costumes. Various changes were made in the execution of the costumes, some of which Burne-Jones approved of and others which he emphatically did not. He designed a sapphire blue cloak for Guinevere. Alice Comyns Carr, Ellen's costume adviser, persuaded him that a silver cloak embroidered with gold and turquoises would look better. It was prepared and looked splendid, Burne-Jones approving, but was too heavy for Ellen and many of the jewels had to be removed.[82]

It was Irving who changed the costume for Morgan Le Fay. Alice Comyns Carr recalled: 'Geneviève Ward, as Morgan Le Fay, was crossing the stage in the heavy robes and truly magnificent head-dress which had seemed to me to accord well with her Eastern type, when Henry suddenly shouted, "Moses and Aaron rolled into one! Take the thing off!" The remark was so queer that both Burne-Jones and I had to laugh, in spite of the fact that it meant a hurried designing of another head-dress.'[83] There was a major row with Irving over Merlin. Burne-Jones had designed an austere, semi-monastic costume of silver-grey tunic, blue-grey cloak and black cap, but Irving had substituted something which Burne-Jones thought made him look like one of the witches in *Macbeth*. Burne-Jones hated it. One of the great costume successes was Irving's black armour, which was much commented on, though in Burne-Jones's original design it had been blue-grey. It seems to have been another suggestion of Irving's that the colour be changed. Alice Comyns Carr had her own problems with Irving. She had designed the outfits for a mermaid chorus. 'In order to make them look like fish under the sea I covered their faces with frosted gauze. Yet at the last rehearsal Henry calmly cut out the whole scene!'[84] For Irving, nothing and no one was sacred; the effect of the play was all.[85]

Burne-Jones had very mixed feelings about the play in the end. He did not attend the first night, although the newspapers reported him present. He outlined his feelings in a letter to a friend:

No – I didn't say a word about the *King Arthur*, not quite knowing what to say, for friends are involved in it: Irving is loveable, and Carr is an old friend now. And I can't expect people to feel about the subject as I do, and have always. It is such a sacred land to me that nothing in the world touches it in comparison. If people wanted to act Calvary I couldn't help it. Somebody was bound to do it I suppose. I don't like plays – don't like the theatre at all. I see that people like the pageant in it and are civil to me about that – it only shows how useless it is to make pictures for them, they need to be roared at or they can't hear; sickening thoughts be these. The pageant looks rather bonny now and then; when the knights gather for the San Graal there is a moment of beauty – of real beauty. It is gone before you can measure it. Irving is a dear fellow and I have an affection for him. He thinks it is better for people to see an Arthurian play than not – that there are enough people who like romance and they might be fed – and perhaps he is right; also I know it is a matter of mood with me how I feel about that. In the main I should like to keep all the highest things secret and remote from people; if they wanted to look they should go a hard journey to see.[86]

His statement that he did not like the theatre is contradicted by his own professions of admiration for Irving and Ellen Terry in *Macbeth, The Dead Heart, Henry VIII* and *The Corsican Brothers.* But it is clear that he believed that the mystic and elevated Arthurian vision that he cherished simply could not be realized on stage.[87] Alice Comyns Carr recognized Burne-Jones' disappointment:

> When he attended one of the first rehearsals he was shocked to discover how much that was purely theatrical had unavoidably crept into the execution of his poetic conception. But however far short of Burne-Jones' expectations the settings for *King Arthur* fell, they created a very real sensation, for nothing like them had ever been seen before, even on Irving's stage, which held the palm for such effects. The artist himself was pleased with the rich Byzantine hall of Camelot, with its three great rounded arches at the back through which the river could be seen winding to the sea. It was an excellent background for setting off the shining plate armour, uplifted spears, and flying pennants of the knights as they gathered for their fond farewell to Arthur. A peculiar religious feeling seemed to inspire the whole scene, and it had a harmony which academic correctness alone could never have achieved.[88]

The holistic view of the stage found its most perfect expression in *King Arthur*. One critic wrote:

> The glory of all the blended arts that he gives us – poetry, acting, music, painting all – surely this is a new thing, a thing only now possible on the stage and realised as yet only by Irving at the Lyceum and Wagner at Bayreuth. Bayreuth I have not seen, but it is inconceivable that it should have anything to show more beautiful than the series of 'Burne-Jones' picture which go to make up *King Arthur*. The mind is thronged with their memories – the dark blue of the Magic Mere, with that glowing vision of Guinevere, gold against silver, in its midst: the sober brown and grey of the heavy masonry, rough hewn with earliest Norman ornament: the knights with glaive and burnie – 'clad in complete steel' as they clashed round the usurper king – or in their robes of solemn hues, purple and russet and sombre red; white maidens singing through the wood of ash and blossoming may, cool with the green of leaves and the grey tree-trunks, and the clouded sky beyond: the orange sunset, dying behind deep blue hills, and sky of pale green, barred with grey clouds and edged with smouldering red. Throughout these pictures held and charmed one.[89]

One collaboration that failed to reach fruition was with Royal Academician Edwin A Abbey. In 1896 Irving decided that *Richard III* would be his next Shakespearean revival. During 1897 he prepared a version of the text ready for acting and scheduled 1899 for the production. He approached Abbey to act as designer. Abbey was an old friend of Irving. They were fellow members of an Anglo-American dining club, The Kinsmen. Irving admired his illustrations for Shakespeare's plays which had appeared in *Harper's Magazine* and he had 'realized' Abbey's great painting 'Richard Duke of Gloucester and Lady Anne' in his 1896 revival of *Richard III*. Abbey recalled for Stoker the nature of their discussions:

> Irving came to him with every detail of the play ready, so that he could get into his mind at one time both the broad dominating ideas and the necessary requirements and limitations of the scenes. The whole play was charted for him at the start. Irving could defend every position he had taken; knew the force and guidance of every passage; and had so studied the period and its history that he could add external illumination to the poet's intention. In addition, the painter found that his own suggestions were so quickly and so heartily seized that he felt from the first that he himself and his work were from the very start prime factors in the creation of the *mise-en-scène*.

Stoker wrote with appreciation of Abbey's designs, which he thought embodied the nature of medieval life:

> What he implied as well as what he showed told at a glance the conditions and restrictions – the dominant forces of that strenuous time: the fierceness and cruelty; the suspicion and distrust; the horrible crampedness of fortress life; the contempt of death which came with the grim uncertainties of daily life.[90]

Irving had spent over £1600 on scenery alone when in 1898 he was taken ill and reluctantly abandoned the production. Tree staged it in 1903 and Irving never returned to it.

In every case, Irving selected artists who had made the subject of his plays their own. Alma-Tadema was the premier painter of the ancient world, Burne-Jones of the Arthurian myths, and Ford Madox Brown had a life-long obsession with *King Lear*. In doing so, he indicated a precise knowledge of Romantic painting and how it could be deployed to realize his own artistic vision.

Although some eminent composers, such as Beethoven, Schubert and *Music* Mendelssohn, had written overtures and incidental music for plays, which had subsequently achieved an independent performance life, theatre music did not initially have a high status in nineteenth-century England. It was associated with melodrama and the 'illegitimate theatre' of the years before the 1843 Theatre Regulation Act ended the monopoly of legitimate drama by the three patent theatres (Drury Lane, Covent Garden and the Haymarket).

In a 1911 lecture to the Musical Association, the composer and conductor Norman O'Neill attributed the rise of quality theatre music directly to Irving:

> I should like to mention Hatton's music written for Charles Kean's Shakespeare and other productions in the 'fifties. These were, as far as I know, the first productions of modern times in England in which a well-known musician of the day was specially engaged to write special music for a play. This has in our own day become a regular practice. Most of our composers have written music for plays at some time or other. It is to Sir Henry Irving, who did so much to improve the artistic conditions of the theatre,

we are indebted for this. He saw the need of something better than the so-called 'hurries', 'tremolos', and sentimental hymn-like tunes which were being served up again and again in our theatres to an easily imposed-upon public.[91]

John Hatton (1808–1886) had indeed provided the scores for a succession of Charles Kean's spectacular productions at the Princess's Theatre: *Sardanapalus*, *Faust and Margaret*, *Henry VIII*, *Richard II*, *King Lear*, *Macbeth*, *The Winter's Tale* and *The Tempest*. In this as in so much else, Kean's theatrical regime prefigured Irving's. Earlier Sir Henry Bishop (1786–1855) had contributed songs and incidental music to countless productions when he was musical director successively of Drury Lane and Covent Garden, but, although regarded in the nineteenth century as a major composer, he was dismissed in the twentieth as 'negligible'.[92]

The young Arthur Sullivan, who was far from 'negligible', provided music for Charles Calvert's Manchester productions of *The Merchant of Venice* (1871) and *Henry VIII* (1877), and Calvert was another of the precursors of Irving in the style and splendour of his productions and his advocacy of the holistic approach to theatre. Sullivan also scored John Hollingshead's London production of *The Merry Wives of Windsor* (1874).

Each theatre in Victorian England had a resident orchestra and a musical director whose job it was to compose incidental music for the plays, select appropriate overtures and *entr'actes* from existing scores, and to conduct the orchestra. When Irving first became a star at the Lyceum under the management of 'Colonel' Hezekiah Bateman and later his wife Mrs Sidney Bateman, the musical director was Robert Stoepel, who had previously been the musical director for Charles Kean at the Princess's Theatre. Apart from the epoch-making production of *The Bells*, which made Irving a star overnight in 1871 and for which Bateman utilized the score composed for the French production of the play by Etienne Singla, Stoepel composed overtures and incidental music for all the other Bateman productions. Stoepel's technique seems to have been to arrange the overtures from selections of musical tunes from the period of the play, to compose his own marches and dances, and to select *entr'actes* from the current stock of Romantic standards, notably the works of Wagner, Gounod and Meyerbeer. Typical of his work was the score he provided for the 1874 production of *Hamlet*, which included a specially composed overture anachronistically incorporating the Danish national hymn, *Souvenirs from Denmark* – a potpourri of Danish folk tunes, the polonaise from Meyerbeer's incidental music to the Danish play *Struensee* and a fantasia on the various settings of Ophelia's songs.

When in 1878 Irving took over the lease of the Lyceum from Mrs Bateman, he cleared out many of the Bateman company employees and replaced them with his own people. The removals included Robert Stoepel, who was replaced by James Hamilton Clarke (1840–1912), the only one of the Lyceum musical directors to make it into the New Grove.[93] Irving had met Clarke some years before while touring in the North. They had discussed music in general and theatre music in particular and Irving had been impressed by 'the freshness and practical character of these views'. Recalling their conversation, Irving engaged Clarke to succeed Stoepel at what Percy Fitzgerald calls 'the handsome salary of some six hundred a year'.[94] At the same time, Irving renamed as the 'orchestra' what had previously been billed as the Lyceum band – clear evidence of the seriousness with which he regarded the musical element of his productions. At a time when many theatres employed no more that a dozen musicians, Irving maintained an orchestra of thirty to thirty-five.[95] Sir Alexander Mackenzie described the orchestra as 'excellent and complete' and the *Musical Times* called it 'efficient'.[96] The orchestra was eventually joined by a chorus of nine and a ballet corps of eight.[97] It has been calculated that between 1879 and 1899 Irving spent £47,000 on the orchestra.[98]

Although Irving promptly dispensed with most of Stoepel's scores, he was still using his overture to *The Lyons Mail* in the 1883 revival; and Stoepel's 'ghost melody', written for Charles Kean's production of *The Corsican Brothers*, remained an integral part of Irving's revival of the play. His music may not have been as negligible as its large-scale abandonment suggests. Clement Scott recorded, for instance, of the 1877 production of *Richard III*: 'the musical introductions, which added greatly to the effect of the representation, entitle … Stoepel to a full tribute of acknowledgment'.[99]

Hamilton Clarke provided new overtures and scores for most of the Bateman productions that Irving revived under his own management. Clarke had been organist at Queen's College, Oxford, and in 1872 had succeeded Arthur Sullivan as organist at St Peter's, South Kensington. He was also a composer in his own right and, as composer and conductor, functioned as musical director at the Lyceum from 1878 to 1881. Percy Fitzgerald, writing in 1906, recalled him as 'a composer of great distinction. His fine, picturesque overtures and incidental music to *The Merchant of Venice* and other Lyceum pieces, still linger in the memory.'[100] Ellen Terry, Irving's co-star, describing him as 'a most gifted composer', singled out Clarke's *Danish March* in *Hamlet*, his 'Brocken' music in *Faust* and his score for *The Merchant of Venice* as 'exactly right'.[101] Irving evidently shared this view, as he continued to use Clarke's music composed for the 1879 production of *The Merchant of Venice* until his death in 1905 and, after Clarke had left the Lyceum, engaged him as a composer in his own right to provide musical scores for such Lyceum productions as *Faust* (1884), *King Lear* (1892) and *Cymbeline* (1896).

For the 1892 production of *King Lear* the composing duties were shared. Musical director Meredith Ball provided the incidental music and a 'barbaric

march' for the opening scene. Hamilton Clarke provided the overture and
entr'actes. The *Musical Times* (1 December 1892) noted that: 'Though not
intended to be specially illustrative of the phases of the action they respectively
precede, the five pieces are in keeping with the subject generally.' Thus
the overture in C minor, the *Allegro moderato* in F minor, the *Allegro agitato*
(B minor), prefacing the storm act; the subdued *Agitato expressivo* (F minor),
suggesting Cordelia tending her demented father; and the vigorous *Allegro*
(D minor), relieved by a plaintive passage for oboe, ushering in the final section
of the tragedy, had 'the merit of appropriateness'. A final comment, 'Doubtless
Mr Clarke will eventually bind together the movements as an Orchestral suite',
demonstrates a recognition that the practice of creating orchestral suites from
incidental music was now well-established.

For his 1896 production of *Cymbeline*, Irving utilized what the *Musical Times*
(1 November 1896) called 'an excellent selection of music'. The main score (an
overture and four *entr'actes*) was by the German composer and conductor Albert
Dietrich (1829–1908) and dated from 1880. The *Musical Times* thought the
pieces 'distinguished by earnestness of purpose and musician-like qualities', all
illustrative of the sentiments of the scenes they preceded. But these pieces had
been supplemented by music by Hamilton Clarke, who wrote incidental music
to accompany many of the act drops, a dance at Philario's house, 'solemn music'
for the supposed death of Imogen and a madrigal, 'Hark, Hark the Lark'.

After he left the Lyceum, Clarke toured with the D'Oyly Carte Opera
Company, scoring several of Sullivan's overtures, and was subsequently chief
conductor of the Carl Rosa Opera Company. From 1889 to 1891 he was in charge
of the Victorian National Orchestra in Melbourne. Returning to Britain, he
resumed his theatrical work until, says the New Grove, 'ill-health obliged him to
retire prematurely'.[102] Ellen Terry puts it more starkly: 'The brilliant gifts of
Clarke, before many years had passed, 'o'er – leaped' themselves, and he ended
his days in a lunatic asylum.'[103]

The relationship between Irving and his musical director, and Irving's
understanding of the role of music, was vividly summed up by Ellen Terry.

> Although [Irving] did not understand a note of music, he felt, through intuition, what
> the music ought to be, and would pull it about and have alterations made. Noone was
> cleverer than Hamilton Clarke, Henry's first musical director ... at carrying out his
> instructions. Hamilton Clarke often grew angry and flung out of the theatre, saying that
> it was quite impossible to do what Mr Irving required. 'Patch it together, indeed!' He
> used to say to me indignantly, when I was told off to smooth him down. 'Mr Irving
> knows nothing about music, or he couldn't ask me to do such a thing.' But the next day
> he would return with the score altered on the lines suggested by Henry, and would confess
> that the music was improved. 'Upon my soul, it's better! The "Guv'nor" was perfectly
> right.'[104]

Sir Alexander Mackenzie, who composed several scores for Irving, confirmed Clarke's view, writing of Irving that 'while not professing any knowledge of music, his unerring instinct for what was fitting or unfitting to a dramatic situation was remarkable'.[105]

When Clarke left the Lyceum, he was replaced as musical director by John Meredith Ball, who had been with the Bancrofts at the Prince of Wales's Theatre. He retained his post from 1881 until Irving lost personal control of the Lyceum in 1899. He provided overtures and incidental music to such productions as *Two Roses, Much Ado About Nothing, Jingle, Werner, Robert Macaire* and *Peter the Great*. But on other occasions his duties were confined to conducting, as Irving began to employ the talents of leading composers to provide scores for his plays.

W.H. Reed, who joined the Lyceum orchestra as a violinist in 1892, recalled those years in a 1939 radio talk:

> The rehearsals at the Lyceum Theatre in those days were rather a trial. If the Guv'nor [Henry Irving] wanted any particular piece of incidental music or a suitable extract to go before a certain scene the band would be summoned to attend at any time in the morning for this purpose. Henry Irving was a very great artist in every way. To watch him rehearsing his colleagues for a new production, as I did on innumerable occasions was an education in itself. His incidental knowledge was immense ... he would come to the footlights, and looking over into the Orchestra he would say, 'Ball, what music do you propose for the entrance of so and so in the second act?' 'Well, I thought this', Meredith Ball would say. Then we would be requested to play No. 9a or something of that sort for Irving to hear. Quite likely he would walk off in the middle as some other idea with regard to the production had occurred to him, and would return later to say, 'I didn't think much of that piece Ball, what was it?' 'It was the music you asked to hear for the second Act.' 'Well, it won't do, let me hear something else.' So we played No. 10b over, and this contained a melody played by a solo viola. We hadn't got very far with this when Irving interrupted with, 'What instrument is that, Ball?' 'It is a solo viola', answered Meredith Ball. 'Oh, is it', said Irving, 'well, cut it out, it sounds like some old cow.' Ball sat back and sighed. Irving strolled of to the back off the stage; eventually 9a was turned on again with complete satisfaction for this particular scene ... At the production of a scene based upon an incident in the story of Don Quixote, we were rehearsing an Overture to go before this when in walked Irving. 'What is that Overture, Mr Ball?' said he. 'That is the Overture to so and so', said Mr Ball. 'Oh, is it?' said Irving, 'I wanted something in the Spanish manner for this. That piece might be the Overture to Westminster Bridge.' So the Overture was changed to Espana by Chabrier, or some similar piece. That was Irving all over and a very characteristic remark – he was a sore trial as I've said, but everyone loved him, from the stars to the call boy.[106]

Irving wanted something special for his 1882 production of *Romeo and Juliet*, the first of the spectacular Shakespeare productions that were to make the Lyceum renowned around the world. With a characteristic eye to publicity value as well as artistic input, Irving thought that if he could interest a leading British composer in undertaking the incidental music, as Bram Stoker put it: 'Not only would the play as a whole benefit enormously, but even its business aspect be greatly enhanced by the addition of the new strength.'[107]

So Irving invited Sir Julius Benedict to compose the score. Benedict (1804–1885), German-born but a naturalized British subject, knighted in 1871, had been a pupil of Weber and had composed a symphony, two piano concertos and four overtures, as well as popular operas, notably *The Lily of Killarney* (1862), a perennial favourite of the Victorians. Even more appropriately, he had been musical director at Drury Lane from 1838 to 1848 and so he knew what was required. Clement Scott, reviewing the play, noted: 'The music of Sir Julius Benedict increases in charm with familiarity. The Chorale that is supposed to awaken Juliet on her bridal morning is a number of special excellence and grace.'[108] Percy Fitzgerald recalled that 'not the least pleasurable part of the whole was the romantic music written in a flowing, tender strain by Sir Julius Benedict, full of juvenile freedom and spirit, thoroughly Italian in character, and having something of the grace and character of Schubert's *Rosamunde*.'[109] Ellen Terry, who played Juliet, noted that the music was 'exactly right. There was no *leit-motiv*, no attempt to reflect the passionate emotion of the drama, but a great deal of Southern joy, of flutes, and wood and wind.'[110]

Up until 1882, the music for theatrical productions was generally accorded a few lines in the review of the play. But once Irving started to employ leading composers, there was a change in the attitude of the press. Increasingly the scores were accorded separate reviews and the papers began to run interviews with the composers about their approach and intentions. Even more significantly in terms of the status of stage music, the august *Musical Times* began to take serious note of Lyceum scores. It did not deign to review Sir Julius Benedict's score for *Romeo and Juliet* in 1882. But by 1885 Lyceum music had become important enough to prompt a full-length article in the *Musical Times* (1 January 1886) on the incidental music to Irving's 'marvellous production' of *Faust* which had opened in the previous September.

The article argued that 'to invest the Lyceum productions with true artistic dignity and worth, music specially written by our foremost composers, and efficiently rendered by a real orchestra and vocalists, is absolutely necessary'. But three factors, it suggested, militated against this: the fact that the actual musical conductor of the theatre could properly supply the incidental music to the play; the expense of such an operation; and the 'entire and absolute indifference of an English theatrical audience as to what music is played'. For *Faust* the incidental music was composed by Hamilton Clarke and Meredith Ball. There were *entr'actes* entitled 'Mephistopheles' and 'Margaret' specially composed by Clarke. 'These as well as the greater part of the incidental music, can be unreservedly commended', said the *Musical Times*. The article concluded:

> The music then as a whole can be highly praised, though it was amusingly despised by
> the audience ... *Entr'acte* music is simply not listened to ... Under this state of things,
> there is no practical necessity for Mr Irving to do as much as he has done in the musical
> accompaniment to his piece, and he, therefore, deserves all the more praise for his sense
> of artistic propriety.

Irving was to follow the advice of the *Musical Times* when in 1888 he
commissioned Sir Arthur Sullivan (1842–1900) to provide the music for his
revival of *Macbeth*. Irving admired Sullivan's music, particularly *The Mikado*,
which he called 'the greatest triumph of light opera-British or foreign – in his
memory'.[111]

In 1885 Irving had invited Sullivan to provide overture and incidental music
to his revival of W.G. Wills's *Olivia*. Sullivan agreed to the use of the song 'Happy
Morn', which he had written for the original 1878 production, but he expressed
reservations about providing a full score: 'overture and *entr'acte* involve a great
deal of thought and labour which would be thrown away. You cannot get the
audience (even on a first night) to consider them as part of the piece and to
listen to them ... consequently it is most ungrateful and disheartening for the
composer.'[112] In the event, overture and incidental music were provided by
musical director Meredith Ball. But *Macbeth* was a major prestige project and
Irving was offering financial terms of unparalleled generosity.

Irving knew what he wanted and following preliminary discussions sent
Sullivan some outline notes to guide him:

> My Dear Sullivan:
> Trumpets and drums are the things behind scenes.
> Entrance of *Macbeth*, *only drum*.
> Distant march would be good for Macbeth's exit in third
> scene – or drum and trumpets as you suggest.
> In the last act there will be several flourishes of trumpets.
> 'Make all our trumpets speak' etc.
> Roll of drum sometimes.
> Really anything you can give of a stirring sort can be easily brought in.
> As you say, you can dot these down at rehearsals – but one player would be good to
> tootle, tootle, so that we could get the exact tune.[113]

When Sullivan had completed his score, he arrived at the Lyceum to play it
through. When he had done so, he asked Irving if he liked it. 'Oh, as music, it's
very fine', said Irving, 'but for our purpose it is no good at all. Not in the least like
it.' Sullivan asked him what he wanted and Irving, by a combination of hand and
body movements and vowel sounds without words, conveyed an impression of
what he required. Sullivan grasped the point, saying 'Much better than mine,

Irving ... I'll rough it out at once', and went off and worked out a theme and got the orchestra to play it and Irving declared it 'Splendid! That is all I could wish for. It is fine.' This story, recounted by both Bram Stoker and Ellen Terry, echoes the account of Hamilton Clarke's experiences with Irving, confirming that, while not musical, Irving knew what he wanted and where he wanted it.[114] Sullivan eventually supplied the overture, preludes to four acts, two choruses for the witches and substantial passages of incidental music in acts 1, 3, 4 and 6.

The *Musical Times* (1 February 1889), praising 'the happy thought which suggested to Mr Irving the propriety of enlisting the genius of one of our foremost English composers, Sir Arthur Sullivan, to adorn the revival of *Macbeth* at the Lyceum theatre', declared: 'If the *Macbeth* music is not the most important of all the productions of the gifted composer, it is without doubt no 'unfit mate' for the several beautiful additions to the Shakespeare music which have from time to time flowed from his expressive, fanciful and skilful pen.'

The *Saturday Review* (5 January 1889) praised the 'singularly fine and effective' overture, the 'masterly' development of the march which heralded Macbeth's approach in Act 1 scene iii, and the variety of Sullivan's art demonstrated by the contrast of the 'charming music which heralds Duncan's arrival, and the freshness and beauty of the Prelude to the Fifth Act' with 'the strangely demoniac nature of the Incantation music'. The *Illustrated Sporting and Dramatic News* (5 January 1889) predicted that Sullivan's *Macbeth* music would live on after *Pinafore* and *Mikado* were forgotten, a prediction that turned out to be somewhat wide of the mark. Only the overture was published and it was later played as a separate concert piece.[115]

Irving called on Sullivan again to provide incidental music to his 1895 production of Joseph Comyns Carr's drama, *King Arthur*. Recalling no doubt the audience's notorious indifference to overtures and preludes, Sullivan supplied these from his existing stock of compositions, his overture *Marmion* as a prelude to the prologue, his *Imperial March* before Act 1, movements from *The Tempest* suite before Acts 2 and 4 and part of the *Irish Symphony* to introduce Act 3. He confined himself to incidental music, mainly vocal. There was a chorus of Lake Spirits, the Chorus of Unseen Spirits, the Chaunt of the Grail, the May Song and the Funeral March and Final Chorus, all of it delicate, atmospheric and Romantic. Dissatisfied with the finale he had provided for the prologue, Sullivan wrote and scored a new finale two days before the opening, which he himself conducted on 12 January 1895.[116] Clement Scott wrote of the music: 'The music is exactly what was wanted – ever subordinate to dramatic effect, and yet always assisting it.'[117] After Sullivan's death, his secretary Wilfred Bendall edited the incidental music to produce a suite.[118] Sullivan, like Irving, had long contemplated an Arthurian subject, and he asked Carr to provide him with a libretto for an Arthurian opera as a successor to his previous chivalric grand opera *Ivanhoe*, but death supervened before the project could be taken further.[119]

The *Musical Times* (1 February, 1895) expressed its regret that Sullivan had not composed the preludes and *entr'actes*:

> The heroic sentiment and wild passion of Mr Comyns Carr's version of the Arthurian legend ... lends itself so sympathetically to music painting that it is to be regretted Sir Arthur Sullivan has not written a special series of *Entr'actes* for this most artistic and sumptuously mounted play ... In the absence of introductions specially for the various scenes, Sir Arthur has done, perhaps, the next best possible by his selection from his previous compositions ... More satisfactory is the incidental music proper. The most effective portion of this is heard during the prologue, the impressiveness of which is greatly enhanced by the graceful choral song sung by the spirits as they float in the magic mere, and the subdued instrumental accompaniment to the spoken text, during the recital of which themes are heard subsequently associated with the sword Excalibur and the Queen, Guinevere. The number next in importance is the 'Chaunt of the Grail', written for mixed voices, and appropriately founded upon a broad, church-like subject. This is developed at some length, ultimately becoming jubilant in character as the knights depart, full of confidence, in search of the Holy Grail. A charming May Song, written in three parts, sung by the Queen's handmaidens, much increases the enjoyment of the beautiful scene, when the curtain rises upon Act 2, and the 'Sleep' chorus which accompanies the 'Passing of Arthur' also heightens the dramatic effect. The skill of the composer is especially noticeable in the suggestive rise and fall of the soft instrumental music which follows, with remarkable faithfulness, the speeches of Merlin, in some instances the rhythm of the verse being most happily echoed by the music.

Sir Alexander Mackenzie (1847–1935), described by Stoker as 'one of the oldest and closest of Irving's friends', provided the scores for *Ravenswood* and *Coriolanus* and was commissioned for two further productions, *Manfred* and *Richard II*, which remained unproduced.[120] Mackenzie, Principal of the Royal Academy of Music, knighted in 1895, had also written many pieces reflecting his Scottish heritage (the Scottish Rhapsodies, the suite 'In the Scottish Highlands', the *Pibroch* suite etc.). He would therefore have seemed highly appropriate as the composer for Irving's production of Herman Merivale's stage version of Scott's *The Bride of Lammermoor*, entitled *Ravenswood* (1890). Mackenzie pronounced it 'a congenial subject offering many opportunities to the musician, but pervaded with gloom, for it began with a funeral and ended with a double tragedy'. But Mackenzie ended his score with the love theme for Edgar and Lucy, implying their union in death, his intention being to signal 'an apotheosis of love'. Irving objected that he had envisaged the final scene as a cold, desolate moonlit scene with a black plume lying on the sands. Having thought about it overnight, however, he conceded the rightness of Mackenzie's interpretation and changed the finale from moonlight to sunrise, writing to Mackenzie: 'Faust does, we hope, go the Heaven in the second part – and Edgar and Lucy I am sure go together.'[121] Less felicitous was the blast of trombones Mackenzie introduced to accompany the shooting of a mad bull by Edgar. This produced titters of laughter in the first night audience. Mackenzie apologized to Irving, who told him not to worry: 'I got the best laugh in the piece.'[122]

The *Musical Times* (1 October 1890) declared the play 'a singularly picturesque and effective melodrama'. The paper attributed its success to a variety of causes: 'the beauty and elaborateness of the scenic effects' with the final tableau of the sable feather on the sands pronounced 'a masterpiece' that 'cannot be witnessed without emotion'; the acting of Irving, Ellen Terry, William Terriss, Miss Marriott and Mr Mackintosh; and 'the really admirable incidental music composed by Dr Mackenzie'. It applauded the choice of Mackenzie for the role, proclaiming him 'peculiarly well qualified' by virtue of his nationality and by the 'descriptive talent' he had displayed in such works as *The Dream of Jubal*, *The Rose of Sharon* and *La Belle Dame Sans Merci*. 'It is our pleasing duty to have to record the fact that his latest effort is at once as workmanlike and attractive as anything he has ever composed.' His prelude and three *entr'actes*, adapted as a concert suite, were scheduled to be played at the Norwich Festival. When the suite was duly performed there, conducted by Mackenzie, the *Musical Times* (1 November 1890) announced that it 'very well stood the test of separation from the acted drama and its production as music *per se*' and declared that the movements of the suite 'charm by the beauty of their themes and by extremely picturesque and masterful treatment'.

Irving commissioned Mackenzie to provide a score for his long-mooted production of Byron's *Manfred* and to provide solo vocalists and chorus from the Royal Academy of Music. Mackenzie completed much of the music, leaving only the scene of the 'Hall of Arimanes' to be completed. Irving intended it to surpass the Brocken scene in *Faust*. In the event, he several times announced and then abandoned plans to produce it. Three preludes from the Manfred music, *Astarte*, *Pastorale* and *The Flight of the Spirits*, were performed at Robert Newman's London Festival in 1899. Irving also commissioned a score for *Richard II*, for which he had prepared an acting edition, but Mackenzie had only sketched 'a small portion of the music' before the production was abandoned.[123]

Mackenzie did, however, provide the score for Irving's last new Shakespearean production, *Coriolanus* (1901). A few nights before opening, Irving requested additional music for the Forum scene which was duly supplied and was thought to be 'one of the most effective "bits"'.[124] Mackenzie found the orchestra inferior, now that a syndicate ran the Lyceum, to what it had been when Irving had personal control. It was plagued by the unwelcome presence of deputies. Mackenzie said he had never seen 'the "Chief" so keenly anxious about the staging of any play' and with justification. Famously, a tired stage hand, observing a poster billing Sir Henry Irving, Sir Lawrence Alma-Tadema and Sir Alexander

Mackenzie, remarked: 'Three knights! That's about all I'll give it.' In the event it ran for thirty-six nights, far below the usual Lyceum run. Mackenzie next heard his funeral march from *Coriolanus* played at the funeral service for Irving in Westminster Abbey on 20 October 1905.[125]

As was now the custom with Lyceum productions, the *Coriolanus* music was extensively reviewed in the press. The *Daily News* (16 April 1901) reported:

> Except that now and again the general style is unquestionably Scotch, which, as the Scottish musical style is claimed to be very ancient, may or may not be considered an anachronism in Rome five centuries before the Christian era, the music exactly serves its purpose, the prelude and *entr'actes* as a preparation for the incidental music to cover a change of scene, or to support the action … The prelude is an effective and rather elaborate piece of orchestral music, mainly based upon two themes, one doubtless representing the imperious and scornful character of Coriolanus himself, and the other the gentler nature of his wife and mother. In the working out, the two, by a happy idea, seem to be contending for mastery. One *entr'acte* 'Voces Populi' presages the popular conspiracy that drives him out, and the other, a solemn march, suggests his final tragedy.

For his 1892 production of Lord Tennyson's play *Becket*, Irving turned to Sir Charles Stanford (1852–1924). When the Lyceum was producing Tennyson's *Queen Mary* under the Bateman regime, Tennyson asked that the young Charles Villiers Stanford, a friend of his sons Hallam and Lionel, should write the incidental music. This was agreed and Stanford provided a score of seven numbers, including an overture, four *entr'actes*, character sketches of Sir Thomas Wyatt, Philip II, Archbishop Cranmer and Queen Mary respectively, the third of which introduced Tallis's ordination hymn, and two songs. However Robert Stoepel, the music director, jealous of the commission and wanting to write the incidental music himself, obstructed Stanford. Stoepel complained that the score was simply too large for the size of band he had at his disposal and Mrs Bateman, the proprietress, said she had not commissioned an overture and *entr'actes*. Tennyson offered to pay for the removal of the first two rows of stalls to accommodate a larger orchestra but Mrs Bateman refused and the Stanford score was withdrawn, apart from the songs. When it opened with a score by Stoepel, on 18 April 1876, Stanford discovered that the orchestra contained enough players to have performed his score. 'It was my first experience (and unhappily not my last) of stage intrigue', he commented in his memoirs.[126] In the event, the characters of Wyatt and Cranmer were cut from the performing version of the play, rendering their preludes redundant.[127] Stoepel's score included an overture *Queen Mary*, a *marche du nuit* and a *chant du soldat*, supplemented by 'Adieu donc, Belle France' (a song composed by Mary, Queen of Scots), Gounod's *Serenade* and the prelude to Wagner's *Lohengrin*.

Stanford went on to become a prolific writer of symphonies, oratorios, cantatas, operas, songs and church music. He was professor of music at

Cambridge and professor of composition at the Royal College of Music, where he was a notable and inspiring teacher. He was knighted in 1902. Stanford acquitted Irving of any blame in the *Queen Mary* matter and acknowledged that he made amends when Irving, under his own management, produced his adaptation of Tennyson's *Becket* in 1893. Bram Stoker visited Stanford to offer him the commission and Stanford offered to do it for nothing out of respect and affection for Tennyson. Stoker was adamant that Irving insisted on paying him for the score, and despite his protests, Irving paid him 300 guineas. He allowed him as many rehearsals as he wanted and the result of Irving's dedication and labours was that Irving, in Stanford's opinion, played *Becket* 'with greater insight and picturesqueness than any of his parts'. He became imbued with 'the spirit of the play' and told Stanford that he never missed coming down behind the curtain to hear the last *entr'acte* (the funeral march).[128]

Stanford provided ten numbers, including an overture, four *entr'actes*, *King Henry*, *Rosamund's Bower*, *Becket's Rest*, *The Martyrdom*, and a duet 'Is It the Wind of Dawn?' And he added an intermezzo to follow *King Henry* in August 1894. Stanford's biographer, Jeremy Dibble, considers it Stanford's finest incidental music, and Stanford arranged a suite from the incidental music, of which *The Martyrdom* was a favourite of Sir Adrian Boult.[129]

The *Musical Times* (1 March 1893) was less impressed:

> Thanks to the enlightened and liberal policy of modern managers, with Mr Irving at their head, the supply of incidental music to the poetic drama by composers of the highest rank among us multiplies with gratifying rapidity. We wish it were possible to chronicle a corresponding increase, among audiences, of appreciation in such work; but the truth that music requires to be listened to, as well as heard, has not yet been realised by theatre-goers in general. At any rate our impressions of Professor Stanford's music to *Becket* were acquired, as to the overture and *entr'actes*, through a hubbub of conversation. To this perhaps we may attribute the fact that it hardly realised our expectations, based as these were on the composer's previous achievements. Of the four *entr'actes* 'King Henry', 'Rosamund's Bower', 'Becket's Rest', and 'The Martyrdom', the first and the last seem to us to show most inventive power. The grace and fitness of the other two are obvious, but distinction seems wanting. The overture appears to need a larger orchestra for its due effect, which is agitated and stormy. The music heard during the progress of the play gives evidence of abundant tact, but surely the clap of thunder which follows the death of Becket did not need an orchestral accompaniment!

In January 1894 Stanford travelled to Glasgow to conduct the suite he had arranged from the *Becket* music, which elicited from the *Musical Times* (1 February 1894) the brief put down: 'It can hardly be said that this music is so interesting on the concert platform as when associated with the play.'

The *Times* (7 February 1893) took a more positive view. Complaining about 'the incessant buzz of conversation' which continued during the intervals, making it difficult to concentrate on the *entr'actes*, the critic concluded that the music was 'marked in an eminent degree by artistic feeling and thoughtfulness'. The review proceeded to analyse the score. Noting that the overture was constructed on themes associated with the principal characters – the plain chant melody 'Telluris ingens conditor' for Becket, a restless figure for violins for Henry, the song 'over! the sweet summer closes,' for Queen Eleanor – the critic continued:

> Professor Stanford's music is full of interest and plays an important part in illustrating and accompanying the tragedy; but throughout he has kept it within judicious limits as never to be obtrusive or over-powering, as is too often the case with music of this description. The charming melodrama, accompanying the close of the scene in Rosamund's bower in Act 2, is an excellent example of the composer's discretion in this respect. In the more extended movements, such as the introduction to the last act, in which the martyrdom is illustrated, he has given fuller rein to his power, and there can be no doubt that when these portions of the music to *Becket* are heard under more favourable circumstances they will prove fully worthy of Professor Stanford's high reputation. The vocal music is unimportant, the duet: 'Is it the Wind of the Dawn?' having had to be omitted in adapting the play for stage representation.

Georges Jacobi (1840–1906) (originally Georg Jacobi) was a German-born composer and conductor who had earned a reputation as a violinist and later conductor in Paris. In 1869 he became conductor of the Bouffes-Parisiens, where he conducted many Offenbach performances. At the outbreak of the Franco-Prussian War he moved to London, and from 1872–1898 (except for 1883–84) was conductor and musical director of the Alhambra Theatre. During that time he composed the music for forty-five Alhambra ballets, scores which have been described as 'competently written and eminently danceable.' This made him, 'the most important ballet composer working in London in his day.'[130] It was doubtless the French background that persuaded Irving to engage Jacobi to provide incidental music for his production of the French Revolution drama, *The Dead Heart* (1889).

The involvement of Jacobi was considered significant enough for the music to be reviewed separately and for newspapers to carry interviews with Jacobi. One article went so far as to say: 'One of the chief features of Mr Irving's revival of *The Dead Heart* is the music, which accompanies the progress of the drama, almost from beginning to end. For it Mr Irving has wisely come to Mr Jacobi – the presiding genius of the Alhambra ballets for many a long year past – than whom, for tunefulness and dramatic quality, it would be difficult to name a superior, while for orchestration in his own speciality of work he stands alone.' Revealing that he had composed the score, which was longer than his usual ballet scores, during the mornings of his three weeks holiday at Herne Bay, Jacobi explained to an interviewer who asked him what the music consisted of:

There is the opening movement … light, melodious, and well-marked, intended to reflect the spirit of the garden scene which ends with the graceful dance. And, of course, there is the undercurrent of mystery in it to accompany the ominous beginnings of the Revolution. After the prologue is over comes the real overture, in which the numbers foreshadow the events and passions of the play, so full of action and colour – especially the taking of the Bastille. In it I have introduced and woven together several of the revolutionary songs of the period – Méhul's 'Chant du Départ', written in 1792 … 'The Marseillaise' and others. Then of course there is the usual musical accompaniment to the dramatic action of the play, the music having to be set to the words in many places as carefully as in opera.[131]

The score was interestingly not deemed worthy of a *Musical Times* review but was considered in detail in the newspapers. The *Observer* (29 September 1889) reported:

For the musical illustration and accompaniment of the drama, recourse has been had to Mr Jacobi, who has executed his happily allotted task with a spirit and significance seldom imparted to such work. The change from the light melodies introducing the garden-scene of the prologue to the stormy and passionate overture of the final act must be singled out for special praise, as must also the deft employment of such revolutionary themes as the *Chant du Départ* and the inevitable *Marseillaise* as the keynotes of the thrilling scenes before the Bastille. This is the kind of aid from the orchestra in which the late Charles Reade would have delighted, and the high service which it rendered last night demands instant recognition.

Another review was equally enthusiastic:

Mr Irving never neglects the musical opportunities of a new production. *The Dead Heart* affords no great scope in this direction, such, for instance, as did the revival of *Macbeth*, wherein the genius of Sir Arthur Sullivan was so worthily employed. The value of music as an adjunct to a drama like Mr Watts Phillips's may be said to depend in no slight measure upon the intelligence and insight brought to bear upon the disposition of varied, subtle effects at each significant point in the play. The task of supplying these effects was entrusted by Mr Irving to M. Georges Jacobi, a musician whose wide experience in the art of illustrating dramatic situations by orchestral means eminently fitted him for the duty. As the result proved, a better man could not have been selected. Every note of melodrama heard last night told well, and helped by its appropriate colour to enhance the effect of the scene. Never obtrusive, but always subdued to the proper pitch, it was melodrama in the true sense of the word and served its purpose to perfection.[132]

The reviewer singled out for praise the prelude which combined the sombre theme for brass, foreshadowing the tragic fate of the hero and an 'elegant passepied characteristic of the period', the overture which included by turn Méhul's *chant du départ*, the *Ça ira* in minor key and the *Marseillaise* and a 'bright original theme in 6–8 time (a genuine bit of Jacobian melody)' and 'the beautiful Nocturne for the horns, with an alternative unison passage for strings, that precedes the final act'.

Irving did not just call upon the great names of the musical world but was willing to try younger musicians. When the young Edward German (1862–1936) heard in 1891 that Irving was planning to produce *Henry VIII*, he wrote at the urgent prompting of his sister to Irving offering his services and reminding him that he had composed the incidental music for Richard Mansfield's production of *Richard III* at the Globe Theatre in 1889. Irving sent for him and told him he had been 'much impressed' by the *Richard III* music and wanted him to write the incidental music for *Henry VIII* and would pay him the same as he had given Mackenzie for *Ravenswood*, namely 300 guineas, remarkably generous for a young composer. Irving could have utilized Sullivan's 1877 incidental music to *Henry VIII*, but opted for a new score from an up and coming composer. German produced an intermezzo in G minor, a coronation march, 'The Death of Buckingham', the Thanksgiving Hymn and Three Dances, Morris Dance, Shepherd's Dance and Torch Dance, and set 'Orpheus with his Lute' to be sung by Queen Katherine's three waiting maids. Irving, anxious that German's music should reflect the spirit of the sixteenth century, suggested several old airs of the period, but German preferred to compose his own and caught the 'Old English' idiom perfectly. The Three Dances became immediately popular and brought German worldwide fame.[133]

The *Musical Times* (1 February 1892), still complaining that 'The average playgoer … seems to regard music as something to be admired rather that enjoyed', thought German's music 'far too good … for the majority of its hearers'. The music was identified as having a 'straightforward' Old English character with the dance music 'being of a particular "taking" kind. The Entr'actes … and certain short passages which occur as the scenes are changed … touch the tragic note to the play; they have a rich sombre colour that is in admirable keeping.' The critic thought German had set 'Orpheus with his Lute' very happily and produced a Procession March that was 'effective and should become popular'.

In general German's incidental music was much admired. One critic remarked that 'the incidental music … reflects the highest credit upon the composer, whose little melodies and phrases are delightfully suggestive of "Old England"'. Another observed, 'Mr Edward German's music is one of the most noticeable features of the production … The incidental music has the charm of perfect fitness as well as of absolute beauty. The Morris dance music is quaintly delightful, and the trio setting of "Orpheus with his Lute" is lovely.'[134] There was particular interest in German's new setting of 'Orpheus With His Lute', best known in Sullivan's setting. German set it for a trio of female voices. 'The new setting is extremely pretty, and the part-writing is wonderfully effective and interesting', was a typical review.[135] German was to rework and add to his *Henry VIII* processional march to provide a *Coronation March* for the coronation of King George V in 1911.

For his ill-fated and short-lived 1898 production of *The Medicine Man*, Irving commissioned Maude Valérie White (1855–1937), perhaps the leading woman composer of her age. But like many other women in the nineteenth century, her talents were largely confined to the setting of songs and short instrumental pieces, the genres considered appropriate for women. She wrote some two hundred songs, characterized by 'an appealing if at times sentimental lyricism'.[136] It was at the behest of her friend Robert Hichens, the co-author of the play, that Irving engaged her. White later revealed to Hichens that 'she never thought much of it' as a play and she was proved right.[137] Maud Valérie White herself recalled: 'I liked Sir Henry Irving very much. His kindness and courtesy were unfailing and it was a real pleasure to have anything to do with him.' But she also recalled: 'Oh, what agonies it is to write incidental music for a play! At every instant the orchestra was stopped and some one would say, even if they were playing pianissimo – "We can't hear ourselves speak. Please take out all the wind instruments and put mutes on the violins." No sooner had this been done than another objection was raised. 'Heavens! How dull it sounds! Isn't something wanting?'[138] Her music included the prelude 'The Medicine Man,' a waltz 'Nocturne Serene' and two *entr'actes*, which were supplemented by the ballet music from Reinecke's opera *King Manfred* and the ballet music from Johann Strauss the Younger's comic opera *Ritter Pazman* as the other *entr'actes*.

It is clear that Irving gave considerable thought to the choice of composers and sought to match the subject to the talent. For *Macbeth*, he went to a composer with a proven track record of setting Shakespearean themes to music (Sullivan), and chose for *King Arthur* the same composer, who had achieved success in grand opera with a chivalric subject (*Ivanhoe*). For the Scottish play *Ravenswood* he went to the Scottish composer Mackenzie and for *Becket* to a notable composer of church music, Stanford. For his French plays *The Dead Heart* and *Robespierre* he chose a composer who had lived and worked in France and could capture a French idiom in his music, Georges Jacobi.

Irving was also willing to pay handsomely for the services of the big name composers. This rate steadily increased over the years. Sir Julius Benedict received 100 guineas for the *Romeo and Juliet* score in 1882.[139] Jacobi received £200 for the score of *The Dead Heart*. This did not cover two already composed pieces, *Silver Wedding March* and *Nocturne*, played by permission as *entr'actes*.[140] Hamilton Clarke received £200 for his *Faust* music in 1885.[141] He agreed to £200 for the *King Lear* score in 1892 but received a further £30 when asked to provide extra music.[142] He received £250 for his *Cymbeline* score and the associated *Imogen* waltz in 1896.[143] Irving paid 300 guineas to Mackenzie for the *Ravenswood* score, to Stanford for *Becket* and to German for *Henry VIII*.[144] But the biggest winner in the payment stakes was Sir Arthur Sullivan. Irving agreed to pay Sullivan £540 for all rights to perform his *Macbeth* music for a first run and one revival and if performed thereafter a royalty of £5 per performance.[145] It was an arrangement that recognized Sullivan's status as Britain's leading composer.

Irving was adamant that the music should be tailored to the production rather than vice-versa. The texts of the plays he performed never remained static and he cut, added to and reshaped the works in his repertoire over the years in response to their impact upon audiences. So although Etienne Singla's score for *The Bells* was played complete in the early performances, it was continually pruned and reworked as Irving honed and polished the text. He removed many pieces of incidental music which did not integrate with and enhance the action of the drama. The entrance music for all but the characters of Mathias the burgomaster and the Mesmerist, for instance, disappeared over time.[146]

Most composers understood his demands. But not all. The play agent Elizabeth Marbury, who represented the authors Sardou and Moreau, recalled problems on the 1903 production of *Dante*. The French composer Xavier Leroux had been selected to provide the score and travelled to London to supervise its performance. But he was reluctant to make cuts in it. Marbury noted:

> When cuts were found necessary in the manuscript, Irving could never understand why in the world Leroux should not blue-pencil his orchestral score in the same way. He insisted that when dialogue was shortened, the corresponding bars of music should be also taken out. We had many futile arguments with him on the subject, with the result that Leroux returned to Paris, a very disgruntled and disappointed composer.[147]

But Irving was generally appreciated by the musical world. Stoker recalled that 'Musicians always took a deep interest in Irving's work both as actor and manager. They seemed to understand in a peculiarly subtle way the significance of everything he did.'[148] Leading composers figured regularly as guests at Irving's celebrity suppers in the Beefsteak Room. Among then were Arrigo Boito, who thought Irving 'the greatest artist he had ever seen', Paderewski, who offered to write the music for an Irving production, Charles Gounod, the Abbé Liszt, who stayed talking until four o'clock in the morning, and Sir George Henschel, singer, conductor and composer, who was promised the commission to score *Julius Caesar*, a production eventually abandoned.

It is clear that the run of distinguished composers willing to set plays at the Lyceum conferred a new respectability on the genre of theatre music. Edward German (knighted in 1928) followed up his scores for *Richard III* and *Henry VIII* with scores for West End productions of *Romeo and Juliet* (1895), *As You Like It* (1896), and *Much Ado About Nothing* (1898). Sir Hubert Parry regularly provided musical scores not only for the classical plays performed at Oxford and Cambridge Universities, *The Birds* (1883), *The Frogs* (1891), *Agamemnon* (1900), *The Clouds* (1905) and *The Achamians* (1914), but also for the West End production *Hypatia* (1893), for which his score was described by the *Musical Times* (1 February 1893) as 'elaborate, extensive and important' and containing enough matter for two symphonies. Their lead was followed by Elgar with his scores for *Grania and Diarmid* (1901), *The Starlight Express* (1915), *King Arthur* (1923) and *Beau Brummel* (1928), by Frederick Delius with *Hassan* (1923) and by Samuel Coleridge-Taylor with his scores for Herbert Beerbohm-Tree's productions, *Herod* (1900), *Nero* (1906), *Faust* (1908) and *Othello* (1911). The result was the addition to the musical repertoire of some engaging and tuneful pieces which, but for the demands of the stage, might otherwise not have existed.

9

Celebrity Culture

Irving was more than just an actor-manager; he was that new phenomenon, a Victorian celebrity. What is a celebrity? It was the American historian Daniel Boorstin in a caustic analysis of the media-dominated modern world, called *The Image* (1963), who wrote: 'The celebrity is a person who is well known for his welknownness', a phrase that over the years since 1963 has been glossed as 'a celebrity is someone who is famous for being famous'.[1] Boorstin saw the celebrity as the dominant cultural form of the modern world 'as characteristic of our culture and our century as was the divinity of the Greek gods in the sixth century BC or the chivalry of knights and courtly lovers in the Middle Ages'.[2]

Since the beginning of recorded history, there have been famous people, warriors and rulers, saints and sinners, artists and prophets, people who have stood out from the crowd, who have been set apart, looked up to, promoted as special. They were the 'doers of great deeds' – political, military, spiritual, artistic, whose names and achievements lived long after their deaths. Boorstin gives as examples St Francis of Assisi, Moses, Julius Caesar, the prophet Mohammed, Shah Jehan, Joan of Arc, Napoleon, Shakespeare, Washington and Lincoln. He makes the point that fame and greatness were never exactly the same but nearly so. Now, he argues, the two are totally separated and that to Shakespeare's three categories of greatness – those who are born great, those who achieve greatness, and those who have greatness thrust upon them – a fourth must be added: 'those who hire press agents and public relations experts to make them look great'.[3]

In the world of the mass media, argues Boorstin, 'we can fabricate fame, we can at will … make a man or woman well known but we cannot make him great. We can make a celebrity but we can never make him a hero.'[4] So this introduces us to another category – the hero, defined by the Oxford English Dictionary as 'one who does brave or noble deeds; an illustrious warrior', or more generally 'a man admired and venerated for his achievements and noble qualities'. Boorstin unflatteringly compares the celebrity and the hero:

> The hero was distinguished by his achievement; the celebrity by his image. The hero created himself; the celebrity is created by the media. The hero is a big man; the celebrity is a big name … the hero is made by folklore, sacred texts and history books; but the celebrity is the creation of gossip, of public opinion, of magazines, newspapers, and the ephemeral images of movie and television screens. The passage of time which creates

and establishes the hero destroys the celebrity. One is made, the other unmade by repetition ... No-one is more forgotten than the last generation's celebrity. The dead hero becomes immortal. He becomes more vital with the passing of time. The celebrity even in his lifetime becomes passé.[5]

It is a powerful passage, achieving its effect by a set of stark contrasts. But like many such statements is true only in parts and exaggerated in others. Boorstin may be making a false antithesis between achievement and image. Heroes had images as well as achievements. Some celebrities have achievements as well as images. Heroes could be promoted just as much as celebrities. Like celebrities, heroes do not last for ever. Some of society's past heroes, Victorian generals and imperial explorers for instance, are now profoundly out of fashion as the world has changed, and new values dominate.

Boorstin's view of the celebrity as a shallow, evanescent, media artefact – an empty, pathetic substitute for real heroes and real greatness – is not shared by other commentators. Leo Braudy sees celebrities as embodiments of the audience's aspirations, as shapers of society's values, as the ultimate individualists in a mass society.[6] Richard Schickel sees celebrity as 'the principal motive power in putting across ideas of every kind – social, political, aesthetic, moral. Famous people are used as symbols of these ideas or become famous for being symbols of them.'[7] Jib Fowles in a study of one hundred current celebrities sees them as cultural icons – 'one of the essential things that hold us together'.[8] Chris Rojek suggests that the rise of celebrity culture is secular society's response to the decline of religion, with worship, relic collection and pilgrimage to the sacred sites associated with the object of adoration transferred from saints and martyrs to the heroes and heroines of popular culture.[9] All these definitions seem to me to be true. Each age gets the celebrities it deserves. They represent its dominant ideas about what is important.

It is undoubtedly true that an extra dimension has been added to the nature of fame by the mass media. Leo Braudy argues that desire for fame has been a feature of western society since its earliest days. But it has taken different forms. In the classical Ancient World, fame was gained by public service, civic virtue and military glory and achieved by generals, legislators and rulers. In the Christian period, the idea of special people as mediators between God and Man, exemplars of humility, spirituality and devotion, brought fame to saints, priests and martyrs.[10]

These co-existed in the pre-industrial world but the industrial world created both a mass market and the technology of mass production as it moved either by evolution or revolution towards democracy and later populism. The French and American revolutions promoting 'the myth of the Common Man' and the Romantic movement celebrating heroic individualism reinforced each other. Concern at the rapid pace of social and economic change led influential nineteenth-century thinkers like Carlyle and Ruskin to look back to the middle ages for models and value systems to counteract what they saw as the malign effects of industrialisation, urbanisation and mass culture.

Carlyle, in an influential series of lectures on heroes and hero-worship (1840), argued the need for heroes as leaders and role models. 'The history of what man has accomplished in this world … is at bottom the History of the Great Men who have worked here. They were the leaders of men, these great ones; the modellers, patterns and in a wide sense creators, of whatsoever the general mass of men contrived to do or attain.'[11] His choice of heroes was the hero as prophet (Mohammed), the hero as poet (Dante and Shakespeare), the hero as priest (Luther, Knox), the hero as man of letters (Rousseau, Johnson, Burns) and the hero as king (Cromwell, Napoleon). In 1850 Ralph Waldo Emerson published *Representative Men*, which like *On Heroes* introduced a key nineteenth-century term, discussing the men who symbolized what was best about Man – 'the genius of humanity' – and through whom one could interpret and understand the age and the environment and what makes humankind function best. Emerson cited Plato, Swedenborg, Montaigne, Shakespeare, Goethe and Napoleon as his 'representative men'.[12]

Certainly the nineteenth century, as much as previous ages, was a century of heroes and hero-worship. Its heroes were drawn from a wide range of activities: generals, statesmen, philanthropists, military leaders, empirebuilders and explorers, writers and thinkers, even some great women – Gladstone and Disraeli, Ruskin and Carlyle, General Havelock and General Gordon, Dr. Livingstone and Henry M. Stanley, Cardinal Newman and General Booth, Dickens and Tennyson, Florence Nightingale and Grace Darling. These were some of the heroes and heroines of the nineteenth century and they fitted Carlyle's definition of heroes as role models and leaders and Emerson's interpretation as 'representative men and women' who improved you by contemplation of their lives and thoughts.

The twentieth century has seen a marked decline in heroes for as variety of reasons. First, democratic societies have been suspicious of overmighty individuals, heroes have been regarded as elitist – and often came from elite groups anyway – and as democracy has given way to populism, we have seen the prediction of Andy Warhol 'that in future everyone will be famous for fifteen minutes' coming true – with the current vogue for so-called 'people' shows, phone-ins, reality television, the ubiquity of the camcorder and the celebration of 'ordinariness'. Secondly, Marxism, a powerful intellectual force in the twentieth century, stressed classes and masses, economic movements and forces rather than individuals or 'great men'. Thirdly, the historical trend of the twentieth century – from Lytton Strachey onwards – to debunk as part of the reaction against all things nineteenth century led to historians seeking to prove that all heroes were in fact drunkards, dunces or lechers, a tendency taken up by the tabloid press, which builds up and then tears down celebrities.

The dilemma posed by the conflict between the need for heroes (as myth figures, icons and role models) and the desire to emphasize ordinariness, the heroism of Everyman and Everywoman in the century of the Common Man, has been resolved by the media in the twentieth century by the development of the star system. As has been observed: 'the basic psychological machinery through which most people relate to film involves some combination of identification and projection' and what the audience identified with and projected themselves onto was the stars.[13] Stars had to fulfil a need and represent an ideal. They had to accomplish the difficult task of being both ordinary – for the purposes of identification – and extraordinary – for the purpose of admiration.

There can be no doubting the influence of stars. They set fashions in clothes, hairstyles, speech, deportment, even lovemaking. They exist as objects of desire, ideal archetypes, role models, wish fulfilment fantasy projections. But their success is not based on great deeds or achievements. It is based on looks or talent or success in some form of artistic endeavour – music, sport, acting – the achievement of an image that pleases, appeals, entertains, rather than the accomplishing of deeds that change the course of history, politics or belief. The star is a product of the leisure society, the kind of society where people have more money and more time and more access to the means of fulfilling their dreams, feeding their imaginative inner lives, rather than changing the world. With the establishment in the twentieth century of a self-centred, gratification-directed consumer society, the star has become the ultimate symbol of the market economy, made and broken by the mass consumer.

The counterpart of the star is the fan. It is commonly asserted that the fan is a product of modern culture, a direct reaction to mass industrial society, the desperate desire to identify being a response to the alienation and anonymity bred by that society. But this is not entirely true. There have always been fans – medieval preachers had them, so did Byzantine charioteers. The existence of fandom is something deep and enduringly psychological. In a collection of essays on fandom, Joli Jenson indignantly rejects what she sees as the predominant notion that fans are obsessed individuals or participants in a hysterical crowd: 'the fan is seen as being irrational, out of control and prey to a number of external forces. There is very little literature that explores fandom as a normal everyday cultural and social phenomenon.'[14]

This is true up to a point. There is a spectrum of fandom but it has a pathological extreme. There are some fans so deranged that they seek immortality by killing the person they worship – as Mark Chapman killed John Lennon. There are hysterical crowds of fans. How else can you explain the crowds of pubescent girls at rock concerts screaming and wetting themselves into a state of hysteria out of frustrated lust for the idol who remains forever beyond their reach? There are quietly devoted but single-minded fans who collect obsessively fan magazines, memorabilia, who write to and dress and speak like their idols. It is a complex phenomenon but it is hard to escape the conclusion that it is in part physical desire for the person, in part the wish to identify with success, in part a recognition of someone who stands for or embodies the kind of person or set of values to which the fan aspires, in part the need to give structure and purpose to life. It is also part of the process of constructing an identity, something most easily done by taking one ready-made from the mass media.

The fan magazines seek to maintain the link with the fans by ensuring that they realize that the stars become stars only by sacrifice, hard work and loneliness; that, although they live lives of conspicuous consumption and luxury, it is attained at a price. They also stress the humble origins and hard climb of the stars. So they remain both ordinary and extraordinary, fulfilling two needs. Articles about their homes, cars, parties, friends, holidays, create what has been called 'an illusion of intimacy,' which is a necessary feature of stardom.

We can identify three objects of admiration: the celebrity, the hero and the star. The hero predates the nineteenth century and goes back to ancient times. But what of star and celebrity? That we should trace both to the middle of the nineteenth century is clear etymologically. Celebrity – the condition of being talked about – famousness, notoriety, is recorded first in 1600, according to the *Oxford English Dictionary*. But *a* celebrity, meaning a person of celebrity, was first used in 1849. Similarly the word 'star' is first found in its theatrical sense as 'an actor, singer, etc. of exceptional celebrity or one whose name is prominently advertised as a special attraction to the public' in 1724, but in a general sense a star as 'one who 'shines' in society or is distinguished in some branch of art or science' is first found in 1850. So, both words became current simultaneously around the middle of the nineteenth century. It is precisely to the middle of the nineteenth century that historians date the development of a popular mass readership for newspapers. The nature of the newspapers changed too, in particular with the development of 'the New Journalism', racier, more populist and more celebrity-driven than their more staid and formal predecessors.

In the changing nature of the press certain journals took a lead and one was the highly influential weekly, the *World*. Its founder and editor was Edmund Yates (1831–1894). A typical Victorian man of letters – novelist, playwright, newspaper columnist, journalist, Bohemian, he conceived the idea of a new journal. Joseph Hatton in his book *Journalistic London* (1882) recalled: 'He always believed that the supposed horror of the British public for what is called 'personal journalism' was a sham, and that, provided it was not vulgar or scurrilous, kept free from mere tittle tattle about women, and from anything like a rowdy element it was certain to be acceptable.'[15] Yates himself says in his autobiography:

I had after much laborious excogitation come to the idea that a new and original journal, wholly differing in style from anything then existent, might have a tolerable chance of success. I never for one moment thought that frivolous chatter … was sufficient in itself to constitute a newspaper … but my opinion was that all the light and gossipy news of the day, properly winnowed and attractively set forth, backed by good political and social articles, written in a bolder, freer and less turgid style than that in which such topics were commonly handled, with first rate dramatic, literary and musical criticism, all laid on different lines from those then existing would form a journalistic amalgam which would most probably hit the public taste.[16]

So he was seeking a half-way house between total avoidance of 'personal journalism' (gossip, human interest, profiles, interviews) such as existed in the early nineteenth century and a total exploitation of the personal such as we get now with the tabloid press.

Yates had entertained his view of a new paper for twenty years, encouraged by the success of the regular column he had contributed to the *Illustrated London News* (1855). He had tried an earlier version, the *Train*, in 1856 but it folded after two years. Now times had changed and in 1874 he launched the *World: A Journal for Men and Women*. It was a sixpenny weekly. Its prospectus stated that 'it will contain a summary of everything worth notice in literature, art and society'; 'will recognize women as a reasonable class of the community whose interests should be equitably considered, and their errors explained without levity or hysterics'. It would 'publish that rarest of all things – candid reviews of good books, good plays, good pictures, and discoveries in science', 'the latest intelligence from the turf, the hunting field and the stock exchange', plus entertaining new fiction 'without any admixture of twaddle'.[17] He attracted a circle of able young journalists and some seasoned veterans and was greatly helped by a sensational libel case when the *World* early on ran a series 'exposing the tricks of west End usurers' and was sued by two moneylenders. The *World* won.

One of most successful features of the *World* was 'celebrities at home', a weekly interview column which talked to celebrities in their own homes, encouraging that illusion of intimacy which is a regular feature of the celebrity culture. Yates insisted in his 1884 autobiography that it involved nothing underhand or intrusive:

The silly idea that any system of espionage would be unduly obtained, and that there would be a general disclosure of skeletons in cupboards, was at once set at rest. By the regulations laid down and insisted upon from the first, that no person would be made the subject of these articles without his or her consent having been obtained and without full liberty, if they wished it, to inspect the article in proof before it was published – with these safeguards, and with a jealous care that the spirit with which they had been written should always be maintained, it appears to me that for the historian of the future, these articles will supply a want which must have been keenly felt by the Macaulays and the Froudes; will enable our descendants to picture to themselves all the exact social surroundings and daily lives and labours, the habits and manners, the dress and appearance of the men of mark in the present day, such as is inadequately afforded even by the diaries of Evelyn and Pepys, or the letters of Walpole.[18]

He noted that there had been four hundred such profiles to date. They were so popular that three series of the full interviews were issued in book form in 1878 and 1879. The lists are instructive as evidence of who was regarded as a celebrity:

Series 1

HRH The Prince of Wales at Sandringham
Mr Tennyson at Haslemere (the Poet Laureate)
Mr John Bright at One Ash (radical politician)
Mr Gladstone at Hawarden (the Liberal leader and former Prime Minister)
Mr Henry Irving at Bond Street (the actor-manager)
Earl of Beaconsfield at Hughenden (the Conservative Prime Minister)
Mr Charles Haddon Spurgeon at Nightingale Lane (Baptist minister and leading
   preacher of the day)
Mr Lowe at Sherbrooke (Robert Lowe, later Lord Sherbrooke; Gladstone's Home
   Secretary and Chancellor of the Exchequer, a controversial Liberal politician and
   albino)
Duke of Beaufort at Badminton (Master of the Horse and a leading courtier)
Mr. W.G. Grace at Downend (the cricketer)
Gustave Doré at Rue St. Dominique St. Germain (the artist)
President Grant at the White House (United States President)
Empress Eugenie at Chislehurst (French Empress in exile)
Thomas Carlyle at Cheyne Row (historian and sage)
Marquess of Salisbury at Hatfield (future Conservative Prime Minister and current
   Foreign Secretary)
Duc Decazes at Quai d'Orsay (French Foreign Minister)
Sir Rowland Hill at Hampstead (postal pioneer)
Earl of Shaftesbury at St. Giles' House (philanthropist)
Ouida at Villa Farinola (popular novelist)
Marshal de MacMahon at the Elysee (French President)
Captain Shaw at Watling Street (Eyre Massey Shaw, chief of Metropolitan Fire Brigade
   1861–91, handsome, well educated, ex-army officer, friend of Prince of Wales,
   knighted on retirement)
Dr John Henry Newman at Birmingham (leading Catholic clergyman)
Mr Charles Mathews at Belgravia (veteran comic actor)
Earl Granville at Walmer Castle (currently Lord Warden of the Cinque Ports and
   former Foreign Secretary)
Miss Mary Elizabeth Braddon at Richmond (popular novelist)
Earl Russell at Pembroke Lodge (former Prime Minister;)
Rev. Henry Ward Beecher at Brooklyn (American preacher)

Series 2

Duke of Richmond and Gordon at Goodwood House (Conservative grandee; Lord President of the Council, former President of Board of Trade and Poor Law Board and future Secretary of State for Scotland)

Sir Henry Thompson at Wimpole Street (fashionable surgeon)

Pope Pius IX in the Vatican

Victor Hugo in the Rue de Clichy (author)

Mr J.L. Toole at Orme Square (leading comic actor)

Dr Pusey at Christchurch (Anglican cleric)

Mr Frederic Leighton at Kensington (painter)

Richard Wagner at Bayreuth (composer)

Professor John Tyndall at Albemarle Street (scientist)

Mr Matthew Dawson at Heath House (racehorse trainer)

M. Jules Simon in Place de la Madeleine (ex French Prime Minister)

Mr George Augustus Sala in Gower Street (journalist)

Lord Houghton at Fryston Hall (poet)

Mr Charles Santley at St. John's Wood (singer)

M. Gambetta at Chausee d'Antin (French journalist and politician)

Father Ignatius at Llanthony (Abbot of Llanthony, Catholic divine)

Mr Charles Darwin at Down (scientist)

Prince Bismarck in the Wilhelmstrasse (German statesman)

Cardinal Manning at Archbishop's House, Westminster (English Catholic leader)

Mr J.J. Mechi at Tiptree Hall (farmer and in 1877 Chairman of London Farmers Club)

Mr George Lewis at Ely Place (barrister)

Sir William Thomson at Gilmore Hill (scientist)

Professor Ruskin at Brantwood (art historian and sage)

Mr George Payne in Queen Street (devotee of turf, gambling, dandy, old-fashioned country squire)

Kaiser Wilhelm at Babelsberg (German Emperor)

Bishop Fraser of Manchester at Bishops Court (Anglican prelate)

Sir Joseph Whitworth at Stancliffe (engineer and industrialist)

Series 3

Marquis of Hartington at Hardwick Hall (Liberal grandee, former Chief Secretary for Ireland and future Secretary of State for India and for War, currently Lord Rector of Glasgow University)

Sir George Airy at Greenwich (the Astronomer Royal)

Robert Peck at Russley ('He is called Robert by half of England') (racehorse trainer)

Mr Archibald Forbes at Maida Vale (war correspondent)

Mr Sims Reeves at Beulah Hill (singer)

Field Marshal von Moltke at the German General Staff

Colonel Henderson at Scotland Yard (Chief Commissioner of Police)

Mr Jowett at Balliol (Oxford academic)

Lord Chief Justice Cockburn at Hertford Street

M. Emile de Girardin in Rue de la Perouse (editor and proprietor of *La France* – leading French newspaper)

Mark Twain at Hartford (American novelist)

Wilkie Collins at Gloucester Place (novelist)

Mlle Sarah Bernhardt in Avenue de Villiers (actress)

Mr Frank Buckland in Albany Street (scientist, naturalist and explorer)

Earl of Wilton at Egerton Lodge (courtier, Lord Steward of the Household)

Mr John Arthur Roebuck at Ashley Place (radical politican)

M. de Lesseps in Rue Richepanse (builder of Suez Canal)

Sir Robert Peel at Drayton Manor (son of the Prime Minister and himself a former Chief Secretary for Ireland)

Lord Napier at the Convent, Gibraltar (Governor of Gibraltar and commander of Abyssinian expeditionary force)

Earl of Carnarvon at Highclere (Colonial Secretary)

Duke of Marlborough at Dublin Castle (Viceroy of Ireland)

Sir Garnet Wolseley in Portman Square (general)

Earl of Rosebery at the Durdans (Liberal grandee and future Prime Minister; currently Lord Rector of Aberdeen University)

W. Harrison Ainsworth at Little Rockley (novelist)

Lord Derby at Knowsley (Tory grandee, former Foreign Secretary)

Monsignor Capel at Kensington (popular Catholic cleric)

Earl of Dufferin at Rideau Hall (Governor General of Canada and later Viceroy of India)

Fascinatingly and revealingly Irving is the fifth of the celebrities, one ahead of the Prime Minister, Lord Beaconsfield. On the scope of the celebrities Yates noted: 'with the exception of our Most Gracious Majesty there is scarcely one personage of importance in the present day who does not find a niche in this series'. And his definition of celebrities: 'The leading members of nearly every reigning family in Europe, presidents and statesmen of the French and American republics, army and navy officers, poets, peers, publicists, leaders in all kinds of sport, members of the Bar and lights of the pulpit, owners, jockeys and trainers of racehorses.'[19] It reflects a strongly hierarchical and deferential society (crown, church, parliament, peerage, the law, the armed forces) but with a leavening of figures from sport and the arts, which signals the beginnings of the acceptance of the leisure culture as an integral part of mass society (actors, singers, popular writers, journalists, sportsmen). But the choice also symbolizes the preoccupations of the age – the crisis of religious faith, war and imperial expansion, the emergence of democracy.

It is worth noting that Yates's new gossip-centred world carried its dangers. In 1858 he had been expelled from the Garrick Club for reporting in a newspaper the contents of a private conversation involving the novelist Thackeray, and in

1885 he spent four months in Holloway Prison following a libel action against the *World* for suggesting the imminent elopement of a peer of the realm.

The success of the *World* was such that it inspired a host of imitations – the *Whitehall Review, Mayfair, Life, Pan, Society* and most notably and successfully of all *Truth*, owned and edited by the Liberal MP Henry Labouchere, who had formerly been a contributor to the *World*. Joseph Hatton calls it 'bitter, personal, brilliant, chatty, impudent, sometimes reckless, always amusing'.[20] The influence in style and content of the *World* percolated down to the dailies and helped to stimulate 'the New Journalism'. By the 1880s periodicals devoted solely to celebrities were being launched: *Celebrities of the Day, Our Celebrities, The Weekly Gallery of Celebrities*.

Significantly the *World* celebrities did not resemble Daniel Boorstin's definition at all. They had both image and achievement for the most part and they included heroes, stars and leaders, though there are a handful who would survive in today's world of non-achieving celebrities.

The idea that with celebrity came responsibility to set an example and to stand up for the highest social values informed one of the most influential best-sellers of the Victorian Age, Samuel Smiles' *Self-Help*. First published in 1859, it had run to fifty editions by 1901 and made its author a celebrity. The object of the book, as stated in the preface, was:

> To re-inculcate those old fashioned but wholesome lessons – which perhaps cannot be too often urged, – that youth must work in order to enjoy, – that nothing creditable can be accomplished without application and diligence, – that the student must not be daunted by difficulties, but conquer them by patience and perseverance, – and that above all he must seek elevation of character, without which capacity is worthless and worldly success is naught.[21]

Smiles saw Character as central to life:

> The crown and glory of life is Character. It is the noblest possession of a man, constituting a rank in itself, and an estate in the general goodwill; dignifying every station, and exalting every position in society ... Character is human nature in its best form. It is moral order embodied in the individual ... The strength, the industry, and the civilization of nations – all depend upon individual character; and the very foundations of civil security rest upon it.[22]

Truthfulness, integrity and goodness were, in Smiles's view, 'the essence of manly character', and they made a man a gentleman. For gentlemanliness was not a matter of birth or wealth but of character.[23]

It was not only the great and famous who embodied Smiles's virtues: 'even the humblest person, who sets before his fellows an example of industry, sobriety, and upright honestly of purpose in life, has a present as well as a future influence upon the well-being of his country'. Yet 'Biographies of great, but especially of good men, are nevertheless most instructive and useful as helps, guides, and incentives to others. Some of the best are almost equivalent to gospels, teaching high living, high thinking and energetic action for their own and the world's good.'[24] Smiles drew not just on politicians and generals but on science, literature and art for his exemplary lives. They included David Wilkie, William Etty, Augustus Pugin, Michael Faraday, Sir Humphry Davy, Dr Livingstone, John Howard, Handel, Disraeli, Bulwer Lytton, Lord Brougham, James Watt, Sir Roderick Murchison and so forth. Irving would have been delighted to see Shakespeare, acknowledged to have been an actor, included among the historical examples. Had Smiles been writing later than 1859 he might even have included Irving, whose life was a classic example of self-help, who had risen from humble origins to fame, turned himself into a gentleman, and uttered regular pronouncements about work, character and chivalry that might well have come from Smiles.

Who was the first celebrity? The most likely candidate is George Gordon, Lord Byron, who in the celebrated phase of the time 'awoke to find himself famous' with the publication of his poem *Childe Harold* in 1812. He had many of the attributes that we would associate with the modern celebrity – he had striking good looks, enhanced by the congenital lameness that gave him an extra air of mystery; he was a self-publicist (retrospectively dubbed 'the showman of the Romantic movement'); his poems caught the mood of the moment; he also fed that element of gossip that goes with celebrity (his amours were notorious and much discussed; his poems were believed to be autobiographical and were pored over for clues); he himself embodied many of the qualities that made his heroes so congenial to the age and who were thus dubbed Byronic, the tormented, solitary, brooding, restless wanderer with a secret sorrow, the espouser of heroic causes, the self-conscious exotic, the perfect identification figure for the young. Byron and his poems became a cult. The Duchess of Devonshire wrote to her son in 1812: 'The subject of conversation, of curiosity, of enthusiasm almost, one might say, of the moment is not Spain or Portugal, warriors or patriots, but Lord Byron ... [*Childe Harold*] is on every table and himself courted, visited, flattered, and praised wherever he appears.'[25] Byron once said that the three greatest men of the nineteenth century were Beau Brummell, himself and Napoleon in that order. All were heroic individualists, all distinguished in their fields – fashion, poetry, war. They also attracted the attention of the fledgling media. We are talking in Byron's case about a small circulation press, but the secret of Byron's success was that his celebrity percolated down. There was a flourishing underground press, connected with the radical movement. The young radical writers and printers pirated Byron's poems, imitated his dress and lifestyle, and publicized his private life, as in the anonymous 1816 volume: *The Private Life of Lord Byron, Comprising his Voluptuous Amours*. Byron was very much the pop star of his day: his image attracted, his works were avidly devoured, he was aped and imitated, and he even appeared during his lifetime thinly disguised in novels and stories. These included Lady Caroline Lamb's *Glenarvon* (1816), Eaton Stannard Barrett's *Six Weeks at Longs* (1817) and Thomas Love Peacock's *Nightmare Abbey* (1818). It was a pattern that was to be followed in the case of other public figures.

If Byron was the poet of the era of Romanticism and Radicalism, the poet of the mid-Victorian heyday was Alfred, Lord Tennyson. By 1850 he was recognized as 'the outstanding poet of his generation' but he had also become a celebrity – and as such an early interviewee of the *World*. *In Memoriam* with its message of faith, hope and love, was an instant success in 1850, selling 60,000 copies within a few months. This coincided with the death of Wordsworth and led to the offer of the poet laureateship, thanks in part to the enthusiasm for his work of Prince Albert. As Laureate he was involved in the production of official verse for particular occasions. Patriotic, royalist, imperialist and Protestant, he caught the dominant mood of the age in 'The Charge of the Light Brigade' and 'The Relief of Lucknow'. The controversy attending the publication of 'Maud', denounced as immoral in some quarters, did him no harm. *The Idylls of the King* was an enormously popular exposition of chivalry as the ideology for the Victorian age and *Enoch Arden* was a tear-jerking best seller: both of them very much in tune with the spirit of the times and of the middle-class readership for fiction, poetry and newspapers. The popularity of his poems, the controversy surrounding 'Maud', the laureateship, and his well-publicized friendship with the Queen, with whom he regularly corresponded, all served to make him a celebrity.

In addition to the body of work and its popularity, the public role and association with the Queen, there was the striking appearance, enhanced by cape and sombrero, made familiar by the photographs of leading portrait photographer Julia Margaret Cameron, who became a worshipper and represents the way in which photography assisted in the creation of a celebrity. Justin McCarthy, writing about the leading figures of the 1860s, noted of Tennyson, attending a reception for Garibaldi:

> There were many Englishmen of great distinction there, and Tennyson was the most conspicuous among the guests. Tennyson's appearance was very striking, and his figure might have been taken as a living illustration of romantic poetry. He was tall and stately, wore a great mass of thick, long hair ... his frame was slightly stooping, his shoulders were bent as if with the weight of thought; there was something entirely out of the common and very commanding in his whole presence and a stranger meeting him in whatever crowd would probably have assumed at once that he must be a literary king ... when he happened to be in London he was a familiar figure in some of the quieter recesses of the Parks, more especially of St James's Park, and nobody to whom he was personally unknown could have passed him without turning to look back on him and

without taking it for granted that he must be a man of distinction and importance. Those who knew him only by sight and happened thus to meet him were sure to tell their friends that they had just seen Tennyson in the park.[26]

This striking appearance and popular achievement was enhanced – contrary to Byron's attitude – by Tennyson's apparent hatred of publicity and desire to avoid it. But it pursued him. Tourists sought out his house, requests for autographs inundated him – Prince Albert was among those writing to ask for one, and people went to extraordinary lengths to catch a glimpse of him, climbing trees to peer into his house. On one occasion he arrived home complaining he had been pursued along the road by two fat ladies and sixteen children. He announced to Julia Margaret Cameron that:

> he believed that every crime and every vice in the world were connected with the passion for autographs and anecdotes and records; that the desire for acquaintance with the lives of great ones was treating them like pigs to be ripped open for the public ... He thanked God Almighty with his whole heart that he knew nothing and the world knew nothing of Shakespeare but his writing.[27]

He was particularly hostile to Americans who he believed 'crossed the ocean with no purpose save to intrude on him'.[28] But his grandson and biographer Charles Tennyson believed he was secretly flattered by all the attention. A later biographer R.B. Martin records:

> Tennyson's name was so well known that when he stayed in a hotel, he had to wait until leaving to sign the register for fear of being mobbed, and he was surely the only poet in history whose name was frequently used without permission in advertisements in the sure knowledge that it would sell goods. He found a grim amusement in telling how Cockles' Pills printed an entirely fictitious letter reading: 'Dear Sir, like most literary men I am subject to violent constipation and your pills I find of the greatest possible comfort. A. Tennyson.'[29]

S.J. Perelman once said: 'In the aristocracy of success there are no strangers' and one of the hallmarks of the celebrity society is that celebrity calls to celebrity.[30] Celebrities reinforce each other – today by attending each others parties, performing together in productions and television programmes, appearing in chat shows, having well-publicized sexual encounters, even marrying. The extent to which a celebrity associates with other celebrities is a measure of his or her status. Tennyson was so celebrated that he revolved within a celebrity world: Garibaldi visited him at Faringford; Queen Emma of the Sandwich Islands came to stay; he corresponded with Queen Victoria and dedicated *The Idylls of the King* to the memory of the Prince Consort. Edward Lear, Edward Fitzgerald, Robert Browning and W.E. Gladstone were friends. General Gordon, Thomas Hardy, Henry James, George Eliot, Coventry Patmore,

Benjamin Jowett, Thomas Carlyle and W.M. Thackeray visited him. He was painted (reluctantly) by Hubert von Herkomer, G.F. Watts and Sir John Millais. His plays *Queen Mary*, *The Cup* and *Becket* were triumphantly staged by Sir Henry Irving. He became the first poet to be awarded a peerage. The other arts had a long time to wait: in painting Frederic Leighton (1896), in music Benjamin Britten (1976), both on their death beds, and in acting Laurence Olivier (1970)

Henry Irving's celebrity is amply attested by the contemporary press. The comic magazine *Moonshine* ran a cartoon series *Days with Celebrities*. No. 8 was Henry Irving (13 August 1881). It shows Irving caricatured with pince-nez, top hat, stick insect legs and long flowing locks. He opens a bazaar, lays a foundation stone, receives an address, makes a speech, visits the strangers gallery at the Commons, researches a forthcoming production in the library, addresses 'a few words of encouragement' to the critics and occupies a theatre box. His photograph appeared in *Figaro*'s weekly gallery of celebrity portraits and he was No. 5 in *The World's Celebrities at Home* series. These are just a few examples culled from the huge acreage of his celebrity coverage.

Perhaps there is no surer evidence of Irving's celebrity than his appearance in 1898 in *The Big Budget*, Dan Leno's comic journal. In one comic strip, Airy Alf and Bouncing Billy, a couple of cockney japesters visit the Lyceum and meet Irving and Ellen Terry in their *Peter the Great* costumes, before falling through an open trapdoor on stage and being carried off in a wheelbarrow amid a crowd of jeering onlookers. Equally telling is the appearance of an Irvingesque figure as Hamlet advertising Beecham's tablets with the line 'To Beecham or not to Beecham, that is the question', which appeared, 'with apologies to our greatest poet and most renowned actor', in the *Illustrated Sporting and Dramatic News* (6 July 1880).

Similar evidence can be found in George and Weedon Grossmith's comic masterpiece *The Diary of a Nobody* (first published in book form in 1892), recounting the lives of the lower middle-class Pooters in Holloway. Their son Lupin brings home his friend, Mr Burwin-Fosselton, the amateur actor, who, says Mr Pooter, 'not only looked rather like Mr Irving but seemed to imagine he was the celebrated actor'. The whole evening is taken up with his Irving imitations and Mr Cummings, one of the other guests, declares that 'Mr Burwin-Fosselton was not only *like* Mr Irving but was in his judgement in every way as *good* or even *better*'. Mr Pooter insists that it is just an imitation and a quarrel develops until Carrie Pooter saves the situation by declaring: 'I'll be Ellen Terry.' Pooter records, 'Dear Carrie's imitation wasn't a bit liked, but she was so spontaneous and so funny that the disagreeable discussion passed off.'[31]

The role of the press in all this is crucial and was recognized at the time. In a critical study of Irving, published in 1883, William Archer, who had a less than adulatory view of Irving's abilities, wrote:

> The Press sways the masses and the masses in turn sway the Press. The criticism which does not actually proceed from devotees by conviction, echoes the plaudits of the first night audiences. The critic is tired of enumerating the old faults and limitations, so leaves them out of sight and sets himself to discover merits by which to explain the indubitable success. In this word lies both the enigma and its key. Nothing succeeds like success, for success is its own advertisement ... He is of all living Englishmen the best advertised at the smallest relative cost. The Prince of Wales, Mr Gladstone, Mrs Langtry, Mr Bradlaugh, are not more in evidence. All the forces of art, literature and society are leagued to give him the puff direct, preliminary, collateral, collusive, and oblique ... Even the scoffs and cavillings of the rabidest infidels ... merely serve the purpose of the puff collusive ... Mr Irving is no longer a celebrated actor, he is the *actor-celebrity* [*my italics*] of the day. It was undoubtedly his talent as an actor, manager and diplomatist, so to speak, that gained him his vogue, but his vogue now reacts upon his talent, and throws it into startling relief. A snowball once set fairly rolling under certain conditions of temperature, and on a declivity of a certain angle, will grow into an avalanche by its own impetus, absorbing and waxing fat upon the very obstructions in its path.[32]

It is important to stress here the interaction of the public and the papers. There was a symbiotic process at work, each side feeding the other.

The fame as an actor is undoubted and it was overnight fame in terms of the West End. He had been a respected character actor in London and the provinces for some years when he opened in *The Bells* at the Lyceum in 1871, mesmerized the audience with his study of the guilt-ridden Alsatian burgomaster and became a star. As one newspaper put it on 26 November 1892: 'On this morning twenty-one years ago, Mr Irving, like Byron, awoke to find himself famous.' The link with the first celebrity is thus made.

The Times records the way in which his instant stardom was greeted. Covering the opening of W.G. Wills's *Charles the First* which followed the run of *The Bells*, the drama critic John Oxenford declared that '*The Bells* was one of the leading topics of the theatrical world during the season 1871–72', and reported 'it is scarcely too much to say that everybody in town who takes a special interest in theatrical matters, and was not professionally engaged elsewhere, was present at the first performance of Mr W.G. Wills's new play *Charles the First*'. He went on to pronounce it a 'triumphant success'.[33] By the time Irving came to play the lead in Bulwer Lytton's *Richelieu* (1873), *The Times* (29 September 1873) was reporting unprecedented scenes:

> Never did aristocratic statesman leap with greater agility into favour with a multitude, which comprised idolators of every class, than did Armand du Plessis-Richelieu on the night of Saturday last. The feat is to be attributed wholly and solely to the genius of Mr Irving ... Enthusiastic sounds of approval came from every part of the house. The pit

not only rose, but it made the rising conspicuous by the waving of countless hats and handkerchiefs. Not bare approval, but hearty sympathy was denoted by this extraordinary demonstration.

Irving's theatrical pre-eminence was cemented in 1874 by his appearance in *Hamlet*. *The Times* (2 November 1874) declared:

> The great event which has been expected with eagerness by the whole theatrical world came off on Saturday night ... The amount of expectation by which the event had been preceded was in itself so remarkable that many persons will find it difficult to account for. Mr Irving has 'done' his Shakespeare in the provinces, and *Hamlet* has been among his parts; but no particular account has come to us as to the manner in which he filled it before he had become a London *celebrity* [*my italics*] ... The crowds which besieged the pit entrance of the Lyceum long before the doors were opened, the numbers who, after the doors opened, were turned back when ... they could not produce a ticket ... showed that the London public had been stimulated to a degree to which it would be difficult to provide a precedent.

His *Hamlet* was an enormous success and ran for an unprecedented two hundred performances, after which Irving never looked back.

Joseph Knight, writing of Irving's 1875 Lyceum *Macbeth*, noted with some bemusement a phenomenon occurring:

> Actor and piece were received with an enthusiasm that may best be described as passionate. A sight such as is now presented is quite unprecedented in stage history, and is worth taking into account by those who study the age in its various manifestations. We have here a man whom a large portion of the public, and by no means the least cultivated section, receives as a great actor. The manifestations are, moreover, such as we read of in the case of the greatest of his predecessors, and contain that mixture of admiration and personal regard which men like Kean and Kemble were able to inspire in their admirers. Yet criticism holds itself aloof, discontented and unsympathetic, and the actor's own profession, though it is, of course, sensible of merit, fails to partake the enthusiasm of the public.[34]

Irving qualifies for celebrity in a number of respects. Firstly, he had a distinctive appearance. Percy Fitzgerald writes: 'Irving was extraordinarily fortunate in his figure and general appearance. It was truly picturesque and quite remarkable. It used to be said that there were only three or four men whom people would turn to look after in the street – Mr. Gladstone, Cardinal Manning and Irving.' This was caused by the hair worn long, the ascetic appearance, the pince-nez and what Fitzgerald calls 'a slightly eccentric style of dress' – a tall, broad brimmed hat, a low collar and a curiously cut coat with 'flowing' collar and skirt.[35]

Frank Harris, buccaneering editor of *The Evening News*, *The Fortnightly Review* and *The Saturday Review*, wrote in his memoirs:

Irving always gave the impression of being more than an actor: he had a great personality; his marked peculiarities of figure, face and speech set him apart and gave him unique place and distinction. Of the three or four chief personages of the eighties, he was the most singular – more arresting even than Parnell. Randolph Churchill and Gladstone had to be seen in the House of Commons to win full recognition, but Irving, like Disraeli, took the eye everywhere and excited the imagination.[36]

Irving had fans. A newspaper clipping from 1880 records:

Henry Irving is decidedly the fashion of the hour. He has succeeded in becoming the pattern of the young men and the idol of the young women. Wherever I turn I detect traces of Irving mania. At the universities the cultus of the long-haired tragedian has succeeded the rage for medieval ritual. In my time undergraduates of a pronounced type were Puseyites, now they are Irvingites. The 'eminent one' in every conceivable character and attitude has supplanted bell, book and candle. Instead of oratories and missals, incense and Oxford frames, the boys adorn their rooms with scenes and characters illustrative of the favourite's most recent successes. The youth of today affects long hair tucked behind the ears, cultivates eye-brows and wears a pince-nez with affectionate regularity.[37]

W.P. Frith the painter recalled the occasion when a group of young ladies from an unnamed college attended a play at the Lyceum:

The play was over, and the young ladies – about a round dozen in number – found their way to the stage door in full determination to see their idol in his habit as he lives, on his exit from the scene of his triumphs. The great actor appeared and found an avenue of young ladies through which he had to walk to his carriage, the door of which was already in possession of ... one of the boldest. The poor actor was dreadfully embarrassed – a pretty young lady transforming herself into a footman! Profuse was his sorrow that she should give herself such trouble; the young ladies were really too kind and so on. So saying, with doffed hat, my friend shook hands with the lady footman, and wishing the fair bevy goodnight, the actor drove away. Of course the lady-footman's hands were gloved. No sooner had the carriage disappeared than ... the hand grasped by Irving was denuded of its glove, a pair of scissors was produced, the glove was cut to pieces, each worshipper receiving a portion, which is very likely a cherished possession to this hour.[38]

In connection with *The Cup* (1881), *Truth* recorded of Irving: 'the ladies ... squabbled for his autograph. I was seriously asked the other day if I could obtain the end of one of the cigars that the great tragedian had smoked.'[39] This is when fashion takes on religious connotations – with provision of holy relics. It was done on a grand scale by Sir Merton Russell-Cotes, an Irving worshipper, who established an Irving Museum at Bournemouth full of memorabilia associated with him, including a lock of his hair.

Many a fan described him or herself as a worshipper. To give just one example. The artist Percy Bradshaw, looking back at his youth, wrote in 1958:

Irving … was something infinitely more important than a great actor. From the first time I saw him on the stage – as Becket – I regarded him as an exalted spiritual being who belonged to another world. I am still certain, having seen him in most of his parts, that no other human being in my time has possessed a tithe of Irving's distinction or hypnotic power. He converted a theatre into a cathedral and I continue to worship at the shrine which is erected in my memory.[40]

We are not yet in the era of the crazed fan, but celebrity was already dangerous. For in 1897 William Terriss, the most popular melodramatic actor of his day, was stabbed to death at the door of his theatre by a deranged small part actor, Richard Prince, who on his arrest was found to have a list of other theatrical notables on him.[41]

One of the groups of fans who turned their Irving worship to practical effect was the Irving Dramatic Club, a society of enthusiastic amateur actors. The club, which was set up in 1879, staged an elaborate Shakespeare production every season, starting with *Hamlet*. The society, reported its honorary secretary Herbert Swears, 'received the approval and support of the Lyceum chief'. Their production of *Henry IV Part One* was so well received that Irving offered to lend them the Lyceum so that they could put it on for the benefit of the Actors' Association. This took place on Sunday 29 March 1890, with Irving and Ellen Terry watching from a box. Irving was so impressed by Frank Macey, who played Hotspur, that he asked him to join the Lyceum company. But Macey, who already had a good job in business, preferred to stick to that rather than risk the hazards of the acting profession. Interestingly, Swears reports: 'Most members of the Irving Club tried to look like their President. I was at a disadvantage because my hair began to thin at an early age. But I remember that one of our number called Wellesley Forbes succeeded in training his locks well over the collar of his coat. This accomplishment filled us all with envy.'[42]

In Irving's career celebrity called to celebrity. One of the greatest painters of the age, W.P. Frith, painted *The Private View of the Royal Academy*, 1881, which centres on Oscar Wilde holding forth to his disciples about the paintings. But the room is full of celebrities. Frith described them in his memoirs.

Near them stands Anthony Trollope, whose homely figure affords a striking contrast to the eccentric forms near him. The rest of the composition is made up of celebrities of all kinds, statesmen, poets, judges, philosophers, musicians, painters, actors, and others. Miss Braddon – close to her Sir Julius Benedict – is talking to a friend. Mr Gladstone shakes hands with Sir Stafford Northcote, Sir William Harcourt and Mr Bright standing by. Mr Browning talks to an aesthetic lady, whose draped back affords a chance of showing that view of the costume. Sir F. Leighton is in earnest conversation with Lady Lonsdale, who sits on one of the ottomans in the gallery not far from Lady Diana Huddleston, Baroness Burdett-Coutts, and others. Professor Huxley is prominent, as are also the Archbishop of York, Lord Coleridge, and Mrs Langtry, Mr Agnew (then

MP), Baron Huddleston – by the latter stand Messrs Tenniel and Du Maurier – and many others; amongst whom I must not forget Miss Ellen Terry and my old friends Irving and Sala. I received the kindest assistance from all these eminent persons, many of whom came to see me at great sacrifice of time and engagements.[43]

On 12 December 1878 Alfred Bryan published a cartoon in the *World* showing much of fashionable society attending an Irving performance at the Lyceum. It was to an extent symbolic because it depicts Disraeli there and he only visited the Lyceum once in 1880 and thought Irving 'third rate'.[44] But certainly much of fashionable society went to the Lyceum and if they did not go, Irving might go to them – as when he did command performances for Queen Victoria and King Edward VII at Windsor and Sandringham. Irving had a shrewd appreciation of the publicity value of such occasions. In 1893 Irving was rehearsing his company for a command performance of *Becket* at Windsor and having all the scenery redone on a small scale to fit the performance space at the castle. Graham Robertson remarked that it would cost a great deal. Irving agreed but said that it was worthwhile in the light of his forthcoming tour of America. He observed: 'For one American who will go to see a play by a great poet, twenty will go to see a play that had been given at Windsor Castle before the Queen.'[45]

Edward VII as Prince of Wales was a regular theatregoer and in 1883 after a performance of *Much Ado* he was entertained to an intimate supper on the stage of the Lyceum by Irving. Irving gave celebrity suppers in the Beefsteak Room, a specially equipped dining room backstage which could seat thirty-six. Bram Stoker lists one thousand notables whom Irving entertained there and they included such celebrities as Paderewski, Adelina Patti, Anthony Hope, Mr and Mrs H.H. Asquith, A.J. Balfour, the Duke of Fife, Sarasate, William Howard Russell, Sarah Bernhardt, Lord and Lady Randolph Churchill, Jerome K. Jerome, the Duke of Devonshire, Hall Caine, P.T. Barnum, Barney Barnato, W.P. Frith, Fridjof Nansen, Franz Liszt, Mary Elizabeth Braddon, Lillie Langtry, Sir Edward Burne-Jones, the Duke of Saxe-Meiningen, the Ranee of Sarawak, the Maharajah Gaekwar of Baroda, Lord Wolseley, Sir Arthur and Lady Conan Doyle, Samuel Smiles, Ethel Barrymore, Sir Charles and Lady Stanford, Sir Charles Hallé, General Sir Hector Macdonald, the Duke and Duchess of Sutherland, Carl Rosa, Dean Farrar, James McNeill Whistler, General William T. Sherman, Sir Henry Morton Stanley and Lady Stanley, Thomas Hardy, Sir Arthur Sullivan, 'Buffalo Bill' Cody, Mark Twain, W.E. and Mrs Gladstone, Judge Thomas Hughes, Sir Luke Fildes and Charles Gounod.[46] The whole cumulative effect of this was to confirm Irving as an undoubted celebrity.

Irving was fully aware of the value of publicity in maintaining his name and fame before the public and in this he followed on the work of 'Colonel' Hezekiah Linthicum Bateman, the original lessee of the Lyceum, who gave him his starring break in *The Bells* in 1871 and managed the theatre until his death in 1875. *The*

Bells was produced in November 1871 and in February 1872 the Queen and the Prince of Wales proceeded in state to St Paul's Cathedral to give thanks for the Prince's recovery from typhoid fever. 'Colonel' Bateman hung a banner decorated with gigantic silver bells from the Lyceum roof to the house opposite – ostensibly to celebrate the Prince's recovery but also to advertise his current hit. When Wills's *Charles the First* was a hit, there was considerable press comment and controversy about the hostile depiction of Cromwell, who was a hero of liberals and radicals, and so 'Colonel' Bateman 'salted the pit and gallery with a small claque who declared now for Cromwell, now for Charles, with excellent results'.[47]

In January 1876 Irving brought a libel action against *Fun*, a weekly comic paper which published a satirical piece attacking Irving on the grounds that he 'undermined the constitution of society and familiarized the masses with the most loathsome details of crime and bloodshed' and that, with 'the hireling portion of the press' at his command, he had 'induced the vulgar and unthinking to consider [him] a model of histrionic ability and the pioneer of an intellectual and cultured school of dramatic art'. The offending journalist, the young George R. Sims, travelled up from Cornwall, made a fulsome apology in court and the case was dropped. Sims subsequently became a celebrated playwright, poet and writer. In his autobiography *My Life* (1917) he suggested that 'Colonel' Bateman brought the case – 'he saw in the undoubted libel the article contained a chance for bold advertisement' – but in fact 'Colonel' Bateman had died the previous March and it seems likely that Irving, with his high sense of his calling and the moral tone of the theatre he was seeking to establish brought the case, but with a clear understanding of its publicity value. The leading comic actor J.L. Toole, the composer Frederic Clay and the playwright Dion Boucicault gave evidence for Irving, and Sims recalled: 'Boucicault arrived late and had to fight his way into the court through the mob which had gathered outside to see the *celebrities*.'[48]

Irving turned his first nights into major celebrity gatherings. Writing in 1923 and looking back on the Irving first nights, the cartoonist Harry Furniss recalled:

> Many years must elapse before we have anything in theatrical London so imposing as a first night of the Lyceum Theatre when Sir Henry Irving presided. Now he is gone the truth is plain to everyone, then realized by a few, that the outlay of 'booming' Sir Henry ate away all subsequent profits. Irving's success was a first-night success, something big, something important, and an audience wholly representative. He was never a failure, the house was always filled through the prescribed run, the press announced record houses, the fiftieth night was heralded with a flourish and the hundredth night with a cannonade of eulogistic artillery. But power of that kind can be bought too dearly, and, in the end, the Lyceum ammunition ran dry. Irving was an artist, a genius, above all, a Bohemian, he cared little for the day of reckoning so long as he pleased and impressed a first-night audience. There was always the anticipation of surprise, the genuine feeling that something out of the common would probably occur on these first nights. The

audience was as important as the play, every one present was taking part in an epoch-making event in the history of the English stage.[49]

The newspaper account of the first night of the revival of *Macbeth* on 29 December 1888 confirms Furniss's recollection of these first nights. Columns are devoted to the account of the celebrities present:

> We hear nowadays of representative gatherings, representative dinners, representative men and women and so forth. It may be conceded … that 'the word is overdone'; yet no other may so easily be found to describe more accurately the audience that came together on Saturday night to witness the production of *Macbeth* at the Lyceum Theatre. Wonderful stories were told of the eagerness of all sorts of people to obtain seats, or even standing room. We were told of the crowd that had already begun to picnic at the pit door at eleven in the forenoon, and that the traffic in the Strand had been seriously impeded all the afternoon; of an American journalist who had made a 'purpose journey' from New York to be present; of a well-known MP who had unavailingly offered 'Mitchells' five guineas that morning for a stall, and so on … when, punctually at the appointed time of a quarter to eight, the curtain rose … it may be doubted whether a more distinguished company has ever before assembled within the walls of a playhouse.

Noting that only royalty was 'wanting to add a finishing touch', the report surveyed the audience in detail. The royal box was occupied by the American Minister and Mrs Phelps, 'the popular representative of our Transatlantic cousins, who are to our lasting regret so soon to leave us'. In the O.P. box were the Earl and Countess of Londesborough. In the stalls were Sir Edward Clarke, the Solicitor General, Lord Fife, Lord Cheylesmore, the Earl of Onslow 'enjoying one more evening out before his departure for his Antipodean Proconsulate' (the Governorship of New Zealand), W.S. Gilbert, Mr and Mrs Oscar Wilde, the fashionable surgeon Sir Morell Mackenzie, the painters Edwin Abbey, Val Prinsep, William Orchardson, Hubert von Herkomer, the actress Geneviève Ward, the actor Squire Bancroft and his son 'Master George' 'during an interval in his round of exams', the impresario Augustus Harris, the war correspondent William Howard Russell, the editor Edmund Yates, the singer George Henschel, Richard D'Oyly Carte ('the only manager whose first nights can compare with this'), the playwrights Arthur Wing Pinero, Hamilton Aidé and Henry Arthur Jones, the sculptor Onslow Ford, the cartoonist Harry Furniss, the artist Linley Sambourne and many more. After the play, 'Mr Irving received a large party on the stage for supper, including most of those whose names we have given and many more'. So it was a typical Irving celebrity first night.[50]

Further publicity was gained by the introduction of the concept of the celebrity dinner. Giving an account of a supper to celebrate the hundredth night of *La Fille de Madame Angot* in Paris in 1872, Percy Fitzgerald noted in 1881: 'This agreeable fashion of celebrating success is rarely practised in England.'[51]

But 'Colonel' Bateman was on to it and the hundredth night of *Hamlet* was celebrated by a banquet at the theatre after the play, attended by 'authors, actors, poets, painters, journalists, publishers, and well known powers of dramatic art'.[52] The dinner was a novelty and was extensively covered in the press. In 1880 the hundredth night of *The Merchant of Venice* was marked by a similar dinner attended by a glittering company (three hundred guests from the arts and letters), though marred by an inappropriate speech by Lord Houghton attacking Irving's interpretation of Shylock as too sympathetic. But this in itself created extra publicity as the newspapers debated the pros and cons of the argument. The hundredth performance of *Romeo and Juliet* in 1882 saw a dinner for one hundred with this time a graceful speech by the Earl of Lytton, the former Viceroy of India and a well known poet under the pseudonym Owen Meredith. Perhaps the most spectacular dining occasion occurred on 4 July 1883 at the St James's Hall when on the eve of Irving's first tour of the United States, five hundred leading figures of the day gathered to pay tribute to him, presided over by the Lord Chief Justice Lord Coleridge, who made one of the speeches in which he paid tribute to Irving's artistic success but also his moral influence. 'The general tone and atmosphere of the theatre wherever Mr Irving's influence is predominant, has been uniformly higher and purer. The pieces which he has acted, and the way he has acted them, have always been such that no husband need hesitate to take his wife, no mother to take her daughter, where Mr Irving is the ruling spirit.'[53]

Speeches were also made by James Russell Lowell, the American Minister in London and a distinguished poet himself, Viscount Bury, J.L. Toole, Lawrence Alma-Tadema, Professor John Tyndall and Irving himself; songs were sung by Sims Reeves and Charles Santley. It is once again celebrity calling to celebrity. The *World* (11 July 1883) declared: 'the Irving dinner of 1883 is really an historical event, and may mark a new point in the national position of English letters as well as of the English stage'. Such extensively reported dinners remained a feature of Irving's career until the end. In addition to which much further publicity was obtained when Irving put on lavish dinners at the Lyceum for visiting dignitaries. In 1897 and 1902 he hosted dinners for the colonial premiers and Indian princes in London for the Diamond Jubilee of Queen Victoria and the coronation of King Edward VII.[54] They were just the most splendid of such regular occurrences.

Another publicity gathering form of activity involved Irving's casting. He regularly co-starred at the Lyceum with Ellen Terry, who was the best loved actress of her age, and the source of as much reporting as Irving himself. But he also invited in guest stars. In one publicity garnering episode he invited the leading American actor of the day, Edwin Booth, then in London and playing to poor houses, at the run-down Princess's Theatre, to join him at the Lyceum and to alternate the roles of Othello and Iago in a revival of *Othello*. It doubled the interest in the play as people came twice to see the stars in the two roles. Irving also brought in for leading roles stars who had established followings of their own – the powerful tragic character actress Geneviève Ward (who later became the first theatrical Dame) and William Terriss, popularly known as 'Breezy Bill', and the best-loved and most popular melodrama star of the day. He also persuaded out of retirement to play leading roles on special occasions such theatrical favourites of the past as Walter Lacy (*Lady of Lyons*), Squire Bancroft (*The Dead Heart*) and Mrs Fanny Stirling (*Romeo and Juliet* and *Faust*). They always gained warm applause, attracted extra spectators and generated newspaper comment. All the publicity surrounding Irving was orchestrated and promoted by his own staff and a coterie of sympathetic journalists who ensured constant coverage of all his on-stage and off-stage activities.

We can conclude that the celebrity was a creation of the nineteenth-century mass media but that in the nineteenth century celebrities included both heroes and stars. The pre-industrial criteria for heroism ensured that churchmen, statesmen and generals were celebrities in the nineteenth century, as were the representatives of the new mass culture such as actors, singers, writers and sportsmen. In the twentieth century, with the eclipse of the hero and the rise of the leisure society, it was mainly stars who became celebrities and the requirements to become a celebrity were a distinctive appearance, regular media exposure, fans, publicity and an image that embodied individuals 'dreams and aspirations'.

Irving contrived to be at the same time hero, star and celebrity. He was a hero as the leading actor-manager of the day and a distinguished public figure. He was a star because he came from humble origins and rose to the top by dedicated effort and remained a solitary and lonely genius, as the publicity had it. He was a celebrity by appearance, publicity, media exposure and hobnobbing with other celebrities. But he used his celebrity not just to advance himself but to advance the cause of his profession. It is in part due to his untiring efforts that actors and actresses, 'rogues and vagabonds' at the start of the nineteenth century, had become by the end of it respected artists, with no fewer than seven actors knighted between 1897 and 1914. The profession had well and truly arrived.

10

Critics and the Press

In the mid nineteenth century there was a rapid expansion of the press, with daily and Sunday papers proliferating. In the first half of the nineteenth century, there had been severe legal and financial restraints on newspapers which were feared by the government as vehicles for sedition, and there was a long-running battle to free the press from these restrictions. Advertising duty was repealed in 1853, stamp duty in 1855 and the duty on paper in 1861. This left the press free for the first time since the reign of Queen Anne.

In the 1850s and 1860s there was a combination of circumstances that were right for the explosion of mass newspaper readership. There was a large concentrated population with a high degree of literacy in urban centres – the 1851 census revealed that for the first time the majority of British people lived in towns and cities, something not achieved in France until the 1920s. Technological change greatly facilitated production and distribution of newspapers and the process of newsgathering. The railway network was in place for distribution and it was linked with the telegraph network with its cheap rates for press telegrams. This made the transmission of news much easier, and by 1852 not only was Britain linked by telegraph with London but in direct communication with all the chief cities of the Continent. There were new, improved, cheaper and faster methods of producing paper and of printing (the rotary steam press in the 1860s, the mechanical typesetter in the 1890s) and there was the subsidizing and promoting of new newspapers, particularly in the provinces by the political parties. By 1900 most big cities had Liberal and Conservative papers. All these developments allowed prices to fall. In 1855 the *Daily Telegraph* reduced its price to a penny; and the *Standard* did so in 1858. It was price above all that facilitated the spread of newspapers. The result was a massive burgeoning of papers. In 1860 there were nine morning and six evening dailies in London and sixteen dailies in the provinces. By the 1880s there were 150 dailies in London and the provinces.

In the early part of the century daily newspapers tended to be restricted to factual information – details of stock market prices, times of ships sailings, announcements of events in the news, advertisements for jobs, reports of parliamentary debates, foreign diplomacy and military engagements. Circulation was small. The seven London morning papers had a combined circulation of

28,000 in the early nineteenth century. The middle decades of the century saw a great growth in middle-class readership. By the 1870s the *Daily Telegraph* alone had a readership of around 200,000. The working classes did not take a daily paper until the 1890s, when the Harmsworth press aimed its papers specifically at the upper working and lower middle classes, but from mid century onwards they took a Sunday paper (notably *Reynolds's Weekly Newspaper*, *Lloyd's Weekly Newspaper* and the *News of the World*).

In the 1880s there was a recognizable movement dubbed 'The New Journalism' and pioneered by W.T. Stead and T.P. O'Connor, which centred on readability (shorter paragraphs, larger headlines, more colloquial English); innovation (parliamentary sketches, interviews, stop press, human interest stories); more crime and more sport; and by the end of the century greater use of illustrations. All this was aimed to widen the appeal and maximize the readership of large circulation dailies.[1] This in its turn meant the serious and systematic coverage of theatre in the press. Compared to the present day, theatre received many column inches devoted to all aspects of the subject with productions being described in the kind of minute detail that is a godsend to theatre historians.

At the same time as there was a major growth in newspapers, there was a similar expansion in the periodical press. Nineteenth-century Britain has been described as 'uniquely the age of the periodical'.[2] There were 630 different titles current in 1873 for instance. More periodicals were devoted to the stage in this century than at any other time. Forty-nine different titles have been identified between 1880 and 1890. Many were short lived, but, with the expansion of theatre in London after the ending of the official monopoly by Covent Garden and Drury Lane in 1843, there was abundant material and stage periodicals tended to combine news, gossip, reviews and verse. They were often written anonymously or pseudonymously since everyone tended to know everyone else in this world and there was a danger of feuds. When Mrs Madge Kendal attacked the theatrical press in an 1884 conference paper for substituting 'insolent and untrue gossip' for 'honest reviews', she was in her turn attacked by almost every stage paper.[3] The two standard papers for the theatrical profession were the *Era*, founded in 1838, and the *Stage*, founded in 1880. But the *Illustrated Sporting and Dramatic News* and the *Theatre* were also influential.

The insatiable hunger of this flood of newspapers and journals for material was fed by a tribe of scribblers, hard-drinking, poorly paid, generous, improvident, clubbable, but also from time to time quarrelsome, perpetually in debt and willing to turn their hands to anything: reviews, descriptive articles, profiles, humorous journalism, verse, but also novels, plays and short stories. They rejoiced in the appellation of 'Bohemians' and dubbed their world of pubs, supper rooms and late night clubs 'Bohemia'. Bohemia figures regularly in the titles of memoirs of the period.[4]

Sir Frank Burnand (1836–1917), the humorous writer and the editor of *Punch* from 1880 to 1906, recalled the Bohemians as 'a convivial fraternity, living from hand to mouth, doing odd journalistic jobs, knowing something of everything: a kindly lot, of little profit to themselves but of marketable value to newspaper editors'.[5] Edmund Yates, a journalist and novelist and the founder of the *World*, recalled that he first encountered the British Bohemia in 1855 when he was twenty-four and, although he was never a full member of it – due to an early marriage and the regular habits required of someone holding an appointment in the Post Office, he shared many of their tastes and pursuits and became close friends with Bohemians. He recalled them as 'young, gifted, and reckless'; and recalled that 'they worked only by fits and starts, and never except under the pressure of necessity; that they were sometimes in the height of happiness, sometimes in the depths of despair, but that ordinarily they passed their lives 'Little caring what might come [and] they had a thorough contempt for the dress, usage and manners of ordinary middle-class civilisation.'[6]

Some of the most prolific journalists actually had civil service day jobs (Clement Scott at the War Office, Tom Taylor at the Board of Health, Edmund Yates and A.B. Walkley at the Post Office), further evidence of the small remuneration to be gained from journalism. Even the drama critic of *The Times* in the middle of the nineteenth century was paid a mere £5 a week.[7] But many journalists were full-time denizens of Bohemia, sitting up long into the night, drinking, smoking and talking, actors, writers and critics mingling freely. Thackeray described Bohemia in his novel *The Adventures of Philip* (1861–62) as 'a land over which hangs an endless fog, occasioned by much tobacco ... a land of chambers, billiard rooms and oyster suppers ... a land of song ... a land of tin dish-covers from taverns, and foaming porter: a land of lotos-eating ... a land where all men call each other by their Christian names; where most are poor, where almost all are young'.[8]

The Arundel, on the corner of Arundel Street overlooking the Thames, permitted smoking in all its rooms, and was characterized by Burnand as a club for 'thorough Bohemians' as opposed to the Garrick, which was for 'a superior order of dramatic authors, actors and theatrical members'.[9] Its members included the actors Irving, Bancroft and Toole, the writers Gilbert, Wills and Swinburne, and the critics John Oxenford, Clement Scott and Joseph Knight.[10] The close friendships that existed between actors and critics are regularly attested. This sometimes inevitably coloured critical reactions towards theatrical productions. The actor J.H. Barnes wrote that Joseph Knight 'was a true friend of actors, though not a fulsome one. A fine specimen of manhood, a thorough Bohemian, but a brilliant, well-read scholar with a kindly nature ... erudite and thoughtful, he had held the balance fairly between praise and blame and had earned and greatly enjoyed the love of all.'[11]

John Oxenford (1812–1877), drama critic of *The Times* from 1850 to 1875, was actually ordered to mute his criticism of actors. Edmund Yates, a friend of Oxenford, recalled that Oxenford told him that when he first became drama critic of *The Times* he freely criticized both plays and actors. But an actor wrote to the editor, J.T. Delane, protesting, and Delane told him:

> I have no doubt you were perfectly right in all you wrote, but that is not the question. The real fact is that these matters are of far too small importance to become subjects for discussion. Whether a play is good or bad, whether a man acts well or ill, is of very little consequence to the great body of our readers, and I could not think of letting the paper become the field for argument on the point. So in future, you understand, my good fellow, write your notices so as much as possible to avoid these sort of letters being addressed to the office. You understand?[12]

In consequence *The Dictionary of National Biography* recorded of Oxenford that he was 'amiable to weakness and the excessive kindliness of his disposition' caused him to err on the side of weakness as to render his opinion as a critic practically valueless.' It was his own boast that 'none of those whom he had censured ever went home disconsolate or despairing on account of anything he had written.'[13] But then like so many of his tribe Oxenford had a foot in both camps. In addition to his dramatic criticism, he wrote sixty-eight plays, and libretti for the operas *Robin Hood* and *Helvellyn* by George A. Macfarren and *Richard Coeur de Lion* and *Lily of Killarney* by Sir Julius Benedict. This was typical of the time.

For all his intellectuality, moralism and hauteur, Irving was a fully paid up member of the Bohemian world. Judicially separated from his wife after only a few years of marriage, he essentially lived a bachelor life and the habits and mores of clubland suited him perfectly. He was elected a member of the Savage Club in 1871, the Garrick Club in 1874, the Green Room Club in 1877, the Athenaeum in 1882 and the Reform Club in 1884. He was also a member of the Arundel Club. The Green Room Club in Leicester Square, set up in 1877, had a membership exclusively of actors. But the other clubs catered for a broader social and artistic range of members. Irving was elected to the Athenaeum under Rule 2 – by nomination of the committee – avoiding the ordinary ballot, which might have blackballed a mere actor.

In 1891 Irving was elected to the Marlborough Club. The Marlborough had been set up with the Prince of Wales as a prime mover when in 1866 White's Club refused to rescind its rule against smoking in the drawing room. The Marlborough allowed unrestricted use of tobacco. Membership was by invitation only and Irving was proposed by the Prince of Wales and seconded by the Duke of Fife. According to his grandson Laurence, Irving rarely used any of them apart from the Garrick; but the fact of his election to such prestigious bodies was recognized as a signal honour for the acting profession.[14] He annually gave a small dinner party at the Reform for particular journalistic friends.[15]

The Savage Club had been founded in 1857 at the instigation of the journalist George Augustus Sala in order to provide a convivial meeting place for authors, artists and journalists. Members included the actors J.L.Toole, Benjamin Webster, E.A. Sothern, John Hare, Charles Wyndham, Barry Sullivan, William Terriss, Wilson Barrett, George Alexander and Beerbohm Tree, the writers Charles Lever, Clement Scott, H.J. Byron, Tom Taylor, G.A. Henty and W. S. Gilbert, the painters Luke Fildes and Hubert Herkomer, the cartoonist Phil May and the composers Frederic Cowen and Alexander Mackenzie. In 1882 the Prince of Wales was elected a member.

The Garrick Club was founded in 1831, as a place 'in which actors and men of education and refinement might meet on equal terms ... Easy intercourse was to be promoted between artists and patrons ... patrons of the drama and its professors were to be brought together, and a rendezvous offered to literary men'.[16] Irving was nominated in 1873 by J. L. Toole and W.P. Frith but blackballed. The identity of the blackballer was recently established as actor James Anderson, apparently jealous of Irving's success at thirty-five.[17] But in 1874, fifty members supported his nomination, including Anthony Trollope, Charles Reade, John Hare and Sir Arthur Sullivan. By 1880, there were still only thirteen actors among the club members, but by 1900, there were thirty-eight.[18]

Two of Irving's journalist friends, both members of the Garrick, wrote about clubs, stressing the good companionship, good conversation, good humour and general conviviality. Joseph Hatton in *Clubland* (1890) stressed that 'an English-man's club for the time being is his private house. The members represent his family and friends.'[19] Percy Fitzgerald, in his 1904 history of the Garrick Club, noted that Irving presented the club with a painting of the Prince of Wales which he had commissioned, George Clint's painting of Edmund Kean as Sir Giles Overreach in *A New Way to Pay Old Debts* and Collier's portrait of J.L. Toole. He also sat for a portrait by Millais, which the painter presented to the club.[20] Fitzgerald records of Irving that 'At the Garrick he was a power. There he received his friends to dinner and supper and there he knew everyone.'[21] Not all actors were such inveterate clubmen as Irving. Sir George Alexander, who had a delicate constitution and was of a shy and reserved nature, preferred to go home after the theatre rather than linger in the club. Sir Charles Wyndham, who suffered from nervous insomnia, walked home to St John's Wood in order to tire himself rather than stay up at the club.[22]

In addition to clubs there were informal dining groups like 'The Knights of the Round Table', who met at Simpsons in the Strand, and whom J.H. Barnes, a long-standing member, described as 'a coterie of jolly friends who had the run of Simpson's fine English food and Simpson's fine cooking in a good, large, private room'. Among the actors and managers who were regular attenders were Henry Irving, David James, Thomas Thorne and John Hollingshead. 'We had the largest round table in the world made from a single piece of wood', recalled Barnes.[23] Another such group was 'The Kinsmen', half – British and half – American in membership. The American Ambassador in London was the ex-officio president. They had bases in both London and New York and a membership which included the actors Irving, Hare and Bancroft, the painters Edwin Abbey, John Singer Sargent, Sir David Murray, Frank Millet and Alfred Parsons, and the writers J.M. Barrie, Anthony Hope and Bret Harte.[24] The Rabelais Club, which flourished from 1879 to 1889, was a literary dining club which met about six times a year. Founded by the novelist Sir Walter Besant, it had seventy or eighty members in its heyday, including Thomas Hardy, Oliver Wendell Holmes, Bret Harte, Henry James, Lord Lytton, George Augustus Sala, Robert Louis Stevenson, John Everett Millais, Lord Houghton and Irving.

Irving was also a freemason. Freemasonry was another form of club life which created friendship networks among the middle and upper classes. The Prince of Wales was Grand Master of the United Grand Lodge of English freemasonry from 1874 until his accession in 1901. Notable freemasons in the world of theatre and music included William Terriss, W.S. Penley, Edward Terry, Sir Augustus Harris, Sir Michael Costa, Carl Rosa, Douglas Jerrold and Sir Henry Lytton. Irving was initiated into the prestigious Jerusalem Lodge no. 197 in 1877. He became a master mason in 1883 and continued to subscribe to the lodge until his death. But he was also one of a group of members who petitioned for a lodge to be established at the Savage Club. It was set up in 1887 and Irving became its first treasurer, relinquishing the job after a year to fellow actor Edward Terry. He remained a member for the rest of his life, as he did also of the St Martin's Lodge, which he joined in 1893. Irving contributed regularly to Masonic charities but, while he warmly supported freemasonry, never took a very active part in it.[25] This was almost certainly due to the demands on his time as actor-manager and leader of the profession.

Irving's affection for that old Bohemian life comes through in a speech he made at a Savage Club Annual dinner held in 'the ornate King's Hall of the Holborn Restaurant' in 1895:

> My memory of the Savage Club goes back to the old days under the Piazza in Covent Garden, and if a man could not be a Bohemian under the piazza, then the most enchanting state of human existence was not for him. Those were the days when we cultivated literature and drama on a chop and a tankard, and came out of Covent Garden at the witching hour when the vegetables were coming in. I daresay some of you – old stagers like myself – can never walk that way even now – that leafy way under the piazza – without reminiscences of old times. Well, gentlemen, you wear your Bohemianism now, with a difference. I look around the boards and see no traces of the chop and tankard. Time was when the literary savage was radiant if he made a guinea by translating a play – or by chance writing one – and he spent it royally in what we used to call under

the piazza 'a jolly little crib'. But now guineas are so plentiful that he can spend one of them, without missing it, on a dinner in a chamber to which such an expression as 'crib' would not be applied without lamentable irreverence ... But though the material conditions are mostly changed and though many of us are grown into that form of external respectability which comes with a larger responsibilities and grey hairs, I am glad and proud to see that the spirit of our dear old club survives, and that we are friends and comrades under these conditions of overwhelming grandeur, just as we were in other days.[26]

Victorian dramatic criticism rose and fell with the fortunes of the theatre. At the start of the nineteenth century, there had emerged two notable critics concerned to explore and understand the mechanics and mystique of acting: Leigh Hunt (1784–1859) and William Hazlitt (1778–1830). They wrote at the time of two great and sharply contrasted actors, Edmund Kean and John Philip Kemble. In the mid-Victorian period, the leading theatrical critic was George Henry Lewes (1817–1878), but he retired from theatre criticism in 1854. As the press expanded, so theatre critics rose in influence and significance. Many were prolific and long-lived. After Lewes retired the three most notable critics of the 1860s, 1870s and 1880s were Edward Dutton Cook, Joseph Knight and Clement Scott. They were critics in an era when, according to George Rowell, theatrical criticism 'displayed more respectability than distinction'.[27]

Edward Dutton Cook (1829–1883) was the son of a solicitor and began his career as an articled clerk to his father. Later he became a clerk in the London offices of the Madras Railway Company. But he left business to take up a career in the arts. He studied painting and later wrote on art for a variety of newspapers and journals. He began a literary career, writing a melodrama, *The Serpent and the Dove*, with Leopold Lewis, which was successfully produced on the stage. Later he wrote ten novels and a collection of short stories. But he was chiefly known as a drama critic, first for the *Pall Mall Gazette* (1867–75) and later the *World* (1875–83). He was married to a celebrated concert pianist. The Bancrofts described Dutton Cook as 'one of the ablest, as he was certainly one of the most difficult to please, of the dramatic critics of the time'.[28] Clement Scott, his fellow critic, concurred in an obituary notice in the *Theatre*:

> If deficient in fervour and enthusiasm, he never wanted decision and judgment. He was not an actor or actress maker, and his praise and blame were alike limited in quantity and quality; but when Dutton Cook did praise it is probable that one word of it was more consoling to an artist than columns of more elaborate flattery. When he did condemn severely, his words bit into the sensitive actor's plate like acid.[29]

He was evidently able to maintain the necessary critical distance because, unlike Knight and Scott, 'he had but little personal acquaintance with actors or actresses'.

Joseph Knight (1829–1907) was born in Leeds, the son of a cloth merchant.

Initially he joined his father in the business but in 1860 left for a literary career. He became drama critic of the *Literary Gazette* in 1860 but later was drama critic of the *Athenaeum* from 1869 to 1907. He also wrote dramatic criticism for the *Globe*, the *Sunday Times* and the *Daily Graphic*. He was editor of *Notes and Queries* from 1883 until his death. The journalist and critic W.L. Courtney, writing in 1925 of the pre-war Garrick Club, with its suppers which used to extend into the small hours, 'and its free and joyous conversational life' recalled that Joseph Knight, 'Joe Knight as he was affectionately called', was 'the life and soul of every meeting'. Courtney claims that he 'did more, perhaps than any other member to keep the whole system of club life together as a jovial institution and a very seed plot for epigrams'.

> Joe Knight ... had many ambitions of a literary and dramatic character. But I think his principal love was for his boon companions who on most nights, and especially after the first night of a play, used to assemble and discuss topics in which they were all more or less interested ... He was a very learned man, more learned than most of his fellow-members imagined ... He wore his learning very lightly ... He knew the history of the stage exceedingly well ... I remember well the robust figure of a genial type, the comrade who loved nothing better than to talk and chaff ... He was a great man for all-night vigils, for nothing seemed to hurt him. He was a strong-limbed, strong-headed Yorkshire man ... He was really distressed if anyone ventured to leave the supper-room early.

Courtney's verdict on him as a critic was that he was 'sound without being brilliant, and perhaps wrote a little too much on the side of good temper'.[30] Knight was recognized as the senior serving dramatic critic by a dinner held in his honour by the acting profession at the Savoy Hotel in 1905. Irving took the chair on that occasion.

Although Knight was the senior critic, perhaps the most influential critic of this era was Clement Scott (1841–1904). Although his career ended in controversy, he was for more or less the duration of Irving's career a major arbiter of theatrical success. He was the son of the curate of Christ Church, Hoxton, and born there in the vicarage. His father, 'Parson Scott of Hoxton' was daily leader writer on the *Morning Chronicle* and editor of the *Christian Remembrancer*. Educated at Marlborough, Scott began his career as a clerk at the War Office (1860–79), retiring from there on a pension without ever having been promoted. From 1863 to 1865 he was drama critic of the *Sunday Times*, but was replaced because of his 'excessive frankness' and succeeded by Joseph Knight. But from 1871 to 1898 he was drama critic of the *Daily Telegraph*, first as assistant to senior drama critic E.L. Blanchard and later his successor. According to *The Dictionary of National Biography* he was the 'best known drama critic of his day ... largely leading popular opinion in theatrical matters'.[31]

In the way of the critics of the day, Scott adapted several French plays for the English stage (*Peril*, *Diplomacy*, *The Vicarage*, *Denise*), co-wrote some original plays (*The Swordsman's Daughter, Jack in the Box*), wrote lyrics for pantomime, comic opera and the music halls, and wrote reams of light verse and descriptive articles. He discovered and popularized 'Poppyland', the area around Cromer in Norfolk. His descriptive account *Poppyland* (1885), much reviewed, made the area a major tourist attraction. His publisher Arthur Greening wrote that he 'deserved the thanks of thousands of jaded workers who have regained health, strength and vitality from a holiday in beautiful "Poppyland".' Aside from dramatic criticism, 'he wrote innumerable eloquent leaders on all sorts of subjects, and his vivid descriptions of Royal weddings, Royal funerals, drawing-rooms, levees, cricket matches, races, celebrated criminal trials and such-like events and functions added not a little to the popularity of the *Daily Telegraph*. All the most important ceremonies of the never-to-be forgotten Jubilee were entrusted to Clement Scott.' He discovered and encouraged 'the budding genius of Miss Marie Corelli'. In 1892 he was assigned by the *Telegraph* to cover the Chicago World's Fair and, on the eve of his departure, was entertained by the Garrick Club at a banquet, 'where all the most notable people in the theatrical and journalistic world were present to give him a hearty send off'.[32]

Vain, passionate, quarrelsome and partisan, Scott made many enemies, though he was devoted to Irving and sedulously promoted his cause. In the 1890s he was plunged into a succession of battles against the dominant trends in theatre. He attacked Wildean 'decadence' in a 'withering' article called 'The Cult of the Green Carnation'. He detested Pinero's popular society plays, *The Second Mrs Tanqueray*, *The Notorious Mrs Ebbsmith* and *The Gay Lord Quex*, believing that Pinero had been infected by Ibsenism – 'its unloveliness, its want of faith, its hopeless, despairing creed, its worship of the ugly in art, and its grim and repulsive reality'.[33] Most of all Scott loathed Ibsen, and the plays of the Norwegian playwright provided the cause which divided the old critics from the new.

Scott had made many enemies and, when he fell from grace, there was rejoicing in some quarters. In 1898 he gave an interview to *Great Thoughts* in which he denounced the morality of the stage as a profession for women. There was a storm of outrage as he was apparently seeking to set back half a century of efforts to make the stage respectable. In 1899 he resigned from the *Daily Telegraph* and retired to Biarritz to complete his *magnum opus, The Stage of Yesterday and the Stage of Today*. He subsequently took up the post of drama critic of the *New York Herald*, cabling his reviews across the Atlantic but later sailing with his wife to New York to be welcomed as 'the great English critic'. But the days of his pre-eminence were over. He, nevertheless, founded a new journal, the *Free Lance*, which survived for a decade, outliving its founder and run by his widow Margaret until its demise. He published collections of his dramatic criticism. But by the time he died he was already being dismissed. *The Dictionary of National Biography* declared that 'Scott's habit of mind was neither impartial not judicial', and that he was opposed to modern schools of acting and writing, in particular Ibsen. He 'never moved beyond the ideals of Robertson and Sardou'.[34] The obituary in the *Daily Telegraph* (where he had reigned supreme only six years before) declared him 'A brilliant impressionist and unflinching advocate, a fearless partisan ... but not, in the true significance of the word, a critic'.[35]

Interestingly, the 'Young Turks' of the new criticism recognized his importance. William Archer thought that 'Scott represents to a nicety the average middle-class Englishman. He found the stage, in the 'sixties, beneath his intellectual level, and sought to raise it. From 'seventy to 'ninety it exactly came up to his intellectual and artistic requirements, and he was happy. In ninety it took a fresh start and left him behind; and he now shrieks to it to come back and 'mark time' for he cannot follow it into 'an atmosphere that is mephitic.'[36]

The critic of the *Star* (presumably A. B. Walkley), writing in 1890, summed up the secret of Scott's success with the reading public:

> Mr Scott is the actors' critic. Important as he is as a dramatic critic, he is even more important as a critic of histrionics. For him it is not so much the play which is the thing, as the player ... It is for this reason that the players swear by (when they don't swear at) Mr Clement Scott, and justly ... He came at the right time. He appealed to the right people. Add that he brought the right mood. It has the inestimable advantage of being a thoroughly English mood. It had the true English preference for the comfortable, the conventional, the pleasant, for things 'of good report' ... To him the playhouse is not a dissecting-room, but an apartment in the House Beautiful. This mood you may or may not approve; but you cannot deny that it is characteristically English ... There is nothing esoteric about him. He has 'opted' for the popular ticket. Like the people, he is ... a sentimentalist. One feels that his criticisms are affairs of the heart quite as much as of the head.[37]

Bernard Shaw, reviewing Scott's collected criticisms of Irving, *From 'The Bells' to 'King Arthur'*, in 1896 agreed with this judgement:

> Mr Clement Scott is not the first of the great dramatic critics; but he is the first of the great dramatic reporters. The main secret of Mr Scott's popularity is that he is above all a sympathetic critic. His susceptibility to the direct expression of human feeling is so strong that he can write with positive passion about an exhibition of it which elicits from his colleagues only some stale, weary compliment in the last sentence of a conventional report ... The excellence of Mr Scott's criticisms lies in their integrity as expressions of the warmest personal feeling and nothing else ... The public believes in Mr Scott because he interprets the plays by feeling *with* the actor ... and giving his feeling unrestrained expression in his notices.

His shortcomings Shaw listed as 'a desire to give pleasure and gain affectionate goodwill', an inability to appreciate the production values of music and painting, and an inability to recognize thoughts and ideas as opposed to feelings.[38]

J.T. Grein, the man who had staged Ibsen's *Ghosts* at the Independent Theatre and received a deluge of critical vituperation, paid tribute to Scott in similar terms when he resigned from the *Daily Telegraph* in 1899:

> His record is a brilliant one. For he was a worker, and until the year 1889 he was ... in the vanguard of dramatic progress. He has brought our stage in contact with the French geniuses of the third quarter of this century, Augier, Dumas *fils*, Sardou ... and when the Scandinavian made its entry with the problem play ... Clement Scott lost his balance. The man of progress of yesterday became the man of retrogression ... Thus, it is not as a critic of plays that Clement Scott's name will shine in the history of our modern stage ... But it is as a judge of actors and acting that Clement Scott's activity on the *Daily Telegraph* will be remembered. Among all the men who have wielded the sceptre of criticism, there has been no one in these last five-and twenty years who equalled him in experience and thoroughness of knowledge in this department ... On the whole, Clement Scott has, therefore, deserved well of our stage.[39]

W.L. Courtney, who succeeded Scott as theatre critic of the *Daily Telegraph*, recalled of him:

> Clement Scott was the most interesting critic in London, and his verdict was of more importance to theatrical managers than that of any other man. The average playgoer accepted Scott's attitude without question and read his criticisms because they appealed to the great middle class ... But the brilliant success of Clement Scott as a critic did not depend wholly on his ability to interpret the voice of the man in the street ... During his career he was far and away the best judge of acting in London ... He wrote a marvellous style, a style which could not be ignored, so considerable was its range and so persuasive its appeal ... Scott's prose was a very rhythmical affair; it was often on the verge of blank verse when its business was to encourage or upbraid, and when it desired to rend an opponent to pieces it became a lyrical scream. It could be pompous and rhetorical, bombastic and full of rodomontade, sentimental and sickly, with a kind of eloquence which was Scott's own. For there was nothing like it in London.[40]

In the 1880s and 1890s a new generation of critics, mainly young men in their thirties, had appeared, marked by high seriousness and scholarly rigour. They remained aloof from the Bohemians and campaigned for the play of ideas, adult serious plays, rather than virtuoso acting vehicles. Interestingly, many of the key critics were not English: William Archer was Scottish, Bernard Shaw Irish and J.T. Grein Dutch. They championed in particular the plays of Ibsen as the way forward for English theatre.

William Archer became the leading light of the new criticism. He was temperamentally, intellectually and in every other way the antithesis of Clement Scott. His style, as Shaw put it, was fastidious and intellectual.[41] Archer (1856–1924) was born in Perth, trained as a lawyer but entered journalism in Edinburgh. Coming to London in 1878 he became drama critic of the *London Figaro* (1879–81). From 1884 to 1905 he was drama critic of the *World*, and despite his misgivings about its frivolous tone, his serious criticism had by the 1890s established him as one of the leading drama critics. He became drama critic on the newly founded Liberal journal the *Tribune* (1906–1908) and later on the Liberal weekly the *Nation* (1908–1910). He was drama critic of the *Star* from 1913 to 1920, after which he gave up journalism. He was a man of wide culture and varied interests, spoke many languages, travelled extensively and campaigned for a national theatre, the abolition of theatrical censorship and the acceptance of Ibsen and 'the play of ideas'. He edited a series of translations of the major Ibsen plays. He wrote studies of the psychology of acting, the ethics of criticism and the state of English drama. He became a friend of Shaw, Grein and Walkley, helped to get *A Doll's House* staged in 1889 and supported Grein's production of *Ghosts*, which, with its theme of hereditary syphilis, caused a storm. A rationalist, a feminist, a moralist and a Liberal, Archer came across as unbendingly austere. *The Dictionary of National Biography* noted that 'as a critic he may have been somewhat harsh in his principles, too rigid in his logic and lacking in the elasticity of mind of his contemporary Arthur Bingham Walkley, but his emphasis on good dramatic structure and his hatred of slovenliness in any form were a necessary and vital help to all young dramatists'.[42] But beneath the rigorous exterior lurked a secret romantic as, although married, he embarked on a love affair with the feminist actress and writer Elizabeth Robins. Late in life he penned one of the last of the great stage melodramas, an exotic imperial thriller called *The Green Goddess*. It ran for two and a half years in New York and a year in London and was filmed three times by Hollywood.[43]

George Bernard Shaw (1856–1950), the Dublin born playwright and intellectual, pioneer Fabian Socialist and vegetarian, burst upon the London critical scene in the 1880s. He had set out to become a novelist but failed to secure publishers for five novels in succession, but he made the friendship of William Archer and, thanks to him, was appointed book reviewer of the *Pall Mall Gazette* (1885–88) and art critic of the *World* (1886–89). He subsequently became music critic of the *Star* (1888–90) and drama critic of the *Saturday Review* (1895–98). After the failure of his early plays, he achieved a success with *The Devil's Disciple* (1897) and was then launched on a full-time playwrighting career. A fervent partisan of the Ibsenites, he published *The Quintessence of Ibsen* in 1891, supported the production activities of the Independent Theatre and campaigned ceaselessly for 'the play of ideas'.[44]

J.T. 'Jack' Grein (1862–1935) was a Dutchman who went to London in 1885 aged twenty-two to work for a Dutch company. He had already been writing drama criticism in the Netherlands and carried on writing for Dutch journals on the state of English theatre. He highlighted what were to become recurrent themes of his critical writing: the lack of original new plays, dishonest and incompetent criticism, bad acting, and the deleterious influence of the censor.

He began writing for English journals, contributing to the *Playgoer* and then starting his own short-lived theatrical journals, the fortnightly *Comedy* and the *Weekly Comedy*. He founded and edited from 1896 to 1898 *To-morrow* which attacked 'the social, intellectual and artistic pretensions of English actors and the whole system of the London theatre'. He founded and ran the weekly *Hollandia* (1897–1900). From 1890 to 1893 he was drama critic of the weekly *Life*. From 1898 to 1918 he was drama critic of the *Sunday Special* (renamed the *Sunday Times* in 1903). In 1891 he founded the Independent Theatre to produce plays rejected by the censor. They produced plays by Ibsen (*Ghosts, A Doll's House, The Wild Duck*) and Zola (*Thérèse Raquin*). He brought German theatre companies to England, and he founded the Anglo-Continental Dramatic Club, the Dramatic Debates Society and the Premieres Club, all aimed at promoting the new drama.[45]

Archer, Shaw and Grein were joined in their Ibsenite campaigning by Arthur Bingham Walkley (A.B. Walkley) (1855–1926). Born in Bristol, educated at Oxford University, Walkley worked as a clerk at the Post Office from 1877 to 1919. But he also had a second career as critic and journalist. He became a drama critic (writing as 'Spectator) on the new daily paper the *Star* (1888–1900) and on the weekly the *Speaker* (1890–99). From 1900 until 1926 he was drama critic of *The Times*. He published several volumes of his collected essays from journals and newspapers. *The Dictionary of National Biography* praised his style for 'his sensitiveness to impression, his accurate and retentive memory, his ease and grace of manner, and his playfulness and wit'.[46] He was one of the few critics to speak up on behalf of *Ghosts*. But later in life he turned against the works of Ibsen and Shaw and the play of ideas, preferring light comedy.

When *Ghosts* was produced, Clement Scott went on the attack. Writing in the *Daily Telegraph* (14 March, 1891), he called *Ghosts*: 'a dull, undramatic, verbose, tedious, and utterly uninteresting play … It is a wretched, deplorable, loathsome history, as all must admit.' The *Daily Telegraph* also ran a leading article on the play on the same day, famously declaring: 'the play performed last night is 'simple' enough in plan and purpose, but simple only in the sense of an open drain; of a loathsome sore un-bandaged; of a dirty act done publicly; or of a lazar-house with all its doors and windows open.' Scott and the *Telegraph* were not alone in their detestation of *Ghosts*. The *Daily News* called it 'a most dismal and repulsive production', the *Daily Chronicle* said the play was 'revolting, suggestive and blasphemous', the *News of the World* 'the work of a crazy foreigner which is neither fish nor flesh, but is unmistakable foul', the *Observer* 'a putrid drama the details of which cannot appear with any propriety in any column save those of a medical journal.'[47]

Irving lined up firmly with the anti-Ibsenites. The 1889 London production of *A Doll's House* had inaugurated a dramatic revolution in England with leading figures of the avant-garde proclaiming the gospel of Ibsenism. Bernard Shaw in his 1891 book *The Quintessence of Ibsenism* wrote:

> Ibsen's message to you is – if you are a member of society, defy it; if you have a duty, violate it; if you have a sacred tie, break it; if you have a religion, stand on it instead of crouching under it; if you have bound yourself by a promise or an oath, cast them to the winds; if the lust of self-sacrifice seize you, wrestle with it as with the devil; and if, in spite of all, you cannot resist the temptation to be virtuous, go drown yourself before you have time to waste the lives of those about you with the infection of that disease.[48]

Irving's philosophy was the exact opposite of this and he struck back on his provincial tour of 1891, making speeches in both Liverpool and Glasgow against this philosophy. He denounced the Independent Theatre as being independent only of modesty and good taste:

> If those of 'the new movement' imagine that they are going to create literature for the British stage which shall be absolutely foreign to British codes of morals, manners, and social usage, they are making, I am sure, an egregious error. Ibsen, it is said, is in the future to be our dramatic teacher, and I learn from one of his prophets that his plays have abolished God, duty, the devotion of a mother to her children, and the obligation of man to his fellow-man; though perhaps it may be that this achievement may not be regarded as quite complete by the rest of the world. Is any English playwright going to expound this philosophy to the public? The English drama must be an exposition of English life and character, and I fail to recognise in these new notions any resemblance to the sentiments which prevail amongst the great mass of our countrymen.[49]

He gave full vent to his horror of the new drama, referring obliquely to *Ghosts*, with a rousing affirmation of belief in the old in a speech to the annual dinner of the Royal General Theatrical Fund, reported by *The Times* (26 May, 1893):

> he noticed that certain gentlemen seemed devoted to the idea that there ought to be a very thin and movable partition between the theatre and the hospital. He was in favour of a broad sphere of dramatic enterprise, but the craving for the physically horrible on the plea that it enlarged the domain of art in the study of human suffering appeared to him not unlikely to stimulate a morbid appetite for horrors on the stage which very few people would be particularly anxious to defend. (*Cheers*) Surely we already had a drama which in its highest expression could not be charged with lack of humanity. It was the greatest glory of our dramatic literature that it was the most broadly humanizing influence in the world. (*Cheers*) Sympathy, tolerance, serene and sustaining wisdom were preached in the plays of Shakespeare as they had never been preached in the pulpit.

The new breed of critics found fault with the old school. Writing in *English Dramatists of To-Day* (1882), William Archer argued that while newspaper dramatic criticism was honest, in the sense of not being influenced by direct or indirect pecuniary considerations, 'it is nowhere more empirical, more superficial, more warped by considerations of personal friendship or enmity towards authors, managers and actors'. For this he blamed in part the life of the clubs: 'theatrical clubs which bring together authors, managers, actors and critics are the bane of critical frankness and impartiality', in other words the exact milieu within which Irving moved.[50]

In his collection of essays *About the Theatre* (1886) Archer returned to the theme. He outlined the duties of the critic as honesty, catholicity of taste, sanity of judgement and alertness of moral sense. He also urged the avoidance of too close an intimacy with actors and writers. He argued that criticism of plays and their ideas was more profitable than criticism of acting. He thought that the role of criticism was to help foster the drama of the future.[51] This view is strikingly contrasted with that of Clement Scott, who believed criticism of the acting was central to his role, something that very much reflected the theatre as an actors' theatre rather than the writers' theatre which Archer sought to foster. Significantly, of the new critics, Grein ran a theatre and Shaw became a prolific playwright and they too placed great weight on the writing.

Stung by the critical reception of his Independent Theatre productions, Grein too launched an attack on the prevailing critical standards in an essay 'The Grave Responsibilities of Dramatic Criticism'. He complained that 'dramatic criticism in this country, with a very few laudable exceptions, is dry, stale and unprofitable; is entirely devoid of intellectual force; is neither elevating nor educating, but simply dull. The best that can be said for it is that it is honest – at least honest in the sense that there is no evidence of traffic in money or even baser coin.' But he thought there was a too cosy intimacy between critics and managers. He asked 'is it honest, I ask, to clink champagne glasses with the manager after a first night, and then to rush to the office to write a notice?' But more seriously he indicted 'the bankruptcy of intelligence' that characterized their hostile reaction to productions of Ibsen and Maeterlinck, a reaction which showed 'That the majority of our critics are unfit to hold the scales. That in their little bourgeois souls there is no comprehension of the great battles that move human life ... It is not only want of breadth and tolerance which debases our dramatic criticism; it is insularity, stupidity, and levity.' He claimed that to many critics 'the duties of dramatic criticism are irksome; they go to the theatre because they are paid for it. They do not love their work. No enthusiasm swells their breast. They know well enough that the majority of new productions are not worth the money wasted, nor the ink spilled, on them.' The whole wealth of continental drama was a closed book to them. They pander to the presumed prejudices of their audience. They lack seriousness of approach.[52]

Irving was only too aware of the importance of the critics and he sought to use them where possible to further his ambitions for the theatre. Laurence Irving recalls his attitude:

Irving had been perfectly instructed by Bateman in the art of handling the more venal sections of the press and … was capable of holding his own with those who attacked him out of personal spite or in sincere belief that they were the champions of reform. While studying carefully the criticism of the few whose opinion he valued and respected, in the main he regarded critics and paragraphists with indifference or contempt. He looked upon himself as the public's humble servant. If he was able to win their support and approval without lowering the high standard he had set himself, he accepted their verdict as that worthy of consideration. Directly his popularity with the public was beyond doubt, he exploited with cynical amusement the venality of the press in furthering his aims and in publishing his activities, while striking ruthlessly at those journalists who, by the vulgar or scandalous nature of their comments, undermined his conception of the dignity of the actor's profession.[53]

Irving's attitude to the critics en masse was summed up with characteristic humour in his after dinner speech to the Royal General Theatrical Fund annual dinner on 25 May 1893. *The Times* (26 May 1893) reported him as saying to his audience of eminent actors and playwrights:

A new drama in these days was no light undertaking. They had to face the tribunal of certain independent spirits who unmade old ideals and created new standards by the stroke of a pen and who amused their intervals of leisure by tracing the philosophy of impressionism to the eccentricities of digestion. (*Laughter*) He received the other day a letter containing a curious request. His correspondent said, 'Can you tell me where I can find a thoroughly sound work on the elements of dramatic criticism?' He might as well have asked any innocent citizen, who found his beautiful new greenhouse smashed by a storm, to put his hand complacently on some thoroughly sound work on the beneficence of hailstones. (*Laughter*)

According to his grandson, Irving divided the critics into three groups: 'the respected and incorruptible', who included Edward R. Russell of the *Liverpool Daily Post*, Alfred Watson of the *Standard* and Joseph Knight of the *Athenaeum*, 'whose integrity and love of the theatre was beyond dispute, and with whom he could be on terms of intimate friendship without being suspected of any ulterior motive'; the 'corruptible', 'who by flattery, entertainment or the purchase of options on their un-actable plays could be counted upon to provide him with a measure of dignified publicity' and to act as mercenaries in his battles with the third but waning group of 'those who, impervious to his magnetism or jealous of his success, were ever ready to heave a brick through the windows of the noble edifice which he was labouring to build'.[54]

Edward R. Russell (1834–1920) was born in London and originally intended for the ministry. But he became a journalist and at twenty-three was editor of the *Islington Daily Gazette*. He later worked on the *Morning Star* but was appointed editor of the *Liverpool Daily Post and Mercury* in 1865 and held the post for fifty years. A keen Liberal and supporter of Gladstone, he was MP for

Glasgow Bridgeton from 1885 to 1887 but, finding it impossible to combine his parliamentary and journalistic activities, gave up his seat. He wrote dramatic criticism as 'An Old Hand'. He was a strong supporter of Irving, reviewed all his productions and wrote lengthy and appreciative analyses of his work for the periodical press, notably the *Fortnightly Review* and *Macmillan's Magazine*. He was knighted in 1893 and created Baron Russell of Liverpool in 1919.

Alfred Watson (1849–1922) was for more than thirty years the musical and dramatic critic of the *Standard*, a staunchly Conservative paper. He was editor of the *Illustrated Sporting and Dramatic News* from 1880 to 1895, writing many articles under the pen name 'Rapier', and he was a regular contributor to the *Saturday Review* from 1885 to 1894. Early in his career he had written a three act drama, *Pendarvon*, for the Alexandra Theatre, Liverpool, where H.J. Loveday, later stage manager of the Lyceum, was stage manager and orchestra conductor, and the libretto of an opera *The Elfin Tree* for the Carl Rosa Opera Company. He also wrote several books on hunting and racing.

In his 1918 autobiography, *A Sporting and Dramatic Career*, Watson recalled his relationship with Irving. They had not met until after Watson had seen his *Hamlet*, which thrilled him. The play had been generally well received but there had been a critical article in *Macmillan's Magazine* by 'A Templar', a pseudonym widely thought to conceal the identity of Sir Theodore Martin, who believed that the retirement of his wife, the actress Helen Faucit, from the stage, 'had put an end to the true interpretation of Shakespeare in the theatre' and in consequence 'resented praise bestowed on any other player'.[55] He had accused Irving by his textual cuts and performance style of turning *Hamlet* into a melodrama. Watson was so outraged that he wrote a point by point refutation of the article for *London Society*, which he reproduced in his autobiography. He concluded by saying: 'It seems to me that Mr Irving *realises* the character, and by art, which is never apparent, conveys his realisation to the audience; that he is absolutely consistent from beginning to end, and that the performance is, in short – what I for one never expected to see – an *embodiment* of Shakespeare's Hamlet.'[56] On the basis of this, their friendship developed and it was Irving who suggested his pen-name 'Rapier'. Watson recalled:

> My acquaintance with Henry Irving rapidly grew to a friendship which has been among the chief pleasures of my life. He never confused the friend and the critic, never for a moment resented what he knew was the honest expression of opinion, and though I had a very genuine affection for him I always wrote what I thought without hesitation. He did nothing without a reason which he had convinced himself was sound, and when we have discussed Shakespearian tragedy I never knew him unable to support his reading by references to the text.[57]

He cited his criticisms of *Macbeth* ('there is a great deal to admire and not a little to condemn, but it may be said at once that Mr Irving's interpretation of *Macbeth* will not be so great a popular success as was that of *Hamlet*) and *Othello* ('The effect of Mr. Irving's pronunciation is as though an artist painted a beautiful picture and deliberately smudged it with his sleeve') as evidence of his critical independence.[58] Nevertheless he regarded Irving as 'the finest artist I ever saw.'

As part of his publicity for his view of himself and the theatre, Irving purchased the *Theatre* magazine. Originally founded as a weekly in January 1877, it was acquired by Irving in August 1878 and transformed into a monthly. It turned out to be highly unprofitable and in December 1879 Irving, having cleared debts of £300 on it, handed it over to Clement Scott. It was valued at £1000, 'which was never paid', and Irving was promised a quarter share of future profits, 'which never materialized'. In 1889 Scott sought to sell it and Irving wrote to him resigning all shares in it so that he could dispose of it. The *Theatre*, under Scott's editorship, acted as an upmarket pro-Irving journal. But it was only one of various ways in which Irving kept himself before the public. There were books by sympathetic journalists with which Irving cooperated, his various addresses on the drama were published and collections of press reviews were published.[59]

Several journalists were dedicated Irvingites. Austin Brereton (1862–1922), born in Liverpool, arrived in London at the age of nineteen. He became private secretary to Clement Scott and assistant editor of the *Theatre* (1881–87). He edited *Dramatic Notes* from 1882 to 1887 and was dramatic critic of the *Stage*. He cooperated with Irving on *Henry Irving: A Biographical Sketch* (1883) and his history of the Lyceum, *The Lyceum and Henry Irving* (1903). In 1908 he published his two-volume biography of Irving, for which he had had access to Irving's scrapbooks covering the years 1858–74; the book in which his father Samuel Brodribb had recorded the incidents of his son's career from 1866 to 1874; Irving's account books for 1878–1905; the Russell-Cotes collection of printed Irvingiana; two hundred letters; and the reminiscences via interview of surviving associates. From 1898 until Irving's death in 1905 Brereton formally acted as his press agent. He wrote biographies of Ellen Terry, Cyril Maude, Peg Woffington and Sarah Bernhardt. In addition he was dramatic and art critic for the *Sydney Morning Herald* (1885–91), drama critic of the *Sphere* (1901 to 1906) and drama critic and assistant editor of the *Illustrated American* (1893–94).

The 'Frederic Daly' who wrote *Henry Irving in England and America, 1838–1884* (1884) was in fact Irving's private secretary, Louis F. Austin, who was also a practising journalist. Louis F. Austin (1852–1905), although born in Brooklyn, the son of an Irishman, Captain Thomas Austin of Dublin, was described by fellow journalist Clarence Rook as a 'Londoner – a Londoner of the West End, the theatres, the clubs, the restaurants, the dinner parties – and the periodicals'. He acted informally at one stage as the private secretary of Baroness Burdett-Coutts, moving on from her to occupy a similar position with Irving, assisting in particular in drafting the after dinner speeches which made Irving by general consent one of the best after dinner speakers in England. But he was mainly known as a journalist. 'His industry and fertility were amazing', recalled Rook, a colleague on the *Daily Chronicle*. He was essentially a columnist and essayist, writing 'Our Note Book' for the *Illustrated London News*, 'The Passing Mood' (under the pen-name Jaques) for the *Daily Chronicle*, 'At Random' for the *Sketch* and the weekly 'Points of View' for the Manchester *Daily Dispatch*. He also wrote leading articles for a syndicate that supplied the provincial press. This daily activity left him no leisure for longer work and his only book-length study was the biography of Irving written under the pseudonym Frederic Daly. Of his journalism (of which two volumes of selections, *At Random* and *Points of View*, were published, the latter posthumously), Rook wrote that Austin was 'the essayist of wide information, of large sympathies, with humorous eyes and a knowledge of the value of words set one against the other'. Austin died suddenly at the Metropole Hotel, Brighton, in evening dress; beside him were the proofs of his final article, an appreciation of Irving, intended for the *North American Review*, a typical piece of promotional publicity ahead of Irving's intended American visit in 1906, a visit that Irving never lived to make, dying soon after Austin himself.[60]

The two-volume *Henry Irving's Impressions of America* (1884), a series of sketches, chronicles and conversations, was by the journalist Joseph Hatton who accompanied Irving on his first American tour. Joseph Hatton (1841–1907), the son of a Derbyshire printer and publisher and at first intended for the law, took up journalism and became editor of the *Bristol Mirror* (1863–68). He came to London in 1868 and set out to make a career as novelist and journalist. The publisher William Tinsley recalled that he had never met a 'more energetic or reliable' author than Hatton. He became editor of the *Gentleman's Magazine*, *School Board Chronicle* and *Illustrated Midland News*, for Messrs Grant & Co. Retiring from his editorships in 1874, he became the London correspondent of the *New York Times*, *Sydney Morning Herald* and *Berlin Kreuz-Zeitung*. For a time he edited the *Sunday Times*. In 1881 the *Standard* sent him to New York to establish an independent telegraph service and he scooped the British press with news of the assassination of President Garfield. He was a member of the Garrick Club and became a close friend of Irving and Toole, writing not just *Irving's Impressions of America* but also ghosting Toole's *Memoirs*. He wrote a thirty-two page pamphlet on the Lyceum *Faust*. In 1892 he became editor of the *People*, a Conservative Sunday newspaper. He contributed a column to it called *Cigarette Papers* in which he regularly referred to Irving. He was also a prolific and successful novelist (he wrote thirty). His greatest successes were *Clytie* (1874), which he dramatized successfully for the stage, *By Order of the Czar* (1890) and *When Rogues Fall Out* (1899). *By Order of the Czar* which dealt with the plight of the Jews in Russia was billed as 'banned in Russia' and carried an endorsement from Mr Gladstone, expressing the hope that the 'book would help alleviate the plight of the Jews in Russia'.[61]

A collection of press reviews of Irving's first American tour was published in 1884 and the *New York Tribune* reviews, by the dedicated Irvingite William Winter, were published as *Henry Irving* in 1885. Clement Scott's reviews of Irving from the *Observer, Daily Telegraph* and *Illustrated London News* were published as *From 'The Bells' to' King Arthur'* in 1896.

Irving regularly gave interviews both to those favoured journalists and to others but, as Stoker recorded, 'he always required that the proof should be submitted to him and that his changes, either by excision or addition, should be respected. He would sign the proof if such were thought desirable. I never knew a case where the interviewer or the newspaper did not loyally hold to this undertaking.'[62] There were, however, criticisms of the amiability and inter-action between Irving and members of the press. One of the most notorious came from Mowbray Morris, who succeeded John Oxenford as dramatic critic of *The Times*. The journalist J.B. Booth recalled the circumstances:

> he retained the post for about six years, as he paraded his intolerant prejudices too palpably, and his attacks on Henry Irving as an actor, artist and public man went beyond the bounds of legitimate criticism. After resigning his newspaper duties he published a book which was described at the time as '226 pages of aggressive "biliousness"' and also 'a silly, prejudiced, unnecessary and misleading work, written evidently by a soured and disappointed man'. Mowbray Morris was a good writer but a slow journalist, and he regarded with mingled envy and contempt those colleagues who outpaced him in what he deprecated as the press and hurry of criticism: and he was mean enough to accuse of subserviency and venality those who succeeded in a task at which he failed.[63]

In this 'bilious' volume, *Essays in Theatrical Criticism* (1882), he denounced the critics for their lack of impartiality: 'How can it be preserved when the relations between the critic and the object of his criticism are so very intimate and personal as they now, it is notorious, too often are.'

In a direct tilt at Irving, Morris declared that 'when the critic is bound by ties of personal friendship, or, as may possibly happen, by ties of personal interest, to the actor, it is surely inevitable that his judgement' should be affected. He thought it 'inevitable' with regard to the critic's relationship with Irving that 'he should regard his Macbeth not as the brave weak man overthrown by ambition and his terrible wife, but as a charming liberal dispenser of champagne and chicken, and other things, perhaps even more convenient'.[64] Booth refuted Morris's charges:

> There is no doubt that Henry Irving was kind to the press. But the suppers that he used to give on 'first nights' were not exclusively for critics, and a newspaper man was not invited on account of his official position, but because he was a personal friend of the

host. Irving loved to gather together in friendship and good fellowship his supporters, and the representatives of every form of literature and art in London, and his supper parties in the Beefsteak Room at the Lyceum were not 'Press Feasts'. Out of fifty guests not more than half a dozen, as a rule, were critics.[65]

All of this is true but there were other inducements than dinners to woo the press. Stephen Coleridge, the son of the Lord Chief Justice, Lord Coleridge, and a long time friend of Irving, recalled in his memoirs:

> In the early days of Irving's long reign at the Lyceum, I remember after a first night when I remained behind to have a chat with him, he asked me to stay and have supper upstairs in the Beeksteak Club-room and 'help him with some critics'. There turned up three of them, making up a party of five. After a pleasant supper Irving placed in the middle of the table a large box of immense cigars. They looked about ten inches long, and were no doubt very choice, rare and precious. The box must have contained a hundred, at, I suppose, about half a crown each. When we rose to depart and the critics donned their overcoats, Irving proceeded with both hands to ladle out the cigars into their deep and large pockets, 'Here, old friend,' he said, 'where is your pocket?' His face was a picture of solemn solicitude for his good friends comfort and welfare, but just as the big bundle of cigars disappeared into the pocket of one of them, having glanced round, and seeing that the others had their backs turned, he looked swiftly at me, shut one eye and glanced at me with the drollest and most informing expression … Many years afterwards, I remember Irving saying to me that if the Press took bribes, he was bound to pay them, disgusting as such business was, but that primarily he must make the theatre pay its way or he could not go on at all; and if to obtain that primary end, the Press had to be bought, money must in a business-like way be set aside for the purpose. He said that one critic, whom he named to me, had 'cost him' since he began quite ten thousand pounds. Of course it was done indirectly by buying plays which were never performed and such-like elegant transactions.[66]

The novelist Henry James, a life-long theatregoer, contributed essays on various aspects of English theatre to a variety of newspapers and periodicals, mainly American, between 1872 and 1901. Writing in 1877, he summed up the position in the London theatre as he saw it. The theatre was dominated by Irving, who enjoyed a pre-eminence unequalled since Macready.

> I am told that London is divided, on the subject of his merits, into two fiercely hostile camps; that he has sown dissention [sic] in families, and made old friends cease to 'speak'. His appearance in a new part is a great event; and if one has the courage of one's opinion, at dinner tables and elsewhere, a conversational godsend … Before attempting Hamlet, which up to this moment has been his greatest success, he had attracted much attention as a picturesque actor of melodrama, which he rendered with a refinement of effect not common upon the English stage. Mr Irving's critics may, I suppose, be divided into three categories: those who justify him in whatever he attempts, and consider him an artist of unprecedented brilliancy; those who hold that he did very well in melodrama, but that

he flies too high when he attempts Shakespeare; and those who, in vulgar parlance, can see nothing in him at all.[67]

This was an accurate account of the situation. James ranked himself with the sceptics and described what he saw as Irving's defects:

> Nature has done very little to make an actor of him. His face is not dramatic, it is the face of a sedentary man, a clergyman, a lawyer, an author, an amiable gentleman – of anything other than a possible Hamlet or Othello. His figure is of the same cast, and his voice completes the want of illusion. His voice is apparently wholly unavailable for purposes of declamation. To say that he speaks at all – in any way that, in an actor, can be called speaking ... Of what the French call diction – of the art of delivery – he has apparently not a suspicion. This forms three fourths of an actor's obligations, and in Mr Irving's acting these three fourths are simply cancelled. What is left to him with the remaining fourth is to be 'picturesque'; and this even his partisans admit he has made his speciality.[68]

In 1880 James elaborated on what he meant by 'picturesque':

> He is what is called a picturesque actor ... and evidently bestows an immense deal of care and conscience upon his work; he meditates, elaborates, and, upon the line of which he moves, carries the part to a very high degree of finish. But it must be affirmed that this is a line with which the especial art of the actor, the art of utterance, of saying the thing, has almost nothing to do. Mr Irving's peculiarities and eccentricities of speech are so strange, so numerous, so personal to himself, his views of pronunciation, of modulation, of elocution so highly developed, the tricks he plays with the divine mother-tongue so audacious and fantastic, that the spectator who desires to be in sympathy with him finds himself confronted with a bristling hedge of difficulties.[69]

James's view of Irving never changed. He wrote, for instance, of Irving's Romeo, 'How little Mr Irving is Romeo it is not worth while even to attempt to declare', and of Irving's manner as Mephistopheles, that it differed 'only in degree from that of the star of a Christmas burlesque'.[70]

James's criticisms were echoed by others in the sceptical camp. They were even shared by some actors. Frank Archer, for example, wrote in his memoirs:

> I never acted with Irving, nor did I ever make any engagement with him. I suspect that a half-heartedness on my own part ... was to some extent the reason that I never joined him. I am afraid I was not always able to be just with regard to the higher gifts he possessed. His elocution was to me so utterly faulty that I could rarely feel myself impressed by him. I suppose it was not affectation, but it conveyed that idea to me. From the back of the pit at the Lyceum one evening I witnessed The Cup ... I really could not, strain my hearing as I might, distinguish Irving's words ... His performance in The Bells was a splendid piece of melodramatic acting ... There were fine things in his Charles the First ... The grim, the weird, and the fateful, of which he was master, were shown, I thought, wonderfully, in Vanderdecken; but as a critic of Irving, for the reasons given, I must, I suppose, be ruled out of court.[71]

Perhaps inevitably Irving became a prime target for criticism from the 'Young Turks' who had a different agenda for theatre from the one pursued by Irving. Irving, super-conscious of the dignity of his profession and of his own hard-won standing within it, was not one to let major critical assaults go without response. Any such assault was usually met with a reply, either from Irving himself or more usually from one of his circle put up to it by Irving. In the most serious cases, Irving threatened the culprits with recourse to the law.

In 1877 William Archer, only twenty-one and yet to make his name as a leading dramatic critic, and two friends he had made as an undergraduate at Edinburgh University, Robert Lowe, an insurance clerk and a future theatrical historian, and George Halkett, a caricaturist and the future art editor of the *Pall Mall Gazette*, collaborated on an anonymous twenty-four page pamphlet entitled *The Fashionable Tragedian*, published in Edinburgh and Glasgow. Lowe provided the ideas, Halkett the caricature illustrations, and Archer did the writing.[72] It was a typical young man's squib, setting out to ridicule one of the acknowledged lions of the day. They began by claiming:

> No actor of this, or indeed any other, age has been so much and so indiscriminately belauded as Mr Henry Irving. For more than five years he has been the 'bright particular star of the British dramatic firmament'. Night after night he has filled the dingy old Lyceum, from the front row of the stalls to the back row of the gallery, with audiences which applauded every jerk, every spasm, every hysteric scream – we almost said every convulsion – in which he chose to indulge. In the provinces he has met with the same success and the same laudation. Newspaper 'critics' have ransacked and exhausted their by no means limited vocabulary in the search for words in which to express his greatness. He is, we are told, the resuscitator of all the past glories of the British drama, with the addition of new glories peculiarly his own. He is the 'interpreter of Shakespeare to the multitude', the apostle of popular dramatic culture. Criticism has not been entirely silent, it is true, but its voice has been drowned in the plaudits of enthusiasm.[73]

They accurately listed the attributes which Irving was said by favourable critics to possess: he was the most intellectual of actors, he was original in that he did not cling to stage tradition but invented new conceptions of character and modes of expression, he was picturesque in attitude, motion and bearing, he was a master of a psychological subtlety hitherto unknown, he elaborated his performances with carefully studied gestures and expressions and, 'possessed of a most delicate and exquisite taste', he presented Shakespeare as it should be presented.

They admitted that Irving had once showed promise ('His Digby Grant was excellent. His first performances as Mathias in *The Bells* were certainly wonderful'.) But since the two hundred night run of *Hamlet* he had gone downhill, long runs and indiscriminate adulation causing all his inherent defects to be exaggerated. They disclaimed any personal knowledge of Irving and any professional connection with the stage and said they were speaking purely as spectators of his performances. They set about listing his defects.

> The first requisite for histrionic greatness is power to move and speak like a normal and rational human being. A man may have intellect, 'picturesqueness', taste, and all the rest of it, but if he walks like an automaton whose wheels need oiling, and speaks alternately from the pit of his stomach and the top of his head, he will never be a great, or a good, or even a passable actor.[74]

They complained that Irving dragged one leg after him as if limping, jerked his shoulders spasmodically, constantly nodded his head backwards and forwards, alternated between *basso profundo* and *falsetto*, and so mangled his pronunciation of English words that it needed a new phonetic system to write them down.

> Apart from his fatal mannerisms of motion and speech, he has physical defects which nothing but the most marked genius could hide. A weak, loosely-built figure, and a face whose range of expression is very limited, are the two principal disadvantages under which he has had to labour. Abject terror, sarcasm, and frenzy are the only passions which Mr Irving's features can adequately express … His figure, again, utterly precludes the possibility of dignity, grace or even ease … So far from struggling against and mastering his natural defects, he has merely exaggerated them, until his admirers have come to look upon them as the beauties of his 'style'.[75]

They then dismissed each of his alleged virtues. Of his intellectuality they said such of his speeches and addresses as they have read, they regarded as 'commonplace'. His originality and picturesqueness lay alike in the strange mannerisms: 'some of his readings are ingenious, though very few of them are strictly original'. As to his psychological subtlety, his Hamlet was 'vulgar', his Macbeth, played as a 'writhing poltroon', was 'liker a horrible nightmare than a Shakespearian tragedy' and his Othello 'simply ghastly'. His Richard III was his most successful role and this was because his defects fitted the part. 'So much then for his psychological subtlety. If it be this which makes of Hamlet a weak-minded puppy, of Macbeth a Uriah Heep in chain armour, of Othello an 'infuriated Sepoy' and of Richard III a cheap Mephistopheles, all we can say is, the less we have of psychological subtlety on the English stage the better.'[76] He elaborated but that was merely a conscientious approach to his job. His taste was 'questionable'.

They concluded by saying that Irving had the makings of an excellent actor, and might have been unsurpassed in certain lines of comedy and melodrama, though he would never make a tragedian. But what he needed was careful training in a good dramatic school 'where he could have learned proper stage-bearing, good elocution, and artistic self-containment'; instead what he actually received was 'the slovenly, haphazard training of provincial and minor metropolitan theatres' and he was then ruined by long runs and excessive adulation. They called for a national theatre 'with good endowment, good traditions, good government'.[77]

It was not the kind of attack that Irving could leave unanswered and a reply appeared, an eighteen-page pamphlet entitled *A Letter Concerning Mr Henry Irving*, published in Edinburgh, Glasgow and London, attributed to 'Yorick'. Laurence Irving discovered that the final paragraph of this *Letter* was drafted in Irving's own hand on his personal notepaper.[78] The reply, attacking *The Fashionable Tragedian*, for claiming that 'Mr Irving is one of the worst actors that ever trod the British stage' set out by reasoned argument to refute the criticisms one by one. On the claim that no actor has been so 'indiscriminately' belauded, Yorick argued that on the contrary 'no actor of this, or indeed of any other age, had been so much or so indiscriminately traduced' and that some critics had been consistently hostile. But their very vituperation was testimony of the originality of his work. They claimed that Irving has been praised by scientists, poets, philosophers and bishops. But was not that a good thing, argued Yorick? Surely, 'the admiration of a Huxley, a Gladstone, a Tennyson, and a Blackie, is not to be despised, nor the testimony of bishops to be disregarded. They prove at least that if Mr Irving is not a perfect actor ... he is a highly distinguished one, and whose performances are worthy of study and earnest consideration.'[79] As to the attacks on his gait, appearance and pronunciation, admittedly his physique was not conspicuously well-suited to the more heroic parts of tragedy but it was particularly suitable for Hamlet, Mathias and Charles I. He had his mannerisms but all great actors do, for instance Kemble, Macready and Charles Kean. 'As for not speaking like a "rational human being", the British public was perhaps the best judge of that. Mr Irving has for many years delighted that public, and Mr Irving is, if we are not deceived, a scholar and a gentleman; certainly he can write good English.' He had moved the public by his rounded performances: 'He throws tradition aside, and gives us the fruit of his own thought and study. The result ... is, in the majority of instances, remarkably successful.'[80] His performances were singularly 'picturesque' and 'vivid'. The critics attacked his 'psychological subtlety' but his Hamlet was 'psychologically consistent' and his Richard III was Shakespeare's and not Colley Cibber's and 'the general effect is wonderfully fine'. Yorick rejected the idea of a national theatre ('twaddle'), which if charged with training all actors would make acting uniform and dull. He concluded that 'No living native artist has so wide a range; and he could therefore maintain, by reason only of his versatility, the high position which he has secured as an exponent of Shakespeare and the romantic drama. Regarded from all sides, he is, without exception, the foremost dramatic artist of his country.'[81] The final paragraph, drafted by Irving himself, suggested that the authors might well be young men who in time would regret ridiculing 'an artist who has given pleasure and instruction to hundreds of thousands of his countrymen'. He ended with a quote from Carlyle: 'Good breeding lies in human nature and is due from all men towards all men.'[82]

Lowe prepared a second edition of *The Fashionable Tragedian*, muting some of his criticisms of Irving's Richard III, about which he had had second thoughts, but rumours of a threatened legal action against the young authors caused him to withdraw it. There for a moment, the battle paused.

The pamphlet war had provoked widespread press comment. But another, more measured round in the battle occurred six years later, when William Archer, by now established as a leading critic in London, published *Henry Irving: Actor and Manager*. His aim in this new work, he said, was 'to diagnose the two diseases of Irving-mania and Irving-phobia which are raging among the public; the former endemic, the latter sporadic, but none the less violent where it does break out. Shunning the contagion of these almost equally pestilent heresies, I wish to suggest the conditions of a sane and healthy criticism.'[83]

Archer began by recognising the pre-eminence and popularity of the Lyceum under Irving: 'It is scarcely too much to say that the Lyceum is as prominent an element in the social life of London as the Théâtre Français in that of Paris … But the Lyceum is more than fashionable, it is popular.'[84] But Archer is critical of Irving's failure to put on modern plays at the Lyceum, believing that the drama of the past could never reflect contemporary reality. Though he would concede in his conclusion that 'it is impossible to doubt that his influence on the English drama is on the whole for good'. Accepting Irving's 'brilliant' and unprecedented success in making the Lyceum the social, financial and artistic centre of British theatrical life, he then identified an anomaly:

> There has probably never been an actor of equal prominence whose talents, nay, whose mere competence, has been so much contested. He is the ideal of a select circle of devotees but even this is small, and its fervour is apt to be tempered with apology. The great public regards him with interest and respect rather than with enthusiasm … in no single part has general consent pronounced him ideal; in many it has emphatically pronounced him quite the reverse … in general society, one needs far more courage to praise than to condemn Mr Irving. To admire him without reserve is held eccentric to the verge of affectation. The orthodox dilate upon the splendour of the scenery, admire Miss Ellen Terry, and are reticent about Mr Irving … On a first night the devotees of course muster largely, and enthusiasm is the order of the evening; but it is otherwise after a piece has run for a week or so. This I can vouch from repeated personal observation. The crowded audiences at the Lyceum as a rule applaud but feebly, and the attendants in front of the house are not above contributing to the rapturous ovations … The true explanation is that the great majority of the audience are intellectually interested, not emotionally excited. There is often as much applause when the curtain rises on an elaborate 'set' as when it falls on a thrilling situation.[85]

Four fifths of the audience were of this type with one fifth comprising 'ebullient devotees' and 'frigid sceptics'. Archer outlined the view of the sceptics.

11. Irving as Shylock in *The Merchant of Venice*.

12. Irving and Ellen Terry in *Olivia*. The only photograph showing Irving and Terry together on stage.

13. Irving as Mathias in *The Bells*.

14. Irving in the title role of *Jingle*.

15. Irving as Mephistopheles.

16. Irving as Dante.

17. Irving as Wolsey.

18. Irving as Robespierre

19. A scene from *King Arthur*.

20. A scene from *Becket*.

21. A scene from *King Lear*.

22. As Lear, with Ellen Terry as Cordelia.

23. Statue of Irving as Hamlet, by E. Onslow Ford.

There is understandably a minority, small but not unimportant, who can see nothing but faults in Mr Irving, who consider his popularity an extraordinary delusion, and who go to the Lyceum as they would to a Chinese joss-house, curious to witness a set of superstitious rites incomprehensible to their intellect and remote from their sympathies.[86]

This, Archer felt, was because they did not go often enough to become familiar with his mannerisms. The press did and made allowances for the mannerisms, looking beyond them. Archer admitted that he began as an unbeliever but seeing Irving regularly 'could recognize the thoughtfulness, the ingenuity, the earnestness that shone through this unhappy veil of mannerism'.[87]

Archer conceded certain qualities to Irving: 'a magnetic personality', an intensity and a physique and physiognomy appropriate to some though not all his parts:

> There have been many better stage-faces than Mr Irving's, but few more remarkable. The high narrow forehead, the marked and overhanging but flexible eye-brows, the dark eyes which can be by turns so penetrating, so dreamy, so sinister, and so melancholy, the thin straight mouth, the hollow cheeks and marvellously mobile jaw, combine to form an incomparable vehicle for the expression of a certain range of character and emotion. To me I confess the face under certain aspects seems absolutely beautiful but its beauty is ascetic, not sensuous.[88]

So in sensuous parts, such as Romeo and Claude Melnotte 'he is painfully out of his element'. His face was perfectly suited for Hamlet, Eugene Aram, the Corsican Brothers, Synorix and Charles I. He thought Irving's physiognomy better suited to character parts rather than heroic parts and interestingly made the distinction not as some critics did between Shakespeare and melodrama but between character parts and heroic parts. Charles I was both ('his portrait of the traditional gentleman king is noble and beautiful'). But for the rest the distinction was clear: Othello, Hamlet, Romeo, Macbeth, Lesurques and Eugene Aram were heroic parts; Iago, Shylock, Richard III, Mathias, Dubosc, Richelieu, Louis XI and Digby Grant were character parts. The range of emotion in these parts was completely within Irving's sphere:

> Hatred, malignity and cunning dwell familiarly in his eye, his jaw can express at will indomitable resolve or grotesque and abject terror. Grim humour lurks in his eyebrows and cruel contempt in the corners of his mouth. No actor had ever fuller command of the expression which has been happily called 'a lurid glance' – witness his Richard and Louis.[89]

In pure comedy, 'there is a monotony about his sardonic smile and the arch side-glances from under his never-resting eyebrows with which he emphasizes every point'. This made his Benedick 'amusing ... but in no sense exhilarating'. There was a lack of spontaneity in this and his other comic creations (Jingle, Jeremy Diddler, Doricourt).

But when he came to list Irving's defects he was once again rehearsing the list from *The Fashionable Tragedian*. Irving, he claimed, neglected the basic rules of acting – to stand still on stage, to move with grace, to speak 'his mother tongue with purity', to manage his voice 'so that it may produce the maximum effect in the auditorium with the minimum of effort to the lungs and the throat'. His restlessness, his walk (head depressed, shoulders thrust forward, spasmodic movements), his mangling of the English language: these mannerisms have increased rather than diminished with success. They heightened his individuality but marred the individuality belonging to his roles, thus making Hamlet, Romeo, Benedick, Eugene Aram and Claude Melnotte 'mere phases of Irving, and nothing but Irving'.

> Each of his characters is a fresh development of his own individuality, not, as is the case with mimetic actors, a study from the life, or a generalization of many studies from the life. He creates rather than imitates. His greatest triumphs are projections of himself, not reflections of the world around him. This characteristic combines with his mannerisms to impart a certain sameness to his style.[90]

He is the least inspired of all distinguished actors ('He never carries us away on the wings of his passion or his pathos ... He never brings us face to face with the very soul of pure humanity'). Archer recalled being lifted out of himself by the acting of Salvini, Jefferson, Sarah Bernhardt, Delaunay, Edwin Booth and Mrs Kendal, but never by Irving. 'In all parts Mr Irving interests his audience; in his better parts he moves them; but he leaves them always conscious of the motive mechanism. He grasps them but they are not rapt away.'[91]

Irving, Archer believed, dominates the stage by the force of intellect. 'He is a restlessly innovating spirit. His intellect is strictly that of the executive artist-eager, earnest, rapid and instinctive, rather than logical or profound ... Edmund Kean read Shakespeare by flashes of lightning: Mr Irving reads him by the student's midnight oil. He is great in new glosses and daring in conjectural emendations. The stalls are startled by his critical acumen, the boxes thrilled by his archaeological scholarship. He throws succulent bones of contention to the critics, which they learnedly discuss to their own infinite satisfaction and his no small advantage.'[92] Archer believed that Irving succeeded best in characters that called for an intellectual rather than a histrionic approach, so his Hamlet was better than his Macbeth and Othello, his Shylock than his Hamlet, his Richard III than his Shylock and his Iago 'comes as near perfection as anything has done'. He acknowledged Irving's excellence as a 'stage manager' (director) and his qualities of 'patient, intelligent elaboration'.

Mr Irving, as a manager, has known how to adapt himself to every art tendency of the day. Foremost among these is a craving for what may be called technical realism of detail … Mr Irving has the art of inspiring to the verge of genius his scenic artists and machinists, which may possibly be the reason why he has so little inspiration left over for himself. As one thinks of the past five years at the Lyceum there rises to the mind's eye a whole gallery of scenic pictures, each as worthy of minute study as any canvas of the most learned archaeological painter. To take only two instances, I venture to say that scenic art at home or abroad has done nothing more perfect than the Temple in *The Cup* and the Cathedral in *Much Ado*. They have been surpassed in mere splendour, but never in minute artistic realism. It seems as if the art of the stage-architect could no further go.[93]

As for Ellen Terry, Irving had turned her into a tragedienne to great acclaim, something Archer regretted for he did not think this played to her strengths, best seen in comic or pathetic roles such as Laetitia Hardy, Iolanthe and Ruth in *Eugene Aram*. But he congratulated Irving on his perception in 'discerning in Miss Terry the almost necessary complement to his own talent'.

Like *The Fashionable Tragedian* this prompted an immediate response, *Henry Irving, Actor and Manager: A Criticism of a Critic's Criticism by an Irvingite*. The pseudonym concealed the identity of Irving's friend and collaborator, the critic and playwright Frank Marshall. He recalled that Archer had been co-author of *The Fashionable Tragedian* 'in which Mr Irving was caricatured with the crude coarseness of one of those boyish artists who attempt frescoes on our street walls, and abused in terms which would have done honour to any female graduate of Billingsgate'.[94]

He rejected each of Archer's anti-Irving observations. He refuted Archer's interpretation of the Lyceum audience as indifferent:

I maintain that the audiences at the Lyceum are, on other nights, quite as attentive and quite as enthusiastic, as on the first night. In the pit, upper boxes and gallery, the applause is hearty and sincere; but what is more important is the close and fixed attention they give to the play; every word is followed with intelligent care; no movement or gesture escapes the eye; but they never applaud at inconvenient points, so as to interrupt the dialogue or action, nor do they allow others to do so.'[95]

On Irving's deficiencies, he noted Archer's comments on Irving's mannerisms of speech and movement. But Marshall replied that acting involved more than walking and talking. Acting consisted of

the power of projecting your own thoughts and feelings into another nature than your own; in so closely identifying yourself, not physically, but mentally and morally, with some other human being, that not only in what you speak and do, but in what you think and feel, you are for the time that other human being, and not yourself … It is because Mr Irving possesses this greatest quality of an actor in the highest degree … he yet succeeds in transforming himself into so many different natures all with such distinct, minute, and consistent characteristics.[96]

He agreed that Irving had his faults, all great artists do. But his merits far outweighed his faults and the harping on about his jerky gait had been overdone. He agreed with Archer about Irving's intensity ('Intensity is a quality, even more useful than graceful gesture or faultless elocution; nay it is the very greatest quality an actor can possess') and he conceded the restlessness, which he attributed to this very intensity and to first night nerves. He also agreed that Irving was a 'great stage manager', lavishing minute care on the production, having thought out every character precisely. He went on to give detailed accounts of individual performances criticized by Archer, stressing their positive, creative and innovatory nature.

George Bernard Shaw was one of the most relentless critics of Irving and the Lyceum, for both ideological and personal reasons. He was a proponent of the new drama, the play of ideas and Ibsenism, and saw the West End, symbolized by Irving's regime at the Lyceum, as resistant to this. But in addition he was in love with Ellen Terry and sought constantly to detach her from her allegiance to the Lyceum. Later in life he wrote about his animosity to Irving in a 1929 preface to the published edition of his correspondence with Ellen Terry. He recalled that he had first seen Irving in Dublin playing Digby Grant in *Two Roses*:

> I instinctively felt that a new drama inhered in this man, though I had by then no conscious notion that I was destined to write it; and I perceive now that I never forgave him for baffling the plans I made for him (always be it remembered, unconsciously) ... He was utterly unlike anyone else: he could give importance and a noble melancholy to any sort of drivel that was put into his mouth; and it was this melancholy, bound up with an impish humour, which forced the spectator to single him out as a leading actor. Here, I felt, is something that leaves the old stage and its superstitions and staleness completely behind, and inaugurates a new epoch in the theatre.[97]

Later, when he saw Ellen Terry in *New Men and Old Acres* in London, 'which was made a success by her performance as *The Two Roses* had been made a success by Irving's', he was completely convinced that here was the woman for the new drama. 'If ever there were two artists apparently marked out by nature to make a clean break with an outworn past and create a new stage world they really were Ellen Terry and Henry Irving.'[98]

But to his lasting annoyance, they did not become the standard-bearers of the new drama. Irving became an overnight star with *The Bells* but

> he immediately turned back to the old Barry Sullivan repertoire of mutilated Shakespear [*sic*] and Bulwer Lytton ... From the public point of view he never looked back: from my point of view he never looked forward. As far as the drama was concerned he was

more old-fashioned than the oldest of his predecessors, and apparently more illiterate than the most ignorant of them.

Shaw reiterated the criticisms made by Archer:

He seemed the most pedantic of elocutionists, because his peculiar nasal method of securing resonance obliged him to pronounce our English diphthongs as vowels; and though he delivered Shakespear's lines (what he left of them) like one who had a sense of their music he would cut a purple passage even out of his own parts quite callously ... He took no interest in the drama as such: a play was to him a length of stuff necessary to his appearance on the stage, but so entirely subordinate to that consummation that it could be cut to his measure like a roll of cloth ... He composed his acting with extraordinary industry and minuteness: his Matthias in *The Bells* and his Charles I were wonderful mosaics of bits of acting thought out touch by touch. His Macaire and Louis XI will hardly be surpassed: they were limited achievements in their *genre*. Even in his Shakespearean impostures ... there were unforgettable moments. But he composed his parts not only without the least consideration for the play as a whole, or even for the character as portrayed by the author (he always worked out some fancy of his own), but without any for the unfortunate actors whom he employed to support him.

His final verdict on the Lyceum regime under Irving was that is was:

an exasperating waste of the talent of the two artists who had seemed to me peculiarly fitted to lift the theatre out of its old ruts and head it towards unexplored regions of drama. With Lyceum Shakespear I had no patience. Shakespear, even in his integrity, could not satisfy the hungry minds whose spiritual and intellectual appetites had been whetted and even created by Ibsen ... The shreds and patches which Irving and his predecessors tore out of his plays and tacked crudely together for performances which were interrupted four or five times by intolerable intervals ... were endurable only by people, who knowing no better, thought they were assisting at a very first-rate solemnization. I knew better. Irving, wasting his possibilities in costly Bardicide, was wasting Ellen Terry's as well.[99]

This considered statement actually conceals two of Shaw's hobby-horses. He detested Shakespeare and he loved Ellen Terry. He wrote to Ellen (28 August 1896): 'Shakespear is as dead dramatically as a doornail.' He described him as 'sixth-rate Kingsley' and he told Ellen: 'I utterly refuse to concern myself with your Beatrices and Portias and the like. *Anybody* can play Shakespear: you are wanted for other things.'[100] On March 26 1896 he wrote to her, complaining that Irving insisted on producing Shakespeare when Ibsen's *Peer Gynt* was available to him. 'Is H.I. blind? Is he deaf? Or is he no actor at all, but only a Shakespear-struck antiquary that he passes by the great chances of his life as if they were pieces of orange peel laid in his path expressly to capsize him.'[101] Replying, on 10 July 1896, Ellen defended Irving's inclusion of Shakespeare in the Lyceum repertoire on hard-headed practical grounds, with a characteristically self-deprecating reference to herself:

> Ah you mad (angry) thing. With justice you might scream out against a woman of my
> age playing the parts I do. I only do it to please H.I. and because I 'draw'. Facts are
> stubborn. Why do you object to Shakespear drawing the people to us better than anything
> else? We have had a good long success in it, you know … 'Fashionable crazes' don't last
> for over twenty years, and London, America and the great English provinces have
> responded to our call in greater numbers during the past two years than ever before, and
> the warmth of the people makes one glad to live! … Why even on the common necessary
> grounds that it pays H.I. to pay so many people in his employment you should
> discontinue a 'goin' on so against Shakespear.[102]

Shaw's critical stance was complicated by the fact that he was in love with
Ellen Terry. Michael Holroyd summarized their relationship:

> 'I really do love Ellen', he was to write. They played at love. He loved her for helping to
> move his romantic feelings from a bruising world on to the stage, from the body to the
> page. She gave him love without threat of death; she gave him consolation in a world
> where real love was too dangerous. They *acted* love.[103]

But he also sought to free her from the Lyceum and deploy her in the new drama.
He wrote to her of Irving on 28 August 1896: 'The man has no artistic sense
outside his own person: he is an ogre who has carried you off to his cave; and
now Childe Roland is coming to the dark tower to rescue you.'[104] He used his
Saturday Review columns to lay into Irving and his misuse of Terry's talents.
Reviewing *King Arthur*, he praised the sets, costumes and scene-painting but
damned the script ('in poetry Mr Comyns Carr is frankly a jobber and nothing
else') and lamented the waste of Ellen:

> As to Miss Ellen Terry, it was the old story, a born actress of real women's parts
> condemned to figure as a mere artist's model in costume plays which, from the woman's
> point of view, are foolish flatteries written by gentlemen for gentlemen … What a theatre
> for a woman of genius to be attached to! Obsolete tomfooleries like *Robert Macaire*,
> schoolgirl charades like *Nance Oldfield*, blank verse by Wills, Comyns Carr, and Calmour,
> with intervals of hashed Shakespeare; and all the time a stream of splendid women's
> parts pouring from the Ibsen volcano and minor craters, and being snapped up by the
> rising generation.[105]

Then came his review of Irving's Corporal Gregory Brewster in *A Story of
Waterloo*, a view completely at odds as Shaw conceded with the general opinion:

> Any one who consults recent visitors to the Lyceum or who seeks for information in the
> Press as to the merits of Mr Conan Doyle's *Story of Waterloo* will in nineteen cases out of
> twenty learn that the piece is a trifle raised into importance by the marvellous acting of
> Mr Irving as Corporal Gregory Brewster. As a matter of fact, the entire effect is contrived
> by the author, and is due to him alone. There is absolutely no acting in it – none whatever.

There is make-up in it, and a little cheap and simple mimicry which Mr Irving does indifferently because he is neither apt nor observant as a mimic of doddering old men, and because his finely cultivated voice and diction again and again rebel against the indignity of the Corporal's squeakings and mumblings and vulgarities of pronunciation.[106]

This spiteful verdict, deliberately setting out to wound, going against the general critical and popular reaction, also indicates the way in which he lined up with the writer against the actor consistently.

When Irving put on *Cymbeline*, Shaw dismissed the play with characteristic vehemence as 'stagey trash of the lowest melodramatic order'. But to his evident surprise he liked Irving's Iachimo:

this Iachimo was quite fresh and novel to me. I witnessed it with unqualified delight: it was no longer a vulgar bagful of 'points', but a true impersonation, unbroken in its life-current from end to end, varied on the surface with the finest comedy, and without a single lapse in the sustained beauty of its execution.

Admitting that Ellen Terry 'invariably fascinates me so much that I have not the smallest confidence in my own judgement respecting her', he nevertheless declared her Imogen to be played 'with infinite charm and delicacy of appeal'.[107]

On the 1897 revival of *Olivia*, in which Hermann Vezin played Dr Primrose opposite Ellen Terry, Shaw after praising Ellen's performance, denounced Irving for stifling her talent.

When I think of the originality and modernity of the talent she revealed twenty years ago, and of its remorseless waste ever since in 'supporting' an actor who prefers *The Iron Chest* to Ibsen, my regard for Sir Henry Irving cannot blind me to the fact that it would have been better for us twenty-five years ago to have tied him up in a sack with every existing copy of the works of Shakespeare, and dropped him into the crater of the nearest volcano. It really serves him right that his Vicar is far surpassed by Mr Hermann Vezin's. Handling the part skilfully and sincerely … Mr Hermann Vezin brings the play back to life on the boards where Sir Henry Irving, by making it the occasion of an exhibition of extraordinary refinement of execution and personality, very nearly killed it as a drama.

Throughout the body of his theatrical criticism, run the same themes: Shakespeare is a waste of time; Ellen Terry can do nothing wrong; and Irving can do almost nothing right.

But behind the scenes there was a brief and uneasy coming together of Irving and Shaw, engineered by Ellen. In 1896, Shaw's one-act play *Man of Destiny*, featuring Napoleon, was offered through Ellen to the Lyceum. She told him 'H.I. quite likes it, and will do it finely'. Irving offered Shaw £50 to keep the acting rights for a year. Shaw later complained: 'Irving's princely manner of buying literary courtiers … was well known to me. The sequel proved that Irving, although contemptuously willing to pay me for control of the play, never had any serious intention of producing it.'[108] Ellen insisted that Irving had intended to produce it in a double bill with Voss's *Schuldig*, of which Sydney Grundy had prepared an English version. But Shaw became furious when he learned that Irving planned to do another Napoleon play, Sardou's *Madame Sans-Gêne* followed by *Richard III*. In a letter to Ellen, dated 23 September 1896, he wrote angrily:

> Oh very well, Sir Henry Irving. A homemade Napoleon isn't good enough for you, isn't it? Very good! We shall see. And you are going to play Richard III, are you? Then I think I know who is going to play Richmond: that's all.[109]

This suggests an intention deliberately to damn *Richard III*, which he did in his review in terms which Irving believed implied that he was drunk on stage: 'he was not, it seemed to me, answering his helm satisfactorily'.[110] Deeply offended, Irving returned *Man of Destiny* and the brief relationship came to an end.

Jack Grein, another young critic, initially joined in the critical assault on Irving. In an essay in the *London Playgoer*, he attacked Irving for not promoting original new plays and pronounced his work at the Lyceum 'dead art'.[111] He wrote a lengthy attack on the acting and staging of *Cymbeline* in *To-morrow*.[112] Like most of the other critics, he denounced *Peter the Great* and *The Medicine Man* but he responded enthusiastically to Irving in his 1896 revival of *Richard III*.

> It is many years since I enjoyed an English theatrical performance so thoroughly as that of *Richard III* at the Lyceum. It was a performance that showed, as I have constantly proclaimed, that the art of acting does indeed run high in England when those who take the lead in it rid themselves of the fatal idea that a theatre is a cheap bazaar to which the public flocks in search of gaudy wares, indifferent as to their quality. It was a performance that charmed the eye, that stimulated the intelligence, that sometimes made the heart beat quicker; a performance that lingers in the memory, as though one would retain it through life, and look forward to saying to a younger generation, 'And in my time, when there were still actors who understood the great art of tragedy, Henry Irving played Richard III as none of my contemporaries played it before him, as none have played it since. It was a masterly presentment, and Irving was a great actor …'[113]

He welcomed the 1899 production of *Robespierre* as a spectacular return to form:

> There is great rejoicing in the theatrical world, for Sir Henry has come back to the old home, and a brilliant success has inaugurated the new chapter of his illustrious career. Such evenings as that of yesterday are unforgettable; they are rare even in the lives of great actors; they have the deep meaning that the popularity of real genius is no ephemeral thing, that a great artist, by the grace of the Muses, is as dear to the public as their very household gods. And it was a glorious return. The play was intensely interesting; the display was unsurpassed in grandeur; above all the actor appeared younger, stronger, and more brilliant than for many days past. That all London will rush

to see Irving in *Robespierre* and do homage to the master of the dramatic profession is a foregone conclusion. But it is equally sure that the play will travel across the globe, for it has all the characteristics of cosmopolitanism. Sardou knows full well what pleases the world is ever sure to please London, the city of all tastes.

Of Irving's performance, Grein wrote:

> Sir Henry himself was throughout at his best. His voice was clear, his articulation distinct, and his bearing as elastic as if he had been granted a fresh lease of life. As usual, he had his episodes of greatness, as in the second act, when he harangued the crowd; in the third, when a mere flash in his eyes betrayed that Robespierre had recognised his son; in the last when delivering his curfew speech in the Convention when he had to rally the faithful round his ragged banner.[114]

Shortly before *Robespierre* Grein had reported on the end of Irving's lesseeship of the Lyceum and the taking over of the theatre by a joint stock company, which would retain his services as leading actor and dramatic adviser. Grein paid a great tribute to the Lyceum regime which he called 'the National theatre of the English world':

> The Lyceum was the embodiment of all that is refined, sumptuous and noble in English histrionic art. It was scarcely progressive, perhaps old-fashioned in its methods, but 'noblesse oblige' was writ large over its porch, and inside there reigned, since Irving was its ruler, faultless decorum wedded to impressive respect of tradition. Sir Henry Irving himself united in his personality all the gifts which are becoming to the leader of a great profession … He ruled with tact and with taste … nothing but perfect order, discipline, and calmness. First nights at the Lyceum were something more than mere theatrical novelties. Their importance was second only to great political events. All London awaited them with keen interest; countless pens were ready to chronicle the history of the evening; the cables spread the news of the trial and the verdict across the oceans, and the next day millions would eagerly devour and discuss the reports of the play and players.

Grein argued that the new company would take the burden of administration off his shoulders, he could devote himself fully to the artistic side of his activities and this could prove his 'Rejuvenescence'.

> And the result will be that he will conquer many who are slow to recognise his greatness … His detractors were principally people who rarely went to the Lyceum, or those who only saw our great actor in his creations of Romeo, of Hamlet, of Benedick, parts he felt bound to perform in order to maintain the motto of his house and the standard of the first theatre in the English world. They only saw Irving at his worst, and under the yoke of personal peculiarities; his grandeur in *Louis XI*, his humour in *Robert Macaire*, his magnificent dignity in *Becket* and *Richelieu*, all that was unknown to them, for Irving often changed his programmes, and his best known parts were by no means his best. In the future, I believe, unhampered by the desire of establishing a record of versatility, and (it is hoped) by the necessity of dividing honours with Miss Ellen Terry by the selection

of plays particularly suited to her, Sir Henry will be able to neglect plays which provide him with no part.[115]

One matter which can be cleared up by empirical research is the criticism of Irving's voice. Among the most celebrated facts about Irving is that he had a very odd pronunciation of English, was sometimes inaudible and could be mannered. Edward Gordon Craig, who wrote one of the best and most closely observed studies of Irving, noted:

> He would say 'Gud' for 'God'; 'Cut-thrut dug' for 'Cut-throat dog' (Shylock); 'Tack the rup frum mey nek' for 'Take the rope from my neck' (Mathias in *The Bells*); 'Ritz' for 'Rich' (Mathias) ... for 'good', Irving said 'god'; sight was 'seyt'; stood was 'stod'; smote became 'smot'; hand was often 'hond' or 'hend'.[116]

Irving was sufficiently conscious of the repeated criticisms to ask Ellen Terry if he really did say 'Gud' for 'God' and all the rest. She replied: 'I said straight out that he *did* say his vowels in a peculiar way.'[117]

No films of Irving exist or ever existed but almost miraculously there are very early Edison cylinder recordings by Irving of three speeches, two, dating from 1898, from *Richard III* and *Becket* and one from *Henry VIII* (recording date unknown), as well as two poems, Monk Lewis's *The Maniac* and Sir Edwin Arnold's *The Feast of Belshazzar*, dating from 1888. They were traced and identified by BBC producer Bennett Maxwell and actor Richard Bebb. Their findings were broadcast in a fascinating Radio 3 programme in the 1960s and the story was told again in Bennett Maxwell's lecture to the Irving Society in 1999.[118] Extraordinarily there is absolutely no evidence of any of these vocal peculiarities on the recordings. While it is the voice of an elderly man, the delivery and pronunciation are normal. Why then, since this odd delivery was not natural to him, did he persist in it, when it caused such continued and indeed virulent criticism?

Richard Bebb believes that he adopted his peculiar method of voice projection in order to conquer the serious stammer from which he suffered in his youth. The playwright Henry Arthur Jones has left a vivid description of Irving's voice:

> The words were sparingly ejaculated from the roof of the mouth and the base of the nose through narrowed teeth and lips, in a hard, thin, supercaustic tone, as bloodless and dry as the caked grey pumice. The open vowels were instinctively avoided and clipped down in his own private way; many of the o's and broad a's became almost i's and e's; not a word came from the throat or chest, much less from the heart; every syllable in the short sentences was precise, calculated, barbed, and reached its mark. This method of utterance could not, of course, be used to convey frank, generous utterance, or to deal wholeheartedly with any subject. But it was tremendously effective, searching, withering, forbidding, exclusive, dominating, unanswerable. It was like a jet of carbolic acid.[119]

Lena Ashwell, the actress, who worked with Irving, recalled:

> He had a high, thin voice, and when he needed depth of tone to express the seething passion that was in him he had no quality of sound to carry the message to his audience. So he prolonged the vowel sounds in a peculiar and sometimes irritating way. Added to this he suffered from catarrh.[120]

Here we have all the elements of an answer. As a sufferer from catarrh myself, I can testify to the fact that you clip your words in order to avoid swallowing them. Irving spoke from the back of the throat and from the nose, and not from the chest, like most actors. He could not project his voice as far as those who used the chest, hence the inaudibility. So he made a virtue of it by changing the stress of words for effect. As Craig said: 'his tendency was to enrich the sounds of words to make them more expressive rather than refined'.[121] We have an example of this in the *Richard III* recording when he growls: 'Dogs *bark* at me as I halt by them'. When researching the role of Richard III during the 1940's, Laurence Olivier talked to old actors who had seen Irving and he listened to their impersonations of him.[122] That high, clipped, narrow, nasal voice used by Olivier as Richard III, preserved in the 1955 film version of the play, can be seen as Olivier's version of Irving's Richard III voice. It fits exactly the description of the Irving voice recorded by Henry Arthur Jones. The reason that the mannerisms do not appear on the recordings is simple. Irving was not projecting his voice to the back of the stalls and did not need to have recourse to his old vocal devices. This particular vocal quality does much to explain his success in certain roles and his failure in others.

Theatre Royal, Bradford.

Lessee - - JOHN HART.

MONDAY, OCTOBER 9TH. 1905, FOR SIX NIGHTS.

FAREWELL TO HENRY IRVING

TUESDAY and FRIDAY NIGHTS, Oct. 10th and 13th at 7.30

❧ BECKET ❧

By ALFRED LORD TENNYSON.

ADAPTED FOR THE STAGE BY HENRY IRVING.

Thomas Becket { Chancellor of England, afterwards Archbishop }	**HENRY IRVING**
Henry II. (King of England)	Mr. GERALD LAWRENCE
King Louis of France	Mr. H. B. STANFORD
Gilbert Foliot (Bishop of London)	Mr. H. ASHETON TONGE
Roger (Archbishop of York)	Mr. WILLIAM LUGG
John of Salisbury } Friends of {	Mr. MARK PATON
Herbert of Bosham } Becket {	Mr. JAMES HEARN
John of Oxford (Called the Swearer)	Mr. T. REYNOLDS
Sir Reginald Fitzurse } The Four Knights of {	Mr. FRANK TYARS
Sir Richard de Brito } the King's Household, {	Mr. G. GRAYSTONE
Sir William de Tracy } Enemies of {	Mr. L. BELMORE
Sir Hugh de Morville } Becket {	Mr. LESLIE PALMER
Richard de Hastings (Grand Prior of Templars)	Mr. J. ARCHER
The Youngest Knight Templar	Mr. STEVENS
Lord Leicester	Mr. VINCENT STERNROYD
Philip de Eleemosyna (The Pope's Almoner)	Mr. W. J. YELDMAN
Herald	Mr. H. R. COOK
Monk	Mr. A. GURNEY
Geoffrey (Son of Rosamund and Henry)	Master TONGE
Retainers {	Mr. A. FISHER / Mr. HAYES
Countrymen {	Mr. CHARLES DODSWORTH / Mr. R. BRENNAN
Servant	Mr. W. MARION
Eleanor of Aquataine { Queen of England, divorced from Louis of France }	Mrs. CECIL RALEIGH
Margery	Miss GRACE HAMPTON
Rosamund de Clifford (Fair Rosamund)	Miss EDITH WYNNE MATTHISON

Knights, Monks, Heralds, Soldiers, Retainers, &c.

Synopsis of Scenery

PROLOGUE.

Scene 1—A Castle in Normandy,   Scene 2—The Same:

ACT I.   Scene 1—Becket's House in London.   Scene 2—Street in Northampton leading to the Castle.   Scene 3—The Same: Scene 4—The Hall in Northampton Castle.

ACT II.   Scene—Rosamund's Bower,

ACT III.   Scene I—Montmirail, "The Meeting of the Kings,"   Scene 2—Outside the Wood, near Rosamund's Bower.   Scene 3—Rosamund's Bower.

"At 'Merton the Archbishop assumed the ordinary habit of the black canons of the Augustinian Rule, which dress he wore to the end of his life."—GRIM,

ACT IV: Scene I—Castle in Normandy—King's Chamber.   2—A Room in Canterbury Monastery.   Scene 3—North Transept of Canterbury Cathedral.   Period—12th Century.

The Scenery has been Specially Painted by Mr. Joseph Harker.
The Overture and Incidental Music by Sir Charles Villiers Stanford.
The Costumes, &c., from designs by Mrs. Comyns Carr and Mr. Charles Cattermole, R.I., executed by Mrs. Nettleship, August et Cie, and Messrs. L. and H. Nathan. Wigs by W. Clarkson.

Playbill from Tennyson's *Becket*, Bradford, 10 and 13 October 1905.

11

English History

More enduring and more influential than almost any academic history is popular memory. There is a popular memory of history which runs alongside and frequently eclipses academic history. It is a heady amalgam of popular painting, poetry, novels, plays and films, a version of history that is essentially unconcerned with causes and consequences, economics and statistics, but centres firmly on the colourful and the arresting, the personal and the emotional, on battles and boudoirs. It remains a fact that there are more historical films about king's mistresses than about the rise of the gentry, the Great Reform Act and the Reformation all put together. It may also influence public opinion in a way that academic history rarely does.

In his inspiring and illuminating book *Theatres of Memory*, Raphael Samuel sought to rescue popular memory from what another great historian called 'the enormous condescension of posterity'. Samuel wrote:

> The starting point of *Theatres of Memory* … is that history is not the prerogative of the historians, nor even, as postmodernism contends, an historian's 'invention'. It is rather, a social form of knowledge, the work, in any given instance, of a thousand different hands. If this is true, the point of the address in any discussion of historiography should not be the work of an individual scholar, nor yet the rival schools of interpretation, but rather the ensemble of activities and practices in which ideas of history are embedded or a dialectic of past-present relations is rehearsed.[1]

He points among other example to popular ballads, legends and local lore, novels and poems, nineteenth-century history readers, *Robinson Crusoe*, Brother Cadfael, the *Good Old Days*, the *Eagle* comic and *Blackadder*, as much historical documents, he asserts, as cartularies and pipe rolls. For the student of Victorian theatre, historical plays are part of this common store of popular historical knowledge.

The past was central to Victorian culture. As Carlyle wrote in his lectures on heroes and hero-worship:

> the whole Past … is the possession of the Present; the Past had always something *true*, and is a precious possession. In a different time, in a different place, it is always some other *side* of our common Human Nature that has been developing itself. The actual True is the *sum* of all these; not any one of them by itself constitutes what of Human Nature is hitherto developed.[2]

The past for the Victorians thus held the key to understanding both the present and human nature. It was Carlyle too who powerfully advanced 'The Great Man' theory of history.[3] This became an article of faith in nineteenth-century culture.

The Romantic movement had had a major impact upon history. One of the key characteristics of Romanticism was a passion for history. History permeated literature and painting and the representation of history became the function of new modes of popular spectacle such as the panorama and the diorama. According to Stephen Bann: 'An irreversible shift had occurred, and history – from being a localized and specific practice within the cultural topography – became a flood that overrode all disciplinary barriers, and, finally, when the barriers were no longer easy to perceive, became a substratum in almost every type of cultural activity.'[4] The eighteenth-century cult of the picturesque stimulated the rise of a new kind of history prominent in the 1820s, 1830s and 1840s. Strongly influenced by Sir Walter Scott, it was a fusion of the antiquarian and the picturesque. The 1840s and 1850s, in particular, saw the mushrooming of antiquarian societies. Their activities were prodigious. They published antique documents, undertook archaeological excavations, collected coins, manuscripts, relics and artefacts, published scholarly journals, compiled local histories and guide-books, charted the histories of churches and castles, drew up family genealogies, studied and interpreted heraldry, collected folk-tales, superstitions and traditions and corresponded voluminously. The antiquarians sought 'to collect, to preserve, and to transmit the memory of the past'.[5] Their method was one of collection, description and classification. Their activities were characterized by a strong sense of place and a strong sense of the visual. They inspired a whole school of historical novelists, notably W. Harrison Ainsworth, who in a succession of best-selling novels such as *The Tower of London* (1840), *Windsor Castle* (1843) and *The Lancashire Witches* (1849) married historical narrative with romantic melodrama and drenched both in antiquarian detail about costume, diet, buildings and customs. Novelists and antiquarians alike were stimulated by the destruction wrought by the Industrial Revolution, by the desire to celebrate provincial pride and regional identity and by the concern for the loss of customs and traditions which bound together the community and transcended emerging class tensions.

The dominance of picturesque antiquarian history was short-lived. A major split developed from the 1850s onwards between historians and antiquarians, between professionals and amateurs. Influenced by intellectual developments in Germany, a class of professional historians emerged in Britain. Their methods were critical, scientific and analytical, their approach professedly objective. They were committed to archival research, increasingly specialized in choice of subject and concentrated in particular on the political and constitutional history of Britain. Developments such as the opening of the Public Record Office, the creation of the Historic Manuscripts Commission, publication of the Calendars of State Papers and the Rolls series, and the development of academic history teaching at the ancient universities led to the creation of an intellectual hegemony by an exclusive elite dominated by the Golden Triangle of Oxford, Cambridge and London, that remains with us to this day. They disparaged and marginalized the antiquarians, deriding them as 'picturesque compilers'. So 'picturesque', which at the start of the 19th century had been a term of approbation, had become a term of disapproval by the end of the century. The emerging split was apparent to Lord Macaulay as early as 1828 when he wrote:

> To make the past present, to bring the distant near, to place us in the society of a great man or on the eminence which overlooks the field of a mighty battle ... to call up our ancestors before us with all their peculiarities of language, manners and garb, to show us over their houses, to seat us at their tables, to rummage their old-fashioned wardrobes, to explain the uses of their ponderous furniture, these parts of the duty which properly belongs to the historian, have been appropriated by the historical novelist. On the other hand, to extract the philosophy of history, to direct our judgment of events and men, to trace the connections of causes and effects, and to draw from the occurrences of former times the general lessons of moral and political wisdom, has become the business of a distinct class of writers.[6]

He went on to compare the work of the historian to a map and the work of the historical novelist to the painted landscape, the one scientific, the other imaginative. Nothing better demonstrates the split than the derision with which professional historians greeted the appointment of the historical novelist Charles Kingsley as Regius Professor of History at Cambridge in 1860, though as a matter of fact his lectures were packed, suggesting the preference of Victorian undergraduates for paintings over maps.

After this, however, there was no going back. Real history was for the specialists and the professionals, for the small circulation scholarly journals, for even smaller circulation academic monographs, for learned conferences and for heavily footnoted articles. Popular history was drawn from elsewhere – from poetry, paintings, novels and articles. As Roy Strong has argued, up to the 1950s history meant for most British children a set of visual images, powerful, romantic, anecdotal. History was taught as a romantic and nationalistic saga of heroes and heroines, kings and queens, wars and conquests, and the steady unfolding of Britain's destiny as both a parliamentary democracy and the mightiest empire since the fall of Rome. History became a mental panorama, defined by Strong as:

> Boadicea rallying the Ancient British against the autocratic forces of Rome, valiant Anglo-Saxons repelling Danish invaders from the shore of Britain, King John signing the Great Charter, the foundation of our liberties, innocent child Princes murdered in the Tower, beautiful tragic Queens making their way towards the scaffold, heroic

Cavaliers on the battlefield, Jacobites fighting for a lost cause ... the Saxon hero-king Alfred, the valiant crusader Richard I, the wicked hunchback Richard III, bluff King Hal, magnificent Elizabeth, innocent Jane Grey, doomed Mary of Scotland, sad-faced Charles I and stern-countenanced Cromwell, the Merry Monarch and Bonnie Prince Charlie.[7]

These were indelibly fixed in the minds of the young because history text books were regularly illustrated with the best examples of Victorian history painting, whose heyday was 1840–70 but which flourished throughout the nineteenth century. It was particularly preoccupied with the middle ages and the Tudor and Stuart periods. The paintings were characterized by an antiquarian accuracy in costumes and settings, the instilling of moral lessons – the history painter Benjamin West saw his work as providing 'invaluable lessons in religion, love of country and morality'– and the foregrounding of human interest stories to make the past come alive.[8] Typical of these paintings were Paul Delaroche's poignant 1830 study of the Princes in the Tower contemplating their fate, Millais' 1870 painting *The Boyhood of Raleigh* in which two sixteenth-century boys are held spellbound by a seaman's stories of his voyages across the oceans, and Frederick Goodall's *An Episode from the Happier Days of Charles I*, an 1853 painting depicting a carefree Stuart royal family on an outing on the Thames. Such paintings did not just remain in galleries but were widely disseminated in cheap prints. They provided a permanent visual memory of a highly selective and romanticized past.

Just as in paintings, so too in the Victorian theatre history was a staple subject, suggesting that Victorian playhouses might well deserve the nickname 'theatres of memory'. As theatre historian Richard Schoch has written: 'Performance was a powerful agent of historical consciousness in the nineteenth century ... greater than that of literature, painting or even photography'.[9] The visual imagery of these historical plays was often directly inspired by famous paintings and plays were staged, framed and lit like paintings. Performance and visual imagery combined to create a popular memory of British history, but one which was often at odds with the academic consensus.

Irving's productions at the Lyceum were almost exclusively historical. But this did not mean a rejection of the present, for Irving, like so many Victorians, saw history as a mirror to hold up to the present. Irving's view of history was consistent and characteristically Victorian. The political upheaval initiated by the French Revolution and the social upheavals set in train by the Industrial Revolution created in the Victorian age a powerful fear of chaos, the fear that everything good and desirable and worthwhile might be lost, and so, along with the imperial self-confidence, went a sense of the essential fragility of order, a consciousness of how thin was the crust of civilization. Therefore concern for order, social, moral and political, underlies his history plays. Irving also believed that drama sprang from character, character as the nineteenth century, and in particular Samuel Smiles, defined it: 'character is human nature in its best form, it is moral order embodied in the individual ... The strength, the industry and the civilization of nations all depend on individual character.'[10] Both these beliefs are embodied in Irving's production of *Charles the First*.

It was Irving's suggestion to W.G. Wills, the bohemian Irish painter and playwright, who was the Lyceum's resident dramatist, that he write a play based on the engraving of Frederick Goodall's painting *An Episode from the Happier Days of Charles I*. This, one of the most popular paintings of the nineteenth century, was a lyrical picture of mother, father, children, servants and dogs on a pleasure barge on the Thames with swans floating gracefully around them. The central theme of the play was to be the evocation of this picture of domestic bliss and its destruction by Cromwell. It was Irving's instruction that audience sympathy was to remain with Charles throughout and this harmonized with Wills's own inclination. His brother and biographer described him as a Royalist and a Tory, and he had the true Irishman's hatred of Cromwell.[11] Wills's play thus not only showed Charles I as saint and martyr but Cromwell as villain and hypocrite.

The play, which opened on 28 September 1872, was in four acts. It made plain that opposition to the king was treason and that Charles I was defending the constitution against rebellion and anarchy. Act 1 at Hampton Court establishes Charles as a loving and devoted husband and father. In Act 2, Cromwell brings parliament's demand – that he surrender his advisers – to the King at Whitehall. But privately he offers to drop his opposition in return for an earldom. When Charles rejects his proposal, Cromwell treacherously tries to seize the King, who is rescued by loyal cavaliers. In Act 3, Charles is betrayed by Moray and the other Scottish lords at Newark and is captured by Cromwell and the parliamentary forces. Act 4 has Queen Henrietta Maria interceding in vain with Cromwell for her husband's life, a final touching meeting between the King and his wife and younger children, and his departure for execution with the single word 'Remember'.

The critical reaction to the play is instructive. It was generally seen as a succession of rather static tableaux rather than a fully integrated and dramatically coherent work. It was criticized for the total absence of humour and of large-scale action scenes, the prevailing tone of unrelieved melancholy and the inadequate characterization of Cromwell. But the stage pictures, the scenery and the settings, some of Wills's poetry and above all Irving's performance as Charles I won universal praise. J.H. Barnes, attending the opening night, recalled that when the curtain rose on the first scene, a glade at Hampton Court, it was so beautifully painted that the audience refused to allow the play to continue until the painter, Hawes Craven, had taken a bow. 'I have never seen this occur on any other occasion.'[12] Irving's dignity and pathos as the King regularly reduced audiences to tears. The *Daily News* (30 September 1872) reported of the first night: 'During the last act there was scarcely a dry eye in the house. Women sobbed openly, and even men showed emotion which comported ill with the habitual serenity of the stalls.'

The *Observer* thought Charles I 'incomparably' Irving's best performance. The *Morning Post* declared that he had 'placed himself at the head of the school of character actors'. The *Daily Telegraph* thought he had 'never done anything better' and the *Standard* enthused: 'A more complete and more deserved triumph has rarely ever been gained, and by his perfect … realisation of an historical character so familiar to all … Mr Irving has unquestionably asserted his right to take the foremost place among tragedians of the day.'[13]

Even more interesting than the aesthetic judgements is that a fierce controversy arose about the historical accuracy of the play, in particular the depiction of Cromwell. The situation was not helped by the fact that, as all the critics agreed, George Belmore, a bluff comedian, was badly miscast as Cromwell. He was eventually replaced in the role by Henry Forrester. Wills was forced to defend himself in print. He wrote to the *Morning Post* citing a series of exclusively Liberal historians to support his factual accuracy. But, in an article in the *Theatre* in April 1880, he defended dramatic license as vital to the dramatization of history:

> History, as it actually falls out, shows a lamentable want of dramatic art; events are strung, and people are brought together, in a promiscuous fashion, and are not compacted into a plot suited for representation.

So the dramatist must rearrange events and provide structure.

> There is certainly nothing sacred in history, but yet we must set one limit to dramatic licence in dealing with facts. The author may shake them in his kaleidoscope as much as he pleases, provided he keeps within the boundary of not shocking the historical conscience of the public. There is a certain common acquaintance with history which he may assume his audience to possess; this he must respect, or … he will break the illusion of his historical tableaux.

Yet he claims value for such dramatized versions of history: 'surely there is some educating use in it – some teaching of national self-respect – some awakening of interest in the past'.[14] But some critics were outraged by the depiction of Cromwell. Dutton Cook in the *Pall Mall Gazette* called Wills 'faithless as a historian' and 'weak to insipidity as a dramatist', and scorned his characterization of Charles I. 'Of his sins against his people, of his perfidy and tyranny … no word is breathed … the play is mainly occupied with the sublimation of the 'Royal Martyr', reasonable enough in a cavalier writer of the time but in a modern author, with a History of England at his elbow, hardly to be tolerated.'[15]

The *Spectator* described as 'utterly unhistorical' the picture of Charles I as 'a magnanimous, gallant, chivalrous, right royal king, loving to his people, faithful to his friends, pious and patriotic, passionately devoted to his wife and children, as firmly attached to his duties as to his rights'.[16] This view of the play as a play persisted. As late as 1899 Charles Hiatt, in his biography of Irving, was calling the play 'a libel on a great hero and what is more, it is libel at once foolish and feeble'; and, in his 1906 biography of the actor, Haldane McFall called the play a 'snob's lie, and a vulgar one, that wasn't fit to gull even the ignorant'.[17] This passionate engagement with the play was due to the transformation in the standing of Cromwell during the nineteenth century. *The Times* (30 September 1872) acknowledged this, reporting: 'When the oldest among us were boys, any amount of abuse might be heaped at pleasure on the memory of the protector, and though at the present day, everybody does not acknowledge his right to the niche assigned to him in Mr Carlyle's Pantheon, few will be satisfied to find him such an abject rascal as he appears in this new play.'

The English Civil War was still a live issue in the nineteenth century, reflecting as it did both the anxieties and aspirations of the Victorians: the fear of rebellion and revolution, the continuing conflict between Anglicanism and Dissent, and the renewed fear of Catholicism.[18] 'We are cavaliers or roundheads before we are conservatives or liberals', wrote the Victorian historian W.E.H. Lecky, testifying to the Civil War's centrality.[19]

The reaction to the play *Charles the First* has to be seen in particular in the context of the reputation of Cromwell.[20] The 1840s – the bicentenary of the Civil War – had seen a major rehabilitation of the Lord Protector in novels, poems, songs, essays, sermons, paintings and editorials. In the eighteenth and early nineteenth centuries he had been reviled by conservatives as a tyrant, regicide and fanatic and by radicals as a hypocrite and dictator. But Thomas Carlyle's *Letters and Speeches of Cromwell* (1845) initiated a hero-worshipping cult by depicting him as the classic English leader, sincere, zealous and resolute, devoted to duty and to his country, and seeking the fulfilment of God's purpose on earth and the maintenance of the moral order. Carlyle was in part constructing the image of the idealized leader as a reproach to the governing elites of his own time. But as S.R. Gardiner, the doyen of Civil War historians, was to write, Carlyle 'changed our whole conception of English history at its most heroic period'.[21] After this, Cromwell became the hero of Dissenters as the epitome of the Nonconformist conscience, the great Protestant. He became the hero of imperialists as the supreme patriot, the man who promoted the navy, conquered Ireland, acquired Jamaica and repulsed foreign foes. Whigs saw him as the hero of the onward march of progress and parliamentary democracy, the proto-Victorian liberal, defender of religious toleration, the constitution and England's national interests. He even became a middle-class role model, included by Samuel

Smiles in his book *Character* as an embodiment of character and conscience. Although the Tories and the Irish never accepted this, S.R. Gardiner by the end of the century could describe him as 'the national hero of the nineteenth century' and 'the most typical Englishman of all time'.[22] The Interregnum had been shorn of revolutionary significance. Cromwell had been assimilated to the prevailing ideologies of the age – Evangelicalism, Liberalism and Imperialism – and now transcended the narrow sectarian divides.

Cromwell's apotheosis as popular hero came in 1899 when on the three hundredth anniversary of his birth a statue of the Lord Protector was unveiled just outside the House of Commons by the Prime Minister, Lord Rosebery. Several previous proposals to erect a statue had failed.[23] But by 1899 Cromwell was widely accepted as an English national hero like Drake and Nelson. It was this heroic image that was enshrined in the popular paintings of the time, paintings like T. Maguire's *Cromwell Refusing the Crown of England*, exhibited throughout England in 1859 and 1860 to great acclaim; and Augustus Egg's *The Night before Naseby* (1859), with Cromwell at prayer in his tent. The heroic image was reinforced later in the century by such canvasses as Ford Madox Brown's *Cromwell Discussing the Protection of the Vaudois with Milton and Andrew Marvell* (1878), David Wilkie Wynfield's *The Death of Oliver Cromwell* (1867), with its long catalogue quotation from Carlyle on the Lord Protector's last moments, and A.C. Gow's *Cromwell at Dunbar* (1886) with Cromwell leading his troops in singing 'The Old Hundredth'.

Nevertheless partisanship prevailed, with the King a particular hero to conservatives and royalists, and Cromwell a hero to radicals and liberals. In the context of the play *Charles the First*, the partisanship took the form of the staging of a rival play. *Cromwell* by Colonel Alfred Bate Richards opened on 21 December 1872 at the Queen's Theatre. Colonel Richards (1820–1876), barrister, journalist, playwright and one of the leading proponents of the Volunteer Movement, had written a series of five act tragedies in the 1840s; *Cromwell* dated from 1847. He had gone on to a career in journalism, being briefly the first editor of the *Daily Telegraph* (1855) and later from 1870 until his death, the editor of the *Morning Advertizer*. The play was dedicated to Thomas Carlyle, who, according to Richards, had 'with labour and eloquence and vehement truth-telling, made CROMWELL and his work apparent to this generation, and given him his right place in all right-thinking minds'. Richards was slightly put out when Carlyle replied saying that he had got the character of Cromwell right but tried to pack too much into the play.[24] The play celebrated Cromwell as the great Protestant hero, the man who defended the Vaudois from persecution, as the Liberal hero who readmitted the Jews to England, as the patriot hero who built up the Navy and extended the British Empire. He was seen as a reluctant revolutionary, driven to execute the King only because of the perfidy of Charles and claiming not to be opposed to kingship in principle, only the tyranny of the Stuarts. The play included a 'realization' of Paul Delaroche's famous painting of Cromwell looking into the coffin of Charles I. But it flopped.

Colonel Richards promptly reissued his play with a new preface, indignantly explaining the play's failure. He praised the actors, including George Rignold 'for his noble conception of Cromwell', performed even though at the time he was 'labouring under a severe and trying illness, which at last induced me to urge him to give up the part, and thereby stop the run of the piece'. But he denounced the production:

> The Play had not been rehearsed for time, and had never had a complete and satisfactory rehearsal at all. It was prematurely announced for representation without my privity or consent. The management paid me the high but perilous compliment of doing little indeed for *Cromwell*, in the way of scenery or mounting, which in these days is almost too severe a test ... I conceive that an historical play of the style and pretensions of *Cromwell* should have the full benefit of scenic art and display which is so freely accorded to the sensational melodramas and burlesques. *Cromwell* was not even allowed a moon, a chorus of Spirits ... nor a numerically respectable army of supers; and the fleet, which should have been pictured within sight of the Old Palace of Greenwich, and whose guns should have sounded ... 'England's proud reply' to the Ambassadors, was simply rendered ludicrous. In short, the Play was starved.[25]

Dutton Cook pronounced it clumsy, prolix and at four hours interminably protracted. He reported that:

> Weariness, perplexity and depression afflicted the spectators at a very early period of the performance. Unable to approve and yet anxious for amusement, they sought to find opportunities of expressing their derision, and visited upon the players the defects of the play. Further they formed themselves into two parties, hissing or cheering according as the sentiment expressed by the characters was Royalist or Republican.[26]

Partisanship also manifested itself during the visit to *Charles the First*, on 22 October 1872, of the Prince and Princess of Wales. The *Standard* reported that one-third of the audience were staunch Royalists, one-half interested in the play and not politics, and a small minority devoted Liberals, 'jealous of every touch that seemed to blot the fair fame of the radical idol'.[27] The two sides cheered and hissed alternately but the Royalist cheers drowned out the Radical hisses during the crucial confrontations. The play ran in the first instance for 180 nights and it remained in Irving's repertoire, regularly performed not just in London but in the provinces and America, until his death in 1905. Whatever the critics and the historians thought, the public loved it and took Irving's *Charles the First* to their hearts.[28] But arguably it had more than just an effect on the popular memory of history.

Charles the First became the only one of Wills's more than twenty-five plays to be published, a clear indication of its perceived significance. The text was published by Blackwoods in 1873, the editor of the text noting that it 'appealed to the sympathies of the public more strongly than any new poetical work brought out within the memory of living men. People not generally used to the melting mood felt themselves compelled to shed tears, not over the words of some respectable half-comic paterfamilias in a domestic tale, but over the sorrows of a king who perished considerably more than two centuries ago.' He defended the author against charges of inaccuracy:

> The aim and mission of the historical dramatist were not the same of those of the historians; but his main purpose was the exhibition of historical characters strongly and sharply defined, and to effect this purpose minor circumstances might be modified. When history is to be represented on the stage it is of more importance that the incidents should be typical than they should accurately copy facts.

But what is more interesting is that the editor acknowledged the importance of the play in restoring support for the monarchy.

> If Mr Wills's play derives interest from the period to which it refers, there is no doubt that it also derived interest from the period of its production. Within a comparatively short time the people of this country seem to have recovered that respect for ancient national institutions to which England owes her greatness, but which, under hostile influences, threatened not long ago to become weakened, if not extinct. Avoiding political phrases, we may fairly say that we are living in a day of wholesome 'constitutional reaction' and that the revived feeling of loyalty finds its expression in *Charles I*. The declaration of the unfortunate monarch that he died a martyr to the Constitution has been borne in mind by Mr Wills. It is as the guardian of the constitution against the irruptions of the Anarchy, and also as the pattern of the true English gentleman that he places Charles upon the stage.[29]

This comment is highly significant. For in the early 1870s the monarchy had hit a lowpoint in popularity. The Queen's long seclusion in Windsor, rumours of an affair with her highland *ghillie* John Brown, and the Prince of Wales's involvement in an unsavoury divorce scandal, all combined to give a boost to republicanism. There were anti-monarchy demonstrations in London, eighty-four republican clubs were set up, a new journal the *Republican*, was launched, a much-read pamphlet, *What Does She Do With It?*, criticized royal finances and leading politicians declared republican sympathies. But the Prince of Wales's near fatal illness and his recovery from typhoid fever and the Queen's return to public life scotched the republican movement. By the last decade of her life Victoria had become a venerable and revered national icon.[30] The production of *Charles the First* tapped into and strongly endorsed this changing national mood.

What *Charles the First* was doing was reviving successfully on the stage the bourgeois domestic interpretation of monarchy which had developed strongly during the lifetime of Victoria and Albert. Victoria and Albert and their nine children had been depicted as a devoted family unit, celebrated in the paintings of F.X. Winterhalter. They were celebrated, too, for their family Christmases and their family summer holidays at Balmoral (their essence conveyed in the best-selling selections from the Queen's journals of 'our life in the Highlands' published in 1868 and 1884). It was all part of a process that has been called 'the domestication of majesty', a process that developed powerfully in the late eighteenth century, a response to the rise of the bourgeois sensibility, a reaction to the destruction and disorder of the French Revolution and a substitution of universal domestic sentiment for specifically and exclusively dynastic imagery.[31] *Charles the First* powerfully reinforced the domestic interpretation of monarchy that was in tune with these middle-class sensibilities, which made 'Home, Sweet Home' virtually a second national anthem.

It also drew on an established and strongly romantic pictorial tradition. More works of art dealing with Charles I, Oliver Cromwell, Henrietta Maria and the Civil War were produced than on any other period in British history.[32] One hundred and seventy-five pictures on these themes were hung in the Royal Academy between 1820 and 1900.[33]

One strong theme was that of Charles I and his family. Daniel Maclise's *An Interview between Charles I and Cromwell* (*c.* 1836) shows a melancholy Charles with children and dogs and a sinister Cromwell; Charles Lucy painted in 1850 the parting of Charles I from his two younger children on the day prior to his execution; and Frederick Goodall painted 'an episode from the happier days of Charles I' in 1853. The play *Charles the First* thus drew on familiar and recognized visual images for part of its impact. Act 1 ended with a 'realization' or stage recreation of Goodall's painting as the family boarded the royal barge for the river trip; and the parting of Charles I and Henrietta Maria in Act 4 was modelled on Millais' popular 1852 painting *A Huguenot Refusing to Seek Safety by Wearing the Roman Catholic Badge*, paralleling Charles's refusal of the proposal that he gain his life by abdicating and handing over his son, the Prince of Wales, to the Roundheads.[34] It also underlined Charles's firm statement to his Catholic wife: 'Our English land is Protestant' and warning her against intriguing with the Jesuits. Irving was also made up to resemble the famous Van Dyck portrait of Charles I and *The Times* (30 September 1872) noted that at his first appearance 'a burst of applause rose on every side' because 'a painting of Van Dyck's seemed to have started living from its frame'. It is worth noting too that Paul Delaroche's *The Mockery of Charles I by Roundhead Soldiers* (1837) deliberately evokes the mocking of Christ. Wills's play evoked a similar comparison in Charles's powerful speech denouncing Moray as Judas. The family idea is foregrounded too in popular literature with Charles I projected as ideal monarch and paterfamilias in Scott's *Woodstock* (1826) and Captain Marryat's *Children of the New Forest*

(1847). This literary and pictorial tradition is at odds with the historical tradition which had developed by the end of the nineteenth century.[35]

The Whig theory of English constitutional history was to be found in most history textbooks.[36] It interpreted English history as a gradually unfolding story of constitutional government and parliamentary rule, in which the Anglo-Saxon Witan, Magna Carta and the development of Parliament in the fourteenth and fifteenth centuries, the English Civil War and the Glorious Revolution were the highlights. According to Valerie Chancellor, 'opinions about the struggles between the King and parliament in the seventeenth century were, on the whole, well disposed to the latter. Most authors depicted the Royalists as the revolutionaries or at least those who were too short-sighted to understand the real meaning of the constitution. A typical judgement of the reign of Charles I is that "The struggle in this reign was between absolute and constitutional monarchy. And the latter prevailed."' Cromwell, despite being the architect of the King's execution, gets 'on the whole a favourable reception from textbooks,' being depicted as champion of law and order and religious toleration, and a courageous and skilful soldier.[37]

Typical perhaps of the judgements of historians on the protagonists in the struggle is the verdict of T.F. Tout, the eminent Professor of Medieval and Modern History at Manchester, who in his Longman textbook *A History of Britain* (1907) wrote that Charles I was 'dignified, good-looking, grave, temperate and religious. But he was neither clever nor clear-headed and he was unable to understand any viewpoint but his own. He had much faith in himself, but little in his people', but 'he died so nobly and piously that his incurable faults were almost forgotten'. Cromwell 'always efficient and honest' was 'one of the best and wisest rulers England ever had', a promoter of religious toleration and overseas expansion. 'But for all his greatness we must never forget that he ruled by the sword and not with the consent of the people.'[38] We are here almost in Sellar and Yeatman territory, but it is worth remembering that in the admirable *1066 and All That* Sellar and Yeatman were satirizing the 'givens' of several generations of textbook which distilled the wisdom of the academics who really did think the 'the cavaliers were wrong but romantic and the roundheads right but repulsive'. So what are we getting in the Victorian theatre as exemplified by *Charles the First* is the extension of a popular mythic version of history that runs alongside and differs markedly from academic history.

The significance of *Charles the First* (1872) was, as Stephen Watt points out, that, together with Tom Taylor's *'Twixt Axe and Crown* (1870), it represented the rebirth of the serious historical play which had fallen out of favour in the 1850s and 1860s.[39] *The Times* (23 December 1872), describing the play as epoch-making, declared that 'our authors, since the time of Lord Lytton's *Richelieu*, seemed almost to have forgotten the possibility of placing really prominent figures of history upon theatrical boards'. *Richelieu* and *Louis XI* had entered the repertoire, but new history plays such as Charles Kean's production of *The First Printer* and Phelps's production of *James the Sixth* had failed, and henceforth Phelps avoided new historical plays and Kean concentrated on Shakespeare. As a result, the legitimate historical drama was largely absent from the stage. *'Twixt Axe and Crown* and *Charles the First* re-established the history play as a viable theatrical attraction.

There was, in addition to box office failure, the question of censorship. Censorship was a problem in the turbulent early decades of the century when the fear of revolution at home and abroad was a preoccupation of the authorities. Charles I had been successfully depicted on stage in William Havard's *The Tragedy of Charles I* (1737), in which, prefiguring Wills, Havard had depicted the King as a devoted husband and father who succumbs to the machinations of a villainous Cromwell. But when Mary Russell Mitford wrote her *Charles I* (1827), covering the imprisonment and trial of the King but featuring the same domestic elements, it was banned by the Lord Chamberlain's office, which deemed it too dangerous to show such a subject at the time. The play was produced in 1834 at the Victoria Theatre, outside the Chamberlain's jurisdiction. But its fate boded ill for historical dramas with any contemporary resonance.

The key to an avoidance of the censorial interference was to follow the precedent of the eighteenth-century playwrights John Banks and Nicholas Rowe, who had concentrated on the private lives of historical figures, avoiding the political history of their times as far as possible. This became the formula for success in the nineteenth century. As Matthew H. Wikander defined it:

> Nostalgia about the past, pity for the passionate ruler, assertions of pastoral and domestic longings are all features of historical drama throughout the nineteenth century. Despite lip-service to authenticity and historicity – in practice, usually limited to pedantic accuracy in set design – playwrights ... devoted their attentions to love intrigue rather than to the rich historical contexts available to them in the age of Macaulay.[40]

This was the model taken up by W.G. Wills and Tom Taylor. By 1870, Taylor had written some seventy plays, only rarely historical (*The Fool's Revenge*, a version of Hugo's *Le Roi S'Amuse* notably). But he followed *'Twixt Axe and Crown* with *Joan of Arc* (1871), *Lady Clancarty* (1874) and *Ann Boleyn* (1876). Significantly they all feature women. *'Twixt Axe and Crown* (1870) ran for two hundred performances. A five act blank verse tragedy, it was sympathetic to Queen Mary Tudor and depicted her as a love-starved recluse, rejected both by Edward Courtenay and her husband King Philip, dying alone and abandoned. She became in Taylor's version a submissive wife, anxious only to please her husband, yet another of the devoted wives of domestic melodrama and historical drama in the 1870s, the counterpart of Henrietta Maria in *Charles the First*, Jane Shore and

Lady Clancarty. The villains of Taylor's play were fanatical Catholics, Bishop Gardiner and Spanish Ambassador Renard. It combined domesticity, melodrama, elevated language, anti-Catholicism and a taste for national history (volumes 5 and 6 of Froude's *History of England*, covering Wolsey to the Armada, were published the day the play opened). Wikander argues that this play and others are part of a theatre of pathos and victimization: 'Their aesthetic remains affective and pathetic; their historiography remains passivist. The historical figure is dramatized as victim, of her evil counsellors or her unhappy childhood.'[41]

Taylor's plays provided starring roles for leading actresses: 'the beautiful Mrs Rousby' as Elizabeth in *'Twixt Axe and Crown*, Ada Cavendish in *Lady Clancarty* and Adelaide Neilson in *Ann Boleyn*. (Irving's failure to revive any of them perhaps stems from their lack of dominant male roles.) The success of *Charles the First*, which provided Irving with a memorable star role, was also due, says Watt, to the combination of Wills's poetic language and scrupulously accurate stage settings and costumes.[42] The programme noted: 'The scenery and appointments have been prepared from portraits of historical personages.' Wills and Taylor rediscovered and refined the important ground rules for the late Victorian dramatist. They included the selection of the best known historical figures and episodes; an emphasis on domestic activity and family life; moments of sentiment; a melodramatic opposition of hero and villain; historically accurate costumes and sets; and the 'realization' of famous paintings. They appealed to all classes by showing the human side of historical figures. Just as Wills published *Charles the First*, Taylor published his historical dramas as a collection, indicating their cultural importance.

The most notable and prestigious provider of historical plays was Alfred, Lord Tennyson. Tennyson's first play was *Queen Mary*, published in 1875. It was the first of what Tennyson called his historical trilogy, adding 'this trilogy pourtrays [*sic*] the making of England'.[43] Each play focused on a major period of conflict which shaped the history of England. *Queen Mary* (1875) dealt with the downfall of Catholicism and the birth of Protestant England; *Harold* (1876) dealt with the conflict of Saxons, Danes and Normans for supremacy and forecast 'the greatness of our composite race'; and *Becket* (1879) covered the struggle between crown and church for predominance.

Why did Tennyson at the age of sixty-five embark on the writing of plays? It has been plausibly suggested that it was his consciousness of his public role as Poet Laureate, a role which led him to 'a monumental and public meditation of England's past, on the history of the empire and civilization of which he believed himself to be the appointed voice'.[44] He sought therefore to do for English history in the nineteenth century what Shakespeare had done for it in the sixteenth, to clothe it in inspiring poetry and vivid imagery.

Having toyed with the ideas of the Armada, Lady Jane Grey and William the

Silent, Tennyson settled on *Queen Mary* after reading volume 6 of J.A. Froude's *History of England*. The play was heavily indebted to Froude, who having read a proof copy wrote enthusiastically to Tennyson to say:

> Beyond the immediate effect, you will have hit Manning and Co. a more fatal blow than a thousand pamphleteers and controversialists – besides this you have reclaimed one more section of English history from the wilderness and given it a form in which it will be fixed for ever. No one since Shakespeare has done that.[45]

The context of this was the extreme anxiety felt by Protestants in the 1870s at the steady rise of the English Catholic priests and churches since the Catholic Emancipation Act of 1829, the affirmation of Papal infallibility at the 1870 Vatican Council, and parliamentary moves to disestablish the Anglican Church. The play was a powerful reminder of the persecution of the Protestants in the reign of 'Bloody Mary'. But Hallam Tennyson recorded that his father also thought that Mary had had a raw deal from history and tradition: 'He pitied the poor girl who not only was cast down by her father from her high estate, but treated with shameless contumely by the familiar friends of her childhood.' She was therefore to become another heroine of the 'theatre of pathos'.[46]

Like Froude, Irving had read a proof copy of the play. 'Colonel' Bateman of the Lyceum took an option on it but died on 22 March 1875. His widow, who took over the lease of the theatre, agreed at Irving's prompting to produce the play. Irving announced its intended production from the Lyceum stage on 29 June 1875 to 'thunderous applause'.[47] But the play was unstageable as it stood. It ran to twenty-three scenes and forty-four characters. Although it was praised by Browning and Gladstone, and respectfully received by the serious press, Henry James pronounced it 'simply a dramatized chronicle ... it has no shape, it is cast into no mould; it has neither beginning, middle nor end'.[48]

It would have to be cut and Mrs Bateman evidently refused to sign a contract until the cuts were made – to Tennyson's annoyance. Tennyson, Irving and James Knowles, the editor of the *Contemporary Review* and a confidant of Tennyson, consulted on how it would be cut. Tennyson sent Mrs Bateman the comments and suggestions on the text by Thomas James Serle, a dramatist and the editor of the *Weekly Dispatch*.[49] But she eventually wrote back on 9 December 1875, asking Tennyson to make the cuts himself. He did so, doubtless bearing in mind the earlier discussions with Irving.[50] The cut version was received and accepted by Mrs Bateman on 14 January 1876.[51]

It was a very different play from the version published the year before that appeared on the Lyceum stage on 18 April 1876. Tennyson had reduced it by half and eliminated twenty-seven characters. The broad political and religious sweep of the Marian age had gone and the play had been 'transformed from a record of the fierce religious passions of the period to an attenuated psychological study'.[52]

Tennyson had seen and admired Irving in the roles of Cardinal Richelieu (1873) and Hamlet (1874). He had pronounced Irving in the latter role 'not a perfect *Hamlet*: the pathetic side of him well done, and the acting original. I liked it much better than Macready's'.[53] He envisaged Irving taking the part of the Cardinal Pole. But the role disappeared entirely in the cutting and Irving played Philip II of Spain instead. It was a comparatively small role but in it Irving secured a personal triumph. The play had evidently been envisaged by the Batemans as a vehicle for their three daughters, who all appeared: Kate Bateman (Mrs Crowe) as Mary Tudor, Virginia Francis (Bateman) as Princess Elizabeth and Isabel Bateman as Alice the maid. But they were all eclipsed by Irving. John Oxenford wrote in *The Times*:

> Philip is only a subordinate character: he appears in but two scenes, that are curiously alike: in each he is required to rebuff the Queen's fondness and to express his resolve to leave England. As Philip, Mr Irving secures an easy victory. Nothing indeed could be better than his performance of this character. He has carefully copied the traditional appearance of the King, and conveys very admirably his airs of frigid arrogance, heartless cruelty, and intense selfishness; the fanaticism and gross superstition which were also characteristic of Philip the author has not required the actor to demonstrate.[54]

In his biography of Irving, Percy Fitzgerald wrote (quoting his own *Whitehall Review* account of the play):

> The King in Tennyson's play-poem *Queen Mary*, I have always thought one of the best, most picturesque, of Irving's impersonations, from the perfect realisation it offered of the characters, impressions, feelings of the historic figure he represented: it was complete in every point of view. As regards its length it might be considered trifling; but it is important because of the *largeness* of the place it fitted. Profound was the impression made by the actor's Philip – not what he had to say, which was little, or by what he had to do, which was less, or by the dress or 'makeup', which was remarkable. He seemed to speak by the expression of his figure and glances; and apart from the meaning of his spoken words, there was another meaning beyond – viz., the character, the almost diseased solitude, the heartless indifference, and the other odious historical characteristics of the Prince, with which it was plain the actor had filled himself.[55]

This intense visual impression, the result in part of Irving's meticulous care over costume and makeup, based on Titian, is captured in Whistler's celebrated portrait of Irving as Philip II and confirmed by the recollection of the playwright Louis N. Parker, recorded in 1939:

> while I have vivid recollections of all other plays he produced I recall nothing whatever of this particular play, except the figure of Philip standing before a great fireplace, sinister and terrifying, the very embodiment of a Velasquez. But what he said or did, or what the play was about … had so entirely gone from me that I had to read the play just now to remind myself of it. Small wonder I couldn't recall it; it is perverse as drama and a perversion of history.[56]

Browning was present on the opening night in a celebrity artistic audience including George Eliot, John Everett Millais, Frederic Leighton and Tom Taylor. He wrote to Tennyson that it was 'a complete success ... Irving was very good indeed, and the others did their best, nor so badly. The love as well as admiration for the author was conspicuous.' Tennyson saw it two weeks later and, according to his son Hallam, 'enjoyed it – Papa was very much pleased with Irving and Mrs Crowe's acting.'[57] Ellen Terry went to see it and recalled of Irving 'he never did anything better to the day of his death ... It was the perfection of quiet malignity and cruelty ... I was just spellbound by a study of cruelty, which seemed to me a triumphant assertion of the power of the actor to create as well as to interpret, for Tennyson never suggested half of what Henry Irving did.'[58] But audiences fell off, and, although it had been anticipated to run for the whole season, after twenty-three performances it was withdrawn by Mrs Bateman. She wrote to Tennyson regretfully that she would gladly have kept it on the stage 'for the honour of the taste of the British public, the dignity of the stage and the respect due to the greatest English poet' but simply could not afford to do so.[59] It was replaced by a revival of those surefire hits *The Bells* and *The Belle's Stratagem*.

The importance of Tennyson and the significance of the play are confirmed by the detailed comparisons which the critics made between the play as staged and the printed version. John Oxenford in *The Times* (20 April 1876) declared: 'a poem *Queen Mary* was from the first and a poem it will remain to the last – a dramatic poem, but not in the truest meaning of the word, a drama'. Joseph Knight, who found it 'impressive rather than dramatic', regretted that with the cuts 'much that is the best and most striking in the poetry' had disappeared.[60] Clement Scott concluded that 'theatrically considered, the drama is even less dramatic on the stage, than it was found to be in the book'. It required audiences to be familiar with the history and the published poem 'otherwise the story of *Queen Mary* will not be presented in a very clear light'.[61]

The full published version of the play opened in Act 1 with political and religious uncertainty. In Scene 1 ordinary people discuss in perplexity the previous parliamentary bastardization of both Mary and Elizabeth in the context of Mary's accession, though they unite in calling 'Long Live Queen Mary'. Two gentlemen discuss her marriage prospects and express concern at the possibility of a marriage with Philip of Spain. In Scene 2 the bishops flee but Archbishop Cranmer remains and is arrested. In Scene 3 the French Ambassador and his agent stir up popular hostility against the preaching of Catholicism and the prospect of the Spanish marriage. In Scene 4 Edward Courtenay, the vain and foppish Earl of Devon, the last of the Plantagenets, defeated in competition for Mary's hand, courts Elizabeth with an eye to the throne. Elizabeth sardonically fends off his advances and retires from the court to study and preserve her life. In Scene 5 Mary, obsessed by Philip's portrait, determines to have him as her husband. Bishop Gardiner, the Chancellor, and the French Ambassador de Noailles seek to dissuade her and the Spanish Ambassador Simon Renard to encourage her. The offer of marriage arrives and the Council is persuaded to agree.

Act 2 opens with Sir Thomas Wyatt raising his rebellion with a stirring patriotic speech not against the crown but against Spanish tyranny. In Scene 2 the Queen visits the Guildhall and wins a pledge of support from the Mayor and the citizens, rallies them with a powerful speech calling on their loyalty and pledging to defend English interests. In Scene 3 Wyatt and his men attack London. In Scene 4 the Queen refuses to flee. Word comes that Wyatt is defeated and captured. The Queen orders his imprisonment along with Courtenay and Elizabeth, who are implicated. The threats to England and the Spanish marriage have been removed.

In Act 3, Scene 1, Sir Ralph Bagenhall recounts the execution of the Lady Jane Grey, the reprisals after the rebellion and the arrival of Philip. In Scene 2, Cardinal Pole returns from exile and Mary believes herself pregnant and ecstatically prophecies the birth of a son who will defend the true faith. Scene 3 sees the official submission of England to Rome, Pole announces his mission to reconcile and heal, and Sir Raph Bagenhall rejects the settlement and is arrested and taken to the Tower. Scene 4 sees the initiation of the persecution of Protestants. There is a great debate between Gardiner and Pole about the pros and cons of persecution. In Scene 6 Philip reveals his hatred of England, the English and Mary to Renard, and his impatience to get away.

In Act 4, Scene 1, the Queen refuses petitions calling for mercy for Cranmer. In Scene 2, Cranmer recants his Protestantism. In Scene 3, Cranmer is condemned to die, recants his recantation and denounces the Pope. He is taken to his death. Paget and Howard discuss the deaths of Bishop Latimer and Ridley. Two old women, Tib and Joan, recount the death of Bishop Gardiner following the burning of Latimer and Ridley. They opine that the burning of the Archbishop will burn the Pope out of England for ever. Peters describes the burning of Cranmer.

Act 5, Scene 1 has Philip behaving coldly towards Mary, predicting her death and considering wooing Princess Elizabeth. In Scene 2 comes news that the new Pope Paul IV, a hard line anti-Spaniard, has deprived Pole of his legateship. Pole is broken-hearted, his hopes of peaceful reconciliation in England dashed. Calais is reported lost. Mary now abandoned, and embittered, begins to fall ill and deranged. In Scene 3 Philip's envoy visits Elizabeth and hints at the possible marriage. She resolves to remain single and defies him. In Scene 4 there are reports of the persecution of the Protestants and that both Pole and the Queen are dying. In Scene 5, the death of Mary is reported and Elizabeth is proclaimed Queen. Bagenhall declares 'God save the crown! The papacy is no more'. Paget, in a contemporary nineteenth-century aside, comments: 'Are we so sure of that?'

The play in full highlights the tyranny of the Papacy, though several times a distinction is made between the Catholics and papists, and Gardiner warns the Queen that the English people will brook neither 'Pope nor Spaniard here to play the tyrant'. The play opposes the idea of revolt against legitimate authority. Elizabeth refuses to participate in plots against Mary. Wyatt raises his revolt not against the Queen but against the Spanish marriage. It is strongly patriotic. When Gardiner suggests saving money by reducing the Calais garrison, Mary exclaims: 'I am Queen of England; take mine eyes, mine heart, but do not lose me Calais'. In Act 1 the audience cheered Mary's line, 'I am English Queen not Roman Emperor,' indicating how much in tune with the audience were Tennyson's patriotic sentiments.

Although some modern critics have defended the play, much of it reads like imitation Shakespeare.[62] There are some notable passages of poetry and individually effective scenes (Elizabeth resisting the advances of Courtenay; the debate about pros and cons of persecution; Philip's scenes; Mary's scenes of obsession, embitterment, disillusionment and illness) but the narrative itself is too cluttered and unwieldy to convey dramatic power or cohesion.

Tennyson in cutting opted to eliminate most of the religious and political scenes, including the characters of Cranmer, Pole and Bonner, and all of Act 4. He added a new final scene keeping Mary on stage for her deathbed scene and having her reconciled with Elizabeth (Hallam Tennyson includes the scene in his biography). The fact that the reverberations of these events still echoed three hundred years later is evidenced by a letter to Tennyson from Sir Henry Bedingfield Bt complaining at the unfair treatment of his ancestor during the play. Tennyson replied, saying that for the stage version the character would be referred to merely as 'Governor of Woodstock' and he would add an extra line for Princess Elizabeth: 'Out, girl, you wrong a noble gentleman.'[63]

Clement Scott concluded that, despite the omission of many characters, two new speeches and a new ending to the last act, the stage version of *Queen Mary* was seriously flawed. The elimination of the Wyatt rebellion 'destroys one of the foundation stones of drama', the elimination of Cranmer and Pole 'robs the play of much of its colour', and the plight of Princess Elizabeth was not linked either to 'the troubles of the time or the domestic trials of the Queen'.

Act 1 of the stage version comprised parts of Scene 4 and 5 of the printed Act 1. A long first scene concentrated on the rival ambassadors, Chancellor and lady-in-waiting discussing with Mary the merits and demerits of Philip. Scott commented: 'The long conversations … are, no doubt, historically interesting, and examples of spirited poetry, but they are not apparently designed with any end tending to assist the dramatic idea'. Act 2 of the stage version, in which Mary rallies support and receives news of Wyatt's defeat, embraces Scenes 2 and 4 of the original act: it covers Wyatt's Rebellion but with Wyatt's scenes excised. Scott found the act without Wyatt had 'a hurried and scrambling effect' with 'few opportunities for acting'.

Act 3 had two scenes. The first one of them (Act 3, Scene 5) has Elizabeth a prisoner at Woodstock 'full of charming poetical conceits and idyllic beauty but unnecessary for stage purposes, in as much as the Princess has the faintest possible connection with the story, and it is not included in the main thread of the plot. The milkmaid's song and the long speech in which Elizabeth wishes she were a milkmaid, so that she might escape the horrors and dangers surrounding her, might advantageously be omitted.' The second scene combined elements of Act 3, Scene 2 and 6 featuring Philip of Spain and, said Clement Scott, 'a favourable feeling is awakened by the Titian picture presented by Mr Henry Irving, and by his admirable assumption of coldness in love and determination in policy'. But Scott observed: 'Experience warns us that the third act is a critical point in the play and this particular act is not helping us on to the end … In the fourth act matters do not improve and it would be difficult to account for the necessity of Joan and Tib, and their account of Gardiner's death in Oxfordshire dialect, seeing that the religious controversy is so carefully eliminated from the story.' But for the most part in Act 4, 'Mary still pleads and Philip still sneers'. Act 5 of the play was made up of Scenes 3 and 5 of the printed text. Scott commented: 'The fifth act has arrived and it is high time that any dramatic power held in reserve should at once be expanded. The interest must be revived now or never. But the grief of the Queen has been too indefinitely postponed. The interest, so long delayed, has gone out of England with Philip, and a source of relief is felt when the Princess Elizabeth hurries on the scene, and is enabled to close the eyes of the dead Queen Mary'. The net result of all this, according to Scott, was that 'instead of a succession of dramatic positions, we are treated to a series of domestic pictures in which Mary pleads for affection and Philip coldly disregards her prayers'.[64] Dutton Cook in the *World* pulled no punches when he wrote:

> Upon the stage the Laureate's *Queen Mary* is probably assured of the sort of success that comes of curiosity and of respect legitimately due to a great writer … but that an enduring addition has been made to the dramatic repertory of the country is not to be believed. Nor should it be charged against the spectators that they remained almost unmoved by the representation of Mr Tennyson's tragedy, or betrayed lack of power to appreciate the merits of the production submitted to their judgment. As a theatrical exhibition *Queen Mary* fails, owing to its deficiency in dramatic quality. It can hardly have been devised originally with the most remote view to representation upon the stage … More is needed than dialogue to constitute a drama; the audience have to be entertained and excited by action no less that speech … much of the stir and action distinguishing the original has been eliminated from the stage edition of the work. *Queen*

Mary has been wrecked indeed, and its least dramatic constituents are among the salvage ... Almost the entire weight of the drama ... devolves upon a heroine who cannot command the sympathies of a theatrical audience, or move them to interest in her proceedings. Practically Mary wearies the spectators not less than she wearies her husband, while his indifference to her seems throughout far more reasonable and intelligible than her devotion to him ... the art of Miss Bateman has strict limitations. Her voice is hollow, her delivery is monotonous, her manner is conventional; her histrionic method altogether is wanting in variety and in light and shade.[65]

Why did Tennyson cut the play the way he did? Clement Scott noted that 'the religious controversy is ... carefully eliminated from the story'. This was undoubtedly prudent. The theatrical censors were very concerned to preserve the religious sensibilities of Victorian audiences. Adaptations of stories from the Bible were completely banned. Depictions of Anglican clergymen were discouraged, though occasionally permitted when the characterization was saintly, like the Vicar of Wakefield in *Olivia*. Anti-Catholic allusions were excised from the English version of Meyerbeer's opera *Les Huguenots*. Even Moslem sensibilities were respected, so that Irving's proposed production *Mahomet* was banned.[66] The likelihood is that the lengthy dramatisation of the persecution of the English Protestants by the Catholics at a time when anti-Catholic feeling was running high in Britain would have invited an immediate ban.

The censors were also eagle-eyed for anything likely to bring the monarchy into disrepute. So there was no harm in softening the character of Mary Tudor by introducing a deathbed reconciliation with Elizabeth. The elimination of the detail of the religious controversy and the political revolt, and the concentration on the domestic and romantic concerns of the crown, therefore lined *Queen Mary* up with *Charles the First* as part of the 'domestication of majesty', an important development which concentrated on the unhappiness of monarchs and reinforced the view that the job of ruling should be left to those trained for it and that it was not for ordinary folk. So the combination of her patriotic assertions of Englishness, which prompted cheers on the opening night, and the stress of her unhappy marriage and childlessness, served an important propaganda purpose on behalf of monarchy, something which neither Tennyson nor Irving would have regretted.

Tennyson's *Harold* was destined not to reach the stage until 1928. In 1879 he offered the completed *Becket* to Irving. Irving reluctantly declined it – on the grounds of costs of staging. But in reality because, as it stood, it was too long and too unplayable. Tennyson published it in 1884. Irving was powerfully drawn to the play, considering it superior to Shakespeare's *King John*, popular in mid-Victorian England for its patriotic and anti-Catholic sentiments. Bram Stoker recalled:

Irving took the main ideas of the play into his heart and tried to work it out. He kept it by him for more than a year. He took it with him to America in the tour of 1884–5; and in the long hours of loneliness, consequent on such work as his, made it part of his mental labour. But it was all without avail; he could not see his way to a successful issue. Again he took it in hand when going to America in 1887–8; for the conviction was still with him that the play he wanted was there, if he could only unearth it. Again long months of effort; and again failure. This time he practically gave up hope.[67]

But then, during the 1891 run of *Henry VIII* and with, Stoker surmises, Irving being 'tuned to sacerdotalism' by playing Cardinal Wolsey, he turned again to the play. The official version given by Stoker of the evolution of *Becket* omits one important fact. In 1889 Tennyson, with Irving's blessing, offered the performing rights in *Becket* to the American actor-manager Lawrence Barrett. When Barrett died in 1891, leaving his stage version unperformed, Tennyson forwarded it to Irving and this gave him the clue he needed for his own version.[68] By Easter 1892 Irving had made up his mind. He called Stoker and his stage manager H.J. Loveday to a meeting in the Beefsteak Room of the Lyceum, and produced a set of foolscap sheets on which he had cut and pasted his version of the play, which was about five-sevenths of the original length. He read it out to Stoker and Loveday: 'I think I have got it at last.' They stayed until four in the morning discussing their plans for production of the play, deciding on Charles Villiers Stanford as the composer of the score. Irving said: 'it was a true "miracle" play – a holy theme: and that he had felt already in studying it that it made him a better man.'[69] Stoker was dispatched to the Isle of Wight and there agreed with Tennyson royalties and the purchase of the rights of the play for a number of years. He asked Tennyson if Irving could cut the play for performance. Tennyson said: 'Irving may do whatever he pleases with it.' He was shown the cut version and, after reading it, agreed to it and also to Irving's request to write a new speech for Becket for the end of the scene at Northampton Castle. Tennyson wrote it and sent it to Irving a few days later.[70] Tennyson asked if Irving could spare from the cutting a favourite character, Walter Map. Irving tried to do so but could not without unbalancing the play and Map went.[71] Tennyson endorsed the choice of Stanford for the score. Irving's acting version was published by Macmillan in 1893.

But Tennyson was already ailing and he died on 6 October 1892 eleven days after his meeting with Stoker. Knowing he would never live to see *Becket* produced, Tennyson told his doctor: 'I can trust Irving – he will do me justice.'[72] He was buried on 12 October at Westminster Abbey, with Irving among the mourners. The play was produced on 6 February 1893, Irving's fifty-fifth birthday, playing 112 times. There was a new production in 1904 and altogether it was produced in Britain and America 308 times.[73] It starred Irving as Becket, with Ellen Terry as Fair Rosamund, William Terriss as Henry II and Geneviève Ward as Queen Eleanor. Hallam Tennyson wrote: 'Assuredly Irving's interpretation of the many-sided, many-mooded, statesman-soldier-saint was as vivid and subtle a piece of acting as has been seen in our day.'[74]

Geneviève Ward had performed the part of Queen Eleanor in an open-air charity performance of *Becket* put on by dedicated amateurs in the presence of the Prince and Princess of Wales in 1886. Tennyson witnessed a rehearsal and was so enthusiastic about her Queen Eleanor that, according to Ward, her subsequent appearance in the play with Irving 'was due to an expressed wish on the author's part'.[75] Ward, who said of the original that 'its dramatic capabilities left much to be desired', noted that in Irving's version it 'underwent an extraordinary change ... to make it suitable for the stage. The words were all the poet's, but the sequence and disposition were wholly the actor's.'[76] She quoted with approval a contemporary critic's account of the differences. The five acts of the original were condensed to four. The prologue remained but the order was changed. The play now began with Queen Eleanor and Fitzurse talking in a Norman castle, not with Henry and Becket talking as in the original. This was because no Victorian actor-manager ever appeared in the first scene when the curtain rose, but required an entrance and applause. So the prologue was divided into two and the order of appearance reversed to conform to this convention.

The whole of Act 1, Scene 4 was cut. In it leprous beggars, invited by Becket to dine, drive off the four knights seeking to murder him, and thus cover Becket's flight to France: 'a fine scene in the tragedy but a whiff too pungent for any sort of attempt at realisation'.[77] A short scene taken from Act 5, Scene 1 was added to Act 1 to allow the knights to explain why they hate Becket. Act 2, which merged Scene 1 of Tennyson's Act 2 and Scene 1 of his Act 3, was set entirely in Rosamund's bower and concentrated on the Fair Rosamund subplot. Act 3 opened with the meeting of Henry II of England and Louis VII of France. Act 2, Scene 1 and Act 3, Scene 2 became Act 3, Scene 1. Ward said that in Scenes 2 and 3, 'the most magnificently dramatic passages Tennyson ever wrote, were passed in and outside Rosamund's Bower and culminated in the intensely thrilling moment when Elinor's dagger as it grazed Rosamund's white bosom, was arrested by the sudden steel clip of the archbishop's hand. Melodrama furnishes no situation more breathtakingly sensational, more unexpected.'[78] Acts 3, 4 and 5 were telescoped and culminated in the dramatic martyrdom finale. Ward said of the Rosamund scene:

> In this, as in every other case, we saw the essential difference between an acting and a literary play. Again and again, what the poet was obliged to describe Mr. Irving had to act. The latter crystallised words into action; descriptions became deeds ... The political matter concerning the young prince had been wisely cut away. Elsewhere we traced the touch of Mr Irving's blue pencil, deleting here lines and half-lines, intensifying the dramatic significance at all times, pruning the strong phrase of Tennyson ... to the squeamish ears of a London audience.[79]

So Irving carved out a playable text by cutting, condensing, tightening and rearranging. He persuaded the Laureate to write him a new curtain speech for the end of Act 1, of which he only used half. Cutting gave him a splendid exit line for Act 4, Scene 2: 'The Pall! I go to meet my King.' Irving cut superfluous dialogue, superfluous historical detail, superfluous characters and subplots to clarify and strengthen the dramatic line.

The play became an undoubted hit with the public in Britain and America. It was done as a command performance for Queen Victoria at Windsor. Irving read the play at the chapter house of Canterbury Cathedral in 1893, in aid of church restoration funds, and in Winchester in 1901, as part of the King Alfred Millenary celebrations. The success of *Becket* is significant because he was of course a Roman Catholic saint murdered at the behest of an English king. Becket, a major cultic figure of veneration in the Middle Ages, had fallen from favour at the time of the Reformation when his shrine at Canterbury had been destroyed. He once again became a figure of historical controversy in the nineteenth century. In the 1840s the beliefs, actions, and racial identities of both Henry and Thomas were seen as having a direct relevance to current crises in thought. 'The opposed figures provided a means of exploring the significance of being – or not being – English. But in this instance, the question of identity was associated more closely with the role of religion.'[80] In the 1820s, French historian Augustin Thierry, constructing a theory on English history essentially from the ideas of Scott's *Ivanhoe*, argued that Becket was a Saxon and his conflict with Norman King Henry II took on a racial as well as a class element. But by the 1840s the Saxon origins of Becket were very largely exploded. English Catholic writers now depicted Becket as saint and martyr, defender of the Papacy and church rights against the state; whereas Protestant writers saw him as a decidedly unEnglish figure whose celibacy, austerity (his daily scourgings, for instance) and Popish sympathies rendered him unsympathetic. As late as 1878, in his biography of Thomas, the historian J.A. Froude could call him 'the impersonation not of what was highest and best in the Catholic church, but of what was falsest and worst'.[81] Into this controversial area stepped the Poet Laureate. One of his objectives always was historical accuracy, and to that end he studied the contemporary sources and visited the scene of Becket's martyrdom. Hallam Tennyson wrote: 'The play is so accurate a representation of the personages and of the time, that J.R. Green [the historian] said that all his researches into the annals of the twelfth century had not given him "so vivid a conception of the character of Henry II and his court as was embodied in Tennyson's *Becket*".'[82] Hallam Tennyson defined his father's view of Becket:

> Becket was a really great and impulsive man, with a firm sense of duty, and, when he renounced the world, looked upon himself as the head of that Church, which was the people's 'tower of strength, their bulwark against throne and baronage'. This idea is

so far wrought in his dominant nature as to betray him into many rash acts; and later he lost himself in the idea. His enthusiasm reached a spiritual ecstasy which carries the historian along with it; and his humanity and abiding tenderness for the poor, the weak and the unprotected, heighten the impression so much as to make the poet feel passionately the wronged Rosamund's reverential devotion for him (most touchingly rendered by Ellen Terry) when she kneels praying over his body in Canterbury Cathedral.[83]

There were many critics who could not see the purpose of the Rosamund subplot and felt that it detracted from the power of the main narrative. But in fact, as Irving appreciated, the Rosamund plot was integral to Tennyson's conception. Queen Eleanor is motivated throughout by her hatred of Rosamund. She offers to support Becket against the King in return for the map of the bower, where the King keeps Rosamund concealed, tries to kill Rosamund and, when foiled by Becket, gets her revenge by informing Henry that Becket has made Rosamund into a nun thus provoking the outburst of rage as 'Will no man rid me of this pestilent priest?' Her presence also softens the character of Becket, allowing him to display compassion. All of this is in line with the treatment of historical events on the Victorian stage with the foregrounding of 'human interest' and sentiment to appeal to the susceptibilities of the Victorian audience.

It is significant that the play opens with Queen Eleanor and Reginald Fitzurse discussing their shared hatred of Becket, who is dismissed as a plebeian, and Eleanor encouraging Fitzurse, who is the rejected lover of Rosamund, to help her remove Rosamund. The fates of Rosamund and Becket are thus linked from the outset. In the second scene of the prologue, Henry II plays chess with his Chancellor, Thomas Becket. The King lays out his plans to limit the powers and jurisdiction of the church. The King asks Becket to protect his mistress, Rosamund de Clifford, and expresses his wish that Becket should succeed the dying archbishop Theobald of Canterbury. Becket is resistant.

In Act 1, Scene 1 Becket, now archbishop of Canterbury, expresses to his confidant Herbert his inner turmoil at taking the position but describes a dream in which God has subdued and chosen him. Rosamund, who has left her protective bower, enters pursued by Fitzurse. Becket defies Fitzurse and sends Rosamund back to her bower. In Scene 2, at Northampton, Eleanor offers to side with Becket against the King if he will give her the map to the bower. He refuses and she vows vengeance on him. The three knights express their hatred of Becket. In Northampton Castle, at the great council, the Constitutions of Clarendon are read out, and Becket's assent is sought. The clergy are to answer charges in royal rather than church courts, the King is to receive revenues from vacant bishoprics, and elections to bishoprics are to take place under the eye of the King in the chapel royal. Becket refuses to seal the Constitutions and appeals to the Pope.

Act 2 is a romantic tryst between Henry and Rosamund in her bower. She intercedes for Becket but the King declares he has exiled all Becket's relatives. In Act 3, in a meeting at Montmirail, King Louis of France brokers an uneasy truce between Henry and Becket, with the Constitutions left on one side. Eleanor finds her way into the bower, tries to stab Rosamund and is stopped by Becket. He takes Rosamund to Godstow Nunnery. Act 4 has Eleanor telling Henry that Becket has consigned Rosamund to a nunnery. He calls upon the knights to rid him of Becket. Rosamund in nun's dress comes to Becket to ask him not to excommunicate the King; Becket agrees. He gives her his blessing. The knights arrive and murder Becket during a thunderstorm.

The story is given a particularly English inflection. Becket is not the tool of the Papacy and the play has a definite anti-papal bias. The Pope's Almoner asks Becket to conciliate the King because the Pope fears Henry will side with the Anti-Pope. Becket thunders: 'If Rome be feeble, then I should be firm', and he denounces the cardinals for taking royal bribes ('Rome is venal even to rottenness'). Similarly the monks flee in terror at the end. So this cannot be seen as a pro-Catholic play. If anything Becket's contempt for Rome and his abandonment by the Canterbury monks suggest we should see him as a proto-Protestant. Becket is portrayed as a principled opponent of royal despotism. He calls the church 'a tower of strength, a bulwark against the throne and baronage' in Act 1. The particular Constitutions that are read out show the crown interfering in legitimate church customs. The people support him as he cries 'the voice of God is the voice of the people'. In Act 3 Becket denounces the bishops and the barons for driving a wedge between him and the King and 'trampling on the rights of Englishmen'. All this gives us a Becket who is a nineteenth-century English constitutionalist, not a mouthpiece for papal Rome. He stands against a despotic crown and an overmighty aristocracy, of the kind which Britain had dispensed with in favour of parliamentary government ('the voice of the people') and middle-class rule. The despising of Becket for his low birth is another mark against the Queen and Fitzurse.

Then there is Rosamund, technically a fallen woman, but one whom the play is keen to show redeemed. Becket protects her throughout, blesses her at the end and ensures her entry into a nunnery. She is shown to be a loving mother to her little son Geoffrey, willing to intercede with Becket for the King and with the King for Becket. As played by Ellen Terry, she became another embodiment of womanliness and tenderness. What Becket, the man of inflexible principle and strong religious faith, defender of the rights of Englishmen and protector of the fallen women, suggested was an analogue of Mr Gladstone rather than a medieval Catholic saint. Irving wrote to Hallam in 1893 to say:

> To me *Becket* is a very noble play, with something of that lofty feeling and that far-reaching influence, which belong to a 'passion play'. There are in it moments of passion and pathos which are the aim and end of dramatic art, and which, when they exist,

atone to an audience for the endurance of long acts. Some of the scenes and passages, especially in the last act, are full of sublime feeling, and are with regard to both their dramatic effectiveness and their poetic beauty as fine as anything in our language. I know that such a play has an ennobling influence on both the audience who see it and the actors who play in it.[84]

Charles Hiatt concluded in his biography of Irving that:

To many persons, Irving's supreme achievement, both as actor and manager, was the production of Tennyson's *Becket* ... Henry Irving seemed to feel that he had a sacred duty to perform to the poet who was then recently buried ... and he performed that duty right nobly. *Becket* was put on the stage with no undue magnificence of spectacle. All in the matter of scenic display, that could help the imagination was there, but, on the other hand, there was no parade of scenery for its own sake. Irving's performance of the chief person of the play was as near perfection as anything he has done ... He was a great actor interpreting a great part in a great manner. The statesman-priest was presented to us in most convincing fashion. The old, immortal history lived before our eyes.[85]

Joseph Hatton, writing in the *Art Journal*, stressed the value of the play to education:

The English history most popularly known among the people is our history as Shakespeare has told it ... It is the stage history of men and things that is best known by the people ... Through the medium of the new play the general public will learn more of the rivalry of Church and Crown in Henry's days than they ever knew before, while the shrine of Becket at Canterbury will for many a summer come to be visited by an increased and increasing number of pilgrims. Not alone is Art indebted to such productions as *Becket*, but literature, poetry, education find in it a national advancement.[86]

Percy Fitzgerald thought that 'One of the most remarkable things connected with *Becket* was the unanimous applause and approbation of the entire press', something that rarely attended Irving's productions.[87]

Clement Scott considered it 'the very greatest of all Henry Irving's stupendous achievements at the Lyceum'. He praised the adaptation: 'In the first place ... Mr Henry Irving has created a play out of an undramatic poem. He has formed, fashioned, and modelled a dramatic substance out of an undramatic cloud'. He thought Irving's performance 'the crowning point of his artistic career ... Mr Henry Irving has never done anything so subtle, so delicate, or so artistically graduated, as this merging of the statesman into the saint ... if ever an actor lived in a part, Mr Henry Irving does in that of Becket'. He praised its historical accuracy and archaeological authenticity:

I cannot see that history has been falsified by the Lyceum production ... Then as regards dress, scenery and archaeological detail, it is very doubtful if it could be improved upon. Charles Kean, with all his passion for archaeology and his student researches, never did anything at the Princess's Theatre better than *Becket*.[88]

Enthusiasm from such a dedicated Irvingite as Scott might have been expected. But his enthusiasm was matched by that of one of Irving's sternest and most consistent critics, William Archer. He declared unambiguously in the *World* (15 February 1893): 'Mr Irving's production of *Becket* is one of the triumphs of his career. In point of artistic delicacy and strength, his Becket deserves to rank with his Charles I. So long as he is on the stage, we are interested, fascinated, moved; and if there are one or two bad quarters of an hour when he is *not* on the stage, that is Tennyson's fault not his.'

Archer's strictures are reserved for the play itself, 'a singularly bad play' in which the poet 'has missed the historical interest, the psychological problem, of his theme. What was it that converted the splendid warrior-diplomat into the austere prelate? The cowl, we are told, does not make the monk; but in Lord Tennyson's psychology it seems that it does'. He complained that 'of the process of thought, the development of feeling, which leads Becket to break with ... the friend of his heart ... we have no hint. The social and political issues are left equally in the vague.' As for the Rosamund subplot, he dismissed it as 'unhistorical, inconceivable and profoundly uninteresting'. He declared himself 'moved and thrilled' by the Council at Northampton and the murder scene, adding 'it is many a day since I, for my part, have felt any kindred emotions within the walls of the Lyceum'. He conceded that Irving was perfectly cast for Becket: 'It would be almost impossible for Mr Irving to fail as an ascetic, a sacerdotal character. His cast of countenance, his expression, his manner, are all prelatical in the highest degree. Nature designed him for a Prince of the Church'. But there was more than just personality to Irving's performance, 'there is imagination, there is composition, there is ... DICTION!'

He noted how Irving had very carefully differentiated his Wolsey, 'the statesman-priest' from Becket, 'the hero-priest'.

> Crafty policy, personal ambition, love of power, were the ruling forces of the Cardinal; the Archbishop is animated by an intense, simple-minded, almost fanatical devotion to the Church, untainted by either subtlety or self-seeking. This may or may not be the Becket of history; it is certainly the Becket of Tennyson, whom Mr Irving embodies with infinite sympathy, fidelity and charm ... In three or four really vital scenes of the play, Tennyson has sketched a noble and touching figure, assigning to him many noble and touching speeches, full of true Tennysonian melody. The history may be bad, the dramatic quality ... none of the highest – but the writing is exquisite. And to this exquisite writing, Mr Irving does ample, almost perfect, justice. Oh, the difference between his diction in *Becket* and *Lear!* Here he gives us – or at any rate gave us on the first night – clear-cut, beautiful English speech in smooth-flowing, delicately cadenced, poetic periods. Many of his lines and sequences of lines were a joy to the ear.

Archer took to task a fellow critic on the *Pall Mall Gazette* for suggesting that Irving's success in the role was due to the fact that it was a melodramatic part.

'This is, I think, unjust both to the poet and the actor. They have cooperated, in the strict sense of the word, in a character-creation of remarkable beauty. It cannot, perhaps, be called tragic, but melodramatic still less. How about "poetic"? I think that is the word that meets the occasion.'

Terriss's Henry II was deemed to have been eclipsed by Irving's Becket, but then he had lost his big speech at Northampton, excised in Irving's version. Ellen Terry was 'graceful, tender and altogether charming' as Rosamund, but the character was 'futile and out of place'; Geneviève Ward was the 'ideal Eleanor of tradition.'

The question of history was never far from the minds of the critics. The *Daily Chronicle* observed that 'Englishmen are once more indebted to Mr Irving for a brilliant and scholarly dramatic transcript of a great period in our history'.[89] But the *Daily News* had wondered: 'Would the hearts of an audience in these "most brisk and giddy-paced times" be stirred by far-off echoes of the strife between the great Plantagenet King and the indomitable champion of the Church's independence of the civil power? Of historical pictures, rich in colour and in tokens of the splendours of Courtly, ecclesiastical and military life in that pictorial epoch, there was certain to be enough to spare; but what of the conflicting principles 'embodied in the persons of the King and the Archbishop.' Mr Irving has rightly said that these two striking personalities give a 'vividly human interest to the contest', at least on the pages of history; but the question was whether this was the sort of human interest to engage the sympathies of modern audiences, who are apt to look for a story with some ingenuity of intrigue, and have little of the appetite for 'chronicle plays' which characterized playgoers in the days when there was no Froudes or Greens to satisfy their cravings ... only actual experiment could perhaps determine. The experiment, however, has been made; and with the results that would have left on the mind of no one who was present at the magnificent demonstration at the Lyceum last night the faintest shadow of a doubt of the success of the performance'. It was not just the applause that greeted the end of each act or even calls at the end. 'It was still more the wrapt attention with which scene after scene was followed, together with that subtle feeling which pervades the house when a play really holds the sympathy of the spectator. In brief, the great gathering of last night were deeply interested'.[90] So the existence of popular histories by the likes of J.A. Froude and J.R. Green did not in any way preclude success for a stage version of the story which they had told in print.

The St. James's Budget (10 February 1893) had its reservations about both the drama and the history. It proclaimed the play:

> among Tennyson's comparative failures ... and though it has some fine passages of poetry, its literary merit is on the whole much below that of *The Falcon* and *The Cup*. Its defects for stage purposes are easily seen. The plot is weak and badly constructed; the scenes are loosely strung together; and the connection of the love interest with the main

motive is not at all close. Moreover the action of the piece is static rather than dynamic; there is little growth or development of character ... Miss Agnes Lambert, writing in the *Nineteenth Century* for this month, tells us that she comes to the conclusion, after a careful examination of the original authorities, that the portrait of Becket in this play is better than that given by any historian. This may be; but good history does not always make good drama. The play largely consists of passages from Mr Freeman's *Essays* and the valuable introduction to the Rolls Series put into blank verse. To many readers it must have seemed doubtful whether this sort of metrical version of Dr Stubbs's *Constitutional History* would prove anything but wearisome on the stage, or whether a modern English audience, be it of the Philistine or the Ibsenite variety, would not yawn over it. The doubts were dispelled before the Lyceum curtain had been up many minutes on Monday. From the first the play carried the audience with it.

The critic praised the sets, the staging and the acting, seeing the Council of Northampton as a particular high point. 'Up to this point the audience were carried along on a current of full and unbroken interest. The sense of participation in great and momentous events – such as we supposed filled the Elizabethan audiences when they sat out the long Shakspearian [*sic*] *Histories* – was notably maintained, and this elaborate illustration of the complicated medieval struggle between Church and State roused a genuine and unmistake-able enthusiasm.' But then, interestingly, the critic observed that:

after all this pomp of pageantry and stately eloquence ... the second Act, which passes in Rosamund's Bower, beautiful as it was, fell a trifle flat. It is a pretty love scene, and Miss Terry was tender and charming in it; but after Northampton Castle, and the fierce feuds of Barons and Churchmen, Priest and King, it seemed strangely modern, and a little tame. We were transported as it were, from ... Angevin England to West Kensington. The love-making of the King and his mistress looks commonplace, the domesticities of the Rosamund establishment ... almost suburban; and when the King finally tells Rosamund to "put on her hood" and go with him to the bounds of the forest, it is as if he was asking her to walk with him to the station and see him off.

But this may well be precisely what appealed to the contemporary audiences about it. The critic warmed much more to the final scenes, culminating in the martyrdom.

The Times (7 February 1893) shared the view of many commentators about the flaws in the play: 'As a drama, pure and simple ... *Becket* cannot ... be described as a masterpiece. For its theme is not only the barren question of the jurisdiction of the Archbishop as opposed to that of the King, but the struggle for supremacy between these rival forces in the politics of the twelfth century is carried on without any attempt on the part of the author to lay bare the springs of action, human and personal, of his characters.' But, having summarized the weaknesses, it went on: 'All these points, however, are merely so many reasons why in other hands, *Becket* might have proved less successful than it undoubtedly is. They do not detract from the commanding merit of Mr Irving's *mise-en-scène* or his fine embodiment of the title-character.' This was because 'a Lyceum play must be judged from more than one standpoint; it must be considered, first and foremost no doubt, as a dramatic study, but secondly, and in an important degree, as a vehicle for spectacular and musical effect ... There can be no doubt in the latter respect at least, *Becket* stands high among Mr Irving's achievements. No finer succession of resplendent pictures has ever been unfolded upon the boards than Mr Irving's representation of Medieval England, an England peopled by rude and warlike barons and ruled by an imperious King still ignorant of the restraints of constitutional government.'

Irving had a particular attachment to the play. When Mrs Walter Pollock said that he had made the play, he replied that 'the play made me. It changed my whole view of Life.' Laurence Irving perceptively noted that there were three Irvings, each of which was authentic: 'the raffish and companionable Irving, known only to his closest friends; the stern autocratic, yet loveable Chief ... the Irving of the Lyceum; and Irving, the figure-head of his profession, courteous, condescending and reticent'. It was this third Irving that 'underwent a subtle change after the production of *Becket*. His manner became slightly pontifical, though without a hint of pomposity'. Laurence Irving concluded: 'Unquestionably in *Becket*, Irving established a closer affinity with his public than in any other piece he played; he promoted, in a sense, a spiritual rather than emotional exhilaration in his audience ... he persuaded himself that in the performance of Becket, spanning the gulf between Church and Stage, he and his audience united in an act of worship.'[91]

SIR HENRY IRVING, TO NAPOLEON OF THAT ILK:—" WELL, UPON MY LIFE!
I HARDLY KNOW MYSELF."

Irving in *Madame Sans-Gêne*, cartoon by Alfred Bryan, *Entr'acte*, 24 April 1897.

12

Foreign History

Irving's historical productions underlined the prevailing values of nineteenth-century Britain. His choice of subjects fascinatingly echoes Carlyle's choice in his seminal volume *On Heroes, Hero-Worship and the Heroic in History*. Carlyle cited the hero as prophet (Mahomet), the hero as poet (Dante and Shakespeare), the hero as priest (Luther and Knox), and the hero as king (Cromwell and Napoleon). Irving commissioned a play on Mahomet but was banned by the censors from performing it. He commissioned and starred in a play about Dante and vigorously promoted the Shakespeare canon. He did not play either Luther or Knox. But the hero as priest was a recognized part of his repertoire and he played Becket, Wolsey and Richelieu. There was no heroic Cromwell but Napoleon was an obsession. Irving kept a bust of Napoleon in his rooms and had many books about his career. Stoker recalled that Irving 'was always delighted to talk of him'.[1] Despite his physical unsuitability – he was too tall – he played Napoleon in Diamond Jubilee Year 1897 in *Madame Sans-Gêne*.

Irving played a succession of tyrants: Shakespeare's Richard III and Macbeth, but also Louis XI, Peter the Great and Robespierre. Their excesses were the antithesis of the parliamentary democracy and constitutional monarchy which were deemed to be the bedrock of Britain's greatness. But they gave the great actor ideal opportunities for bravura performance. A major element in the Victorian psyche was hatred of the French Revolution, which loomed over the nineteenth century as an awful warning in the same way that the Bolshevik Revolution was to loom over the twentieth. The bloodlust of the mob and the tyranny of the revolutionary demagogues had already been graphically highlighted in such key nineteenth-century texts as Thomas Carlyle's *The French Revolution* and Charles Dickens's *A Tale of Two Cities*. They were to be joined in the Edwardian era by Baroness Orczy's *The Scarlet Pimpernel*, the third of a trilogy whose thrust was powerfully anti-revolutionary. Irving's contribution to this historical strand was his production of the plays *The Dead Heart*, *Robespierre* and *Madame Sans Gêne*. Lastly the Italian Renaissance, a powerful aesthetic and cultural influence on the nineteenth century, was celebrated in *Dante* and in the spectacular Renaissance recreations for *Romeo and Juliet* and *Much Ado*.

Perhaps the most enduring of Irving's non-Shakespearian tyrants was Louis XI, 'the Spider King' (1461–83). A contemporary of Richard III and something of a French counterpart, Louis acquired a mythic existence in the nineteenth century when he figured in three major literary works of the Romantic period as the archetype of the cruel, scheming and superstitious medieval tyrant: Sir Walter Scott's *Quentin Durward* (1823), Victor Hugo's *Notre Dame de Paris* (1831) and Casimir Delavigne's play *Louis XI* (1832). These key works were joined in 1902 by Justin Huntly McCarthy's *If I Were King*, in which Louis encountered François Villon.

In the way of the mid-Victorian theatre, which shamelessly plundered the hits of the French stage to create 'new' English plays, Dion Boucicault prepared an English version of Delavigne's play as a vehicle for Charles Kean. It was produced at the Princess's Theatre in 1855 and was an instant hit. *The Times* (15 January 1855) said: 'We can scarcely conceive anything more perfect.' The part was a gift for a character actor and even Samuel Phelps, who normally avoided melodrama, succumbed and played it in 1861. Boucicault himself took the role in New York in 1879 and, playing it in his broad Irish brogue, was laughed off the stage. Irving inevitably took it on, first playing it at the Lyceum on 9 March 1878. It remained part of his repertoire until the end of his career.

The background of the play was the dispute between Louis XI of France and his great vassal, Charles the Bold, Duke of Burgundy. The Duc de Nemours (whose father had been executed by Louis) comes in disguise as Burgundy's envoy carrying a treaty setting out Charles's demands. If they are not met, he is to challenge Louis or his champion to single combat, to settle the dispute. Louis agrees to the treaty but plots to have the envoy ambushed on the way back to Burgundy and the treaty stolen. Not only does he fear the power of Burgundy, he fears the popularity of his own son, the Dauphin Charles. Louis tricks Marie de Commines, who is in love with Nemours, into revealing his identity. Louis is about to sign the treaty when news arrives that the Duke of Burgundy has been killed in battle. Louis now unmasks and arrests Nemours and orders his captains to seize Burgundy. The King's physician Coitier helps Nemours escape. Louis orders his arrest. Seeking help from holy man Francis de Paule, Louis confesses to having poisoned his own brother and to having unjustly executed the father of Nemours. Nemours returns, intending to kill Louis, but seeing his terror and guilt tells him to live on in torment. Louis orders him to be seized but collapses in convulsions. The Dauphin is about to be proclaimed King when Louis revives. He orders that Nemours should be executed. Marie intervenes and pleads for Nemours. In the hope of saving his soul, Louis spares him and dies, ordering everyone to pray for him. The Dauphin is proclaimed King.

The play is essentially a character study of the King, who is by turns crafty, cruel, suspicious, superstitious and terrified of death. Clement Scott described Irving's performance: 'His thin, drawn, cruel face, his curiously crafty eye, his uncertain voice, broken, petulant and shrill, his restless manner, give the first idea of the character.' He called it 'his most complete and scholarly study' and praised his death scene ('impressive without being morbid').[2]

Cardinal Richelieu (1585–1642) as a character was not a straightforward dictator. He was the indispensable first minister of France and his actions, cunning, bold and unorthodox, were dictated by his overwhelming love of France and his desire to centralize authority on the crown and defeat the destructive and selfish ambitions of the nobles. He became a familiar figure in the culture of Romanticism, thanks to his appearances in Alfred de Vigny's novel *Cinq-Mars* (1826) and Alexandre Dumas' *The Three Musketeers* (1844).

The play *Richelieu* in its final form emerged from the productive collaboration of the writer Edward Bulwer Lytton and the actor William Charles Macready, which ensured that at least three of Lytton's plays held the stage throughout the nineteenth century. In 1838 Lytton had produced for Macready the first draft of a play about the political machinations of Richelieu, intending that Macready should play the romantic lead, eventually called the Chevalier de Mauprat. But Macready immediately saw that Richelieu was by far the most interesting character in the play and persuaded Lytton to rewrite it and focus the dramatic interest on the Cardinal. As it was being rewritten, Lytton and Macready constantly exchanged notes about the action and dramatic structure. Once it was completed, Macready studied histories of the period to get his interpretation right and sought accuracy in costumes and settings.[3]

The play was performed in 1839 and was acclaimed an instant hit. The role remained in Macready's repertoire until he retired. Samuel Phelps then took it on and, from 1845 until his death in 1878, he played the role and was widely seen as the definitive interpreter of it. 'Colonel' Bateman at the Lyceum particularly wanted Irving to play the role and physically he was perfect for it. But Irving was reluctant and only agreed to please Bateman. Although it was popular with audiences, and he performed it on tour in 1878 and occasionally thereafter, he did not retain the role in his permanent repertoire. Irving did not say why he was reluctant to play the role for which, on the face of it, he was ideally suited. But the reason is likely to be that in 1873 when he first played it, Phelps was still performing. As Irving admitted to Chance Newton, he 'funked' playing Wolsey for years because of Phelps's success in the role. Newton also suggests that Irving demanded and got a payrise from £35 to £50 a week from Bateman to play it.[4]

When Lytton published the text of the play, he restored in brackets all the passages cut by Macready, added learned footnotes and defended his alterations from historical fact. He said he was claiming 'that license with dates and details which poetry permits'. He admitted to amalgamating the conspiracy of the Duc de Bouillon with the 'Day of Dupes', and the treason of Cinq-Mars with the fate of the earlier favourite Baradas. It is clear Lytton was concerned with the question of historical accuracy and the educational value often posited for historical drama, explaining of the cuts 'an important consequence of these suppressions, is that Richelieu himself is left, too often and too unrelievedly, to positions which place him in an *amiable* light, without that shadowing forth of his more sinister motives and his fiercer qualities, which is attempted in the written play'. He concluded: 'To judge the author's conception of Richelieu fairly, and to estimate how far it is consistent with historical portraiture, the play must be *read*.'[5] He was revealingly here drawing a distinction between the theatrical version of history in which concessions were made to the demands of the drama and the authentic version of history, which above all needed to be read and studied.

But it was the theatrical version which captured the public imagination. The play interweaves political machinations and a conventional romantic subplot. Act 1 begins with the King's brother the Duc d'Orleans and his favourite Count Baradas plotting with other nobles the overthrow of the King, Louis XIII, and his chief minister, Richelieu, and the installation of Orleans on the throne with the aid of Spanish troops. The Cardinal's ward Julie de Mortmar is loved by both Baradas and the King, but she loves Chevalier Adrien de Mauprat. Richelieu has Mauprat arrested, but only to marry him to Julie in order to keep her out of the hands of the King. He explains his aim to recreate France from her 'old feudal and decrepit carcase'. In Act 2, the King forbids the marriage of Julie and Mauprat. Baradas tells Mauprat that Richelieu contrived the marriage to humiliate him and urges him to assassinate Richelieu. The King sends for Julie to live at court. Richelieu retires to his castle at Ruelle to escape attack by the conspirators.

In Act 3, Julie arrives at Ruelle, having resisted the King's advances but having been told by Baradas that Mauprat approved of them. Mauprat arrives to assassinate Richelieu but the Cardinal produces Julie and exposes the lies of Baradas. Learning that his own guard are part of the plot against him, Richelieu gets Mauprat to claim to have strangled him, feigns death and deceives the plotters. In Act 4, Richelieu reappears and tells the King about the nobles' plot against him. Louis refuses to believe him. He has Mauprat arrested and sends for Julie. Richelieu places her under the protection of the church and launches the curse of Rome on any who touch her. He then defies Baradas and collapses. In Act 5, Richelieu is rumoured to be dying. Julie appeals to the King for Mauprat's life. Baradas presses his suit on her. Richelieu secures evidence incriminating the plotters and brings it to the King, who has Baradas arrested. Mauprat and Julie are reunited and pardoned. Richelieu is restored to power.

The power of the play is attested by the memoirs of George Arliss. Contracted in 1935 by 20th Century Pictures to play Richelieu, Arliss concluded:

> It was very soon obvious to me that it would be wise for us to found the picture on the old play. I had no idea that there were so many people still alive who had read Bulwer Lytton or who had seen his five-act drama *Richelieu or The Conspiracy*. But whenever I

mentioned that I was going to do *Richelieu* somebody would say, 'Ah, Baradas, what a part!' or 'That scene between Richelieu and Louis – great!' and all the old playgoers mentioned the 'Magic Circle' scene. If these flashes of memory had come only from actors I should not have been surprised, but so many of the older people who were merely theatre-goers seemed equally familiar with the play. So I realized an important section of the audience would be disappointed if we broke away entirely from Lytton's formula. When I told Mary Anderson that I was going to do Richelieu, she said: 'Oh wonderful! The Magic Circle – I can see Irving now!' and to my surprise she reeled off the entire speech.[6]

The resulting film simplified the plot, added extra historical episodes, but included all the big scenes from the play in what became a stylish, fast-moving political thriller in costume. All that now remains of the play in the public consciousness is Richelieu's line: 'The pen is mightier than the sword.'

Dutton Cook, writing in the *World*, was unimpressed by Irving's Richelieu. He began by pointing to the deficiencies of the play itself. The lovers are conventional. The frustration of the conspiracy is a foregone conclusion, the plot itself weak and the 'measures taken to frustrate it are almost ludicrously inapt'. But the play 'is by no means lacking in stir and incident … while of skilful dialogue and of high-sounding rhetoric there is a most liberal supply'. But the central interest is the character of Richelieu, 'a curious amalgam of lofty patriotism and low cunning … alternately a grim jester and an enthusiast of most exalted aims … now calm and sarcastic as Iago, and anon furious and impassioned as Lear'.

Dutton Cook praised the staging: 'The play has never before enjoyed such splendour or completeness of decoration. The costumes are notably rich and tasteful; the characters wear the aspect of animated Vandycks.' But he goes on: 'in other respects the representation leaves much to be desired'. He damns the acting ability of the Lyceum company: 'The Lyceum company numbers few actors of any note, and occasionally the drama suffered gravely from the incompetence of its exponents.' Only John Clayton as the King earns praise: 'the actor's appearance is most picturesque, and he declaims his speeches with excellent effect. Of the other actors little can be said in the way of commendation.'

Of Irving's Richelieu, he wrote: 'Mr Irving plays with care and intelligence, his physical gifts, with the assistance of appropriate costume, enabling him to present a striking resemblance to the well-known portraits of the Cardinal. His performance on the whole, however, is deficient in sustained force and fails to impress.' He itemized Irving's failings, his 'system of elocution is somewhat monotonous, and his longer speeches appear to tax him severely, their effect upon the audience being oppressive; while his sarcastic utterances lose point from his too deliberate manner and his lack of a penetrating and resonant quality of voice'. He lays too little stress on the humorous side of the character and is 'spiritless enough' for three acts but 'permits himself a grand burst of passion at the close of the fourth', where 'the actor's genuine ardour evoked storms of applause' (this will be the Curse of Rome speech). 'His most successful effort was in the last scene, which was in many respects very finely rendered.'[7]

It is interesting to compare this notice with Cook's review of Edwin Booth's performance of Richelieu at the Princess's Theatre in November 1880. Cook repeated his complaints about the defects of the play but acknowledged that it remains popular with actors because 'it provides so many opportunities for histrionic flourish and parade'. He thought that Booth's performance was 'remarkable both for its elaboration and its force'.

> A trained elocutionist, and gifted with a voice of rare power and compass, he is always audible; his sagacity as an actor enabling him to give keen point and singular significance to his speeches … In the earliest passages of the play Mr Booth wins applause by his adroitness and ingenuity as an actor of defined and almost humorous character, and his power to personate; in the later scenes he demonstrates his fine command of tragic vehemence and passion. Richelieu's great speeches denouncing Baradas, and invoking the powers of the Church in aid of the persecuted Julie are delivered with extraordinary vigour and virulence, the oratorical frenzy of the actor's manner exercising an electrical effect upon the audience, greatly exciting them, and urging them to most enthusiastic applause.[8]

It is clear Booth succeeded in those areas in which Cook deemed Irving to have failed: the contrast between the humour and the passion, and the vigour, vividness and variety of delivery of the lines. The criticisms of Irving were those that were to become familiar: inaudibility, a too deliberate delivery, and lack of necessary vocal force for the big speeches. Although Brereton says that Cook was frequently grudging towards Irving,[9] Clement Scott, who was to become a devoted Irvingite, and who had praised his performance in *The Bells*, *Charles the First* and *Eugene Aram*, was even more critical. They were all expecting a great performance and it did not come. Conceding that Irving was intelligent and picturesque, he uses similar terms to Cook. The delivery of the verse was 'monotonous and stilted', the performance lacked power and passion. When he finally rose to it in 'The Curse of Rome' speech: 'Voice, strength, and energy overtaxed; a speech delivered so incoherently, that few could follow one syllable'. Yet Scott goes on to admit he was in a minority and points to the fact that the audience were willing Irving to succeed: 'The principal actor was cheered and feted with such triumph as has fallen to few actors in our time. Hats and handkerchiefs were waved; the pit and gallery leaped up on the benches; the house shook and rang with the applause, but the excitement was unwholesome and the cheers were forced. It was the wild delirium of a revival meeting, an excited, earnest enthusiast having previously created slaves, bent them all to his imperious will. The greater the shouting on the stage, the more the cheering of the audience. It was a triumph of din, an apotheosis of incoherence.'[10] Whatever the critics might think, the passionate support of the audience, developed in three short years, shows that Irving was now an undoubted star.

Another historical tyrant, Peter the Great, was the subject of one of Irving's later plays and one of several short-lived failures from the latter part of his career. It was written by his son Laurence and Irving had lavished particular care on it to ensure its success. Although it was a tragedy, it was written not in blank verse but in prose and it centred on the conflict between father and son and between opposing views of the role of the Czar, Peter's autocratic reformer being contrasted with Alexis's humane reactionary.

Audiences were willing the play to succeed when it opened on 1 January 1898. The *Weekly Sun* (2 January 1898) declared:

> 'Welcome back' was the sentiment uppermost in every mind at the Lyceum last night. Sir Henry Irving has developed a love of travel that his admirers in London do not encourage. Long absences in America, and in the English provinces, are not agreeable to the countless friends of the pre-eminent actor, however admirable his *locum tenens* may be. But the King is on his throne again, and the tithe of his subjects able to assemble in the Lyceum last night received him with shouts of acclamation. That many a month may elapse ere he sets forth on his travels again, and that success of *Peter the Great* may help to maintain him in the Lyceum programme is their ardent desire.

The play *Peter the Great* was in five acts. Act 1 is set in Moscow in the Kremlin. Czar Peter is away fighting the Turks and rumours arrive of his defeat and capture. The priests and aristocratic reactionaries, whose powers have been eclipsed by Peter's reforms, encourage his son, the Czarevich Alexis, who is acting as regent in his father's absence, to proclaim himself Czar and seize the throne. Alexis is opposed to his father's reforms: 'His work! His work! Go down into the street and you shall see a row of festering heads on spikes … That is my father's work'. His mother, Peter's ex-wife Eudoxia, divorced and imprisoned in a nunnery by the Czar, encourages him to stand by his father and assist him in his schemes. But Alexis allows himself to be proclaimed Czar. Unexpectedly, Peter returns, determined to suppress opposition to himself. His second wife, the peasant-born Czarina Catherine, to whom Eudoxia has appealed for help, intercedes for Alexis and his friends and Peter pardons them. He resolves to leave Moscow to build a new capital at St. Petersburg. Peter tells Alexis that he knows he has neglected him but is willing to make amends if his heir will make an effort to equip himself to succeed:

> You mustn't think I'm going to love you because you're my son. That's all very well for common people but that is no law for emperors. Emperors don't have sons: they have successors! Love Russia and you love me.

Act 2 takes place three months later. Pausing from building his new capital of

St Petersburg and fighting off the Swedes, Peter comes to Alexis and seeks to examine him on the two books – on fortifications and shipbuilding – he has set him to study, to equip him for rulership. But Alexis, who has been dallying with the beautiful Euphrosyne rather than studying, makes various excuses for not having read the books. Peter strikes him and tells him he must choose between taking up Peter's work or entering a monastery. Alexis begs to be allowed to marry Euphrosyne; Peter refuses. Alexis agrees to enter a monastery. Instead, at the urging of his friends, Alexis flees to Naples with Euphrosyne.

Act 3 takes place in Naples where Alexis and Euphrosyne have taken refuge in the castle of St Elmo. News arrives that Catherine has had a son. Count Tolstoy, Peter's envoy, urges Euphrosyne to persuade Alexis to return to Russia, promising that Peter will look favourably on a marriage between them. He tells Alexis that Peter wants him to become Czarevich again. Alexis agrees to return.

Act 4, in the hall of the Senate in St Petersburg, sees Alexis on trial for treason, the chief witness against him being Euphrosyne, her complicity bought by the promise of a wealthy husband. Alexis denounces Peter's tyranny and is condemned to death. Catherine, unable to bear the thought that her newly-born child may be 'baptized in his brother's blood', intercedes for Alexis. Peter meditates on the various options but signs the death warrant. In Act 5, Peter visits his son in prison, Alexis asks forgiveness for having failed in his duty and Peter asks forgiveness for failing in his love towards his son. Alexis goes willingly to his death, administered by poison. Peter learns that his new child has died and that now he is childless. Outside the anniversary of his great victory of Poltava is being celebrated, but he refuses to allow his private sorrow to suspend the festivities: 'He made the fullest atonement at the last. I honour him. Let Russia honour him. He was my son, my own, my very son.' The contrast between personal grief and national rejoicing ends the play.

Opinion about Irving's acting was, as ever, divided. One critic noted:

> Not the least recommendation of the play is that it gives Sir Henry Irving a part in more than one respect new to him. The brutal callousness of the Czar, his rough good humour so quickly changed to the grimmest ferocity, afford rare opportunity for the actor's mastery of variety of mood. Peter, who is nothing more than a barbarian, is not the same five minutes together ... Sir Henry Irving depicts every phase of the part in the most skilful manner, making each stand out, yet bringing the whole into perfect harmony ... It is a performance marked by exceptional finish and spirit, the grim comedy portions of which are singularly telling.[11]

But for other critics this variety of mood was a weakness rather than a strength:

> Sir Henry Irving fumes and blusters in the character with an amazing expenditure of physical energy. All to little purpose however: for the inherent weakness of the character is only thrown into relief by the force of the language and gesture assigned to it. Peter is

never two moments in the same mood or under the sway of the same idea. He veers about like a weathercock, and finding the dramatist's language an inadequate medium for the expression of his volcanic temperament, growls and roars like a wild beast. The actor's performance in this respect is all too suggestive of a steam hammer employed in cracking a nut.[12]

Several critics noted that Ellen Terry's Catherine, the goodhearted, down-to-earth, peasant-born second wife of Peter, was essentially a rerun of Madame Sans-Gêne, one brutally but accurately dismissing the role as 'short and unimportant'. The American actor Robert Taber, imported to play Alexis after Johnston Forbes-Robertson, perhaps scenting disaster, turned it down, was widely praised. There were two other Americans in the cast, Ethel Barrymore as Euphrosyne and Miss Rockman as Eudoxia. This suggests that Irving was looking deliberately at the American market to retrieve his failing fortunes.

There was an evident desire on the part of many critics to be generous to Laurence. The *Westminster Budget* (7 January 1898) called it 'an interesting, strange drama rich in life and power'. The *St James' Gazette* (3 January 1898) said: 'with all its faults the play is, notwithstanding, a remarkable achievement for a dramatist of Mr Irving's years'. J.T. Grein, however, pulled no punches when he wrote: 'it has no local colour, for none of the characters are typically Russian, and nothing but the names remind us that Muscovite blood flows in their veins … the dialogue scarcely ever rose to the occasion. It was all very colloquial, common-place, and lacking in grip'. He dismissed it as imitation Sardou, 'a nondescript panorama – an ocean of useless speech – a texture of enormous conception, but loosely knit, slow in motion, full of rhetoric but devoid of humanity'.[13]

Whatever their views of the quality of the play, the critics were pessimistic about its prospects. One critic wrote:

> A less promising field there could hardly be for the aspiring dramatist to cultivate. In its dramatic aspects Russian life is gloomy, harsh, dismal; and the pleasure-seeking public are apt to be intolerant of a bleak and cheerless atmosphere, as Mr Laurence Irving himself ought to have learnt from the reception accorded a few years ago to an earlier play of his – clever enough but Russian – entitled *Love, Hunger and the Law*.[14]

Another observed:

> It is a long time since a modern play with such a harrowing theme was produced in a West End theatre, and its intensity is increased by a liberality of painful detail. The fault of undue length may easily be remedied, but the tone of the piece is scarcely susceptible of alteration.[15]

The word 'gloomy' cropped up constantly in the reviews. Bram Stoker concluded:

The tone of the play did not suit the public taste. It was not altogether the fault of the dramatist, but rather of the originals. History is history and has to be adhered to – in some measure at any rate; and the spectacle of a father hounding his son to death is one to make to shudder those whose instincts and sympathies are normal. The history of the time lent itself to horrors. On the first night in one scene where one of the conspirators who had been tortured – off the stage, but whose screams were heard – was brought in pale and bloody, the effect was too great for some of the audience, who rose quickly and left their seats. On the next night this part of the scene was taken out and other lesser horrors modified. Towards the end of the month it became necessary to prepare for a change of bill.[16]

The play closed after thirty-eight performances.

The French Revolution had initially been greeted with joy by some: 'how much the greatest thing that has ever happened to mankind and how much the best' (Charles James Fox); 'Bliss it was in that dawn to be alive, but to be young was very heaven' (Wordsworth). But the horrors of the 'Reign of Terror' induced a more fearful reaction. David Lodge noted the seminal influence on Victorian novels (in particular Mrs Gaskell's *North and South*, Dickens' *Barnaby Rudge* and *A Tale of Two Cities*, Disraeli's *Sybil* and Charlotte Bronte's *Shirley*) of Carlyle's apocalyptic vision of mob action.[17] He concluded of the Victorian novelists:

> The idea of mass experience, mass consciousness, mass behaviour, frightened them, and their fictional representation of crowds in action is invariably negative. The crowd attracts lawless and violent elements in society, and gives them an opportunity to indulge their evil inclinations; it also releases the evil and destructive potential inherent in all of us ... the French Revolution, especially as represented by Carlyle, had given the idea of power of the crowd a new and nightmarish dimension.[18]

British attitudes towards the French Revolution were conditioned by the fact that there was not just revolution in 1789 but in 1830, 1848 and, in the form of the Paris Commune, 1870. Each of them revived memories of 'The Terror'. It was all seen in pointed contrast to Britain, where there had been a peaceful evolution with the widening of the franchise and the gradual extension of civil liberties to religious and ethnic minorities. The attitude of nineteenth-century British historians to the French Revolution was a conservative one, 'in favour of reforms and violent against violence'.[19] Over eighty plays using characters, events and situations from the French Revolution on the nineteenth century English stage have been identified.[20] Despite the dangers of censorship, authors returned again and again to the subject. While many plays celebrated the victories of Wellington and Nelson over the French, some writers used the French setting to comment on domestic British issues. The subject of class was at the heart of Bulwer Lytton's *The Lady of Lyons*, one of the most popular English romantic dramas of the nineteenth century. Its popularity was enough to ensure that Irving should have wanted to produce it. But there was no reason why he should have chosen to play the hero in the make-up of a young Napoleon, were it not for a certain admiration for the French emperor. It is not perhaps surprising that there was empathy. After all, Napoleon was, like Irving, a poor provincial lad who conquered the world, overcoming all difficulties and enemies until he finally met his Waterloo. The lad from Somerset, like the lad from Corsica, was also to meet his Waterloo.

When Carlyle came to his final form of heroism, kingship, he defined it as follows:

> The Commander over men; he to whose will our wills are to be subordinated, and loyally surrender themselves, and find their welfare in doing so, may be reckoned the most important of Great Men. He is practically the summary for us of *all* the various figures of Heroism; Priest, Teacher, whatsoever of earthly or of spiritual dignity we can fancy to reside in a man, embodies itself here, to *command* over us, to furnish us with constant practical teaching, to tell us for the day and hour what we are to *do*.[21]

This might well be a description of Irving's view of himself. He was the Guv'nor, the commander of the staff of the Lyceum. His will was all. But he saw the Lyceum as a temple of art and himself as its high priest.

Carlyle's first example of hero as King was Cromwell, whose reputation Carlyle did so much to rehabilitate. He was not in Irving's pantheon. He preferred *Charles the First* with Cromwell cast as villain. But Carlyle's second choice, Napoleon, was not as great a man as Cromwell for Carlyle, but like him in bringing order out of the chaos of revolution, to tame the beast. A man of sincerity and faith, he rose naturally to be king and was recognized as such, but at the end succumbed to the 'theatrical paper mantles, tinsel and mummery' of dynasties, sham kingdoms and a hollow alliance with the Pope. The very theatricality which did not appeal to Carlyle may well have further endeared Napoleon to Irving. Irving returned regularly to the period of the French Revolution, starring successively in *The Lady of Lyons*, *The Dead Heart*, *Madame Sans-Gêne*, *Robespierre* and *Waterloo*. The themes that these plays explored were class relations, social mobility, sacrifice and tyranny.

Edward Bulwer Lytton's romantic melodrama *The Lady of Lyons: or Love and Pride*, like *Richelieu* a successful product of the creative partnership between the writer and the actor William Charles Macready, had held the stage since it was first performed in 1838. Bulwer Lytton explained in the preface to the published version of the play that, having long wanted to 'illustrate certain periods of French history', he had selected the early days of the Republic (1795–98), with its possibilities for the rapid advance of young men within the army, as the most appropriate for the story he wanted to tell.

For during the early years of the first and most brilliant successes of the French Republic, in the general ferment of society, and its brief equalization of ranks, Claude's high-placed love, his ardent feelings, his unsettled principles (his struggle between which makes the passion of this drama), his ambition, and his career, were phenomena that characterized the age, and in which the spirit of the nation went along with the extravagance of the individual.[22]

The character of the title is Pauline Deschappelles, the daughter of a merchant and the most beautiful girl in Lyons. At the start of the play Beauseant, a gentleman, applies to marry Pauline and is refused, as is his friend Glavis. Pauline's mother is encouraging her to aim for marriage with a foreign nobleman, titles having been abolished in Revolutionary France. Claude Melnotte, a gardener's son who once worked for the Deschappelles, has fallen hopelessly in love with Pauline. He sends her poems but his advances are cruelly rebuffed. Beauseant and Glavis plot to humiliate Pauline by ensuring her unwitting marriage to the gardener's son. They dress him up and present him to Pauline as the Prince of Como, he courts her and they marry. He takes her back to his cottage where the imposture is revealed. Pauline is mortified but Claude is overcome with remorse. He releases her from marriage and joins the French army leaving for Italy. Two years later, he returns, as Morier, now a colonel, a war hero and a rich man. Pauline is about to marry Beauseant in order to save her father from financial ruin. Introduced to Colonel Morier, Pauline tells him that she loves Melnotte but must marry to save her father. Melnotte produces the money to settle the Deshappelles' debts, reveals his identity, and is united with Pauline. Beauseant slinks away. 'You have won love and honour nobly', declares Pauline's father.

There is a strong and interesting class dimension to the play. Pauline's mother, although only a merchant's wife, is determined her daughter shall marry a nobleman. Beauseant, her original suitor, is the son of a marquis but has lost his title in the Revolution. Throughout he behaves badly, announcing to the audience at the outset 'It is a great sacrifice I make in marrying into a family in trade', thereafter devising the plot to humiliate Pauline and finally seeking to buy her hand in marriage. So, although a gentleman by birth, he is not true gentleman. Claude, on the other hand, though a gardener's son, has turned himself into a gentleman, by learning reading, Latin, fencing, dancing and painting. He is nicknamed 'The Prince' by the locals for his prowess and accomplishments. Then by his own efforts in the army rises from the ranks to become a colonel. In this he mirrors the career of the honest and decent soldier, Damas, Madame Deschappelles' cousin, who at the start of the play has risen from the ranks to become a colonel and ends the play as a general. He had seen through the imposture, challenged Claude to a duel and been beaten in the swordfight, thus becoming convinced that Claude is a gentleman. Pauline puts on airs and acts haughtily but eventually sees the errors of her ways and falls for the self-made gentleman.

These sympathies with the self-made gentleman and hostility to the aristocrat, according well with Bulwer's liberal political beliefs, did not go unnoticed at the time. *The Times* denounced the play for its 'republican' propaganda. Macready from the stage rejected any idea that the play was political: 'There are no political allusions that do not grow out of the piece, and are necessarily conducive to the working story … I trust I shall receive credit for the assertion of the principle upon which I conduct this theatre – that art and literature have no politics.' In the preface to the first 1838 printed version, Lytton declared: 'I can honestly say that I endeavoured, as much as possible, to avoid every political allusion applicable to our own time and land – our own prejudices and passions.'[23]

But it was the fable-like romantic drama that drew audiences and continued to do so. The play made a strong appeal to Irving and it is clear that he identified strongly with Claude Melnotte, the peasant who had consciously turned himself into a gentleman. It had long been a favourite play of his.[24] In the very first week of his acting career at the Royal Lyceum, Sunderland, he played the second officer in *The Lady of Lyons*. Only two years later at the Queen's Theatre, Edinburgh, he chose the play for his benefit performance, playing Claude. He played Claude again at the Theatre Royal, Manchester, in 1862. He also gave public readings of the play in London in 1859 and in Buxton in 1863. So when he revived it early in his own management at the Lyceum in London in 1879 it was because it was a play that was important to him.

Most of his contemporary biographers dismissed his performance. Austin Brereton called the revival 'a managerial mistake … For this drama is opposed to all natural acting. Unless it is played in bombastic style, it has no attraction. Besides, its sentiment is very unreal, not to say mawkish.'[25] Charles Hiatt said it was 'a part for which Irving is both mentally and physically unsuited. Where he should have been buoyant and rapturous he was solemn, and, at times, irritable'.[26] Frederic Daly (Louis F. Austin) wrote:

> Claude Melnotte cannot be ranked amongst Mr Irving's best impersonations. Many an inferior actor might be more at home as the rhetorical but commonplace lover of Lord Lytton's play. Mr Irving's versatility is remarkable; but it is no disparagement to his art to say that, though he can be many things by turns, he cannot be the lover who is perpetually in transports about his mistress' eyebrows.[27]

Certainly Irving and Ellen Terry played the roles differently from Macready and Helen Faucit in the first production. Faucit had played Pauline as proud, scornful and imperious; Macready, Claude as ardently romantic. But, as Clement Scott noted, Ellen played Pauline as 'tenderly fragile … constantly fainting and tearfully pathetic', turning her into 'a French Olivia'. Irving played Claude as 'deeply tragic, absorbed, and highly nervous'.[28] But perhaps the writer who understood best what Irving was trying to do here was Percy Fitzgerald. He recalled that Irving 'was himself in sympathy with the piece, and prepared it on romantic and picturesque lines'. It was part of his conscious mission to rescue melodrama, to refine it and make it suitable for the contemporary audience, just as he did with *The Dead Heart*. Fitzgerald recalled:

> It has usually been presented in a stagey, declamatory fashion, as affording opportunity to the two leading performers for exhibiting a robustious or elocutionary passion. It was determined to tone the whole down, as it were, and present it as an interesting love story, treated with restraint. Nothing could be more pleasing than the series of scenes thus unfolded, set off by the not unpicturesque costumes of the revolutionary era ... In Irving's Claude there was a sincerity and earnestness which went far to neutralise these highly artificial, not to say 'high-flown', passages which have so often excited merriment. Miss Terry, as may be conceived, was perfectly suited to her character – the ever-charming Pauline; and displayed an abundance of spontaneousness, sympathy and tenderness.[29]

Rudolph de Cordova, who saw the play and admired Irving's acting in it, said: 'It is the fashion to say that *The Lady of Lyons* is 'fustian'. It is only fustian when treated in the wrong spirit, without any conviction and enthusiasm. Actually it is a great *acting* vehicle, taxing all the actor's technical skill ... Irving, who probed every part he played for its psychological problems, gave a deep mental maturity to Claude'. He noted too a great *coup de théâtre* devised by Irving when he came on in the last act as Colonel Morier:

> As he came on the stage, Irving looked the image of Napoleon. The effect was electrical. It was not, of course, the Buonaparte of the later days when he had put on flesh, but the Buonaparte of the first Italian campaign ... the Buonaparte of the set mouth, the eagle-like glance, the beautiful, thin face, which Josephine said was too handsome to be disfigured by a moustache.[30]

Irving staged it with faultless taste and visual style. Clement Scott wrote in the *Daily Telegraph*:

> Even those, who are unaffectedly weary of the old-fashioned sentiment of the play, and are bold enough to have formed a very decided opinion on the characteristic of Claude and the pride of Pauline, can gaze contentedly at faultless pictures, at costume raised to the dignity of art, if occasionally astonishing in its accuracy, and at the immeasurable graces of arrangement and movement, which pleased the eye when the ear is out of tune with the passion of the scene.[31]

Irving achieved a memorable effect at the end of Act 4 for, as Melnotte declares to Colonel Damas who has suggested he join his regiment, 'Place me wherever a foe is most dreaded – wherever France most needs a life', Claude rushes out and joins a detachment of French troops marching four abreast as the band plays the

Marseillaise. They marched past with banners flying and drums beating to the correct French military beat and they kept on marching as Irving had the curtain rising and falling over the scene. Irving employed 150 soldiers from the Brigade of Guards as supers. The result, as de Cordova recalled, was 'the curtain comes down to thunderous applause. Up it went. Down it came. Over and over and over again as we kept on applauding, applauding, applauding, with a fevered, almost frenzied, tribute of admiration for a master of climax.'[32] The play ran for forty-one nights plus four special performances and then was withdrawn and Irving, now forty-one, never played Claude again.

The Revolution became on the Victorian stage the vehicle for moral fables of suffering, sacrifice and redemption. It may have been Bulwer Lytton, that inspirer of much in the Romantic canon, who first applied in fiction the idea of someone sacrificing themselves on the guillotine to save the life of a friend or lover. In his novel *Zanoni* (1842) the leading figure goes to the guillotine to save the woman he loves. In Paris in 1847 the stage version of Dumas' novel *Le Chevalier de Maison Rouge* had Geneviève the heroine entering prison to change places with Marie Antoinette and facilitate her escape. But she and her lover Maurice are captured and condemned to death. It is his best friend Lorin who takes their place and dies on the scaffold.

In Ben Webster's play *The Destruction of the Bastille* (1844), produced under his management at the Adelphi, Robespierre sacrifices his life to save and unite two lovers, his daughter Ernestine and a young captain of the Swiss Guard, Victor Rollande. This was followed in 1853 by Boucicault's adaptation of the Dumas play, now titled *Genevieve: or The Reign of Terror*. Then came Watts Phillips with his play *The Dead Heart*, which he offered to Ben Webster. Webster, who thought it resembled *Genevieve* too closely, held it back for three years but when in 1859 Dickens's *A Tale of Two Cities* began appearing in serial form, Phillips pressed Webster to act and Webster put on *The Dead Heart* at the Adelphi on 10 November 1859, playing the lead himself.[33] His erstwhile partner and now rival, Madame Celeste, mounted a rival production at the Lyceum on 18 January 1860, Tom Taylor's adaptation of Dickens's *A Tale of Two Cities* but with Sydney Carton spared the guillotine – Barsad perishes in his place. *The Dead Heart* was proclaimed by the papers 'a most unprecedented hit. The life-like pictures of the French Revolution have never before been equalled, even on the Parisian stage, for correctness of detail and costume, and the acting of the principal characters have received the universal stamp of praise.'[34] It ran for six weeks, being withdrawn in favour of *A Christmas Carol*, and was subsequently revived at intervals.

The similarity of the plot of *The Dead Heart* to that of *A Tale of Two Cities* led the Dickens faction to charge Phillips with plagiarism. Webster responded by saying he had had the Phillips play for two years and had once read it out to a group of friends which included Dickens. So it seems the basic idea came to Dickens from Phillips rather than vice-versa. But Carton may also have been partly inspired by the character of Richard Wardour, who sacrifices his life to save the woman he loves unrequitedly, a role Dickens himself had played in a performance of Wilkie Collins's *The Frozen Deep* in 1857.[35] Both Phillips and Dickens admitted using Carlyle's *French Revolution*, where they would have found the story of a nobleman Lieutenant General Loiserolles, imprisoned in St Lazare, who takes the place of his son on the guillotine, when the son's name is called.[36]

Watts Phillips (1825–1874) was another of those literary Bohemians who turned his hand to anything and everything; he was, as his sister recalled, 'novelist, poet, artist, dramatist, critic, caricaturist, *comique*, and an admirable, spirited, natural letter writer'.[37] With his high forehead, Van Dyke beard and Tudor collar, he cultivated a resemblance to Shakespeare. Abandoning an early ambition to be an actor, he earned his living working as a journalist for the *Daily News* and *Town Talk* but, entranced by the stage, he turned to playwriting. *The Dead Heart* was his first play and his greatest success.

Phillips wrote many other plays (*The Huguenot Captain, Amos Clarke, Marlborough, Lost in London, Paper Wings, Camilla's Husband, Theodora, The Woman in Mauve, Black Mail, Nobody's Child, On the Jury*). At one time he had four plays running simultaneously in London. His friend, the actor John Coleman commented in 1890: 'Many of these dramas took six months of the author's life … yet, as he himself stated, his highest remuneration for a play was three hundred pounds.'[38] In fact Phillips, who lived for many years in Paris, suffered from recurrent ill-health, brought on, his sister suggests, by overwork.

In 1889, a century after the storming of the Bastille, Irving decided on a revival of *The Dead Heart* at the Lyceum. First of all he hired Walter Herries Pollock to adapt it to his own requirements. This meant reducing the knockabout comedy and stylizing and refining the text, so that it was transformed from Adelphi melodrama to Lyceum romantic drama. Irving was to lavish his usual attention on the production: Hawes Craven's beautiful painted scenery; Georges Jacobi arranging and supervising the music of the period; expert research to guarantee the accuracy of the costumes by Alice Comyns Carr, Joseph Grego and W.H. Margetson; the spectacular recreation of the storming of the Bastille.

Irving had long been anxious to act with Squire Bancroft, one of his chief rivals as leading actor-manager of the day, and a prime exemplar of gentlemanly theatre. He invited him to play Chateau Renaud in *The Corsican Brothers* in 1880, but Bancroft was still in management at the Haymarket and busy with his own productions. The Bancrofts retired in 1885 and in 1889 Irving asked Bancroft to emerge from retirement to play the Abbé Latour in his revival of *The Dead Heart*. Subtly increasing the pressure on Bancroft, Irving said he would not undertake the revival unless Bancroft agreed to do it. Bancroft eventually offered to do it for nothing, but Irving insisted on paying him the appropriate rate for a guest star. Bancroft donated £1000 of his fee to the Salvation Army and the rest to other charities.[39] As Irving no doubt anticipated, there was much press comment on the return of Bancroft, and, although on the opening night he was suffering both from a bad cold and first night nerves, he was enthusiastically received by audience and press.

The other publicity coup was in having the real-life mother and son Ellen Terry and Gordon Craig playing a fictional mother and son. Gordon Craig was Irving's godson and he was genuinely devoted to the boy, arranging and paying for elocution lessons for him with veteran actor Walter Lacy and for French lessons, taking him on holiday, arranging his acting debut and on the occasion presenting him with an inscribed eighteenth century silver-topped cane. Craig recalled: 'I had been to Bradfield College – learnt nothing. Then in 1889, Lyceum Theatre and Henry Irving – my real school and my real master.'[40] Terry thought her part 'rather uninteresting' but 'my son Teddy made his first appearance in it, and I soon forgot that for me the play was rather "small beer".'[41] There was to be some criticism that an antique Adelphi melodrama was unworthy of the Lyceum. But Irving was wedded to the form and his mission to refine and elevate it. Terry noted: 'It was only a melodrama, but Henry could always invest a melodrama with life, beauty, interest, mystery, by his methods of production.'[42]

His methods of production involved revising the script, sparing no expense to get sets, costumes and music just right, and creating sweeping and striking stage pictures. He wrote to Ellen:

> I'm full of French Revolution … and could pass an examination. In our play, at the taking of the Bastille we must have a starving crowd-hungry, eager, cadaverous faces. If that can be well carried out, the effect will be very terrible, and the contrast to the other crowd (the red and fat crowd – the blood-gorged ones who look as if they'd been drinking wine – (*red* wine, as Dickens says) would be striking … A letter this morning from the illustrious Blank offering me his prompt book to look at … I think I shall borrow the treasure. Why not? Of course he will say that he has produced the play and all that sort of thing; but what does that matter, if one can only get one hint out of it? The longer we live, the more we see that if we only do our own work thoroughly well, we can be independent of everything else or anything that may be said … I see in Landry a great deal of Manette – the same vacant gaze into years gone by when he crouched in his dungeon nursing his wrongs.[43]

This letter gives us a sharp insight into Irving's approach: steeping himself in research, drawing on Dickens, willing to use anything (such as an old prompt book) to glean extra inspiration, thinking visually.

Ben Webster, the actor grandson of Benjamin Webster of the Adelphi, was in the audience and later recalled his impressions:

There was much surprise that Irving should resuscitate a thirty-year-old melodrama of this type. The centenary of the taking of the Bastille was a good excuse so far as the general public was concerned, but it did not satisfy artistic conscience, and there was much shaking of heads and whispering of lowered prestige, but the end justified the experiment, both artistically and financially. Irving's special gift of giving dignity to any form of drama was again evident. Just as his treatment of *The Lyons Mail* and *The Bells* had raised them almost to the importance of classics, so he was able to perform the miracle once more. As to stage management, it is safe to say that never was such an amazing example of realism as the taking of the Bastille seen in a theatre. The spaciousness of the setting was extraordinary; one felt oneself transported to Paris on that fatal fourteenth of July, a participator in the drama; the heat, the dust, the rolling clouds of smoke from the cannon were present and actual. It was an experience lived, rather than merely witnessed.[44]

The play accurately captured the trajectory of British views of the French Revolution and the move from sympathy to horror, in the context of Britain's view of itself as a parliamentary democracy and constitutional monarchy. The play opens with a prologue set in 1771. In the Café de la Belle Jardinière, disaffected Parisians discuss the plight of the people under the regime of Louis XV (people dying from starvation; the aristocratic corruption at the court of Versailles; and the malign influence of the King's mistress Madame Du Barry). Robert Landry, a young sculptor and radical, dances with his betrothed, the wine merchant's daughter Catherine Duval. She is also loved by Count de St Valery but his proposal of marriage has been rejected. The Count's confidant and adviser, the Abbé Latour, 'the most accomplished scoundrel in Paris', devises a scheme to get rid of Landry and to compromise Catherine. He arranges for the Count to enter Catherine's bedroom via a ladder to propose an elopement and Landry, finding them together, believes she has betrayed him. Latour then appears with a detachment of soldiers and a warrant for Landry's arrest for treason, obtained through the help of Du Barry. He is taken to the Bastille.

Act 1, set in 1789, eighteen years later, opens with the storming of the Bastille. The prisoners are released, among them a broken and distracted Landry. He asks to be taken to Catherine. Catherine, believing Landry dead, has married St Valery and produced a son, Arthur. St Valery himself is dead but young Arthur is now under the corrupting influence of Latour and running up gambling debts. Latour makes advances to Catherine and, when she rejects them, reveals that Landry is alive. Landry, who has been informed of Catherine's situation, encounters Latour and Arthur at the gaming house and swears revenge on them. When Catherine appears and tries to explain to him what happened, he tells her that although he is alive, his heart is dead.

Act 2 is set in 1794 at the height of the terror. The mob surround the Conciergerie prison, cheering news of the names of prisoners marked for execution. Latour and Arthur are on the death list. Landry, now a leading figure in the Convention, has the Abbé brought from his cell and offers him the chance of freedom if he survives a duel. They fight and Latour is killed. In Act 3, Catherine intercedes with Landry for her son's life. She explains that soon after his arrest, St Valery tried to secure his release but Latour convinced them he was dead and that was when she married St Valery. She implores him 'by the memory of our old love ... save my son'. Landry, his heart reawakened to love of her, takes Arthur's place on the scaffold, first ensuring the reunion of mother and son.

The play personalizes the response of the Revolution in Landry. At the outset, there is sympathy with Landry as a young radical who, because of the excesses of the Ancien Régime, refuses to toast the King and pens vitriolic accounts of the corruption of the court. Aristocratic tyranny sees him immured in the Bastille and the people eventually free him. But the Revolution, apparently justified in its initial aims, soon turns to anarchy and massacre. The names of the victims read out include both aristocrats and commoners. Landry, known as 'Cato the Censor' ('as cold as marble and as true as steel') begins to question the indiscriminate slaughter ('And with this grim scaffold they would regenerate mankind? With this ghastly emblem of the madness of the time'). Then, when humanity is reawakened and love reasserts its power, he makes the supreme sacrifice to reunite mother and son.

The corrupting nature of the Revolution is reinforced by the comic character, Toupet, who starts out as an ultra-royalist Versailles barber, but transforms himself into a dedicated supporter of the Revolution and a republican jailer. So the revolution becomes a vehicle for opportunists. As in *A Tale of Two Cities*, the British stance is that the aristocratic Ancien Régime and the republican reign of Terror are equally evil and the implication is that France would have been much better off with the evolutionary progress of the British system.

The success of the play reawakened interest in both Watts Phillips and in the plagiarism controversy, and directly prompted two books. John Coleman, a friend of the author and an actor who played Robert Landry throughout the provinces, notably at York, Leeds and Glasgow ('its attraction was perennial!' he recalled) published *The Truth about The Dead Heart*.[45] Watts Phillips's sister, Emma Watts Phillips, published a biography, *Watts Phillips: Artist and Playwright*, in which she specifically credits Irving's revival of the play with reawakening interest in her brother. Both recorded their impressions of the play. Coleman praised the *mise-en-scène*:[46]

The opening scene – the Garden of the Café de la Belle Jardinière – is superbly beautiful; the dramatic action is animated and appropriate; the dance bright and joyous, and eminently suggestive of the spring time of mirth and joy, of life and love. Taking of the Bastille is the most picturesquely realistic spectacle of that epoch ever presented either on the French or English stage. Every one concerned from the principal actor down to the humblest supernumerary, acts like an artist. Every detail, every figure, every note of music, every costume, every colour, every inflection of the voice, nay, even every whisper, every gesture, and every look, are appropriate to the tremendous strength of the situation, and the result is an *ensemble* which does not fail to satisfy the most exacting standard of criticism.[47]

Of Irving's Landry, he wrote: 'Mr Irving has found in Robert Landry a character probably more after his own heart and his resources than any he has hitherto sustained – a character which commingles the poetic and the picturesque with the pathetic and heroic. Landry is at once hero and martyr, victim and victor, sufferer of wrong and avenger of blood … From the first moment the auditor is held spellbound and captive by the player's potent art, and the entire performance rises in one continuing and ever-increasing crescendo until the climax of the sacrifice is reached, and the hero-martyr passes from the darkness of night to the splendour of eternal morning.' He thought that 'Ellen Terry's Catherine Duval is the quintessence of all that is sweet, and tender and loveable in woman'.[48] He defended it against dismissal as a mere melodrama:

> This play appeals to those who have heads to think and hearts to feel … In three short hours it crystallises three phases of a nation's history. Before the mind's eye arise the joy, the sorrow, the love of love, the hate of hate, the villainy, the revenge, the remorse and the despair, the crime and the punishment, the storm and the strife, the thunder breath of the great upheaval of the old barriers, and the bloody baptism of the mightiest epoch, which has ever burst upon this earth of ours, since the dawning of Creation's day.[49]

Watts Phillips's sister, who also witnessed the revival, regretted 'the almost total elimination of its humours', the comic grotesquerie of Toupet and Cerisette which had provided she thought a necessary counterpoint to the tragedy. 'In its new shape, therefore, the play seemed to present too much unvaried sadness'.[50] But she put her finger correctly on Irving's success in the part.

> Mr Irving … brought the whole into harmony with the times, and imparted to it a true romantic grace. It is admitted that he himself has been rarely fitted with a part so suited to his genius and capacities, or in which he has roused the sympathies of his audience more thoroughly. It is only the romantic actor that understands what may be called the *key* of a play.[51]

She stressed his grace and his magnetism, the 'significance in the face, the bearing, the fashion in which he even wears his clothes', the restraint and reserve which suggested 'quiet, condensed purpose'. She too praised the *mise-en-scène*, in particular the final sequence:

> We venture to say that nothing so beautifully suggestive, as well as effective has been seen on the stage as the last pictures of *The Dead Heart*. There is a darkened chamber in the prison whence Landry goes forth to make his sacrifice, the meeting of the mother

and son following. After an interval the background lightens, and a misty vision is seen behind, of the tumbrel moving on the guillotine, and the admirably-posed figure of Landry standing erect. To most spectators this seemed to be the fitting and sufficient conclusion. But what followed was a true surprise. With a fine, almost imperceptible, progress, the background seemed to dissolve, leaving 'not a wrack behind'; figures began to grow and multiply, a sort of lurid tone came over all, and there was revealed the whole scene of scaffold, with – the most effective of all – the long row of revolutionary soldiers ranged, their backs to the audience. This living shadowy barrier between the reality and the visions seemed wonderfully effective. There was nothing of the usual pretentious 'tableau' in this; the idea was conveyed that this scene was before the mind of the mother and son, which, in those high-strung, nervous days, it might well be. The judicious *reserve* of the whole change, and the perfect repose, made it almost a dreamy, intellectual operation, contrasted with the usual upheavings and 'clatterings' with which such things are usually done.[52]

Reservations about the quality of the play, even as revised by Walter Herries Pollock, remained. One critic commented:

The Dead Heart ... is a profoundly sombre and pathetic melodrama, with a plot that is full of powerful dramatic suggestion. The scheme is admirable, and it is the work of a skilful playwright; but it needs a dramatist to 'write it up'. The dialogue is very poor; and instead of merely allowing Mr Walter Pollock to 'revise it', Mr. Irving should have had the play rewritten. It lacks emotional impulse as it is. There are some scenes that might be full of drama, that might literally vibrate with passionate emotion, if only they were written. Dramatically the play is a rough sketch at present, and consequently its impressiveness is considerably discounted. But it serves.[53]

Another complained:

A vast amount of time, energy, money and artistic labour has been expended by Mr Henry Irving upon an unfortunate experiment. *The Dead Heart* is a play with a spurious reputation. At the time of the original production it was regarded as something unusually excellent, but the Adelphi theatre of half a century ago was not the Lyceum theatre of today. Mr Irving has consistently educated his audience upwards; and his usual insight momentarily forsook him when he elected to place before his patrons a piece that is immeasurably inferior to anything he has ever attempted before. Its garish crudity has been to some extent toned down by the refined pen of Mr Walter Pollock, but the process while modifying colour has nowhere intensified effect, and the present version of *The Dead Heart* presents the regrettable appearance of a 'restored' church.[54]

A third remarked:

The Lyceum production of *The Dead Heart* is an admirable illustration of what a little good acting, and a great deal of excellent stage management will do to make an indifferent play acceptable ... Mr Walter Pollock has improved the play as written by Mr Watts Phillips, he has cut out a lot of unnecessary dialogue, put the tiresome low-comedy element in the background, and adapted a great deal of the high falutin' language into simple and sensible English. With all this, *The Dead Heart* remains, from a dramatic point of view, an unsatisfactory work, thin in plot and improbable in motive ... The play is one that derives most of its value from its setting.[55]

But there was unstinting praise for the acting, the staging, the music and the costumes. The storming of the Bastille and the duel between Landry and Latour were singled out as high points by many critics. One critic observed:

> Mr Irving as manager and dramatic organiser was seen at his best. The scenery, painted and arranged by Mr Telbin and Mr Hawes Craven, may challenge comparison with the famous sets in the *Faust* and the *Macbeth* ... the incidental music has been very skilfully adapted to the action of the piece, and forms a feature of special interest and attractiveness. Above all, there are here presented such stage crowds as have rarely, if ever, been seen in English theatre.[56]

Another critic noted:

> The taking of the Bastille, when the stage is filled with a surging and howling mob, is a spectacle that haunts the mind; but still more impressive, perhaps, are the deliberate methods of the Terror, coupled with the ghastly signs of the guillotine as dimly discerned in the early morning.[57]

In Squire Bancroft's view the duel was the best scene in the play, fought in a moonlit room with sabres. 'The scene remains in the memory, and I often hear from many old playgoers that it was the best thing of the kind they ever saw.'[58] Walter Pollock gave him a miniature rapier in Toledo steel as a memento of the production. But it was not without its hazards. Both Bancroft and Irving were short-sighted and habitually wore glasses. Although they rehearsed in them, they acted without them. Both were good fencers and made a convincing show of it. One critic comments:

> The duel between Landry and Abbé Latour, which is fought with sabres, is one of the most thrilling episodes in the play, will perhaps please the audience more when it is said that it is not a pre-arranged fight; for so consummate a broad-sword fencer is Mr Irving that he lets Mr Bancroft ... lay on with all his might and how he likes, and calmly defends himself against the attack, which is never alike twice. In consequence, for absolute realism, it surpasses Mr Mansfield's tremendous fight in *Richard III*.[59]

It was a play in which the two strongest roles went to Irving and Bancroft. Irving garnered general praise. Typical of the reviews he received was this comment:

> We all know his special talent for the lurid effects of melodrama, and he simply revels in the part of Robert Landry. His deadly impassivity in the duel scene sends a cold shiver down your back. But his great coup is in the scene of Robert's disinternment from the

dungeons of the Bastille. Such a makeup, such a wild unkempt, uncanny figure from Callot or Cruikshank? And his awful, inhuman bloodcurdling screech.[60]

Another critic wrote:

> The three stages of the hero's career – the buoyancy of his youth, the betrayal of all his bright hopes in manhood, and the nobility of his final self-sacrifice – are finely portrayed by Mr Irving, who proves once again his mastery of melodramatic colouring.[61]

Bancroft similarly received plaudits:

> It was a happy thought to cast Bancroft for the part of Abbé Latour. Never has the cynical, faithless, treacherous courtier found a more polished representative. Mr Bancroft's management of the character, with its splendid audacity, its biting sarcasm, its utterly corrupt and depraved selfishness, and its perfect *tenue* is admirable. Very striking is the duel scene between Landry and the Abbé as rendered by Mr Irving and Mr Bancroft; the one, cold, implacable, pitiless, the other haughty, contemptuous and cynical, with a perceptible undercurrent of deadly hate and treachery combined nevertheless with all the pride of caste and the unflinching courage of the *gentilhomme*.[62]

The critics agreed, however, with Ellen Terry's own estimate of her part of Catherine Duval when they wrote: 'Miss Ellen Terry looks very charming, and more Ellen Terry than ever in an absolutely insignificant part'; and 'Miss Ellen Terry has few opportunities as Catherine and scarcely makes the most of them'; and 'it is not a good part, and we scarcely think it is well fitted to Miss Terry's personality'.[63]

The Dead Heart ran for 166 consecutive performances, 183 nights altogether in its Lyceum revival. But it was not revived thereafter and Irving did not tour it in America. As the favourite British stage representation of the French Revolution it was superseded by two other productions, *The Only Way*, a version of *A Tale of Two Cities* by Freeman Wills and Frederick Langbridge, which John Martin-Harvey premiered at the Lyceum in 1899 and which remained in his repertoire for the rest of his career; and *The Scarlet Pimpernel*, Baroness Orczy's stage play which Fred Terry starred in for years after his first appearance in 1903. Irving did it for the chance to stage the French Revolution, and for the chance it gave him to play hero, martyr and avenger, in the same play and for its celebration of heroic self-sacrifice.

Madame Sans-Gêne by Victorien Sardou and Emile Moreau was first seen in Paris in 1893 with the celebrated actress Réjane in the lead. It was an enormous popular success, was regularly revived and by 1900 had received more than 600 performances. Irving saw Madame Réjane and her company play it in London in 1895 and purchased the English rights. Joseph Comyns Carr translated it into English and it was produced at the Lyceum on 10 April 1897. It was later turned into a light opera, *The Duchess of Danzig*, by Ivan Caryll and Henry Hamilton, appearing first in 1903 and enjoying long runs in London and the provinces. Irving saw it as an ideal vehicle for Ellen Terry but also as the opportunity for him to play Napoleon. Its success in France and its subsequent popularity as a light opera suggest that Irving's commercial instincts here were sound, something acknowledged by the usually critical William Archer in his review of the Lyceum production.

Stoker, although he knew of Irving's fascination with Napoleon, had not taken seriously his desire to play the part, particularly in *Madame Sans-Gêne*. For one thing Napoleon did not appear until half way through the play, an unusual thing for an actor-manager to contemplate. 'The part of Napoleon in the play is not one that could appeal to any great actor on grounds of dramatic force. Its relative position in the play is not even one that appeals to the measure of self-value which is, to some degree, in all of us.' There was an even greater problem with the part. 'No two men could be further apart in matter of physique and identity. Napoleon, short and stout, full-faced, aggressive, coarse. Irving, tall, thin, ascetic; with manners of exquisite gentleness; with a face of such high, thoughtful distinction that it stood out in any assemblage of clever men.'[64]

Irving had concluded that his best chance to play a part he clearly wanted to was in a comedy. ('Matters that work against one in serious drama can de made actually to further one's purpose in comedy.') So, if his appearance provoked laughter, it would enhance rather than undermine the production. But Irving spared no pains to turn himself into Napoleon. He had oversize furniture and properties made to help reduce his height. He had fleshings made to pad him out and a costume designed to create the impression of stoutness. As Stoker recalled: 'All that Irving required to satisfy the audience was the *coup d'oeil*; in endeavouring to convince it does not do to start off with antagonism. So long as the first glance did not militate against him, he could depend on himself to realize their preconceived idea – which was of historical truth – by acting.'[65] So Irving's Napoleon was first seen, seated low behind a huge writing table, piled with books, dwarfed by the pillars and pilasters of the room which carried the eye upwards from the floor and surrounded by soldiers, generals and statesmen played by actors chosen for their height. The gasp from the audience that greeted this first appearance told him that his stratagem had worked. Irving's Napoleon was one talking point for audiences; the other was Ellen Terry's impersonation of the washerwoman turned duchess.

The play, which had fifty parts in it and was lavishly staged, costing Irving £3587 3s. 6d., opened on 10 April 1897. Ellen recorded in her diary: 'I acted courageously and fairly well. Extraordinary success.'[66] But Laurence Irving records that 'Irving was disappointed to find that Ellen Terry, for whom he had bought Sardou's play, became more and more out of temper with her part as rehearsals went on. Perhaps it was because her tiresome family and the man Shaw were constantly discouraging her. She was having her usual difficulty in learning her words and had not finally mastered them by the first night.[67]

Madame Sans-Gêne begins with a prologue, set in August 1792, in the laundry of Madame Sans-Gêne, as the beautiful Catherine Hubscher is called, on account of her free and easy manner. It is the day of the storming of the Tuileries. The Garde Nationale are seen marching back and forth in front of her door. Her lover, Sergeant Lefebvre, is in the thick of the fight while Fouché is watching events from the laundry. When Catherine has dismissed the women and closed her shop, she is startled by the entrance through her private door of the Austrian Count de Neipperg, who has escaped from the Tuilleries. He is wounded and pursued, and Catherine hides him in her own bedroom, where Lefebvre discovers him, provoking jealousy. But she proves her innocence and allows Neipperg to escape.

Act 1 begins nineteen years later when Lefebvre is a Marshal of France and Duke of Danzig and Catherine is his wife and the Duchess, though she retains her frank common ways. Fine clothes and the services of a dancing master fail to improve her. She is the laughing stock of her servants and a scandal at the imperial court. The sisters of the Emperor Napoleon, Queen Caroline and Princess Elisa, wait upon her and she astonishes them by her candour and gives them a piece of her mind for adopting a lofty tone towards her.

In Act 2, Napoleon, outraged by her behaviour, her clumsiness and her slang, sends for Lefebvre and suggests that he divorce her or lose imperial favour. He returns to Catherine, tells her about the interview and that he rejected the Emperor's demand. Suspecting the Emperor's sisters of poisoning his mind against her, she consults Fouché, the ex-police chief, who confirms her suspicions, but warns her to keep her temper and hold her tongue. She meets the two sisters, denounces them furiously, and is summoned to see the Emperor. In Act 3, the Emperor is in his library at Compiégne, with his chief of police, generals and courtiers. His sisters apply for a private audience and tell Napoleon that his wife, Marie-Louise, is having an affair with Count de Neipperg. A furious family row ensues, in which they lapse into Corsican, the Emperor rejects their accusations and drives them out.

Madame Sans-Gêne arrives for her interview and Napoleon denounces her for her lack of breeding and urges a divorce. She defends herself with spirit, claims that his sisters sneer at the army, demonstrates her knowledge of his campaigns (which she joined in as a *vivandière*, being wounded at Wagram). She climaxes her defence by presenting him with a bill for his laundry when he was a young lieutenant. He is now attracted to her and makes an advance, but she repels and rebukes him, declaring her love for her husband.

In the next scene, Napoleon, lying in wait at midnight, apprehends Neipperg making his way to the Empress's bedroom. Neipperg draws his sword on the

Emperor, who orders him to be shot. But Catherine and Fouché contrive to prove the innocence of the Empress and to smuggle Neipperg out of France.

The critics praised the spectacle (particularly the opening Revolutionary scenes and the reception at Compiégne), the costumes (several newspapers ran articles just on the dresses) and the novelty of Irving playing Napoleon and Terry playing 'common'. But there was very little praise for the play itself. *Punch* (24 April 1897) observed:

> That the play, not a particularly good one to start with, loses in this translation, is evidenced not only by the adapter having made the French washerwoman of 1792 talk London slang of 1897, but also by the absurdity of retaining the scene where Napoleon and his sisters 'drop into Corsican' when they are having a family squabble ... The piece, which is remarkable neither for striking novelty of plot nor for brilliancy of dialogue, must depend for its success mainly on public curiosity to see how SIR HENRY IRVING contrives to reduce himself to physical Napoleonic proportions, and how delightful is the *Madame Sans-Gêne* of MISS ELLEN TERRY.

William Archer in the *World* (14 April 1897) noted:

> So long as the intrigue is kept in the background, the play is amusing enough, and the scene between the washerwoman-duchess and the sub-lieutenant-Emperor may rank as one of the most ingenious and amusing pieces of quasi-historical comedy ever written. It is not unworthy of the elder Dumas. But the preparations for the Fouché–Neipperg–Rovigo intrigue cause a tedious break in the fun of the first act, while the working out of the miserable invention simply devastates the last act. It seemed to me that the actors were as much bored as I was by the childish futility of this scene, the plots and counterplots that lead to nothing at all, the perpetual movement without the smallest advance. Might not Mr Comyns Carr, I wonder, have spared us some of this tedium?

There was widespread astonishment at Ellen Terry taking on the role of the vulgar French washerwoman. But most critics agreed with the *Westminster Budget* (16 April 1897) that she 'gave one the idea of a civilized person doing it as a 'lark'.' *Punch* said: 'She is a charming Madame Sans-Gêne. Her washerwoman is not quite as vulgar as was that of Madame Réjane, and therefore our English actress's portrayal of the character is not so life-like ... as was the great French actress's impersonation ... But it is Ellen Terry as Madame Sans-Gêne and that, for most playgoers, is enough.' Another critic thought the performance: 'a distinctly English Madame Sans-Gêne; there is not a ha'porth of the French woman in Miss Terry'. A further comment was: 'To see Ellen Terry, the most delicate and refined of our actresses in a part which is one of broad, almost low comedy, is to increase our respect for the art of histrionic illusion ... She does it and with really brilliant success'.[68] Irving convinced his critics by and large. His performance was variously described as 'a marvellous transformation', 'something of a *tour de force*' and 'quite worthy of a place in the gallery of his brilliant creations'.[69]

Even Shaw, admittedly still hoping that Irving was going to take his play *Man of Destiny* then under consideration at the Lyceum, was more amiable than usual to Irving: 'He is nothing but the jealous husband of a thousand fashionable dramas, talking Buonapartiana. Sir Henry Irving seizes the opportunity to show what can be done with an empty part by an old stage hand. The result is that he produces the illusion of the Emperor behind the part ... it is an amusingly crafty bit of business.'[70] One person was unpersuaded. The Prince of Wales told Irving: 'Sir Henry – you should not play Napoleon – Wellington perhaps – but not Napoleon.'[71] This was quite perceptive. Irving would have made a marvellous Wellington: but he never essayed the role.

Stoker, while admiring Irving's acting, thought that his presence in the role unbalanced the play. He recalled:

> And when he did act how real it was. The little short-stepped quick run in which he moved in his restless dominance was no part of general historic record; but it fitted into the whole personality in such a way that, having seen, one cannot dissociate them. The ruthless dominance; the quick blaze of passion which recalled to our memory the whirlwind rush at Lodi or the flame-like sweep over the bridge at Arcola; the conscious acting of a part to gain his end; the typical attack on Neipperg. All these were so vivid that through the midst of their swirling memory loomed the very identity of Napoleon himself. Strange to say that the very excellence of Irving's acting, as well as his magnitude in public esteem, injured the play, *qua* play. To my mind it threw it in a measure out of perspective. The play is a comedy, and a comedy of a woman at that. Napoleon is in reality but an incidental character ... Irving, as the part was written, was too big for the play. It was not in any way his fault ... It was primarily the fault of the dramatists in keeping the Emperor, who was incidental, on the stage too long.[72]

There was a certain degree of dissatisfaction. The *Westminster Budget* (16 April 1897), while conceding the play was 'superbly mounted', complained that Irving appeared only in one and a half of the four acts, and regretted that he should choose to appear in a French play displaying 'little originality'. But William Archer – of all people – came to Irving's defence.

> We are apt to pay Sir Henry Irving the embarrassing compliment of regarding him as a privileged person, and instinctively imposing on him correlative obligations. The Lyceum has for so long been proclaimed, and justly, our leading theatre, and its manager holds by common consent so pre-eminent and representative a position, that we find it difficult to think of the theatre as a commercial enterprise like any other, and the manager as a mere dealer in entertainments ... The Lyceum is no sacred precinct, dedicate from of old to poetic drama; and it is absurd for us to feel injured, humiliated or even surprised if we find Shakespeare, for a season, supplanted by Sardou. In all probability, *Madame Sans-Gêne* will prove a most attractive entertainment for the Jubilee public. It gives Miss Ellen Terry a rollicking part, through which she gambols delightfully ... It presents Sir Henry Irving in a great historic character, for which he has obviously no physical fitness,

so that people are curious to see how he effects the incredible transformation. It involves a lavish display of costumes and uniforms, and a great deal of scenic movement and bustle. In short, it is quite the play for holiday-making pleasure-seekers, and may very well fill the gap left by the departed *Prisoner of Zenda* and the departing *Red Robe*.[73]

The play did not enjoy the success of other Lyceum production. It ran initially for twenty-nine consecutive performances and then was joined in repertory by *The Bells* and *The Merchant of Venice*. That season expenses exceeded receipts at the Lyceum by £10,000. But in an autumn provincial tour that year with *Madame Sans-Gêne* as the chief attraction (fifty-six performances bringing in £16,094 16s. 9d.) a handsome profit of £7095 19s. 2d. helped offset the Lyceum losses.[74] It also played with success in America. The spectacle of the beloved Ellen Terry playing vulgar, which upset some London critics, was something which did not perturb the provinces. Stoker recalled that at the first performance of the play in Sheffield, 'where the audiences were enormous and people hearty', in the scene with the dancing master where she was having trouble with her train, Ellen began to wring it as she had done with heavy articles in her washtub days. 'There was an instantaneous roar of applause. Half the women of the audience did their own washing and half the men knew the action; all throughout the house, both men and women, recognized the artistic perfection from which she utilized the impulse. From that evening the action became an established usage.'[75] This tells us something not only about the play but about Irving's provincial audience.

Robespierre, commissioned by Irving from Sardou, used the historical events of the 'Terror' as background to a story which strongly resembles *The Dead Heart*: former sweetheart intercedes with ruthless revolutionary leader to save her son and he dies to preserve the boy's life. The play, set in July 1794, opens in the forest of Montmorency, with a meeting between Benjamin Vaughan, a Whig MP who has been sent to France with peace proposals for Robespierre, and Clarisse de Maluçon and her niece Marie Thérèse, whose family he has known in London. Clarisse's husband, who fought in the Vendée uprising against the French republic, has died in London, and his widow and her niece are hiding out under assumed names. Clarisse reveals to Vaughan that her son Olivier is really the son of Robespierre, who seduced her when he was still a young lawyer and secretary to a counsellor in the Parlement of Paris. Vaughan has his interview with Robespierre and his proposals are rejected, for Robespierre is now at the height of his dictatorial powers. Robespierre's spies inform him of Vaughan's meeting with the two women and he orders their arrest.

In Act 2, Olivier searches for his mother and cousin and finds them in the prison of Port-Libre. This confirms Olivier in his hatred of Robespierre. On the next day, Robespierre attends the fête of the Supreme Being and is about to make a speech from in front of the statue of Reason when he is denounced as a tyrant by Olivier, who is arrested. In Act 3, Robespierre is enjoying a domestic interlude at the home of the Duplay family. Olivier is brought in for questioning and from papers he is carrying Robespierre deduces that Olivier is his son. Olivier reveals that his mother is in prison and, believing that this has doomed her, he faints and is carried away to prison. In Act 4, Clarisse and her niece, released from prison by Robespierre, are in hiding. Clarisse has a meeting with Robespierre. She reproaches him with his responsibility for the Reign of Terror. But he defends his conduct by appealing to the idealism of his aims. The sound of the tumbrils is heard in the streets conveying victims to the guillotine, and Clarisse begs Robespierre to stop the bloodshed. Robespierre searches for Olivier through a succession of prisons and in one at night has a vision of his various victims. But Olivier has been released by the Committee of Public Safety, who have commissioned him to murder Robespierre if their plan to dethrone him fails. At the Convention Hall, Robespierre is denounced by Tallien and falls from power. He shoots himself in the jaw in time to prevent Olivier killing him. Dying, he tells Clarisse: 'At last the child is saved and you too. At least I have lived to receive your pardon.'

Robespierre was the first production mounted by Irving after his recovery from a serious illness and the first since he surrendered control of the Lyceum to a joint stock company. It was conceived on a massive scale, with a huge cast and major scenes of spectacle: sixty-nine speaking parts and over a hundred supers.

A.B. Walkley in *The Times* (17 April 1899) faithfully recorded the emotion of the occasion:

> Whatever the play had been like ... It would have been well worth while to be at the Lyceum on Saturday evening simply to witness the enthusiasm which welcomed Sir Henry Irving's reappearance ... The deafening cheers meant sympathy as well as welcome and there have not been many occasions in our theatrical history on which welcome and sympathy have been so heartily expressed.

There was a two to three minute ovation when Irving made his first appearance. Walkley went on to evaluate the production:

> All through the hand of a master of stagecraft is seen. The play would probably succeed even as spectacle, since to spectacle is added drama of genuine interest and power the effect is irresistible. Never before, even at the Lyceum, have we had a more beautiful series of stage pictures, more lifelike representations of thrilling quasi-historical incidents. The roll call of doomed prisoners in the prison of Port-Libre is a scene that haunts the memory – the fearless demeanour of some, the piteous struggles of others; the mother torn from her child; the husband and wife imploring to be sent to die together – it is painful even to tears, but it is a scene of great beauty and enthralling interest ... the *Fête* of the Supreme Being is another triumph of stage management with an extraordinary realistic crowd.

The acting throughout was 'well suited to the play' and Irving was equally good as the 'suspicious, anxious tyrant, fearful of footsteps and stirrings of leaves, even while he proclaims himself 'strongest man in the state" and 'as the father whose heart is cruelly wounded by finding his son a bitter and implacable enemy'. He thought Ellen Terry 'womanliness and tenderness itself' and Kyrle Bellew a handsome and energetic Olivier, who 'won all hearts by his youthful looks and manly beauty'.

The *Daily Graphic* (19 April 1899) similarly noted Irving's 'splendid reception' and predicted the play would enjoy 'prodigious success':

> Critics may pretend the piece is of humble value as drama; the public will say that it has thrilling scenes, brilliant acting, and gorgeous spectacular effects which outweigh all that we may urge reluctantly. Certainly the stage has never seen anything more remarkable than the Fête of the Supreme Being on the Place de la Révolution, nor even from the Saxe-Meiningen Company the crowd so intensely individualised as in this or the scene in the Convention. Sir Henry has come back to us seeming younger and more alert than before his illness. Perhaps the diminution of responsibility has assisted to rejuvenate him. Certainly he is at his best, and whether it be as Robespierre urging his son to stay where his mother is, or Robespierre watching beside the mother to see whether Olivier is inside the tumbrels, or Robespierre half mad with terror and remorse at midnight in the Conciergerie, surrounded by the ghosts of his victims, Sir Henry is acting as only he can act.

The *Graphic*'s prediction proved right. There was much grumbling about the literary quality of the play, normally ahead of praise for the spectacle and the acting. One American critic called the play 'a grievous disappointment ... not only the Sardou of Melodrama, but the melodramatic Sardou at his second best'. But he went on to say: 'In his long career, Irving may have done stronger work than he does in *Robespierre*, but never work more finished, more subtle, more true to nature and to the dramatist's intention. His very mannerisms suited the character, and he indicated all its qualities with the firmness and the clearness of a master'.[76]

The *Westminster Budget* (21 April 1899) noted: 'whilst admitting ... that *Robespierre* is a brilliant and interesting entertainment, which will be meat for almost any man's money, and that as spectacle and collection of effective incidents it has remarkable quality, I cannot pretend that it is of much value as a work of dramatic art, though it comes from the pen of the most popular and successful of living playwrights'. This was typical of its reviews.

Several critics were reminded of *The Only Way* in the prison and convention scenes. But several others were reminded of the Dreyfus debates in the Chamber of Deputies which gave the play a certain topicality.[77] Its success was undoubted. It was performed 105 times in London, forty-three times in the provinces and 109 in America: 257 times in all. The popularity of the production prompted

Chapman and Hall to reissue George Henry Lewes's biography of Robespierre and Pearson to publish an English version of a French novel about Robespierre.

An intriguing pendant to the French Revolution series of plays is Arthur Conan Doyle's vignette *A Story of Waterloo* (later just *Waterloo*). Doyle, like Irving, was fascinated by Napoleon and the Napoleonic Wars, which feature regularly in his work (*The Adventures of Brigadier Gerard, Uncle Bernac, The Great Shadow*). In 1892 Doyle had turned his short story 'A Straggler of '15' into a one act play which he submitted to Irving. Irving loved it and purchased the acting rights for one hundred pounds. It was first produced in Bristol on a provincial tour on 17 December 1894. A new characterization by Irving was a significant enough event to bring the London critics down to the West Country to review it. It was first seen in London at a charity matinee on 17 December 1894 and opened at the Lyceum on 4 May 1895.

The play, set in June 1881, is basically an extended character sketch of an octogenarian Napoleonic War veteran Corporal Gregory Brewster. During the course of the play, Brewster's grand niece arrives to keep house for him, a young sergeant calls, anxious to meet the old hero, and the colonel of Brewster's old regiment visits to hear the old man's own version of the Battle of Waterloo. Brewster tells the story of the battle before sinking back exhausted to sleep. Suddenly he rises up with a final burst of martial vigour, crying: 'The guards need powder and by God, they shall have it', before falling back dead. 'I think the Third Guards have a full muster now', says the young sergeant. The story might have been inspired by Hubert von Herkomer's popular 1875 painting *The Last Muster* in which an elderly Chelsea pensioner dies during a church service. The play focused squarely on Irving's performance as the old man, endlessly repeating his old stories, dosing himself with medicine, weeping uncontrollably when he breaks his old clay pipe and constantly invoking the 'Dook' of Wellington as he comments on events before his final blaze of energy recalls the vigour of the war hero.

The play struck a chord with the public and it was to remain in Irving's repertoire to the end. With the predictable exception of Shaw, who poured scorn on both the play and performance, the critics loved the play as much as the public. Typical is the comment of the *Daily News* (22 September 1894): 'Mr Irving's acting throughout kept the house silent except when it was sobbing, and ... Dr Conan Doyle's little play carried all before it with its precisely symmetrical and balanced art.' Doyle noted: 'The house laughed and sobbed, exactly as I had done when I wrote it', though he recorded his resentment that many critics attributed the play's effect entirely to Irving's acting rather than Doyle's own writing ('Certainly every stage effect was indicated in the manuscript').[78] The playwright Henry Arthur Jones succinctly explained the appeal of the play to a late Victorian audience:

His Waterloo veteran was a marvellous picture of dignified senility. The dignity of Irving was there, but it was the dignity of a common soldier, widely different from the dignity of Charles or Becket. Yet it had a universal reference, and subtly and sweetly raised the virtues of patriotism and obedience, vindicated the nobility of common everyday instinctive duty, and reconciled us to patient, poverty-stricken old age. And in this altogether delightful little play Irving did not sink his author or push him aside, but simply illustrated him with a magic of his own. It was a true happy marriage between author and actor.[79]

The play can be seen as part of the process by which in the second half of the nineteenth century the image of Britain's military was transformed from 'brutal and licentious soldiery' into heroic, often Christian and imperial warriors, the embodiment of chivalry, courage and sacrifice, a process which involved the poetry of Tennyson, Kipling and Henley, the annual Drury Lane melodramas, the boys' books of G.A. Henty and his contemporaries, the war reports by the correspondents of the *Daily Mail* and the paintings of Lady Butler.[80] It was therefore the perfect choice to be performed before 2000 colonial troops plus the Indian princes and colonial premiers at a special matinee to celebrate the Diamond Jubilee on 25 June 1897. Bram Stoker recorded:

> No such audience could have been had for this military piece. It sounded the note of the unity of the Empire which was then in celebration; all were already tuned to it. The scene at the end was indescribable. It was a veritable ecstasy of loyal passion.[81]

Irving played the part in all 345 times, eighty times in London, 177 in the provinces and eighty-eight times in America. There was a command performance at Sandringham for King Edward VII. It was also, with symbolic appropriateness, the role in which Irving was last seen in London at a benefit matinee, on 15 June 1905, the year of his death.[82]

The Italian Renaissance was essentially an historical construct developed in the nineteenth century and defined by its interests, aspirations and ideologies.[83] The Renaissance with its sharply delineated heroes (Michelangelo, Leonardo, Dante and Raphael) and villains (Cesare and Lucrezia Borgia, Machiavelli) appealed to that Manichaean dualism in the Victorian world view. It also fascinated for the paradox that it was a major period of artistic and scientific advance, taking place against a background of violence, pestilence and religious and political strife. For some historians of the Renaissance, like Walter Pater and Jules Michelet 'Renaissance art and Renaissance life offered models of freedom of expression, freedom of emotion and intellectual liberty denied to them by Victorian culture'.[84] For those discontented with the present, many turned to the past for ideal societies. Ancient Greece, Ancient Rome, the Middle Ages and the Renaissance each attracted advocates who saw in its structures and values both a model and a warning.

The Italian masters were taken as an ideal by artists, sculptors and builders. Italian Renaissance style banks, hotels, town halls and railway stations sprang up all over nineteenth-century Britain. The canvases of the great Renaissance painters were studied, imitated and referred to in the work of Victorian painters. Raphael, Michelangelo and Leonardo were seen to embody perfection in painting and set the standard to be attained by modern painters. There was a reaction against the idolization of the High Renaissance masters in particular by the Pre-Raphaelite Brotherhood (1848), who turned to an earlier generation of painters who, they claimed, embodied greater realism, moral earnestness and political and religious conviction. Later, the High Renaissance made a comeback, but they were all aspects of the same epoch.

Novelists sought inspiration in the great figures of the Renaissance, with Bulwer Lytton writing *Rienzi* (1835), Emma Robinson *Caesar Borgia* (1846), G.P.R. James *Leonora D'Orco* (1857) and George Eliot *Romola* (1863). Poets like Browning, Landor and Dante Gabriel Rossetti turned to the Renaissance for subjects and inspiration. As Hilary Fraser concludes: 'The principal reason for the prevailing enthusiasm for Renaissance Italy was that Italy, where the present seemed to maintain its links with the past, offered Victorian humanists access to history, and the Renaissance gave them reassurance that the past could be resurrected, and indeed appropriated.'[85]

There were two key figures in Renaissance history to whom the Victorians returned again and again: Rienzi and Dante – and it is no coincidence that Irving was attracted to both. Cola di Rienzi was the Roman tribune who led a popular uprising against aristocratic tyranny in Rome and established a republic in 1347. He was excommunicated and exiled, then assassinated in 1354. But he was seen to prefigure the Italian Risorgimento of the nineteenth century and to be a champion of democracy against aristocratic tyranny. Bulwer Lytton made him the hero of his novel, *Rienzi: Last of the Tribunes* (1835), in which he drew constant comparisons between the events of the past and those of the present. The novel inspired an opera by Wagner, and a painting by Holman Hunt, a scene of Rienzi vowing to secure justice for the death of his brother in a fight with the aristocratic Orsinis: the turning point in his career. Irving commissioned a play from W.G. Wills, but, although he had the text printed up and worked on it, he never produced it.

Dante was a principal interest of the Victorian Renaissance. He inspired the subjects of many painters, notably Edward Poynter, Simeon Solomon, Frederic Leighton, Joseph Noel Paton and John Hancock. He was ever present in Victorian literature by quotation, imitation and invocation. Ruskin called him 'the central man of all the world'. Carlyle named him, along with Shakespeare, in his chapter on 'the Hero as Poet' in *On Heroes, Hero Worship and the Heroic in History*. Carlyle argued that there were in the poet elements of the politician, the thinker, the legislator, whose greatness lay in his ability to penetrate 'into the heart of Being'. In the *Divina Commedia*, he is 'the spokesman of the Middle Ages; the thought they live by stands here, in everlasting music. These sublime ideas of his, terrible and beautiful, are the fount of the Christian meditation of all good men who had gone before him'. His historical importance was that 'Dante speaks to the noble, the pure and the great in all times and places'. While Dante was sent into the world to embody the religion of the Middle Ages, Shakespeare embodied the outer life of Europe, 'its chivalries, courtesies, humours, ambitions, what practical way of thinking, acting, looking at the world, men then had'. He embodied valour, candour, tolerance and truthfulness. Dante represented the Soul, Shakespeare the Body. But, of the two, Shakespeare was the greater because, unlike Dante, he had fought and conquered his own sorrows. Carlyle saw Shakespeare as having unparalleled vision and insight but he also attained tranquillity, calmness and placidity.[86] Dante appealed to the Victorians on every level. For Protestants, he was a proto-Protestant reformer, for Catholics a Catholic mystic; for nationalists, he was an early Italian nationalist and romantics celebrated his doomed love for Beatrice. Dante was also seen as an archetypal exile and outsider. It may have been this which explains why Oscar Wilde, George Eliot and John Henry Newman, outsiders all, compared themselves or were compared to Dante.[87]

Dante was also a long-standing obsession of Irving's. He believed he looked like the poet and had already proposed the subject to Tennyson without success. The fact that Dante was long in his mind is evidenced by the fact that he dressed the Prologue of *Romeo and Juliet* as Dante in his 1882 production for no very good textual reason other than his fascination with the character and the Renaissance. It may have been suggested by Leighton's painting *Dante in Exile* (1864), showing an austere Dante in Verona passing through what looks like a wedding party. Eventually it was Sardou and his writing partner Emile Moreau who were commissioned by Irving to produce a Dante play. *Dante* was to be Irving's last new production.

Sardou and Moreau had researched the subject thoroughly but decided not to dramatize Dante's love for Beatrice (perhaps the most famous fact generally known about him) or to explore the complex political background of the conflicts between the Guelphs and Ghibellines. Sardou wrote: 'I am sick to death of them all! It is a puzzle to me how these people managed to recognize each other and know which party they belonged to.' In a magazine interview, Sardou explained the nature of the play:

> The drama we have written is purely symbolical and in harmony with the poetic tradition of the Middle Ages and with Dante's own works, in which symbolism is to be seen everywhere. My friend Moreau and myself are well aware that Pia de Tolomei and Francesca da Rimini were not the great poet's contemporaries, that Ugolino's death does not coincide with the date of our prologue, that Francesca was not killed in Florence,

and that Dante was not at Avignon when Pope Clement V died there. But we never entertained the idea of writing an historical drama, strictly speaking, and never gave anyone to understand that such was the case with *Dante*. That which struck us most in the personality of the poet were the essentially human side to his character, his quick, impulsive nature, ever ready for the extremes of love or hatred and bursting with indignation at the sight of hypocrisy, corruption and injustice. He whom we wished to depict on the stage was the man who thirsted for justice, though living in an epoch of crime. We have purposely blended history and tradition, truth and fiction, and ignored Dante's marriage with a Donati, his matrimonial differences, and the obscure lot of his seven children. Of his political career and the feuds between the Guelphs and the Ghibellines we have retained but the supreme facts of his exile … No, *Dante* is not a historical drama. We did not intend to evoke in the slightest degree the politician plunged in the discords of his country … we sought something else in the poet's life! We attempted to bring into relief its purely human features. We sought in his works and the vicissitudes of his existence the actions and feelings which find an echo throughout all ages. Politics belong to their day and lose much of their interest with time; but the master idea of the poet's life moves us deeply: his haughty revolt against the injustices of men. Through the darkness of the Middle Ages we see shining in him a ray of the future light of civilization.[88]

Dante opens with a prologue set in Pisa. In the background is 'The Tower of Hunger', in which the fallen tyrant Ugolino with his sons and grandsons are confined to die of starvation. First Dante enters, and meets the mother of his child Gemma, Pia dei Tolomei, the successor to Beatrice in his affections. Then Helen of Swabia, Count Ugolino's daughter-in-law, appears and seeks to obtain mercy from the pitiless crowd, the jailors and the ruthless Archbishop Ruggieri, but in vain. Dante intercedes with the archbishop, but is excommunicated for his pains. The poet in reply prophesies the downfall of Pisa.

The first act opens ten years later with a springtime festival at Florence. Dante enters, disguised as a monk, but is recognized by his friend the painter Giotto. Maddened by jealousy, Malatesta murders his wife Francesca da Rimini and her lover Paolo. Meanwhile Dante has an interview with his natural daughter Gemma. Her mother Pia, who has been married to Nello della Pietra, is confined by her husband in his castle in the Maremma to die of malaria and neglect. The pretended monk is summoned to absolve the dying woman. One result of this interview is the disclosure of the secret of Gemma's birth. Gemma appears, but, before she can reach her father, is hurried off by Nello to some unknown destination.

In the second act Pia dies, and Dante, having discovered the whereabouts of Gemma, goes to the convent of San Pietro to rescue her. The abbess and nuns, who are in league with Nello, strive in vain to persuade Gemma to take the vows. But Nello and his supporters enter with drawn swords, and when he tries to carry off his daughter Dante is severely wounded by Nello and left for dead. But the poet is not dead. His friend Casella staunches his wounds and saves his life. In the third act Dante, at the behest of the spirit of Beatrice, descends to Hades in the company of Virgil. Charon, the City of Dis, the Fiery Tombs and the Circle of Ice are all visited, and the spirits of Ugolino, Ruggieri, Paolo, and Francesca encountered. Then they pass over the Bridge of Rocks into the Valley of Asphodels, where they meet Pia dei Tolomei with her attendant spirits. The fourth act takes place at the Papal palace at Avignon, whither Dante, as a result of his interview with Pia, has gone in pursuit of Gemma. Cardinal Colonna is about to burn Gemma and her lover Bernardino as heretics, but Dante frightens the wicked Cardinal by a message from Hades to the effect that his own hour is come. Colonna falls down dead at the hour foretold, and Gemma and Bernadino are saved.

Dante, which opened at the Theatre Royal, Drury Lane, on 30 April 1903, was a major departure from Irving's commitment to reproducing history on the stage. Therefore a pamphlet by 'an Italian student' explaining what exactly was going on was on sale along with the programme at the theatre. The pamphlet began with a brief summary of the known facts of Dante's life and sought to disentangle fact from fantasy in the play. Then quoting Carlyle's verdict on Dante it went on to explain that the play encapsulated his spirit as derived from his work, 'the moral Dante … a lover of liberty, a fierce hater of persecution, of oppression and clerical domination'. The pamphlet also explained that the painter Giotto and the composer Casella were friends of Dante, that Pia might have been the unnamed noble woman Dante fell for after Beatrice (though this is more likely to have been his eventual wife, Gemma Donati), that Dante's daughter Beatrice may have been illegitimate, but unlike the fictional daughter Gemma, who marries real-life Bernardino da Polenta, Beatrice became a nun. Ugolino, Nello della Pietra and Malatesta were all real-life figures, though there is no evidence of contact with Dante and Dante is not known to have visited Avignon.

A.B. Walkley in *The Times* (1 May 1903), summed up the general reaction to the play. He suggested that the average Drury Lane playgoer was not a Dantist and knew little of Dante. For 'people who know and love their *Divina Commedia*, the Drury Lane *Dante* will not do at all', and he proceeded to point out, giving chapter and verse, all the errors of fact and interpretation. But he followed this by admitting that the play was for playgoers first and foremost, 'the playgoers – there are legions of them – who have fallen under the spell of Sir Henry Irving's magic personality. Whatever he chooses to play is, they feel, good enough for them.' Also, those who like spectacle would be contented. But 'those who cling to the old-fashioned notion that a play should be a play: that it should have strong, continuous and cumulative dramatic interest' would leave disappointed. Walkley suggests that Sardou could either have handled the poet's life and text reverently and faithfully or have invented his own new plot with Dante as the central figure.

But he had tried to do both and had failed. 'He has strung little Dantean episodes, more or less authentic, on a cock and bull story of his own invention.' He found the result 'ramshackle, confusing, rather irritating'. But then there was always the spectacle and Irving: 'it is, of course, obvious that if ever a man was born to look Dante to the life he is the man. The moment he emerges from the porch of the church at Pisa you recognize the fresco profile. And he wanders through the play – for really he is only a wanderer – with just the right air and accent of ascetic severity and melancholy aloofness'.

Irving had poured money into the production. Stoker recalled sadly: 'The labour of the preparation and rehearsal was endless, the expense enormous.'[89] In all, £13,000 had been expended before the curtain went up. Stoker had not read the play or even the scenario before Irving read it out to the company on 12 January 1903: 'I am bound to say that as it went on my heart sank. The play was not a good one. It had too many characters and covered too wide a range. Indeed had it not been for Irving's wonderful reading I should not have been able to follow the plot. When I saw the play on the first night, acted by a lot of people and lacking the concentration of the whole thing passing through one skilled mind, I found a real difficulty of comprehension.' Despite this, Stoker thought Irving was 'superb':

> He did not merely look like Dante – he *was* Dante; it was like a veritable reincarnation. His features had a natural resemblance to the great poet! The high-bred 'eagle' profile; the ascetic gauntness; the deep earnest resonant voice; the general bearing of lofty gloom of the exile – these things one and all completed a representation which can never be forgotten by any one who saw it.[90]

Irving, who had throughout expressed confidence in it, finally conceded the truth. He asked Lena Ashwell, who was playing both Pia and Gemma, what she thought of the play. Although she thought it 'a poor play', she recalled: 'I was dumb. He smiled, a curiously fascinating smile, and said: "Sardou is old, too old; it would take a Dante to write about Dante"'.[91]

Percy Fitzgerald was even more severe, declaring *Dante* 'an utterly disappointing business … It was a poor, skimpy, storyless, passionless thing'. And as to Irving: 'His voice was at this time weak and thin; his speech slow and monotonous – it was more a recitation than acting. In fact he was not Dante. There was little or no passion or action. The character made no impression and seemed to be overpowered by the noisy, riotous crowds that overflowed the piece.'[92]

Despite this, the play ran for eighty-two performances at Drury Lane and this seems to have been based entirely on the audience's love for Irving. Walkley reported that the play was greeted with 'a positive frenzy of enthusiasm'. One journalist, writing for an American periodical, devoted his article almost entirely to an account of Irving's reception by the audience:

'Old favourites' appeal to English men and women with a force that is nowhere else so genuine and so palpable; and of all the actors on the English stage there is no one who even begins to compare in popularity with Irving. He stands, and for twenty years he has stood, in a class apart, both as an actor and as a man ... But it is not only as an actor that English people keep a warm place in their hearts for Irving. His character and personality, his kindliness, modesty, and dignity of his disposition, I will add his misfortunes too, have won for him a popular devotion such as goes out to no English-speaking actor of our time. In the speech which was forced from him that evening he spoke of the 'affectionate' welcome he had just received. The word was well chosen. Indeed, there was something more than affection in the way the house rose to him at his entrance, recalled him again at the end of each act, and thundered its applause at his brief halting words of thanks. There is no need for a claque when Irving's name is on the playbill. The people love him, and that ends the matter. I have emphasized the magnificence of this personal tribute because it was really the feature of the evening. It was not the play that was cheered but Irving.[93]

The failure of the play, however, became apparent on tour. It was included in the repertoire for the autumn provincial tour but given only twenty-one times and in only three towns. It was taken to America and played thirty-four times, but it was obvious that it was much less of a draw than the old repertoire. It was therefore withdrawn and the scenery was stored in Washington and, at the end of the tour, sent to Canada and given away. The public had spoken.

13

Religion

Historians have, rightly, seen Evangelicalism as a vital force in the shaping of Victorian society. Many leading Victorians had devout Evangelical upbringings and were possessed by a high sense of duty, accompanied often by an air of self-righteousness: Queen Victoria, Prime Ministers Gladstone and Peel, the historian Macaulay, Cardinal Newman, Cardinal Manning, Sir Henry Havelock, General Gordon, John Ruskin, Charles Kingsley, the Brontë sisters, Elizabeth Barrett Browning, George Eliot, General Booth, Dr Barnardo, Thomas Cook, scientists Michael Faraday and Joseph Lister, David Livingstone, the great industrialists W. H. Lever, Titus Salt, the Cadburys, the Rowntrees, the Frys. To them we might legitimately add Sir Henry Irving.[1]

The origins of Evangelicalism lay in the religious revival of the mid eighteenth century, when a number of Anglican clergymen, such as John Wesley, underwent conversion experiences. The form of Christianity they practised and preached was intensely emotional and experiential. It was a reaction against the rationalism and deism, the complacency and worldliness of the eighteenth century and a return to the Puritanism of the seventeenth. There was now a split in the Anglican Church, a significant minority leaving to become Methodists and Nonconformists. There was a great growth in membership of the Nonconformist sects: the Congregationalists' numbers doubled between 1750 and 1800 and increased fourfold by 1838; the Baptists tripled their membership between 1750 and 1800 and tripled it again by 1838. The Methodists expanded from 22,642 in 1767 to over half a million by the mid nineteenth century. These groups were all Evangelical. There was also a significant Evangelical presence in the Church of England. They shared a simple, fundamentalist faith and a strong commitment to service and hard work. From 1800 to 1880 the Evangelicals dominated British life, successively though unofficially led by two dynamic and charismatic figures, from 1800 to 1830 William Wilberforce and after 1830 by Lord Shaftesbury. From the 1860s their influence slowly but gradually dwindled. But if the Evangelical grip relaxed, many of their values had penetrated deep into society and would not easily be eradicated.

The Evangelicals believed in total commitment to Christianity as 'the principle of all human actions, the great animating spirit of human conduct' as Hannah More put it.[2] They appealed to emotion rather than reason, and were obsessed by the need for salvation from sin. Above all they believed in the primacy of individual conscience.

As Richard Helmstader has defined it:

> Each individual's active responsibility for the ultimate destiny of his soul began with the awakening of his conscience. The conscience was, indeed, fundamentally important in the Evangelical scheme of salvation, and conscience pervaded the Evangelical view of the world. Conscience, for Evangelicals, was the principal guide for action. Conscience was essential for salvation, and the key to individual improvement and social progress. Without conscience, all would be lost. Every man's concern for salvation began with his own conscience, with his awareness of sin in general and recognition of his own sinful condition in particular. Once aware of the depth of his own depravity and frightened, perhaps terrorised, by the prospect of eternal damnation, the sinner was ripe for reformation. Thus did conscience, or awareness of sin, lie at the base of his subsequent pilgrimage of grace.[3]

But it was not so much a theology, more a way of life, a 'call to seriousness'.[4] Conversion lay at the heart of Evangelical thinking; good works and the fulfilment of Christian teaching were signs of this conversion. The characteristics of the Evangelicals were intense seriousness of purpose, addiction to hard work, hostility to worldliness, censoriousness, an intense missionary impulse and a puritanical abstention from worldly pleasure. Their aim was 'nothing less than a frontal assault on virtually every prevailing assumption and habit of their time and their replacement by the principles and practices of Vital Christianity'.[5] They succeeded in transforming British society in the second half of the nineteenth century. As Harold Perkin has written: 'Between 1780 and 1850 the English ceased to be one of the most aggressive, brutal, rowdy, outspoken, riotous, cruel and bloodthirsty nations in the world and became one of the most inhibited, polite, orderly, tenderminded, prudish and hypocritical.'[6] Society unquestionably became more disciplined and law-abiding in the nineteenth century, thanks to a combination of factors – the imposition of factory discipline, the creation of a police force, the spread of education, and the exertion of social control through a moral transformation in the wake of the rise of Evangelicalism and the revival of chivalry. Each fed into a political party: Evangelicalism into Liberalism and chivalry into Conservatism. Both merged to create the dominant ideology of the last decades of the century, imperialism.

As G. M. Young put it: 'The Evangelicals gave the island a creed which was at once the basis of its morality and the justification of its wealth and power, and within the creed, the state of being an elect people, which, set to a more blatant tune, became a principal element in late Victorian Imperialism.'[7] The Evangelicals succeeded in substantially transforming the attitudes and values of both the middle class and the aristocracy, who had been untouched by the eighteenth-century religious revival but had been largely won over by mid nineteenth century. The middle classes, and in particular middle-class women, became pillars of Evangelical enterprises. The Evangelicals also had a significant impact on the lives of the working classes, both directly and indirectly. The 1851 census revealed that only half the population had attended a place of worship on the Sunday of the census and the bulk of non-attenders were working-class. The Nonconformists and the Anglican Evangelicals made a sustained bid to win over the working classes through distribution of tracts, Evangelical missions targeted at particular groups (seamen, soldiers, costermongers, crossing sweepers, navvies, prostitutes) and the Ragged Schools. The idea behind these schools was to give Bible instruction to those turned away from the day and Sunday Schools because of their filthy appearance and extreme poverty. The Ragged School Union was set up in 1844 and by 1850 there were over one hundred Ragged Schools, regularly attended by more than 100,000 children and by thousands of adults from the lowest classes. In 1844 the YMCA was set up and in 1855 the YWCA. Ian Bradley calls them two of 'the most important agencies for spreading the principles and practices of evangelical religion among young people in Victorian England'.[8]

The Evangelicals actively promoted the cult of respectability and conformity as the code of behaviour for all, setting examples in their own lives, publishing heroic biographies of great Evangelicals, issuing tracts and manuals of behaviour and stressing duty, hard work, home and family. It was the Evangelicals who succeeded in making the home the centre of nineteenth century English life. Home-centred leisure, strict sabbath observance, regular family prayers, rejection of frivolity and promotion of improving and intellectually serious pursuits were the keynote of Evangelical domestic life.

The traditional picture of Evangelicals and culture has been of a narrow philistine existence, gloomily preoccupied with sin. But Doreen Rosman has persuasively argued that the Evangelicals in fact shared the tastes and interests of their more cultivated contemporaries to a greater degree than has been hitherto recognized.[9] They were particularly suspicious of public amusements and the company of the unregenerate and thus frowned on theatregoing, dancing, cardplaying, shooting and field sports. But they were willing to be more relaxed at home. In the family circle, they cultivated reading (particularly favouring devotional poetry and religious novels). Some read the classics and Shakespeare (drama was accepted when read in the home, but not when acted on the stage). But they were critical of the Romantic and Gothic literature as sensationalist. Singing and performance of music was encouraged, particularly of sacred music (Haydn, Mozart, Pergolesi, Handel). Paintings were also acceptable if moral and uplifting. Evangelicals in general justified even an interest in secular culture if it could be seen as an adjunct of civilization and the promotion of the finer feelings. In addition to culture, they also promoted walking, sightseeing, nature study and other 'useful knowledge' as a means of intellectual improvement.

The Evangelicals were great missionaries, both at home and abroad. Abroad they linked the imperial impulse with conversion to Christianity and the abolition of slavery, imbuing British imperialism with a distinctive air of duty and self-righteousness. At home their missionary impulse was devoted both to improving society and to improving the people. Most of the famous human-itarian ventures of the nineteenth century had Evangelical leadership and inspiration, for instance, Elizabeth Fry's work in prisons and prison reform, Josephine Butler's crusade on behalf of prostitutes and Dr Barnardo's mission to deprived children. Lord Shaftesbury was the head of virtually every campaign for humanitarian legislation in the mid nineteenth century: reforming the factory system and working conditions, humanising the laws relating to lunacy, seeking to establish decent housing conditions for the masses, promoting the humanization of the criminal law.

For Evangelicals it was a primary duty to help relieve human suffering. The voluntary charitable society was their preferred vehicle for accomplishing this. By the middle of the nineteenth century there were 500 voluntary philanthropic societies, three quarters of them Evangelical. Socially and politically the Evangelicals were conservative. They believed in Christianising and humanizing the existing social and economic order rather than overturning or reconstructing it. Although they supported legislation when necessary to eliminate social evils, they preferred to deal with poverty and suffering by voluntary charitable efforts rather than handing over this duty to the state because that effectively negated the individual moral responsibility which lay at the heart of their world view.

In 1802 the Evangelicals formed the Society for the Suppression of Vice and for thirty years mounted a crusade to raise the level of public morality. The Evangelicals were instrumental in outlawing the importation, display or publication of obscene material (securing the passing of the Obscene Publications Act of 1857). W.H. Smith, a staunch Methodist and the man who controlled all the station bookstalls, exercised strict censorship over the materials on sale on them and Charles Mudie of Mudie's Circulating Library, which was an arbiter of taste in publishing, also kept questionable literature off the book-shelves. Dr Thomas Bowdler cleaned up Shakespeare for home consumption, giving his name to the activity of removing questionable material from the classics, to 'bowdlerize'. The Evangelicals attacked gambling and got the state lottery abolished in 1826. They campaigned against drunkenness, having licensing hours tightened and persuading employers not in future to pay out wages in the pub. They got beerhouses closed during the time of Sunday services. They got rowdy traditional fairs (including the famous old Bartholomew Fair) closed down, and a Methodist appointed as theatrical censor.

Three of the most successful reformist movements were the Sabbatarians (notably the Lord's Day Observance Society, established in 1831), the Temperance movement (in particular the United Kingdom Alliance and the British Temperance League, which developed after 1829), and the RSPCA (1824). All three movements were predominantly Evangelical in origin and aims, sought to be national in scope, and deployed similar methods of agitation (legislation, prosecution and education). All three combined to attack that recreational network that embraced gambling, drinking, cruel sports, Sabbath-breaking and blasphemy.

The Lord's Day Observance Society saw itself as defending employees' leisure time against employers' rapacity. So there was an alliance of Evangelicals and sections of the working class on this. The Sabbatarians achieved a number of successes. As early as 1780 they had got an Act passed banning Sunday trading and sports and entertainments on a Sunday. In 1849 the delivery of mail on a Sunday was banned. In 1856 Sunday afternoon military band concerts in all London parks were banned. The result was the creation of the Victorian Sunday, which became a byword for boredom and dullness.[10] The temperance movement enjoyed great popular support and there were strong teetotal elements within both the Liberal Party and later the Labour Party.[11] It was Evangelical influence that helped get bullbaiting, bearbaiting, dogfighting and cockfighting banned by law in 1835.

The attack on traditional working class recreations split society but not on class lines. It created alliances between, on the one hand, humanitarians, philanthropists, sentimentalists, paternalists and working-class 'respectables' who were in favour of cleaning up society and, on the other hand, traditionalists, 'roughs', free traders, drinksellers, *bonviveurs*, sportsmen and libertarians, who wanted things left as they were.[12] The net effect of the moral transformation of society wrought in part by the Evangelicals was a decline in drunkenness, crime and violence, the growth of domesticity and the deep rooting at all levels of society of the doctrine of respectability.

The theatre was viewed with intense suspicion not just by Evangelicals but by all churches. The arguments against the stage went back to Plato and the early Church Fathers and were regularly rehearsed – the falsity and untruthfulness of the imitation involved in acting, the belief that the stage lowered morals, exalted sensual pleasure and wasted time. Supporters of the stage argued that at its best it was educational, uplifting and a vehicle for moral instruction. The debate still raged throughout the nineteenth century.

Regular sermons against the stage were delivered throughout the century. The Reverend Thomas Best of Sheffield, annually for forty-seven years from 1817, delivered thunderous denunciations of the stage. In one sermon, he declared the stage to be worse than cholera because while the victims of cholera would go to heaven, frequenters of the theatre were destined for hell. But for every attack, there was an equally spirited defence. The personally devout playwright Sheridan Knowles lectured regularly for thirty years from 1820 on the essentially spiritual nature of the stage, declaring 'The Almighty has employed the drama as a vehicle of Revelation'.[13] W.E. Gladstone, who in his youth had thought theatre-going a sin, became in later life an enthusiastic theatre-goer and admirer of Henry Irving and declared at a dinner in honour of Charles Kean in 1862: 'Religion herself has not always disdained to find in [the drama] a direct handmaid for the attainment of her purpose.' It was a view shared by the Reverend Charles Dodgson (Lewis Carroll), who contributed to the *Theatre* magazine in 1888 an essay entitled 'The Stage and the Spirit of Reverence', arguing something similar.[14]

Richard Foulkes has traced the often troubled relations between church and stage, culminating by the end of the century in something of a rapprochement. Despite the mutual antipathy, there were strong affinities between church and stage. For both involved performance, ritual and declamation. Foulkes points to the intriguing facts that some clergymen (Dean Milman, Charles Maturin, Charles Kingsley) actually wrote plays, some of which were performed on the stage; that the public schools under their clerical headmasters staged plays; and that a failed actor J.C.M. Bellew became a fashionable cleric famous for his public readings of *Hamlet*. The Supreme Governor of the Church of England, the personally devout Queen Victoria, was a passionate theatre-goer and had command performances at Windsor.[15]

But the opprobrium attached to a career on the stage is manifested in the attitude of William Charles Macready. The son of actors, he was sent to Rugby and educated to be a gentleman. He aspired to a career as lawyer or clergyman, but family financial reverses forced him onto the stage. Although a brilliant and successful actor, recognized as the leader of his profession, he was continually embarrassed by his calling and retired from it as soon as he could. He left the stage in 1851 and settled first in Sherborne, where he ran a night school for locals, and later in Cheltenham, where he died on 27 April 1873.

For all his reservations about his calling, Macready began the process of raising the status of the stage and the acting profession, a process continued by the Old Etonian Charles Kean (who was elected a fellow of the Society of Antiquaries) and Samuel Phelps (whose brother was a clergyman and the Master of Sidney Sussex College, Cambridge). They all combined highly respectable lives and irreproachable public careers in which they strove to associate the theatre with taste, decency, education and moral uplift. Similarly the status of actresses was transformed. Regarded as little better than a prostitute at the start of the century, the profession of actress was elevated by the activities of Fanny Kemble, Helen Faucit, Marie Wilton and Dame Madge Kendal, who conducted themselves as ladies, joined fashionable congregations and participated in charitable projects.

By the end of the century it was a profession that vicars' daughters, such as Sybil Thorndike and Violet and Irene Vanbrugh, could safely enter.

Not only the careers of such key figures but also the religious, social and intellectual transformation of the nineteenth century caused attitudes to the theatre slowly but surely to change. The manifestations of this change included the mission of Bishop James Fraser of Manchester to that city's theatres, aiming to purify rather than abolish the stage, the popularity of the Oberammergau Passion Play which inspired home-grown Bible story *tableaux vivants* at inner city churches, and the foundation of student drama societies at both Oxford and Cambridge, where the authorities had previously discouraged theatricals. Perhaps the culmination of these developments was the foundation of the Church and Stage Guild (1879) and the Actors' Church Union (1898), organizations which brought the two institutions together in formal meetings.

While the church was undergoing changes, so too was the theatre. The middle-class audience began to return in large numbers, the professional status of actors rose and the gentility and moral tone of plays began to be stressed. The cult of Shakespeare as the pre-eminent British cultural hero proved as inspiring to clerics as to laymen. The National Shakespeare Committee planning the Shakespeare Tercentenary of 1864 included three archbishops and four bishops. Eventually, after the censor had ensured that religious themes and Bible stories were rigorously excluded from the stage for much of the nineteenth century, there was a breakthrough in the 1890s when the prohibition was relaxed and the religious problem dramas of Henry Arthur Jones (*Judah, Michael and His Lost Angel*), and Hall Caine (*The Christian, The Eternal City*), and above all the spectacular melodrama of the early days of Christianity, Wilson Barrett's *The Sign of the Cross*, which was recommended by clergymen from the pulpit, achieved theatrical and moral success.

The rapprochement between church and stage reached a final consummation in the career of Sir Henry Irving, who came to embody two of the principal distinctive shaping social and ideological forces of the nineteenth century – Evangelicalism and chivalry. Irving embodied the Evangelical world view in almost all its aspects – in his immense industry, enthusiastic missionary spirit and high-mindedness. Physically Irving was, with his frock coat and *pince-nez*, renowned for resembling the traditional Victorian parson. His roots were in Nonconformity. Irving's mother, Mary Behenna, was a devoutly Methodist Cornish woman. So was his maternal aunt Sarah Penberthy, who brought Irving up for ten years while his parents strove to make a living, first in Bristol and later in London. While he was living in Cornwall with the Penberthys, daily Bible readings were part of Irving's life. He professed a Christian conversion during a church service at the age of ten and his aunt hoped that he would enter the ministry. But Irving joined his parents in London in 1848 and was sent to the

City Commercial School where he had elocution lessons, did public readings and at the age of twelve was taken to see Samuel Phelps in *Hamlet* at Sadler's Wells. After this, the ardour for Methodism which he had professed while in Cornwall was transferred to the stage.

Although Irving became a clerk after leaving school, he was acting as an amateur in his spare time. Then in 1856 he abandoned clerking to become a full-time professional actor. His mother believed that he had damned himself by this decision, never forgave him and cast him off. For his new career, he changed his name from John Henry Brodribb to Henry Irving. The new surname was chosen partly after a favourite childhood writer, Washington Irving, but partly after Edward Irving, the popular preacher who had briefly flirted with the stage before deploying his histrionic talents in the pulpit.[16]

Irving, nevertheless, retained a Christian faith. It had mellowed and broadened since his boyhood. He told his old friend, the journalist Chance Newton, that his Aunt Sarah 'frightened us by her terrible 'iron-bound' Calvinism; her awful theories as to its being necessary to be 'Elect' to be saved, and all that kind of awful anti-Christian theology'.[17] Newton recalled his many conversations with Irving about religious belief: 'We each knew that the other had the deepest reverence for that theme of themes and an abiding sense of man's need for a vital faith to sustain him.' He went on 'Henry Irving always displayed what he had so continuously and consistently shown by his deeds in and out of his profession – that is, a real and practical Christianity. John Wesley himself (of whom we sometimes spake) could show no greater sympathy with Universalism as opposed to Calvinism.'[18] Newton claimed that Irving was 'strongly in favour' of the Larger Hope views of Tennyson's *In Memoriam*, and the Eternal Hope views of Dean Farrar. Farrar had earned himself notoriety and scotched his chances of a bishopric by a series of sermons rejecting the traditional idea of hell as a place of torment and fire and brimstone, arguing that 'the virtue which has no better basis than fear of Hell is no virtue at all' and suggesting that heaven is a matter of living a life of principle.[19] This rejection of a narrow Calvinism in favour of a broad and generous though principled faith evidently appealed to Irving.

The breadth of his Christian sympathy extended beyond the Church of England to Roman Catholicism. Percy Fitzgerald recalled:

> Irving had ever a sort of romantic interest in the Roman Catholic Church and its ceremonial grandeur. I often think that he fancied he was somehow affiliated to it, from having so often figured as one of its ecclesiastics on the stage. Cardinals, bishops, priests, religious processions, rites, altars, sanctuaries – all these he was perfectly familiar with, and he had 'made up' by the most careful inquiries [*sic*] all details that were necessary ... At all events there was a tenderness in his bearing towards the Church. He knew the two Cardinals Manning and Vaughan and had many Catholic friends.[20]

For all his Romantic attachment to Catholic forms and rituals, Irving found the kind of practical Christianity he actually lived by in General Booth, founder of the Salvation Army, with whom he became friendly and to whose Army funds he made regular donations, Newton recalled:

> Irving displayed intense interest in the wonderful work of 'the General' and his 'Army' among the masses of the submerged, the starving, the sin-stricken, the degraded, the fallen, the criminal, the despairing, and the dying ... At our last meeting Irving said, 'The General and I met again the other day, and I said to him, 'General we are both towering stars, you and I. You on the Religious Stage and I on the Dramatic. Well, well, it is for us to see that we each give the best thing that is in us in the different departments to which our God has called us'.[21]

Irving's generosity was legendary, particularly to members of the profession. He paid a weekly pension to some forty elderly actors. His generosity even extended to people who disparaged him. G.R. Sims recalled:

> If The Bells made Irving it certainly did not make Leopold Lewis. He did very little afterwards, and remained to the end a disappointed and dissatisfied man. Irving behaved admirably to him, and stood by him to the finish. But the success of The Bells had given poor Lewis a false idea of his own value as a dramatist, and he became a man with a grievance, and gradually drifted out and died at the Royal Free Hospital in February 1890 ... It was not the author who made it the enormous success that it proved, but the actor, a fact which Leopold Lewis failed unfortunately to realise.[22]

But the sequel to this was described by Bram Stoker. Lewis had sold the rights to the play to Samuel French the publisher, from whom Irving purchased them: 'Notwithstanding this ... purchase, Irving used, after the death of Lewis, to allow his widow a weekly sum whenever he was playing – playing not merely The Bells but anything else – up to the time of his death.'[23] Chance Newton recalled a similar story concerning veteran actor Hermann Vezin:

> Irving not only paid Vezin £80 per week to deputize for him at the Lyceum in Macbeth, but sometimes trying though dear old ... Vezin could be, and haughtily as he often bore himself to the Chief, Irving during the remainder of his own life saw that Vezin, though he had ceased to act for him, was largely helped during the trying times that fell upon that noble Shakespearean.[24]

Irving had a particular mission to revive the English poetic drama, hence his encouragement of both W.G. Wills and Lord Tennyson. When he learned that the playwright and poet John Westland Marston, who had kept the tradition of poetic drama going between 1840 and 1870, had fallen on hard times, he organized a benefit for him. On the afternoon of 1 June 1887, he put on a matinee performance of Werner with himself in the lead. He staged it as a fully rehearsed and finished production, complete with new specially designed scenery, costumes and armour. The box office receipts for the performance came to £100 but Irving handed over a cheque for £928 to Marston, a sum that maintained him in comfort until his death in 1890.[25] There were many such benefits. Stoker puts these acts into a broader context:

> All his life long Irving worked for others – for his art; never for himself. If rewards came – and they showered upon him – he took them meekly without undue pride, without arrogance; never as other than tributes beyond his worth. He made throughout years a great fortune but nearly all of it he spent as it came on his art, and in helping his poorer brethren. His own needs were small. He lived in a few rooms, ate sparingly, drank moderately. He had no vices that I know of: he was not extravagant; did not gamble, was not ostentatious, even in his charities. There are many widows and orphans who mourn his loss.[26]

But Irving was anxious above all for recognition by the church of the moral value of the stage. This eventually came towards the end of his career when the Anglican and Catholic churches both invited him to perform. Irving was asked by F.W. Farrar, the Dean of Canterbury, to perform before an invited audience scenes from *Becket* on 31 May 1897 in the Chapter House of Canterbury Cathedral. The proceeds were in aid of the Thirteenth Centenary Fund for the restoration of the cathedral. Special trains were laid on to bring audience members from London. Dean Farrar welcomed him to the event with words which must have warmed his heart:

> Sir Henry is known not only throughout the length and breadth of England, but amongst the English-speaking race throughout the world as one whose genius and steadfast purpose has brought before us, in a way unsurpassed for splendour, many of the glorious dramas of our greatest poet, Shakespeare … and he has throughout all his life endeavoured to purify the stage and to make it what it has been in past ages and with other nations, what it may be and now constantly is among us, not only a source of pleasure and amusement, but a stimulus to the imagination, and an element of thoughtful teaching, brought more vividly home to the mind through the medium of the eyes.

Irving proceeded to read selected scenes from the play in a performance lasting three hours.[27] It was enthusiastically received and raised £215 for the restoration fund. The event was remarkable in two respects: an actor reading a play in a church and also heroizing a Catholic saint who had traditionally had a bad press from Protestant historians and whose standing Irving helped to enhance with his performance.

The following year on 17 May at the invitation of Cardinal Vaughan, Irving delivered at Archbishop's House, Westminster, his lecture on the character of Macbeth in aid of the funds of the Catholic Social Union, whose aims and objects were 'to enlist the personal sympathy and service of the cultured, leisured, and well-to-do class on behalf of their less happily circumstanced brethren'. He concluded with a performance of *The Dream of Eugene Aram*. Cardinal Vaughan himself presided at the event and made a speech of thanks.[28] These invitations represented a welcome recognition of Irving's continuing advocacy of the moral and spiritual value of the stage. It was a career-long mission which he pursued with all the seriousness of purpose, high-mindedness and missionary spirit of the true Evangelical. References to the Lyceum as a temple or cathedral of the dramatic art are numberless and Irving's religious commitment to his calling was legendary. 'To him his art was a religion', said Lena Ashwell, who acted with him in *King Arthur* and *Dante*.[29] It was not just in the content of theatrical performance that Irving strove for moral uplift. He took a leading role in the movement to make the theatre as an institution respectable. His untiring activities to this end have already been explored.

Irving's intellectual and moral predispositions were powerfully reinforced by two personal blows, which cannot but have had the most significant impact psychologically. Not only did his strict Methodist mother cast him off when he went on the stage, his upper-crust wife, Florence, the daughter of an army surgeon-general, famously declared to him as they were driving home after his first-night triumph in *The Bells* in 1871: 'Are you going on making a fool of yourself like this all your life?' He got out of the carriage, left her and never saw her again, though continuing to support both her and his two sons. This may well have added to his drive to bring honour and respectability to his profession. It was also a double tragedy which probably drove him to explore roles involving guilt and remorse so powerfully and convincingly. It was a personal pre-disposition which dramatically reinforced the Evangelicals' ideological promotion of the centrality of conscience to human morality. It may also have left him with a sympathy for the outcast, which, remarkably for a racist age, led him to give notably sympathetic performances as the Jew Shylock, whom he played not as the traditional red-wigged villain but as a tragic hero, symbol of an oppressed race, and Othello, whom he played not as a primeval black savage but as a cultivated Moorish gentleman, protective of his honour.

The power of conscience and the emotional effects of guilt and remorse upon the individual sinner became a recurrent and recognized theme in Irving's art. The play which made Irving an overnight star, *The Bells*, was a prime study of guilt, remorse and retribution. It was a cherished project of Irving. In 1871 'Colonel' Bateman had engaged Irving as leading man at the Lyceum, intending him to partner his daughter Isabel. Irving made it a condition of his engagement that Bateman would produce *The Bells* as a vehicle for him when the opportunity arose. The play had been adapted by Leopold Lewis from a French play based on the novel *Le Juif Polonais* by Erckmann-Chatrian, a double-barrelled name concealing two Alsatian authors Emile Erckmann and Alexandre Chatrian. They

had based it on a real-life crime. It had been produced in Paris in 1869 with the
great French actor Talien in the lead. Lewis, whom George R. Sims called 'a
solicitor of Bohemian habits who combined law with literature and both with
hot rum, for which he had a weakness',[30] had unsuccessfully hawked the play
around the major London managements. But when Irving read it he saw it as the
perfect vehicle for himself. 'Colonel' Bateman was persuaded to acquire the rights
and Irving worked with Lewis reshaping and refining it for the stage.[31]

After the failure in rapid succession of *Fanchette* and *Pickwick*, Irving
reminded Bateman of his promise to stage *The Bells*. Bateman, despite his
misgivings about the play, misgivings doubtless increased when a rival English
version called *Paul Zegers* failed at the Royal Alfred Theatre, Marylebone, only a
couple of weeks before the scheduled opening of *The Bells*, authorized the
production and even imported Monsieur Etienne Singla from Paris to conduct
the original score he had composed for the 1869 Paris production.

Irving directed *The Bells*, overseeing every aspect of the production and
prepared his own performance with infinite care. It opened to a sparse house on
25 November 1871. It made Irving an overnight star and saved the fortunes of
the Bateman regime. It ran for 151 continuous performances. It was, however,
part of a double-bill. *Pickwick* continued to be performed after *The Bells*,
eventually replaced by a revival of the old farce *Raising the Wind* with Irving as
Jeremy Diddler. This established what was to become a feature of Irving's regime
at the Lyceum and was designed to confirm his versatility. For it showed him
playing tragedy and comedy on the same night.

The Bells became a phenomenon of the Victorian theatre. After 1871 it
remained in Irving's repertoire for the rest of his life. He eventually performed it
800 times all over both Britain and America, essaying the role for the last time in
the week of his death in 1905. In 1892 his fellow actors presented him with a
signed testimonial, and a statuette of Irving as Mathias by Onslow Ford, to
celebrate the twenty-first anniversary of the initial production. The longevity of
the production (thirty-four years) and the consistency of its appeal in London
and the provinces, in America and Canada is testimony to its power and appeal.
After Irving's death and in the decades leading up to the Second World War it
was performed by others, notably Irving's son, H.B. Irving, and his most devoted
disciple, Sir John Martin-Harvey. After the Second World War, which can in many
ways be seen to mark the watershed between the Victorian and the post-Victorian
worlds, it largely vanished from the theatrical repertoire and from the popular
consciousness, so much so that the cry 'The bells, the bells', which anyone up to
1939 would have known was a reference to Henry Irving and the play, came to
be recognized thereafter as a reference to Charles Laughton as Quasimodo in the
1939 Hollywood film *The Hunchback of Notre Dame*.

But until the Second World War, the association of Irving with the play remained deeply engrained. When in 1926 a silent film of *The Bells* based on Erckmann-Chatrian rather than Leopold Lewis was produced in Hollywood starring Lionel Barrymore as Mathias with Boris Karloff as the Mesmerist, a foreword announced that there had been many performances of *The Bells* in the previous half century but the most notable exponent of the role of Mathias had been Sir Henry Irving.

What accounts for the durability of the play? One obvious reason is the bravura performance of the leading actor. Ellen Terry, who watched him many times in *The Bells* described the intensity of his death scene:

> Every time he heard the sound of the bells, the throbbing of his heart must nearly have killed him. He used always to turn quite white – there was no trick about it. It was imagination acting physically on the body. His death as Mathias ... was different from all his other stage deaths. He really did almost die – he imagined death with such horrible intensity. His eyes would disappear upwards, his face grow grey, his limbs cold.[32]

It was hailed by almost every critic after the first performance. Dutton Cook in the *Pall Mall Gazette* said: 'Acting at once so intelligent and so intense has not been seen on the London stage for many years ... the actor is thoroughly possessed by his part and depicts its agonizing fear and passionate despair with real artistic force.' The *Athenaeum* said: 'there is no question that the man who could give such portraiture as Mr Irving afforded on the conflict of emotion and passion has histrionic power of the rarest kind'.[33] Reviews of this kind regularly greeted the performance of the role. The uniformity of praise was such that to promote the play 'Colonel' Bateman took a two-inch double-column advertisement in the newspapers, saying that it was impossible to print all the favourable opinions of the new play and its star, so he simply listed in double column the names of the forty-one newspapers and journals that had lauded *The Bells* and Henry Irving.[34]

But there was more to it that this, the conception of the character, the structure and nature of the drama and the moral to be drawn appealed powerfully to the Victorian sensibility and in particular to the dominating idea of the Non-conformist conscience. It is notable that Irving's Mathias differed very greatly from his French counterpart, as performed by the great actor Coquelin. H. Chance Newton, better known at the columnist Carados of *The Referee*, saw both Irving and Coquelin in the role and wrote:

> No two performances could be so opposed to each other as Coquelin's and Irving's. Irving gave a romanticized and inescapably magnetic performance that haunted one for many a day and night after seeing him. Coquelin made this inn-keeping murderer a bullet-headed bully of the most matter-of-fact criminal description. The Irving 'Mathias' was in continual terror at the idea of detection, whereas Coquelin gloried in his gory crime and laughed and chuckled over it. I remember that Irving and I talked to Coquelin

about this strange disparity of view … Coquelin, admitting that Irving's was a very great, penetrating performance asserted roundly that nevertheless it was totally unlike the French murderer that he represented. Coquelin added: 'I play Mathias as I know such murderers would be in parts of my country; Irving's is a great assumption, but it is not a bit like the real thing.'[35]

But that is precisely the point. It is a Mathias for Protestant Victorian England and not for Catholic France.

The American critic William Winter appreciated the importance of the character transformation wrought by Irving, when he wrote of Mathias after Irving's first American production of *The Bells*:

He is a living monument of the retributive vengeance of Divine Justice. It could not be difficult for an experienced actor to play this part effectively, in a professional sense. Mr Irving has accomplished far more than that. By giving this murderer a human heart, by making paternal tenderness the motive and passion of his life, and then by depicting with consummate skill, those agonies of the soul which only such a soul can suffer, he creates an image not less pitiable than horrible of that forlorn humanity which evil has conquered, and which inexorable justice must now destroy … Mr Irving produced the effect of pathos as well as largely the effect of terror, the latter being predominant, and his method, in the latter being wonderfully subtle and picturesque. The feverish alertness engendered by the strife of a strong will against a sickening apprehension, the desperate sense, now defiant and now abject, of impending doom, the slow paralysis of the feelings, under the action of remorse – these, indeed, were given with appalling truth.[36]

The play carefully sets up a classical domestic situation: it is Christmas Eve, the setting is the inn of Mathias with its warmth and good fellowship and Mathias, the respected Alsatian innkeeper and burgomaster, is established as a loving husband and father who is planning the wedding of his daughter to the local gendarme. But he nurses a terrible secret: fifteen years earlier he has murdered and disposed of a Polish Jew for the contents of his money-belt. As people begin to talk of the murder and the gendarme Christian begins to investigate it afresh, the pressure on Mathias grows. He hears ghostly sleighbells, has a vision of himself committing the murder and passes out, and finally in a dream appears before a supernatural court where under the influence of a mesmerist he relives the murder and is sentenced to hang. Awaking from the dream, he screams 'Take the rope from my neck' and dies from the stress of his guilt. Not only has divine retribution followed on from the committing of a heinous crime but the audience has witnessed at first hand the terrible effects of a guilty conscience on someone who had been a good man but had been tempted by poverty into a crime that had ultimately destroyed himself and his happy home. It was a powerful warning to anyone tempted to stray; temptation must be fought and overcome. It also powerfully points up the fragility of respectability, the destruction of domestic bliss and the primacy of conscience.[37]

The success of *The Bells* undoubtedly prompted the suggestion that Irving's grim and powerful party piece, a recitation of Thomas Hood's poem 'The Dream of Eugene Aram', should be turned into a drama, as a vehicle for Irving's particular talents. His recitation of the Hood poem was regularly reported as holding audiences 'spellbound'. 'Colonel' Bateman commissioned an Aram play from W.G. Wills, the resident Lyceum playwright.

The story of Eugene Aram, like that of Mathias and the Polish Jew, was based on fact. He was one of the most celebrated murderers of the eighteenth century. Aram, a self-taught gardener's son had become a scholar, linguist and school-master in Knaresborough. He vanished in April 1745, abandoning his wife and children – there had been eight, two of whom had died. Two months earlier Daniel Clark, a prosperous local shoemaker, had also disappeared without trace. In 1758 a skeleton was found in St Robert's Cave and identified as Clark's. Anna Aram testified that her husband and their neighbour Richard Houseman, a linen weaver, had conspired to murder Clark. It seemed that Clark, Houseman and Aram had been involved in a plot to defraud their neighbours by acquiring many goods on credit, intending to make off with the proceeds, but the partners had fallen out. Houseman turned King's evidence, implicating Aram as the murderer. Aram was traced and arrested in Lynn, Norfolk, where he was working as an usher in the grammar school. Undertaking his own defence and maintaining his innocence to the end, Aram was found guilty and sentenced to death. After a failed attempt at suicide, he was hanged on 6 August 1759. Widely respected in Knaresborough for his gentlemanly refinement and intellectual attainments, he actually wrote several poems while in prison and completed an essay on the etymological links between Celtic and other European languages. Unlike other murderers of the time, Aram did not vanish from public consciousness. He haunted the imagination not only of contemporaries but also of the Romantic movement and later the Victorian age. It was the paradox of an apparent gentleman and scholar who resorts to murder that disturbed a society with a clear perception of the values attached to the concept of respectability.[38]

Aram's skull was preserved for study and ended up at the Royal College of Surgeons. Tourists visited the sites associated with the crime and so many came that the local inn, the White Horse, was renamed the Eugene Aram. Even more significantly, Aram was taken up and transformed into a literary archetype. In 1829 Thomas Hood published his ballad 'The Dream of Eugene Aram'. It became one of the most famous recitation pieces of the nineteenth century. It was apparently inspired by the memories of Admiral James Burney, who as a boy had been a pupil at Lynn Grammar School and recalled Aram pacing the schoolyard with some of the older boys and discussing strange murders, apparently to ease the burden of a guilty conscience. The poem takes the form of a monologue by Aram to one of his child pupils. He talks about a dream that haunts his mind in which he murders an old man and seeks to conceal the body and is thereafter tormented by guilt and a belief in the inevitability of discovery. Although there is no contemporary evidence of the historical Aram being tormented by guilt, Hood turned him into the archetypal anguished anti-hero of the Romantic movement.

Irving became the most celebrated interpreter of the poem. He recited it throughout his career whenever a specialist item was required of him. Bram Stoker witnessed a private performance of it for a dozen friends in a dining room, with Irving in evening dress. He described it in his *Reminiscences of Henry Irving*:

> such was Irving's commanding force, so great was the magnetism of his genius, so profound was the sense of his dominance that I sat spellbound ... That I knew the story and was even familiar with its unalterable words was nothing. The whole thing was new, recreated by a force of passion which was like a new power. Across the footlights amid picturesque scenery and suitable dress, with one's fellows beside and all around one, though the effect of passion can convince and sway it cannot move one personally beyond a certain point. But here was incarnate power, incarnate passion, so close that one could meet it eye to eye, within touch of the outstretched hand. The surroundings became non-existent; the dress ceased to be noticeable, recurring thoughts of self-existence were not at all. Here was indeed Eugene Aram as he was face to face with his Lord; his very soul aflame in the light of his abiding horror. Looking back now, I can realise the perfection of art with which the mind was led and swept and swayed hither and thither as the actor wished. How a change of tone or time denoted the personality of the 'Blood-avenging Sprite' – and how the nervous, eloquent hands slowly moving, outspread fan-like, round the fixed face – set as doom, with eyes as inflexible as Fate – emphasised it till one instinctively quivered with pity! Then came the awful horror on the murderer's face as the ghost in his brain seemed to take external shape before his eyes, and enforced on him that from his sin there was no refuge. After this climax of horror the Actor was able by art and habit to control himself to the narrative mood while he spoke the few concluding lines of the poem. Then he collapsed half-fainting.[39]

The performance reduced Stoker to a 'violent fit of hysterics', and inspired his life-long devotion to 'The Guv'nor'.

But the piece had more than just an emotional effect; it had a perceived moral effect. Cardinal Vaughan, the Archbishop of Westminster, told Irving after a recitation of 'Aram' 'that he could not conceive how any man, however provoked, could possibly bring himself to perpetrate, in hot blood or cold, a murder, after hearing Sir Henry Irving's awesome and agonizing rendering of Hood's poem'.[40]

Inspired in part by Hood's poem, the novelist Edward Bulwer Lytton undertook the next stage of Aram's transformation in his 1832 novel *Eugene Aram*. Embellishing the known facts with his own Romantic imagination, he transformed Aram into a full-blown Byronic hero, solitary, tormented, brooding, tragic, blood brother to Manfred and Faust. Lytton's novel opens in 1758 at

Grassdale, the fictional equivalent of Lynn, where Aram, living as a scholarly recluse, haunted by a guilty secret, falls in love with Madeline Lester daughter of the Squire. He is about to marry her when the murder of Daniel Clarke (rather than Clark) is uncovered. He is arrested and tried, and after a flashback to the crime, he is condemned to death, but commits suicide to avoid the gallows, and Madeline dies of grief. In Lytton's version, Aram, a poor gentleman scholar, seeks funds to finance his scientific research for the benefit of mankind. He debates the pros and cons of robbing and murdering a depraved man for the greater good of society. Daniel Clarke becomes in this version a dissolute minor aristocrat, who has deserted his wife and son and is a robber and a rapist. Aram feels no regret for the murder but does regret the effects on Madeline and her family and reflects on the unpredictable consequences of crime and the essential unreliability of dispassionate reasoning. In Lytton's version, Aram is elevated and romanticized. He has neither wife nor children, wins the love of a good woman and had genuinely sought to do good.

But Lytton's sympathetic picture of the murderer provoked strong and continuing protest at his apparent romanticization and justification of murder. So in 1849 he revised the novel to make it clear that Aram was involved in the robbery but not in the murder. The success of the novel inevitably led to stage versions. There was an authorized adaptation of the novel by W.T. Moncrieff, *Eugene Aram: or St Robert's Cave*, first performed at the Surrey Theatre on 8 February 1832. There were several other unauthorized adaptations in 1832, both in London and Edinburgh, and a further adaptation was seen at the Marylebone Theatre in 1855.

But the most successful stage version was W.G. Wills's *The Fate of Eugene Aram* (usually known simply as *Eugene Aram*) which initially ran at the Lyceum for three months (19 April to 20 June 1873) Wills's brother and biographer, the Reverend Freeman Wills, whom Chance Newton called 'a very "advanced" cleric of the muscular Christian type',[41] noted:

> Purists were forearmed with the objection that it would enlist sympathy for the criminal; but as a vivid picture of the tortures of remorse the drama was little open to objection on ethical grounds. From the first appearance of the haunted man in the old-fashioned vicarage garden it is obvious that his happiness is his misery and his misery is the only alleviation of his remorse. This, surely, is good morality.[42]

It was claimed in the Lyceum programme that the play was based on neither Hood's poem nor Lytton's novel but 'mainly on tradition.' There were, however, elements of both and echoes of *The Bells*. According to William Winter, 'in the construction of the piece Henry Irving made many radical suggestions. The treatment of the character of Aram was devised by him.'[43]

Wills's play took place during the course of one day in 1759 in the vicarage and churchyard of Knaresborough. It had an idyllic opening in the vicarage garden, 'with the old porch smothered with jasmine and redolent of roses'. Clement Scott noted it as 'one of the most natural and poetical summer pictures the stage has ever seen since Mr Bateman took the Lyceum.'[44] From this sunny beginning the mood steadily darkened. Aram is the respected schoolmaster, who receives a testimonial from the local people praising his 'wisdom' and 'spotless life'. He is in love with and about to marry Ruth Meadows, the vicar's daughter. She seeks the reason for his melancholy and he reveals that he had once loved another woman who had died. Houseman, who had witnessed the killing of Clarke by Aram, turns up, seeking to retrieve money that was buried with Clarke fifteen years before. A suspicious gardener follows Houseman to St Robert's Cave and discovers the skeleton of Clarke. Houseman tries to blackmail Aram, who defies him. The gardener now reveals the discovery of the skeleton and denounces Houseman as the murderer. But Houseman implicates Aram, who denies it. The vicar asks Aram and Houseman to accompany him to investigate. But, following inspection of the skeleton, Houseman flees; Aram retires to the churchyard haunted by guilt and, collapsing beneath a cross, confesses to Ruth that he had indeed killed Clarke, who had seduced and abandoned the woman he loved. He dies as the dawn breaks, and church music peals out.

Wills had kept closely to the classical unities of time, place and theme. His play, like much of his work, was strong on poetry and weak on plot. *The Times* (21 April 1873) noted correctly that it was a psychological study, not a sensational melodrama. But it was an ideal vehicle for Irving. It was greeted by an expectant first-night audience with a storm of applause, and there were some enthusiastic reviews. Clement Scott said: '*Eugene Aram* is no ordinary play. The acting of Mr. Irving is no ordinary acting.' He noted that in the scene in which Houseman denounced Aram as the murderer, Irving's acting 'electrified the audience, and the play was deservedly stopped for applause'. He observed that the third act was essentially 'one tremendous soliloquy, and the excellence of Mr Irving's acting is at once pronounced with the statement that it held the audience from the commencement'.[45] William Winter praised Irving for 'investing psychological subtlety with tender human feeling and romantic grace, and making an imaginary experience of suffering vital and heart-rending in its awful reality'.[46] The *Spectator* published a lengthy comparison of Mathias and Aram. It argued that although both performances were studies in guilt and remorse and both involved confessions, Mathias had no enemy but himself, and the pressure came from within and the study 'is finer'; with Aram, the pressure came from without (the arrival of Houseman and the discovery of the body). But it conceded that the acting of Irving was 'wonderfully fine', and 'deeply impressive' as it modulated from melancholy to anguish to terror to contrition; 'the fight of the mind which is torturing with the body which is betraying him' was 'perfect'.[47]

After its initial run, the play was revived briefly in Irving's first two seasons as manager, 1879 and 1880, with Ellen Terry taking over the part of Ruth, but it never gained anything like the hold in the repertoire that *The Bells* did. What is common to both is the fragility of respectability as burgomaster and school-master, pillars of the local community, are destroyed by guilt and by the action of conscience.

It is worth noting that the transformation of Aram, from condemned murderer to sympathetic hero via Hood, Lytton and Wills was completed in 1902 when John Martin-Harvey starred in *After All*, a new version of the Aram story specially written for him by two clergymen, Freeman Wills (W.G.'s brother) and Frederick Langbridge. Aram kills Clarke after he has seduced, abandoned and driven to suicide Aram's sister. When eventually brought to trial, he is found innocent but, tormented by conscience, he leaves his fiancée with her other admirer and departs 'whether to make a public confession or simply vanish, is not made clear'.[48] The play, later retitled *Eugene Aram*, was not a success, and soon dropped out of Harvey's repertoire.

The hero haunted by guilt and in search of redemption turned up again in *Vanderdecken* (1878). The legend of the 'Flying Dutchman' – something of a variation on the age-old tale of 'The Wandering Jew' – derived from a sixteenth-century Dutch legend. It told how a Dutch sea captain, Vanderdecken, was trying to round the Cape of Good Hope in the teeth of a storm in his ship *The Flying Dutchman*. He refuses to seek shelter in the bay, declaring, 'May I be eternally damned if I do, though I should beat about here until the day of judgement'. His blasphemy leads to his condemnation to that eternal life.

The story first appeared in English in *Blackwood's Magazine* in 1821 as 'Vanderdecken's Last Message' and was eventually made the basis of a novel, *The Phantom Ship*, by Captain Marryat in 1839. The *Blackwood's* story was turned into an Adelphi melodrama by Edward Fitzball, first produced in 1826. In the same year the legend inspired a poem by German poet Heinrich Heine, who introduced the idea of the Dutchman being redeemed by the selfless love of a pure woman. The Heine poem inspired Richard Wagner to compose his opera *Der Fliegende Holländer*, first performed in Dresden in 1843. It was first produced in London in 1870 and it was the opera that gave Percy Fitzgerald the idea of a play on the subject as a vehicle for Irving. 'He was,' recalled Fitzgerald 'it was often repeated, the "ideal" Vanderdecken.'[49] Irving himself strongly favoured the idea and 'Colonel' Bateman was persuaded to commission the play, with Fitzgerald providing the dramatic construction and W.G. Wills furnishing the poetic dialogue. The play, however, went through several reworkings with Irving himself contributing ideas. It finally opened after Bateman's death on 8 June 1878, but it ran only a month, its demise being attributed to unusually hot summer weather and the particularly gloomy nature of the play.[50]

The story had Thekla, an imaginative young Norwegian girl, engaged to Olaf, falling in love with a mysterious stranger from the sea, Vanderdecken. The jealous Olaf fights a duel with Vanderdecken, hurling him over a cliff apparently to his death, but the sea washes him up again, still alive. Thekla learns that only if a woman will sacrifice her life for him for love will his endless wandering be brought to an end. She agrees and boards the phantom ship with him. It was essentially a one-part play, allowing Irving to soliloquize at length on his fate: 'What is my doom? Worse than hell! Eternal loneliness! Eternal silence!' Irving won praise from the critics for his performance. Joseph Knight called him 'splendidly picturesque and impressive, his aspect in the stronger scenes being absolutely lurid'.[51] Clement Scott thought him 'a Vanderdecken haunted by the despair of an eternity of life'.[52] He praised the staging and the scenery. But in general critics found the play talky and static. So, too, apparently did the public. But Fitzgerald records that Irving maintained his faith in the idea and urged him to have another go at it.[53] Nothing came of it. Irving's persistent desire to make something of the story tells us, however, much about his dramatic priorities and intellectual preoccupations.

On 27 September 1879, Irving revived George Colman the Younger's *The Iron Chest*. The play was derived from the novel *Caleb Williams* by the radical writer William Godwin. Godwin's novel, published in 1794, was a frankly propagandist work, designed to show the 'tyranny and perfidiousness exercised by the powerful members of the community against those who are less privileged than themselves'. So in the first part of the novel a tyrannical country squire Tyrrel ruins one of his tenants Hawkins for failing to yield to one of his whims. He then quarrels with benevolent squire Falkland, knocks him down in public and is later found murdered. Hawkins and his son are suspected, arrested and executed for the crime. Falkland thereafter becomes a recluse but his humble-born, self-educated secretary Caleb Williams comes to suspect him of the murder. Williams is then persecuted by Falkland, falsely accused of murder and hounded from place to place by Falkland's agents until eventually Caleb lays a formal charge of murder against Falkland, confronts him and Falkland breaks down and confesses.

Colman took the central situation of the novel, changed the names and turned it into a study of conscience. *The Iron Chest* made its debut at Drury Lane in 1796 but on its initial opening failed, a failure for which Colman blamed and roundly denounced the leading actor John Philip Kemble. It was revived later in the year with R.W. Elliston in the lead and became a success. It subsequently became one of Edmund Kean's most brilliant triumphs. This meant that it entered the Romantic repertoire as something which leading actors took on to measure themselves against their predecessors. All the critics rehearsed its stage history at the start of their reviews of Irving's performance. Macready detested the play, as he made clear in his diary, and never played Mortimer, though as a young man he played Wilford.[54] But both Charles Kean and Samuel Phelps took on the leading role of Sir Edward Mortimer. This was enough to persuade Irving to revive it. But more than that it was another of those studies of conscience and guilt in which Irving revelled. Dutton Cook perceptively observed, given its stage history and Irving's predilections:

> Altogether Mr Irving was quite justified, I think, in producing this play at the Lyceum Theatre. Preceding tragedians had bestowed a reputation upon it; and no doubt it occurred to him that, in his turn, he could do something about the character of *Mortimer*. He had indeed served a sort of apprenticeship to the part by his achievement as *Mathias*, as *Eugene Aram*, and as *Philip* in Mr Aidé's play.[55]

Colman's play in fact contains all the elements that made *The Bells* such a powerful vehicle. Set in the New Forest in the early seventeenth century, the play opens by establishing Sir Edward Mortimer's benevolence. He sends his secretary Wilford with money to relieve the poverty of the family of the poacher Rawbold. Wilford says of Mortimer that he is 'one of those judges who, in their office, will never warp the law to save offenders; but his private charity binds him to assist the needy, before their necessities drive them to crimes which his public duty must punish'. Wilford later questions the faithful steward Adam Winterton about the reasons for the reclusive lifestyle adopted by Mortimer, and Winterton tells him that several years before Sir Edward became involved in an incident with the uncle of Lady Helen, the woman he loved. The uncle, a brute hated by all, picked a quarrel with him, knocked him down and was later found murdered. Mortimer was tried but acquitted and thereafter has lived in seclusion, with Lady Helen, in a nearby cottage. Wilford comes to suspect because of Mortimer's strange behaviour that he is in fact the murderer and seeks to open an iron chest in the library, in search of evidence. Mortimer denounces him for questioning his innocence, but later, tormented by conscience, confesses to Wilford that he is the murderer. He swears Wilford to secrecy and Wilford, who owes him everything, agrees to remain silent, but asks to leave his service. Mortimer tells him he must remain. Wilford flees, is attacked and injured in the forest and cared for by a soft-hearted robber, Armstrong, in the abbey ruins, the headquarters of a band of robbers. Mortimer discusses the flight with Helen and vows to pursue Wilford. But Helen urges Mortimer to leave him to his conscience: 'There is no earthly punishment so great, to scourge the evil act, as man's own conscience, to tell him he is guilty.' Mortimer has let it be known that Wilford has fled because he has robbed his employer. Mortimer's half-brother, Captain Fitz-Harding, believing Wilford innocent, persuades him to return. Wilford does return, refusing to say why he fled but proclaiming his innocence. Mortimer insists on Wilford's guilt, has his trunk sent for and reveals hidden there Mortimer's watch and family jewels, but there are other items too, a document and a bloodstained dagger. The document is Mortimer's confession to the murder and the dagger the instrument used. Mortimer confesses his guilt, begs the forgiveness of the wronged Wilford and dies in Helen's arms.

Mortimer resembles Mathias. Outwardly respectable, benevolent, seeking to expiate his sin by doing good, he is also tormented by conscience. Colman omits the fact that innocent men were hanged for the murder. He concentrates only on the second half of the novel and he transforms it from anti-aristocratic propaganda into a study of individual conscience, with big scenes of guilt, suspicion, remorse and expiation for the actors.

In preparing it for the stage, Irving had had virtually to reconstruct the play. The three-act original was recast in four acts and ten scenes. The original had been studded with glees and madrigals by Stephen Storace, making it 'half-opera, half-tragedy'. Irving eliminated all but one of the songs. He also altered the setting. No longer was the play set in the early seventeenth century with the hybrid 'semi-Elizabethan, semi-Caroline costume' of previous productions. It was relocated to 1792, the era of the novel, and in accordance with the prevalent principles of realism and archaeological accuracy, the play, as Clement Scott observed, was 'mounted ... with strict attention to the furniture and architecture of the late eighteenth century, admirable alike in detail and effect, and presenting to the audience very noble and impressive stage pictures'.[56] The result of all these changes was to concentrate attention on the central character and his mental torment.

In reviewing the play, the critics left their readers in no doubt about its imperfections. Dutton Cook thought the play:

> chiefly defective in regard to its coherence; the incidents are all detached or semi-detached ... The scenes devoted to Sir Edward Mortimer and his story have the remotest connection with the scenes occupied by the *Rawbold* family; while between the depressing household and the band of robbers who receive the boy *Wilford* so hospitably the relationship is very hard to discover ... Of course Goodwin's novel [*sic*] of *Caleb Williams* lies at the foundation of *The Iron Chest* and the infirmities of Colman's play result from his attempts to deal dramatically with an undramatic subject. The attractions of the novel were found in its graduality of development and the incessant movement of scenes in which Caleb is hunted from place to place by Falkland; and these are just the qualities which cannot be adequately reflected upon the stage.

He did not have much more time for the novel, declaring it:

> dull and disappointing, after allowance has been made for the originality and the striking nature of its theme. It is written in a rude, crude style, and abounds in absurdly stilted descriptions of scenery, unnatural characters, and most artificial pictures of society.

As for the play:

> Colman's speeches are often eloquent enough, if they incline to verbosity; they are the
> conventional efforts of a skilled playwright contriving occasions for declamation.
> Sincerity, perhaps, is lacking throughout the play, with genuine poetic force, depth,
> and feeling. But the blank verse may be fairly said to be as good or as bad as the late
> Lord Lytton's.[57]

Joseph Knight was even more severe:

> Colman's *The Iron Chest* is one of the worst plays of the worst epoch in our dramatic
> annals. The great central figure which Godwin in his *Caleb Williams* supplied is there.
> And in this is found the attraction which has commended the character to every
> tragedian except Macready. It is sadly dwarfed, however, from the original. For this
> Colman may not be greatly to blame, since the elaborate psychology which is the chief
> feature in the novel is not to be preserved in a play. Such operatic surroundings as
> Colman supplied are contemptible to the last degree. The blank verse would do discredit
> to Tate or Brady and the whole workmanship is pitiful. Still the fact remains that the
> central figure is strong.[58]

Knight's solution was for Irving to have commissioned 'some living dramatist'
to extract a new play from *Caleb Williams*. All, however, were agreed that the role
of Mortimer was a personal triumph for Irving. Dutton Cook declared of Irving:

> He is an adept at depicting remorse ... he has demonstrated also his power of illustrating
> wide and varying ranges of passion and character. It seems to me that his *Mortimer* may
> rank quite among his best performances, in right of its artistic completeness, its
> picturesqueness, its intensity, and moderation. In none of his characters has he exhibited
> more thorough control of himself and of his art, keeping voice and gesture well in
> subjection, repressing habits or tricks of manner, and yet retaining in full his wonted
> power to impress, to awe, and to excite ... he has ... modernised the method of
> impersonation; so that *Sir Edward Mortimer*, becoming more like a gentleman of the
> eighteenth century than he has appeared on former occasions, pertains more to nature
> and reality, less to fiction and stage, than has been his wont hitherto. Some of the old
> traditional points and effects, swift transitions and grand explosions, may have been
> missing; but I do not know that they were much missed. Mr Irving's *Sir Edward Mortimer*
> commands attention and interest from his first discovery upon the scene, the impression
> strengthening and deepening as the play proceeds; the actor's early forbearance and
> repose enhancing by the force of contrast his absolute self-abandonment when the climax
> of the story is reached, and the situation permits, and even demands, a display of a most
> vehement and frantic sort.[59]

So not only does Irving give one of his character studies of conscience but this is
the latest stage in his presentation of the evolving and rounded psychological
portrait, removed from the striking of attitudes and the making of points which
previous interpreters of the part had done. Joseph Knight wrote:

Mr Irving's performance of *Sir Edward Mortimer* in *The Iron Chest* is an instance of absolute realisation. Never, probably, since the days when ... Kemble came on to the boards ... has the play been seen to equal advantage, or the character received with such precise embodiment. As a picture of despair and desolation, sombre and funereal, illumined by bursts of passion which rend and convulse the frame, and are yet as evanescent as they are powerful, the performance is marvellous. The grimmer aspect of Mr Irving's powers has never been seen to equal advantage, and if the performance is not so fine as the Louis XI, it is only because the comic element is wanting. Mr Irving's face is capable of being charged with any amount of tragic expression, and it is not easy to conceive a picture of remorse burning fiercely behind the closed shutters of a resolute will more powerful than that he presents in the scene in which he sets himself to work a cruel and deliberate vengeance on the boy whose curiosity has stirred his fears.[60]

Similarly Clement Scott:

For the success of *The Iron Chest* the direct personal interest of Mr. Henry Irving is alone responsible – and not an influence of tradition, be it remembered, but a direct and immediate sympathy between artist and audience. It is quite true that this favourite actor has played in *The Bells* and *Eugene Aram*, and who can say in how many more plays in which he has represented the tortures of a distressed and disturbed conscience; he has struck the same chord with innumerable variations on the same theme; but we don't believe he has ever been so calm, so poetical, so dignified, and so unrestless, as in Sir Edward Mortimer. The pathetic expression of the face, the strange power of the eye, the extraordinary calm of the features, attracted the audience in spite of themselves. In all the soliloquies a pin might have been heard to drop, for the artist held his audience easily in his hand, and by some strange magnetic power, all who listened discarded for the moment the mere passing fascination of the story, and entered into the thoughts, the mental agony, and the conscience throbs of this most miserable man ... Like so many of Mr Irving's haunted and hunted characters, it is still unlike them, and we do not believe that, under so many disadvantages of subject, he has ever acted so well, so firmly, and so conscientiously.[61]

By contrast with the praise for Irving's Mortimer, Norman Forbes's Wilford was castigated. Dutton Cook called him 'awkward and monotonous and ... curiously epicene', and Scott complained of the 'girlishness' of Forbes's performance: 'There was no truth in the tones of the voice, no appearance of real distress, and the crude formula of art was never concealed.'[62]

The first night audience received Irving's performance rapturously and it looked set fair for a long run. But the gloomy and old-fashioned nature of the play doomed it. Looking back, Brereton called it 'Colman's dreary drama' and Fitzgerald, 'hopelessly old-fashioned'. Even J.H. Barnes, who was in the play as Fitz-Harding, called it 'old-fashioned and turgid' though 'beautifully produced'.[63] It ran for a month before being withdrawn and was never revived. It was succeeded on the stage by one of Irving''s greatest successes, *The Merchant of*

Venice. Irving in his curtain speech had declared himself pleased by the reception of *The Iron Chest* 'because it is my intention to reproduce other old plays'. These undoubtedly included *The Stranger* and *The Gamester*, both of which he abandoned as projects as a result of the *Iron Chest* experience.

Perhaps the crowning achievement of Irving's regime in both artistic and economic terms was *Faust*. It was first performed in the 1885–86 season, revived in the 1886–87 season, and was revived again in 1888, 1894 and 1902. It was acted for the last time in Bristol on 10 December 1902. It was given in all 792 times in Britain and America, a record exceeded only by *The Bells*, and that had begun under the Bateman regime. It brought in an estimated £250,000 in box office receipts during its career.[64]

By the nineteenth century, *Faust* had become a classical Evangelical morality tale, personalizing the Devil and debating the centrally important issues of physical versus spiritual, restraint versus excess. Faust was a real-life sixteenth-century scholar around whom a corpus of legend developed, in particular the story that he had sold his soul to the Devil to regain his youth. As early as 1588 this provided the basis for a classic play, Christopher Marlowe's *Doctor Faustus*. There were several notable versions in the nineteenth century. Charles Kean produced Dion Boucicault's version of the story, *Faust and Margaret* in 1854. Charles Gounod's 1859 opera *Faust* became a staple of the Victorian stage, eclipsing Spohr's opera *Faust* and overshadowing Berlioz's dramatic cantata *The Damnation of Faust*. In 1866, Samuel Phelps had starred at Drury Lane as Mephistopheles in *Faust*, Bayle-Bernard's adaptation of Goethe, the first for the English stage. W.S. Gilbert produced another stage version in blank verse called *Gretchen* (1879). Intriguingly this version starred H.B. Conway as Faust. He was to play the same role in Irving's *Faust* only to fail on the opening night and be replaced by George Alexander, who had scored a first night hit in the lesser role of Valentine.

Irving commissioned W.G. Wills to provide an adaptation of Part 1 of Goethe's celebrated poetic drama, tailored to the Lyceum stage. The fact that it was originally to have been called *Mephisto* leaves little doubt about who was to be the leading character.[65] The play was completed 'two or three years' before its production and, as always, Irving undertook extensive research, including a trip to Germany, in order to ensure the visual accuracy of his stage pictures. It opened on 19 December 1885, to the customary fashionable audience, headed this time by the Prince and Princess of Wales.

The familiar story opens at Easter with the elderly philosopher Faust, jaded and disillusioned after a lifetime of arid study, hating the onset of old age and infirmity, and preparing to take poison. Mephistopheles appears and strikes a bargain with him. Faust will regain his youth and in the future his body and soul will belong to Mephistopheles. Their compact is signed in blood. They embark on a life of 'feverish revelry'. Mephistopheles helps the rejuvenated Faust to seduce the innocent maiden Margaret. He causes Margaret to poison her mother with what she believes to be a sleeping draught. He assists Faust to kill her brother Valentine in a duel. By now, Margaret is pregnant and she is cursed by her dying brother for her fall from grace. Faust abandons her and is taken to the witches' sabbat on the Brocken. Distracted by grief, Margaret drowns her child after its birth and ends up in prison, condemned to death. Faust tries to persuade her to escape but she seeks to expiate her sins in death. She dies at the foot of the cross and her soul is borne away to heaven by a flight of angels.

The moral of the play was clear. It is explained by the American writer William Winter:

> The sin of Faust is a spiritual sin, and the meaning of all his subsequent terrible experiences is that spiritual sin must be – and will be – expiated. No human soul can ever be lost. In every human soul the contest between good and evil must continue until the good has conquered and the evil is defeated and eradicated. Then, when the man's spirit is adjusted to its environment in the spiritual world, it will be at peace – and not till then ... it is the greatest of all delusions to suppose that you can escape from yourself. Judgment and retribution proceed within the soul and not from sources outside it.

Winter thought that this was 'more distinctly indicated in Mr Wills's play ... than in any other play upon the subject that has been presented'.[66]

Irving spared no expense in staging the tale with pictorial magnificence and awe-inspiring spectacle. The scenes on the Brocken long remained in the memories of those who witnessed them.[67] It became one of the great landmarks of Victorian spectacular theatre. There were, however, some who remained unmoved, dismissing it as a mere pantomime. Henry James, writing in *Century* magazine, conceded the production's visual splendours, but witheringly dismissed Wills' text ('so meagre, so common, so trivial') and the acting of Irving as Mephistopheles ('thin'), Ellen Terry as Margaret ('rough and ready') and George Alexander as Faust ('insignificant').[68]

But this was a minority view. William Winter declared Irving's performance as Mephistopheles 'superb in ideal and perfect in execution ... a great work ... this Fiend, towering to the loftiest summit of cold intellect, is the embodiment of cruelty, malice and scorn, pervaded and interfused with grim humour. That ideal Mr Irving made actual.'[69] He was equally impressed by Ellen Terry:

> Ellen Terry in her assumption of Margaret, once more displayed that profound knowledge of human love – that knowledge of it through the soul and not simply the mind – which is the source of her exceptional and irresistible power ... In her embodiment she transfigured the character; she maintained it in an ideal world, and she was the living epitome of all that is fascinating in essential womanhood – glorified by genius.[70]

Clement Scott pronounced Irving's Mephistopheles 'incomparable' and Ellen Terry's Margaret 'one of the most beautiful and remarkable performances Miss Ellen Terry has ever given on the stage'.[71] Ellen herself said that 'Margaret was the part I liked better than any other – outside Shakespeare. I played it beautifully sometimes. The language was often very commonplace … but the character was all right, simple, touching, sublime.' She thought George Alexander 'played it admirably. Indeed he always was like an angel with me.' But added, 'I never cared much for Henry's Mephistopheles – a twopence coloured part, any way. Of course he had his moments … but they were few.'[72] Lewis Carroll (Charles Dodgson) wrote, however: 'Such a picture as Irving gives us of "Mephistopheles" must surely have a healthy influence. Who can see it and not realise, with a vividness few producers could rival, the utter *hatefulness* of sin.'[73]

Audiences loved it, responding to the spectacle, the performances and the message. Alongside *The Bells* (and unlike *Vanderdecken*, *Eugene Aram* and *The Iron Chest*), it remained in his repertoire until almost the end. *The Bells*, as the classic demonstration of the destructive power of the guilty conscience, and *Faust*, as a vivid demonstration of the consequences of choosing the physical over the spiritual and of the need to seek expiation, spoke directly to widely held religious views and saw the stage fulfilling its role as secular pulpit.

14

Shylock and the Jews

Irving's biographer Percy Fitzgerald recounts the story of Irving taking a hansom cab one night during the run of *The Merchant of Venice* at the Lyceum in 1879–80:

> In a fit of absence of mind he tendered a shilling for his fare, whereas it should have been eighteenpence or two shillings. Whereupon the cabby who recognized his man, burst out: 'If yer plays the Jew inside that theayter as well as yer does outside, darned if I won't spend this bob on coming to see yer.' It is said he was so delighted with the retort that he promptly gave the man half a sovereign.[1]

This anecdote illustrates perfectly how deeply entrenched in the society and culture of Victorian England was the stereotyped image of the Jew as miser and skinflint. The irony of the situation is that at the time Irving was playing the most sympathetic Shylock ever seen on the English stage and causing controversy thereby.

The Merchant of Venice was of great cultural significance in the nineteenth century. Linda Rozmovits calls it 'a late Victorian popular obsession.'[2] She argues that it was regarded by scholars as the height of Shakespeare's dramatic achievement and for the public was 'one of the best known and best liked plays in English.' Its late Victorian pre-eminence, she attributes to its relevance to three burning issues of the period: mass education, the debates around feminism and the Jewish question. Following the passing of the 1870 Education Act, it became an important feature in the teaching of English. Over sixty school editions of *The Merchant* were published between 1870 and 1920. It was valued because it was both accessible and morally instructive. The characters of Portia and Shylock became the centre of cultural debate. Portia could be and was seen both as the ideal Victorian wife, subordinating her independence, education and wealth to her husband, and accepting a role of obedience, selflessness and virtue as wife of Bassanio, and as the independent professional woman who foils Shylock in court. Shylock became the focus of debates about the Jews and about usury.

Richard Altick confirms Rozmovits' view of *The Merchant*'s cultural centrality. He discovered that *The Merchant* was one of the most painted Shakespeare plays during the nineteenth century (the others were *Romeo and Juliet, The Tempest, Hamlet, As You Like It* and *A Midsummer Night's Dream*); 150 paintings of scenes from the play are recorded. The most popular scenes to be depicted were Shylock giving instructions to his daughter Jessica about securing his money bags while he is out to dinner; the trial scene and Shylock's defeat; and the casket scenes in which Portia's suitors are tested. Altick concludes that 'Except for Falstaff, no male Shakespearean character on canvas was examined more critically than the usurer.' So Shylock's devotion to his money and his ultimate humiliation were the dominant themes for the painters, underlining the traditional view of Shylock.[3]

The nineteenth century was a century of changing attitudes to the Jews. From 1290 to 1664 the Jews had been officially barred from England. Thereafter, they had returned but only in small numbers. By 1815, there were about 20–30,000 Jews in Britain, two-thirds of them in London. They ranged from pedlars and old clothes men to wealthy financiers, like the Rothschilds. They developed their own institutions: the Board of Deputies (1760), the Jews' Free School (1817), the *Jewish Chronicle* (1841) and the Jewish Board of Guardians (1859).[4]

But ancient prejudices were a long time dying. In 1753 the Jew Bill to allow the Jews naturalization was withdrawn after violent anti-Semitic agitation. During the nineteenth century, however, the Jews made steady progress. The Jews were given the vote in 1835, and permitted to enter Parliament in 1858. The first Jewish barrister was called to the bar in 1833; the first Jewish Lord Mayor of London elected in 1855; the first Jewish government minister appointed in 1871; the first Jewish judge in 1873; and the first Jewish peer in 1885. In 1874 a Jew, Benjamin Disraeli, became Prime Minister. Even though he had converted to Anglicanism, he was regularly depicted as a caricatured Jewish stereotype. *Punch* portrayed him both as Shylock and Fagin.

The process of Jewish emancipation represented the Liberal tradition of toleration, the belief that it was socially undesirable to discriminate against individuals or groups on the grounds of religion, a view which led to the removal of penalties against Protestant Nonconformists in 1828, and the passing of the Catholic Emancipation Act in 1829. It was hoped that the Jews would forsake their tradition of separation and integrate fully into British society. But reservations remained: the belief that Jews had divided loyalties and would always remain outsiders and that their moral character was tainted by their deep involvement with finance.

Anti-Semitism resurfaced dramatically in Britain in the 1870s and 1880s. Initially, it was a response to the foreign policy of Prime Minister Disraeli. The massacre of the independence-seeking Bulgarian Christians by the Turks caused a storm of horrified protest in Britain. Gladstone championed the Bulgarian cause. But Disraeli and his government supported the Turks, Britain's ally against Russia. This caused an outbreak of hostility towards Disraeli which focused on his Jewishness. The historian Goldwin Smith denounced him for leading Britain astray with his 'Hebrew flashiness', the *Church Times* referred to him as the 'Jew premier' and Sir Richard Burton published a pamphlet calling Disraeli 'a Hebrew of Hebrews' and suggesting that Jewish interests and instincts dominated his policies to the detriment of his party and his country. The significance of this hostility is that it extended from Disraeli to the whole Jewish community. It might have blown over but for another and more permanent factor, a massive influx of Jewish refugees.

In 1850 the Jewish population was still only 35,000. But it grew tenfold by 1939, as a result of the arrival of thousands of Jews fleeing the racial pogroms in Eastern Europe between 1881 and 1905. The Jews settled in East London, Leeds and Manchester and were concentrated in particular trades (tailoring, boot and shoe manufacture, moneylending, pawnbroking).

The Jewish influx occurred at a time of acute economic hardship in the East End, with hard winters coinciding with a trade depression in the mid 1880s, and this led some newspapers to claim the Jews were taking English jobs by working for less. The Jews crowded into particular slum areas, exacerbating the housing situation, and constituting inevitably a large group alien in language, dress, religion and customs to those around them, and therefore an obvious target for resentment. The immigrants tended to maintain a separate identity and there were certainly Jews involved in rackrenting and in sweated labour operations, both facts adding to the mounting hostility.

Hostility mounted further with systematic accusations by some anti-Semitic journalists that the Jews were carriers of disease, that they were involved in the 'white slave' trade and big prostitution rackets, and that they contained many anarchists and socialists who were involved in terrorism. Once again there is some truth in some of these accusations. There were Jews involved in crime and prostitution – but so were lots of non-Jews too. There was an element among the Jews of anarchists, socialists and radicals and they were plotting. The Siege of Sidney Street when the police surrounded a houseful of anarchists involved Jews. All of this awakened and revivified the old hatreds and prejudices which had been preserved in the culture.

Prejudice against immigrant groups can arise for a variety of reasons. There is individual inadequacy which leads some people who are psychopathic or paranoid to project their fears, hatreds and anxieties onto a defined group. There is general scapegoatism, blaming particular social problems (crime, unemployment, bad housing) on specific alien groups. There is particular scapegoatism, which involves emotional spasms at specific times of crisis when the majority turn on a minority to vent their rage. There is economic and social competition for jobs, housing and women, for which in the event of shortage, alien groups can be blamed. Finally there are cultural myths, images of 'the other' rooted deep in the collective imagination of the majority. Probably a combination of all these reasons operated to inflame anti-Semitism in the last decades of the nineteenth century.

Pressure groups began to be formed for immigration restriction such as the frankly anti-Semitic British Brothers League (1901) and the Immigration Reform Association, formed in 1903 to keep out paupers, sick and criminal immigrants without specific mention of the Jews. Anti-Jewish feeling began to run high in the East End and there was anti-Semitic violence in Bethnal Green and anti-Jewish riots in South Wales, where the troops had to be sent in to keep order. In 1905, the year of Henry Irving's death, Parliament passed the Aliens Act, to keep out 'undesirable aliens', although there was no specific mention of Jews.

There had been a decline in tolerance of the Jews during the last decade of the nineteenth century. There was periodic violence in certain restricted areas and at particular times. But there were no centrally organized pogroms (as in Russia in the Tsarist period and Germany in the 1930s), no mass expulsions (as in the middle ages) and no official action to restrict the social and economic movement of the Jews. Jewish emancipation was not reversed and 'as far as discriminatory legislation and physical violence were concerned, Jews lived easier lives between 1876 and 1939 than they did in earlier years'.[5] Jews were thus able to rise to the very top of society. Between 1910 and 1919, 16 per cent of all millionaires were Jewish, though Jews never amounted to more than 1 per cent of the population. Jews, the Sassoons, Sir Ernest Cassell, Baron de Hirsch and Lord Burnham, were prominent at the court of King Edward VII. But although never legal or official, there was widespread casual anti-Semitism: 'No Jews need apply' signs involved jobs and housing; Jews were banned from various clubs, and the term 'Jew' was regularly used as a synonym for 'miser'. Cartoons regularly depicted Jews with big hooked noses and greasy ringlets. This anti-Semitism cut across class, gender and party. It resulted in a situation of official tolerance and unofficial intolerance. Attitudes to the Jews were fostered by cultural stereotypes.[6]

The cultural concept of the Jew as villain has a long pedigree and dates back to the earliest days of Christianity. The Jews were seen simply as the killers of Christ and guilty therefore of deicide and over the years, and particularly during the Middle Ages, a cluster of other images attached to them. They were associated with magic, Satanism, poisoning, ritual child murder and usury, and by extension greed, miserliness and extortion. These images found expression on the English stage in the sixteenth century in Marlowe's *The Jew of Malta*, whose central figure Barabas is a poisoner, and in Shakespeare's *The Merchant of Venice*, where Shylock becomes the archetypal Jewish moneylender.

By the early nineteenth century there was a standard Jewish stereotype which appeared regularly in plays, ballads and stories. He is summarized by Edgar Rosenberg as follows:

A fairly thorough going materialist, a physical coward, an opportunist in money-matters, a bit of a wizard in peddling his pharmaceuticals; queer in his religious observance in so far as he still paid attention to them, clannish in his loyalties, secretive in his living habits, servile in his relations with Christians whom he abominated; for physical signposts, he had an outlandish nose, an unpleasant odour and frequently a speech impediment also.[7]

At the end of the eighteenth century for the first time a positive alternative stereotype emerged, an alternative to the negative, the 'the saintly Jew', a product of the Enlightenment. The kindly and philanthropic moneylender in Richard Cumberland's play *The Jew* (1794) and the wise and generous Jewish banker in Maria Edgworth's novel *Harrington* (1817) were consciously created as positive stereotypes. Subsequently the heroes of George Eliot's novel *Daniel Deronda* and of Disraeli's novels were gentleman Jews and Zionists.

But the problem was that Jewish villains created more impact and were longer lasting. The three most noted were Shakespeare's moneylender Shylock, Dickens' Fagin the Jewish fence in *Oliver Twist*, who was based on the real-life fence Ikey Solomons, transported to Van Diemens Land in 1830, and at the end of the century George Du Maurier's Svengali, the dirty, bullying Jewish hypnotist of the novel *Trilby* (1894), which became a celebrated play and later film. When they were criticized for anti-Semitism, both Dickens and Du Maurier sought to make amends by creating sympathetic Jewish characters, Dickens's Mr. Riah in *Our Mutual Friend* and Du Maurier's Leah Gibson in *The Martian*: but nobody noticed them.

Shakespeare's *The Merchant of Venice* (1596) had been conceived as a romantic comedy with Shylock as the archetypal Jewish miser.[8] Shakespeare's own version of the play was absent from the stage from 1660 to 1741. It was supplanted by George Granville's much altered adaptation *The Jew of Venice* (1701), with Shylock played as a comic caricature. In 1741 the Irish actor Charles Macklin revived Shakespeare's original text, playing Shylock as a ferocious villain and holding the stage for the next fifty years in that interpretation. Edmund Kean achieved a triumph in the role in 1814, abandoning the traditional red wig that Shylock had worn, and playing him as a Romantic anti-hero, powerful, passionate, revengeful, so that William Hazlitt who witnessed his performance wrote 'our sympathies are more often with him than with his enemies. He is honest in his vices; they are hypocrites in their virtues.'[9] Kean's electrifying performance dominated the memories of playgoers until Irving took up the role, even though it had been played in the meantime by William Charles Macready, Samuel Phelps and Charles Kean. Act 5 was usually omitted in these years, ending the play with Shylock's exit and thus emphasizing his role as central character, a view that so far prevailed that it was commonly assumed that the title of the play referred to him, when in fact it referred to Antonio.

When Irving came to do *The Merchant of Venice*, he transformed the popular image of Shylock. Gone was the ferocious red-wigged villain of Macklin and the Romantic anti-hero of Kean; Irving's Shylock was, in the words of his co-star Ellen Terry 'a heroic saint'.[10] The play opened on 1 November 1879, and ran for an unprecedented 250 nights. By the time it closed on 31 July 1880, it had been seen by 330,000 people. The role was to remain in Irving's repertoire until his death – he played it eventually a thousand times, and was to alter fundamentally the way Shylock was perceived and played.[11]

Why did Irving choose to do this notably sympathetic Shylock? There were perhaps a combination of personal and professional reasons. Henry Irving was, as his grandson Laurence testifies, 'at heart a liberal',[12] and religious toleration was an axiom of Liberalism. He also had a natural sympathy for outcasts, stemming from his own experience. As an actor, he was a member of a tribe of rogues and vagabonds, to whose social acceptance he devoted much of his career. He had been cast off by his strict Methodist mother when he went on stage and separated from his socially ambitious wife Florence when she disparaged his profession. He showed sympathy for Oscar Wilde after his disgrace and also bestowed dignity and gentility on a black character, Othello.

His patroness, Angela, Baroness Burdett-Coutts, also favoured a sympathetic portrayal of Shylock. Irving was the favourite actor of the leading philanthropist of Victorian England, Baroness Burdett-Coutts, and even more of her long-time companion, Mrs Hannah Brown. Mrs Brown regarded him as a surrogate son, writing to him daily, and he adopted her as something of a surrogate mother. She saw his *Hamlet* thirty times. The Baroness shared his enthusiasm, presenting him with Garrick's ring after his performance as Richard III. It has also been suggested that she may have financially backed some of his productions. In the summer of 1879 Baroness Burdett-Coutts chartered the steam yacht *Walrus* for a Mediterranean cruise. The guests included Irving, the painter Edwin Long and the young American William Ashmead Bartlett, who assisted her in her charitable work. Irving and Long apparently vied for the Baroness's attention but to everyone's astonishment and not a little scandal in Victorian high society, romance blossomed between the Baroness, then sixty-six, and Bartlett, who was half her age. They married in 1881.[13]

Irving had planned to use the trip to research atmosphere, props and settings for his next production, which he projected to be either *Othello* or *Venice Preserved*. The yacht called at Spain, Tangier and Tunis and it was in Tunis that Irving saw the Oriental Jew who gave him his first insight into a possible interpretation of Shylock. He explained to journalist Joseph Hatton:

> I saw a Jew once, in Tunis, tear his hair and raiment, fling himself into the sand, and writhe in a rage, about a question of money – beside himself with passion. I saw him again, self-possessed and fawning; and again, expressing real gratitude for a trifling money courtesy. He was never undignified until he tore at his hair and flung himself

down, and then he was picturesque; he was old, but erect, even stately, and full of resource. As he walked behind his team of mules he carried himself with the lofty air of a king.[14]

Since Irving told the same story to his associates Bram Stoker and Robert Hichens, it seems likely to be true and would be in line with Irving's observation of character and detail. He began to consider a production of *The Merchant of Venice* and was encouraged in this by the Baroness, who according to her biographer 'had many Jewish friends and knew how deeply they were offended by the caricatured Jew of stage and literature. She had been most impressed by Sir Moses Montefiore, the great Jewish philanthropist, and wanted Irving to present a dignified Jew.'[15]

The fact that sympathy for the Jews was overtly an object of the reinterpretation of Shylock is underlined in books about Irving by his press agent Austin Brereton and his secretary Louis Austin (writing as Frederic Daly). Brereton notes that 'several Jewish writers considered it as a vindication of their race' and Daly said, 'The whole Hebrew community was in ecstasies ... Never before had Shylock ... appealed more strongly to the sympathies of all.'[16] In his memoirs Frank Harris, editor successively of the *Fortnightly Review* and the *Saturday Review*, recalled: 'Irving's reading was cheered in London to the echo because it was a rehabilitation of the Jew.'[17] There is a typescript of a speech on *The Merchant* amongst the Stoker papers along with other Irving speeches and addresses, and it looks as if it was intended for delivery by Irving. But there is no indication of if and when it was delivered. In it, the playing of Shylock is directly related to the popular attitude to the Jews. It argues that the strength of race hatred of the Jews explained why the character was played as a low comic character, 'the butt and scorn of all' for two hundred years. Then Macklin showed him in his true form – 'clothed in the dignity of his racial scorn and mantled in individual hate'. The speech concludes 'From that day to this, Shylock stands out as a strong lonely representative of an injured and humiliated race whom no torture, no neglect, no oppression could force to forgo their vital characteristics. With better and more general education came a larger measure of tolerance.'[18]

Then there were the professional reasons. Throughout his career Irving sought to measure himself against his great predecessors in the classic roles. Macready had famously been unable to find the key to Shylock, Phelps performed the role successfully but it was Edmund Kean's impact that Irving wanted to surpass. Irving became known for his radical reinterpretations of the classic roles. His Hamlet, Richard III and Macbeth were distinctively his own interpretations. Shylock would be too.

There may also have been a more personal reason for the choice of interpretation. J.H. Barnes, known as 'Handsome Jack', played Bassanio to Irving's Shylock in the 1879–80 production and left an account of the experience in his autobiography, *Forty Years on the Stage*. He was all too aware that he might offend by his comments. He recorded that 'there is no kind of doubt that Irving was a great actor, a very great actor indeed' and 'it may appear presumptuous in me to attempt to say anything about a man of whom so much has been written by many of the greatest minds of his time', but he added pertinently that 'most of his biographers and commentators have been people from outside his own calling' and therefore a view from someone in the profession would be valuable.

Conceding that Irving's Shylock was 'full of interest and was a really fine study indeed', and Miss Terry's Portia was 'bewitching and artistic in all the scenes at Belmont', he went on to say that her trial scene was less convincing and indeed the whole trial scene presented problems. He rejected the idea that Shylock was intended to be a sympathetic character, particularly in the trial scene. 'If ever a cold-blooded murderer was drawn, in all his hateful intensity, this is the example' and 'the baffled, angry, turbulent, tragic (in other words the traditional exit of Edmund Kean and others) is surely nearer to the author's intention and most certainly more effective to the audience'. Writing in 1914, Barnes said that he had become more convinced of his view over the years and even suggested that in conversation with Irving when he was last on tour with him in 1901 'he was almost disposed to agree with my view'. The reason he advances for Irving's interpretation is to wonder:

> whether or not the Shylock he played and made so famous was absolutely the Shylock he would have played if he had possessed a greater amount of physical power. Of course the Shylock I have in mind depends on the actor's power to play the great scene with Tubal in the earlier act that begins 'You knew, none so well as you, of my daughter's flight'. It is here he must build up the character with graduated awful intensity, and it is here that Edmund Kean and his disciples used 'to lift the audience out of their seats', as they did in the final exit from the trial scene, which I have seen played in a whirlwind of passion. Now, I may be taking a great liberty with the memory of a man for whom I entertain nothing but profound respect, but I have always fancied that at the early rehearsals I saw him 'make shots' at the big scheme and, with his great mentality, recognise that it was out of his reach, and so, by degrees, he came to develop with consummate art a Shylock he could compass.[19]

Barnes received some support in his criticism of the trial scene from none other than Ellen Terry. Generally agreed to be the Portia of her generation, having played it to great acclaim in the Bancrofts' 1875 production opposite an inadequate Shylock (Charles Coghlan), she fervently defended Irving's interpretation of Shylock:

> Henry Irving's Shylock was generally conceded to be full of talent and reality, but some critics could not resist saying that this was *not* the Jew that Shakespeare drew! Now who is in a position to say what *is* the Jew that Shakespeare drew? I think Henry Irving knew as well as most! ... Some said his Shylock was intellectual, and appealed more to the

intellect of his audience. Surely this is talking for the sake of talking. I recall so many things that touched people to the heart![20]

But – and it is a big but – she agreed that Irving's interpretation of Shylock changed the balance of the trial scene.

I found that Henry Irving's Shylock necessitated an entire revision of my conception of Portia, especially in the trial scene ... I had considered, and am still of the same mind, that Portia in the trial scene ought to be very *quiet*. I saw an extraordinary effect in this quietness. But as Henry's Shylock was quiet, I had to give it up. His heroic saint was splendid, but it wasn't good for Portia.[21]

It may well be that all these considerations played a part in Irving's thinking. For Shylock, unusually, we have a detailed record of Irving's own thinking on the subject. The journalist Joseph Hatton accompanied the Lyceum company on its first tour of America and published an account, *Henry Irving's Impressions of America*, in which he included interviews with Irving about his roles. After his first night as Shylock in Boston, Irving told Hatton 'the play has gone well, very well, indeed; but the audience were not altogether with me. I always feel, in regard to this play, that they do not quite understand what I am doing. They only responded at all to-night where Shylock's rage and mortification got the better of his dignity.' He was only too aware of the Shylock that audiences were used to.

They are accustomed to have the part of Shylock strongly declaimed; indeed, all the English Shylocks, as well as American representatives of the part, are very demonstrative in it. Phelps was, so was Charles Kean: and I think American audiences look for the declamatory messages in Shylock, to compare your rendering of them with the readings they have previously heard. You omit much of what is considered great business in Shylock, and American audiences are probably a little disappointed that your view of the part forbids anything like what may be called the strident characteristics of most other Shylocks. Charles Kean ranted considerably in Shylock, and Phelps was decidedly noisy, – both fine, no doubt, in their way. Nevertheless they made the Jew a cruel butcher of a Jew. They filled the stage with his sordid greed and malignant desire for vengeance on the Christian, from his first entrance to his final exit. I never saw Kean's Shylock, nor Phelps's, nor, indeed, any one's. But I am sure Shylock was not a low person; a miser, a usurer, certainly, but a very injured man – at least he thought so. I felt that my audience tonight had quite a different opinion, and I once wished the house had been composed entirely of Jews. I would like to play Shylock to a Jewish audience.[22]

It is of course not true that he had never seen anyone's Shylock. He had acted in *The Merchant* in the roles of Salarino and Bassanio earlier in his career. But his Shylock was his own interpretation. He explained his approach to Joseph Hatton:

I look on Shylock ... as the type of a persecuted race; almost the only gentleman in the play and the most ill-used. He is a merchant who trades in the Rialto, and Bassanio and

Antonio are not ashamed to borrow money off him, nor to carry off his daughter. The position of his child is, more or less, a key to his own. She is a friend of Portia. Shylock was well-to-do a Bible-read man, as his readiness at quotations shows; and there is nothing in his language, at any time, that indicates the snuffling usurer which some persons regard him, and certainly nothing to justify the use the early actors made of the part for the low comedian. He was a religious Jew; learned, for he conducted his case with masterly skilfulness, and his speech is always lofty and full of dignity. Is there a finer speech in Shakespeare than Shylock's defence of his race? Shakespeare's Jew was a type, not a mere individual; he was a type of the great, grand race, – not a mere Houndsditch usurer. He was a man famous on the Rialto; probably a foremost man in his synagogue – proud of his descent – conscious of his moral superiority to many of the Christians who scoffed at him, and fanatic enough, as a religionist, to believe that his vengeance had in it the element of a godlike justice.[23]

This leaves one in no doubt of Irving's sympathy for the Jews in general and Shylock in particular and, that most characteristic Irving touch, to see him as a gentleman. And so he played him. Percy Fitzgerald described his Shylock as 'not the conventional usurer with patriarchal beard and flowing robe, dirty and hooknosed, but a picturesque and refined Italianized Jew, genteelly dressed: a dealer in money, in the country of Lorenzo de' Medici, where there is an aristocracy of merchants'.[24]

Irving elaborated upon his characterization of Shylock, explaining to Joseph Hatton that he had identified various changes of mood, beginning 'quiet, dignified, diplomatic', then becoming satiric and then 'somewhat light and airy in his manner, with a touch of hypocrisy in it'. Irving believed that Shylock conceived of the idea of his 'pound of flesh' bargain the moment Antonio turned on him and said he was 'like to spit on him again' and demanded money nevertheless. After that, Irving believed, there was 'a constant, though vague, suggestion of a desire for revenge, nothing definite or planned, but a continual sense of undeserved humiliation and persecution'. Finally during the trial scene, 'everything indicates a stern, firm, persistent, implacable purpose, which, in all our experience of men is, as a rule, accompanied by an apparently calm manner'. After he loses, Shylock is 'utterly crushed and borne down'.[25]

Irving based his acting version of the play on Charles Kean's published version, but he made significant changes. He cut the Prince of Arragon, shortened the casket scene and the Jessica-Lorenzo idyll, and deleted all the bawdy, but he restored a trimmed fifth act, which had customarily been omitted. He made some significant cuts in the interests of softening Shylock's character. He cut the scene in which Jessica told Launcelot 'our house is hell', and that she is ashamed to be her father's child, and the scene in which she hopes she is illegitimate and not the Jew's daughter and glories in having turned Christian. Irving cut Solanio and Salarino's derogatory remarks about Shylock, the reference to the boys of

Venice pursuing and mocking him for his loss and Shylock's lines giving greater weight to his grief at the loss of his ducats than his daughter. These cuts had the effect of stressing Shylock's domestic tragedy and a scene which Irving added to the play and which was universally praised underlined this. After Jessica and Lorenzo have eloped, swept away amid a tumult of masked revellers, the curtain fell. It rose again after a couple of seconds on an empty stage and Shylock, preceded by the tapping of his stick, was seen returning over the bridge bearing a lantern. He walked slowly to his door, knocked three times, and when no answer came, three times again with greater deliberation, and he raised his lantern to illuminate the darkened upper levels of the house and the curtain fell on him, looking broken and despairing as he realized his daughter had fled.[26] Ellen Terry recorded 'For absolute pathos, achieved by absolute simplicity of means, I never saw anything in the theatre to compare with his Shylock's return home over the bridge to his deserted house after Jessica's flight.'[27]

How was the new interpretation of Shylock received? The three most respected theatrical critics of the day were unanimous in their praise. Clement Scott of the *Daily Telegraph* proclaimed it a 'success' and declared that it would 'bind closer the sympathies of the intelligent public with the name, the fame, the energy and the industry of Henry Irving'. He thought its production :

> presented ... a picture of rare splendour; the character of Shylock personated in a style that rivets the attention, absorbs the interest, and draws out the intellectual faculties of the audience; a Portia who will live beyond the present day as one of the most gracious and charming of Shakespearean memories; an atmosphere of general intelligence and wholesome co-operation; and a scene which fascinates the eye by its colour, its harmony, and its tastes.

He recognized Irving's determination to:

> give us a new Shylock, and to discard theatrical tradition ... a proud, resolute, and religious man, sincere in his ancient faith, tender in his recollections, as hard and inflexible as adamant when his revenge becomes a madness, cold and impassive in the demand for his rights, crushed with horror at the injustice that is his doom.[28]

Joseph Knight of the *Athenaeum* thought it 'remarkable in many respects. Considered as interpretation it is superior to anything of its class that has been seen on the English stage by the present generation, while as a sample of the manner in which Shakspeare [*sic*] is hereafter to be mounted it is of highest interest'. He thought Irving's 'entire performance is thoughtful and scholarly, and likely to raise Mr Irving's reputation ... the final exit of the Jew is one of the most impressive things we can recall'. He also thought Terry's Portia 'remarkable'.[29]

Dutton Cook of the *Pall Mall Gazette*, pronouncing the production 'a success', noted that this was not the Shylock of the patent theatres, with its 'violence of tone, fierceness of gesture, the explosions of passion, so long associated with the part'. He added interestingly in the light of Barnes's comments: 'it is not only that Mr Irving has not sufficient physical force for such clamorous exhibitions, but his conception and treatment of the character are altogether more subdued'. He praised the performance as:

> altogether consistent and harmonious, and displays anew that power of self-control which has come to Mr Irving this season as a fresh possession. Every temptation to extravagance or eccentricity of action was resolutely resisted, and with the happiest results, I never saw a Shylock that obtained more commiseration from the audience; for usually, I think, Shylock is so robustly vindictive and energetically defiant, as to compel the spectators to withhold from him their sympathies. But Mr Irving's Shylock, old, haggard, halting, sordid, represents the dignity and intellect of the play; beside him, the Christians, for all their graces of aspect and gallantry of apparel, seem but poor creatures. His hatred of them finds justification in his race and his religion, and in the fact that they, his mental inferiors, are his tyrants; and when he is plundered by them alike of his child and his gold, his detestation turns naturally not so much to blind fury as to a deadly purpose of revenge. There is something grandly pathetic in the fixed calm of the Jew as he stands in the judgement-hall, a figure of Fate inexorably persistent, demanding the penalty of his bond; he is no mere usurer punishing a bankrupt debtor; if he avenges private injuries, he also represents a nation seeking atonement for centuries of wrong.[30]

All these critics had understood, appreciated and accepted his interpretation. Austin Brereton reported: 'The London and provincial press had many columns of glowing praise, much of which was as discriminating as it was eulogistic.'[31]

The painter W. Graham Robertson was thirteen when he saw *The Merchant* in 1879 and he never forgot Irving's performance, writing in his 1931 autobiography *Time Was*: 'I seem to remember every movement, every tone.' Later he came to feel that Irving's interpretation was wrong. 'His dignified, heroic, intensely aristocratic Martyr was magnificent and unforgettable, but it upset the balance of the play, and it ruined Portia's trial scene. How small and mean sounded her quibbling tricky speeches when addressed to a being who united the soul of Savonarola and the bearing of Charles the First with just a touch of Lord Beaconsfield ... Still, right or wrong, his Shylock was a living thing, a haunting, memorable figure, and I left the theatre with the profoundest sympathy for the noble, ill used Jew.'[32]

But other voices were raised at the time to object to the sympathetic interpretation. Henry James wrote in *Scribner's Magazine*:

> He looks the part to a charm, or shall we say repulsion, and he might be painted as he stands. His conception ... is a sentimental one, and he has endeavoured to give us a sympathetic, and above all, a pathetic Shylock ... The actor struck us as rigid and frigid, and above all as painfully behind the stroke of the clock. The deep-welling malignity, the grotesque horror, the red-hot excitement of the long baffled, sore-hearted member of a

despised trade, who has been all his life at a disadvantage, and who at last finds his hour and catches his opportunity – these elements had dropped out. Mr Irving's Shylock is neither excited nor exciting, and many of the admirable speeches, on his lips, lack much of their incision; notably the outbreak of passion and prospective revenge after he finds that Antonio has become forfeit, and that his daughter has fled from him, carrying her dowry.[33]

Bernard Shaw wrote in the *Saturday Review*:

There was no question then of a bad Shylock or a good Shylock he was simply not Shylock at all; and when his own creation came into conflict with Shakespear's [*sic*], as it did quite openly in the Trial scene, he simply played in flat contradiction of the lines, and positively acted Shakespear off the stage.[34]

Lewis Carroll and Lord Tennyson both privately expressed their disagreement with Irving's interpretation.[35]

The disagreement with his interpretation surfaced even at the celebrations of the hundredth performance. This took place on 14 February 1880 and was the first of what were to become regular and extensively reported celebration dinners. The dinner was scheduled for 11.30 p.m. and within forty minutes of the play ending a red and white striped marquee had been set up on the stage, tables and chairs set up, two chandeliers hoisted and 300 guests seated. They were drawn from 'all that was artistic, literary and fashionable' in London. They included the Earls of Dunraven, Fife and Onslow, the painters Luke Fildes, Lawrence Alma-Tadema, John Tenniel, Edwin Long, Val Prinsep, William Orchardson, the actors J.L. Toole, Squire Bancroft, W.H. Kendal, Hermann Vezin, David James, John Hare, Henry Neville and Charles Kelly, the playwrights W.G. Wills, James Albery, Hamilton Aidé, H.J. Byron, Tom Taylor, Oscar Wilde and Herman Merivale, the composer Sir Julius Benedict, the critics Dutton Cook, Joseph Knight and Clement Scott, the writers and journalists Frank Marshall, Charles Dickens the Younger, Percy Fitzgerald, E.L. Blanchard, Edmund Yates, F.C. Burnand, Joseph Comyns Carr and a scattering of MPs. They were each presented with a copy of Irving's text of *The Merchant* bound in white parchment and lettered in gold, and they sat down to a meal of clear turtle soup, cold salmon and cucumbers, lamb cutlets and mushrooms, sweetbreads, stuffed larks, cold game and salad, ham and peas, Russian salad and aspic of prawns, Parmesan straws, cheese, salad and celery, washed down with magnums of Heidsieck champagne (1874) and Leoville claret of the same year, while a string quintet played softly. The after dinner speech and toast was delivered by the elderly poet and politician Richard Monckton-Milnes, Lord Houghton. He proceeded to deliver a speech which Austin Brereton described as 'not a happy one, nor in good taste for such an occasion'.[36] He began by expressing his dislike for centenaries and the new system of long runs, saying he preferred the old arrangement whereby the same plays were never done more than twice a week and actors could be seen in a variety of roles. He welcomed the improved state of morality now attached to the stage, so that families of good breeding could allow their sons to enter the profession after a university education. 'I recall now the genuine indignation and roughly expressed sentiments of some leading performers and critics who were sitting near me at this very awkward compliment', wrote Percy Fitzgerald later.[37] Houghton went on to criticize the new reading of the role, saying:

> they had seen a rehabilitation … for the old Jew Shylock, who was usually regarded as a ferocious monster, whose sole desire was to avenge himself in the most brutal manner on the Christians of his neighbourhood, had become a gentleman of the Hebrew persuasion, in a voice very like a Rothschild, and not more ferocious than became an ordinary merchant of the period, afflicted with a stupid, foolish servant, and a wilful, pernicious daughter; and the process went on, till the Hebrew gentleman, led by a strange chance into the fault of wishing to vindicate in his own person the injuries of centuries of wrong to his ancestors on the person of the merchant of Venice, is foiled by a very charming woman.[38]

Irving rose to reply and was received 'with loud and continuous cheers and the waving of handkerchiefs' and abandoning his prepared reply delivered an impromptu speech of wit, grace and dignity, during which he paid tribute to his co-star Ellen Terry (who was not present), and expressed his gratitude for the long run 'which he did not think could have been attained if Shylock had been the Whitechapel old gentleman which he has sometimes been represented, and which appeared to be the ideal of the character in the mind of my Lord Houghton, but which was certainly not his own conception'. Irving received a standing ovation and, after the company had retired to the smoking room, to partake of Irving's stock of cigars, J.L. Toole got up and made a further speech 'and a more graceful, earnest, or generous setting forth of the views of himself and his brother actors could not have been given'. Once again hearty applause followed, good feeling was restored and the party continued until dawn.[39]

The Houghton scandal was, however, widely reported and the ensuing publicity did nothing but good for Irving and his production. Further controversy arose after the great Victorian critic and arbiter of taste John Ruskin went to see *The Merchant*. On Friday 28 November 1879 Ruskin went with his disciple Oscar Wilde to see Irving in *The Merchant of Venice* and subsequently criticized the production in a dispute which rumbled on until the middle of 1880. On 1 December 1879 he wrote to Miss Sara Anderson from Herne Hill to say:

> I went to see Mr Irving last Friday in Shylock, and the Doge of Venice – as I heard afterwards – told all the Senators I was there – and Irving sent to ask me to come round after his final discomfiture – so I went and made him a pretty little speech – and have written to him yesterday (Sunday) to ask him to make Portia cast down her eyes when she tells Bassanio what she is good for.[40]

Ruskin's letter was preserved among the Irving papers and reproduced in Laurence Irving's biography of his grandfather:

> My dear Mr Irving, The kind interest you shewed in what I was too awkwardly imperfect in saying when you received me on Friday evening, leads me to write to you with more accuracy and frankness if I can – and may, on what I felt – namely this, that you were a most true and tender and noble actor – but that you had not yet as much love for Shakespeare as for your art, and were therefore not careful enough to be wholly in harmony with his design … I scarcely venture to say more *now*, than that I do not think the greatest actor can ever be seen to full advantage – unless every concurrent or opponent part in the play be at least adequately sustained. Now – and I trust the meritorious actors of the other parts will forgive what I say with pain and in the strictest sense of my duty – your opponent's part of Antonio was not understood by the audience – as it was rendered on Friday evening – still less the brightly opponent part of Bassanio – and though Miss Terry's Portia has obtained so much applause, it greatly surprises me that you have not taught her a grander reading of the part. Portia is chiefly great in her majestic humility (the main sign of her splendid intellect) and – to take only one instance of what I do not doubt to be misinterpretation – the speech, 'You see me Lord Bassanio …', she would, I am certain, produce its true effect on the audience only if spoken with at least half a dozen yards between her and Bassanio – and with her eyes on the ground through most of the lines.
>
> I am going to look carefully through your reading of the play – but as a painter, I protest against the loss of Arragon [the role of the Prince of Arragon had been cut for Irving's staging]. It is like pulling a leaf from a trefoil. I again entreat your patience with me and your trust in my sincere sympathy and admiration.
>
> Believe me, my dear Sir, faithfully and respectfully yours, J. Ruskin[41]

There may be some force in Ruskin's criticism of the performances of Antonio and Bassanio unbalancing the play. Henry James claimed that the supporting performances in *The Merchant* were 'inadequate', and Clement Scott said of the cast: 'For the rest there is some careful and un-ambitious acting', but for the most part they receive the negative compliment of 'doing little harm'.[42] Ruskin had made a particular study of Shakespeare's heroines and his comments on Portia are in line with his view of the character as expressed in *Proserpina* where he stresses her humility, modesty and intellect and says she becomes 'a perfect Christian wife'.[43] But Ruskin's 'pretty little speech' in the Lyceum dressing room, in which he said he found Irving's acting 'noble, tender and true', was reported in the *Theatre* on 1 January 1880, a magazine which Irving had until recently owned but which he had handed over to the journalist Clement Scott, an Irving devotee, who used the magazine assiduously to promote Irving's cause.[44]

Ruskin was very vexed that his dressing room civilities, which in fact did not express his fundamental disagreement with Irving's interpretation of Shylock, should have been made public. Unwilling to become involved personally in a row, he enlisted a third party, a Mr Laister, to write on his behalf to Irving, which he did in a letter dated 9 February 1880:

> Dear Sir, Mr Ruskin writes me on the subject of a paragraph which appeared in *Theatre* magazine for January reporting him to have spoken to you of your representation of Shylock as 'noble, tender and true'.
>
> As I have not the honour of your personal acquaintance I shall perhaps best further his object if I quote from his letter the passages following: 'I have no doubt that whatever Mr Irving has stated that I said, I *did* say. But in personal address to an artist to whom one is introduced for the first time, one does not usually say all that may be in one's mind: and if expressions limited, if not exaggerated by courtesy, be afterwards quoted as a total and carefully expressed criticism, the general reader will be – or may be – easily misled. I did and do much admire Mr Irving's own acting as Shylock: but I entirely dissent (and indignantly as well as entirely) from his general reading and treatment of the play.'

He asked Irving to publish the whole of Ruskin's letter to him to clarify his stance, adding:

> You are probably aware that the Play in question, as revived, has given rise to a vast deal of public teaching, the moral of which Mr Ruskin and others greatly deplore; and he naturally desires to correct any wrong impression which the unqualified publication of the paragraph in *Theatre* might create.[45]

Irving turned to his friend Walter Herries Pollock, journalist and writer, for advice. Pollock drafted the following reply:

> Dear Sir, I beg to acknowledge the receipt of your letter to me of the 8th February. I am at a loss to know in what character you address me, and to understand why Mr Ruskin, from whose letter to yourself you have made quotations, does not write to me in person, if he has any communication to make to me.
>
> I must, therefore, in all courtesy, decline to enter into correspondence with a stranger and will only add that I am in no way responsible for the paragraph in the *Theatre* magazine, to which attention is called at the commencement of your letter. I am Yours faithfully, Henry Irving.[46]

Mr Laister, having pleaded Ruskin's ill health as an excuse for this triangular correspondence, reminded Irving that all Ruskin asked was a simple yes or no to his request. In conclusion he wrote:

> Pray allow me also to repeat on my own account that the verbal truth of the paragraph in *Theatre* is not disputed by Mr Ruskin; but that its meaning is – especially in view of the fact that he had written to you fully *before* that paragraph appeared. Mr Ruskin has not said that you are responsible for what appears in *Theatre* – but as he did not supply the paragraph himself he may infer, perhaps, that you did.

Further *if* Mr Ruskin is under the impression that you are (in one sense) responsible for *Theatre*, he shares it with other people, both private and professional.[47]

On 1 March, 1880, Scott published a letter from Laister in the *Theatre*, repeating the essence of his letter to Irving and referring readers to Ruskin's views on Shylock contained in *Munera Pulveris* (originally published in *Fraser's Magazine* in 1862), of which Laister provided extracts.[48] In *Munera Pulveris*, in the fourth section on Commerce, Ruskin drew a strict contrast between fair trading – 'commerce in kindness' – and profiteering – 'commerce in unkindness', which was a form of usury. Usury was an abomination for Ruskin and this for Ruskin lay at the heart of Shakespeare's play. He wrote:

> This inhumanity of mercenary commerce is the more notable because it is a fulfilment of the law that the corruption of the best is the worst. For as, taking the body natural for the symbol of the body politic, the governing and forming powers may be likened to the brain, and the labouring to the limbs, the mercantile, presiding over circulation and communication of things in changed utilities, is symbolized by the heart; and if that hardens, all is lost. And this is the ultimate lesson which the leader of English intellect meant for us (a lesson, indeed, not all his own, but part of the old wisdom of humanity), in the tale of *The Merchant of Venice*; in which the true and incorrupt merchant, kind and free, beyond every other Shakespearean conception of men, is opposed to the corrupted merchant – or usurer; the lesson being deepened by the expression of the strange hatred which the corrupted merchant bears to the pure one, mixed with intense scorn.[49]

This is the root of Ruskin's objections to Irving's Shylock, an interpretation which became the dominant one to such an extent that Ruskin wrote in a postscript to *St Mark's Rest* (1884) that the modern view of Shylock was erroneous. He said 'the public ... now – consistently and naturally enough but ominously – considers Shylock a victim to the support of the principles of legitimate trade' and Antonio 'a spectacular sentimentalist' thus reversing completely what Ruskin saw as the relative vice and virtue of their positions, and confirming the extent to which Irving's performance had changed the popular perception of Shylock.[50] But unlike Lord Houghton, Ruskin's motivation was not anti-Semitic. In *Val d'Arno* (1874), Ruskin wrote:

> All wholesome indignation against usurers was prevented, in the Christian mind, by wicked and cruel religious hatred of the race of Christ. In the end, Shakespeare himself, in his fierce effort against the madness, suffered himself to miss his mark by making his usurer a Jew.[51]

So Ruskin is hostile both to usury and to anti-Semitism.

The controversy with Irving petered out. Scott invited Ruskin to contribute an essay to *Theatre*, elaborating on his criticism of Irving's interpretation, 'a performance', said Scott, 'that has justly evoked the highest interest of men of intelligence and taste'.[52] But in the issue of 1 April 1880 Scott reported that 'serious pressure of business and overwhelming work' had prevented Ruskin from complying and the matter was allowed to drop.[53]

The *Church Times* (5 March 1880) felt moved to comment on Irving's Shylock in the context of an article on the correspondence in the *Contemporary Review* between Ruskin and the Bishop of Manchester on the subject of usury:

> It is impossible to discuss the subject without a passing reference to the odd perversion of the character of Shylock which has been introduced by Mr Henry Irving into his beautiful presentation of *The Merchant of Venice*. One may imagine the amazement of Shakespere [*sic*], if he could have foreseen the most malignant and the paltriest of his villains transformed into the champion of an oppressed and downtrodden race. The fact is, Shylock's nationality is not of the essence of the character. It is true that he is a Hebrew, but that is because none but a Jew could have been a medieval usurer. Shylock is, however, more than a mere usurer – he is intended to be at every point the exact opposite of the noble Antonio, whose generosity, affectionateness and patriotism are the real causes of 'the lodged hate and the certain loathing' which Shylock bore him. It is difficult to suppose that Shakespere had any serious Intention of writing up either Usury or Judaism. It is true that the play looks for a little time as if it were going to be tragic, but it is pure comedy: … there is no reason to believe that Shakespere had any ulterior motive; but if he had the intention of preaching a sermon on toleration, he could only have meant it to cover it with ridicule … We have lived to see much strange whitewashing, but an apotheosis of usury, in its worst and most detestable form, is a startling phenomenon.

Irving was perfectly happy to keep the controversy about his interpretation going, in the pages of *Theatre*. To coincide with the opening of *The Merchant*, and doubtless in anticipation of criticism from traditionalists, the magazine published an essay by Frederick Hawkins entitled 'Shylock and Other Stage Jews', clearly written from a liberal perspective. After sketching in attitudes towards the Jews up to the reign of Queen Elizabeth I, he went on to argue that *The Merchant* was 'a plea for toleration towards the Jews'. Hawkins stressed the qualities Shakespeare had bestowed on Shylock, 'a generous enthusiasm for his sacred tribe and ancient law', deep veneration for the memory of his dead wife, tender attachment to his daughter, 'many of the graces of intellect'. How has his fine nature become warped and soured? 'As an inevitable consequence of the inherited and personal wrongs he has endured, is enduring and will always have to endure.' He cited the famous 'if you prick us do we not bleed?' speech as 'proof of rare moral courage' on Shakespeare's part and claims that 'the play was written not so much for the sake of its brighter elements as for the purpose of concentrating attention upon an oppressed and insulted Jew'. He went on to give a brief account of the interpretations of Shylock on the stage up until Kean, contextualising them in prevailing attitudes towards Jews in society and actually suggesting that the element of sympathy within Kean's performance 'doubtless added strength to the movement which resulted in the removal of Jewish disabilities' and concluding 'that the stage should have had a share in that triumph of common sense is, I think, a matter of earnest congratulation.'[54]

The Hawkins article was followed up in the next issue of *Theatre* by a symposium on it with a variety of views expressed. Theodore Martin began by flatly contradicting Hawkins's idea that *The Merchant of Venice* was 'a plea for tolerance'. 'I can find no trace of such an intention. Nobody in the play urges anything in the nature of such a plea. Jew and Christian are alike intolerant ... Shakespeare, moreover, never wrote plays to enforce a moral.' The next contribution, billed as being 'by an actor', was from Irving himself, not surprisingly endorsing Hawkins's view that Shakespeare 'consciously enlisted our sympathies on the side of Shylock'.

The Shakespearean scholar F.J. Furnivall rejected the idea that the object of Shakespeare's play was 'a plea for toleration towards the Jews', but accepted that the assertion of Shylock's humanity was intended to include the Jewish race as well as the individual character. Frank Marshall, editor of the Irving Shakespeare, said that 'it is not necessary to suppose that Shakespeare had any special views with regard to the removal of Jewish disabilities in his portrayal of the character of Shylock', but nevertheless argued that because he was a great dramatist he had been able to enter into the feelings of his characters and the audience were therefore led to ask what kind of man the vindictive and narrow-minded Shylock might have been if he had encountered from the Christians around him 'that noble forbearance and mercy which they professed, but did not practice'. Israel Davis, co-proprietor of the *Jewish Chronicle*, took more or less the same view. The Bacon expert James Spedding argued that Shakespeare was a businessman and aimed only to produce a pleasing romantic comedy that would appeal to his audience. The *Daily Telegraph* leader-writer David Anderson, rejected the idea of the play as a plea for toleration, nevertheless found the character of Shylock 'eminently natural and consistent with his historical truth'. Frederick Hawkins had the last word, responding to each of his critics and modifying his view to conclude that in drawing the character of Shylock Shakespeare 'indirectly but deliberately advanced a plea for toleration towards the Jews'.[55]

Perceptive critics such as A.B. Walkley saw Irving's Shylock in the context of contemporary attitudes to the Jews: 'It was the Jew Idealized in the light of the modern occidental reaction against the *Judenhetze*, a Jew already conscious of the Sidonias, the Disraelis, who were to issue from his loins.'[56] Irving's *Merchant* captured the spirit of the age. As James C. Bulman recorded: 'It held the stage until 1905 – a quarter of a century – and spawned a host of imitators. In fact, most productions of the play for the next fifty years paid homage to Irving, directly or indirectly.'[57]

The American actor Edwin Booth had achieved a triumph in New York in 1867 as Shylock. He had no doubt how Shylock was to be played, writing to H.H. Furness:

> My notion of Shylock is of the traditional type, which I firmly believe to be 'the Jew which Shakespeare drew'. Not the buffoon that Dogget gave according to Lord Lansdowne's Version, but the strongly marked and somewhat grotesque character which Macklin restored to the stage, and in which he was followed by Cooke, by Edmund Kean and by my Father ... If we side with him in self-defence, 'tis because we have charity, which he had not; if we pity him under the burthen of his merited punishment 'tis because we are human, which he is not, – except in shape, and even that, I think, should indicate the crookedness of his nature.[58]

This was the Shylock that Booth brought to England in 1880 and 1882 but it was deemed old-fashioned in the light of Irving's reinterpretation. Seeking to demonstrate this, Edward R. Russell, editor of the *Liverpool Daily Post* and Liberal MP, wrote in 1888 of Booth's performance:

> Mr Edwin Booth played Shylock while the recollection of Mr Irving's performance was yet fresh, and it is no exaggeration to say that he played it very finely on the lines which had long been commonly regarded as correct and consistent with the poet's meaning. Now, although Mr Irving had been but moderately praised for his conception Mr Booth was assailed with a chorus of condemnation, not a note of which would have been heard if the performance had been given two years before. It was, they said (*Times*) 'the old and obvious representation of the Hebrew as a detestable but powerless usurer – a degraded being, a prey to sordid love of gain, to fierce love of revenge, redeemed by nothing nobler than a self-assertion which proves futile. The words that are most pathetic in the play were so pronounced as to bring out only their grotesque side, and to raise a laugh.' 'It is too low a view', said an eminent critic (*Observer*) with sudden conviction, 'to make the leading character in the great drama merely villainous and inhuman. The provocation ought to be dwelt on: the innate dignity of the character, even if it be only such dignity in evil as the hero of Milton's Epic, has, should be made emphatic. The absence of all admirable and worthy qualities, of all claim to charity and respect made Mr Booth's Shylock a comparatively uninteresting impersonation, though his wonted skill in clear and picturesque elocution had their effect.'[59]

It was the sympathetic Shylock that Irving took to New York in 1883, a performance much admired and applauded but which provoked some dissent. The *New York Times* (18 November 1883), noting that Irving was presenting a sympathetic Shylock, argued that Shylock should be above all 'miserly and cruel' but 'Mr. Irving's sentimental scheme of the character ... makes Shylock lachrymose and tiresome'.

The interpretation of Shylock did not remain static. John Gross reports: 'it is generally agreed that his interpretation grew less sympathetic over the years'.[60] Linda Rozmovits says that Gross' claim is 'unsupported by any convincing evidence'. She claims that virtually the only critic to express this view was William Winter who had his own conservative agenda. She cites in refutation an 1887 critic of a revival of *Merchant* saying: 'Mr. Irving's view of the character of Shylock and his subtle appeals for sympathy on the Jews behalf ... remain of course unchanged. Right or wrong, his is a noble ideal of the part, and he is not likely in any way to lower it'.[61] But Rozmovits is wrong on two counts. She quotes Gross out of context. For he goes on to say that many accounts of Irving playing Shylock in his later years 'stress the grandeur and pathos that he continued to bring to the part.'[62] But also he was by no means the only person to claim that Irving's interpretation changed over the years. His biographer Austin Brereton said so in 1908: 'Irving's interpretation of Shylock in his first revival differed materially from that of later years', and he will have seen the performances.[63] Richard Dickins published an account of forty years of theatregoing during which he saw two hundred performances of thirty-four of Shakespeare's plays, fifty of them being produced by Irving. He saw many of Irving's Shylocks from the first in 1879 to a final appearance in May 1905 and noted 'in the case of Shylock his alterations were, as time passed, considerable'.[64] The questions that arise are what changes and why. Toby Lelyveld has argued that over the years Irving's Shylock coarsened and became less subtle. She relates it to increasing hostility to the Jews following the influx of Eastern European Jewish refugees, implying that Irving was responding to a changed attitude in the audience and the context.[65] But this may not be the case. Recording that Irving discussed with the novelist Hall Caine his book *The Scapegoat* (1890), which dealt with the persecution of the Jews, Bram Stoker recalled: 'Irving was hugely interested. Any form of oppression was noxious to him; and certainly the Jewish "Exodus" that was just then going on came under that heading.'[66]

On Irving's death in 1905, the *Jewish World* published for the first time a letter that he had written to A Henriques Valentine on 19 February 1893:

> Dear Sir, In reply to your request, I can only say that Shylock illustrates very forcibly the superiority of Shakespeare's humanity to Marlow's [*sic*]. For example Marlow's Barabbas is the typical friend [presumably a misprint for fiend] of superstition, whereas Shylock is intensely human, and, therefore, appeals to us more strongly than he could have appealed to Shakespeare's contemporaries, though we see today (happily not in England) a grievous lapse into that intolerant hatred of the Jews which distinguished the Middle Ages.[67]

This would suggest Irving's interpretation of Shylock was not influenced by the large-scale Jewish immigration into London. It is more likely to have been the result of Irving's perfectionism. According to Ellen Terry:

> Henry Irving never grew tired of a part, never ceased to work at it, just as he never gave up the fight against his limitations ... To this heroic perseverance, he adds an almost

childlike eagerness in hearing any suggestion for the improvement of his interpretation which commended itself to his imagination and his judgement. From a blind man came the most illuminating criticism of his Shylock. The sensitive ear of the sightless hearer detected a fault in Henry Irving's method of delivering the opening line of his part:

'Three thousand ducats – well!'

'I hear no sound of the usurer in that', the blind man said at the end of the performance. 'It is said with the reflective air of a man to whom money means very little.' The justice of the criticism appealed strongly to Henry. He revised his reading not only of the first line, but of many other lines in which he saw now that he had not been enough of the money-lender.[68]

Writing in 1911, William Winter, the American critic called Irving's 'the most thoroughly consistent, absorbingly interesting, and decisively paramount impersonation of Shylock that has been seen within the last sixty years.'[69] Winter confirmed the transformation:

When Irving first acted Shylock he manifested a poetically humanitarian ideal of the part ... he indicated the Jew as the venerable Hebrew patriarch, the lonely, grieved widower, and the affectionate, while austere, father. He failed not, indeed, to present Shylock as the vengeful representative antagonist of intolerant Christian persecution of the Jewish race and religion. but he personated a man, originally humane, who had become embittered by cruel injustice, without having entirely lost the essential attributed of average humanity ... As time passed, however, a radical change in the presentation was, little by little, effected, till at last, without entire abandonment of a purpose and power to awaken sympathy, it became the true Shylock of Shakespeare – hard, merciless, inexorable, terrible.[70]

The *Manchester Guardian* reviews of his visits to Manchester with Shylock provide evidence that he was indeed hardening his interpretation over the years. In 1881, two years after he first played the role at the Lyceum, Irving took his Shylock to Manchester. The *Guardian* critic thought the role 'admirably suited to his special gifts and capacities'. He said: 'Shylock's immense intellectual superiority is one of the chief notes of his character and nothing could have been finer than the way in which Mr Irving conveyed this.' But he went on to say:

Modern modes of thought have naturally influenced our view of the play, and more than one actor, both in England and in Germany, has sought to make Shylock sentimental and sympathetic as the representative and the martyr of an oppressed and down-trodden race ... This will not do. Shakspere [*sic*] does not paint Shylock without redeeming touches, but the notion that he intended the Jew to have the sympathies of an audience is a mere piece of modern sentimentalism. ... Shylock's hatred is not a calculating enmity for definite losses incurred through Antonio, any more that it is an impersonal and almost magnanimous desire to be avenged on the oppressor of his race. Both these elements enter into his feeling, but it is deeper lodged that either of them. The fierce passion which shakes Shylock in the frenzied scene after he has heard of Jessica's disappearance and his utter remorselessness in the trial scene are consistent only with a personal hatred pushed almost to the verge of monomania. It is his success in rendering these which makes Mr Irving's performance one of the truest as well as the grimmest things he has ever done.[71]

The critic noted a change from grotesque to serious in the delivery of the line 'I would not have given it for a wilderness of monkeys' from its delivery at the Lyceum, and described his rage in the Tubal scene: 'there is, indeed, something animal in the Jew's entire loss of self-control, and Mr Irving spares us no detail of the wild eyes, wolfish teeth and foaming mouth'.[72] When Irving played the role again in 1899, the *Guardian* critic called it 'one of the very finest of his accomplishments – a performance full of beauty wrought with perfect discretion, infinitely stimulating and impressive', but argued that 'of his bearing in the trial scene it might be said that it is too implacable and relentless for one to be presently overthrown in ignoble discomfiture'.[73] All this lends support to the idea of a hardening of the interpretation. It looks then as if he came to believe his original interpretation had been too sympathetic and hardened it but retained enough of the sympathy to balance the new hardness.

Conclusive evidence is provided by the *Liverpool Daily Post* (7 October 1891) reviewing the performance of *Merchant* on the Autumn provincial tour. The reviewer says:

We have come to the conclusion, especially about Mr Irving, that he is a progressive, and within limits a changeful actor, and that in certain characters, while he never surrenders the special conceptions which have stamped the original merit of his original performances, he is enabled by subsequent thought to give a more perfect balance to his impersonations, and to satisfy in so doing a greater range of minds. It does not always follow that in so doing he increases the satisfaction of his earliest and readiest admirers. But Mr Irving's admirers are always thoughtful people, and they are easily reconciled to developments which while not sacrificing the essential new truth, weaken objections which may be fairly supposed to have been provoked by the new truth having been made uncompromisingly prominent. Mr Irving's Shylock last night appeared older, more sordid, more ill-favoured, less consciously noble, than the Shylock which he formerly presented. Those who in other days were struck with the fine truth of the idea that Shylock, besides being an offensive usurer, was the depository and embodiment of the grand mystic traditions of Judaism may miss somewhat the very impressive figure which used to advance to the middle of the stage in the first scene of the play. But they will have the candour to admit that Shylock was sordid, and may have been very old, and may have been ill-favoured, and that none of these things conflict with any effect that Shylock ought to produce in the piece, if only the great charm of mystic solemnity in those passages in which, to use a Bulwerian phrase, Shylock's 'wrongs make him sacred' while his representative Jewish character give both his wrongs and his eloquence a lofty and noble interest. That great charm is retained, though the Shylock in the earlier scenes has more savagery and less serenity of mind than formerly, and thus is established a sort of compromise between the old theory according to which Shylock was simply a hateful wretch, and the new and truer theory according to which he was largely the product of cruel persecution acting upon the consciousness of a Hebrew informed and inflamed with all the unparalleled glories of the chosen race.

This review says it all. Irving's penchant for continually reworking his performance, his attention to criticism, his desire to please his audience had resulted in a performance which retained some of its original features but had been hardened and made less noble. This allowed audiences to take from it what they wanted. The same production seen in Bristol elicited from the critic of the *Bristol Mercury* (23 September 1891) the view that Irving's Shylock was 'an abject, hateful creature, thinking of nothing but his money and his revenge, with really no claim upon our kindly feelings' and the critic of the *Western Daily Press* (23 September 1891) observed that 'His Shylock was a man of dignity and bearing, although soured by the indignities to which he had been exposed'.

15

Afterword

Irving was one of the last representatives of a truly organic culture, in which novels, poems, plays, music and paintings overlapped and interpenetrated in a way that they have wholly ceased to do. He made no distinction between high and low brow, alternating happily between Shakespeare and popular melodrama, showing all of them equal respect. His audience was cross-class and truly national. For not only did he perform habitually to a mixed audience at his West End base, the Lyceum, but he toured Britain regularly and extensively, setting standards of taste and performance which all other companies strove to reach and cementing a truly national theatrical taste.

Irving sought not just to entertain but to elevate popular taste, to integrate the arts and to educate and ennoble the nation. This was recognized by *The Times*, which declared that Irving's company had 'gone far towards redeeming the stage for the Anglo-Saxon race as a popular educator' and the architect Alfred Darbyshire wrote that 'The change in public appreciation of the stage as a medium of artistic expression during the latter half of Queen Victoria's reign ... is mainly owing to the gigantic work of Sir Henry Irving'.

For Irving his work was his life and his mission a sacred trust. Sir John Martin-Harvey, who acted with him for many years, recalled: 'He had a concentration upon his work unusually single and powerful. He had no hobbies or distractions. You will remember in *Who's Who* he entered his relaxation as "acting". As he slowly realized where his ideal lay, he pursued it without pause, without hurry and that ideal became the control of a theatre, devoted to the greatest work he could envisage.'

One of Irving's last great productions, long-cherished, was *King Arthur*. Staged in 1895 with music by Sir Arthur Sullivan and designs by Sir Edward Burne-Jones, starring Irving as King Arthur and Ellen Terry as Queen Guinevere, it retold the age-old saga of the Round Table, ending with its break-up and the death of the King. Just as the Round Table was broken and dispersed, so too was the Lyceum lost and Irving's company dissolved. The search for the grail of artistic perfection ended with the elderly actor, racked by emphysema, his heart weakened by pleurisy and pneumonia, embarking on a farewell provincial tour. The tour revealed just how deeply he had etched himself into the heart of the nation. The journalist Austin Brereton who accompanied the tour wrote:

The tour was one continuous triumph. There is no exaggeration in the use of the word. The affection of the public for the player was evident in every town and on every occasion. On almost every night the actor had to make a short speech before the curtain, and many social and other honours were heaped upon him. One of the most remarkable demonstrations took place on the last night of Irving's engagement in Swansea. The applause at the fall of the curtain had hardly subsided when someone in the gallery began to sing 'Lead, Kindly Light' and the hymn was immediately taken up by the whole audience. Some persons tried to stop this extraordinary, demonstration, but Irving, stepping forward, expressed his delight, and with deep emotion, said that scene would be forever graven upon his memory. The incident, which has no parallel in the history of the stage, closed with the singing by the entire audience, all of whom rose to their feet, of 'God Be With You Till We Meet Again'.

The farewell tour was never completed, for Irving died shortly after completing the performance of one of his favourite roles, Becket, at the Theatre Royal, Bradford, on 13 October 1905. The last words he spoke on any stage signified that he had completed his mission: 'Into Thy hands, O Lord, into Thy hands'.

Notes

Notes to Chapter 1: Sir Henry Irving

1   Bram Stoker, *Personal Reminiscences of Henry Irving* (London: Heinemann, 1907), p. 463.

2   Laurence Irving, *Henry Irving: The Actor and his World* (London: Faber, 1951), p. 672.

3   Alan Hughes, 'The Lyceum Staff: A Victorian Theatrical Organisation', *Theatre Notebook*, 28 (1974), pp.11–17.

4   Tracy C. Davis, *The Economics of the British Stage, 1800–1914* (Cambridge: Cambridge University Press, 2000), pp. 215–25. Cf. Alan Hughes, 'Henry Irving's Finances: The Lyceum Accounts, 1878–1899', *Nineteenth-Century Theatre Research*, 1 (1973), pp. 79–87.

5   Irving's introductions to Talma's *Essay on the Actor's Art* and Diderot's *The Paradox of Acting*, and his replies to Constant Coquelin and George Barlow, can be found in Jeffrey Richards, ed., *Sir Henry Irving: Theatre, Culture and Society* (Keele: Keele University Press, 1994), pp. 29–35, 69–74, 135–142.

6   Fitzgerald Collection, x, p. 154.

7   H.A. Saintsbury and Cecil Palmer, eds, *We Saw Him Act* (London: Hurst and Blackett, 1939), pp. 195–96.

8   Saintsbury and Palmer, *We Saw Him Act*, pp. 359–60.

9   Michael Booth, *Theatre in the Victorian Age* (Cambridge: Cambridge University Press, 1991), p. 9.

10 Jim Davis and Victor Emeljanow, *Reflecting the Audience: London Theatregoing, 1840–1880* (Hatfield: University of Hertfordshire Press, 2001), p. 226.

11 Booth, *Theatre in the Victorian Age*, p. 9.

12 William Archer, *Henry Irving: Actor and Manager* (London: Field and Tuer, 1883), pp. 28–31.

13 Douglas Reid, 'Popular Theatre in Victorian Birmingham', in D. Bradby, L. James and B. Sharratt, eds, *Performance and Politics in Popular Drama* (Cambridge: Cambridge University Press, 1980), pp. 65–89; Jeremy Crump, 'The Popular Audience for Shakespeare in Nineteenth-Century Leicester', in Richard Foulkes, ed., *Shakespeare and the Victorian Stage* (Cambridge: Cambridge University Press, 1986), pp. 271–82.

14 Russell Jackson, 'Shakespeare in Liverpool: Edward Saker's Revivals, 1876–81', *Theatre Notebook*, 32 (1978), pp. 100–9; Richard Foulkes, *The Calverts: Actors of Some Importance* (London: The Society for Theatre Research, 1992).

15 Frederick Rogers, *Labour, Life and Literature* (Brighton: Harvester Press, 1973), p. 134.

16 Irving, *Henry Irving*, p. 18.

17 Saintsbury and Palmer, *We Saw Him Act*, pp.122, 126.

18 Ellen Terry, *The Story of My Life* (London: Hutchinson, 1908), p. 337.

19 Thomas Carlyle, *Past and Present* (London: Chapman and Hall, 1905) pp. 172–3.

20 Charles Forshaw, ed., *Tributes to the Memory of the Late Sir Henry Irving* (London: Elliot Stock, 1905), p. x.

21 Forshaw, *Tributes to Irving*, pp. 81, 78, 125, 133.

22 Forshaw, *Tributes to Irving*, pp. 68, 71, 76.

23 The performances praised include Hamlet, Becket, Gregory Brewster and Mathias in *The Bells* (pp. 92–94); Shylock, Hamlet, Lear, Gregory Brewster (pp. 213–14), Hamlet, Jingle, the Vicar of Wakefield, Dubosc, Lesurques, Mathias, Louis XI, Charles I, Romeo, Dante, Mephistopheles, Shylock, Othello, Richard III, Lear, Macbeth (pp. 185–86), Hamlet, Benedick, Shylock, Mathias, Gregory Brewster (pp. 200–1), Mathias, Charles I and Becket (pp. 217–18), Wolsey, Shylock, Lear, Mathias, Benedick, Becket (p. 233), Hamlet, Becket (p. 234), Hamlet, Louis XI, King Arthur, Shylock, Mathias, Becket (pp. 235–37).

24 Forshaw, *Tributes to Irving*, pp. 86, 111–112, 216.

25 Forshaw, *Tributes to Irving*, pp. 116, 134, 158, 170, 171, 248, 245.

26 Forshaw, *Tributes to Irving*, pp. 65, 73–4.

27 Forshaw, *Tributes to Irving*, pp. 169, 228.

28 Forshaw, *Tributes to Irving*, pp. 117–118, 70, 170, 22.

29 Forshaw, *Tributes to Irving*, pp. 244, 184, 187.

30 Forshaw, *Tributes to Irving*, pp. 102, 96, 89, 114–115, 146, 106–107, 160–66, 181, 190, 225, 227–28, 131.

31 Forshaw, *Tributes to Irving*, pp. 72, 157. Cf. pp. 65, 72, 78, 79, 80, 119, 151, 183.

32 Forshaw, *Tributes to Irving*, pp. 79–80.

Notes to Chapter 2: Chivalry

1 E.T. Cook and Alexander Wedderburn, eds, *The Complete Works of John Ruskin* (George Allen: London, 1904), xviii, pp. 121–2.

2 Walter E. Houghton, *The Victorian Frame of Mind, 1830–1870* (New Haven and London: Yale University Press, 1957), p. 343.

3 Alfred, Lord Tennyson, *The Works* (London: Macmillan, 1898), p. 203.

4 Mark Girouard, *The Return to Camelot: Chivalry and the English Gentleman* (New Haven and London: Yale University Press, 1981), p. 260. On the emergence of the chivalric gentleman, see also Philip Mason, *The English Gentleman: The Rise and Fall of an Ideal* (London: Andre Deutsch, 1982).

5 Samuel Smiles, *Self-Help* (London: John Murray, 1911), p. 470.

6 Norman Vance, *The Sinews of the Spirit: The Ideal of Christian Manliness in Victorian Literature and Religious Thought* (Cambridge: Cambridge University Press, 1985).

7 Vance, *Sinews of the Spirit*, p. 47.

8 Thomas Carlyle, *Past and Present* (London: Chapman and Hall, 1905), pp. 163–4.

9 Thomas Hughes, *Tom Brown at Oxford* (London: Macmillan, 1889), p. 99.

10 Thomas Hughes, *Tom Brown's Schooldays* (London: Macmillan, 1889), p. 246.

11 Thomas Hughes, *The Manliness of Christ* (London: Macmillan, 1880), pp. 25–6.

12 See Mark Girouard, *Return to Camelot*, pp. 141–64, on Kingsley, Hughes and Arnold.

13 Girouard, *Return to Camelot*, pp. 56–162.

14 On athleticism see J.A. Mangan, *Athleticism in the Victorian and Edwardian Public School* (Cambridge: Cambridge University Press, 1981).

15 Girouard, *Return to Camelot*, p. 169.

16 Girouard, *Return to Camelot*, p. 164.

17 On the public school story, see Jeffrey Richards, *Happiest Days: The Public Schools in English Fiction* (Manchester: Manchester University Press, 1981).

18 Girouard, *Return to Camelot*, p. 226.

19 Ellen Terry, *The Story of My Life* (London: Hutchinson, 1908), p. 229.

20 H.A. Saintsbury and Cecil Palmer, eds, *We Saw Him Act* (London: Hurst and Blackett, 1939), p. 245.

21 Terry, *Story of My Life*, p. 233.

22 Saintsbury and Palmer, *We Saw Him Act*, p. 248.

23 George Rowell, *Queen Victoria Goes to the Theatre* (London: Paul Elek, 1978), p. 103.

24 On this phenomenon see Beverly Taylor and Elizabeth Brewer, *The Return of King Arthur* (Cambridge: D.S. Brewer, 1983).

25 Stephen Wildman and John Christian, *Edward Burne-Jones, Victorian Artist-Dreamer* (New York: Metropolitan Museum of Art, 1998): Muriel Whitaker, *The Legends of King Arthur in Art* (Cambridge: D.S. Brewer, 1990); Debra Mancoff, *The Arthurian Revival in Art* (New York and London: Garland, 1990).

26 Freeman Wills, *W.G. Wills: Dramatist and Painter* (London: Longmans, Green and Co., 1898), pp. 233–62, summarises the play.

27 Austin Brereton, *The Life of Henry Irving* (London: Longmans, Green and Co., 1908), ii, pp. 210, 247, 248.

28 Fitzgerald Collection, xiv, p. 81.

29 Both reviews are in the Fitzgerald Collection, xiv, p. 87.

30 William Archer, *The Theatrical 'World' of 1895* (London: Walter Scott, 1896), pp. 20–35.

31 Sir John Martin-Harvey, *The Autobiography* (London: Sampson, Low, Marston and Co., 1933), pp. 175–76.

32 Kate Terry Gielgud, *A Victorian Playgoer* (London: Heinemann, 1980), ed. by Muriel St Clare Byrne, pp. 22–23.

33 Laurence Irving, *Henry Irving: The Actor and his World* (London: Faber, 1951), p. 439.

34 Bram Stoker, *Personal Reminiscences of Henry Irving* (London: Heinemann, 1907), p. 167.

35 Both reviews are in The Fitzgerald Collection, xiv, p. 54.

36 Frederick Brown, *Theatre and Revolution: The Culture of the French Stage* (New York: Viking, 1980), p. 116.

37 Brereton, *The Life of Henry Irving*, i, p. 62.

38 Brereton, *The Life of Henry Irving*, i, p. 74.

39 Brereton, *The Life of Henry Irving*, ii, pp. 126, 128.

40 Saintsbury and Palmer, *We Saw Him Act*, pp. 239–40.

41 Saintsbury and Palmer, *We Saw Him Act*, pp. 241–43.

42 Weedon Grossmith, *From Studio to Stage* (London: John Lane, 1913), pp. 170–83.

43 George Bernard Shaw, *Our Theatres in the Nineties* (London: Constable, 1932), i, p. 114.

44 Terry, *Story of My Life*, p. 248.

45 Saintsbury and Palmer, *We Saw Him Act*, p. 29.

46 Saintsbury and Palmer, *We Saw Him Act*, pp. 31–32.

47 Terry, *Story of My Life*, p. 254.

48 Saintsbury and Palmer, *We Saw Him Act*, p. 47.

49 Clement Scott, *From 'The Bells' to 'King Arthur'* (London: John McQueen, 1897), p. 11.

50 Clement Scott and Cecil Howard, *The Life and Reminiscences of E.L. Blanchard* (London: Hutchinson, 1891), ii, p. 385.

51 Brereton, *The Life of Henry Irving*, i, p. 352.

52 Saintsbury and Palmer, *We Saw Him Act*, p. 221.

53 Saintsbury and Palmer, *We Saw Him Act*, p. 32.

Notes to Chapter 3: Ellen Terry

1 T. Edgar Pemberton, *Ellen Terry and Her Sisters* (London: C. Arthur Pearson, 1902), p. 288.

2 Edward Gordon Craig, *Ellen Terry and Her Secret Self* (London: Sampson Low, Marston and Co., 1932), pp. 163–65.

3 Nina Auerbach, *Ellen Terry: Player in Her Time* (London: Phoenix House, 1987), p. 194.

4 Bram Stoker, *Personal Reminiscences of Henry Irving* (London: Heinemann, 1907), p. 363.

5 Ibid.

6 Ellen Terry, *The Story of My Life* (London: Hutchinson, 1908), pp. 73–74.

7 Charles Hiatt, *Ellen Terry and Her Impersonations* (London: George Bell and Sons, 1898), pp. 72–73.

8 Terry, *Story of My Life*, pp. 106–7.

9 Clement Scott, *Ellen Terry: An Appreciation* (New York: Frederick A. Stokes, 1900), pp. 101–2.

10 Hiatt, *Ellen Terry*, p. 97.

11 Freeman Wills, *W.G. Wills: Dramatist and Painter* (London: Longmans, Green and Co., 1898), p. 158.

12 Henry James, *The Scenic Art*, ed. Allan Wade (London: Rupert Hart-Davis, 1949), p. 114.

13 Terry, *Story of My Life*, p. 147.

14 Terry, *Story of My Life*, p. 107.

15 Auerbach, *Ellen Terry*, p. 195.

16 On the relationship between Ellen Terry and G.F. Watts see D. Loshak, 'G.F. Watts and Ellen Terry', *Burlington Magazine*, 105 (1963), pp. 476–85.

17 Tracy C. Davis, *Actresses as Working Women* (London: Routledge, 1991), p. 105.

18 Laurence Irving, *Henry Irving: The Actor and his World* (London: Faber, 1951), pp. 478–80; Roger Manvell, *Ellen Terry* (London: Heron Books 1968), p. 247.

19 Joy Melville, *Ellen and Edy* (London: Pandora, 1988), pp. 94–95.

20 Margaret Webster, The *Same Only Different* (London: Victor Gollancz, 1969), p. 191.

21 John Pick, 'Irving's Knighthood: The Untold Story' (unpublished paper), p. 9.

22 Lucy, Lady Duff Gordon, *Discretions and Indiscretions* (London: Jarrolds, 1932), p. 34.

23 Marguerite Steen, *A Pride of Terrys* (London: Longman, 1962), p. 185.

24 Steen, *A Pride of Terrys*, p. 186.

25 Steen, *A Pride of Terrys*, p. 187–88.

26 Telegram from Irving to Winter, 25 August, 1886, with note from Winter on reverse, (Folger Shakespeare Library, Y.C 485 (128). I owe this reference to Richard Foulkes.

27 Terry, *Story of My Life*, p. 336.

28 On the role of women in Victorian Society, see Carol Dyhouse, *Girls Growing Up in Victorian and Edwardian Britain* (London: Routledge, 1981); Deborah Gorham, *The Victorian Girl and the Feminine Ideal* (London: Croom Helm, 1982); Joan Burstyn, *Victorian Education and the Ideal of Womanhood* (London: Croom Helm, 1980) Martha Vicinus ed., *Suffer and Be Still* (Bloomington: Indiana University Press, 1973) Martha Vicinus ed., *A Widening Sphere: Changing Roles of Victorian Women* (London: Methuen 1980).

29 Christopher St John ed., *Ellen Terry and Bernard Shaw: A Correspondence* (London: Reinhardt and Evans, 1949), p. xvi.

30 Hiatt, *Ellen Terry*, pp. 77–79.

31 Hiatt, *Ellen Terry*, pp. 113–14.

32 Dutton Cook, *Nights at the Play* (London: Chatto and Windus, 1883), p. 376.

33 Hiatt, *Ellen Terry*, p. 153.

34 William Archer, *The Theatrical 'World' of 1895* (London: Walter Scott, 1896), pp. 31–32.

35 Terry, *Story of My Life*, p. 316.

36 Hiatt, *Ellen Terry*, pp. 242–43.

37 Pemberton, *Ellen Terry and Her Sisters*, p. 292.

38 W. Graham Robertson, *Time Was* (London: Hamish Hamilton, 1931), p. 153.

39 William Archer, *The Theatrical 'World' for 1893* (London: Walter Scott, 1894), p. 53.

40 Christopher St John, *Ellen Terry* (London: John Lane, 1907), p. 24.

41 Terry, *Story of My Life*, p. 149.

42 Ellen Terry, *Four Lectures on Shakespeare*, ed. by Christopher St John (London: Martin Hopkinson, 1932), p. 13.

43 William Winter, *Shadows of the Stage* (New York: Macmillan, 1893), pp. 290–91.

44 Auerbach, *Ellen Terry*, p. 226.

45 Terry, *Story of My Life*, p. 162.

46 Terry, *Story of My Life*, p. 163.

47 Terry, *Four Lectures on Shakespeare*, p. 97.

48 Pemberton, *Ellen Terry and Her Sisters*, p. 286.

49 Stoker, *Personal Reminiscences of Henry Irving*, p. 363.

50 Terry, *Story of My Life*, p. 308.

51 St John, ed., *Ellen Terry and Bernard Shaw*, p. 272.

52 Terry, *Story of My Life*, p. 316.

53 Terry, *Story of My Life*, p. 317.

54 Ibid.

55 J.T. Grein, *Dramatic Criticism*, i (London: John Long, 1899), p. 63.

56 Grein, *Dramatic Criticism*, i, p. 281.

57 Terry, *Story of My Life*, p. 164.

58 Terry, *Story of My Life*, p. 162, 235; Laurence Irving, *Henry Irving*, p. 457.

59 Terry, *Story of My Life*, pp. 215–16.

60 E.T. Cook and Alexander Wedderburn, eds, *The Complete Works of John Ruskin* (London: George Allen, 1904), xxv, pp. 416–19.

61 Mrs Anna Jameson, *Characteristics of Women, Moral, Poetical and Historical* (London: Saunders and Otley, 1858), i, pp. 72–73 (Portia), 143 (Beatrice), 161 (Juliet), 233 (Viola), 268 (Ophelia); ii, pp. 32 (Desdemona), 51 (Imogen), 92 (Cordelia), 275 (Katherine), 175 (Volumnia), pp. 312–13 (Lady Macbeth).

62 Terry, *Four Lectures on Shakespeare*, p. 80.

63 Terry, *Four Lectures on Shakespeare*, p. 107.

64 Terry, *Four Lectures on Shakespeare*, p. 83.

65 Terry, *Four Lectures on Shakespeare*, p. 97.

66 Terry, *Four Lectures on Shakespeare*, pp. 116–17.

67 Terry, *Four Lectures on Shakespeare*, pp.125–26.

68 Terry, *Four Lectures on Shakespeare*, p. 129, 139, 153, 160–61.

69 Terry, *Four Lectures on Shakespeare*, p. 159.

70 Terry, *Four Lectures on Shakespeare*, p. 166.

71 Terry, *Story of My Life*, p. 188.

72 Hiatt, *Ellen Terry*, p. 147.

73 Letter from Henry Irving to Clement Scott, 11 June 1880, in the Scott Collection, Huntington Library.

74 Hiatt, *Ellen Terry*, pp. 195–96.

75 Terry, *Story of My Life*, p. 249.

76 Terry, *Story of My Life*, p. 150.

77 Terry, *Story of My Life*, p. 311.

78 Auerbach, *Ellen Terry*, p. 226.

79 Terry, *Story of My Life*, p. 152.

80 Hiatt, *Ellen Terry*, p. 115–16.

81 Sir Theodore Martin, 'Theatrical Reform: *The Merchant of Venice* at the Lyceum', *Blackwoods Magazine*, 126 (December 1879), pp. 641–56.

82 James, *The Scenic Art*, p. 143.

83 Terry, *Story of My Life*, pp. 183–85.

84 Terry, *Four Lectures on Shakespeare*, p. 116.

85 Richard Foulkes, 'Helen Faucit and Ellen Terry as Portia', *Theatre Notebook*, 31 (1977), pp. 27–37, quote on p. 35.

86 St John, ed., *Ellen Terry and Bernard Shaw*, p. 73.

87 Robert Hichens, *Yesterday* (London: Cassell, 1947), p. 115.

88 Terry, *Story of My Life*, p. 169.

89 Terry *Story of My Life*, p. 205.

90 Pemberton, *Ellen Terry and Her Sisters*, p. 247.

91 Terry, *Story of My Life*, p. 209.

92 Hiatt, *Ellen Terry*, p. 166.

93 Hiatt, *Ellen Terry*, p. 167.

94 Hiatt, *Ellen Terry*, p. 167.

95   Her detailed notes on Lady Macbeth are reproduced in Manvell, *Ellen Terry*, pp. 356–66. Cf. also Michael R. Booth, 'Ellen Terry's Rehearsal Copy *of King Lear*', *Theatre Notebook*, 33 (1979), pp. 23–29.

96   Pemberton, *Ellen Terry and Her Sisters*, pp. 262–63.

97   Hiatt, *Ellen Terry*, p. 196.

98   Craig, *Ellen Terry and Her Secret Self*, p. 165.

99   Terry, *Story of My Life*, pp. 154–5.

100   Craig, *Ellen Terry and Her Secret Self*, p. 153.

101   Terry, *Story of My Life*, p. 95.

102   Hiatt, *Ellen Terry*, p. 190.

103   Terry, *Story of My Life*, p. 198.

104   Craig, *Ellen Terry and Her Secret Self*, p. 150.

105   Joseph Knight, *Theatrical Notes* (London: Lawrence and Bullen, 1893), p. 52.

106   Clement Scott, *From 'The Bells' to King Arthur'* (London: John McQueen, 1897), p. 148.

107   Terry, *Story of My Life*, pp. 306–7.

108   Craig, *Ellen Terry and Her Secret Self*, p. 158.

109   St John, *Ellen Terry*, p. 64.

110   Hiatt, *Ellen Terry*, p. 227.

111   Craig, *Ellen Terry and Her Secret Self*, p. 141.

112   Terry, *Story of My Life*, p. 141.

113   Robertson, *Time Was*, pp. 157–58.

114   Manvell, *Ellen Terry*, p. 35.

115   Scott, *Ellen Terry*, p. 17.

116   Robertson, *Time Was*, p. 54.

117   Hiatt, *Ellen Terry*, p. 155.

118   Hiatt, *Ellen Terry*, p. 226

119   Hiatt, *Ellen Terry*, p. 74.

120   Scott, *From 'The Bells' to 'King Arthur'*, p. 148.

121   Knight, *Theatrical Notes*, p. 305.

122   Michael R. Booth, 'Ellen Terry', in John Stokes, Michael R. Booth and Susan Basnett, *Bernhardt, Terry, Duse: The Actress in her Time* (Cambridge: Cambridge University Press, 1988), pp. 79–84.

123   James, *The Scenic Art*, pp. 142–43.

124   Terry, *Story of My Life*, p. 107.

125   Eve Adam, ed., *Mrs J. Comyns Carr's Reminiscences* (London: Hutchinson, 1926), p. 31.

126   Terry, *Story of My Life*, pp. 307, 350.

127   Robertson, *Time Was*, p. 154.

128   Pemberton, *Ellen Terry and Her Sisters*, pp. 263–64.

129   Gail Marshall, *Actresses on the Victorian Stage: Feminine Performance and the Galatea Myth* (Cambridge: Cambridge University Press, 1998).

130   Marshall, *Actresses on the Victorian Stage*, p. 130.

131   Marshall, *Actresses on the Victorian Stage*, p. 55

132   Davis, *Actresses as Working Women*, pp. 97–101.

133   Marshall, *Actresses on the Victorian Stage*, p. 141.

134 St John, *Ellen Terry*, p. 43.

135 Davis, *Actresses as Working Women*, p. 24.

136 Terry, *Story of My Life*, p. 164

137 Auerbach, *Ellen Terry*, p. 257.

138 Terry, *Story of My Life*, p. 78.

139 Kerrison Preston, ed., *Letters from Graham Robertson* (London: Hamish Hamilton, 1953), p. 260.

140 Craig, *Ellen Terry and Her Secret Self*, p. 140.

141 Terry, *Story of My Life*, pp. 304–5.

142 Craig, *Ellen Terry and Her Secret Self*, p. 11.

Notes to Chapter 4: The Victorian Stage

1 T.H.S. Escott, *Social Transformations of the Victorian Age* (London: Seeley and Co., 1897), p. 209.

2 Escott, *Social Transformations*, p. 210.

3 Escott, *Social Transformations*, p. 213.

4 Escott, *Social Transformations*, p. 216.

5 Escott, *Social Transformations*, p. 218.

6 The rise in social status of the actor is traced in Michael Baker's superb book, *The Rise of the Victorian Actor* (London: Croom Helm, 1978). See also Michael Sanderson, *From Irving to Olivier: A Social History of the Acting Profession, 1880–1983* (London: Athlone Press, 1984).

7 Squire and Marie Bancroft, *Recollections of Sixty Years* (London: Thomas Nelson and Sons, 1911), pp. 60, 97.

8 The Bancrofts, *Recollections of Sixty Years*, p. 94.

9 Sanderson, *From Irving to Olivier*, p. 32–33.

10 Jeffrey Richards, ed., *Sir Henry Irving: Theatre, Culture and Society* (Keele: Keele University Press, 1994), pp. 206–12.

11 Sir Frank Benson, *My Memoirs* (London: Ernest Benn, 1930), pp. 295–96.

12 Charles Pascoe, ed., *The Dramatic List* (London: Temple Publishing, n.d.), p. 225.

13 Shirley Allen, *Samuel Phelps and Sadler's Wells Theatre* (Middletown, Connecticut: Wesleyan University Press, 1971), p. 68.

14 H. Chance Newton, *Cues and Curtain Calls* (London: John Lane, 1927), p. 41.

15 Newton, *Cues and Curtain Calls*, pp. 9–10.

16 Allen, *Samuel Phelps*, p. 110.

17 J.H. Barnes, *Forty Years on the Stage* (London: Chapman and Hall, 1914), pp. 69, 71.

18 Allen, *Samuel Phelps*, p. 165.

19 Newton, *Cues and Curtain Calls*, p. 68.

20 Barnes, *Forty Years on the Stage*, pp. 67–69, 102.

21 Sir Johnston Forbes-Robertson, *A Player under Three Reigns* (London: T. Fisher Unwin, 1925), pp. 69–70.

22 Newton, *Cues and Curtain Calls*, pp. 135–36; Richards, ed., *Sir Henry Irving: Theatre, Culture and Society*, p. 179.

23 George Rowell, *Queen Victoria Goes to the Theatre* (London: Paul Elek, 1978), pp. 103, 105. On Queen Victoria's command performances also see Richard W. Schoch, *Queen Victoria and the Theatre of Her Age* (Basingstoke: Palgrave, 2004).

24 Bram Stoker, *Personal Reminiscences of Henry Irving* (London: Heinemann, 1907), p. 376; Richards, *Henry Irving; Theatre, Culture and Society*, p. 179. For the true story behind 'The Poor Box Scandal' see Schoch, *Queen Victoria and the Theatre of Her Age*, pp. 61–69.

25 Rowell, *Queen Victoria Goes to the Theatre*, pp. 105–6; Stoker, *Personal Reminiscences of Henry Irving*, p. 379.

26 Stoker, *Personal Reminiscences of Henry Irving*, pp. 380–83.

27 Sir Sidney Lee, *King Edward VIII* (London: Macmillan and Co., 1925), i, pp. 167–69.

28 Lee, *King Edward VII*, i, pp. 570–72.

29 Squire Bancroft, *Empty Chairs* (London: John Murray, 1925), p. 7.

30 Bancroft, *Empty Chairs*, p. 1.

31 Bancroft, *Empty Chairs*, p. 8; Lee, *King Edward VII*, i, p. 571.

32 Lee, *King Edward VII*, i, pp. 176–77.

33 Stoker, *Personal Reminiscences of Henry Irving*, p. 104.

34 Stoker, *Personal Reminiscences of Henry Irving*, p. 112.

35 Stoker, *Personal Reminiscences of Henry Irving*, pp. 211–17.

36 Stoker, *Personal Reminiscences of Henry Irving*, pp. 216–17.

37 Stoker, *Personal Reminiscences of Henry Irving*, pp. 391–92.

38 Stoker, *Personal Reminiscences of Henry Irving*, p. 185.

39 Stoker, *Personal Reminiscences of Henry Irving*, p. 174.

40 M.R.D. Foot, ed., *The Gladstone Diaries* (Oxford: Clarendon Press, 1968), i, p. 595.

41 H.C.G. Matthew, ed., *The Gladstone Diaries* (Oxford: Clarendon Press, 1978), v, pp. 146, 216, 243, 301, 304, 312, 391, 415.

42 Matthew ed., *The Gladstone Diaries*, v, p. 222.

43 Matthew ed., *The Gladstone Diaries*, v, p. 223.

44 *Times*, 21 July, 1859. On Gladstone and the stage, see Glynne Wickham, 'Gladstone, Oratory and the Theatre', in Peter Jagger, ed., *Gladstone* (London: Hambledon Press, 1998), pp. 1–31.

45 *The Theatre*, 13 March 1878.

46 Stoker, *Personal Reminiscences of Henry Irving*, pp. 107–8.

47 Ellen Terry, *The Story of My Life* (London: Hutchinson, 1908), pp. 54, 352.

48 Stoker, *Personal Reminiscences of Henry Irving*, p. 260.

49 Lucy Masterman, ed., *Mary Gladstone: Her Diaries and Letters* (London: Methuen, 1930), pp. 107, 153, 295.

50 Stoker, *Personal Reminiscences of Henry Irving*, p. 260.

51 H.C.G. Matthew, ed., *The Gladstone Diaries* (Oxford: Clarendon Press 1986), ix, p. 30.

52 Matthew, *The Gladstone Diaries*, vi, p. 50.

53 Matthew, *The Gladstone Diaries*, ix, p. 391.

54 Matthew, *The Gladstone Diaries*, ix, p. 105.

55 Matthew, *The Gladstone Diaries*, ix, p. 216.

56 Matthew, *The Gladstone Diaries*, ix, pp. 296, 422.

57 Matthew, *The Gladstone Diaries*, ix, p. 487.

58 Matthew, *The Gladstone Diaries* (1990), x, p. 2.

59 Matthew, *The Gladstone Diaries*, x, p. 294.

60 Matthew, *The Gladstone Diaries*, x, p. 358.

61 Stoker, *Personal Reminiscences of Henry Irving*, p. 263.

62 Matthew, *The Gladstone Diaries* (1990), xi, pp. 528–9.

63 Matthew, *The Gladstone Diaries* (1994), xii, p. 344; Stoker, *Personal Reminiscences of Henry Irving*, p. 262.

64 Matthew, *The Gladstone Diaries*, xiii, p. 25.

65 Matthew, *The Gladstone Diaries*, xiii, p. 148.

66 Stoker, *Personal Reminiscences of Henry Irving*, p. 264; Matthew, *The Gladstone Diaries*, xiii, p. 208.

67 Masterman, *Mary Gladstone*, p. 103.

68 Masterman, *Mary Gladstone*, p. 133.

69 Masterman, *Mary Gladstone*, p. 147.

70 Masterman, *Mary Gladstone*, p. 148.

71 Masterman, *Mary Gladstone*, p. 194.

72 Masterman, *Mary Gladstone*, p. 215.

73 Masterman, *Mary Gladstone*, p. 216.

74 Masterman, *Mary Gladstone*, p. 227.

75 Masterman, *Mary Gladstone*, p. 246.

76 Masterman, *Mary Gladstone*, pp. 269, 358.

77 Masterman, *Mary Gladstone*, p. 379.

78 Masterman, *Mary Gladstone*, p. 420.

79 Eliza Aria, *My Sentimental Self* (London: Chapman and Hall, 1922), p. 121. On Irving's charitable donations, see also Newton, *Cues and Curtain Calls*, pp. 39, 70–71, and Joe Graham, *An Old Stock Actor's Memories* (London: John Murray, 1930), pp. 221–24.

80 Charles V. Stanford, *Pages from an Unwritten Diary* (London: Edward Arnold, 1914), p. 228.

81 *Times*, 2 July, 1875, announced a record subscription list of over £1000. But Wendy Trewin, *The Royal General Theatrical Fund: A History, 1838–1988* (London: Society for Theatre Research, 1989), p. 50, says the dinner raised £810 16s. 0d., still a substantial sum.

82 Trewin, *The Royal General Theatrical Fund*, pp. 63, 98.

83 Sanderson, *From Irving to Olivier*, pp. 88–89.

84 Austin Brereton, *The Life of Henry Irving* (London: Longmans, Green and Co., 1908), ii, p. 83; Sanderson, *From Irving to Olivier*, p. 89.

85 Laurence Irving, *Henry Irving: The Actor and his World* (London: Faber, 1951), p. 433.

86 Stoker, *Personal Reminiscences of Henry Irving*, p. 196.

87 Irving, *Henry Irving*, p. 432.

88 Irving, *Henry Irving*, p. 433.

89 Ibid.

90 Richards, *Sir Henry Irving: Theatre, Culture and Society*, pp. 82–84.

91 Terry, *Story of My Life*, p. 191.

92 Many of them are reprinted in Richards, *Sir Henry Irving: Theatre, Culture and Society*.

93 Richards, *Sir Henry Irving: Theatre, Culture and Society*, pp. 161–62, 164, 166.

94 Richards, *Sir Henry Irving: Theatre, Culture and Society*, pp. 166–67, 169, 171, 177, 178.

95   Richards, *Sir Henry Irving: Theatre, Culture and Society*, pp. 182, 183, 184, 186–7, 187, 190.

96   Richards, *Sir Henry Irving: Theatre, Culture and Society*, p. 194.

97   Richards, *Sir Henry Irving: Theatre, Culture and Society*, p. 192.

98   Richards, *Sir Henry Irving: Theatre, Culture and Society*, p. 199.

99   Richards, *Sir Henry Irving: Theatre, Culture and Society*, pp. 220–29.

100   The themes were set out again in Irving's articles, 'The Ethics of the Stage', in *Treasure Trove* (8 October 1890) and 'The Mission of the Stage and the Actor', in *Collier's Magazine* (13 December 1902).

101   Henry Neville, *The Stage: Its Past and Present in Relation to Fine Art* (London: Richard Bentley and Son, 1875), pp. 5, 8, 13.

102   Neville, *The Stage*, p. 60.

103   Neville, *The Stage*, pp. 73–74.

104   Neville, *The Stage*, pp. 85–86.

105   Neville, *The Stage*, p. 74.

106   William Archer surveyed the controversy in an essay in *Time*, collected in his William Archer, *About the Theatre* (London: T. Fisher Unwin, 1886), pp. 211–38.

107   *Compact Edition of the Dictionary of National Biography* (Oxford: Oxford University Press, 1975), ii, p. 2728.

108   Mrs Madge Kendal, *The Drama* (London: David Bogue, 1884), pp. 3–4, 8–9, 15, 16.

109   Jessie Millward, *Myself and Others* (London: Hutchinson, 1923), pp. 56–57.

110   Kendal, *The Drama*, pp. 17, 24.

111   Dame Madge Kendal, *Dame Madge Kendal by Herself* (London: John Murray, 1933), p. 197.

112   *Theatre*, new series, 5 (2 February, 1885), pp. 92–93.

113   F.C. Burnand, 'Behind the Scenes', *Fortnightly Review*, 37 (January 1885), pp. 84–94.

114   Hamilton Aïdé, 'The Actor's Calling', *Nineteenth Century*, 17 (1885), pp. 521–26.

115   John Coleman, 'The Social Status of the Actor', *National Review*, 5 (1885), pp. 20–28.

116   Irving, *Henry Irving*, p. 614.

117   Raymond Blathwayt, *Does the Theatre Make for Good? An Interview with Mr Clement Scott* (London: A.W. Hall, 1898).

118   *Great Thoughts* reprinted the interview as a penny pamphlet with a round-up of reactions to it.

119   Irving, *Henry Irving*, p. 615.

120   The essay is reproduced in Frederic Whyte, *The Life of W.T. Stead* (New York and London: Houghton Mifflin / Jonathan Cape, n.d.), ii, pp. 247–54.

121   Alfred Darbyshire, *The Art of the Victorian Stage* (Manchester: Sherratt and Hughes, 1907), p. 81.

122   Roland Quinault, 'The Cult of the Centenary, 1784–1914', *Historical Research*, 71 (October 1998), p. 322.

123   Jonathan Bate, *The Genius of Shakespeare*, (London: Picador, 1997), p. 174.

124   On the emergence of a distinctive English/British culture, see Linda Colley, *Britons* (New Haven: Yale University Press, 1992), and Gerald Newman, *The Rise of English Nationalism, 1740–1830* (London: Weidenfield, 1987).

125   J.C. Trewin, *The Story of Stratford-upon-Avon* (London: Staples Press 1950), p. 47.

126 On the Shakespeare Jubilee see Christian Deelman, *The Great Shakespeare Jubilee* (London: Michael Joseph, 1964), and on the Tercentenary, see Richard Foulkes, *The Shakespeare Tercentenary of 1864* (London: Society of Theatre Research, 1984).

127 Richards, *Sir Henry Irving: Theatre, Culture and Society*, pp. 274–77.

128 Richards, *Sir Henry Irving: Theatre, Culture and Society*, pp. 104–6.

129 Lord Ronald Gower, *Old Diaries, 1881–1901* (London: John Murray, 1902), p. 271.

130 *Times*, 16 July 1896.

131 *Farewell of Sir Henry Irving: Visit to Bath, 16, 17, 18, February 1905* (printed for private circulation at the Herald Office, Bath), pp. 15–16.

132 Richards, *Sir Henry Irving: Theatre, Culture and Society*, pp. 309–11. In 1928, the empty niches on the memorial were finally filled by figures of Dr Faustus, Edward II and Barabas, the Jew of Malta, sculpted by Charles Hartwell, a pupil of Onslow Ford. On the history of the memorial, see Alan Stockwell, 'The Canterbury Marlowe Memorial', *First Knight*, 8 (2004), pp. 23–28.

133 Edward Augustus Freeman, *The History of the Norman Conquest of England* (London: Macmillan, 1877), i, p. 49; J.R. Green, *The Conquest of England* (London: Macmillan, 1906), i, p. 207.

134 Stoker, *Personal Reminiscences of Henry Irving*, p. 160.

135 Stoker, *Personal Reminiscences of Henry Irving*, p. 159.

136 Laurence Irving, *The Precarious Crust* (London: Chatto and Winduss, 1971), p. 178. There is a full account of the unveiling in *The Times*, 6 December 1910.

137 Margaret Baker, *London Statues and Monuments* (Princes Risborough: Shire, 1995).

138 J.C. Trewin, *Benson and the Bensonians* (London: Barrie and Rockliff, 1960), pp. 214–17.

139 *A Tribute to the Genius of William Shakespeare* (London: Macmillan, 1916), p. v.

Notes to Chapter 5: The Victorian Repertoire

1 William Archer, *The Old Drama and the New* (London: Heinemann, 1923), pp. 19, 24, 30, 31, 32.

2 Archer, *The Old Drama and the New*, pp. 246, 245, 254.

3 Archer, *The Old Drama and the New*, pp. 48–49, 254, 255, 256.

4 Archer, *The Old Drama and the New*, pp. 266, 280.

5 Archer, *The Old Drama and the New*, p. 286.

6 Archer, *The Old Drama and the New*, pp. 250, 270.

7 Maurice Willson Disher, *The Last Romantic* (London: Hutchinson, 1948), p. 32.

8 Allan Rodway, *The Romantic Conflict* (London: Chatto and Windus, 1963), p. 8.

9 A.B. Walkley, *Playhouse Impressions* (London: T. Fisher Unwin, 1892), pp. 257–61.

10 Disher, *The Last Romantic*, pp. 62–63.

11 Robert Baldick, *The Life and Times of Frédérick LeMaître* (Fair Lawn, New Jersey: Essential Books, 1959), p. 54.

12 Baldick, *The Life and Times of Frédérick LeMaître*, p. 245.

13 Frank Archer, *An Actor's Notebooks* (London: Stanley Paul, n.d.), p. 291.

14 On Fechter, see Clement Scott, *Thirty Years at the Play* (London: The Railway and General Automatic Library, 1891), pp. 15–19.

15 Willson Disher, *The Last Romantic*, p. 60.

16 Albert W. Halsall, *Victor Hugo and the Romantic Drama* (Toronto: University of Toronto Press, 1994), pp. 63, 68–69.

17 Jeffrey Richards, ed., *Sir Henry Irving: Theatre, Culture and Society* (Keele: Keele University Press, 1994), p. 112.

18 Richards, *Sir Henry Irving: Theatre, Culture and Society*, pp. 176–77.

19 Alan Hughes, *Henry Irving: Shakespearean* (Cambridge: Cambridge University Press, 1981), p. 22.

20 Willson Disher, *The Last Romantic*, p. 32.

21 Gary Taylor, *Reinventing Shakespeare* (London: Vintage, 1991), p. 167.

22 Thomas Carlyle, *On Heroes, Hero-Worship and the Heroic in History* (London: Chapman and Hall, 1907), pp. 95–96.

23 Aron Y. Stavisky, *Shakespeare and the Victorians* (Norman: University of Oklahoma Press, 1969), p. 4.

24 Taylor, *Reinventing Shakespeare*, p. 194.

25 Ellen Terry, *Story of My Life* (London: Hutchinson, 1908), p. 166.

26 Squire and Marie Bancroft, *Recollections of Sixty Years* (London: Thomas Nelson and Sons, 1911), p. 362.

27 On the great tradition of Shakespeare acting see Robert Speaight, *Shakespeare on the Stage* (London: Collins, 1973).

28 Richards, *Sir Henry Irving: Theatre, Culture and Society*, pp. 237–309.

29 Richards, *Sir Henry Irving: Theatre, Culture and Society*, pp. 283–84.

30 Richards, *Sir Henry Irving: Theatre, Culture and Society*, pp. 284–85.

31 Richards, *Sir Henry Irving: Theatre, Culture and Society*, pp. 124–25.

32 Austin Brereton, *The Life of Henry Irving* (London: Longmans, Green and Co., 1908), i, pp. 167–68.

33 Hughes, *Henry Irving, Shakespearean*, p. 27.

34 John Ranken Towse, *Sixty Years of Theatre* (New York: Funk and Wagnalls, 1916), pp. 183–84.

35 Clement Scott, *The Drama of Yesterday and Today* (London: Macmillan, 1899), i, p. 461.

36 Richards, *Sir Henry Irving: Theatre, Culture and Society*, pp. 238–39.

37 Terry, *Story of My Life*, pp. 124–27, 129.

38 Clement Scott, *Some Notable Hamlets* (London: Greening, 1900), pp. 64–65, 68, 69, 76.

39 Joseph Knight, *Theatrical Notes* (London: Lawrence and Bullen, 1893), p. 6.

40 Dutton Cook, *Nights at the Play* (London: Chatto and Windus, 1883), pp. 262–63.

41 Sir Edward R. Russell, *Arrested Fugitives* (London: James Nisbet, 1912), pp. 57–58.

42 Richard Dickins, *Forty Years of Shakespeare on the English Stage* (privately printed), p. 18. Cf. also Eden Philpotts in H.A. Saintsbury and Cecil Palmer, eds, *We Saw Him Act* (London: Hurst and Blackett, 1939), p. 85.

43 Hughes, *Henry Irving: Shakespearean*, pp. 29–30.

44 William Archer, *About the Theatre* (London: T. Fisher Unwin, 1886), pp. 239–40.

45 Archer, *About the Theatre*, p. 241.

46 Archer, *About the Theatre*, pp. 254–55.

47 Clement Scott, *From 'The Bells' to 'King Arthur'* (London: John MacQueen, 1897), p. 84.

48 Knight, *Theatrical Notes*, p. 101.

49 Scott, *From 'The Bells' to King Arthur'*, p. 84.

50 Cook, *Nights at the Play*, pp. 309, 307.

51 Bram Stoker, *Personal Reminiscences of Henry Irving* (London: Heinemann, 1907), p. 55.

52 Cook, *Nights at the Play*, p. 463.

53 Cook, *Nights at the Play*, p. 462

54 Terry, *Story of My Life*, pp. 206, 204.

55 Terry, *Story of My Life*, p. 207.

56 Terry, *Story of My Life*, p. 205.

57 Scott, *From 'The Bells' to 'King Arthur'*, p. 209; William Archer, *Henry Irving: Actor and Manager* (London: Field and Tuer, 1883), p. 92.

58 Richards, *Sir Henry Irving: Theatre, Culture and Society*, p. 240.

59 Terry, *Story of My Life*, p. 206.

60 Richards, *Sir Henry Irving: Theatre, Culture and Society*, p. 254.

61 Hughes, *Henry Irving: Shakespearean*, p. 92.

62 Terry, *Story of My Life*, p. 174.

63 The essay is reprinted as 'Sex in Tragedy', in Joseph Comyns Carr, *Coasting Bohemia* (London: Macmillan, 1914), pp. 162–98. Ellen Terry comments on it in Terry, *Story of My Life*, p. 306.

64 Nancy Lynn Simon, 'Henry Irving and Ellen Terry in *Macbeth*, Lyceum Theatre, 29 December 1888', Ph.D. Thesis, University of Washington, (1975), pp. 161–71.

65 Knight, *Theatrical Notes*, p. 168.

66 Scott, *From 'The Bells' to 'King Arthur'*, p. 106; Cook *Nights at the Play*, p. 328.

67 Cook, *Nights at the Play*, pp. 328–29.

68 Knight, *Theatrical Notes*, p. 168.

69 Scott, *From 'The Bells' to 'King Arthur'*, p. 108.

70 Richards, *Sir Henry Irving: Theatre, Culture and Society*, p. 239.

71 Dickins, *Forty Years of Shakespeare on the English Stage*, pp. 30–31, 83.

72 Kate Terry Gielgud, *A Victorian Playgoer* (London: Heinemann, 1980), p. 47.

73 Scott, *From 'The Bells' to 'King Arthur'*, p. 229.

74 Scott, *From 'The Bells' to 'King Arthur'*, pp. 238–39.

75 Fitzgerald Collection, v, pp. 36, 44.

76 Terry, *Story of My Life*, pp. 212–14.

77 Hughes, *Henry Irving: Shakespearean*, p. 173.

78 William Winter, *Henry Irving* (New York: George J. Coombes, 1885), pp. 59–67.

79 Scott, *From 'The Bells' to 'King Arthur'*, p. 254.

80 Dickins, *Forty Years of Shakespeare on the English Stage*, p. 43.

81 Fitzgerald Collection, vii, pp. 298, 313.

82 Sir John Martin-Harvey, *Autobiography* (London: Sampson Low, Marston and Co., 1933), pp. 79–80; Terry, *Story of My Life*, pp. 232–33.

83 Terry, *Story of My Life*, p. 232.

84 Terry, *Story of My Life*, p. 233.

85   Laurence Irving, *Henry Irving: The Actor and his World* (London: Faber, 1951), p. 441.

86   Fitzgerald Collection, vii, pp. 307.

87   Fitzgerald Collection, vii, pp. 307, 302, 313.

88   Richards, *Sir Henry Irving: Theatre, Culture and Society*, pp. 240–41.

89   J.S. Bratton, ed., *Plays in Performance: King Lear* (Bristol: Bristol Classical Press, 1987), p. 41.

90   Stoker, *Personal Reminiscences of Henry Irving*, p. 76.

91   Fitzgerald Collection, x, p. 99.

92   Fitzgerald Collection, x, pp. 115, 114, 97, 111.

93   Stoker, *Personal Reminiscences of Henry Irving*, p. 356; Saintsbury and Palmer, *We Saw Him Act*, p. 298.

94   Fitzgerald Collection, x, p. 125.

95   William Archer, *The Theatrical 'World' of 1896* (London: Walter Scott, 1897), p. 260.

96   Bernard Shaw, *Our Theatre in the Nineties* (London: Constable, 1948), ii, p. 195.

97   Fitzgerald Collection, xxi, p. 42.

98   *Fortnightly Review*, 60 (1896), pp. 635–47.

99   Archer, *The Theatrical 'World' of 1896*, p. 273.

100 Terry, *Story of My Life*, p. 316.

101 Shaw, *Our Theatre in the Nineties*, ii, p. 199.

102 Archer, *The Theatrical 'World' of 1896*, pp. 272–73.

103 *Daily Telegraph*, 23 September 1896.

104 Scott, *From 'The Bells' to 'King Arthur'*, p. 336.

105 Fitzgerald Collection, x, p. 49.

106 Scott, *From 'The Bells' to 'King Arthur'*, p. 338.

107 Fitzgerald Collection, x, p. 49.

108 Fitzgerald Collection, x, p. 58.

109 Terry, *Story of My Life*, p. 372.

110 Terry, *Story of My Life*, p. 302; The Bancrofts, *Recollections of Sixty Years*, p. 355.

111 Walter H. Pollock, *Impressions of Henry Irving* (London: Longmans, Green and Co., 1908), p. 92.

112 H. Chance Newton, *Cues and Curtain Calls* (London: John Lane, 1927), pp. 39–40.

113 *Daily Telegraph*, 16 October 1905: Newton, *Cues and Curtain Calls*, p. 40, Stoker, *Personal Reminiscences of Irving*, p. 52.

114 Margaret J. Howell, *Byron Tonight* (Windlesham: Springwood Books, 1982), p. 34.

115 Howell, *Byron Tonight*, pp. 5–10.

116 William Ruddick, 'Lord Byron's Historical Tragedies', in Kenneth Richards and Peter Thomson, eds, *Nineteenth-Century British Theatre* (London: Methuen, 1971), pp. 83–94.

117 Howell, *Byron Tonight*, p. 70.

118 Howell, *Byron Tonight*, p. 117.

119 Howell, *Byron Tonight*, p. 104.

120 Howell, *Byron Tonight*, p. 146; Cf. Terry, *Story of My Life*, p. 249.

121 Shirley Allen, *Samuel Phelps and Sadler's Wells Theatre* (Middletown, Connecticut: Wesleyan University Press, 1971), p. 271.

122 Chance Newton, *Cues and Curtain Call*, p. 33.

123 Stoker, *Personal Reminiscences of Henry Irving*, pp. 332–33.

124   Sir Alexander Mackenzie, *A Musician's Narrative* (London: Cassell, 1927), pp. 176–77.

125   Percy Fitzgerald, *Sir Henry Irving* (London: T. Fisher Unwin, 1906), p. 188.

126   Fitzgerald Collection, vii, p. 373.

127   Fitzgerald Collection, vii, p. 277.

128   Fitzgerald Collection, vii, p. 373.

129   Scott, *From 'The Bells' to 'King Arthur'*, pp. 299–304.

130   Fitzgerald Collection, vii, p. 373; viii, p. 277.

131   Terry, *Story of My Life*, p. 249.

132   Fitzgerald, *Sir Henry Irving*, p. 189.

133   Stoker, *Personal Reminiscences of Henry Irving*, p. 136.

134   Harold Nicolson, *Swinburne* (London: Macmillan, 1926), p. 149.

135   Cecil Y. Lang, ed., *The Swinburne Letters* (New Haven: Yale University Press, 1960), iii, pp. 77–78.

136   Nicolson, *Swinburne*, p. 149.

137   Lang, *The Swinburne Letters*, iii, p. 25; v (1962), p. 96.

138   Lang, *The Swinburne Letters*, v, p. 182.

139   Lang, *Swinburne Letters*, iii, p. 43.

140   On the Victorian world view see Walter E. Houghton, *The Victorian Frame of Mind, 1830–1870* (New Haven: Yale University Press, 1957), and David Newsome, *The Victorian World Picture* (London: John Murray, 1997).

141   Michael Booth, *English Melodrama* (London: Herbert Jenkins, 1965), p. 14.

142   Peter Brooks, *The Melodramatic Imagination* (New Haven: Yale University Press, 1976), p. 4.

143   Brooks, *The Melodramatic Imagination*, p. 15.

144   Irving, *Henry Irving*, p. 200.

145   Laurence Irving, *The Precarious Crust* (London: Chatto and Windus, 1971), p.19.

146   Laurence Irving, *The Successors* (London: Rupert Hart-Davis, 1967), p. 109.

147   Irving, *The Precarious Crust*, pp. 19–20.

148   Irving, *The Precarious Crust*, p. 23.

149   Charles Hiatt, *Henry Irving* (London: George Bell and Sons, 1899), p. 15.

150   Richard D. Altick, *Paintings from Books* (Columbia: Ohio State University Press, 1985), p. 149.

151   Altick, *Paintings from Books*, p. 405.

152   Freeman Wills, *W.G. Wills: Dramatist and Painter* (London: Longmans, Green and Co., 1898), p. 157.

153   Wills, *W.G. Wills*, pp. 158–59.

154   Irving, *The Precarious Crust*, p. 24.

155   *Sketch*, 17 April 1901.

156   Hughes, *Henry Irving: Shakespearean*, pp. 168–69.

157   Henry Arthur Jones, *The Shadow of Henry Irving* (London: Richards, 1931), pp. 23, 68.

158   On this subject see Masao Miyoshi, *The Divided Self* (New York: New York University Press, 1969).

159   Saintsbury and Palmer, *We Saw Him Act*, p. 188. On the doubleness see Peter Thomson, '"Weirdness that Lifts and Colours All": The Secret Self of Henry Irving' in Richard Foulkes, ed., *Shakespeare and the Victorian Stage* (Cambridge: Cambridge University Press, 1986),

pp. 97–105; and David Mayer, 'Doubles: Lesurques and Dubosc, Jekyll and Hyde, Svengali and Trilby', in Alan Burton and Laraine Porter, eds, *Crossing the Pond* (Trowbridge: Flicks Books, 2002), pp. 26–33.

160 Saintsbury and Palmer, *We Saw Him Act*, pp. 121–23.
161 Unidentified newspaper clipping in the Dorothea Baird Scrapbook (in possession of John H.B. Irving), p. 26.

Notes to Chapter 6: Playwrights

1 John Russell Stephens, *The Profession of the Playwright: British Theatre, 1800–1900* (Cambridge: Cambridge University Press, 1992), pp. 13–19.
2 *Theatre* new series, 1 (January 1880) for the symposium 'The Dearth of Dramatists: Is It a Fact?' pp. 1–11. On the dramatic year of 1879, see *Theatre*, 1 (February 1880), pp. 125–26.
3 Sir Frank Burnand, *Records and Reminiscences* (London: Methuen, 1904), ii, pp. 176–77.
4 Percy Fitzgerald, *Memoirs of an Author* (London: Bentley, 1895), ii, pp. 42, 45, 46, 47.
5 Jeffrey Richards, ed., *Sir Henry Irving: Theatre, Culture and Society* (Keele: Keele University Press, 1994), pp. 285–87.
6 *Compact Edition of the Dictionary of National Biography* (Oxford: Oxford University Press, 1975), ii, p. 2792.
7 J.B. Booth, *Palmy Days* (London: Richards Press, 1957), p. 84.
8 Sir John Martin-Harvey, *Autobiography* (London: Sampson Low and Marston, 1933), pp. 240–41.
9 William Archer, *English Dramatists of To-Day* (London: Sampson Low, Marston, Searle and Rivington, 1882), pp. 233, 242, 262.
10 *Compact Edition of the Dictionary of National Biography*, ii, p. 2478.
11 Robert Hichens, *Yesterday* (London: Cassell and Co., 1947), pp. 84–85.
12 *Compact Edition of Dictionary of National Biography*, ii, p. 2463.
13 Hichens, *Yesterday*, pp. 114–15.
14 Hichens, *Yesterday*, p. 115.
15 Carr's career is recounted in his two volumes of autobiography, *Some Eminent Victorians* (London: Duckworth, 1908) and *Coasting Bohemia* (London: Macmillan, 1914). Also in Eve Adam, ed., *Mrs J. Comyns Carr's Reminiscences*, (London: Hutchinson, 1926) and in Mrs Comyns Carr's recollections of her husband, *J. Comyns Carr: Stray Memories* (London: Macmillan, 1920).
16 Mrs Comyns Carr, *J. Comyns Carr: Stray Memories*, pp. 116–18.
17 On Courtney, see *Compact Edition of the Dictionary of National Biography*, ii, p. 2582, and Courtney's autobiography, *The Passing Hour* (London: Hutchinson, 1925).
18 Courtney, *The Passing Hour*, p. 241.
19 Austin Brereton, *The Life of Henry Irving* (London: Longmans, Green and Co., 1908), ii, p. 225.
20 Courtney, *The Passing Hour*, pp. 130–32.
21 Jerome A. Hart, *Sardou and the Sardou Plays* (Philadelphia: Lipincott, 1913), p. 114.
22 Joseph I.C. Clarke, *My Life and Memories* (New York: Dodd, Mead and Co., 1925).

23   Freeman Wills, *W.G. Wills: Dramatist and Painter* (London: Longmans, Green and Co., 1898), p. 1.

24   Fitzgerald, *Memoirs of an Author*, ii, pp. 24, 25, 28–29.

25   Wills, *W.G. Wills*, pp. 33, 2, 38.

26   Fitzgerald, *Memoirs of an Author*, ii, p. 25.

27   Wills, *W.G. Wills*, pp. 118, 66.

28   Wills, *W.G. Wills*, p. 118

29   Wills, *W.G. Wills*, pp. 119–20.

30   Wills, *W.G. Wills*, p. 94.

31   Dutton Cook, *Nights at the Play* (London: Chatto and Windus, 1883), p. 152.

32   Wills, *W.G. Wills*, p. 113.

33   Geneviève Ward and Richard Whiteing, *Both Sides of the Curtain* (London: Cassell and Co., 1918), p. 73; Wills, *W.G. Wills*, pp. 123–24.

34   Wills, *W.G. Wills*, p. 216; Mary Anderson, *A Few Memories* (New York: Harper and Bros, 1896), p. 230.

35   Ward and Whiteing, *Both Sides of the Curtain*, p. 73; Wills, *W.G. Wills*, pp. 151–52.

36   Ellen Terry, *The Story of My Life* (London: Hutchinson, 1908), pp. 140–41.

37   Booth, *Palmy Days*, p. 79.

38   Wills, *W.G. Wills*, p. 173.

39   Ward and Whiteing, *Both Sides of the Curtain*, p. 73.

40   Wills, *W.G. Wills*, pp. 150–54, 266–67, 151–52.

41   Wills, *W.G. Wills*, p. 152.

42   Wills, *W.G. Wills*, p. 182.

43   Booth, *Palmy Days*, p. 79.

44   James F. Stottlar, 'A Victorian Stage Adapter at Work: W.G. Wills "Rehabilitates" the Classics', *Victorian Studies*, 16 (1973), pp. 401–32.

45   Archer, *English Dramatists of To-Day*, pp. 352–80.

46   Bram Stoker, *Personal Reminiscences of Henry Irving* (London: Heinemann, 1907), pp. 325–26.

47   Stoker, *Personal Reminiscences of Henry Irving*, pp. 329, 330, 325. Stoker's list of plays includes Wills's *Mephisto* but this seems to have been the working title of *Faust*.

48   John Dickson Carr, *The Life of Sir Arthur Conan Doyle* (New York: Vintage Books, 1975), pp. 125, 140.

49   Stoker, *Personal Reminiscences of Irving*, p. 329.

50   Stoker, *Personal Reminiscences of Irving*, pp. 120–21, 124.

51   Stoker, *Personal Reminiscences of Irving*, p. 137; Peter Thomson, 'Tennyson's Plays and Their Production', in D.J. Palmer ed., *Writers and their Background: Tennyson* (London: G. Bell and Sons, 1973), p. 248; Lang and Shannon, *The Letters of Alfred, Lord Tennyson*, iii, p. 429; William Winter, *Shadows of The Stage*, p. 275.

52   Stoker, *Personal Reminiscences of Irving*, pp. 176–79, 164–66.

53   H. Chance Newton, *Cues and Curtain Calls* (London: John Lane, 1927), pp. 42–43.

54   Clarke, *My Life and Memories*, pp. 289–90.

55   Memorandum of agreement between Henry Irving and J.I.C. Clarke, dated 9 July, 1894, Irving deed box.

56   Letter from Clarke to Irving, 14 July 1894, Irving deed box

57   Letters from Clarke to Irving, 26 March 1895 and 19 July 1895, Irving deed box.

58   Clarke, *My Life and Memories*, p. 291.

59   Stoker, *Personal Reminiscences of Irving*, p. 166.

60   Memorandum of agreement between Irving and Ellen Terry, 4 February 1898, Irving deed box.

61   Stoker, *Personal Reminiscences of Irving*, pp. 162–63.

62   Terry, *Story of My Life*, pp. 308–9.

63   Walter Herries Pollock, *Impressions of Henry Irving* (London: Longmans, Green and Co., 1908), p. 117.

64   There is a lengthy exchange of letters between Traill and Stoker in which ideas for the play and its structure are batted back and forth. They are dated 21 June 1897, 30 June 1897, 3 July 1897, 30 October 1897, 10 November 1897, 5 December 1897, 6 December 1897, 9 December 1897, 20 January 1898, 25 May 1898, 23 June 1898, 30 June 1898. A letter dated 10 September 1897 from Traill accepts Irving's suggestion of a change of name for the leading character from Elton to Tregenna. All the letters are in the Irving deed box.

65   Letters from J.I.C. Clarke to Stoker, 11 September 1896, 5 January 1897, 26 January 1897, 12 February 1897, 10 September 1897; letter from Clarke to Irving, 14 May 1897. Irving deed box.

66   Stoker, *Personal Reminiscences of Henry Irving*, pp. 326–27, Stoker consistently refers to him as Robert Emmett rather than the correct Emmet.

67   On the life, legend and dramatic history of Robert Emmet, see Marianne Elliott, *Robert Emmet: The Making of a Legend* (London: Profile Books, 2003).

68   Stoker's account of the genesis of the play is in Stoker, *Personal Reminiscences of Henry Irving*, pp. 326–28.

69   Newton, *Cues and Curtain Calls*, p. 43; Richard Fawkes, *Dion Boucicault*, (London: Quartet Books, 1979), p. 223. Boucicault's version of *Robert Emmet* [sic] is printed in Andrew Parkin, ed., *Selected Plays of Dion Boucicault* (Gerrard's Cross: Colin Smythe, 1987), pp. 331–97.

70   Fitzgerald, *Memoirs of an Author*, ii, pp. 27–28.

71   Fitzgerald, *Memoirs of an Author*, ii, p. 29.

72   William Winter, *Shadows of the Stage* (New York: Macmillan, 1893), p. 355.

73   Fitzgerald, *Memoirs of an Author*, ii, pp. 29–31.

74   Stoker, *Personal Reminiscences of Henry Irving*, pp. 35–36.

75   Percy Fitzgerald, *Sir Henry Irving* (London: T. Fisher Unwin, 1906), p. 76.

76   Stoker, *Personal Reminiscences of Henry Irving*, p. 320.

77   Stoker, *Personal Reminiscences of Henry Irving*, pp. 316–17.

78   Stoker, *Personal Reminiscences of Henry Irving*, pp. 317–21.

79   Hall Caine, *My Story* (London: Heinemann, 1906), pp. 249–51.

80   Unidentified clipping, Dorothea Baird Scrapbook, p. 26.

81   Stoker, *Personal Reminiscences of Henry Irving*, p. 26.

82   Stephens, *The Profession of the Playwright*, pp. 67–74.

83   Wills, *W.G. Wills*, p. 145.

84   Wills, *W.G. Wills*, p. 149.

85 Letter from Stoker to Wills, 2 July 1880; letter from Wills to Stoker, 19 July 1880, Irving deed box.

86 Wills, *W.G. Wills*, pp. 196–97.

87 Newton, *Cues and Curtain Calls*, p. 42; Wills, *W.G. Wills*, p. 200.

88 Letter from Wills to Irving, 2 March 1891; memorandum from Stoker to Wills, 5 March 1891; memorandum from Stoker to Wills, 25 October 1890; memorandum dated 13 March 1891, Irving deed box.

89 Harry Plunket Greene, *Charles Villiers Stanford* (London: Edward Arnold, 1935).

90 Letter from Stoker to Wills, 17 August, 1883, Irving deed box.

91 Letter from Wills to Stoker, 6 December, 1886; memorandum dated 25 October, 1890; memorandum dated 24 July, 1893; receipt dated 7 July, 1888, Irving deed box.

92 Letter from Merivale to Irving, 21 December 1882; receipt from Frank Marshall to Irving, 27 October 1882; agreement between Irving and Alfred Calmour, 18 July 1887, Irving deed box.

93 Letter from Stoker to Cosmo Logie, 8 January 1881. Irving deed box.

94 Stephens, *The Profession of the Playwright*, pp. 64, 71.

95 Letter from Charles L. Reade to Irving, 6 May 1891, and Stoker's reply and calculations, Irving deed box.

96 Memorandum dated 26 May, 1892, Irving deed box; Stephens, *The Profession of the Playwright*, p. 70.

97 Stephens, *The Profession of the Playwright*, p. 69.

98 Memorandum of agreement with Hichens and Traill, 12 July 1897, Irving deed box.

99 Memorandum of Agreement with Heinrich Conreid, agent of Richard Voss, 14 April 1891; letter from Sydney Grundy to Irving, 23 July 1891, Irving deed box.

100 Memorandum of agreement with J.I.C. Clarke, 27 July 1896; letter from Clarke to Irving, 10 September 1897.

101 Clarke, *My Life and Memories*, p. 290.

102 Stephens, *Profession of the Playwright*, p. 71.

103 Memorandum of agreement with Arthur W. Pinero, 21 November 1879 and 31 July 1880; memorandum of agreement with Egerton Castle and Walter Herries Pollock, 24 May 1893; memorandum of agreement with Laurence Irving, 21 July 1894, Irving deed box.

104 Letter from Mrs Bayle-Bernard to Irving, 14 March 1901; letter from Irving to Mrs Bayle-Bernard, 6 April 1901; letter from Mrs Bayle-Bernard to Irving, 8 April 1901, Irving deed box.

105 Memorandum of agreement with James Mortimer, 10 July 1895; letter from Mortimer to Irving, 8 July 1895, Irving deed box.

106 Letter from Moore to Stoker, 17 February 1881; receipt from Moore to Irving, 19 February 1881, Irving deed box.

107 Letters from Stoker to Burnand and Williams, 23 March 1885; from Irving to Burnand, 14 April 1888, Irving deed box.

108 Stephens, *The Profession of the Playwright*, pp. 72–73.

109 Letters from Stoker to Alfred Calmour, 18 May, 1888; Calmour to Irving, 19 May 1888; Stoker to Calmour, 18 June 1888, Irving deed box.

110 Letters from Wills to Irving, 16 August 1883; Stoker to Wills, 17 August 1883, Irving deed box.

111 Memorandum of agreement with Freeman Wills regarding *Charles the First*, 24 April 1893; regarding *Olivia*, 24 April 1893, £100 for each play, Irving deed box.

112 Letter from Freeman Wills to Stoker, 25 January 1905.

Notes to Chapter 7: Ruskin and Ruskinism

1 E.T. Cook and Alexander Wedderburn, eds, *The Complete Works of John Ruskin* (London: George Allen, 1904), v, pp. 56–59.

2 Jeffrey Richards, ed., *Sir Henry Irving, Theatre, Culture and Society: Essays, Addresses and Lectures* (Keele: Keele University Press, 1994), pp. 81, 179, 101.

3 *Catalogue of a Portion of the Dramatic Library of a Gentleman, to be Sold at Auction by Messrs Christie, Manson and Woods, 21 February 1899*, p. 21.

4 *Catalogue of the valuable library of Sir Henry Irving, Deceased, which will be Sold at Auction by Messrs Christie, Manson and Woods, 18 October 1905*, p. 22.

5 Cook and Wedderburn, *Complete Works of Ruskin*, xxxiii, p. xxx.

6 *Theatre*, new series, 1 (2 April 1883), p. 216.

7 Cook and Wedderburn, *Complete Works of Ruskin*, xxvi, p. 328; Joan Evans and John Howard Whitehouse, eds, *The Diaries of John Ruskin*, iii, (Oxford: Clarendon Press, 1959), p. 841 (16 April 1875), p. 841 (22 April 1875), p. 781 (29 March 1874).

8 Evans and Whitehouse, *Diaries of John Ruskin*, ii (Oxford: Clarendon Press, 1958), p. 566 (1 August 1862), p. 613 (22 March 1867), iii, p. 874 (30 November 1875).

9 Cook and Wedderburn, *Complete Works of Ruskin*, xxxvii, pp. 28–29.

10 Evans and Whitehouse, *Diaries of John Ruskin*, ii, p. 719. (26 January 1872).

11 Cook and Wedderburn, *Complete Works of Ruskin*, xxxiv, p. 549.

12 Cook and Wedderburn, *Complete Works of Ruskin*, xxx, p. 341.

13 Evans and Whitehouse, *Diaries of John Ruskin*, iii, p. 1044 (16 December 1882).

14 Evans and Whitehouse, *Diaries of John Ruskin*, iii, p. 963 (28 June 1877).

15 Elizabeth Marbury, *My Crystal Ball* (London: Hurst and Blackett, 1924), pp. 90–91.

16 Irving, *Theatre, Culture and Society*, p. 78.

17 Margaret Howell, *Byron Tonight* (Windlesham: Springwood Books, 1982), p. 81.

18 Martin Meisel, *Realizations* (Princeton: Princeton University Press, 1983), p. 404.

19 On the toga play genre see David Mayer, ed., *Playing Out the Empire* (Oxford: Clarendon Press, 1994). His book contains the full text of *Claudian*.

20 James Thomas, *The Art of the Actor-Manager: Wilson Barrett and the Victorian Theatre* (Ann Arbor, Michigan: UMI Research Press, 1984), p. 67.

21 Cook and Wedderburn, *Complete Works of Ruskin*, xxxiv, p. 667.

22 Madge Kendal, *Madge Kendal by Herself* (London: John Murray, 1933), p. 169.

23 Gail Marshall, *Actresses on the Victorian Stage: Feminine Performance and the Galatea Myth* (Cambridge: Cambridge University Press, 1998).

24 Mary Anderson, *A Few Memories* (New York: Harper and Brothers, 1896), p. 228.

25 M.H. Spielmann, *John Ruskin* (London: Cassell, 1900), p. 54.

26 J.L. Bradley and Ian Ousby, eds, *The Correspondence of John Ruskin and Charles Eliot Norton* (Cambridge: Cambridge University Press 1987), p. 472.

27 Hallam Tennyson, *Alfred, Lord Tennyson: A Memoir* (London: Macmillan, 1897), ii, p. 259.

28 Austin Brereton, *The Life of Henry Irving* (London: Longmans, Green and Co., 1908), i, pp. 326–27.

29 Bram Stoker, *Personal Reminiscences of Henry Irving* (London: Heinemann, 1907), p. 131.

30 Tennyson, *Alfred, Lord Tennyson*, ii, p. 258.

31 Cecil Y. Lang and Edgar F. Shannon Jr, eds, *The Letters of Alfred, Lord Tennyson* (Oxford: Clarendon Press, 1990), iii, pp. 199–205.

32 Lang and Shannon, *Letters of Tennyson*, iii, pp. 201–2.

33 Stoker, *Reminiscences of Irving*, p. 133.

34 Stoker, *Reminiscences of Irving*, pp. 133–34.

35 Tennyson, *Alfred, Lord Tennyson*, ii, p. 258; Ellen Terry, *The Story of My Life* (London: Hutchinson, 1908), p. 194.

36 Tennyson, *Alfred, Lord Tennyson*, ii, p. 258.

37 Lang and Shannon, *Letters of Tennyson*, iii, pp. 206–7.

38 Tennyson, *Alfred, Lord Tennyson*, ii, p. 258.

39 Terry, *Story of My Life*, pp. 198–99.

40 Stoker, *Reminiscences of Henry Irving*, pp. 133–34.

41 Terry, *Story of My Life*, p. 196.

42 Terry, *Story of My Life*, p. 198.

43 Brereton, *The Life of Henry Irving*, i, p. 327.

44 Clement Scott, *From 'The Bells' to 'King Arthur'* (London: John McQueen, 1897), pp. 201–2.

45 William Archer, *English Dramatists of To-Day* (London: Sampson, Low and Co., 1882), pp. 350–51.

46 Terry, *Story of My Life*, p. 198.

47 Undated clipping, Fitzgerald Collection, iv, p. 125.

48 Percy Fitzgerald, *Sir Henry Irving: A Biography* (London: T. Fisher Unwin, 1906), pp. 121–22.

49 Lang and Shannon, *Letters of Tennyson*, iii, pp. 361, 368, 372, 373.

50 Thomas, *The Art of the Actor-Manager*, p. 67.

51 On rational recreation see Hugh Cunningham, *Leisure in the Industrial Revolution* (London: Croom Helm, 1980) and Peter Bailey, *Leisure and Class in Victorian England* (London: Routledge, 1978).

52 Cook and Wedderburn, *Complete Works of John Ruskin*, xix, p. 221; xxxiv, pp. 247, 251.

53 E. Harcourt Burrage, *J. Passmore Edwards: Philanthropist* (London: Partridge, 1902).

54 Richards, *Sir Henry Irving: Theatre, Culture and Society*, p. 215.

55 Richards, *Sir Henry Irving: Theatre, Culture and Society*, p. 205.

56 Richards, *Sir Henry Irving: Theatre, Culture and Society*, p. 218.

57 Richards, *Sir Henry Irving: Theatre, Culture and Society*, p. 219.

58 Richards, *Sir Henry Irving: Theatre, Culture and Society*, pp. 206–12.

59 Richards, *Sir Henry Irving: Theatre, Culture and Society*, pp. 213–14.

60 Richards, *Sir Henry Irving: Theatre, Culture and Society*, p. 108.

Notes to Chapter 8: The Arts

1 Oscar Wilde, *The Works of Oscar Wilde* (London: Spring Books, 1965), p. 929.

2 Jeffrey Richards, ed., *Sir Henry Irving: Theatre, Culture and Society* (Keele: Keele University Press, 1994), p. 46.

3 Richards, *Sir Henry Irving: Theatre, Culture and Society*, pp. 43–44.

4 Martin Meisel, *Realizations* (Princeton: Princeton University Press, 1983), pp. 43–44.

5 Alfred Darbyshire, *The Art of The Victorian Stage* (Manchester: Sherratt and Hughes, 1907), pp. 1–2.

6 Darbyshire, *Art of the Victorian Stage*, p. 8.

7 Darbyshire, *Art of the Victorian Stage*, p. 1.

8 H.A. Saintsbury and Cecil Palmer, eds, *We Saw Him Act* (London: Hurst and Blackett, 1939), p. 395.

9 Charles Hiatt, *Henry Irving* (London: George Bell and Sons, 1899), p. 263.

10 Edward Gordon Craig, *Henry Irving* (London: J.M. Dent and Sons, 1930), pp. 127–34.

11 Craig, *Henry Irving*, p. 134. H. Chance Newton, *Cues and Curtain Calls* (London: John Lane, 1927), p. 4, lists the Dickens roles.

12 Wilde, *The Works of Oscar Wilde*, p. 905.

13 Susan Weber Soros, ed., *E.W. Godwin: Aesthetic Movement Architect and Designer* (New Haven: Yale University Press, 1999), p. 60.

14 Sir Herbert Beerbohm Tree, *Thoughts and After-Thoughts* (London: Cassell, 1915), p. 44.

15 On Godwin's career and influence, see Soros, ed., *E.W. Godwin* and John Stokes, *Resistible Theatres* (London: Paul Elek Books, 1972), pp. 33–68.

16 Tree, *Thoughts and After-Thoughts*, pp. 44–45.

17 Tree, *Thoughts and After-Thoughts*, p. 56.

18 Richards, *Sir Henry Irving: Theatre, Culture and Society*, p. 46.

19 Craig, *Henry Irving*, p. 115.

20 Bram Stoker, *Personal Reminiscences of Henry Irving* (London: Heinemann, 1907), p. 60.

21 Henry Herman, 'The Stage as a School of Art and Archaeology', *Magazine of Art*, 11 (1888) pp. 332–37.

22 Wilde, *The Works of Oscar Wilde*, p. 911.

23 J.B. Booth, *The Days We Knew* (London: T. Werner Laurie, 1943), p. 99.

24 For detailed accounts of Irving's rehearsals, see Ellen Terry, *The Story of My Life* (London: Hutchinson, 1908), pp. 168–71; Saintsbury and Palmer, *We Saw Him Act*, p. 262; G.B. Burgin, 'The Lyceum Rehearsals', *Idler*, 3 (1893), pp. 122–41.

25 Craig, *Henry Irving*, p. 114.

26 Terry, *Story of My Life*, p. 208.

27 George C. Odell, *Shakespeare from Betterton to Irving* (New York: Charles Scribner's Sons, 1920), ii, pp. 377–78. On the history and significance of the Saxe-Meiningen Company, see Max Grube, *The Story of the Meininger* (Coral Gables, Florida: University of Miami Press, 1963).

28 Austin Brereton, *The Life of Henry Irving* (London: Longmans, Green and Co., 1908), ii, p. 259.

29   On Irving's stage lighting, see Alan Hughes, 'Henry Irving's Artistic Use of Stage Lighting'. *Theatre Notebook*, 33 (1979), pp. 100–9 and Bram Stoker 'Irving and Stage Lighting', *Nineteenth Century*, 69 (May 1911), pp. 903–12. On theatre lighting in general, see Terence Rees, *Theatre Lighting in the Age of Gas* (London: Society for Theatre Research, 1978).

30   Stoker, 'Irving and Stage Lighting', p. 911.

31   Terry, *Story of My Life*, p. 173.

32   Saintsbury and Palmer, *We Saw Him Act*, pp. 262–63.

33   Saintsbury and Palmer, *We Saw Him Act*, p. 263.

34   Saintsbury and Palmer, *We Saw Him Act*, p. 398.

35   Hughes, 'Henry Irving's Artistic Use of Stage Lighting', pp. 106–7.

36   Edward R. Russell, 'Romeo and Juliet at the Lyceum', *Macmillan's Magazine*, 46 (1882), p. 326.

37   *Fortnightly Review*, 36 (September 1884), p. 406.

38   Saintsbury and Palmer, *We Saw Him Act*, pp. 397–8.

39   Seymour Lucas, 'The Art of Dressing an Historical Play', *Magazine of Art*, 17 (1894), pp. 276–81.

40   Fitzgerald Collection, x, p. 70.

41   Fitzgerald Collection, x, p. 65.

42   Fitzgerald Collection, x, p. 58.

43   Fitzgerald Collection, x, p. 63.

44   Herman, 'The Stage as a School of Art and Archaeology', p. 337.

45   On the history of scene-painting, see Sybil Rosenfeld, *A Short History of Scene Design in Great Britain* (Oxford: Basil Blackwell, 1973).

46   J.W. Cole, *The Life and Theatrical Times of Charles Kean FSA* (London: Richard Bentley, 1859), ii, p. 379.

47   Darbyshire, *The Art of the Victorian Stage*, p. 19.

48   W. Moelwyn Merchant, *Shakespeare and the Artist* (London: Oxford University Press, 1959), p. 117.

49   Darbyshire, *The Art of the Victorian Stage*, p. 101.

50   William Telbin, 'Art in the Theatre', *Magazine of Art*, 12 (1889), pp. 92–97, 195–201.

51   Stoker, *Personal Reminiscences of Henry Irving*, pp. 69–70.

52   Oscar Wilde, 'Shakespeare and Scenery', *Dramatic Review*, 14 March 1885; reprinted in John Wyse Jackson, ed., *Aristotle at Afternoon Tea: The Rare Oscar Wilde* (London: Fourth Estate, 1991), pp. 73–74.

53   Percy Fitzgerald, *Sir Henry Irving* (London: T. Fisher Unwin, 1906), pp. 80–81.

54   'Scene Painters and Scene Painting: A Talk with Mr Hawes Craven', *Sala's Journal* (4 March 1893), pp. 208–9. See also *The Compact Edition of the Dictionary of National Biography* (Oxford: Oxford University Press, 1995), ii, p. 2585.

55   Stoker, *Personal Reminiscences of Henry Irving*, p. 165.

56   Terry, *Story of My Life*, p. 172. Cf. Fitzgerald, *Sir Henry Irving*, p. 89.

57   Terry, *Story of My Life*, p. 69.

58   Stoker, *Personal Reminiscences of Henry Irving*, pp. 54–55.

59   Darbyshire, *Art of the Victorian Stage*, p. 101.

60   Fitzgerald, *Sir Henry Irving*, p. 103.

61 Terry, *Story of My Life*, p. 183.

62 Stoker, *Personal Reminiscences of Henry Irving*, p. 425.

63 Stoker, *Personal Reminiscences of Henry Irving*, p. 285–86.

64 Percy Cross Standing, *Sir Lawrence Alma-Tadema* (London: Cassell, 1905), p. 92.

65 Darbyshire, *Art of the Victorian Stage*, p. 105.

66 Vern Swanson, *Sir Lawrence Alma-Tadema* (London: Ash and Grant, 1977), p. 28.

67 Standing, *Sir Lawrence Alma-Tadema*, p. 97.

68 Richard Phené-Spiers, 'The Architecture of *Coriolanus* at the Lyceum Theatre', *Architectural Review*, 10 (1901), pp. 2–21. See also Sybil Rosenfeld, 'Alma-Tadema's Designs for Henry Irving's *Coriolanus*', *Deutsche Shakespeare Gesellschaft West Jahrbuch* (1974), pp. 84–95.

69 Fitzgerald Collection, xv, pp. 41–43, 54.

70 *Sketch*, 17 April 1901; Fitzgerald Collection, xv, p. 54.

71 *Daily News*, 16 April, 1901.

72 Richard Dickins, *Forty Years of Shakespeare on the English Stage* (privately printed, 1907), pp. 99–100.

73 Fitzgerald Collection, xv, p. 54.

74 Saintsbury and Palmer, *We Saw Him Act*, pp. 382–83.

75 Meisel, *Realizations*, pp. 417–32; Helen Borowitz, '*King Lear* in the Art of Ford Madox Brown', *Victorian Studies*, 21 (1978), pp. 309–34.

76 W. Graham Robertson, *Time Was* (London: Hamish Hamilton, 1931), pp. 168–69.

77 Stoker, *Personal Reminiscences of Henry Irving*, p. 289.

78 Georgiana Burne-Jones, *Memorials of Edward Burne-Jones* (London: Macmillan, 1912), ii, p. 248.

79 Stoker, *Personal Reminiscences of Henry Irving*, p. 289.

80 Burne-Jones, *Memorials of Edward Burne-Jones*, ii, p. 247.

81 Stoker, *Personal Reminiscences of Henry Irving*, p. 165.

82 Terry, *Story of My Life*, pp. 350–51; Eve Adam, ed., *Mrs J. Comyns Carr's Reminiscences* (London: Hutchinson, 1926), p. 206.

83 Adam, *Mrs Comyns Carr's Reminiscences*, pp. 207.

84 Adam, *Mrs Comyns Carr's Reminiscences*, pp. 206–7.

85 On the costumes, see Christine Poulson, 'Costume Designs by Burne-Jones for Irving's production of *King Arthur*', *Burlington Magazine*, 128 (1986), pp. 18–24.

86 Burne-Jones, *Memorials of Edward Burne-Jones*, ii, pp. 247–49.

87 Terry, *Story of My Life*, pp. 306–12; Burne-Jones, *Memorials of Edward Burne-Jones*, ii, p. 324.

88 Adam, *Mrs Comyns Carr's Reminiscences*, p. 208.

89 Fitzgerald Collection, xiv, p. 61.

90 Stoker, *Personal Reminiscences of Henry Irving*, pp. 294–95.

91 David Mayer, ed., *Henry Irving and The Bells* (Manchester: Manchester University Press, 1980), p. 109.

92 Stanley Sadie, ed., *The New Grove Dictionary of Music and Musicians* (London: Macmillan, 1980), ii, pp. 741–43.

93 Sadie, *The New Grove Dictionary of Music and Musicians*, iv, p. 444.

94 Fitzgerald, *Sir Henry Irving*, p. 91.

95 Cyril Ehrlich, *The Music Profession in Britain since the Eighteenth Century* (Oxford: Clarendon Press, 1985), p. 58.

96 Sir Alexander Mackenzie, *A Musician's Narrative* (London: Cassell, 1927), p. 176; *Musical Times*, 1 January, 1886.

97 Alan Hughes, 'The Lyceum Staff: A Victorian Theatrical Organization', *Theatre Notebook*, 28 (1974), pp. 13–14.

98 John Pick, *The West End: Mismanagement and Snobbery* (Eastbourne: John Offord Publications, 1983), p. 89.

99 Clement Scott, *From 'The Bells' to 'King Arthur'* (London: John MacQueen, 1897), p. 109.

100 Fitzgerald, *Sir Henry Irving*, p. 91.

101 Terry, *Story of My Life*, pp. 153–54.

102 Sadie, *The New Grove Dictionary of Music and Musicians*, iv, p. 444.

103 Terry, *Story of My Life*, p. 154.

104 Terry, *Story of My Life*, pp. 153–54.

105 Mackenzie, *A Musician's Narrative*, p. 175.

106 W.H. Reed, 'Looking Back: Many Years in the Orchestra', broadcast on 28 July 1939 on BBC Regional Programme. I owe this reference to Peter Horton.

107 Stoker, *Personal Reminiscences of Henry Irving*, p. 60.

108 Scott, *From 'The Bells' to 'King Arthur'*, p. 244.

109 Fitzgerald, *Sir Henry Irving*, p. 161.

110 Terry, *Story of My Life*, p. 210.

111 Herbert Sullivan and Newman Flower, *Sir Arthur Sullivan: His Life, Letters and Diaries* (London: Cassell, 1950), p. 158. On Sullivan's Shakespeare scores see Arthur Jacobs, 'Sullivan and Shakespeare', in Richard Foulkes, ed., *Shakespeare and the Victorian Stage* (Cambridge: Cambridge University Press, 1986), pp. 196–206.

112 Laurence Irving, *Henry Irving: The Actor and his World* (London: Faber, 1951), pp. 456–57.

113 Sullivan and Flower, *Sir Arthur Sullivan*, p. 182.

114 Stoker, *Personal Reminiscences of Henry Irving*, pp. 70–71; Terry, *Story of My Life*, p. 304.

115 A suite from the incidental music has now been recorded. Marco Polo, 8. 223635.

116 Sullivan and Flower, *Sir Arthur Sullivan*, p. 233.

117 Arthur Jacobs, *Arthur Sullivan: A Victorian Musician* (Aldershot: Scolar Press, 1992), p. 359.

118 Now recorded. Marco Polo 8. 223635.

119 Jacobs, *Arthur Sullivan*, p. 360.

120 Stoker, *Personal Reminiscences of Henry Irving*, p. 337.

121 Mackenzie, *A Musician's Narrative*, pp. 174–75.

122 Mackenzie, *A Musician's Narrative*, p. 175.

123 Mackenzie, *A Musician's Narrative*, p. 177.

124 Mackenzie, *A Musician's Narrative*, p. 178.

125 Mackenzie, *A Musician's Narrative*, p. 179.

126 Charles V. Stanford, *Pages from an Unwritten Diary* (London: Edward Arnold, 1914), p. 229.

127 Jeremy Dibble, *Charles Villiers Stanford: Man and Musician* (Oxford: Oxford University Press, 2002), pp. 76–77.

128 Stanford, *Pages from an Unwritten Diary*, pp. 230–31.

129 Dibble, *Charles Villiers Stanford*, p. 245.

130 Ivor Guest, *Ballet in Leicester Square* (London: Dance Books, 1992), p. 27.

131 Fitzgerald Collection, ix, p. 108.

132 Fitzgerald Collection, ix, p. 97.

133 William Herbert Scott, *Edward German* (London: Chappel and Co., 1932), pp. 54–59.

134 Fitzgerald Collection, x, pp. 57, 73.

135 Fitzgerald Collection, x, p. 58.

136 Sadie, *The New Grove Dictionary of Music and Musicians*, xx, p. 384.

137 Robert Hichens, *Yesterday* (London: Cassell, 1947), p. 118.

138 Maud Valérie White, *Friends and Memories* (London: Edward Arnold, 1914), p. 373.

139 Receipt from Sir Julius Benedict to Irving, 1 August 1882, H.B. Irving deed box.

140 Memorandum of agreement between Irving and Georges Jacobi, 3 October 1889, Irving deed box.

141 Letters from Hamilton Clarke to Irving, 2 July and 3 July 1885, Irving deed box.

142 Memorandum of Agreement between Irving and Clarke, 8 February 1892; letter from Clarke to Bram Stoker, 19 October, 1892, Irving deed box.

143 Memorandum of Agreement between Irving and Clarke, 8 October 1896. Irving deed box.

144 Memorandum of agreement between Irving and Mackenzie, 30 October 1890; Stanford, *Pages from an Unwritten Diary*, p. 230; Memorandum of Agreement between Irving and German, 11 January 1893, Irving deed box.

145 Memorandum of Agreement between Irving and Sullivan, 15 May 1889, Irving deed box.

146 For a full account of the evolution of the Singla score see David Mayer, *Henry Irving and The Bells*, pp. 108–31.

147 Elizabeth Marbury, *My Crystal Ball* (London: Hurst and Blackett, 1924), p. 101.

148 Stoker, *Personal Reminiscences of Henry Irving*, p. 331.

Notes to Chapter 9: Celebrity Culture

1 Daniel Boorstin, *The Image* (Harmondsworth: Penguin, 1963), p. 67.

2 Boorstin, *The Image*, p. 66.

3 Boorstin, *The Image*, p. 55.

4 Boorstin, *The Image*, p. 58.

5 Boorstin, *The Image*, pp. 70–71.

6 Leo Braudy, *The Frenzy of Renown* (New York: Oxford University Press, 1986), p. 6.

7 Richard Schickel, *Intimate Strangers: The Culture of Celebrity* (New York: Doubleday, 1985), p. viii.

8 Jib Fowles, *Starstruck* (Washington, DC: The Smithsonian Institute, 1985), p. 28.

9 Chris Rojek, *Celebrity* (London: Reaktion Books, 2001), p. 57.

10 Braudy, *The Frenzy of Renown*, p. 585.

11 Thomas Carlyle, *On Heroes, Hero Worship and the Heroic in History* (London: Henry Frowde, 1904), pp. 1–2.

12 Ralph Waldo Emerson, *Representative Men* (London: Henry Frowde, 1903).

13 Andrew Tudor, *Image and Influence* (London: George Allen and Unwin, 1975), p. 76.

14 Lisa D. Lewis, ed., *The Adoring Audience: Fan Culture and Popular Media* (London: Routledge, 1992), p. 13.

15 Joseph Hatton, *Journalistic London* (London: Sampson Low, 1882), p. 85.

16 Edmund Yates, *Recollections and Experiences* (London: Richard Bentley and Son, 1885), p. 447.

17 Yates, *Recollections*, p. 455.

18 Yates, *Recollections*, p. 463.

19 Yates, *Recollections*, p. 464.

20 Hatton, *Journalistic London*, p. 96.

21 Samuel Smiles, *Self-Help* (London: John Murray, 1911), pp. vii–viii.

22 Smiles, *Self-Help*, p. 449–50.

23 Smiles, *Self-Help*, p. 470.

24 Smiles, *Self-Help*, pp. 6–7.

25 Leslie A. Marchand, *Byron: A Portrait* (London: John Murray, 1971), p. 121. It was Peter Quennell who dubbed Byron 'the showman of the Romantic movement', *Byron: The Years of Fame* (London: Collins, 1950), p. 77.

26 Justin McCarthy, *Portraits of the Sixties* (London: T. Fisher Unwin, 1903), pp. 56, 58.

27 Charles Tennyson, *Alfred Tennyson* (London: Macmillan, 1950), pp. 339–40.

28 Robert Bernard Martin, *Tennyson: The Unquiet Heart* (Oxford: Faber and Faber and Oxford University Press, 1983), p. 565.

29 Martin, *Tennyson*, p. 467.

30 Schickel, *Intimate Strangers*, p. 259.

31 George and Weedon Grossmith, *The Diary of a Nobody* (Harmondsworth: Penguin, 1965), pp. 119–20. Weedon Grossmith had of course acted with Irving in *Robert Macaire*.

32 William Archer, *Henry Irving: Actor and Manager. A Critical Study* (London: Field and Tuer, 1883), pp. 41–43.

33 *Times*, 30 September 1872.

34 Joseph Knight, *Theatrical Notes* (London: Lawrence and Bullen, 1893), p. 165.

35 Percy Fitzgerald, *Sir Henry Irving: A Biography* (London: T. Fisher Unwin, 1906), p. 291.

36 Frank Harris, *My Life and Loves* (London: W.H. Allen, 1964), p. 375.

37 A unidentified newspaper clipping in the Fitzgerald Collection, iv, p. 209. Since it is surrounded by reviews of *The Corsican Brothers*, it can be assumed to date from 1880.

38 W.P. Frith, *My Autobiography and Reminiscences* (New York: Harper and Brothers, 1888), ii, p. 212.

39 Undated clipping in the Fitzgerald Collection, iv, p. 175.

40 Percy V. Bradshaw, *'Brother Savages and Guests': A History of the Savage Club, 1857–1957* (London: W.H.Allen, 1958), p. 27.

41 George Rowell, *William Terriss and Richard Prince: Two Players in an Adelphi Melodrama* (London: The Society for Theatre Research, 1987).

42 H.A. Saintsbury and Cecil Palmer, eds, *We Saw Him Act* (London: Hurst and Blackett, 1939), p. 195.

43 Frith, *My Autobiography and Reminiscences*, i, pp. 441–42.

44 The Marquess of Zetland ed., *Letters of Disraeli to Lady Bradford and Lady Chesterfield* (London: Ernest Benn, 1929), ii, p. 300.

45   W. Graham Robertson, *Time Was* (London: Hamish Hamilton, 1931), p. 286.

46   Bram Stoker, *Personal Reminiscences of Henry Irving* (London: Heinemann, 1906), i, pp. 315–26.

47   Laurence Irving, *Henry Irving: The Actor and his World* (London: Faber, 1951), p. 220.

48   Laurence Irving, *Henry Irving*, pp. 270–71; George R. Sims, *My Life* (London: Eveleigh Nash, 1917), pp. 14–15.

49   Harry Furniss, *Some Victorian Women: Good, Bad and Indifferent* (London: John Lane, 1923), pp. 73–74.

50   Fitzgerald, Collection, v, p. 338.

51   Percy Fitzgerald, *The World Behind the Scenes* (London: Chatto and Windus, 1881), p. 147.

52   *The Hornet*, 3 March 1875.

53   There is a detailed account of the dinner plus speeches and guest list in Austin Brereton, *Henry Irving: A Biographical Sketch* (London: David Bogue, 1883), appendix, pp. 98–112.

54   Kristan Tetens, 'A Grand Informal Durbar': Henry Irving and the Coronation of Edward VII', *Journal of Victorian Culture*, 8 (Autumn 2003), pp. 257–91.

Notes to Chapter 10: Critics and the Press

1   On the growth, nature and influence of the Victorian press, see Alan J. Lee, *The Origins of the Popular Press, 1855–1914* (London: Croom Helm, 1976); Lucy Brown, *Victorian News and Newspapers* (Oxford: Clarendon Press, 1985); Aled Jones, *Powers of the Press* (Aldershot: Scolar Press, 1996); George Boyce, James Curran and Pauline Wingate, eds, *Newspaper History: From the Seventeenth Century to the Present Day* (London: Constable, 1978).

2   J. Don Vann and Rosemary T. Van Arsdel, *Victorian Periodicals and Victorian Society* (Toronto: University of Toronto Press, 1995), p. 7.

3   *Theatre*, new series, 5 (2 February 1885), pp. 92–93.

4   See, for example, Mrs Margaret Clement Scott, *Old Days in Bohemian London* (New York: Frederick A. Stokes, 1919); Joseph Comyns Carr, *Coasting Bohemia* (London: Macmillan, 1914); William Mackay, *Bohemian Days in Fleet Street by a Journalist* (London: John Long, 1913). For a good modern account of this world, see Nigel Cross, *The Common Writer: Life in nineteenth-century Grub Street* (Cambridge: Cambridge University Press, 1985).

5   Sir Frank Burnand, *Records and Reminiscences* (London: Methuen, 1904), ii, p. 41.

6   Edmund Yates, *Recollections and Experiences* (London: Richard Bentley, 1885), pp. 205–6.

7   Yates, *Recollections and Experiences*, p. 212.

8   Yates, *Recollections and Experiences*, p. 206.

9   Burnand, *Records and Reminiscences*, ii, p. 231.

10   J.B. Booth, *Palmy Days* (London: Richards Press, 1957), p. 74.

11   J.H. Barnes, *Forty Years on the Stage* (London: Chapman and Hall, 1914), pp. 274–75.

12   Yates, *Recollections and Experiences*, pp. 211–12.

13   *Compact Edition of the Dictionary of National Biography* (Oxford: Oxford University Press, 1975), ii, p. 1569.

14   Laurence Irving, *Henry Irving: The Actor and his World* (London: Faber, 1951), p. 324.

15 Austin Brereton, *The Life of Henry Irving* (London: Longmans, Green and Co., 1908), ii, p. 324.

16 Guy Boas, *The Garrick Club, 1831–1947* (London: The Garrick Club, 1948), p. 16.

17 *Irvingite*, 25 (October 2003), p. 1.

18 Michael Sanderson, *From Irving to Olivier: A Social History of the Acting Profession, 1880–1983* (London: the Athlone Press, 1985), p. 137.

19 Joseph Hatton, *Clubland* (London: Virtue and Co., 1890), p. iii.

20 Percy Fitzgerald, *The Garrick Club* (London: Elliot Stock, 1904), pp. 231–32.

21 Percy Fitzgerald, *Sir Henry Irving* (London: T. Fisher Unwin, 1906), p. 293.

22 W.L. Courtney, *The Passing Hour* (London: Hutchinson, 1925), pp. 200, 204.

23 Barnes, *Forty Years on the Stage*, pp. 62–63.

24 Fred Kerr, *Recollections of a Defective Memory* (London: Thornton Butterworth, 1930), pp. 226–28; Eve Adam, ed., *Mrs J. Comyns Carr's Reminiscences* (London: Hutchinson, 1926), p. 119.

25 Andrew Prescott, 'Brother Irving: Sir Henry Irving and Freemasonry', *First Knight*, 7 (December 2003), pp. 13–22.

26 Fitzgerald Collection, xiv, p. 60.

27 George Rowell, *Victorian Dramatic Criticism* (London: Methuen, 1971), p. xvi.

28 Marie and Squire Bancroft, *Recollections of Sixty Years* (London: Thomas Nelson and Sons, 1911), p. 233.

29 *Theatre*, new series, 2 (1 October 1883), pp. 213–14.

30 Courtney, *The Passing Hour*, pp. 181–83.

31 *Compact Edition of the Dictionary of National Biography*, ii, p. 2877.

32 L. Arthur Greening, 'Clement Scott: An Appreciation', pp. 21–23, foreword to Clement Scott, *Some Notable Hamlets of the Present Time* (London: Greening and Co., 1900).

33 Margaret Clement Scott, *Old Days in Bohemian London*, p. 185.

34 *Compact Edition of the Dictionary of National Biography*, p. 2877.

35 Max Beerbohm, *Last Theatres, 1904–1910* (London: Rupert Hart-Davis, 1970), p. 80.

36 James Agate, *Those Were the Nights* (London: Hutchinson, 1946), p. 24.

37 *Star*, 29 March 1890, quoted in Agate, *Those Were The Nights*, pp. 32–33.

38 George Bernard Shaw, *Dramatic Opinions and Essays* (New York: Brentano's 1928), i, pp. 442–49.

39 J.T. Grein, *Dramatic Criticism* (London: John Long, 1899), i, pp. 170–72.

40 Courtney, *The Passing Hour*, pp. 213–20.

41 Shaw, *Dramatic Opinions and Essays*, i, p. 443.

42 *Compact Edition of the Dictionary of National Biography*, ii, p. 2485.

43 On Archer's career and influence see Lieutenant-Colonel Charles Archer, *William Archer: His Life, Work and Friendships* (London: Allen and Unwin, 1931), and Peter Whitebrook, *William Archer* (London: Methuen, 1993).

44 On Shaw, see Michael Holroyd, *Bernard Shaw*, i (London: Penguin, 1990), and ii (1991).

45 On Grein, see Michael Orme, *J.T. Grein* (London: John Murray, 1936), and N. Schoonderwoerd, *J.T. Grein, Ambassador of the Theatre, 1862–1935* (Assen: Van Gorcum and Co., 1963).

46 *Compact Edition of the Dictionary of National Biography*, ii, p. 2945.

47 On the reception of *Ghosts*, see Orme, *J.T. Grein*, pp. 86–89.

48 Jeffrey Richards, ed., *Sir Henry Irving: Theatre, Culture and Society* (Keele: Keele University Press, 1994), p. 130.

49 Richards, *Sir Henry Irving: Theatre, Culture and Society*, p. 134. The complete speeches are reprinted on pp. 129–35.

50 William Archer, *English Dramatists of To-Day* (London: Sampson Low, Marston, Searle and Rivington, 1882), pp. 12–13.

51 William Archer, *About the Theatre* (London: T. Fisher Unwin, 1886), pp. 172–202.

52 Grein, *Dramatic Criticism*, i, pp. 192–201.

53 Irving, *Henry Irving*, pp. 350–51.

54 Irving, *Henry Irving*, p. 351.

55 Alfred Watson, *A Sporting and Dramatic Career* (London: Macmillan, 1918), p. 62.

56 Watson, *A Sporting and Dramatic Career*, p. 70.

57 Watson, *A Sporting and Dramatic Career*, p. 70.

58 Watson, *A Sporting and Dramatic Career*, pp. 70–71.

59 Irving, *Henry Irving*, pp. 349–50.

60 L.F. Austin, *Points of View* (London: Bodley Head, 1906), introduction by Clarence Rook, pp. v–x.

61 Joseph Hatton, *Cigarette Papers* (London: Anthony Treherne, 1902), advertisement in endpapers for *By Order of the Czar*.

62 Bram Stoker, *Personal Reminiscences of Henry Irving* (London: Heinemann, 1907), p. 196.

63 J.B. Booth, *The Days We Knew* (London: T. Werner Laurie, 1945), p. 102.

64 Mowbray Morris, *Essays in Theatrical Criticism* (London: Remington and Co., 1882), pp. 6, 8.

65 Booth, *The Days We Knew*, pp. 102–3.

66 Stephen Coleridge, *Memories* (London: John Lane, 1913), pp. 147–49.

67 Henry James, *The Scenic Art*, ed., Allan Wade (London: Rupert Hart-Davis, 1949), pp. 102–3.

68 James, *The Scenic Art*, p. 104.

69 James, *The Scenic Art*, p. 139.

70 James, *The Scenic Art*, pp. 164–220.

71 Frank Archer, *An Actor's Notebooks* (London: Stanley Paul, n.d.), p. 291.

72 Archer, *William Archer*, pp. 68–69.

73 Anonymous (William Archer, R.W. Lowe and George Halkett), *The Fashionable Tragedian* (Edinburgh: Thomas Gray, 1877), p. 1.

74 Anonymous, *The Fashionable Tragedian*, pp. 6–7.

75 Anonymous, *The Fashionable Tragedian*, pp. 9, 10, 11.

76 Anonymous, *The Fashionable Tragedian*, pp. 19–20.

77 Anonymous, *The Fashionable Tragedian*, pp. 23–24.

78 Irving, *Henry Irving*, p. 290.

79 'Yorick', *Letter Concerning Mr Henry Irving* (Edinburgh: Edinburgh Publishing Company; London: Simpkin, Marshall and Co. and Glasgow: John Menzies and Co., 1877), pp. 6–7.

80 'Yorick', *Letter Concerning Mr Henry Irving*, pp. 8, 9, 10.

81 'Yorick', *Letter Concerning Mr Henry Irving*, p. 17

82   'Yorick', *Letter Concerning Mr Henry Irving*, p. 18.

83   William Archer, *Henry Irving: Actor and Manager* (Field and Tuer, 1883), p. 26.

84   Archer, *Henry Irving*, pp. 28–31.

85   Archer, *Henry Irving*, pp. 32–35.

86   Archer, *Henry Irving*, pp. 35–36.

87   Archer, *Henry Irving*, p. 40.

88   Archer, *Henry Irving*, pp. 47–48.

89   Archer, *Henry Irving*, pp. 51–52.

90   Archer, *Henry Irving*, pp. 77–78.

91   Archer, *Henry Irving*, pp. 81, 82.

92   Archer, *Henry Irving*, pp. 88–89.

93   Archer, *Henry Irving*, pp. 96–97.

94   'An Irvingite: (Frank Marshall), *Henry Irving: Actor and Manager. A Criticism of a Critic's Criticism* (London: Routledge, 1883), p. 14.

95   'An Irvingite', *Henry Irving*, pp. 24–25.

96   'An Irvingite', *Henry Irving*, pp. 34–35.

97   Christopher St John, ed., *Ellen Terry and Bernard Shaw: A Correspondence* (London: Reinhardt and Evans, 1949), pp. xxiv–xxv.

98   St John, *Ellen Terry and Bernard Shaw*, pp. xxv–xxvi.

99   St John, *Ellen Terry and Bernard Shaw*, pp. xxvi–xxx.

100 St John, *Ellen Terry and Bernard Shaw*, pp. 16, 38; Bernard Shaw, *Our Theatres in the Nineties* (London: Constable, 1948), ii, p. 268.

101 St John, *Ellen Terry and Bernard Shaw*, p. 23.

102 St John, *Ellen Terry and Bernard Shaw*, p. 32.

103 Holroyd, *Bernard Shaw*, i, p. 348.

104 St John, *Ellen Terry and Bernard Shaw*, p. 52.

105 Shaw, *Our Theatres in the Nineties*, i, p. 17.

106 Shaw, *Our Theatres in the Nineties*, i, p. 115.

107 Shaw, *Our Theatres in the Nineties*, ii, pp. 195–202.

108 St John, *Ellen Terry and Bernard Shaw*, p. 19–20.

109 St John, *Ellen Terry and Bernard Shaw*, p. 71.

110 Shaw, *Our Theatres in the Nineties*, ii, pp. 285–92.

111 *London Playgoer*, 4 (June 1890), pp. 57–91.

112 *To-morrow*, 2 (1896), pp. 292–94.

113 Grein, *Dramatic Criticism*, i, p. 185.

114 Grein, *Dramatic Criticism*, i, pp. 278, 282.

115 Grein, *Dramatic Criticism*, i, pp. 260–63.

116 Edward Gordon Craig, *Henry Irving* (London: J.M. Dent and Sons, 1930), p. 63.

117 Ellen Terry, *The Story of My Life* (London: Hutchinson, 1908), p. 155.

118 Michael Kilgarriff, 'Henry Irving and the Phonograph: The Bennett Maxwell Lecture', *First Knight*, 3, no. 1 (June 1999), pp. 26–29.

119 Jones, *The Shadow of Henry Irving*, pp. 91–92.

120 Lena Ashwell, *Myself a Player* (London: Michael Joseph, 1936), p. 72.

121 Craig, *Henry Irving*, p. 63.

122 Scott Colley, *Richard's Himself Again: A Stage History of Richard III* (New York: Greenwood Press, 1992), p. 11.

Notes to Chapter 11: English History

1 Raphael Samuel, *Theatres of Memory* (London: Verso, 1994), p. 8.
2 Thomas Carlyle, *On Heroes, Hero-Worship and the Heroic in History* (London: Chapman and Hall, 1905), p. 41.
3 Carlyle, *On Heroes*, pp. 1–2.
4 Stephen Bann, *Romanticism and the Rise of History* (New York: Twayne, 1995), pp. 6–7.
5 Philippa Levine, *The Amateur and the Professional: Antiquarians, Historians and Archaeologists in Victorian England, 1838–1886* (Cambridge: Cambridge University Press, 1986), p. 70.
6 Thomas Babington Macaulay, *Critical and Historical Essays* (London: Methuen, 1903), i, pp. 115–16.
7 Roy Strong, *And When Did You Last See Your Father?* (London: Thames and Hudson, 1978), p. 11.
8 Strong, *And When Did You Last See Your Father?*, pp. 16–17.
9 Richard Schoch, *Shakespeare's Victorian Stage: Performing History in the Theatre of Charles Kean* (Cambridge: Cambridge University Press, 1998), p. 2.
10 Samuel Smiles, *Self-Help* (London: John Murray, 1911), p. 450.
11 Freeman Wills, *W.G. Wills: Dramatist and Painter* (London: Longmans, Green and Co., 1898), p. 118.
12 J.H. Barnes, *Forty Years on the Stage* (London: Chapman and Hall, 1914), p. 111.
13 Reviews cited in Austin Brereton, *The Life of Henry Irving* (London: Longmans, Green and Co., 1908), i, pp. 135–36.
14 *Theatre*, 1 (April 1880), pp. 199–202.
15 Dutton Cook, *Nights at the Play* (London: Chatto and Windus, 1883), pp. 157–58.
16 Brereton, *Life of Henry Irving*, i, p. 133.
17 Charles Hiatt, *Henry Irving* (London: George Bell and Sons, 1899), p. 108; Haldane MacFall, *Henry Irving* (Edinburgh: T.N. Foulis, 1906), p. 123.
18 Timothy Lang, *The Victorians and the Stuart Heritage* (Cambridge: Cambridge University Press, 1995), p. xi.
19 A. Dwight Culler, *The Victorian Mirror of History* (New Haven and London: Yale University Press), p. 37.
20 On Cromwell's image and reputation see Peter Karsten, *Patriot Heroes in England and America* (Madison: University of Wisconsin Press, 1978), pp. 139–63; Blair Worden, *Roundhead Reputations* (London: Allen Lane, 2001), pp. 215–315; R.C. Richardson, ed., *Images of Oliver Cromwell* (Manchester: Manchester University Press, 1993).
21 Karsten, *Patriot Heroes*, p. 118.
22 Worden, *Roundhead Reputations*, p. 254.
23 Worden, *Roundheads Reputations*, pp. 296–315.
24 Alfred Bate Richards, *Oliver Cromwell* (London: Effingham Wilson, 1873), pp. 5–6.

25 Richards, *Oliver Cromwell*, pp. iii–iv.

26 Cook, *Nights at the Play*, pp. 168–69.

27 Brereton, *The Life of Henry Irving*, i, pp. 136–37.

28 Wills, *W.G. Wills*, p. 118.

29 W.G. Wills, *Charles the First* (Edinburgh and London: Blackwood, 1873), pp. vii–x.

30 Richard Williams, *The Contentious Crown* (Aldershot: Ashgate, 1997).

31 Simon Schama, 'The Domestication of Majesty: Royal Family Portraiture, 1500–1850', *Journal of Interdisciplinary History*, 17 (Summer 1986), pp. 155–83.

32 Strong, *And When Did You Last See Your Father?*, p. 137.

33 Strong, *And When Did You Last See Your Father?*, p. 141.

34 *Times*, 30 September 1872.

35 On the place of *Charles the First* in the literary and pictorial tradition, see Martin Meisel, *Realizations* (Princeton: Princeton University Press, 1983), pp. 239–44.

36 Valerie Chancellor, *History for Their Masters* (Bath: Adams and Dart, 1970), p. 50.

37 Chancellor, *History for Their Masters*, pp. 52–53.

38 T.F. Tout, *A History of Great Britain from the Earliest Times to the Death of Queen Victoria* (London: Longman), pp. 261, 277, 283.

39 Stephen Watt, 'Historical Drama and the "Legitimate" Theatre: Tom Taylor and W.G. Wills in the 1870s', in Judith Fisher and Stephen Watt, eds, *When They Weren't Doing Shakespeare* (Athens: University of Georgia Press, 1989), pp. 187–211.

40 Matthew H. Wikander, *The Play of Truth and State: Historical Drama from Shakespeare to Brecht* (Baltimore: Johns Hopkins University Press, 1986), p. 4.

41 Wikander, *The Play of Truth and State*, p. 133.

42 Watt, 'Historical Drama and the "Legitimate" Theatre', p. 200.

43 Hallam Tennyson, *Alfred, Lord Tennyson* (London: Macmillan, 1897), ii, p. 173.

44 Valerie Pitt, *Tennyson Laureate* (London: Barrie and Rockliff, 1962), p. 221.

45 Phyllis Grosskurth, 'Tennyson, Froude and Queen Mary', *Tennyson Research Bulletin*, 2 (November 1973), p. 45.

46 Tennyson, *Alfred, Lord Tennyson*, ii, p. 178.

47 Cecil Y. Lang and Edgar F. Shannon Jr. eds, *The Letters of Alfred, Lord Tennyson* (Oxford: Clarendon Press, 1990), iii, p. 105.

48 Henry James, *Views and Reviews* (Boston: Ball Publishing, 1908), p. 183.

49 Lang and Shannon, *Letters of Tennyson*, iii, pp. 107, 111.

50 Laurence Irving, *Henry Irving: The Actor and His World* (London: Faber, 1951), pp. 266–67.

51 Lang and Shannon, *Letters of Tennyson*, iii, p. 119.

52 Grosskurth, 'Tennyson, Froude and Queen Mary', p. 52.

53 Lang and Shannon, *Letters of Tennyson*, iii, p. 95.

54 H.A. Saintsbury and Cecil Palmer, eds, *We Saw Him Act* (London: Hurst and Blackett, 1939), p. 103.

55 Percy Fitzgerald, *Sir Henry Irving* (London: T. Fisher Unwin, 1906), p. 67.

56 Saintsbury and Palmer, *We Saw Him Act*, p. 103.

57 Irving, *Henry Irving*, p. 273.

58 Ellen Terry, *The Story of My Life* (London: Hutchinson, 1908), pp. 122–23.

59 Irving, *Henry Irving*, p. 274.

60 Joseph Knight, *Theatrical Notes* (London: Lawrence and Bullen, 1893), pp. 115–16.

61 Clement Scott, *From 'The Bells' to 'King Arthur'* (London: John McQueen, 1897), p. 91.

62 Defenders of the play include Peter Thomson, 'Tennyson's Plays and Their Production', in D.J. Palmer, ed., *Writers and Their Background: Tennyson* (London: G. Bell and Sons, 1973), pp. 226–54; and Dennis M. Organ, *Tennyson's Dramas: A Critical Study* (Lubbock, Texas: Texas Tech Press, 1979).

63 Tennyson, *Alfred, Lord Tennyson*, ii, p. 184.

64 Scott, *From 'The Bells' to 'King Arthur'*, pp. 91–95.

65 Cook, *Nights at the Play*, pp. 310–13.

66 John Russell Stephens, *The Censorship of English Drama, 1824–1901* (Cambridge: Cambridge University Press, 1980), pp. 92–114.

67 Bram Stoker, *Personal Reminiscences of Henry Irving* (London: Heinemann, 1907), p. 137.

68 Thomson, 'Tennyson's Plays and their Production', p. 244; Laurence Irving, *Henry Irving*, p. 534.

69 Stoker, *Reminiscences of Irving*, p. 144.

70 It is printed in Tennyson, *Alfred, Lord Tennyson*, ii, p. 197.

71 Stoker, *Reminiscences of Irving*, p. 150.

72 Stoker, *Reminiscences of Irving*, p. 156.

73 Stoker, *Reminiscences of Irving*, p. 157.

74 Tennyson, *Alfred, Lord Tennyson*, ii, p. 195.

75 Geneviève Ward and Richard Whiteing, *Both Sides of the Curtain* (London: Cassell, 1981), p. 135.

76 Ward and Whiteing, *Both Sides of the Curtain*, pp. 134–36.

77 Ward and Whiteing, *Both Sides of the Curtain*, p. 136.

78 Ward and Whiteing, *Both Sides of the Curtain*, pp. 136–37.

79 Ward and Whiteing, *Both Sides of the Curtain*, pp. 137–38.

80 Clare A. Simmons, *Reversing the Conquest: History and Myth in Nineteenth-Century British Literature* (New Brunswick: Rutgers University Press, 1990).

81 Simmons, *Reversing the Conquest*, p. 136.

82 Tennyson, *Alfred, Lord Tennyson*, ii, p. 193.

83 Tennyson, *Alfred, Lord Tennyson*, ii, p. 195.

84 Tennyson, *Alfred, Lord Tennyson*, ii, p. 196

85 Hiatt, *Henry Irving*, pp. 240, 243.

86 Fitzgerald Collection, xii, p. 173.

87 Fitzgerald, *Sir Henry Irving*, p. 228.

88 Scott, *From 'The Bells' to 'King Arthur'*, pp. 355–58.

89 Fitzgerald Colletion, x, p. 129.

90 Fitzgerald Collection, x, p. 154.

91 Irving, *Henry Irving*, pp. 559–60.

Notes to Chapter 12: Foreign History

1   Bram Stoker, *Personal Reminiscences of Henry Irving* (London: Heinemann, 1907), p. 169.
2   Clement Scott, *From 'The Bells' to 'King Arthur'* (London: John MacQueen, 1897), pp. 124, 127, 129.
3   Charles H. Shattuck, ed., *Bulwer and Macready* (Urbana: University of Illinois Press, 1958).
4   H. Chance Newton, *Cues and Curtain Calls* (London: John Lane, 1927), p. 13.
5   Lord Lytton, *The Dramatic Works* (Freeport, New York: Books for Libraries Press, 1972), pp. 180–82.
6   George Arliss, *George Arliss by Himself* (London: John Murray, 1940), p. 204.
7   Dutton Cook, *Nights at the Play* (London: Chatto and Windus, 1883), pp. 209–12.
8   Cook, *Nights at the Play*, pp. 426–29.
9   Austin Brereton, *The Life of Henry Irving* (London: Longmans, Green and Co., 1908), i, p. 157.
10 Scott, *From 'The Bells' to 'King Arthur'*, pp. 37–43.
11 Fitzgerald Collection, xxii, p. 45.
12 Fitzgerald Collection, xxii, p. 41.
13 J.T. Grein, *Dramatic Criticism* (London: John Long, 1899), i, pp. 22–23.
14 Fitzgerald Collection, xxii, p. 41.
15 Fitzgerald Collection, xxii, p. 48.
16 Stoker, *Personal Reminiscences of Irving*, p. 174.
17 David Lodge, 'The French Revolution and the Condition of England: Crowds and Power in the Early Victorian Novel', in Ceri Crossley and Ian Small, eds, *The French Revolution and British Culture* (Oxford: Oxford University Press, 1989), pp. 123–40.
18 Lodge, 'The French Revolution and the Condition of England', p. 139.
19 Hedva Ben-Israel, *English Historians on the French Revolution* (Cambridge: Cambridge University Press, 1968), p. 278.
20 Kate Newey, 'The Drama of History: The French Revolution and the English Stage', unpublished conference paper, p. 7.
21 Thomas Carlyle, *On Heroes, Hero-Worship and the Heroic in History* (London: Chapman and Hall, 1905), p. 197.
22 Lytton, *Dramatic Works*, p. 105.
23 J.C. Trewin, *Mr Macready* (London: Harrap, 1955), p. 142.
24 Stoker, *Personal Reminiscences of Irving*, p. 241.
25 Brereton, *Life of Henry Irving*, i, p. 283.
26 Charles Hiatt, *Henry Irving* (London: George Bell and Son, 1899), p. 168.
27 Frederic Daly, *Henry Irving in England and America, 1838–84* (London: T. Fisher Unwin, 1884), p. 58.
28 Scott, *From 'The Bells' to 'King Arthur'*, pp. 148–9.
29 Percy Fitzgerald, *Sir Henry Irving* (London: T. Fisher Unwin, 1906), pp. 97, 99.
30 H.A. Saintsbury and Cecil Palmer, eds, *We Saw Him Act* (London: Hurst and Blackett, 1939), pp. 153, 155.
31 Scott, *From 'The Bells' to 'King Arthur'*, p. 146.
32 Saintsbury and Palmer, *We Saw Him Act*, p. 155; Stoker, *Personal Reminiscences of Irving*,

pp. 101–2; Laurence Irving, *Henry Irving: The Actor and his World* (London: Faber, 1951), p. 324.

33 Margaret Webster, *The Same, Only Different* (London: Victor Gollancz, 1969), pp. 79–80.

34 Webster, *The Same, Only Different*, p. 79.

35 Peter Ackroyd, *Dickens* (London: Sinclair-Stevenson, 1990), pp. 771–77.

36 Thomas Carlyle, *The French Revolution* (London: Chapman and Hall, 1837), iii, book 6, p. 240.

37 E. Watts Phillips, *Watts Phillips: Artist and Playwright* (London: Cassell, 1891), p. 12.

38 John Coleman, *The Truth about The Dead Heart* (London: Henry J. Drane, 1890), p. 101.

39 Marie and Squire Bancroft, *The Bancrofts: Recollections of Sixty Years* (London: Thomas Nelson and Sons, 1911), pp. 358–59.

40 Edward Gordon Craig, *Index to the Story of My Days* (London: The Hulton Press, 1957), p. 103.

41 Ellen Terry, *The Story of My Life* (London: Hutchinson, 1908), p. 308.

42 Ibid.

43 Ibid.

44 Saintsbury and Palmer, *We Saw Him Act*, p. 276.

45 Coleman, *The Truth about The Dead Heart*, p. 55.

46 Phillips, *Watts Phillips*, p. v.

47 Coleman, *The Truth about The Dead Heart*, pp. 108–9.

48 Coleman, *The Truth about The Dead Heart*, pp. 111–13.

49 Coleman, *The Truth about The Dead Heart*, pp. 118–19.

50 Phillips, *Watts Phillips*, p. 52.

51 Phillips, *Watts Phillips*, pp. 53–54.

52 Phillips, *Watts Phillips*, pp. 60–61.

53 Fitzgerald Collection, ix, p. 97.

54 Fitzgerald Collection, ix, p. 103.

55 Fitzgerald Collection, ix, p. 108.

56 Fitzgerald Collection, ix, p. 94.

57 Fitzgerald Collection, ix, p. 99.

58 Marie and Squire Bancroft, *The Bancrofts*, p. 362.

59 Fitzgerald Collection, ix, p. 107.

60 Fitzgerald Collection, ix, p. 100.

61 Fitzgerald Collection, ix, p. 99.

62 Fitzgerald Collection, ix, p. 99.

63 Fitzgerald Collection, ix, pp. 100, 108, 97.

64 Stoker, *Reminiscences of Henry Irving*, p. 171.

65 Stoker, *Reminiscences of Henry Irving*, p. 171.

66 Terry, *Story of My Life*, p. 369.

67 Irving, *Henry Irving*, p. 602.

68 Both reviews are in the Fitzgerald Collection, xviii, p. 65.

69 Fitzgerald Collection, xviii, pp. 40, 65, 69.

70 *Saturday Review*, 17 April 1897.

71 Irving, *Henry Irving*, p. 602.

72   Stoker, *Reminiscences of Henry Irving*, pp. 171–72.

73   *World*, 14 April 1897.

74   Brereton, *The Life of Henry Irving*, ii, p. 266.

75   Stoker, *Personal Reminiscences of Henry Irving*, pp. 172–73.

76   Bram Stoker Collection, box 24, item 172.

77   *Westminster Budget*, 21 April 1899; *Today*, 27 April 1899.

78   Arthur Conan Doyle, *Memories and Adventures* (London: John Murray, 1930), p. 141.

79   Henry Arthur Jones, *The Shadow of Henry Irving* (London: Richards Press, 1931), p. 45.

80   On this process see J.M. MacKenzie, ed., *Popular Imperialism and the Military* (Manchester:
     Manchester University Press, 1992); J.W.M. Hichberger, *Images of the Army: The Military in
     British Art* (Manchester: Manchester University Press, 1988).

81   Stoker, *Personal Reminiscences of Henry Irving*, p. 164.

82   On the play, its reception and significance see the excellent book by W.D. King, *Irving's
     Waterloo* (Berkeley: University of California Press, 1993). It contains a reprint of the text of
     the play and Shaw's spiteful review.

83   Hilary Fraser, *The Victorians and Renaissance Italy* (Oxford: Blackwell, 1992), and J.B. Bullen,
     The Myth of the Renaissance in Nineteenth-Century Writing (Oxford: Clarendon Press, 1994).

84   Bullen, *The Myth of the Renaissance*, p. 10.

85   Fraser, *The Victorians and Renaissance Italy*, p. 42.

86   E.T. Cook and Alexander Wedderburn, eds, *The Complete Works of John Ruskin* (London:
     George Allen, 1903), xi, p. 187; Carlyle, *On Heroes, Hero-Worship and the Heroic in History*,
     pp. 93, 98, 100, 101.

87   Fraser, *The Victorians and Renaissance Italy*, p. 145; Alison Milbank, *Dante and the Victorians*
     (Manchester: Manchester University Press, 1998), pp. 1–2.

88   M.T. Beaugeard-Durand, 'How the Play of *Dante* Was Written', *English Illustrated Magazine*,
     new series, 3 (June 1903), pp. 227–36.

89   Stoker, *Personal Reminiscences of Henry Irving*, p. 177

90   Stoker, *Personal Reminiscences of Henry Irving*, p. 178.

91   Sainstbury and Palmer, *We Saw Him Act*, p. 327.

92   Fitzgerald, *Sir Henry Irving*, pp. 268–69.

93   Stoker Collection, box 23, item 189.

Notes to Chapter 13: Religion

1   On nineteenth-century Evangelicalism see Ian Bradley, *The Call to Seriousness: The
    Evangelical Impact on the Victorians* (London: Jonathan Cape, 1976); James Munson, *The
    Nonconformists* (London: SPCK, 1991); D.W. Bebbington, *Evangelicalism in Modern Britain*
    (London: Unwin Hyman, 1989); and T.W. Laqueur, *Religion and Respectability* (New Haven
    and London: Yale University Press, 1976).

2   Bradley, *Call to Seriousness*, p. 19.

3   Richard Helmstader, 'The Nonconformist Conscience' in Peter Marsh, ed., *The Conscience
    of the Victorian State* (Hassocks; Harvester Press, 1979), p. 142.

4   Bradley, *Call to Seriousness*, p. 22.

5   Bradley, *Call to Seriousness*, p. 22.

6   Harold Perkin, *The Origins of Modern English Society, 1780–1880* (London: Routledge, 1969), p. 280.

7   G.M. Young, *Victorian England: Portrait of an Age* (Oxford: Oxford University Press, 1977), pp. 4–5.

8   Bradley, *Call to Seriousness*, p. 48.

9   Doreen Rosman, *Evangelicals and Culture* (London: Croom Helm, 1984).

10   John Wigley, *The Rise and Fall of the Victorian Sunday* (Manchester: Manchester University Press, 1988).

11   Brian Harrison, *Drink and the Victorians* (Keele: Keele University Press, 1994); Lilian Lewis Shiman, *The Crusade Against Drink in Victorian England* (London: Macmillan, 1988).

12   J.M. Golby and A.W. Purdue, *The Civilisation of the Crowd: Popular Culture in England, 1750–1900* (London: Batsford, 1984), p. 86.

13   Richard Foulkes, *Church and Stage in Victorian England* (Cambridge: Cambridge University Press, 1997), pp. 22–27. This is the outstanding study of the subject.

14   Lewis Carroll, 'The Stage and the Spirit of Reverence', *Theatre*, 11 (June 1888), pp. 285–94.

15   Foulkes, *Church and Stage in Victorian England*, pp. 8–9, 15–17, 35–49, 60–61, 81–82.

16   Laurence Irving, *Henry Irving* (London: Faber, 1951), p. 62.

17   H. Chance Newton, *Cues and Curtain Calls* (London: John Lane, 1927), p. 70.

18   Chance Newton, *Cues and Curtain Calls*, p. 69.

19   Foulkes, *Church and Stage in Victorian England*, pp. 226–27.

20   Percy Fitzgerald, *Sir Henry Irving: A Biography* (London: T. Fisher Unwin, 1906), pp. 293–94.

21   Chance Newton, *Cues and Curtain Calls*, p. 72.

22   G.R. Sims, *My Life* (London: Eveleigh Nash, 1917), p. 98.

23   Bram Stoker, *Personal Reminiscences of Henry Irving* (London: Heinemann, 1907), p. 93.

24   Chance Newton, *Cues and Curtain Calls*, p. 24.

25   Irving, *Henry Irving*, p. 281.

26   Stoker, *Reminiscences of Irving*, p. 449.

27   Austin Brereton, *The Life of Henry Irving* (London: Longmans, Green and Co., 1908), ii, pp. 261–64.

28   Brereton, *The Life of Henry Irving*, ii, pp. 271–76.

29   H.A. Saintsbury and Cecil Palmer, eds, *We Saw Him Act* (London: Hurst and Blackett, 1939), p. 329.

30   David Mayer, ed., *Henry Irving and The Bells* (Manchester: Manchester Univesity Press, 1980), p. 6.

31   On the rights situation, see Mayer, *Henry Irving and The Bells*, p. 10.

32   Ellen Terry, *The Story of My Life* (London: Hutchinson, 1908), p. 338.

33   Both reviews are quoted in Brereton, *The Life of Henry Irving*, i, p. 119.

34   Brereton, *The Life of Henry Irving*, i, p. 114.

35   H. Chance Newton, *Crime and the Drama* (London: Stanley Paul, 1927), p. 64.

36   *New York Tribune*, 31 October 1883.

37   For a full account of the production, see David Mayer, *Henry Irving and The Bells*.

38 On the life and literary fortunes of Aram see Nancy Jane Tyson, *Eugene Aram: The Literary History and Typology of the Scholar Criminal* (Hamden, Connecticut: Archon Books, 1983).

39 Stoker, *Reminiscences of Irving*, p. 19.

40 Brereton, *The Life of Henry Irving*, ii, p. 274.

41 Chance Newton, *Crime and the Drama*, p. 35.

42 Freeman Wills, *W.G. Wills: Dramatist and Painter* (London: Longmans, Green and Co., 1898), p. 128.

43 William Winter, *Shadows of the Stage* (New York and London: Macmillans 1893), p. 355.

44 Clement Scott, *From 'The Bells' to 'King Arthur'* (London: John McQueen, 1897), p. 27.

45 Scott, *From 'The Bells' to 'King Arthur'*, p. 30.

46 Winter, *Shadows of the Stage*, p. 349.

47 Brereton, *The Life of Henry Irving*, i, pp. 143–45.

48 Nicholas Butler, *John Martin-Harvey* (Wivenhoe: Nicholas Butler, 1997), p. 70.

49 Fitzgerald, *Sir Henry Irving*, p. 75.

50 Brereton, *The Life of Henry Irving*, i, p. 75. On the play, see also Wills, *W.G. Wills*, pp. 133–42, and Fitzgerald, *Sir Henry Irving*, pp. 75–77.

51 Joseph Knight, *Theatrical Notes* (London: Lawrence and Bullen, 1893), p. 226.

52 Scott, *From 'The Bells' to 'King Arthur'*, p. 140.

53 Fitzgerald, *Sir Henry Irving*, p. 77.

54 Sir Frederick Pollock, ed., *Macready's Reminiscences* (London: Macmillans, 1876), p. 428.

55 Dutton Cook, *Nights at the Play* (London: Chatto and Windus, 1883), p. 386.

56 Scott, *From 'The Bells' to 'King Arthur'*, p. 155.

57 Dutton Cook, *Nights at the Play*, pp. 385–86.

58 Knight, *Theatrical Notes*, p. 300.

59 Dutton Cook, *Nights at the Play*, p. 387.

60 Knight, *Theatrical Notes*, p. 300.

61 Scott, *From 'The Bell' to 'King Arthur'*, pp. 156, 158.

62 Dutton Cook, *Nights at the Play*, p. 387; Scott, *From 'The Bells' to 'King Arthur'*, p. 158.

63 Brereton, *The Life of Henry Irving*, i, p. 301, Fitzgerald, *Sir Henry Irving*, p. 101; J.H. Barnes, *Forty Years on the Stage* (London: Chapman and Hall, 1914), p. 100.

64 For a detailed account of this production see Michael Booth, *Victorian Spectacular Theatre, 1850–1910* (London: Routledge, 1981), pp. 93–126.

65 Wills, *W.G. Wills*, p. 201.

66 Winter, *Shadows of the Stage*, pp. 34–35.

67 Saintsbury and Palmer, *We Saw Him Act*, pp. 259–65; Fitzgerald, *Sir Henry Irving*, p. 176.

68 Henry James, *The Scenic Art*, ed., Allan Wade (London: Rupert Hart-Davis, 1949), pp. 217–25.

69 Winter, *Shadows of the Stage*, pp. 39–40.

70 Winter, *Shadows of the Stage*, pp. 42–43.

71 Scott, *From 'The Bells' to 'King Arthur'*, pp. 294–95.

72 Terry, *Story of My Life*, pp. 239–43.

73 *Theatre*, new series, 11 (June 1888), p. 292.

Notes to Chapter 14: Shylock and the Jews

1 Percy Fitzgerald, *Sir Henry Irving: A Biography* (London: T. Fisher Unwin, 1906), p. 253.

2 Linda Rozmovits, *Shakespeare and the Politics of Culture in Late Victorian England* (Baltimore and London: the Johns Hopkins University Press, 1998), p. 3.

3 Richard Altick, *Paintings from Books: Art and Literature in Britain, 1760–1900* (Columbus: Ohio State University Press, 1985), pp. 259, 267.

4 On the Jews in nineteenth-century Britain and attitudes to them, see Cecil Roth, *A History of Jews in England* (Oxford: Clarendon Press, 1964); Israel Finestein, *Jewish Society in Victorian England* (London: Vallentine Mitchell, 1993); Colin Holmes, *Anti-Semitism in British Society, 1876–1939* (London: Edward Arnold, 1979); Colin Holmes, *A Tolerant Country? Immigrants, Refugees and Minorities in Britain* (London: Faber, 1991).

5 Holmes, *Anti-Semitism in British Society*, p. 220.

6 On cultural constructions of the Jew, see Edgar Rosenberg, *From Shylock to Svengali: Jewish Stereotypes in English Fiction* (Stanford: Stanford University Press, 1960); Bryan Cheyette, *Constructions of 'the Jew' in English Literature: Racial Representations, 1875–1945* (Cambridge: Cambridge University Press, 1995).

7 Rosenberg, *From Shylock to Svengali*, p. 35.

8 On the stage history of *The Merchant of Venice*, see John Gross, *Shylock* (London: Chatto and Windus, 1992); Toby Lelyveld, *Shylock on the Stage* (London: Routledge, 1961); James C. Bulman, *The Merchant of Venice* (Manchester: Manchester University Press, 1991).

9 Bulman, *Merchant of Venice*, p. 26.

10 Terry, *Story of My Life*, p. 26.

11 Laurence Irving, *Henry Irving: The Actor and His World* (London: Faber, 1951), p. 357.

12 Irving, *Henry Irving*, p. 521.

13 Edna Healey, *Lady Unknown: The Life of Angela Burdett-Coutts* (London: Sidgwick and Jackson, 1978), pp. 192–97.

14 Joseph Hatton, *Henry Irving's Impressions of America* (London: Sampson Low, Marston, Searle and Rivington, 1884), p. 175.

15 Healey, *Lady Unknown*, p. 192.

16 Austin Brereton, *The Life of Henry Irving* (London: Longmans, Green and Co., 1908), i, p. 303; Frederic Daly, *Henry Irving in England and America, 1838–84* (London: T. Fisher Unwin, 1884), p. 60.

17 Frank Harris, *My Life and Loves* (London: W.H. Allen, 1964), p. 49.

18 Stoker Collection, box 8, item 522.

19 J.H. Barnes, *Forty Years on the Stage* (London: Chapman and Hall, 1914), pp. 101–8.

20 Terry, *Story of My Life*, p. 186.

21 Terry, *Story of My Life*, p. 163.

22 Hatton, *Henry Irving's Impressions of America*, pp. 171–72.

23 Hatton, *Henry Irving's Impressions of America*, pp. 173, 175.

24 Fitzgerald, *Sir Henry Irving*, p. 103.

25 Hatton, *Henry Irving's Impressions of America*, pp. 173–79.

26   For detailed discussions of the production, see James C. Bulman, *The Merchant of Venice*, pp. 28–52, and Alan Hughes, *Henry Irving: Shakespearean* (Cambridge: Cambridge University Press, 1981), pp. 224–41.

27   Terry, *Story of My Life*, p. 186.

28   Clement Scott, *From 'The Bells' to 'King Arthur'* (London: John McQueen, 1897), pp. 163, 185.

29   Joseph Knight, *Theatrical Notes* (London: Lawrence and Bullen, 1893), p. 302.

30   Dutton Cook, *Nights at the Play* (London: Chatto and Windus, 1883), pp. 391–93.

31   Brereton, *The Life of Henry Irving*, i, p. 303.

32   W. Graham Robertson, *Time Was* (London: Hamish Hamilton, 1931), pp. 55–56.

33   Henry James, *The Scenic Art*, ed., Allan Wade (London: Rupert Hart-Davis, 1949), pp. 140–41.

34   George Bernard Shaw, *Our Theatres in the Nineties* (London: Constable, 1932), ii, p. 198.

35   Lewis Carroll, *Selected Letters*, ed., Morton Cohen (New York: Panther Books 1982), pp. 94–95; William Allingham, *Diary, 1847–1889* (London: Centaur Press, 2000), p. 287.

36   Brereton, *The Life of Henry Irving*, i, p. 316.

37   Fitzgerald, *Sir Henry Irving*, p. 109.

38   Brereton, *The Life of Henry Irving*, i, p. 315.

39   Brereton, *The Life of Henry Irving*, i, p. 318.

40   E.T. Cook and Alexander Wedderburn, eds, *The Complete Works of John Ruskin* (London: George Allen, 1904), xxxvii, p. 303.

41   Irving, *Henry Irving*, p. 346.

42   Henry James, *The Scenic Art*, p. 147; Clement Scott, *From 'The Bells' to 'King Arthur'*, p. 169.

43   Cook and Wedderburn, eds, *The Complete Works of John Ruskin*, xxv, pp. 417–18.

44   *Theatre*, new series, 1 (1880), p. 63.

45   Irving, *Henry Irving*, p. 348.

46   Irving, *Henry Irving*, p. 349.

47   Irving, *Henry Irving*, p. 349.

48   *Theatre*, new series, 1 (1880), p. 169.

49   Cook and Wedderburn, eds, *The Complete Works of John Ruskin*, xvii, pp. 222–24.

50   Cook and Wedderburn, eds, *The Complete Works of John Ruskin*, xxiv, p. 418.

51   Cook and Wedderburn, eds, *The Complete Works of John Ruskin*, xxiii, p. 161.

52   *Theatre*, new series, 1 (1880), p. 169.

53   *Theatre*, new series, 1 (1880), p. 249.

54   Frederick Hawkins, 'Shylock and Other Stage Jews', *Theatre*, 3 (1879), pp. 191–98.

55   'The Round Table', *Theatre*, 3 (1879), pp. 253–61.

56   A.B. Walkley, *Playhouse Impressions* (London: T. Fisher Unwin, 1892), pp. 259–60.

57   Bulman, *The Merchant of Venice*, p. 51.

58   H.H. Furness, *New Variorum Edition of Shakespeare's The Merchant of Venice* (Philadelphia: J.B. Lippincott and Co., 1888), pp. 383–84.

59   Edward R. Russell, *The Merchant of Venice* (Liverpool, 1888), pp. 6–7.

60   Gross, *Shylock*, p. 141.

61   Rozmovits, *Shakespeare and the Politics of Culture*, p. 133.

62   Gross, *Shylock*, p. 141.

63 Brereton, *The Life of Henry Irving*, i, pp. 302–3.

64 Richard Dickins, *Forty Years of Shakespeare on the English Stage* (privately printed, 1907), p. 35.

65 Lelyveld, *Shylock on the Stage*, pp. 91–95.

66 Bram Stoker, *Personal Reminiscences of Henry Irving* (London: Heinemann, 1907), p. 320.

67 Fitzgerald Collection, xv, p. 99.

68 Terry, *Story of My Life*, p. 187.

69 William Winter, *Shakespeare on the Stage* (New York: Moffat, Yard and Company, 1911), pp. 174–75.

70 Winter, *Shakespeare on the Stage*, pp. 177–78.

71 *The Manchester Stage*, 1880–1900 (London: Archibald Constable, 1900), pp. 90–93.

72 *The Manchester Stage*, p. 96.

73 *The Manchester Stage*, pp. 101–7.

Index

Note: For ease of reference, actors are entered under the entry 'actors', playwrights under the entry 'playwrights', and plays under the entry 'plays'.